(ex•ploring)

SERIES

1. To investigate in a systematic way: examine. 2. To search into or range over for the purpose of discovery.

(ex•ploring)
SERIES

1. To investigate in a systematic way: examine. 2. To search into or range over for the purpose of discovery.

Microsoft® Office

PowerPoint® 2007
COMPREHENSIVE

Robert T. Grauer

Cynthia Krebs | Keith Mulbery

PEARSON

Prentice Hall

**Upper Saddle River
New Jersey 07458**

Library of Congress Cataloging-in-Publication Data

Grauer, Robert T., 1945–
  Exploring Microsoft Office PowerPoint 2007 comprehensive / Robert T. Grauer, Cynthia Krebs, Keith Mulbery.
    p. cm.
  ISBN-13: 978-0-13-232847-0
  ISBN-10: 0-13-232847-X
  1. Presentation graphics software. 2. Microsoft PowerPoint (Computer file) I. Krebs, Cynthia. II. Mulbery, Keith.
III. Title.
  T385.G737442 2007
  005.5'8—dc22

                                                                            2007023427

Vice President and Publisher: Natalie E. Anderson
Associate VP/ Executive Acquisitions Editor, Print: Stephanie Wall
Executive Acquisitions Editor, Media: Richard Keaveny
Sr. Acquisitions Editor: Melissa Sabella
Product Development Manager: Eileen Bien Calabro
Sr. Editorial Project Manager/Development: Eileen Clark
Editorial Project Manager/Assistant Editor: Jenelle J. Woodrup
Market Development Editor: Claire Hunter
Editorial Assistant: Rebecca Knauer
Executive Producer: Lisa Stritc
Content Development Manager: Cathi Profitko
Project Manager, Media: Ashley Lulling
Director of Marketing: Margaret Waples
Sr. Marketing Manager: Scott Davidson
Sr. Sales Associate: Rebecca Scott
Sr. Managing Editor: Cynthia Zonneveld
Associate Managing Editor: Camille Trentacoste
Production Project Manager: Lynne Breitfeller
Sr. Operations Supervisor: Nick Sklitsis
Design Director: Maria Lange
Art Director/Interior and Cover Design: Blair Brown
Cover Illustration/Photo: Courtesy of Getty Images/Laurent Hamels
Composition: GGS Book Services
Project Management: GGS Book Services
Project Manager: Kevin Bradley
Production Editors: Blair Woodcock and Andrea Shearer
Cover Printer: Phoenix Color
Printer/Binder: Banta/Menasha

10 9 8 7 6 5 4 3 2 1
ISBN-13: 978-0-13-232847-0
ISBN-10: 0-13-232847-X

Dedications

To Marion—my wife, my lover, and my best friend.

Robert Grauer

I dedicate this book to those I love in thanks for the joy and support they give me:
My wonderful children: Marshall, Jaron, Jenalee, and Michelle who make it all
worthwhile, and Bradley Behle—my newest son and a welcome addition to our family.

My granddaughter, Ava—her baby cuddles make life a pleasure.
My parents, Neal and Zola Mulhern, who continually do all they can to make life easier.
And to those who have gone before: my father, Reed J. Olsen, and my
Grandparents Waddoups. I would like to dedicate this book to my siblings: my sister, Vicki O. Ridgway,
and my brothers Randy J. and Michael R. Olsen. Thank you for always being there for me.

Cynthia Krebs

I would like to dedicate this book to my family and close friends who provided a
strong community of emotional support and patience as I completed my doctorate program
and worked on this edition of the Exploring series.

Keith Mulbery

About the Authors

Dr. Robert T. Grauer

Dr. Robert T. Grauer is an Associate Professor in the Department of Computer Information Systems at the University of Miami, where he has been honored with the Outstanding Teacher Award in the School of Business. He is the vision behind the Exploring Series, which is about to sell its 3 millionth copy.

Dr. Grauer has written more than 50 books on programming and information systems. His work has been translated into three foreign languages and is used in all aspects of higher education at both national and international levels.

Dr. Grauer also has been a consultant to several major corporations including IBM and American Express. He received his Ph.D. in operations research in 1972 from the Polytechnic Institute of Brooklyn.

Cynthia Krebs

Cynthia Krebs is a professor in the Digital Media Department at Utah Valley State College, where she has taught since 1988. In addition to teaching classes in basic computer proficiency using Microsoft Office, she teaches classes in business presentations, business graphics, and an introduction to multimedia. She has received the Teacher-of-the-Year Award in the School of Business twice during her tenure at UVSC.

She has written chapters for many texts, co-authored a text on advanced word processing, and has presented locally and nationally. A graduate of Utah State University, Cynthia lives in Springville, Utah.

She has four children and one granddaughter. When she isn't teaching or writing, she enjoys spending time with her children and spoiling her granddaughter.

Dr. Keith Mulbery

Dr. Keith Mulbery is an Associate Professor in the Information Systems and Technology Department at Utah Valley State College, where he teaches computer applications, programming, and MIS classes. He has written more than 15 software textbooks and business communication test banks. In January 2001, he received the Utah Valley State College Board of Trustees Award of Excellence for authoring *MOUS Essentials Word 2000*. In addition to his series editor and authoring experience, he also served as a developmental editor on two word processing textbooks. In 2007, he received the UVSC School of Technology and Computing Scholar Award.

He received his B.S. and M.Ed. (majoring in Business Education) from Southwestern Oklahoma State University and earned his Ph.D. in Education with an emphasis in Business Information Systems at Utah State University in 2006. His dissertation topic was computer-assisted instruction using TAIT to supplement traditional instruction in basic computer proficiency courses.

Contributing Author

Barbara Stover

Barbara Stover is a professor of Information Technologies at Marion Technical College in Marion, Ohio. She teaches Web design courses and manages the Blackboard and student e-mail systems at the college and is also an adjunct faculty member at the George Washington University. She received a M.A. in Education and Human Development, with a major in Educational Technology Leadership from the George Washington University. She has 31 years of teaching experience.

Brief Contents

Contents

Microsoft Office PowerPoint 2007

CHAPTER TWO | Presentation Development: Planning and Preparing a Presentation   143

CHAPTER THREE | Presentation Design: Enhancing with Illustrations   205

CHAPTER FOUR | PowerPoint Multimedia Tools: Enhancing with Multimedia   287

CHAPTER FIVE | Charts and Graphs: Working with Text and Statistical Charts and Graphs   353

CHAPTER SIX | Presentation Customization: Customizing the Slideshow   427

CHAPTER SEVEN | Web Presentations: Adding Interactivity and Using Web Features   493

CHAPTER EIGHT | Collaborate and Distribute: Reviewing, Securing, and Publishing a Presentation   555

Acknowledgments

The success of the Exploring series is attributed to contributions from numerous individuals. First and foremost, our heartfelt appreciation to Melissa Sabella, senior acquisitions editor, for providing new leadership and direction to capitalize on the strength and tradition of the Exploring series while implementing innovative ideas into the Exploring Office 2007 edition. Scott Davidson, senior marketing manager, was an invaluable addition to the team who believes in the mission of this series passionately and did an amazing job communicating its message.

During the first few months of the project, Eileen Clark, senior editorial project manager, kept the team focused on the vision, pedagogy, and voice that has been the driving force behind the success of the Exploring series. Claire Hunter, market development editor, facilitated communication between the editorial team and the reviewers to ensure that this edition meets the changing needs of computer professors and students at the collegiate level. Keith Mulbery gave up many nights and weekends (including Thanksgiving) to jump in and help out with anything that was asked of him, including assisting with topical organization, reviewing and revising content, capturing screenshots, and ensuring chapter manuscripts adhered to series guidelines.

Jenelle Woodrup, editorial project manager/assistant editor, masterfully managed the flow of manuscript files among the authors, editorial team, and production to ensure timely publication of series. Laura Town, developmental editor, provided an objective perspective in reviewing the content and organization of selected chapters. Eileen Calabro, product development manager, facilitated communication among the editorial team, authors, and production during a transitional stage. The team at GGS worked through software delays, style changes and anything else we threw at them to bring the whole thing together. Art director Blair Brown's conversations with students and professors across the country yielded a design that addressed the realities of today's students with function and style.

A special thanks to the following for the use of their work in the PowerPoint section of the text: Cameron Martin, Ph.D., Assistant to the President, Utah Valley State College, for the use of the Institutional Policies and Procedures Approval Process flowchart; Nick Finner, Paralegal Studies, Utah Valley State College, for the use of his research relating to the elderly population residing in the prisons of Utah; Ryan Phillips, Xeric Landscape and Design (XericUtah.com), for sharing Xeric's concepts for creating beautiful, drought-tolerant landscapes and for the photographs illustrating these concepts; Jo Porter, Photographer, Mapleton, Utah, for allowing the use of her beautiful engagement and wedding photographs; and David and Ali Valeti for the photographs of their baby and their family.

The following organizations and individuals generously provided data and structure from their organizational databases: Replacements, Ltd., Shweta Ponnappa, JC Raulston Arboretum at North Carolina State University, and Valerie Tyson. We deeply appreciate the ability to give students a feel for "real" data.

The new members of the Exploring author team would like to especially thank Bob Grauer for his vision in developing Exploring and his leadership in creating this highly successful series.

Maryann Barber would like to thank Bob Grauer for a wonderful collaboration and providing the opportunities through which so much of her life has changed.

The Exploring team would like to especially thank the following instructors who drew on their experience in the classroom and their software expertise to give us daily advice on how to improve this book. Their impact can be seen on every page:

Barbara Stover, Marion Technical College

Bob McCloud, Sacred Heart University

Cassie Georgetti, Florida Technical College

Dana Johnson, North Dakota State University

Jackie Lamoureux, Central New Mexico Community College

Jim Pepe, Bentley College

Judy Brown, The University of Memphis

Lancie Anthony Affonso, College of Charleston

Mimi Duncan, University of Missouri – St. Louis

Minnie Proctor, Indian River Community College

Richard Albright, Goldey-Beacom College

We also want to acknowledge all the reviewers of the Exploring 2007 series. Their valuable comments and constructive criticism greatly improved this edition:

Aaron Schorr
Fashion Institute of Technology

Alicia Stonesifer
La Salle University

Allen Alexander, Delaware
Tech & Community College

Amy Williams, Abraham
Baldwin Agriculture College

Annie Brown
Hawaii Community College

Barbara Cierny
Harper College

Barbara Hearn
Community College of Philadelphia

Barbara Meguro
University of Hawaii at Hilo

Bette Pitts
South Plains College

Beverly Fite
Amarillo College

Bill Wagner
Villanova

Brandi N. Guidry
University of Louisiana at Lafayette

Brian Powell
West Virginia University – Morgantown
Campus

Carl Farrell
Hawaii Pacific University

Carl Penzuil
Ithaca College

Carole Bagley;
University of St. Thomas

Catherine Hain
Central New Mexico CC

Charles Edwards
University of Texas of the Permian Basin

Christine L. Moore
College of Charleston

David Barnes
Penn State Altoona

David Childress;
Ashland Community College

David Law, Alfred
State College

Dennis Chalupa
Houston Baptist

Diane Stark
Phoenix College

Dianna Patterson
Texarkana College

Dianne Ross
University of Louisiana at Lafayette

Dr. Behrooz Saghafi
Chicago State University

Dr. Gladys Swindler
Fort Hays State University

Dr. Joe Teng
Barry University

Dr. Karen Nantz
Eastern Illinois University.

Duane D. Lintner
Amarillo College

Elizabeth Edmiston
North Carolina Central University

Erhan Uskup
Houston Community College

Fred Hills, McClellan
Community College

Gary R. Armstrong
Shippensburg University of Pennsylvania

Glenna Vanderhoof
Missouri State

Gregg Asher
Minnesota State University, Mankato

Hong K. Sung
University of Central Oklahoma

Hyekyung Clark
Central New Mexico CC

J Patrick Fenton
West Valley College

Jana Carver
Amarillo College

Jane Cheng
Bloomfield College

Janos T. Fustos
Metropolitan State College of Denver

Jeffrey A Hassett
University of Utah

Jennifer Pickle
Amarillo College

Jerry Kolata
New England Institute of Technology

Jesse Day
South Plains College

John Arehart
Longwood University

John Lee Reardon
University of Hawaii, Manoa

Joshua Mindel
San Francisco State University

Karen Wisniewski
County College of Morris

Karl Smart
Central Michigan University

Kathryn L. Hatch
University of Arizona

Krista Terry
Radford University

Laura McManamon
University of Dayton

Laura Reid
University of Western Ontario

Linda Johnsonius
Murray State University

Lori Kelley
Madison Area Technical College

Lucy Parker,
California State University, Northridge

Lynda Henrie
LDS Business College

Malia Young
Utah State University

Margie Martyn
Baldwin Wallace

Marianne Trudgeon
Fanshawe College

Marilyn Hibbert
Salt Lake Community College

Marjean Lake
LDS Business College

Mark Olaveson
Brigham Young University

Nancy Sardone
Seton Hall University

Patricia Joseph
Slippery Rock University.

Patrick Hogan
Cape Fear Community College

Paula F. Bell
Lock Haven University of Pennsylvania

Paulette Comet
Community College of Baltimore County,
Catonsville

Pratap Kotala
North Dakota State University

Richard Blamer
John Carroll University

Richard Herschel
St. Joseph's University

Richard Hewer
Ferris State University

Robert Gordon
Hofstra University

Robert Marmelstein
East Stroudsburg University

Robert Stumbur
Northern Alberta Institute of Technology

Roberta I. Hollen
University of Central Oklahoma

Roland Moreira
South Plains College

Ron Murch
University of Calgary

Rory J. de Simone
University of Florida

Ruth Neal
Navarro College

Sandra M. Brown
Finger Lakes Community College

Sharon Mulroney
Mount Royal College

Stephen E. Lunce
Midwestern State University

Steve Schwarz
Raritan Valley Community College

Steven Choy
University of Calgary

Susan Byrne
St. Clair College

Thomas Setaro
Brookdale Community College

Todd McLeod
Fresno City College

Vickie Pickett
Midland College

Vipul Gupta
St Joseph's University

Vivek Shah
Texas State University - San Marcos

Wei-Lun Chuang
Utah State University

William Dorin
Indiana University Northwest

Finally, we wish to acknowledge reviewers of previous editions of the Exploring series—we wouldn't have made it to the 7th edition without you:

Alan Moltz
Naugatuck Valley Technical Community
College

Alok Charturvedi
Purdue University

Antonio Vargas
El Paso Community College

Barbara Sherman
Buffalo State College

Bill Daley
University of Oregon

Bill Morse
DeVry Institute of Technology

Bonnie Homan
San Francisco State University

Carl M. Briggs
Indiana University School of Business

Carlotta Eaton
Radford University

Carolyn DiLeo
Westchester Community College

Cody Copeland
Johnson County Community College

Connie Wells
Georgia State University

Daniela Marghitu
Auburn University

David B. Meinert
Southwest Missouri State University

David Douglas
University of Arkansas

David Langley
University of Oregon

David Rinehard
Lansing Community College

David Weiner
University of San Francisco

Dean Combellick
Scottsdale Community College

Delores Pusins
Hillsborough Community College

Don Belle
Central Piedmont Community College

Douglas Cross
Clackamas Community College

Ernie Ivey
Polk Community College

Gale E. Rand
College Misericordia

Helen Stoloff
Hudson Valley Community College

Herach Safarian
College of the Canyons

Jack Zeller
Kirkwood Community College

James Franck
College of St. Scholastica

James Gips
Boston College

Jane King
Everett Community College

Janis Cox
Tri-County Technical College

Jerry Chin
Southwest Missouri State University

Jill Chapnick
Florida International University

Jim Pruitt
Central Washington University

John Lesson
University of Central Florida

John Shepherd
Duquesne University

Judith M. Fitspatrick
Gulf Coast Community College

Judith Rice
Santa Fe Community College

Judy Dolan
Palomar College

Karen Tracey
Central Connecticut State University

Kevin Pauli
University of Nebraska

Kim Montney
Kellogg Community College

Kimberly Chambers
Scottsdale Community College

Larry S. Corman
Fort Lewis College

Lynn Band
Middlesex Community College

Margaret Thomas
Ohio University

Marguerite Nedreberg
Youngstown State University

Marilyn Salas
Scottsdale Community College

Martin Crossland
Southwest Missouri State University

Mary McKenry Percival
University of Miami

Michael Hassett
Fort Hayes State University

Michael Stewardson
San Jacinto College – North

Midge Gerber
Southwestern Oklahoma State University

Mike Hearn
Community College of Philadelphia

Mike Kelly
Community College of Rhode Island

Mike Thomas
Indiana University School of Business

Paul E. Daurelle
Western Piedmont Community College

Ranette Halverson
Midwestern State University

Raymond Frost
Central Connecticut State University

Robert Spear, Prince
George's Community College

Rose M. Laird
Northern Virginia Community College

Sally Visci
Lorain County Community College

Shawna DePlonty
Sault College of Applied Arts and Technology

Stuart P. Brian
Holy Family College

Susan Fry
Boise State Universtiy

Suzanne Tomlinson
Iowa State University

Vernon Griffin
Austin Community College

Wallace John Whistance-Smith
Ryerson Polytechnic University

Walter Johnson
Community College of Philadelphia

Wanda D. Heller
Seminole Community College

We very much appreciate the following individuals for painstakingly checking every step and every explanation for technical accuracy, while dealing with an entirely new software application:

Barbara Waxer
Bill Daley
Beverly Fite
Dawn Wood
Denise Askew
Elizabeth Lockley

James Reidel
Janet Pickard
Janice Snyder
Jeremy Harris
John Griffin
Joyce Neilsen

LeeAnn Bates
Mara Zebest
Mary E. Pascarella
Michael Meyers
Sue McCrory

Preface

The Exploring Series

Exploring has been Prentice Hall's most successful Office Application series of the past 15 years. For Office 2007 Exploring has undergone the most extensive changes in its history, so that it can truly move today's student "beyond the point and click."

The goal of Exploring has always been to teach more than just the steps to accomplish a task – the series provides the theoretical foundation necessary for a student to understand when and why to apply a skill. This way, students achieve a broader understanding of Office.

Today's students are changing and Exploring has evolved with them. Prentice Hall traveled to college campuses across the country and spoke directly to students to determine how they study and prepare for class. We also spoke with hundreds of professors about the best ways to administer materials to such a diverse body of students.

Here is what we learned

Students go to college now with a different set of skills than they did 5 years ago. The new edition of Exploring moves students beyond the basics of the software at a faster pace, without sacrificing coverage of the fundamental skills that everybody needs to know. This ensures that students will be engaged from Chapter 1 to the end of the book.

Students have diverse career goals. With this in mind, we broadened the examples in the text (and the accompanying Instructor Resources) to include the health sciences, hospitality, urban planning, business and more. Exploring will be relevant to every student in the course.

Students read, prepare and study differently than they used to. Rather than reading a book cover to cover students want to easily identify what they need to know, and then learn it efficiently. We have added key features that will bring students into the content and make the text easy to use such as objective mapping, pull quotes, and key terms in the margins.

Moving students beyond the point and click

All of these additions mean students will be more engaged, achieve a higher level of understanding, and successfully complete this course. In addition to the experience and expertise of the series creator and author Robert T. Grauer we have assembled a tremendously talented team of supporting authors to assist with this critical revision. Each of them is equally dedicated to the Exploring mission of **moving students beyond the point and click.**

Key Features of the Office 2007 revision include

- **New** **Office Fundamentals Chapter** efficiently covers skills common among all applications like save, print, and bold to avoid repetition in each Office application's first chapter, along with coverage of problem solving skills to prepare students to apply what they learn in any situation.

- **New** **Moving Beyond the Basics** introduces advanced skills earlier because students are learning basic skills faster.

- **White Pages/Yellow Pages clearly** distinguish the theory (white pages) from the skills covered in the Hands-On exercises (yellow pages) so students always know what they are supposed to be doing.

- **New** **Objective Mapping** enables students to skip the skills and concepts they know, and quickly find those they don't, by scanning the chapter opener page for the page numbers of the material they need.

- **New** **Pull Quotes** entice students into the theory by highlighting the most interesting points.

- **New** **Conceptual Animations** connect the theory with the skills, by illustrating tough to understand concepts with interactive multimedia.

- **New** **More End of Chapter Exercises** offer instructors more options for assessment. Each chapter has approximately 12–15 exercises ranging from Multiple Choice questions to open-ended projects.

- **New** **More Levels of End of Chapter Exercises,** including new Mid-Level Exercises tell students what to do, but not how to do it, and Capstone Exercises cover all of the skills within each chapter.

- **New** **Mini Cases with Rubrics** are open ended exercises that guide both instructors and students to a solution with a specific rubric for each mini case.

Instructor and Student Resources

Instructor Chapter Reference Cards

A four page color card for every chapter that includes a:

- *Concept Summary* that outlines the KEY objectives to cover in class with tips on where students get stuck as well as how to get them un-stuck. It helps bridge the gap between the instructor and student when discussing more difficult topics.

- *Case Study Lecture Demonstration Document* which provides instructors with a lecture sample based on the chapter opening case that will guide students to critically use the skills covered in the chapter, with examples of other ways the skills can be applied.

The Enhanced Instructor's Resource Center on CD-ROM includes:

- **Additional Capstone Production Tests** allow instructors to assess all the skills in a chapter with a single project.

- **Mini Case Rubrics** in Microsoft® Word format enable instructors to customize the assignment for their class.

- **PowerPoint® Presentations** for each chapter with notes included for online students.

- **Lesson Plans** that provide a detailed blueprint for an instructor to achieve chapter learning objectives and outcomes.

- **Student Data Files**

- **Annotated Solution Files**

- **Complete Test Bank**

- **Test Gen Software with QuizMaster**

TestGen is a test generator program that lets you view and easily edit testbank questions, transfer them to tests, and print in a variety of formats suitable to your teaching situation. The program also offers many options for organizing and displaying testbanks and tests. A random number test generator enables you to create multiple versions of an exam.

QuizMaster, also included in this package, allows students to take tests created with TestGen on a local area network. The QuizMaster Utility built into TestGen lets instructors view student records and print a variety of reports. Building tests is easy with Test-Gen, and exams can be easily uploaded into WebCT, BlackBoard, and CourseCompass.

Prentice Hall's Companion Web Site

www.prenhall.com/exploring offers expanded IT resources and downloadable supplements. This site also includes an online study guide for student self-study.

Online Course Cartridges

Flexible, robust and customizable content is available for all major online course platforms that include everything instructors need in one place.
www.prenhall.com/webct
www.prenhall.com/blackboard
www.coursecompass.com

my**it**lab

my**it**lab for Microsoft Office 2007, is a solution designed by professors that allows you to easily deliver Office courses with defensible assessment and outcomes-based training.

The new *Exploring Office 2007* System will seamlessly integrate online assessment and training with the new my**it**lab for Microsoft Office 2007!

Integrated Assessment and Training

To fully integrate the new my**it**lab into the *Exploring Office 2007* System we built my**it**lab assessment and training directly from the *Exploring* instructional content. No longer is the technology just mapped to your textbook.

This 1:1 content relationship between the *Exploring* text and my**it**lab means that your online assessment and training will work with your textbook to move your students beyond the point and click.

Advanced Reporting

With my**it**lab you will get advanced reporting capabilities including a detailed student click stream. This ability to see exactly what actions your students took on a test, click-by-click, provides you with true defensible grading.

In addition, my**it**lab for Office 2007 will feature. . .

Project-based assessment: Test students on Exploring projects, or break down assignments into individual Office application skills.

Outcomes-based training: Students train on what they don't know without having to relearn skills they already know.

Optimal performance and uptime: Provided by a world-class hosting environment.

Dedicated student and instructor support: Professional tech support is available by phone and email when you need it.

No installation required! my**it**lab runs entirely from the Web.

And much more!

www.prenhall.com/myitlab

Visual Walk-Through

Office Fundamentals Chapter

efficiently covers skills common among all applications like save, print, and bold to avoid repetition in each 1st application chapter.

chapter 1 | Office Fundamentals

Using Word, Excel, Access, and PowerPoint

objectives

After you read this chapter you will be able to:

1. Identify common interface components **(page 4)**.
2. Use Office 2007 Help **(page 10)**.
3. Open a file **(page 18)**.
4. Save a file **(page 21)**.
5. Print a document **(page 24)**.
6. Select text to edit **(page 31)**.
7. Insert text and change to the Overtype mode **(page 32)**.
8. Move and copy text **(page 34)**.
9. Find, replace, and go to text **(page 36)**.
10. Use the Undo and Redo commands **(page 39)**.
11. Use language tools **(page 39)**.
12. Apply font attributes **(page 43)**.
13. Copy formats with the Format Painter **(page 47)**.

Hands-On Exercises

Exercises	Skills Covered
1. IDENTIFYING PROGRAM INTERFACE COMPONENTS AND USING HELP (page 12)	• Use PowerPoint's Office Button, Get Help in a Dialog Box, and Use the Zoom Slider • Use Excel's Ribbon, Get Help from an Enhanced ScreenTip, and Use the Zoom Dialog Box • Search Help in Access • Use Word's Status Bar • Search Help and Print a Help Topic
2. PERFORMING UNIVERSAL TASKS (page 28) Open: chap1_ho2_sample.docx Save as: chap1_ho2_solution.docx	• Open a File and Save it with a Different Name • Use Print Preview and Select Options • Print a Document
3. PERFORMING BASIC TASKS (page 48) Open: chap1_ho3_internet.docx Save as: chap_ho3_internet_solution.docx	• Cut, Copy, Paste, and Undo • Find and Replace Text • Check Spelling • Choose Synonyms and Use Thesaurus • Use the Research Tool • Apply Font Attributes • Use Format Painter

chapter 3 | **Access**

Customize, Analyze,
and Summarize Query Data
Creating and Using Queries to Make Decisions

bjectives

After you read this chapter you will be able to:

1. Understand the order of precedence (page 679).
2. Create a calculated field in a query (page 679).
3. Create expressions with the Expression Builder (page 679).
4. Create and edit Access functions (page 690).
5. Perform date arithmetic (page 694).
6. Create and work with data aggregates (page 704).

Hands-On Exercises

Exercises	Skills Covered
1. CALCULATED QUERY FIELDS (PAGE 683) **Open:** chap3_ho1-3_realestate.accdb **Save:** chap3_ho1-3_realestate_solution.accdb **Back up as:** chap3_ho1_realestate_solution.accdb	• Copy a Database and Start the Query • Select the Fields, Save, and Open the Query • Create a Calculated Field and Run the Query • Verify the Calculated Results • Recover from a Common Error
2. EXPRESSION BUILDER, FUNCTIONS, AND DATE ARITHMETIC (page 695) **Open:** chap3_ho1-3_realestate.accdb (from Exercise 1) **Save:** chap3_ho1-3_realestate_solution.accdb (additional modifications) **Back up as:** chap3_ho2_realestate_solution.accdb	• Create a Select Query • Use the Expression Builder • Create Calculations Using Input Stored in a Different Query or Table • Edit Expressions Using the Expression Builder • Use Functions • Work with Date Arithmetic
3. DATA AGGREGATES (page 707) **Open:** chap3_ho1-3_realestate.accdb (from Exercise 2) **Save:** chap3_ho1-3_realestate_solution.accdb (additional modifications)	• Add a Total Row • Create a Totals Query Based on a Select Query • Add Fields to the Design Grid • Add Grouping Options and Specify Summary Statistics

Access 2007   677

Objective
Mapping
allows students to skip the
skills and concepts they
know and quickly find those
they don't by scanning the
chapter opening page for
the page numbers of the
material they need.

Case Study

begins each chapter to provide an effective overview of what students can accomplish by completing the chapter.

CASE STUDY

West Transylvania College Athletic Department

The athletic department of West Transylvania College has reached a fork in the road. A significant alumni contingent insists that the college upgrade its athletic program from NCAA Division II to Division I. This process will involve adding sports, funding athletic scholarships, expanding staff, and coordinating a variety of fundraising activities.

Tom Hunt, the athletic director, wants to determine if the funding support is available both inside and outside the college to accomplish this goal. You are helping Tom prepare the five-year projected budget based on current budget figures. The plan is to increase revenues at a rate of 10% per year for five years while handling an estimated 8% increase in expenses over the same five-year period. Tom feels that a 10% increase in revenue versus an 8% increase in expenses should make the upgrade viable. Tom wants to examine how increased alumni giving, increases in college fees, and grant monies will increase the revenue flow. The Transylvania College's Athletic Committee and its Alumni Association Board of Directors want Tom to present an analysis of funding and expenses to determine if the move to NCAA Division I is feasible. As Tom's student assistant this year, it is your responsibility to help him with special projects. Tom prepared the basic projected budget spreadsheet and has asked you to finish it for him.

Case Study

Your Assignment

- Read the chapter carefully and pay close attention to mathematical operations, formulas, and functions.
- Open *chap2_case_athletics*, which contains the partially completed, projected budget spreadsheet.
- Study the structure of the worksheet to determine what type of formulas you need to complete the financial calculations. Identify how you would perform calculations if you were using a calculator and make a list of formulas using regular language to determine if the financial goals will be met. As you read the chapter, identify formulas and functions that will help you complete the financial analysis. You will insert formulas in the revenue and expenditures sections for column C. Use appropriate cell references in formulas. Do not enter constant values within a formula; instead enter the 10% and 8% increases in an input area. Use appropriate functions for column totals in both the revenue and expenditures sections. Insert formulas for the Net Operating Margin and Net Margin rows. Copy the formulas.
- Review the spreadsheet and identify weaknesses in the formatting. Use your knowledge of good formatting design to improve the appearance of the spreadsheet so that it will be attractive to the Athletic Committee and the alumni board. You will format cells as currency with 0 decimals and widen columns as needed. Merge and center the title and use an attractive fill color. Emphasize the totals and margin rows with borders. Enter your name and current date. Create a custom footer that includes a page number and your instructor's name. Print the worksheet as displayed and again with cell formulas displayed. Save the workbook as **chap2_case_athletics_solution**.

Key Terms

are called out in the margins of the chapter so students can more effectively study definitions.

Pull Quotes

entice students into the theory by highlighting the most interesting points.

Tables

A *table* is a series of rows and columns that organize data.

A *cell* is the intersection of a row and column in a table.

> The table feature is one of the most powerful in Word and is the basis for an almost limitless variety of documents. It is very easy to create once you understand how a table works.

A *table* is a series of rows and columns that organize data effectively. The rows and columns in a table intersect to form *cells*. The table feature is one of the most powerful in Word and is an easy way to organize a series of data in a columnar list format such as employee names, inventory lists, and e-mail addresses. The Vacation Planner in Figure 3.1, for example, is actually a 4x9 table (4 columns and 9 rows). The completed table looks impressive, but it is very easy to create once you understand how a table works. In addition to the organizational benefits, tables make an excellent alignment tool. For example, you can create tables to organize data such as employee lists with phone numbers and e-mail addresses. The Exploring series uses tables to provide descriptions for various software commands. Although you can align text with tabs, you have more format control when you create a table. (See the Practice Exercises at the end of the chapter for other examples.)

Vacation Planner			
Item	Number of Days	Amount per Day (est)	Total Amount
Airline Ticket			449.00
Amusement Park Tickets	4	50.00	200.00
Hotel	5	120.00	600.00
Meals	6	50.00	300.00
Rental Car	5	30.00	150.00
Souvenirs	5	20.00	100.00
TOTAL EXPECTED EXPENSES			$1799.00

Figure 3.1 The Vacation Planner

In this section, you insert a table in a document. After inserting the table, you can insert or delete columns and rows if you need to change the structure. Furthermore, you learn how to merge and split cells within the table. Finally, you change the row height and column width to accommodate data in the table.

Inserting a Table

You can create a table from the Insert tab. Click Table in the Tables group on the Insert tab to see a gallery of cells from which you select the number of columns and rows you require in the table, or you can choose the Insert Table command below the gallery to display the Insert Table dialog box and enter the table composition you prefer. When you select the table dimension from the gallery or from the Insert Table dialog box, Word creates a table structure with the number of columns and rows you specify. After you define a table, you can enter text, numbers, or graphics in individual cells. Text

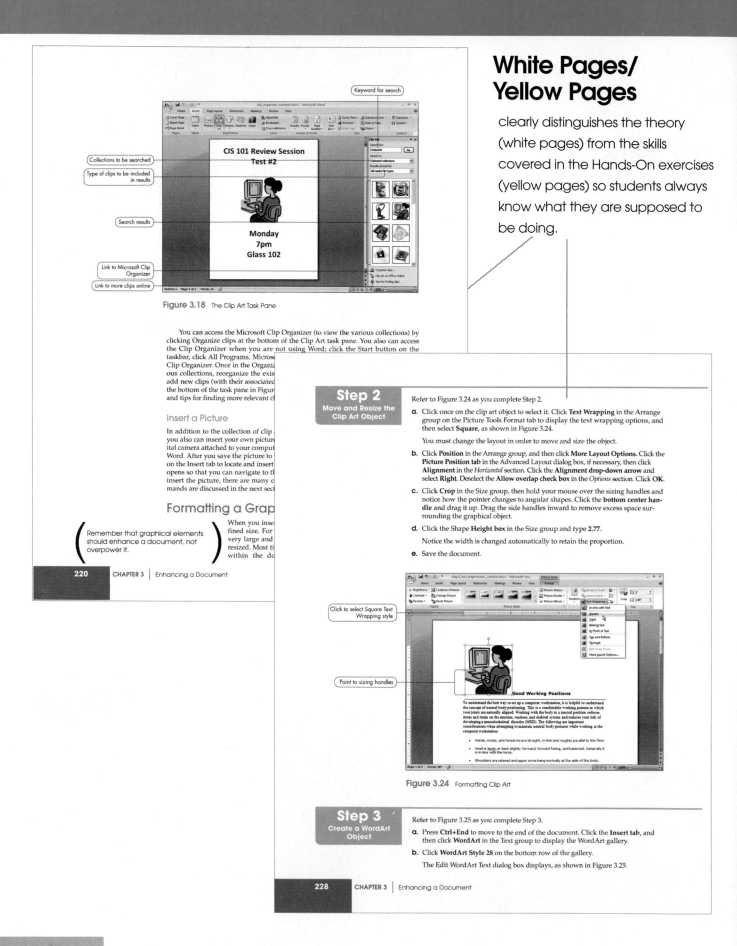

White Pages/ Yellow Pages

clearly distinguishes the theory (white pages) from the skills covered in the Hands-On exercises (yellow pages) so students always know what they are supposed to be doing.

Keyword for search

CIS 101 Review Session
Test #2

Monday
7pm
Glass 102

Collections to be searched
Type of clips to be included in results
Search results
Link to Microsoft Clip Organizer
Link to more clips online

Figure 3.18 The Clip Art Task Pane

You can access the Microsoft Clip Organizer (to view the various collections) by clicking Organize clips at the bottom of the Clip Art task pane. You also can access the Clip Organizer when you are not using Word; click the Start button on the taskbar, click All Programs, Micros... Clip Organizer. Once in the Organiz... ous collections, reorganize the exis... add new clips (with their associated the bottom of the task pane in Figur... and tips for finding more relevant c...

Insert a Picture

In addition to the collection of clip... you also can insert your own pictur... ital camera attached to your compu... Word. After you save the picture to... on the Insert tab to locate and inser... opens so that you can navigate to th... insert the picture, there are many c... mands are discussed in the next sect...

Formatting a Grap...

When you inse...
fined size. For...
Remember that graphical elements should enhance a document, not overpower it.
very large and...
resized. Most ti...
within the do...

220 CHAPTER 3 | Enhancing a Document

Step 2
Move and Resize the Clip Art Object

Refer to Figure 3.24 as you complete Step 2.

a. Click once on the clip art object to select it. Click **Text Wrapping** in the Arrange group on the Picture Tools Format tab to display the text wrapping options, and then select **Square**, as shown in Figure 3.24.

You must change the layout in order to move and size the object.

b. Click **Position** in the Arrange group, and then click **More Layout Options.** Click the **Picture Position tab** in the Advanced Layout dialog box, if necessary, then click **Alignment** in the *Horizontal* section. Click the **Alignment drop-down arrow** and select **Right**. Deselect the **Allow overlap check box** in the *Options* section. Click **OK.**

c. Click **Crop** in the Size group, then hold your mouse over the sizing handles and notice how the pointer changes to angular shapes. Click the **bottom center handle** and drag it up. Drag the side handles inward to remove excess space surrounding the graphical object.

d. Click the Shape **Height box** in the Size group and type **2.77.**

Notice the width is changed automatically to retain the proportion.

e. Save the document.

Click to select Square Text Wrapping style

Point to sizing handles

Good Working Positions

Figure 3.24 Formatting Clip Art

Step 3
Create a WordArt Object

Refer to Figure 3.25 as you complete Step 3.

a. Press **Ctrl+End** to move to the end of the document. Click the **Insert tab**, and then click **WordArt** in the Text group to display the WordArt gallery.

b. Click **WordArt Style 28** on the bottom row of the gallery.

The Edit WordArt Text dialog box displays, as shown in Figure 3.25.

228 CHAPTER 3 | Enhancing a Document

Summary

1. **Create a presentation using a template.** Using a template saves you a great deal of time and enables you to create a more professional presentation. Templates incorporate a theme, a layout, and content that can be modified. You can use templates that are installed when Microsoft Office is installed, or you can download templates from Microsoft Office Online. Microsoft is constantly adding templates to the online site for your use.

2. **Modify a template.** In addition to changing the content of a template, you can modify the structure and design. The structure is modified by changing the layout of a slide. To change the layout, drag placeholders to new locations or resize placeholders. You can even add placeholders so that elements such as logos can be included.

3. **Create a presentation in Outline view.** When you use a storyboard to determine your content, you create a basic outline. Then you can enter your presentation in Outline view, which enables you to concentrate on the content of the presentation. Using Outline view keeps you from getting buried in design issues at the cost of your content. It also saves you time because you can enter the information without having to move from placeholder to placeholder.

4. **Modify an outline structure.** Because the Outline view gives you a global view of the presentation, it helps you see the underlying structure of the presentation. You are able to see where content needs to be strengthened, or where the flow of information needs to be revised. If you find a slide with content that would be presented better in another location in the slide show, you can use the Collapse and Expand features to easily move it. By collapsing the slide content, you can drag it to a new location and then expand it. To move individual bullet points, cut and paste the bullet point or drag-and-drop it.

5. **Print an outline.** When you present, using the outline version of your slide show as a reference is a boon. No matter how well you know your information, it is easy to forget to present some information when facing an audience. While you would print speaker's notes if you have many details, you can print the outline as a quick reference. The outline can be printed in either the collapsed or the expanded form, giving you far fewer pages to shuffle in front of an audience than printing speaker's notes would.

6. **Import an outline.** You do not need to re-enter information from an outline created in Microsoft Word or another word processor. You can use the Open feature to import any outline that has been saved in a format that PowerPoint can read. In addition to a Word outline, you can use the common generic formats Rich Text Format and Plain Text Format.

7. **Add existing content to a presentation.** After you spend time creating the slides in a slide show, you may find that slides in the slide show would be appropriate in another show at a later date. Any slide you create can be reused in another presentation, thereby saving you considerable time and effort. You simply open the Reuse Slides pane, locate the slide show with the slide you need, and then click on the thumbnail of the slide to insert a copy of it in the new slide show.

8. **Examine slide show design principles.** With a basic understanding of slide show design principles you can create presentations that reflect your personality in a professional way. The goal of applying these principles is to create a slide show that focuses the audience on the message of the slide without being distracted by clutter or unreadable text.

9. **Apply and modify a design theme.** PowerPoint provides you with themes to help you create a clean, professional look for your presentation. Once a theme is applied you can modify the theme by changing the color scheme, the font scheme, the effects scheme, or the background style.

10. **Insert a header or footer.** Identifying information can be included in a header or footer. You may, for example, wish to include the group to whom you are presenting, or the location of the presentation, or a copyright notation for original work. You can apply footers to slides, handouts, and Notes pages. Headers may be applied to handouts and Notes pages.

Summary

links directly back to the objectives so students can more effectively study and locate the concepts that they need to focus on.

More End-of-Chapter Exercises with New Levels of Assessment

offer instructors more options for assessment. Each chapter has approximately 12-15 projects per chapter ranging from multiple choice to open-ended projects.

Practice Exercises

reinforce skills learned in the chapter with specific directions on what to do and how to do it.

New Mid-Level Exercises

assess the skills learned in the chapter by directing the students on what to do but not how to do it.

New Capstone Exercises

cover all of the skills with in each chapter without telling students how to perform the skills.

Mini Cases with Rubrics

are open ended exercises that guide both instructors and students to a solution with a specific rubric for each Mini Case.

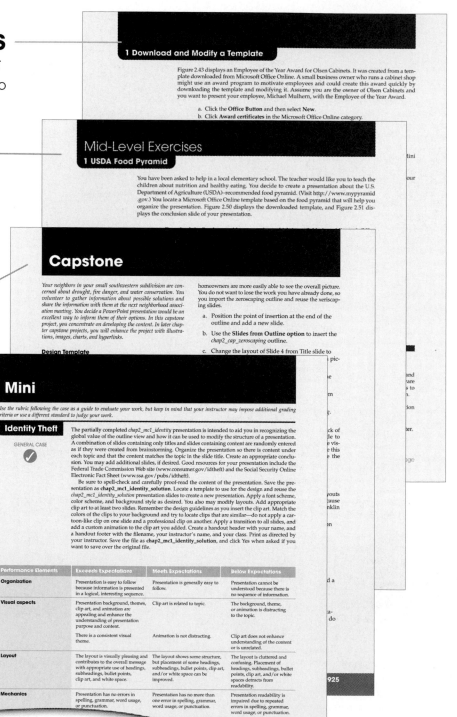

Using Word, Excel, Access, and PowerPoint

bjectives

After you read this chapter, you will be able to:

1. Identify common interface components **(page 4)**.

2. Use Office 2007 Help **(page 10)**.

3. Open a file **(page 18)**.

4. Save a file **(page 21)**.

5. Print a document **(page 24)**.

6. Select text to edit **(page 31)**.

7. Insert text and change to the Overtype mode **(page 32)**.

8. Move and copy text **(page 34)**.

9. Find, replace, and go to text **(page 36)**.

10. Use the Undo and Redo commands **(page 39)**.

11. Use language tools **(page 39)**.

12. Apply font attributes **(page 43)**.

13. Copy formats with the Format Painter **(page 47)**.

Hands-On Exercises

Exercises	Skills Covered
1. IDENTIFYING PROGRAM INTERFACE COMPONENTS AND USING HELP (page 12)	• Use PowerPoint's Office Button, Get Help in a Dialog Box, and Use the Zoom Slider • Use Excel's Ribbon, Get Help from an Enhanced ScreenTip, and Use the Zoom Dialog Box • Search Help in Access • Use Word's Status Bar • Search Help and Print a Help Topic
2. PERFORMING UNIVERSAL TASKS (page 28) **Open:** chap1_ho2_sample.docx **Save as:** chap1_ho2_solution.docx	• Open a File and Save It with a Different Name • Use Print Preview and Select Options • Print a Document
3. PERFORMING BASIC TASKS (page 48) **Open:** chap1_ho3_internet_docx **Save as:** chap_ho3_internet_solution.docx	• Cut, Copy, Paste, and Undo • Find and Replace Text • Check Spelling • Choose Synonyms and Use Thesaurus • Use the Research Tool • Apply Font Attributes • Use Format Painter

CASE STUDY
Color Theory Design

Natalie Trevino's first job after finishing her interior design degree is with Color Theory Design of San Diego. Her new supervisor has asked her to review a letter written to an important client and to make any changes or corrections she thinks will improve it. Even though Natalie has used word processing software in the past, she is unfamiliar with Microsoft Office 2007. She needs to get up to speed with Word 2007 so that she can open the letter, edit the content, format the appearance, re-save the file, and print the client letter. Natalie wants to suc-

cessfully complete this important first task, plus she wants to become familiar with all of Office 2007 because she realizes that her new employer, CTD, makes extensive use of all the Office products.

In addition, Natalie needs to improve the appearance of an Excel workbook by applying font attributes, correcting spelling errors, changing the zoom magnification, and printing the worksheet. Finally, Natalie needs to modify a short PowerPoint presentation that features supplemental design information for CTD's important client.

Your Assignment

- Read the chapter and open the existing client letter, *chap1_case_design*.
- Edit the letter by inserting and overtyping text and moving existing text to improve the letter's readability.
- Find and replace text that you want to update.
- Check the spelling and improve the vocabulary by using the thesaurus.
- Modify the letter's appearance by applying font attributes.
- Save the file as **chap1_case_design_solution**, print preview, and print a copy of the letter.
- Open the *chap1_case_bid* workbook in Excel, apply bold and blue font color to the column headings, spell-check the worksheet, change the zoom to 125%, print preview, and print the workbook. Save the workbook as **chap1_case_bid_solution**.
- Open the *chap1_case_design* presentation in PowerPoint, spell-check the presentation, format text, and save it as **chap1_case_design_solution**.

Microsoft Office 2007 Software

(Which software application should you choose? You have to start with an analysis of the output required.)

Microsoft Office 2007 is composed of several software applications, of which the primary components are Word, Excel, PowerPoint, and Access. These programs are powerful tools that can be used to increase productivity in creating, editing, saving, and printing files. Each program is a specialized and sophisticated program, so it is necessary to use the correct one to successfully complete a task, much like using the correct tool in the physical world. For example, you use a hammer, not a screwdriver, to pound a nail into the wall. Using the correct tool gets the job done correctly and efficiently the first time; using the wrong tool may require redoing the task, thus wasting time. Likewise, you should use the most appropriate software application to create and work with computer data.

Choosing the appropriate application to use in a situation seems easy to the beginner. If you need to create a letter, you type the letter in Word. However, as situations increase in complexity, so does the need to think through using each application. For example, you can create an address book of names and addresses in Word to create form letters; you can create an address list in Excel and then use spreadsheet commands to manipulate the data; further, you can store addresses in an Access database table and then use database capabilities to manipulate the data. Which software application should you choose? You have to start with an analysis of the output required. If you only want a form letter as the final product, then you might use Word; however, if you want to spot customer trends with the data and provide detailed reports, you would use Access. Table 1.1 describes the main characteristics of the four primary programs in Microsoft Office 2007 to help you decide which program to use for particular tasks.

Table 1.1 Office Products

Office 2007 Product	Application Characteristics
Word 2007	*Word processing software* is used with text to create, edit, and format documents such as letters, memos, reports, brochures, resumes, and flyers.
Excel 2007	*Spreadsheet software* is used to store quantitative data and to perform accurate and rapid calculations with results ranging from simple budgets to financial analyses and statistical analyses.
PowerPoint 2007	*Presentation graphics software* is used to create slide shows for presentation by a speaker, to be published as part of a Web site, or to run as a stand-alone application on a computer kiosk.
Access 2007	*Relational database software* is used to store data and convert it into information. Database software is used primarily for decision-making by businesses that compile data from multiple records stored in tables to produce informative reports.

Word processing software is used primarily with text to create, edit, and format documents.

Spreadsheet software is used primarily with numbers to create worksheets.

Presentation graphics software is used primarily to create electronic slide shows.

Relational database software is used to store data and convert it into information.

In this section, you explore the common interface among the programs. You learn the names of the interface elements. In addition, you learn how to use Help to get assistance in using the software.

Identifying Common Interface Components

A **user interface** is the meeting point between computer software and the person using it.

A **user interface** is the meeting point between computer software and the person using it and provides the means for a person to communicate with a software program. Word, Excel, PowerPoint, and Access share the overall Microsoft Office 2007 interface. This interface is made up of three main sections of the screen display shown in Figure 1.1.

Office Button, Quick Access Toolbar, and title bar

Ribbon

Status bar

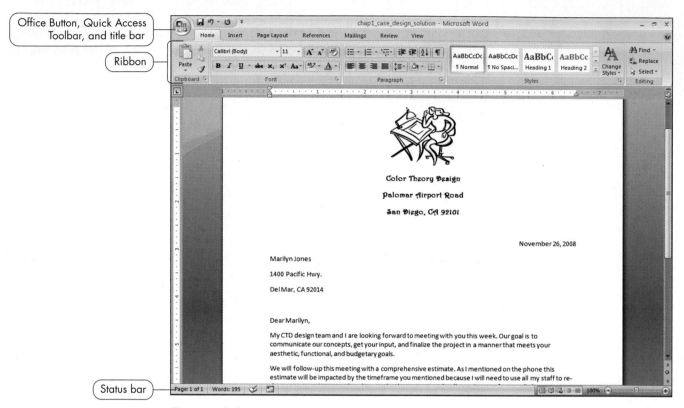

Figure 1.1 Office 2007 Interface

Use the Office Button and Quick Access Toolbar

The first section of the Office 2007 interface contains three distinct items: the Microsoft Office Button (referred to as Office Button in the Exploring series), Quick Access Toolbar, and the title bar. These three items are located at the top of the interface for quick access and reference. The following paragraphs explain each item.

Click the **Office Button** to display the Office menu.

The **Office menu** contains commands that work with an entire file or with the program.

The **Office Button** is an icon that, when clicked, displays the **Office menu**, a list of commands that you can perform on the entire file or for the specific Office program. For example, when you want to perform a task that involves the entire document, such as saving, printing, or sharing a file with others, you use the commands on the Office menu. You also use the Office menu commands to work with the entire program, such as customizing program settings or exiting from the program. Some commands on the Office menu perform a default action when you click them, such as Save—the file open in the active window is saved. However, other commands open a submenu when you point to or click the command. Figure 1.2 displays the Office menu in Access 2007.

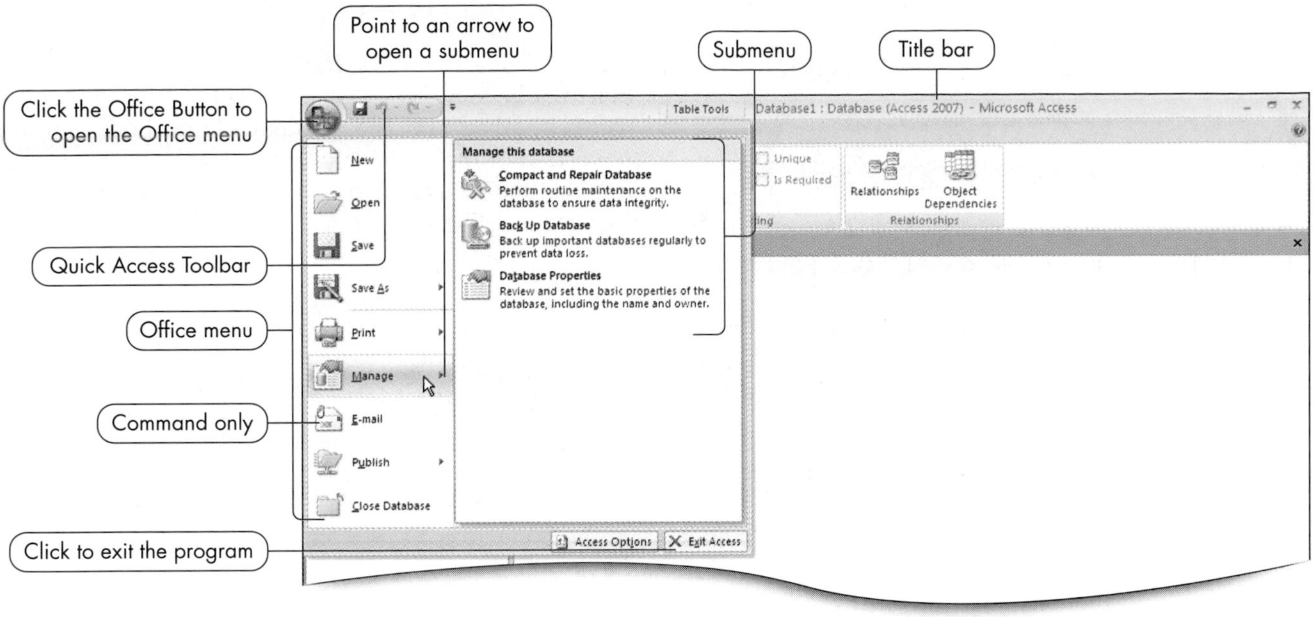

Figure 1.2 Access Office Menu

TIP Displaying the Office Menu from the Keyboard

If you prefer to use a keyboard shortcut to display the Office menu instead of clicking the Office Button, press Alt+F.

The ***Quick Access Toolbar*** contains buttons for frequently used commands.

The second item at the top of the window is the ***Quick Access Toolbar***, which contains buttons for frequently used commands, such as saving a file or undoing an action. This toolbar keeps buttons for common tasks on the screen at all times, enabling you to be more productive in using these frequently used commands.

TIP Customizing the Quick Access Toolbar

As you become more familiar with Microsoft Office 2007, you might find that you need quick access to additional commands, such as Print Preview or Spelling & Grammar. You can easily customize the Quick Access Toolbar by clicking the Customize Quick Access Toolbar drop-down arrow on the right end of the toolbar and adding command buttons from the list that displays. You also can customize the toolbar by changing where it displays. If you want it closer to the document window, you can move the toolbar below the Ribbon.

A ***title bar*** displays the program name and file name at the top of a window.

The third item at the top of the screen is the ***title bar***, which displays the name of the open program and the file name at the top of a window. For example, in Figure 1.1, *chap1_case_design_solution* is the name of a document, and *Microsoft Word* is the name of the program. In Figure 1.2, *Database1* is the name of the file, and *Microsoft Access* is the name of the program.

The **Ribbon** is a large strip of visual commands that enables you to perform tasks.

> The Ribbon is the command center of the Microsoft Office 2007 interface, providing access to the functionality of the programs.

Familiarize Yourself with the Ribbon

The second section of the Office 2007 interface is the **Ribbon**, a large strip of visual commands that displays across the screen below the Office Button, Quick Access Toolbar, and the title bar. The Ribbon is the most important section of the interface: It is the command center of the Microsoft Office 2007 interface, providing access to the functionality of the programs (see Figure 1.3).

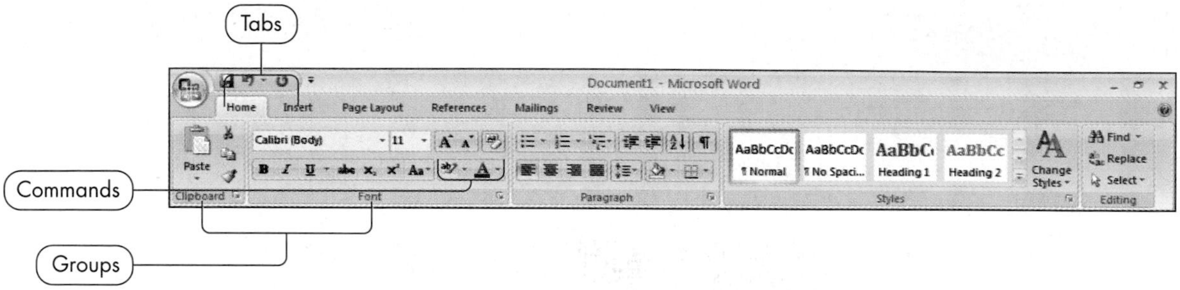

Figure 1.3 The Ribbon

The Ribbon has three main components: tabs, groups, and commands. The following list describes each component.

Tabs, which look like folder tabs, divide the Ribbon into task-oriented categories.

- **Tabs**, which look like folder tabs, divide the Ribbon into task-oriented sections. For example, the Ribbon in Word contains these tabs: Home, Insert, Page Layout, Reference, Mailings, Review, and View. When you click the Home tab, you see a set of core commands for that program. When you click the Insert tab, you see a set of commands that enable you to insert objects, such as tables, clip art, headers, page numbers, etc.

Groups organize similar commands together within each tab.

- **Groups** organize related commands together on each tab. For example, the Home tab in Word contains these groups: Clipboard, Font, Paragraph, Styles, and Editing. These groups help organize related commands together so that you can find them easily. For example, the Font group contains font-related commands, such as Font, Font Size, Bold, Italic, Underline, Highlighter, and Font Color.

A **command** is a visual icon in each group that you click to perform a task.

- **Commands** are specific tasks performed. Commands appear as visual icons or buttons within the groups on the Ribbon. The icons are designed to provide a visual clue of the purpose of the command. For example, the Bold command looks like a bolded B in the Font group on the Home tab. You simply click the desired command to perform the respective task.

The Ribbon has the same basic design—tabs, groups, and commands—across all Microsoft Office 2007 applications. When you first start using an Office 2007 application, you use the Home tab most often. The groups of commands on the Home tab are designed to get you started using the software. For example, the Home tab contains commands to help you create, edit, and format a document in Word, a worksheet in Excel, and a presentation in PowerPoint. In Access, the Home tab contains groups of commands to insert, delete, and edit records in a database table. While three of the four applications contain an Insert tab, the specific groups and commands differ by application. Regardless of the application, however, the Insert tab contains commands to *insert something*, whether it is a page number in Word, a column chart in Excel, or a shape in PowerPoint. One of the best ways to develop an understanding of the Ribbon is to study its structure in each application. As you explore each program, you will notice the similarities in how commands are grouped on tabs, and you will notice the differences specific to each application.

The Ribbon provides an extensive sets of commands that you use when creating and editing documents, worksheets, slides, tables, or other items. Figure 1.4 points out other important components of the Ribbon.

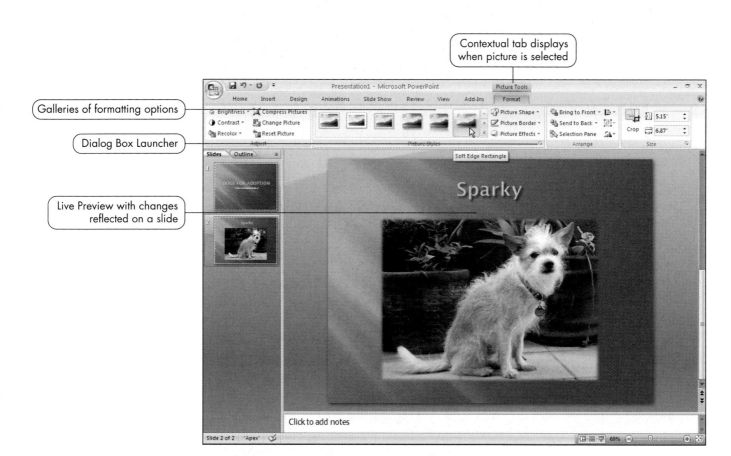

Figure 1.4 PowerPoint with Ribbon

A ***dialog box*** is a window that provides options related to a group of commands.

A ***Dialog Box Launcher*** is a small icon that, when clicked, opens a related dialog box.

A ***gallery*** is a set of options that appears as thumbnail graphics.

Live Preview provides a preview of the results for gallery options.

Figure 1.4 shows examples of four other components of the Ribbon. These components include a Dialog Box Launcher, a gallery, Live Preview, and a contextual tab. The following list describes each component:

- A ***Dialog Box Launcher*** is a small icon located on the right side of some group names that you click to open a related ***dialog box***, which is a window that provides options related to a group of commands.

- A ***gallery*** is a set of options that appear as thumbnail graphics that visually represent the option results. For example, if you create a chart in Excel, a gallery of chart formatting options provides numerous choices for formatting the chart.

- ***Live Preview*** works with the galleries, providing a preview of the results of formatting in the document. As you move your mouse pointer over the gallery thumbnails, you see how each formatting option affects the selected item in your document, worksheet, or presentation. This feature increases productivity because you see the results immediately. If you do not like the results, keep moving the mouse pointer over other gallery options until you find a result you like.

A *contextual tab* is a tab that provides specialized commands that display only when the object they affect is selected.

• A *contextual tab* provides specialized commands that display only when the object they affect is selected. For example, if you insert a picture on a slide, PowerPoint displays a contextual tab on the Ribbon with commands specifically related to the selected image. When you click outside the picture to deselect it, the contextual tab disappears.

A *Key Tip* is the letter or number that displays over each feature on the Ribbon and Quick Access Toolbar and is the keyboard equivalent that you press.

TIP Using Keyboard Shortcuts

Many people who have used previous Office products like to use the keyboard to initiate commands. Microsoft Office 2007 makes it possible for you to continue to use keyboard shortcuts for commands on the Ribbon. Simply press Alt on the keyboard to display the Ribbon and Quick Access Toolbar with shortcuts called Key Tips. A *Key Tip* is the letter or number that displays over each feature on the Ribbon or Quick Access Toolbar and is the keyboard equivalent that you press. Notice the Key Tips that display in Figure 1.5 as a result of pressing Alt on the keyboard. Other keyboard shortcuts, such as Ctrl+C to copy text, remain the same from previous versions of Microsoft Office.

Press the letter on the keyboard to initiate a command

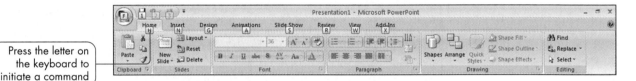

Figure 1.5 Key Tips Displayed for Ribbon and Quick Access Toolbar

Use the Status Bar

The *status bar* displays below the document and provides information about the open file and buttons for quick access.

The third major section of the Office 2007 user interface is the status bar. The *status bar* displays at the bottom of the program window and contains information about the open file and tools for quick access. The status bar contains details for the file in the specific application. For example, the Word status bar shows the current page, total number of pages, total words in the document, and proofreading status. The PowerPoint status bar shows the slide number, total slides in the presentation, and the applied theme. The Excel status bar provides general instructions and displays the average, count, and sum of values for selected cells. In each program, the status bar also includes View commands from the View tab for quick access. You can use the View commands to change the way the document, worksheet, or presentation displays onscreen. Table 1.2 describes the main characteristics of each Word 2007 view.

Table 1.2 Word Document Views

View Option	Characteristics
Print Layout	Displays the document as it will appear when printed.
Full Screen Reading	Displays the document on the entire screen to make reading long documents easier. To remove Full Screen Reading, press the Esc key on the keyboard.
Web Page	Displays the document as it would look as a Web page.
Outline	Displays the document as an outline.
Draft	Displays the document for quick editing without additional elements such as headers or footers.

The **Zoom slider** enables you to increase or decrease the magnification of the file onscreen.

The **Zoom slider**, located on the right edge of the status bar, enables you to drag the slide control to change the magnification of the current document, worksheet, or presentation. You can change the display to zoom in on the file to get a close up view, or you can zoom out to get an overview of the file. To use the Zoom slider, click and drag the slider control to the right to increase the zoom or to the left to decrease the zoom. If you want to set a specific zoom, such as 78%, you can type the precise value in the Zoom dialog box when you click Zoom on the View tab. Figure 1.6 shows the Zoom dialog box and the elements on Word's status bar. The Zoom dialog box in Excel and PowerPoint looks similar to the Word Zoom dialog box, but it contains fewer options in the other programs.

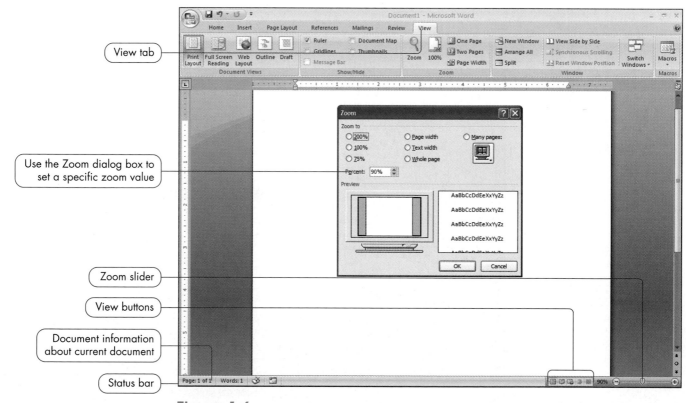

Figure 1.6 View Tab, Zoom Dialog Box, and the Status Bar in Word

Using Office 2007 Help

(Help is always available when you use any Office 2007 program.)

Have you ever started a project such as assembling an entertainment center and had to abandon it because you had no way to get help when you got stuck? Microsoft Office includes features that keep this type of scenario from happening when you use Word, Excel, Access, or PowerPoint. In fact, several methods are available to locate help when you need assistance performing tasks. Help is always available when you use any Office 2007 program. Help files reside on your computer when you install Microsoft Office, and Microsoft provides additional help files on its Web site. If you link to Microsoft Office Online, you not only have access to help files for all applications, you also have access to up-to-date products, files, and graphics to help you complete projects.

Use Office 2007 Help

To access Help, press F1 on the keyboard or click the Help button on the right edge of the Ribbon shown in Figure 1.7. If you know the topic you want help with, such as printing, you can type the key term in the Search box to display help files on that topic. Help also displays general topics in the lower part of the Help window that are links to further information. To display a table of contents for the Help files, click the Show Table of Contents button, and after locating the desired help topic, you can print the information for future reference by clicking the Print button. Figure 1.7 shows these elements in Excel Help.

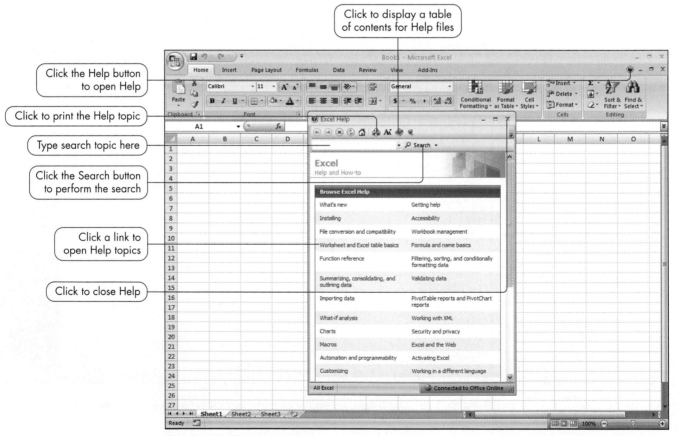

Figure 1.7 Excel Help

Use Enhanced ScreenTips

An *Enhanced ScreenTip* displays the name and brief description of a command when you rest the pointer on a command.

Another method for getting help is to use the Office 2007 Enhanced ScreenTips. An *Enhanced ScreenTip* displays when you rest the mouse pointer on a command. Notice in Figure 1.8 that the Enhanced ScreenTip provides the command name, a brief description of the command, and a link for additional help. To get help on the specific command, keep the pointer resting on the command and press F1 if the Enhanced ScreenTip displays a Help icon. The advantage of this method is that you do not have to find the correct information yourself because the Enhanced ScreenTip help is context sensitive.

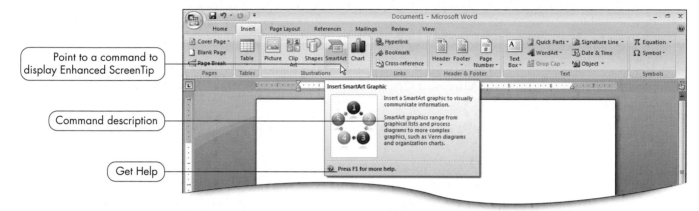

Figure 1.8 Enhanced ScreenTip

Get Help with Dialog Boxes

As you work within a dialog box, you might need help with some of the numerous options contained in that dialog box, but you do not want to close the dialog box to get assistance. For example, if you open the Insert Picture dialog box and want help with inserting files, click the Help button located on the title bar of the dialog box to display specific help for the dialog box. Figure 1.9 shows the Insert Picture dialog box with Help displayed.

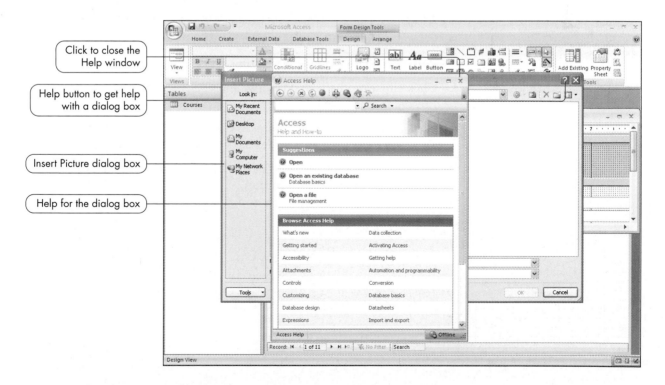

Figure 1.9 Help with Dialog Boxes

Hands-On Exercises

1 | Identifying Program Interface Components and Using Help

Skills covered: 1. Use PowerPoint's Office Button, Get Help in a Dialog Box, and Use the Zoom Slider **2.** Use Excel's Ribbon, Get Help from an Enhanced ScreenTip, and Use the Zoom Dialog Box **3.** Search Help in Access **4.** Use Word's Status Bar **5.** Search Help and Print a Help Topic

Step 1 **Use PowerPoint's Office Button, Get Help in a Dialog Box, and Use the Zoom Slider**	Refer to Figure 1.10 as you complete Step 1. **a.** Click **Start** to display the Start menu. Click (or point to) **All Programs**, click **Microsoft Office**, then click **Microsoft Office PowerPoint 2007** to start the program. **b.** Point to and rest the mouse on the Office Button, and then do the same to the Quick Access Toolbar. As you rest the mouse pointer on each object, you see an Enhanced ScreenTip for that object. **TROUBLESHOOTING:** If you do not see the Enhanced ScreenTip, keep the mouse pointer on the object a little longer. **c.** Click the **Office Button** and slowly move your mouse down the list of menu options, pointing to the arrow after any command name that has one. The Office menu displays, and as you move the mouse down the list, submenus display for menu options that have an arrow. **d.** Select **New**. The New Presentation dialog box displays. Depending on how Microsoft Office 2007 was installed, your screen may vary. If Microsoft Office 2007 was fully installed, you should see a thumbnail to create a Blank Presentation, and you may see additional thumbnails in the *Recently Used Templates* section of the dialog box. **e.** Click the **Help button** on the title bar of the New Presentation dialog box. PowerPoint Help displays the topic *Create a new file from a template*. **f.** Click **Close** on the Help Window and click the **Cancel** button in the New Presentation dialog box. **g.** Click and drag the **Zoom slider** to the right to increase the magnification. Then click and drag the **Zoom slider** back to the center point for a 100% zoom. **h.** To exit PowerPoint, click the **Office Button** to display the Office menu, and then click the **Exit PowerPoint button**.

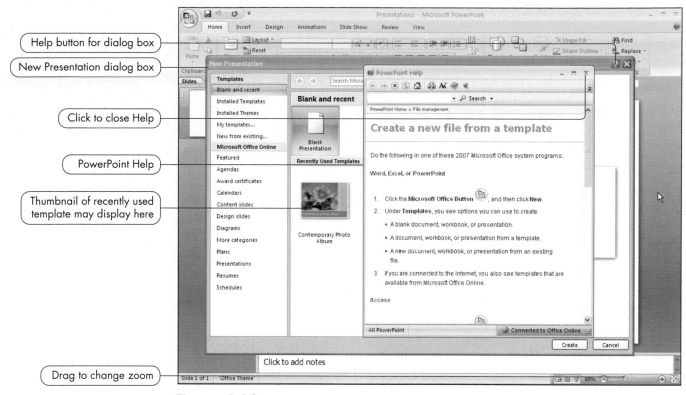

Help button for dialog box

New Presentation dialog box

Click to close Help

PowerPoint Help

Thumbnail of recently used template may display here

Drag to change zoom

Figure 1.10 PowerPoint Help for New Presentations Dialog Box

Step 2
Use Excel's Ribbon, Get Help from an Enhanced ScreenTip, and Use the Zoom Dialog Box

Refer to Figure 1.11 as you complete Step 2.

a. Click **Start** to display the Start menu. Click (or point to) **All Programs**, click **Microsoft Office**, then click **Microsoft Office Excel 2007** to open the program.

b. Click the **Insert tab** on the Ribbon.

The Insert tab contains groups of commands for inserting objects, such as tables, illustrations, charts, links, and text.

c. Rest the mouse on **Hyperlink** in the Links group on the Insert tab.

The Enhanced ScreenTip for Hyperlinks displays. Notice the Enhanced ScreenTip contains a Help icon.

d. Press **F1** on the keyboard.

Excel Help displays the *Create or remove a hyperlink* Help topic.

TROUBLESHOOTING: If you are not connected to the Internet, you might not see the context-sensitive help.

e. Click the **Close button** on the Help window.

f. Click the **View tab** on the Ribbon and click **Zoom** in the Zoom group.

The Zoom dialog box appears so that you can change the zoom percentage.

g. Click the **200%** option and click **OK**.

The worksheet is now magnified to 200% of its regular size.

h. Click **Zoom** in the Zoom group on the View tab, click the **100%** option, and click **OK**.

The worksheet is now restored to 100%.

i. To exit Excel, click the **Office Button** to display the Office menu, and then click the **Exit Excel button**.

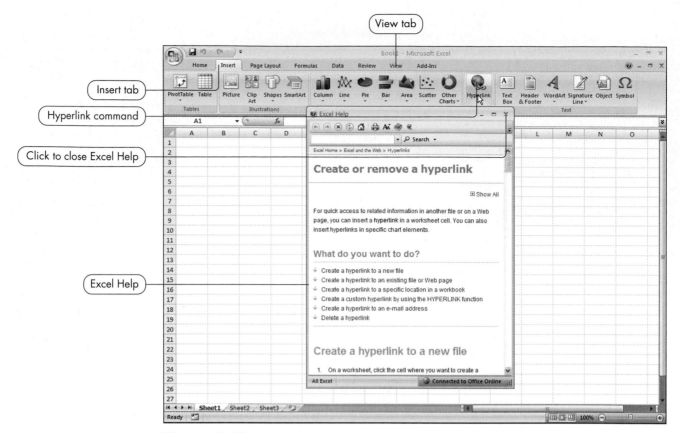

Figure 1.11 Excel Ribbon with Help

Refer to Figure 1.12 as you complete Step 3.

a. Click **Start** to display the Start menu. Click (or point to) **All Programs**, click **Microsoft Office**, then click **Microsoft Office Access 2007** to start the program.

Access opens and displays the Getting Started with Microsoft Access screen.

TROUBLESHOOTING: If you are not familiar with Access, just use the opening screen that displays and continue with the exercise.

b. Press **F1** on the keyboard.

Access Help displays.

c. Type **table** in the Search box in the Access Help window.

d. Click the **Search** button.

Access displays help topics.

e. Click the topic **Create tables in a database**.

The help topic displays.

f. Click the **Close** button on the Access Help window.

Access Help closes.

g. To exit Access, click the **Office Button** to display the Office menu, and then click the **Exit Access button**.

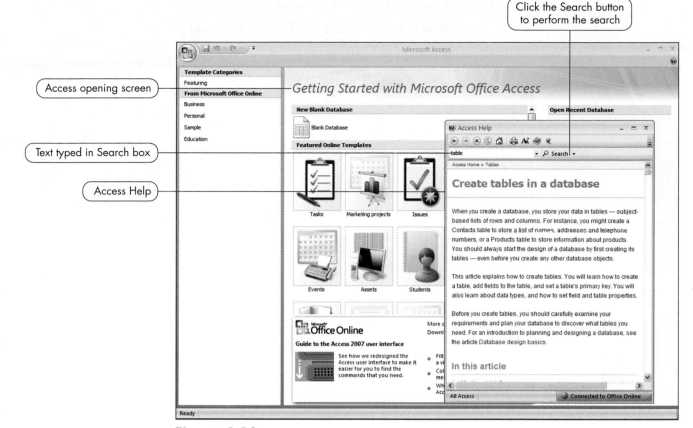

Figure 1.12 Access Help

Refer to Figure 1.13 as you complete Step 4.

a. Click **Start** to display the Start menu. Click (or point to) **All Programs**, click **Microsoft Office**, then click **Microsoft Office Word 2007** to start the program.

Word opens with a blank document ready for you to start typing.

b. Type your first name.

Your first name displays in the document window.

c. Point your mouse to the **Zoom slider** on the status bar.

d. Click and drag the **Zoom slider** to the right to increase the magnification.

The document with your first name increases in size onscreen.

e. Click and drag the slider control to the left to decrease the magnification.

The document with your first name decreases in size.

f. Click and drag the **Zoom slider** back to the center.

The document returns to 100% magnification.

g. Slowly point the mouse to the buttons on the status bar.

A ScreenTip displays the names of the buttons.

h. Click the **Full Screen Reading button** on the status bar.

The screen display changes to Full Screen Reading view.

i. Press **Esc** on the keyboard to return the display to Print Layout view.

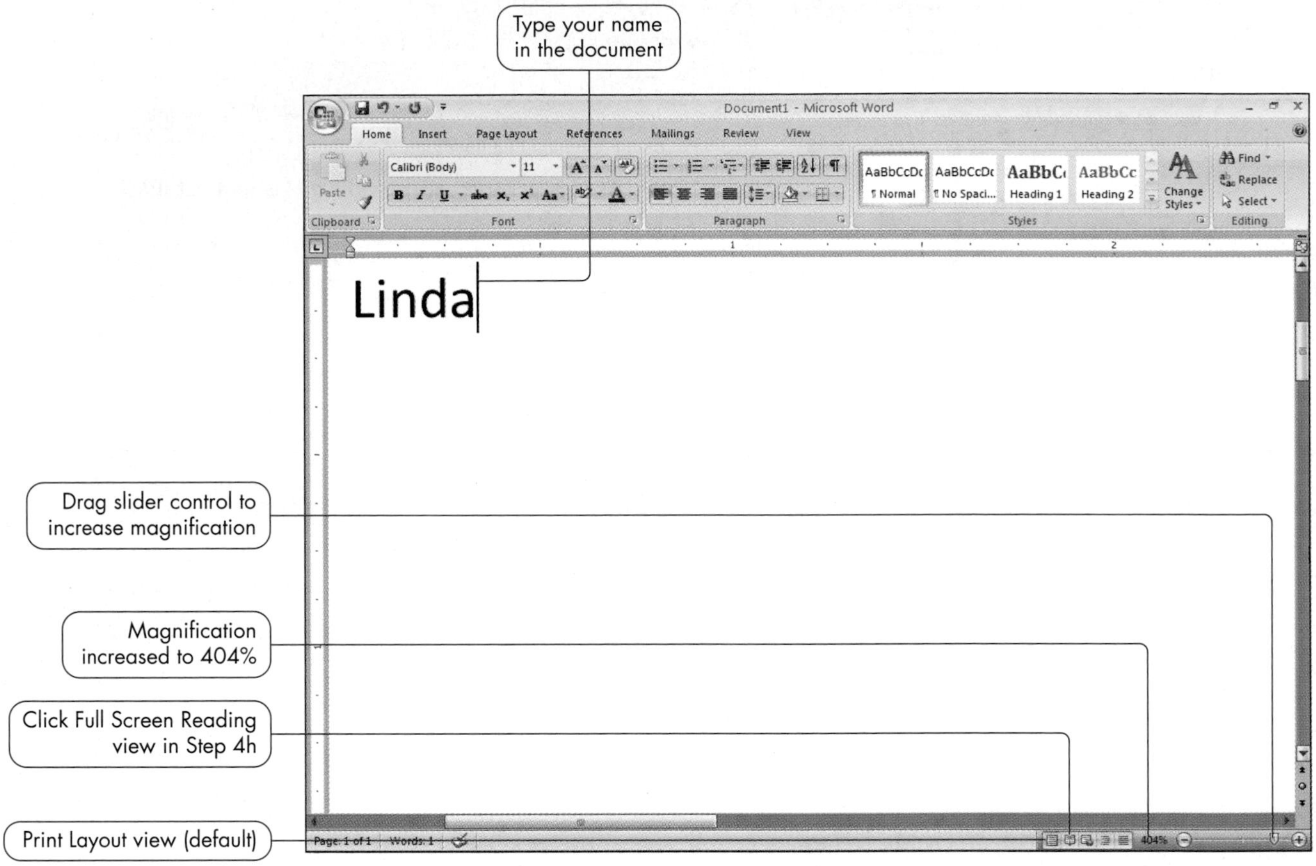

Figure 1.13 The Word Status Bar

Step 5

Search Help and Print a Help Topic

Refer to Figure 1.14 as you complete Step 5.

a. With Word open on the screen, press **F1** on the keyboard.

Word Help displays.

b. Type **zoom** in the Search box in the Word Help window.

c. Click the **Search** button.

Word Help displays related topics.

d. Click the topic **Zoom in or out of a document**.

The help topic displays.

TROUBLESHOOTING: If you do not have a printer that is ready to print, skip Step 5e and continue with the exercise.

e. Turn on the attached. printer, be sure it has paper, and then click the Word Help **Print** button.

The Help topic prints on the attached printer.

f. Click the **Show Table of Contents** button on the Word Help toolbar.

The Table of Contents pane displays on the left side of the Word Help dialog box so that you can click popular Help topics, such as *What's new*. You can click a closed book icon to see specific topics to click for additional information, and you can click an open book icon to close the main Help topic.

g. Click the **Close** button on Word Help.

Word Help closes.

h. To exit Word, click the **Office Button** to display the Office menu, and then click the **Exit Word button**.

A warning appears stating that you have not saved changes to your document.

i. Click **No** in the Word warning box.

You exit Word without saving the document.

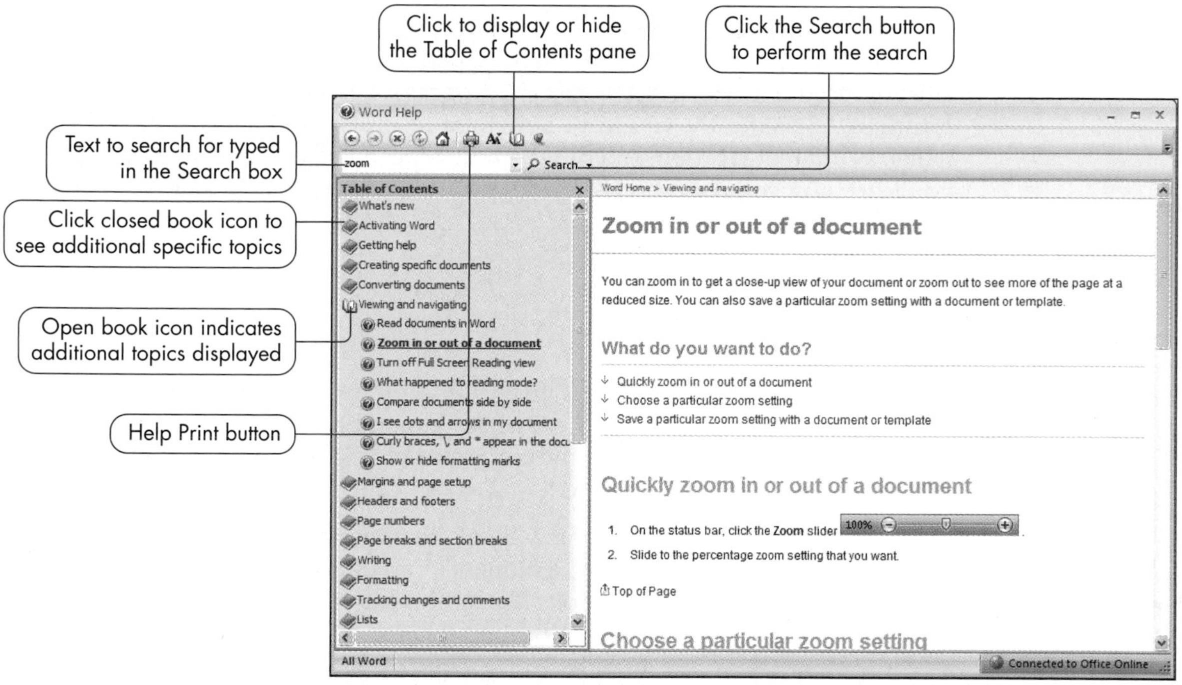

Figure 1.14 Word Help

Universal Tasks

Today, storing large amounts of information on a computer is taken for granted, but in reality, computers would not have become very important if you could not save and re-use the files you create.

One of the most useful and important aspects of using computers is the ability to save and re-use information. For example, you can store letters, reports, budgets, presentations, and databases as files to reopen and use at some time in the future. Today, storing large amounts of information on a computer is taken for granted, but in reality, computers would not have become very important if you could not save and re-use the files you create.

Three fundamental tasks are so important for productivity that they are considered universal to most every computer program, including Office 2007:

- opening files that have been saved
- saving files you create
- printing files

In this section, you open a file within an Office 2007 program. Specifically, you learn how to open a file from within the Open dialog box and how to open a file from a list of recently used files in a specific program. You also save files to keep them for future use. Specifically, you learn how to save a file with the same name, a different name, a different location, or a different file type. Finally, you print a file. Specifically, you learn how to preview a file before printing it and select print options within the Print dialog box.

Opening a File

When you start any program in Office 2007, you need to start creating a new file or open an existing one. You use the Open command to retrieve a file saved on a storage device and place it in the random access memory (RAM) of your computer so you can work on it. For example:

- When you start Word 2007, a new blank document named Document1 opens. You can either start typing in Document1, or you can open an existing document. The *insertion point*, which looks like a blinking vertical line, displays in the document designating the current location where text you type displays.

The *insertion point* is the blinking vertical line in the document, cell, slide show, or database table designating the current location where text you type displays.

- When you start PowerPoint 2007, a new blank presentation named Presentation1 opens. You can either start creating a new slide for the blank presentation, or you can open an existing presentation.

- When you start Excel 2007, a new blank workbook named Book1 opens. You can either start inputting labels and values into Book1, or you can open an existing workbook.

- When you start Access 2007—unlike Word, PowerPoint, and Excel—a new blank database is not created automatically for you. In order to get started using Access, you must create and name a database first or open an existing database.

Open a File Using the Open Dialog Box

Opening a file in any of the Office 2007 applications is an easy process: Use the Open command from the Office menu and specify the file to open. However, locating the file to open can be difficult at times because you might not know where the file you want to use is located. You can open files stored on your computer or on a remote computer that you have access to. Further, files are saved in folders, and you might need to look for files located within folders or subfolders. The Open dialog box, shown in Figure 1.15, contains many features designed for file management; however, two features are designed specifically to help you locate files.

- **Look in**—provides a hierarchical view of the structure of folders and subfolders on your computer or on any computer network you are attached to. Move up or down in the structure to find a specific location or folder and then click the desired location to select it. The file list in the center of the dialog box displays the subfolders and files saved in the location you select. Table 1.3 lists and describes the toolbar buttons.

- **My Places bar**—provides a list of shortcut links to specific folders on your computer and locations on a computer network that you are attached to. Click a link to select it, and the file list changes to display subfolders and files in that location.

Table 1.3 Toolbar Buttons

Buttons	Characteristics
Previous Folder	Returns to the previous folder you viewed.
Up One Level	Moves up one level in the folder structure from the current folder.
Delete	Deletes the selected file or selected folder.
Create New Folder	Creates a new folder within the current folder.
Views	Changes the way the list of folders and files displays in the File list.

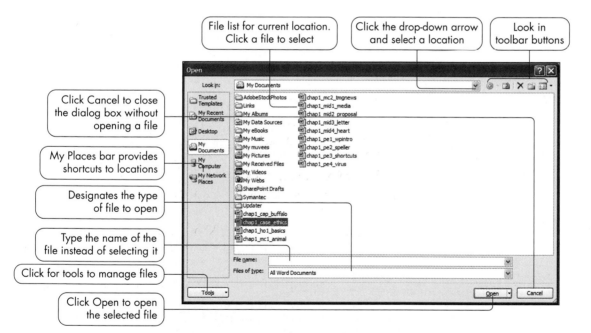

Figure 1.15 Open Dialog Box in Word

After you locate and select the file, click the Open button in the dialog box to display the file on the screen. However, if, for example, you work as part of a workgroup that shares files with each other, you might find the need to open files in a more specialized way. Microsoft Office programs provide several options for opening files when you click the drop-down arrow on the Open button. For example, if you want to keep the original file intact, you might open the file as a copy of the original. Table 1.4 describes the Open options.

Table 1.4 Open Options

Open Options	Characteristics
Open	Opens the selected file with the ability to read and write (edit).
Open Read-Only	Opens the selected file with the ability to read the contents but prevents you from changing or editing it.
Open as Copy	Opens the selected file as a copy of the original so that if you edit the file, the original remains unchanged.
Open in Browser	Opens the selected file in a Web browser.
Open with Transform	Opens a file and provides the ability to transform it into another type of document, such as an HTML document.
Open and Repair	Opens the selected file and attempts to repair any damage. If you have difficulty opening a file, try to open it by selecting Open and Repair.

Open Files Using the Recent Documents List

Office 2007 provides a quick method for accessing files you used recently. The Recent Documents list displays when the Office menu opens and provides a list of links to the last few files you used. The list changes as you work in the application to reflect only the most recent files. Figure 1.16 shows the Office menu with the Recent Documents list.

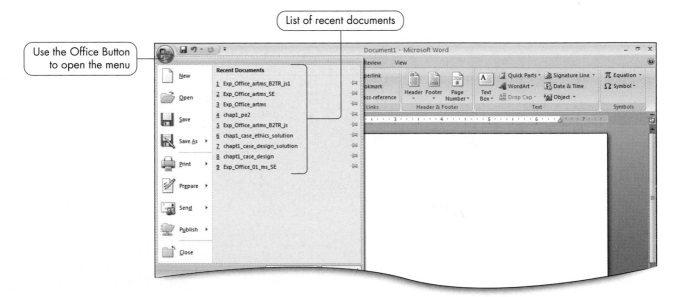

Figure 1.16 The Recent Documents List

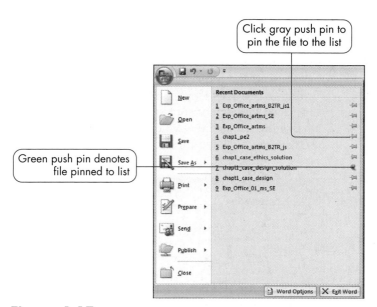

Figure 1.17 The Recent Documents List

Saving a File

As you work with any Office 2007 application and create files, you will need to save them for future use. While you are working on a file, it is stored in the temporary memory or RAM of your computer. When you save a file, the contents of the file stored in RAM are saved to the hard drive of your computer or to a storage device such as a flash drive. As you create, edit, and format a complex file such as a report, slide show, or budget, you should consider saving several versions of it as you work. For example, you might number versions or use the date in the file name to designate each version. Using this method enables you to revert to a previous version of the document if necessary. To save a file you create in Word, PowerPoint, or Excel, click the Office Button to display the Office menu. Office provides two commands that work similarly: Save and Save As. Table 1.5 describes the characteristics of these two commands.

> As you create, edit, and format a complex file such as a report, slide show, or budget, you should consider saving several versions of it as you work.

Table 1.5 Save Options

Command	Characteristics
Save	Saves the open document: • If this is the first time the document is being saved, Office 2007 opens the Save As dialog box so that you can name the file. • If this document was saved previously, the document is automatically saved using the original file name.
Save As	Opens the Save As dialog box: • If this is the first time the document is being saved, use the Save As dialog box to name the file. • If this document was saved previously, use this option to save the file with a new name, in a new location, or as a new file type preserving the original file with its original name.

When you select the Save As command, the Save As dialog box appears (see Figure 1.18). Notice that saving and opening files are related, that the Save As dialog box looks very similar to the Open dialog box that you saw in Figure 1.15. The dialog box requires you to specify the drive or folder in which to store the file, the name of the file, and the type of file you wish the file to be saved as. Additionally, because finding saved files is important, you should always group related files together in folders, so that you or someone else can find them in a location that makes sense. You can use the Create New Folder button in the dialog box to create and name a folder, and then save related files to it.

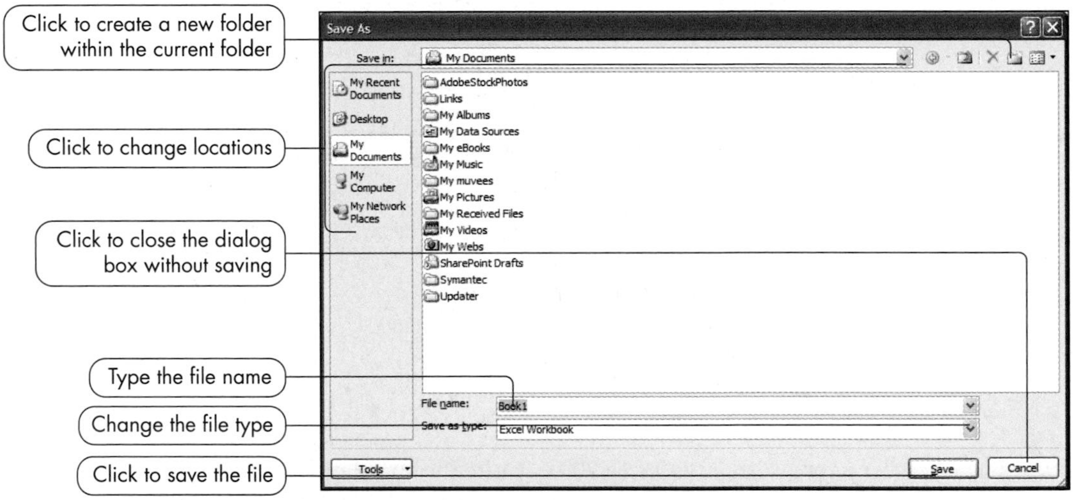

Figure 1.18 Save As Dialog Box in Excel

All subsequent executions of the Save command save the file under the assigned name, replacing the previously saved version with the new version. Pressing Ctrl+S is another way to activate the Save command. If you want to change the name of the file, use the Save As command. Word, PowerPoint, and Excel use the same basic process for saving files, which include the following options:

• naming and saving a previously unsaved file

• saving an updated file with the same name and replacing the original file with the updated one

• saving an updated file with a different name or in a different location to keep the original intact

• saving the file in a different file format

TIP Saving from the Office Menu

You should select the Save As command on the Office menu rather than pointing to the arrow that follows the command. When you point to the arrow, menu options display for saving the file in an alternative format. Always check the Save as type box in the dialog box to be sure that the correct file type is specified.

A ***macro*** is a small program that automates tasks in a file.

A ***virus checker*** is software that scans files for a hidden program that can damage your computer.

Office 2007 saves files in a different format from previous versions of the software. Office now makes use of XML formats for files created in Word, PowerPoint, and Excel. For example, in previous versions of Word, all documents were saved with the three-letter extension .doc. Now Word saves default documents with the four-letter extension .docx. The new XML format makes use of file compression to save storage space for the user. The files are compressed automatically when saved and uncompressed when opened. Another important feature is that the XML format makes using the files you create in Office 2007 easier to open in other software. This increased portability of files is a major benefit in any workplace that might have numerous applications to deal with. The new file format also differentiates between files that contain *macros*, which are small programs that automate tasks in a file, and those that do not. This specification of files that contain macros enables a virus checker to rigorously check for damaging programs hidden in files. A ***virus checker*** is software that scans files for a hidden program that can damage your computer. Table 1.6 lists the file formats with the four-letter extension for Word, PowerPoint, and Excel, and a five-letter extension for Access.

A ***template*** is a file that contains formatting and design elements.

Table 1.6 Word, PowerPoint, Excel, and Access File Extensions

File Format	Characteristics
Word	.docx—default document format .docm—a document that contains macros .dotx—a template without macros (a **template** is a file that contains formatting and design elements) .dotm—a template with macros
PowerPoint	.pptx—default presentation format .pptm—a presentation that contains macros .potx—a template .potm—a template with macros .ppam—an add-in that contains macros .ppsx—a slide show .ppsm—a slide show with macros .sldx—a slide saved independently of a presentation .sldm—a slide saved independently of a presentation that contains a macro .thmx—a theme used to format a slide
Excel	.xlsx—default workbook .xlsm—a workbook with macros .xltx—a template .xltm—a template with a macro .xlsb—non-XML binary workbook—for previous versions of the software .xlam—an add-in that contains macros
Access	.accdb—default database

Access 2007 saves data differently from Word, PowerPoint, and Excel. When you start Access, which is a relational database, you must create a database and define at least one table for your data. Then as you work, your data is stored automatically. This powerful software enables multiple users access to up-to-date data. The concepts of saving, opening, and printing remain the same, but the process of how data is saved is unique to this powerful environment.

TIP   Changing the Display of the My Places Bar

Sometimes finding saved files can be a time-consuming chore. To help you quickly locate files, Office 2007 provides options for changing the display of the My Places bar. In Word, PowerPoint, Excel, and Access, you can create shortcuts to folders where you store commonly used files and add them to the My Places bar. From the Open or Save As dialog box, select the location in the Look in list you want to add to the bar. With the desired location selected, point to an empty space below the existing shortcuts on the My Places bar. Right-click the mouse to display a **shortcut menu**, which displays when you right-click the mouse on an object and provides a list of commands pertaining to the object you clicked. From the shortcut menu, choose Add (folder name)—the folder name is the name of the location you selected in the Look in box. The new shortcut is added to the bottom of the My Places bar. Notice the shortcut menu in Figure 1.19, which also provides options to change the order of added shortcuts or remove an unwanted shortcut. However, you can only remove the shortcuts that you add to the bar; the default shortcuts cannot be removed.

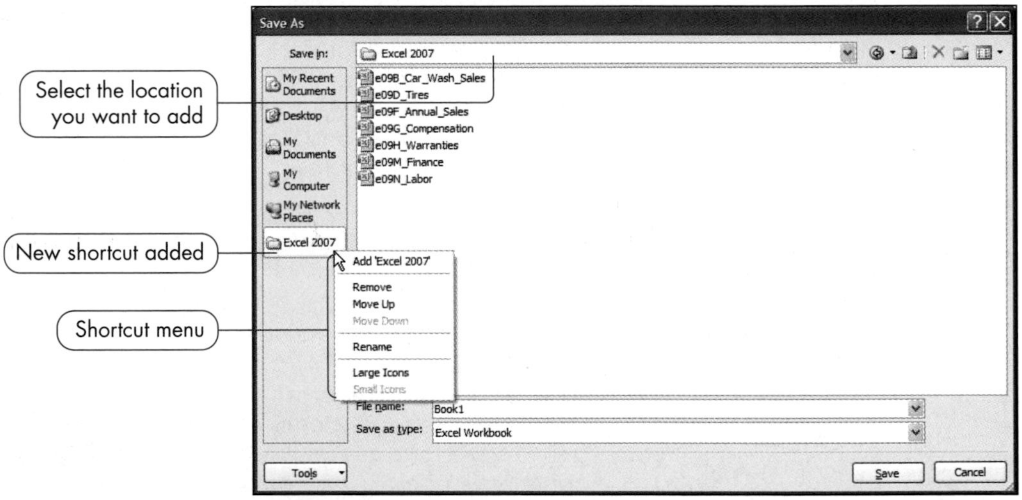

A **shortcut menu** displays when you right-click the mouse on an object and provides a list of commands pertaining to the object you clicked.

Select the location you want to add

New shortcut added

Shortcut menu

Figure 1.19   Save As Dialog Box with New Shortcut Added to My Places Bar

Printing a Document

As you work with Office 2007 applications, you will need to print hard copies of documents, such as letters to mail, presentation notes to distribute to accompany a slide show, budget spreadsheets to distribute at a staff meeting, or database summary reports to submit. Office provides flexibility so that you can preview the document before you send it to the printer; you also can select from numerous print options, such as changing the number of copies printed; or you can simply and quickly print the current document on the default printer.

Preview Before You Print

It is highly recommended that you preview your document before you print because Print Preview displays all the document elements, such as graphics and formatting, as they will appear when printed on paper. Previewing the document first enables you to make any changes that you need to make without wasting paper. Previewing documents uses the same method in all Office 2007 applications, that is, point to the arrow next to the Print command on the Office menu and select Print Preview to display the current document, worksheet, presentation, or database table in the Print Preview window. Figure 1.20 shows the Print Preview window in Word 2007.

> It is highly recommended that you preview your document before you print because Print Preview displays all the document elements, such as graphics and formatting, as they will appear when printed on paper.

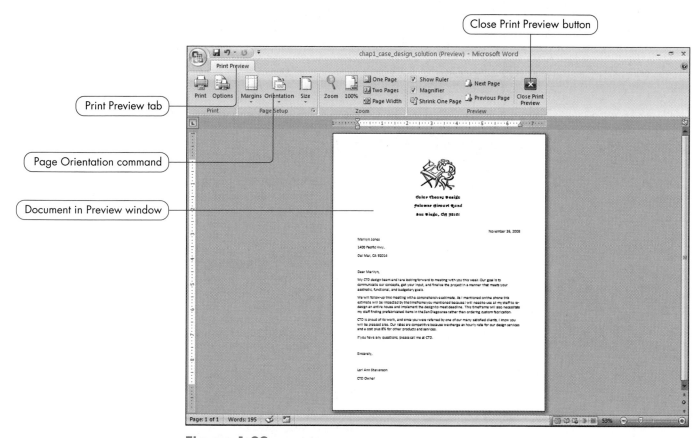

Figure 1.20 Print Preview Window

As you preview the document, you can get a closer look at the results by changing the zoom. Notice that the mouse pointer displays in the Preview window as a magnifying glass with a plus sign, so that you can simply click in the document to increase the zoom. Once clicked, the plus sign changes to a minus sign, enabling you to click in the document again to decrease the zoom. You also can use the Zoom group on the Print Preview tab or the Zoom slider on the status bar to change the view of the document.

Other options on the Print Preview tab change depending on the application that you are using. For example, you might want to change the orientation to switch from portrait to landscape. Refer to Figure 1.20. **Portrait orientation** is longer than it is wide, like the portrait of a person; whereas, **landscape orientation** is wider than it is long, resembling a landscape scene. You also can change the size of the paper or other options from the Print Preview tab.

Portrait orientation is longer than it is wide—like the portrait of a person.

Landscape orientation is wider than it is long, resembling a landscape scene.

If you need to edit the document before printing, close the Print Preview window and return to the document. However, if you are satisfied with the document and want to print, click Print in the Print group on the Print Preview tab. The Print dialog box displays. Figure 1.21 shows Word's Print dialog box.

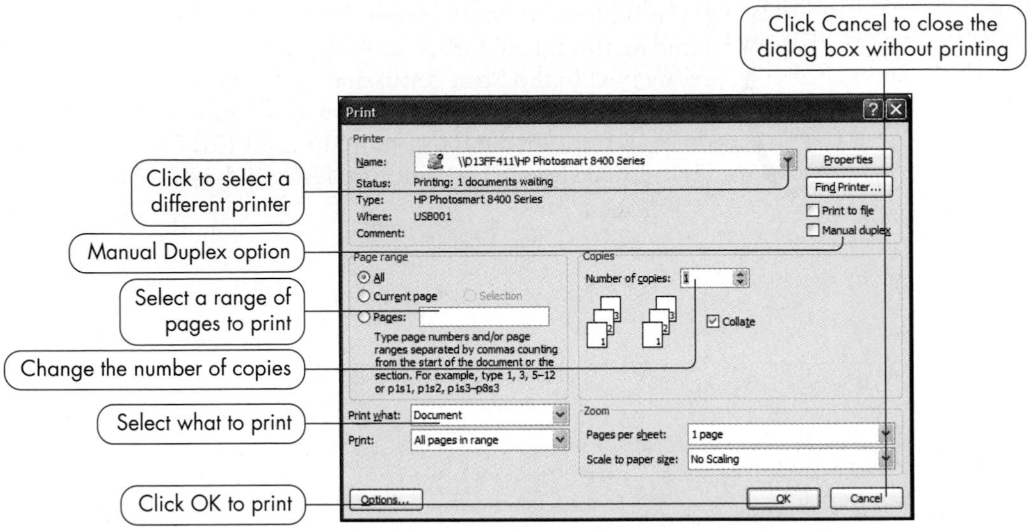

Figure 1.21 Print Dialog Box

The Print dialog box provides numerous options for selecting the correct printer, selecting what to print, and selecting how to print. Table 1.7 describes several important and often-used features of the Print dialog box.

Table 1.7 Print Dialog Box

Print Option	Characteristics
All	Select to print all the pages in the file.
Current page/slide	Select to print only the page or slide with the insertion point. This is a handy feature when you notice an error in a file, and you only want to reprint the corrected page.
Pages	Select to print only specific pages in a document. You must specify page numbers in the text box.
Number of Copies	Change the number of copies printed from the default 1 to the number desired.
Collate	Click if you are printing multiple copies of a multi-page file, and you want to print an entire first copy before printing an entire second copy, and so forth.
Print what	Select from options on what to print, varying with each application.
Selection	Select to print only selected text or objects in an Excel worksheet.
Active sheet(s)	Select to print only the active worksheet(s) in Excel.
Entire workbook	Select to print all worksheets in the Excel workbook.

As you work with other Office 2007 applications, you will notice that the main print options remain unchanged; however, the details vary based on the specific task of the application. For example, the *Print what* option in PowerPoint includes options such as printing the slide, printing handouts, printing notes, or printing an outline of the presentation.

A *duplex printer* prints on both sides of the page.

A *manual duplex* operation allows you to print on both sides of the paper by printing first on one side and then on the other.

TIP Printing on Both Sides of the Paper

Duplex printers print on both sides of the page. However, if you do not have a duplex printer, you can still print on two sides of the paper by performing a **manual duplex** operation, which prints on both sides of the paper by printing first on one side, and then on the other. To perform a manual duplex print job in Word 2007, select the Manual duplex option in the Print dialog box. Refer to Figure 1.21. With this option selected, Word prints all pages that display on one side of the paper first, then prompts you to turn the pages over and place them back in the printer tray. The print job continues by printing all the pages that appear on the other side of the paper.

Print Without Previewing the File

If you want to print a file without previewing the results, select Print from the Office menu, and the Print dialog box displays. You can still make changes in the Print dialog box, or just immediately send the print job to the printer. However, if you just want to print quickly, Office 2007 provides a quick print option that enables you to send the current file to the default printer without opening the Print dialog box. This is a handy feature to use if you have only one printer attached and you want to print the current file without changing any print options. You have two ways to quick print:

- Select Quick Print from the Office menu.
- Customize the Quick Access toolbar to add the Print icon. Click the icon to print the current file without opening the Print dialog box.

Hands-On Exercises

2 | Performing Universal Tasks

Skills covered: 1. Open a File and Save It with a Different Name **2.** Use Print Preview and Select Options **3.** Print a Document

<table>
<tr>
<td>

Step 1

Open a File and Save It with a Different Name

</td>
<td>

Refer to Figure 1.22 as you complete Step 1.

a. Start Word, click the **Office Button** to display the Office menu, and then select **Open**.

The Open dialog box displays.

b. If necessary, click the **Look in drop-down arrow** to locate the files for this text-book to find *chap1_ho2_sample*.

TROUBLESHOOTING: If you have trouble finding the files that accompany this text, you may want to ask your instructor where they are located.

c. Select the file and click **Open**.

The document displays on the screen.

d. Click the **Office Button**, and then select **Save As** on the Office menu.

The Save As dialog box displays.

e. In the *File name* box, type **chap1_ho2_solution**.

f. Check the location listed in the **Save in** box. If you need to change locations to save your files, use the **Save in drop-down arrow** to select the correct location.

g. Make sure that the *Save as type* option is Word Document.

TROUBLESHOOTING: Be sure that you click the **Save As** command rather than pointing to the arrow after the command, and be sure that Word Document is specified in the Save as type box.

h. Click the **Save button** in the dialog box to save the file under the new name.

</td>
</tr>
</table>

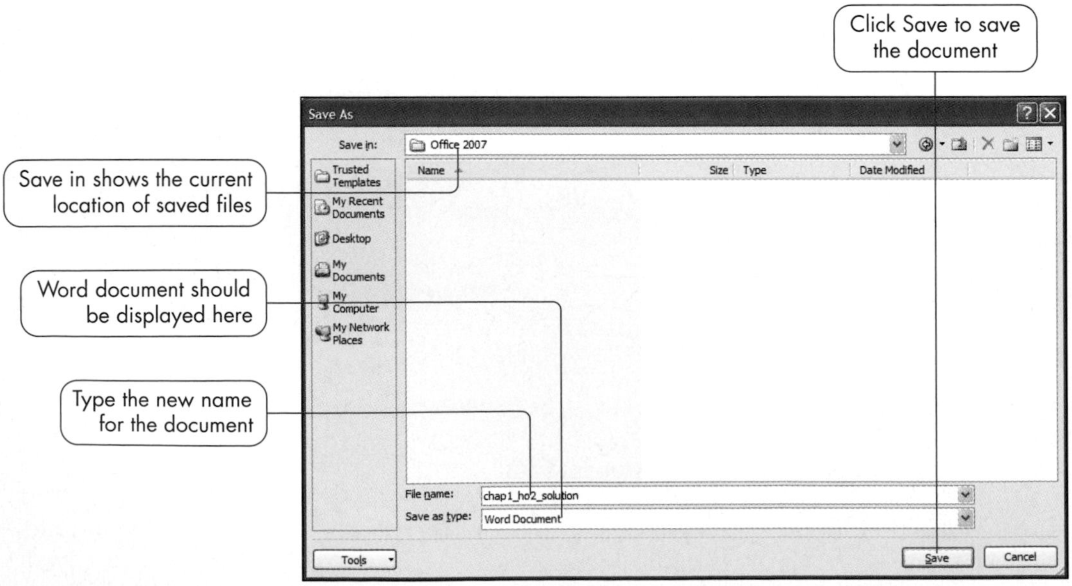

Click Save to save the document

Save in shows the current location of saved files

Word document should be displayed here

Type the new name for the document

Figure 1.22 Save As Dialog Box

Step 2
Use Print Preview and Select Options

Refer to Figure 1.23 as you complete Step 2.

a. With the document displayed on the screen, click the **Office Button** and point to the arrow following **Print** on the Office menu.

The Print submenu displays.

b. Select **Print Preview**.

The document displays in the Print Preview window.

c. Point the magnifying glass mouse pointer in the document and click the mouse once.

TROUBLESHOOTING: If you do not see the magnifying glass pointer, point the mouse in the document and keep it still for a moment.

The document magnification increases.

d. Point the magnifying glass mouse pointer in the document and click the mouse again.

The document magnification decreases.

e. Click **Orientation** in the Page Setup group on the Print Preview tab.

The orientation options display.

f. Click **Landscape**.

The document orientation changes to landscape.

g. Click **Orientation** a second time, and then choose **Portrait**.

The document returns to portrait orientation.

h. Click the **Close Print Preview** button on the Print Preview tab.

i. The Print Preview window closes.

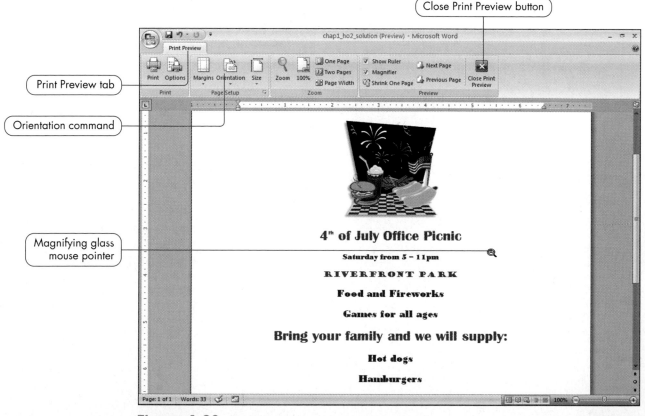

Figure 1.23 Print Preview

Step 3
Print a Document

Refer to Figure 1.24 as you complete Step 3.

a. Click the **Office Button**, and then point to the arrow next to **Print** on the Office menu.

The print options display.

b. Select **Print**.

The Print dialog box displays.

TROUBLESHOOTING: Be sure that your printer is turned on and has paper loaded.

c. If necessary, select the correct printer in the **Name box** by clicking the drop-down arrow and selecting from the resulting list.

d. Click **OK**.

The Word document prints on the selected printer.

e. To exit Word, click the **Office Button**, and then click the **Exit Word button**.

f. If prompted to save the file, choose **No**.

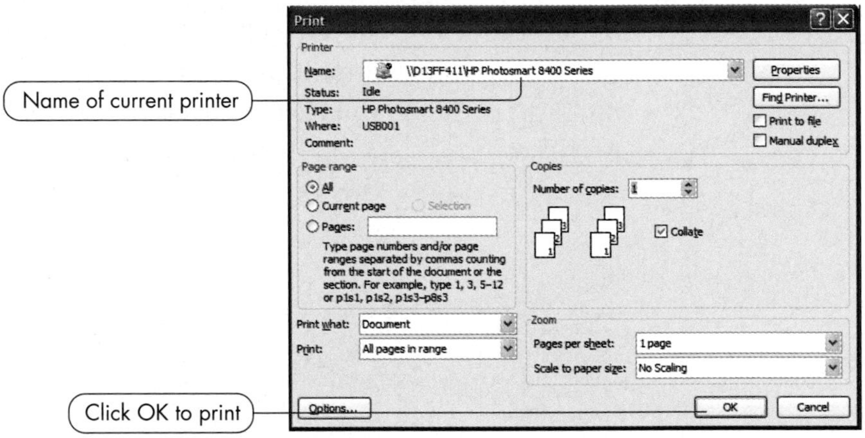

Figure 1.24 The Print Dialog Box

Basic Tasks

Many of the operations you perform in one Office program are the same or similar in all Office applications. These tasks are referred to as basic tasks and include such operations as inserting and typing over, copying and moving items, finding and replacing text, undoing and redoing commands, checking spelling and grammar, using the thesaurus, and using formatting tools. Once you learn the underlying concepts of these operations, you can apply them in different applications.

Most basic tasks in Word fall into two categories:

- editing a document
- formatting a document

Most successful writers use many word processing features to revise and edit documents, and most would agree that the revision process takes more time than the initial writing process. Errors such as spelling and grammar need to be eliminated to produce error-free writing. However, to turn a rough draft into a finished document, such as a report for a class or for a business, requires writers to revise and edit several times by adding text, removing text, replacing text, and moving text around to make the meaning clearer. Writers also improve their writing using tools to conduct research to make the information accurate and to find the most appropriate word using the thesaurus. Modern word processing applications such as Word 2007 provide these tools and more to aid the writer.

> Most successful writers use many word processing features to revise and edit documents, and most would agree that the revision process takes more time than the initial writing process.

The second category of basic tasks is formatting text in a document. Formatting text includes changing the type, the size, and appearance of text. You might want to apply formatting to simply improve the look of a document, or you might want to emphasize particular aspects of your message. Remember that a poorly formatted document or workbook probably will not be read. So whether you are creating your résumé or the income statement for a corporation's annual report, how the output looks is important. Office 2007 provides many tools for formatting documents, but in this section, you will start by learning to apply font attributes and copy those to other locations in the document.

In this section, you learn to perform basic tasks in Office 2007, using Word 2007 as the model. As you progress in learning other Office programs such as PowerPoint, Excel, and Access, you will apply the same principles in other applications.

Selecting Text to Edit

Most editing processes involve identifying the text that the writer wants to work with. For example, to specify which text to edit, you must select it. The most common method used to select text is to use the mouse. Point to one end of the text you want to select (either the beginning or end) and click-and-drag over the text. The selected text displays highlighted with a light blue background so that it stands out from other text and is ready for you to work with. The *Mini toolbar* displays when you select text in Word, Excel, and PowerPoint. It displays above the selected text as semitransparent and remains semitransparent until you point to it. Often-used commands from the Clipboard, Font, and Paragraph groups on the Home tab are repeated on the Mini toolbar for quick access. Figure 1.25 shows selected text with the Mini toolbar fully displayed in the document.

The *Mini toolbar* displays above the selected text as semitransparent and repeats often-used commands.

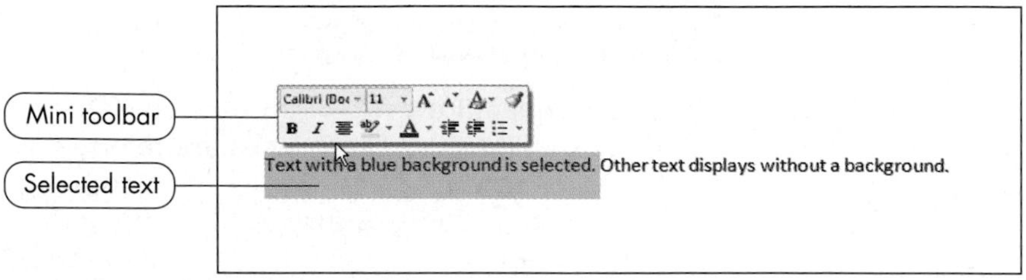

Figure 1.25 Selected Text

Sometimes you want to select only one word or character, and trying to drag over it to select it can be frustrating. Table 1.8 describes other methods used to select text.

Table 1.8 Easy Text Selection in Word

Outcome Desired	Method
Select a word	Double-click the word.
One line of text	Point the mouse to the left of the line, and when the mouse pointer changes to a right-pointing arrow, click the mouse.
A sentence	Hold down Ctrl and click in the sentence to select.
A paragraph	Triple-click the mouse in the paragraph.
One character to the left of the insertion point	Hold down Shift and press the left arrow key.
One character to the right of the insertion point	Hold down Shift and press the right arrow key.

TIP | Selecting Large Amounts of Text

As you edit documents, you might need to select a large portion of a document. However, as you click-and-drag over the text, you might have trouble stopping the selection at the desired location because the document scrolls by too quickly. This is actually a handy feature in Word 2007 that scrolls through the document when you drag the mouse pointer at the edge of the document window.

To select a large portion of a document, click the insertion point at the beginning of the desired selection. Then move the display to the end of the selection using the scroll bar at the right edge of the window. Scrolling leaves the insertion point where you placed it. When you reach the end of the text you want to select, hold down Shift and click the mouse. The entire body of text is selected.

Inserting Text and Changing to the Overtype Mode

Insert is adding text in a document.

As you create and edit documents using Word, you will need to *insert* text, which is adding text in a document. To insert or add text, point and click the mouse in the location where the text should display. With the insertion point in the location to insert the text, simply start typing. Any existing text moves to the right, making room for the new inserted text. At times, you might need to add a large amount of text in a document, and you might want to replace or type over existing text instead of inserting text. This task can be accomplished two ways:

- Select the text to replace and start typing. The new text replaces the selected text.

Overtype mode replaces the existing text with text you type character by character.

- Switch to *Overtype mode*, which replaces the existing text with text you type character by character. To change to Overtype mode, select the Word Options button on the Office menu. Select the option Use Overtype Mode in the Editing Options section of the Advanced tab. Later, if you want to return to Insert mode, repeat these steps to deselect the overtype mode option. Figure 1.26 shows the Word Options dialog box.

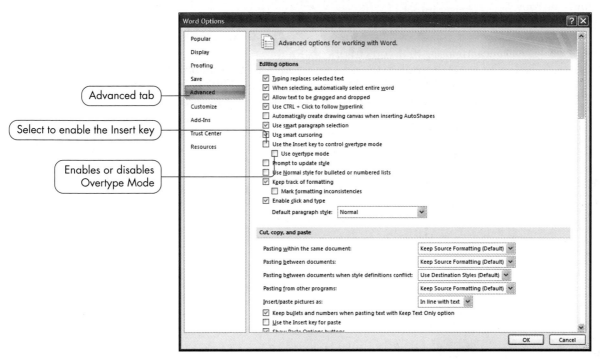

Figure 1.26 The Word Options Dialog Box

> ### TIP   Using the Insert Key on the Keyboard
>
> If you find that you need to switch between Insert and Overtype mode often, you can enable Insert on the keyboard by clicking the Word Options button on the Office menu. Select the option Use the Insert Key to Control Overtype Mode in the Editing Options section on the Advanced tab. Refer to Figure 1.26. You can now use Insert on the keyboard to switch between the two modes, and this option stays in effect until you go back to the Word Options dialog box and deselect it.

Moving and Copying Text

As you revise a document, you might find that you need to move text from one location to another to improve the readability of the content. To move text, you must cut the selected text from its original location and then place it in the new location by pasting it there. To duplicate text, you must copy the selected text in its original location and then paste the duplicate in the desired location. To decide whether you should use the Cut or Copy command in the Clipboard group on the Home tab to perform the task, you must notice the difference in the results of each command:

Cut removes the original text or object from its current location.

Copy makes a duplicate copy of the text or object, leaving the original intact.

Paste places the cut or copied text or object in the new location.

- **Cut** removes the selected original text or object from its current location.
- **Copy** makes a duplicate copy of the text or object, leaving the original text or object intact.

Keep in mind while you work, that by default, Office 2007 retains only the last item in memory that you cut or copied.

You complete the process by invoking the Paste command. **Paste** places the cut or copied text or object in the new location. Notice the Paste Options button displays along with the pasted text. You can simply ignore the Paste Options button, and it will disappear from the display, or you can click the drop-down arrow on the button and select a formatting option to change the display of the text you pasted. Figure 1.27 shows the options available.

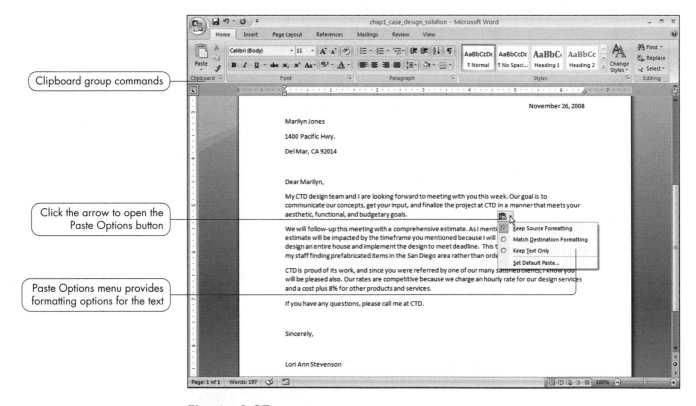

Figure 1.27 Text Pasted in the Document

TIP Moving and Copying Using Shortcuts

You can use alternative methods instead of using the commands located on the Home tab to cut, copy, and paste text. Office 2007 provides the following shortcuts:

- After selecting text, point back to the selected text and right-click the mouse. The shortcut menu displays, allowing you to choose Cut or Copy. Move the insertion point to the desired location, right-click the mouse again, and choose Paste from the shortcut menu.

- After selecting text, use the keyboard shortcut combinations Ctrl+C to copy or Ctrl+X to cut text. Move the insertion point to the new location and press Ctrl+V to paste. These keyboard shortcuts work in most Windows applications, so they can be very useful.

- After selecting text, you can move it a short distance in the document by dragging to the new location. Point to the selected text, hold down the left mouse button, and then drag to the desired location. While you are dragging the mouse, the pointer changes to a left-pointing arrow with a box attached to it. Release the mouse button when you have placed the insertion point in the desired location, and the text displays in the new location.

Use the Office Clipboard

The **Clipboard** is a memory location that holds up to 24 items for you to paste into the current document, another file, or another application.

Office 2007 provides an option that enables you to cut or copy multiple items to the **Clipboard**, which is a memory location that holds up to 24 items for you to paste into the current file, another file, or another application. The Clipboard stays active only while you are using one of the Office 2007 applications. When you exit from all Office 2007 applications, all items on the Clipboard are deleted. To accumulate items on the Clipboard, you must first display it by clicking the Dialog Box Launcher in the Clipboard group on the Home tab. When the Clipboard pane is open on the screen, its memory location is active, and the Clipboard accumulates all items you cut or copy up to the maximum 24. To paste an item from the Clipboard, point to it, click the resulting drop-down arrow, and choose Paste. To change how the Clipboard functions, use the Options button shown in Figure 1.28. One of the most important options allows the Clipboard to accumulate items even when it is not open on the screen. To activate the Clipboard so that it works in the background, click the Options button in the Clipboard, and then select Collect without Showing Office Clipboard.

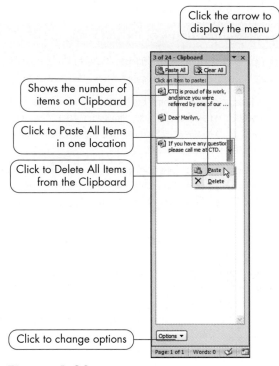

Figure 1.28 Clipboard

Finding, Replacing, and Going to Text

You can waste a great deal of time slowly scrolling through a document trying to locate text or other items. Office 2007 provides features that speed up editing by automatically finding text and objects in a document, thus making you more productive. Office 2007 provides the following three related operations that all use the Find and Replace dialog box:

Find locates a word or group of words in a document.

Replace not only finds text, it replaces a word or group of words with other text.

Go To moves the insertion point to a specific location in the document.

- The *Find* command enables you to locate a word or group of words in a document quickly.

- The *Replace* command not only finds text quickly, it replaces a word or group of words with other text.

- The *Go To* command moves the insertion point to a specific location in the document.

Find Text

To locate text in an Office file, choose the Find command in the Editing group on the Home tab and type the text you want to locate in the resulting dialog box, as shown in Figure 1.29. After you type the text to locate, you can find the next instance after the insertion point and work through the file until you find the instance of the text you were looking for. Alternatively, you can find all instances of the text in the file at one time. If you decide to find every instance at once, the Office application temporarily highlights each one, and the text stays highlighted until you perform another operation in the file.

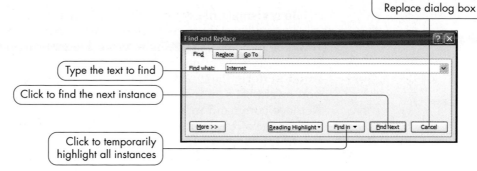

Click to exit Find and
Replace dialog box

Type the text to find

Click to find the next instance

Click to temporarily
highlight all instances

Figure 1.29   Find Tab of the Find and Replace Dialog Box

TIP   Finding and Highlighting Text in Word

Sometimes, temporarily highlighting all instances of text is not sufficient to help you edit the text you find. If you want Word to find all instances of specific text in a document and keep the highlighting from disappearing until you want it to, you can use the Reading Highlight option in the Find dialog box. One nice feature of this option is that even though the text remains highlighted on the screen, the document prints normally without highlighting. Figure 1.30 shows the Find and Replace dialog box with the Reading Highlight options that you use to highlight or remove the highlight from a document.

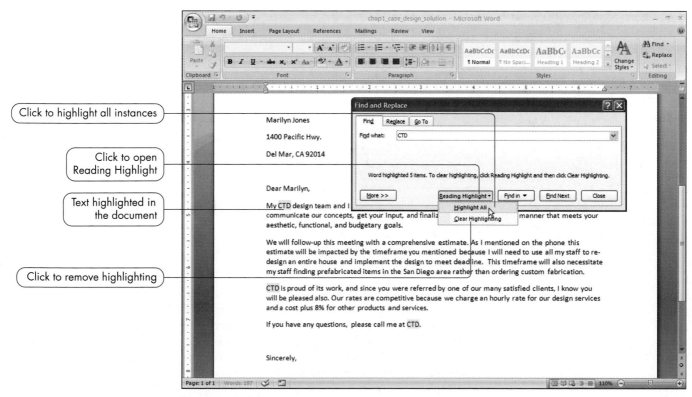

Click to highlight all instances

Click to open
Reading Highlight

Text highlighted in
the document

Click to remove highlighting

Figure 1.30   Find and Replace Dialog Box with Highlighting Options

Replace Text

While revising a file, you might realize that you have used an incorrect term and need to replace it throughout the entire file. Alternatively, you might realize that you could be more productive by re-using a letter or report that you polished and saved if you replace the previous client's or corporation's name with a new one. While you could perform these tasks manually, it would not be worth the time involved, and you might miss an instance of the old text, which could prove embarrassing. The Replace command in the Editing group on the Home tab can quickly and easily replace the old text with the new text throughout an entire file.

In the Find and Replace dialog box, first type the text to find, using the same process you used with the Find command. Second, type the text to replace the existing text with. Third, specify how you want Word to perform the operation. You can either replace each instance of the text individually, which can be time-consuming but allows you to decide whether to replace each instance one at a time, or you can replace every instance of the text in the document all at once. Word (but not the other Office applications) also provides options in the dialog box that help you replace only the correct text in the document. Click the More button to display these options. The most important one is the Find whole words only option. This option forces the application to find only complete words, not text that is part of other words. For instance, if you are searching for the word *off* to replace with other text, you would not want Word to replace the *off* in *office* with other text. Figure 1.31 shows these options along with the options for replacing text.

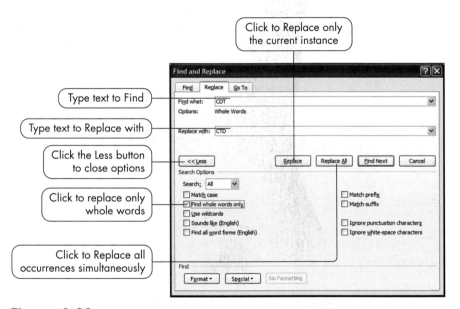

Figure 1.31 Find and Replace Dialog Box

Go Directly to a Location in a File

If you are editing a long document and want to move within it quickly, you can use the Go To command by clicking the down arrow on the Find command in the Editing group on the Home tab rather than slowly scrolling through an entire document or workbook. For example, if you want to move the insertion point to page 40 in a 200-page document, choose the Go To command and type 40 in the *Enter page number* text box. Notice the list of objects you can choose from in the Go to what section of the dialog box in Figure 1.32.

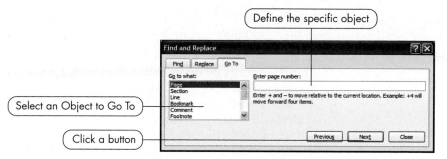

Figure 1.32 Go To Tab of the Find and Replace Dialog Box

Using the Undo and Redo Commands

The **Undo** command cancels your last one or more operations.

The **Redo** command reinstates or reverses an action performed by the Undo command.

As you create and edit files, you may perform an operation by mistake or simply change your mind about an edit you make. Office applications provide the **Undo** command, which can cancel your previous operation or even your last few operations. After using Undo to reverse an action or operation, you might decide that you want to use the **Redo** command to reinstate or reverse the action taken by the Undo command.

To undo the last action you performed, click Undo on the Quick Access Toolbar. For example, if you deleted text by mistake, immediately click Undo to restore it. If, however, you deleted some text and then performed several other operations, you can find the correct action to undo, with the understanding that all actions after that one will also be undone. To review a list of the last few actions you performed, click the Undo drop-down arrow and select the desired one from the list—Undo highlights all actions in the list down to that item and will undo all of the highlighted actions. Figure 1.33 shows a list of recent actions in PowerPoint. To reinstate or reverse an action as a result of using the Undo command, click Redo on the Quick Access Toolbar.

The **Repeat** command repeats only the last action you performed.

The **Repeat** command provides limited use because it repeats only the last action you performed. To repeat the last action, click Repeat on the Quick Access Toolbar. If the Office application is able to repeat your last action, the results will display in the document. Note that the Repeat command is replaced with the Redo command after you use the Undo command. For example, Figure 1.33 shows the Redo command after the Undo command has been used, and Figure 1.34 shows the Repeat command when Undo has not been used.

Figure 1.33 Undo and Redo Buttons

Using Language Tools

Documents, spreadsheets, and presentations represent the author, so remember that errors in writing can keep people from getting a desired job, or once on the job, can keep them from getting a desired promotion. To avoid holding yourself back, you should polish your final documents before submitting them electronically or as a hard copy. Office 2007 provides built-in proofing tools to help you fix spelling and grammar errors and help you locate the correct word or information.

Check Spelling and Grammar Automatically

By default, Office applications check spelling as you type and flag potential spelling errors by underlining them with a red wavy line. Word also flags potential grammar errors by underlining them with a green wavy line. You can fix these errors as you enter text, or you can ignore the errors and fix them all at once.

To fix spelling errors as you type, simply move the insertion point to a red wavy underlined word and correct the spelling yourself. If you spell the word correctly, the red wavy underline disappears. However, if you need help figuring out the correct spelling for the flagged word, then point to the error and right-click the mouse. The shortcut menu displays with possible corrections for the error. If you find the correction on the shortcut menu, click it to replace the word in the document. To fix grammar errors, follow the same process, but when the shortcut menu displays, you can choose to view more information to see rules that apply to the potential error. Notice the errors flagged in Figure 1.34. Note that the Mini toolbar also displays automatically.

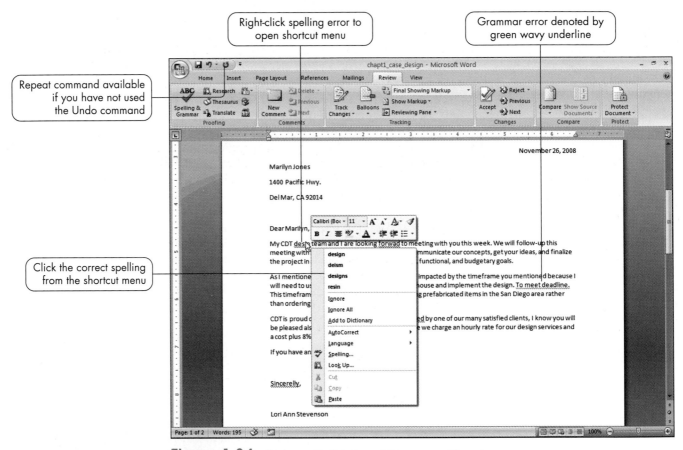

Figure 1.34 Automatic Spell and Grammar Check

Check Spelling and Grammar at Once

Some people prefer to wait until they complete typing the entire document and then check spelling and grammar at once. To check for errors, click Spelling & Grammar in Word (Spelling in Excel or PowerPoint) in the Proofing group on the Review tab. As the checking proceeds through the file and detects any spelling or grammar errors, it displays the Spelling dialog box if you are using Excel or PowerPoint, or the Spelling and Grammar dialog box in Word. You can either correct or ignore the changes that the Spelling checker proposes to your document. For example, Figure 1.35 shows the Spelling and Grammar dialog box with a misspelled word in the top section and Word's suggestions in the bottom section. Select the correction from the list and change the current instance, or you can change all instances of the error throughout the document. However, sometimes the flagged word might be a specialized term or a person's name, so if the flagged word is not a spelling error, you can ignore it once in the current document or throughout the entire document; further, you could add the word to the spell-check list so that it never flags that spelling again.

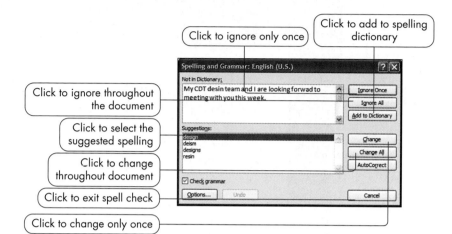

Figure 1.35 Spelling and Grammar Dialog Box

TIP   **Proofreading Your Document**

The spelling and grammar checks available in Word provide great help improving your documents. However, you should not forget that you still have to proofread your document to ensure that the writing is clear, appropriate for the intended audience, and makes sense.

Use the Thesaurus

As you edit a document, spreadsheet, or presentation, you might want to improve your writing by finding a better or different word for a particular situation. For example, say you are stuck and cannot think of a better word for *big*, and you would like to find an alternative word that means the same. Word, Excel, and PowerPoint provide a built-in thesaurus, which is an electronic version of a book of synonyms. Synonyms are different words with the same or similar meaning, and antonyms are words with the opposite meaning.

The easiest method for accessing the Thesaurus is to point to the word in the file that you want to find an alternative for and right-click the mouse. When the shortcut menu displays, point to Synonyms, and the program displays a list of alternatives. Notice the shortcut menu and list of synonyms in Figure 1.36. To select one of the alternative words on the list, click it, and the word you select replaces the original word. If you do not see an alternative on the list that you want to use and you want to investigate further, click Thesaurus on the shortcut menu to open the full Thesaurus.

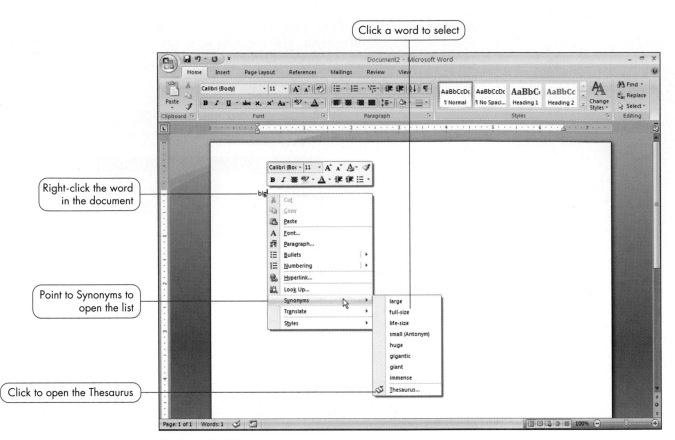

Figure 1.36 Shortcut Menu with Synonyms

An alternative method for opening the full Thesaurus is to place the insertion point in the word you want to look up, and then click the Thesaurus command in the Proofing group on the Review tab. The Thesaurus opens with alternatives for the selected word. You can use one of the words presented in the pane, or you can look up additional words. If you do not find the word you want, use the Search option to find more alternatives. Figure 1.37 shows the Thesaurus.

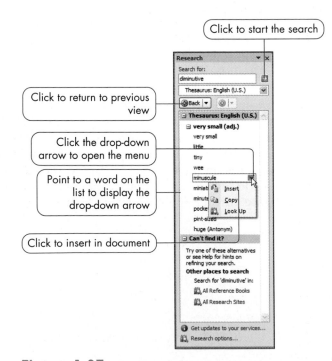

Figure 1.37 The Thesaurus

Conduct Research

As you work in Word, Excel, or PowerPoint, you might need to find the definition of a word or look up an item in the encyclopedia to include accurate information. Office 2007 provides quick access to research tools. To access research tools, click the Research button in the Proofing group on the Review tab. Notice in Figure 1.38 that you can specify what you want to research and specify where to Search. Using this feature, you can choose from reference books, research sites, and business and financial sites.

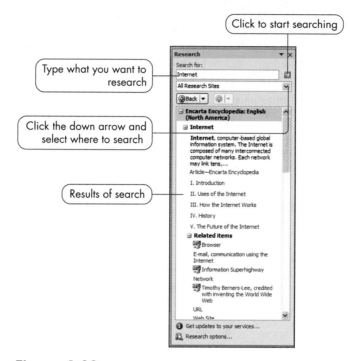

Click to start searching

Type what you want to research

Click the down arrow and select where to search

Results of search

Figure 1.38 Research Task Pane

Applying Font Attributes

Taking the time to format text helps the reader find important information in the document by making it stand out and helps the reader understand the message by emphasizing key items.

After you have edited a document, you might want to improve its visual appeal by formatting the text. **Formatting text** changes an individual letter, a word, or a body of selected text. Taking the time to format text helps the reader find important information in the document by making it stand out and helps the reader understand the message by emphasizing key items. You can format the text in the document by changing the following font attributes:

Formatting text changes an individual letter, a word, or a body of selected text.

- font face or size

- font attributes such as bold, underline, or italic

- font color

The Font group on the Home tab—available in Word, Excel, PowerPoint, and Access—provides many formatting options, and Office provides two methods for applying these font attributes:

- Choose the font attributes first, and then type the text. The text displays in the document with the formatting.
- Type the text, select the text to format, and choose the font attributes. The selected text displays with the formatting.

You can apply more than one attribute to text, so you can select one or more attributes either all at once or at any time. Also, it is easy to see which attributes you have applied to text in the document. Select the formatted text and look at the commands in the Font group on the Home tab. The commands in effect display with a gold background. See Figure 1.39. To remove an effect from text, select it and click the command. The gold background disappears for attributes that are no longer in effect.

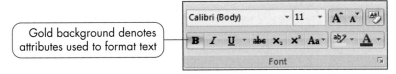

Figure 1.39 Font Group of the Home tab

Change the Font

A **font** is a named set of characters with the same design.

A **font** is a named set of characters with the same design, and Office 2007 provides many built-in fonts for you to choose from. Remember that more is not always better when applied to fonts, so limit the number of font changes in your document. Additionally, the choice of a font should depend on the intent of the document and should never overpower the message. For example, using a fancy or highly stylized font that may be difficult to read for a client letter might seem odd to the person receiving it and overpower the intended message.

Remember that more is not always better when applied to fonts, so limit the number of font changes in your document.

One powerful feature of Office 2007 that can help you decide how a font will look in your document is Live Preview. First, select the existing text, and then click the drop-down arrow on the Font list in the Font group on the Home tab. As you point to a font name in the list, Live Preview changes the selected text in the document to that font. Figure 1.40 shows the selected text displaying in a different font as a result of Live Preview.

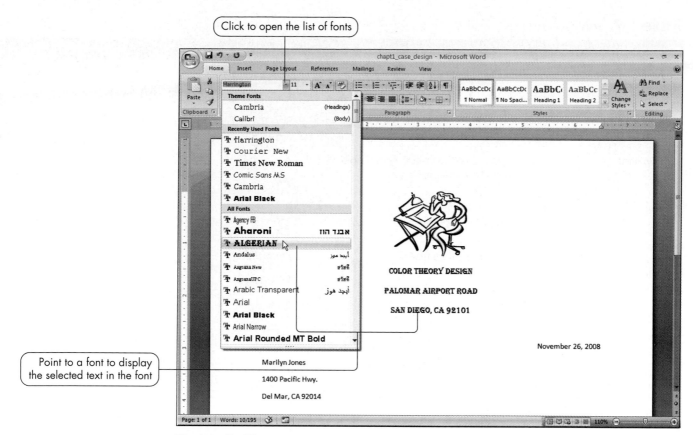

Figure 1.40 Font List

Change the Font Size, Color, and Attributes

Besides changing the font, you also can change the size, color, and other attributes of text in a document. Because these formatting operations are used so frequently, Office places many of these commands in several places for easy access:

- in the Font group on the Home tab
- on the Mini toolbar
- in the Font dialog box

Table 1.9 describes the commands that display in the Font group of the Home tab and in the Font dialog box.

Table 1.9 Font Commands

Command	Description	Example
Font	Enables you to designate the font.	Arial **Comic Sans MS**
Font Size	Enables you to designate an exact font size.	Size 8 Size 18
Grow Font	Each time you click the command, the selected text increases one size.	A **A**
Shrink Font	Each time you click the command, the selected text decreases one size.	B **B**
Clear Formatting	Removes all formatting from the selected text.	***Formatted*** Cleared
Bold	Makes the text darker than the surrounding text.	**Bold**
Italic	Places the selected text in italic, that is, slants the letters to the right.	*Italic*
Underline	Places a line under the text. Click the drop-down arrow to change the underline style.	<u>Underline</u>
Strikethrough	Draws a line through the middle of the text.	~~Strikethrough~~
Subscript	Places selected text below the baseline.	Sub$_{script}$
Superscript	Places selected text above the line of letters.	Super^{script}
Change Case	Changes the case of the selected text. Click the drop-down arrow to select the desired case.	lowercase UPPERCASE
Text Highlight Color	Makes selected text look like it was highlighted with a marker pen. Click the drop-down arrow to change color and other options.	Highlighted
Font Color	Changes the color of selected text. Click the drop-down arrow to change colors.	Font Color

If you have several formatting changes to make, click the Dialog Box Launcher in the Font group on the Home tab to display the Font dialog box. The Font dialog box is handy because all the formatting features display in one location, and it provides additional options such as changing the underline color. Figure 1.41 shows the Font dialog box in Word.

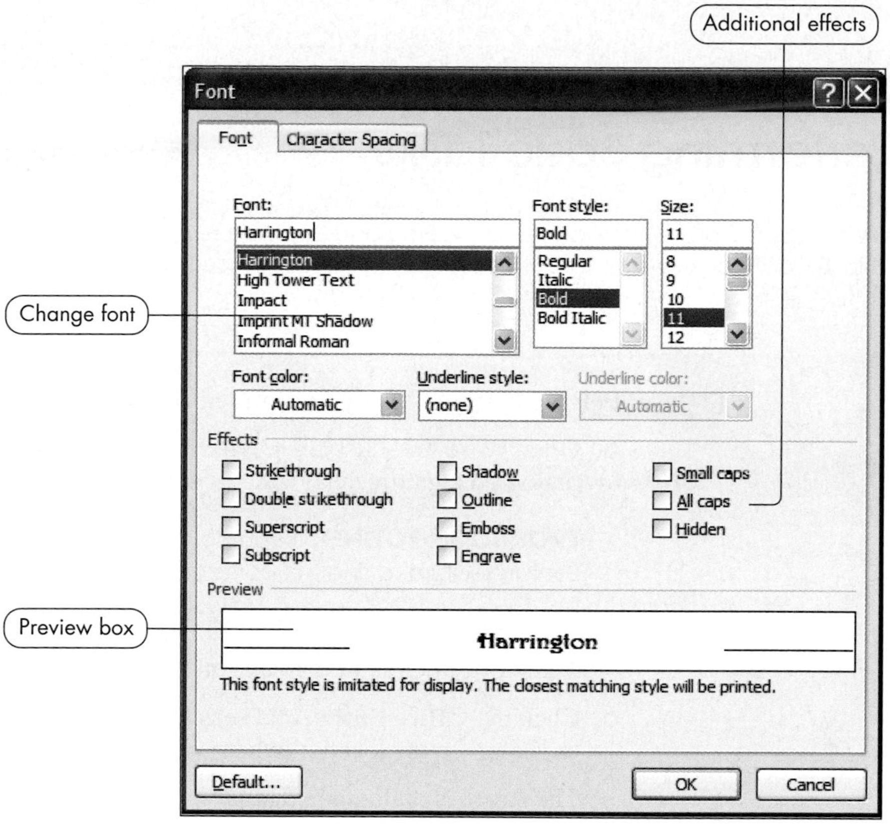

Figure 1.41 Font Dialog Box

Copying Formats with the Format Painter

After formatting text in one part of a document, you might want to apply that same formatting to other text in a different location in the document. You could try to remember all the formatting options you selected, but that process would be time-consuming and could produce inconsistent results. Office 2007 provides a shortcut method called the *Format Painter*, which copies the formatting of text from one location to another.

Select the formatted text you want to copy and click the Format Painter in the Clipboard group on the Home tab to copy the format. Single-click the command to turn it on to copy formatting to one location—the option turns off automatically after one copy—or double-click the command to turn it on for unlimited format copying—you must press Esc on the keyboard to turn it off.

The ***Format Painter*** copies the formatting of text from one location to another.

Hands-On Exercises

3 | Performing Basic Tasks

Skills covered: 1. Cut, Copy, Paste, and Undo **2.** Find and Replace Text **3.** Check Spelling **4.** Choose Synonyms and Use Thesaurus **5.** Use the Research Tool **6.** Apply Font Attributes **7.** Use Format Painter

Refer to Figure 1.42 as you complete Steps 1 and 2.

a. Open Word and click the **Office Button**, click **Open**, and then using the Open dialog box features, navigate to your classroom file location.

> **TROUBLESHOOTING:** If you have trouble finding the file, remember to use the Look in feature to find the correct location.

b. Select the file *chap1_ho3_internet* and click the **Open** button.

The Word document displays on the screen.

c. Click the **Office Button** and select **Save As**. If necessary, use the **Look in** feature to change to the location where you save files.

The Save As dialog box displays.

d. Type the new file name, **chap1_ho3_internet_solution**, be sure that *Word Document* displays in the *Save as type* box, and click **Save**.

The file is saved with the new name.

e. Click to place the insertion point at the beginning of the second sentence in the first paragraph. Type **These developments brought together**, and then press **Spacebar**.

The text moves to the right, making room for the new inserted text.

f. Press and hold down **Ctrl** as you click this sentence below the heading The World Wide Web: *The Netscape browser led in user share until Microsoft Internet Explorer took the lead in 1999.*

g. Click **Cut** in the Clipboard group on the Home tab.

The text disappears from the document.

h. Move the insertion point to the end of the last paragraph and click **Paste** in the Clipboard group on the Home tab.

The text displays in the new location.

i. Reselect the sentence you just moved and click **Copy** in the Clipboard group on the Home tab.

j. Move the insertion point to the end of the first paragraph beginning *The idea* and click the right mouse button.

The shortcut menu displays.

k. Select **Paste** from the shortcut menu.

The text remains in the original position and is copied to the second location.

l. Click **Undo** on the Quick Access Toolbar to undo the last paste.

Refer to Figure 1.42 to complete Step 2.

a. Press **Ctrl + Home** to move the insertion point to the beginning of the document. Click **Replace** in the Editing group on the Home tab.

The Find and Replace dialog box displays.

b. Type **Internet** in the *Find what* box and type **World Wide Web** in the *Replace with* box.

c. Click the **Replace All** button. Click **OK** to close the information box that informs you that Word has made seven replacements. Click **Close** to close the Find and Replace dialog box.

All instances of Internet have been replaced with World Wide Web in the document.

d. Click **Undo** on the Quick Access Toolbar.

All instances of *World Wide Web* have changed back to *Internet* in the document.

e. Click **Replace** in the Editing group on the Home tab.

The Find and Replace dialog box displays with the text you typed still in the boxes.

f. Click the **Find Next** button.

The first instance of the text *Internet* is highlighted.

g. Click the **Replace** button.

The first instance of Internet is replaced with World Wide Web, and the next instance of Internet is highlighted.

h. Click the **Find Next** button.

The highlight moves to the next instance of Internet without changing the previous one.

i. Click the **Close** button to close the Find and Replace dialog box.

The Find and Replace dialog box closes.

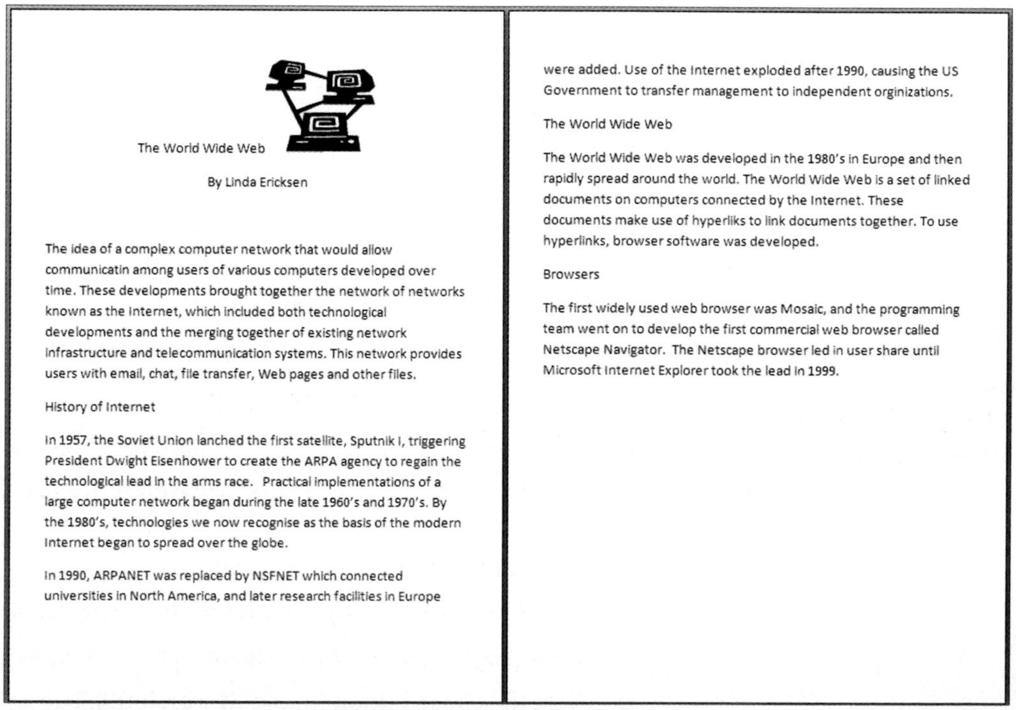

The World Wide Web

By Linda Ericksen

The idea of a complex computer network that would allow communicatin among users of various computers developed over time. These developments brought together the network of networks known as the Internet, which included both technological developments and the merging together of existing network infrastructure and telecommunication systems. This network provides users with email, chat, file transfer, Web pages and other files.

History of Internet

In 1957, the Soviet Union lanched the first satellite, Sputnik I, triggering President Dwight Eisenhower to create the ARPA agency to regain the technological lead in the arms race. Practical implementations of a large computer network began during the late 1960's and 1970's. By the 1980's, technologies we now recognise as the basis of the modern Internet began to spread over the globe.

In 1990, ARPANET was replaced by NSFNET which connected universities in North America, and later research facilities in Europe

were added. Use of the Internet exploded after 1990, causing the US Government to transfer management to independent orginizations.

The World Wide Web

The World Wide Web was developed in the 1980's in Europe and then rapidly spread around the world. The World Wide Web is a set of linked documents on computers connected by the Internet. These documents make use of hyperliks to link documents together. To use hyperlinks, browser software was developed.

Browsers

The first widely used web browser was Mosaic, and the programming team went on to develop the first commercial web browser called Netscape Navigator. The Netscape browser led in user share until Microsoft Internet Explorer took the lead in 1999.

Figure 1.42 Edited Document (Shown in Full Screen Reading View)

Step 3
Check Spelling

Refer to Figure 1.43 as you complete Steps 3–5.

a. Right-click the first word in the document that displays with the red wavy underline: *communicatin*.

> **TROUBLESHOOTING:** If the first word highlighted is the author's last name, ignore it for now. The name is spelled correctly, but if it is not listed in the spell check, then Word flags it.

The shortcut menu displays with correct alternatives.

b. Click **communication** to replace the misspelled word in the document.

The incorrect spelling is replaced, and the red wavy underline disappears.

c. Click the **Review tab**, and then click **Spelling & Grammar** in the Proofing group.

The Spelling and Grammar dialog box opens with the first detected error displayed.

d. Move through the document selecting the correct word from the suggestions provided and choosing to **Change** the errors.

e. Click **OK** to close the Spelling and Grammar checker when the process is complete.

Step 4
Choose Synonyms and Use Thesaurus

a. Place the insertion point in the word **complex** in the first sentence and right-click the mouse.

The shortcut menu displays.

b. Point to **Synonyms** on the shortcut menu.

The list of alternative words displays.

c. Click the alternative word **multifaceted**.

The new word replaces the word *complex* in the document.

d. Click in the word you just replaced, *multifaceted*, and click the **Thesaurus** button on the Review tab.

The Thesaurus displays with alternatives for **multifaceted**.

e. Scroll down the list and point to the word *comprehensive*.

A box displays around the word with a drop-down arrow on the right.

f. Click the drop-down arrow to display the menu and click **Insert**.

The word *comprehensive* replaces the word in the document.

Step 5
Use the Research Tool

Refer to Figure 1.43 to complete Step 5.

a. Place the insertion point in the Search for text box and type **browser**.

b. Click the drop-down arrow on the **Reference** list, which currently displays the Thesaurus.

The list of reference sites displays.

c. Click **Encarta Encyclopedia: English (North American)** option.

A definition of the browser displays in the results box.

d. Click the **Close** button on the Research title bar.

The Research pane closes.

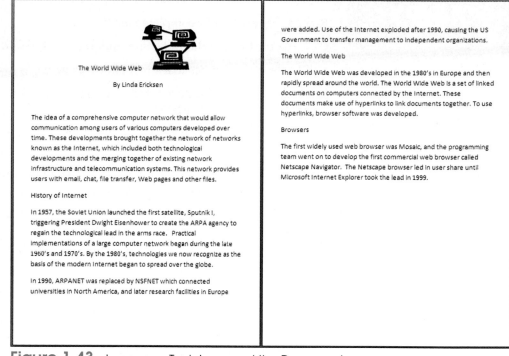

The idea of a comprehensive computer network that would allow communication among users of various computers developed over time. These developments brought together the network of networks known as the Internet, which included both technological developments and the merging together of existing network infrastructure and telecommunication systems. This network provides users with email, chat, file transfer, Web pages and other files.

History of Internet

In 1957, the Soviet Union launched the first satellite, Sputnik I, triggering President Dwight Eisenhower to create the ARPA agency to regain the technological lead in the arms race. Practical implementations of a large computer network began during the late 1960's and 1970's. By the 1980's, technologies we now recognize as the basis of the modern Internet began to spread over the globe.

In 1990, ARPANET was replaced by NSFNET which connected universities in North America, and later research facilities in Europe were added. Use of the Internet exploded after 1990, causing the US Government to transfer management to independent organizations.

The World Wide Web

The World Wide Web was developed in the 1980's in Europe and then rapidly spread around the world. The World Wide Web is a set of linked documents on computers connected by the Internet. These documents make use of hyperlinks to link documents together. To use hyperlinks, browser software was developed.

Browsers

The first widely used web browser was Mosaic, and the programming team went on to develop the first commercial web browser called Netscape Navigator. The Netscape browser led in user share until Microsoft Internet Explorer took the lead in 1999.

Figure 1.43 Language Tools Improved the Document

Step 6
Apply Font Attributes

Refer to Figure 1.44 as you complete Steps 6 and 7.

a. Select the title of the document.

The Mini toolbar displays.

b. Click **Bold** on the Mini toolbar and then click outside the title.

TROUBLESHOOTING: If the Mini toolbar, is hard to read, remember to point to it to make it display fully.

The text changes to boldface.

c. Select the title again and click the drop-down arrow on the **Font** command in the Font group on the Home tab.

The list of fonts displays.

d. Point to font names on the list.

Live Preview changes the font of the selected sentence to display the fonts you point to.

e. Scroll down, and then select the **Lucinda Bright** font by clicking on the name.

The title changes to the new font.

f. With the title still selected, click the drop-down arrow on the **Font Size** command and select **16**.

The title changes to font size 16.

g. Select the byline that contains the author's name and click the **Underline** command, the **Italic** command, and the **Shrink Font** command once. All are located in the Font group on the Home tab.

The author's byline displays underlined, in italic, and one font size smaller.

h. Select the first heading *History of Internet* and click the **Font Color** down arrow command in the Font group on the Home tab. When the colors display, under Standard Colors, choose **Purple**, and then click outside the selected text.

The heading displays in purple.

i. Select the heading you just formatted as purple text and click **Bold**.

Refer to Figure 1.44 to complete Step 7.

a. Click the **Format Painter** command in the Clipboard group on the Home tab.

The pointer changes to a small paintbrush.

b. Select the second unformatted heading and repeat the process to format the third unformatted heading.

The Format Painter formats that heading as purple and bold and automatically turns off.

c. Press **Ctrl** while you click the last sentence in the document and click the **Dialog Box Launcher** in the Font group.

d. Select **Bold** in the Font style box and **Double strikethrough** in the *Effects* section of the dialog box, then click **OK**.

e. Click outside the selected sentence to remove the selection and view the effects, and then click back in the formatted text.

The sentence displays bold with two lines through the text. The Bold command in the Font group on the Home tab displays with a gold background.

f. Select the same sentence again, click **Bold** in the Font group on the Home tab, and then click outside the sentence.

The Bold format has been removed from the text.

g. Click **Save** on the Quick Access Toolbar.

The document is saved under the same name.

h. To exit Word, click the **Office Button**, and then click the **Exit Word** button.

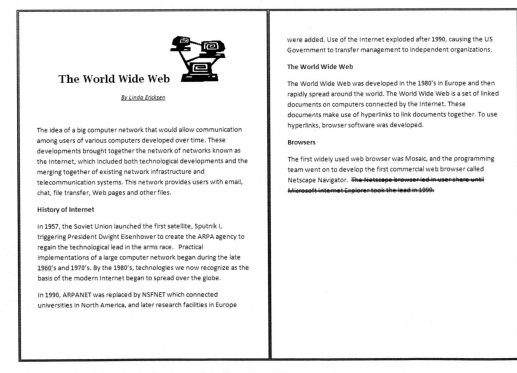

Figure 1.44 Formatted Document

Summary

1. **Identify common interface components.** You learned to identify and use the common elements of the Office 2007 interface and apply them in Word, PowerPoint, Excel, and Access. The top of the application window contains the Office Button that, when clicked, displays the Office menu. The Quick Access Toolbar provides commonly used commands, such as Save and Undo. The primary command center is the Ribbon, which contains tabs to organize major tasks. Each tab contains groups of related commands. The bottom of the window contains a status bar that gives general information, view options, and the Zoom slider.

2. **Use Office 2007 Help.** When you need help to continue working with Office 2007, you can use the Help feature from your computer or get help at Microsoft Office Online. You can position the mouse pointer on a command to see an Enhanced ScreenTip. You can click some Enhanced ScreenTips to display help. You can get context-sensitive help by clicking Help within dialog boxes.

3. **Open a file.** To retrieve a file you have previously saved, you use the Open command. When you open a file, it is copied into RAM so that you can view and work on it.

4. **Save a file.** As you create and edit documents, you should save your work for future use. Use the Save or Save As command to save a file for the first time, giving it a name and location. To continue saving changes to the same file name, use Save. To assign a new name, location, or file type, use Save As.

5. **Print a document.** Producing a perfect hard copy of the document is an important task, and you can make it easier by previewing, selecting options, and printing. You can select the printer, how many copies to print, and the pages you want to print. In addition, each program has specific print options.

6. **Select text to edit.** In order to edit text, you have to identify the body of text you want to work with by selecting it first. You can select text by using the mouse.

7. **Insert text and change to the Overtype mode.** To edit text in the document, you need to be able to insert text and to replace text by typing over it. The Insert mode inserts text without deleting existing text. The Overtype mode types over existing text as you type.

8. **Move and copy text.** You can move text from one location to another to achieve a better flow in a document, worksheet, or presentation. You can use the Copy command to duplicate data in one location and use the Paste command to place the duplicate in another location.

9. **Find, replace, and go to text.** Another editing feature that can save you time is to find text by searching for it or going directly to a specific element in the document. You can also replace text that needs updating.

10. **Use the Undo and redo Commands.** If you make a mistake and want to undo it, you can easily remedy it by using the Undo feature. Likewise, to save time, you can repeat the last action with the Redo command.

11. **Use language tools.** Office 2007 provides tools to help you create and edit error-free documents. You can use the spelling check and grammar check, the built-in thesaurus, and even conduct research all from your Word document. You can check spelling and conduct research in Excel and PowerPoint as well.

12. **Apply font attributes.** Applying font formats can help make the message clearer. For example, you can select a different font to achieve a different look. In addition, you can adjust the font size and change the font color of text. Other font attributes include bold, underline, and italic.

13. **Copy formats with the Format Painter.** You might want to copy the format of text to another location or to several locations in the document. You can easily accomplish that with the Format Painter.

Key Terms

Multiple Choice

1. Software that is used primarily with text to create, edit, and format documents is known as:

   (a) Electronic spreadsheet software
   (b) Word processing software
   (c) Presentation graphics software
   (d) Relational database software

2. Which Office feature displays when you rest the mouse pointer on a command?

   (a) The Ribbon
   (b) The status bar
   (c) An Enhanced ScreenTip
   (d) A dialog box

3. What is the name of the blinking vertical line in a document that designates the current location in the document?

   (a) A command
   (b) Overtype mode
   (c) Insert mode
   (d) Insertion point

4. If you wanted to locate every instance of text in a document and have it temporarily highlighted, which command would you use?

   (a) Find
   (b) Replace
   (c) Go To
   (d) Spell Check

5. The meeting point between computer software and the person using it is known as:

   (a) A file
   (b) Software
   (c) A template
   (d) An interface

6. Which of the following is true about the Office Ribbon?

   (a) The Ribbon displays at the bottom of the screen.
   (b) The Ribbon is only available in the Word 2007 application.
   (c) The Ribbon is the main component of the Office 2007 interface.
   (d) The Ribbon cannot be used for selecting commands.

7. Which element of the Ribbon looks like folder tabs and provides commands that are task oriented?

   (a) Groups
   (b) Tabs
   (c) Status bar
   (d) Galleries

8. Which Office 2007 element provides commands that work with an entire document or file and displays by default in the title bar?

   (a) Galleries
   (b) Ribbon
   (c) Office Button
   (d) Groups

9. If you needed the entire screen to read a document, which document view would you use?

   (a) Outline view
   (b) Draft view
   (c) Print Layout
   (d) Full Screen Reading

10. The default four-letter extension for Word documents that do not contain macros is:

    (a) .docx
    (b) .pptx
    (c) .xlsx
    (d) .dotm

11. Before you can cut or copy text, you must first do which one of the following?

    (a) Preview the document.
    (b) Save the document.
    (c) Select the text.
    (d) Undo the previous command.

12. What is the name of the memory location that holds up to twenty-four items for you to paste into the current document, another document, or another application?

    (a) My Places bar
    (b) My Documents
    (c) Ribbon
    (d) Clipboard

Multiple Choice continued

13. Word flags misspelled words by marking them with which one of the following?

   (a) A green wavy underline

   (b) Boldfacing them

   (c) A red wavy underline

   (d) A double-underline in black

14. Which of the following displays when you select text in a document?

   (a) The Mini toolbar

   (b) The Quick Access Toolbar

   (c) A shortcut menu

   (d) The Ribbon

15. Formatting text allows you to change which of the following text attributes?

   (a) The font

   (b) The font size

   (c) The font type

   (d) All of the above

a. Open Access. Click the **Office Button**, and then select **Open**. Use the Look in feature to find the *chap1_pe1* database, and then click **Open**.

b. At the right side of the Ribbon, click the **Help** button. In the Help window, type **table** in the **Type words to search for** box. Click the **Search** button.

c. Click the topic *Create tables in a database*. Browse the content of the Help window, and then click the **Close** button in the Help window.

d. Double-click the **Courses table** in the left pane. The table opens in Datasheet view.

e. Click the **Office Button**, point to the arrow after the **Print** command, and select **Print Preview** to open the Print Preview window with the Courses table displayed.

f. Point the mouse pointer on the table and click to magnify the display. Compare your screen to Figure 1.45.

g. Click the **Close Print Preview** button on the Print Preview tab.

h. Click the **Office Button**, and then click the **Exit Access button**.

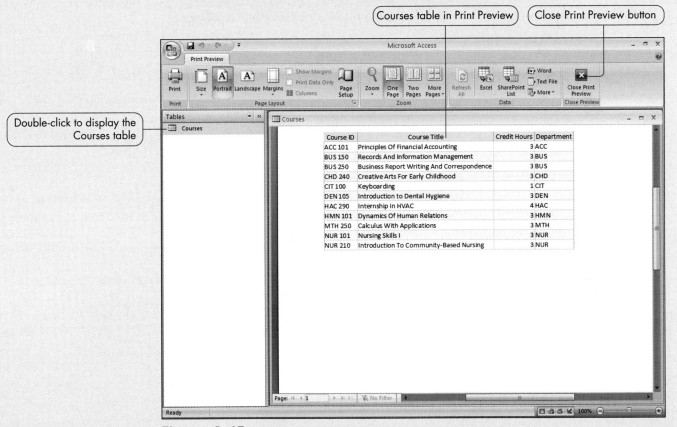

Figure 1.45 Access Print Preview

...continued on Next Page

As part of your Introduction to Computers course, you have prepared an oral report on phishing. You want to provide class members with a handout that summarizes the main points of your report. This handout is in the rough stages, so you need to edit it, and you also realize that you can format some of the text to emphasize the main points.

a. Start Word. Click the **Office Button**, and then select **Open**. Use the *Look in* feature to find the *chap1_pe2* document, and then click **Open**.

b. Click the **Office Button**, and then select **Save As**. In the *File name* box, type the document name, **chap1_pe2_solution**, be sure that Word document displays in the *Save as type* box, and use the *Look in* option to move to the location where you save your class files. Click **Save**.

c. In the document, click after the word Name and type **your name**.

d. Select your name, and then click **Bold** and **Italic** on the Mini toolbar—remember to point to the Mini toolbar to make it display fully. Your name displays in bold and italic.

e. Move the insertion point immediately before the title of the document and click the **Replace** button in the Editing group on the Home tab.

f. In the *Find what* box of the Find and Replace dialog box, type **internet**.

g. In the *Replace with* box of the Find and Replace dialog box, type **email**.

h. Click the **Replace All** button to have Word replace the text. Click **OK**, and then click **Close** to close the dialog boxes.

i. To format the title of the document, first select it, and then click the **Font arrow** in the Font group on the Home tab to display the available fonts.

j. Scroll down and choose the **Impact** font if you have it; otherwise, use one that is available.

k. Place the insertion point in the word *Phishng*. Right-click the word, and then click **Phishing** from the shortcut menu.

l. To emphasize important text in the list, double-click the first **NOT** to select it.

m. Click the **Font Color** arrow and select Red, and then click **Bold** in the Font group on the Home tab to apply bold to the text.

n. With the first instance of NOT selected, double-click **Format Painter** in the Clipboard group on the Home tab.

o. Double-click the second and then the third instance of **NOT** in the list, and then press **Esc** on the keyboard to turn off the Format Painter.

p. Compare your document to Figure 1.46. Save by clicking **Save** on the Quick Access Toolbar. Close the document and exit Word or proceed to the next step to preview and print the document.

...continued on Next Page

Email Scams

Name: *Student name*

Phishing is fraudulent activity that uses email to scam unsuspecting victims into providing personal information. This information includes credit card numbers, social security numbers, and other sensitive information that allows criminals to defraud people.

If you receive an email asking you to verify an account number, update information, confirm your identity to avoid fraud, or provide other information, close the email immediately. The email may even contain a link to what appears at first glance to be your actual banking institution or credit card institution. However, many of these fraudsters are so adept that they create look-alike Web sites to gather information for criminal activity. Follow these steps:

Do **NOT** click any links.

Do **NOT** open any attachments.

Do **NOT** reply to the email.

Close the email immediately.

Call your bank or credit card institution immediately to report the scam.

Delete the email.

Remember, never provide any information without checking the source of the request.

Figure 1.46 Phishing Document

3 Previewing and Printing a Document

You created a handout to accompany your oral presentation in the previous exercise. Now you want to print it out so that you can distribute it.

a. If necessary, open the *chap1_pe2_solution* document that you saved in the previous exercise.
b. Click the **Office Button**, point to the arrow after the Print command, and select **Print Preview** to open the Print Preview window with the document displayed.

...continued on Next Page

c. Point the mouse pointer in the document and click to magnify the display. Click the mouse pointer a second time to reduce the display.

d. To change the orientation of the document, click **Orientation** in the Page Setup group and choose **Landscape**.

e. Click **Undo** on the Quick Access Toolbar to undo the last command, which returns the document to portrait orientation. Compare your results to the zoomed document in Figure 1.47.

f. Click **Print** on the Print Preview tab to display the Print dialog box.

g. Click **OK** to print the document.

h. Close the document without saving it.

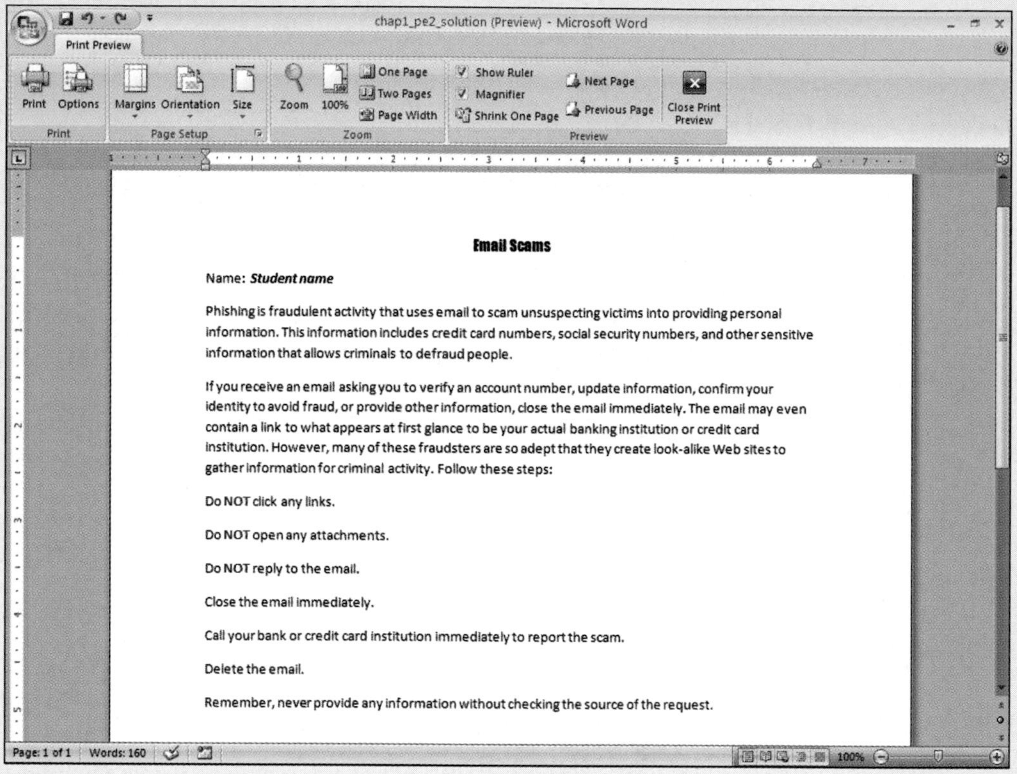

Figure 1.47 Document in Print Preview Window

4 Editing a Promotion Flyer

You work for Business Express, formerly known as Print Express, a regional company specializing in business centers that design and produce documents for local businesses and individuals. Business Express has just undergone a major transition along with a name change. Your job is to edit and refine an existing flyer to inform customers of the new changes. Proceed as follows:

a. Open Word. Click the **Office Button**, and then select **Open**. Use the *Look in* feature to find the *chap1_pe4* document.

b. Click the **Office Button** again and select **Save As**. Type the document name, **chap1_pe4_solution**, be sure that Word document displays in the *Save as type* box, and use the *Look in* option to move to the location where you save your class files.

c. Place the insertion point at the beginning of the document, and then click **Spelling & Grammar** in the Proofing group on the Review tab to open the Spelling and Grammar dialog box.

d. Click the **Change** button three times to correct the spelling errors. Click **OK** to close the completion box.

...continued on Next Page

e. Place the insertion point at the end of the first sentence of the document—just before the period. To insert the following text, press **Spacebar** and type **that offers complete business solutions**.

f. Place the insertion point in *good* in the first sentence of the third paragraph and right-click the mouse.

g. Point to **Synonyms**, and then click **first-rate** to replace the word in the document.

h. Place the insertion point in *bigger* in the last sentence of the third paragraph and click **Thesaurus** in the Proofing group on the Review tab. Point to **superior** and click the drop-down arrow that displays. Click **Insert** from the menu to replace the word in the document, and then click the **Close** button on the Thesaurus.

i. Select the last full paragraph of the document and click **Cut** in the Clipboard group on the Home tab to remove the paragraph from the document.

j. Place the insertion point at the beginning of the new last paragraph and click **Paste** in the Clipboard group on the Home tab to display the text.

k. Click **Undo** on the Quick Access Toolbar twice to undo the paste operation and to undo the cut operation—placing the text back in its original location.

l. Place the insertion point after the colon at the bottom of the document and type **your name**.

m. Compare your results to Figure 1.48, and then save and close the document.

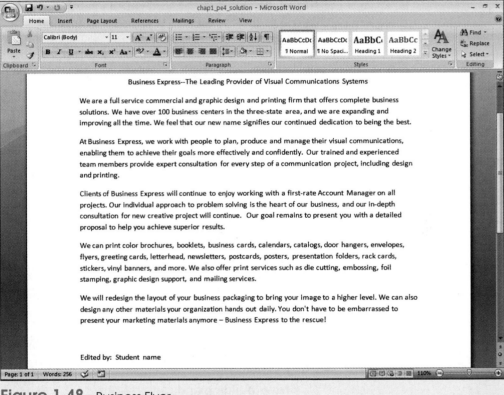

Figure 1.48 Business Flyer

Mid-Level Exercises

1 Updating a Training Document

Your position as trainer for a large building supply company involves training all new employees. It is your job to familiarize new employees with the services provided by Castle Home Building Supply. You distribute a list at the training session and you realize that it needs updating before the next session, so you decide to edit and format it.

a. Start Word. Open the *chap1_mid1* file and save it as **chap1_mid1_solution**.

b. Change the title font to Arial Rounded MT Bold size 16 and change the font color to dark brown.

c. Make the subtitle Arial Unicode MS and italic.

d. Cut the item *Help with permits* and make it the second item on the list.

e. In the first list item, insert **and** after the word *fair*.

f. Change the word *help* in the last list item to **Assistance**.

g. Select the list of items excluding the heading, Services Provided.

h. Bold the list and change the font size to 16.

i. Save the document and compare it to Figure 1.49.

Castle Home Building Supply

Where the Customer Comes First

Services Provided:

Fair and accurate estimates

Help with permits

Free delivery on all orders over $100

Design help

Professional Installation available

Custom work

Professional assistance

New building and renovations

Assistance with inspections

Figure 1.49 Training Document

...continued on Next Page

The owner of the Bayside Restaurant wants your help formatting his menu so that it is more pleasing to customers; follow the steps below:

a. Open the *chap1_mid2* document and save it as **chap1_mid2_solution**.

b. Format the menu title as Broadway size 16.

c. Format the three headings: Appetizers, Soups and Salads, and Lunch or Dinner Anytime! as Bodoni MT Black, size 12, and change the font color to Dark Red. Remember to format the first one and use the Format Painter for the second two headings.

d. Format all the dish names, such as Nachos, using the Outline Font Effects.

e. Bold all the prices in the document.

f. Preview the document, compare to Figure 1.50, and then print it.

g. Save and close the document.

Bayside Menu - Great Food & Prices!

APPETIZERS

NACHOS: tri-color tortilla chips, melted cheddar cheese topped with tomato, onion and jalapeno **$ 9.00**

CHICKEN WINGS: baked, served with celery sticks and blue cheese dip **$ 9.00**

MOZZARELLA STICKS: baked, then served with a hearty marinara sauce **$ 9.00**

CRAB & ARTICHOKE DIP: a creamy blend of artichoke hearts, lump meat crab meat and cheese, served with toasted bread **$ 12.00**

STEAMED SHRIMP: half-pound of extra large shrimp, served with cocktail sauce **$14.00**

SOUPS and SALADS

CHILE: beef and bean chili with tortilla chips on the side **$ 7.00**

HOUSE SALAD: mixed greens and garden vegetables **$ 5.00**

LUNCH or DINNER ANYTIME!

CRAB CAKE SANDWICH: jumbo crab meat on a toasted roll served with chips and dip **$ 15.00**

CLASSIC CLUB: turkey, ham, cheddar and provolone cheese, bacon, lettuce, tomato and mayo on toasted bread, served with chips and dip **$ 10.00**

DOUBLE BURGER: half-pound Black Angus beef burger, cooked the way you order it, topped with American cheese, bacon, onion, lettuce and tomato on a toasted roll with French fries **$ 11.00**

BBQ PULLED PORK SANDWICH: pulled pork with BBQ sauce served on a toasted roll with chips **$ 10.00**

SWISS CHICKEN: breast topped with Swiss cheese, bacon and tomato with ranch dressing, served on a toasted roll and French fries **$ 10.00**

TURKEY WRAP: sliced turkey breast, lettuce, tomato and mayo, rolled on a flour tortilla, served with chips and dip **$ 10.00**

RUEBEN: corned beef, sauerkraut, Swiss cheese and Russian dressing on toasted rye, served with French fries **$ 10.00**

CHICKEN TENDERS: breaded and baked just right, served with BBQ sauce, honey mustard and French Fries **$ 10.00**

ITALIAN PIZZA: mozzarella, pepperoni, and marinara **$ 8.00**

Figure 1.50 The Formatted Menu

...continued on Next Page

3 Enhance the Insurance Letter

Your job duties at Health First Insurance, Inc., involve maintaining the correspondence. You need to update the welcome letter you send to clients to reflect the company's new name, new address, and other important elements, and then address it to a new client. Proceed as follows.

a. Open the *chap1_mid3* document and save it as **chap1_mid3_solution**.

b. Run the Spelling check to eliminate the errors.

c. Use Replace to change **University Insurance, Inc**. to **Health First Insurance, Inc**. throughout the letter.

d. Change the Address from **123 Main St**. to **1717 N. Zapata Way**.

e. Change the inside address that now has **Client name, Client Address, Client City, State and Zip Code** to **your name and complete address**. Also change the salutation to your name.

f. Move the first paragraph so that it becomes the last paragraph in the body of the letter.

g. Preview the letter to be sure that it fits on one page, compare it with Figure 1.51, and then print it.

h. Save and close the document.

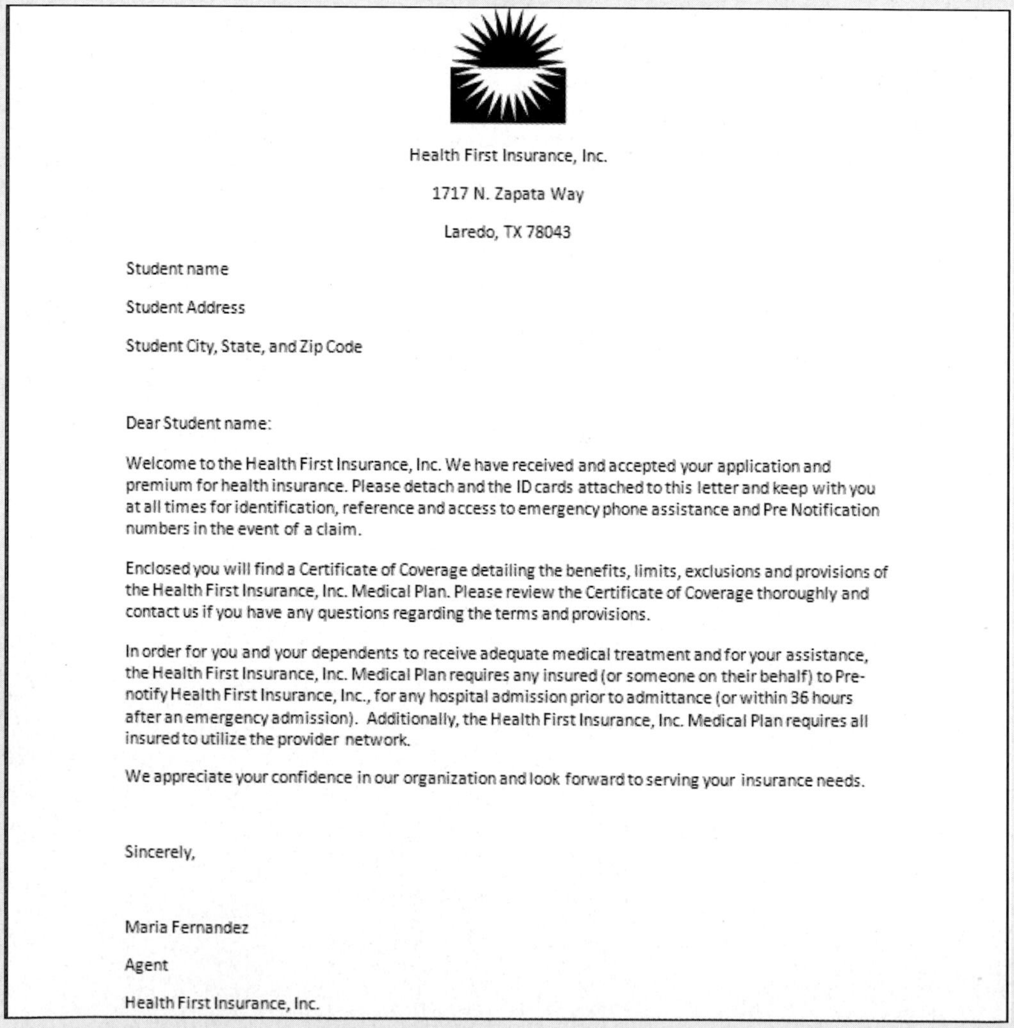

Health First Insurance, Inc.

1717 N. Zapata Way

Laredo, TX 78043

Student name

Student Address

Student City, State, and Zip Code

Dear Student name:

Welcome to the Health First Insurance, Inc. We have received and accepted your application and premium for health insurance. Please detach and the ID cards attached to this letter and keep with you at all times for identification, reference and access to emergency phone assistance and Pre Notification numbers in the event of a claim.

Enclosed you will find a Certificate of Coverage detailing the benefits, limits, exclusions and provisions of the Health First Insurance, Inc. Medical Plan. Please review the Certificate of Coverage thoroughly and contact us if you have any questions regarding the terms and provisions.

In order for you and your dependents to receive adequate medical treatment and for your assistance, the Health First Insurance, Inc. Medical Plan requires any insured (or someone on their behalf) to Pre-notify Health First Insurance, Inc., for any hospital admission prior to admittance (or within 36 hours after an emergency admission). Additionally, the Health First Insurance, Inc. Medical Plan requires all insured to utilize the provider network.

We appreciate your confidence in our organization and look forward to serving your insurance needs.

Sincerely,

Maria Fernandez

Agent

Health First Insurance, Inc.

Figure 1.51 The Updated Letter

Capstone Exercise

In this project, you work with a business plan for Far East Trading Company that will be submitted to funding sources in order to secure loans. The document requires editing to polish the final product and formatting to enhance readability and emphasize important information.

Editing the Document

This document is ready for editing, so proceed as follows:

a. Open the *chap1_cap* document. Save the document as **chap1_cap_solution**.

b. Run the Spelling and Grammar check to eliminate all spelling and grammar errors in the document.

c. Use the Thesaurus to find a synonym for the word **unique** in the second paragraph of the document.

d. Use the Go To command to move to page 3 and change the $175,000 to $250,000.

e. Move the entire second section of the document (notice the numbers preceding it) now located at the end of the document to its correct location after the first section.

f. Insert the street **1879 Columbia Ave.** before Portland in the first paragraph.

g. Copy the inserted street address to section 2.3 and place it in front of Portland there also.

h. Replace the initials **FET** with **FETC** for every instance in the document.

i. Type over 1998 in the third paragraph so that it says 2008.

Formatting the Document

Next, you will apply formatting techniques to the document. These format options will further increase the readability and attractiveness of your document.

a. Select the two-line title, and change the font to Engravers MT, size 14, and change the color to Dark Red.

b. Select the first heading in the document: 1.0 Executive Summary, then change the font to Gautami, bold, and change the color to Dark Blue.

c. Use the Format Painter to make all the main numbered headings the same formatting, that is 2.0, 3.0, 4.0, and 5.0.

d. The first three numbered sections have subsections such as 1.1, 1.2. Select the heading 1.1 and format it for bold, italic, and change the color to a lighter blue—Aqua, Accents, Darker 25%.

e. Use the Format Painter to make all the numbered subsections the same formatting.

Printing the Document

To finish the job, you need to print the business plan.

a. Preview the document to check your results.

b. Print the document.

c. Save your changes and close the document.

Mini Cases

Use the rubric following the case as a guide to evaluate our work, but keep in mind that your instructor may impose additional grading criteria or use a different standard to judge your work.

A Thank-You Letter

GENERAL CASE

As the new volunteer coordinator for Special Olympics in your area, you need to send out information for prospective volunteers, and the letter you were given needs editing and formatting. Open the *chap1_mc1* document and make necessary changes to improve the appearance. You should use Replace to change the text (insert your state name), use the current date and your name and address information, format to make the letter more appealing, and eliminate all errors. Your finished document should be saved as **chap1_mc1_solution**.

Performance Elements	Exceeds Expectations	Meets Expectations	Below Expectations
Corrected all errors	Document contains no errors.	Document contains minimal errors.	Document contains several errors.
Use of character formatting features such as font, font size, font color, or other attributes	Used character formatting options throughout entire document.	Used character formatting options in most sections of document.	Used character formatting options on a small portion of document.
Inserted text where Instructed	The letter is complete with all required information inserted.	The letter is mostly complete.	Letter is incomplete.

The Information Request Letter

RESEARCH CASE

Search the Internet for opportunities to teach abroad or for internships available in your major. Have fun finding a dream opportunity. Use the address information you find on the Web site that interests you, and compose a letter asking for additional information. For example, you might want to teach English in China, so search for that information. Your finished document should be saved as **chap1_mc2_solution**.

Performance Elements	Exceeds Expectations	Meets Expectations	Below Expectations
Use of character formatting	Three or more character formats applied to text.	One or two character formats applied to text.	Does not apply character formats to text.
Language tools	No spelling or grammar errors.	One spelling or grammar error.	More than one spelling or grammar error.
Presentation	Information is easy to read and understand.	Information is somewhat unclear.	Letter is unclear.

Movie Memorabilia

Use the following rubrics to guide your evaluation of your work, but keep in mind that your instructor may impose additional grading criteria.

Open the *chap1_mc3* document that can be found in the Exploring folder. The advertising document is over-formatted, and it contains several errors and problems. For example, the text has been formatted in many fonts that are difficult to read. The light color of the text also has made the document difficult to read. You should improve the formatting so that it is consistent, helps the audience read the document, and is pleasing to look at. Your finished document should be saved as **chap1_mc3_solution**.

Performance Elements	Exceeds Expectations	Meets Expectations	Below Expectations
Type of font chosen to format document	Number and style of fonts appropriate for short document.	Number or style of fonts appropriate for short document.	Overused number of fonts or chose inappropriate font.
Color of font chosen to format document	Appropriate font colors for document.	Most font colors appropriate.	Overuse of font colors.
Overall document appeal	Document looks appealing.	Document mostly looks appealing.	Did not improve document much.

Introduction to PowerPoint

Presentations Made Easy

bjectives

After you read this chapter, you will be able to:

1. Identify PowerPoint user interface elements **(page 75)**.
2. Use PowerPoint views **(page 80)**.
3. Open and save a slide show **(page 85)**.
4. Get Help **(page 88)**.
5. Create a storyboard **(page 93)**.
6. Use slide layouts **(page 96)**.
7. Apply design themes **(page 96)**.
8. Review the presentation **(page 98)**.
9. Add a table **(page 105)**.
10. Insert clip art **(page 105)**.
11. Use transitions and animations **(page 107)**.
12. Run and navigate a slide show **(page 116)**.
13. Print with PowerPoint **(page 118)**.

Hands-On Exercises

Exercises	Skills Covered
1. **INTRODUCTION TO POWERPOINT** (page 89) **Open:** chap1_ho1_intro.pptx **Save as:** chap1_ho1_intro_solution.pptx	• Start PowerPoint • Open an Existing Presentation • Type a Speaker's Note • View the Presentation • Save the Presentation with a New Name • Locate Information Using Help
2. **CREATING A PRESENTATION** (page 99) **Open:** none **Save as:** chap1_ho2_content_solution.pptx	• Create a New Presentation • Add Slides • Check Spelling and Use the Thesaurus • Modify Text and Layout • Reorder Slides • Apply a Design Theme
3. **STRENGTHENING A PRESENTATION** (page 110) **Open:** chap1_ho2_content _solution.pptx (from Exercise 2) **Save as:** chap1_ho3_content_solution.pptx (additional modifications)	• Add a Table • Insert, Move, and Resize Clip Art • Apply a Transition • Animate Objects
4. **NAVIGATING AND PRINTING** (page 121) **Open:** chap1_ho3_content_solution.pptx (from Exercise 3) **Save as:** chap1_ho4_content_solution.pptx (additional modifications)	• Display a Slide Show • Navigate to Specific Slides • Annotate a Slide • Print Audience Handouts

CASE STUDY

Be a Volunteer

While watching television one evening, you see a public service announcement on the volunteer organization Big Brothers Big Sisters. The Big Brothers Big Sisters organization seeks to help children ages 6 through 18 reach their potential by providing mentors through their growing years. The organization matches "Bigs" (adults) with "Littles" (children) in one-on-one relationships with the goal of having the mentor make a positive impact on the child's life. Being intrigued, you attend an informational open house where volunteers and board members give an overview of the program and share personal experiences. At the open house you discover that the organization has been helping at-risk children for more than 100 years and that in 2003 Big Brothers Big Sisters was selected by *Forbes Magazine* as one of its top ten charities that it believes are worthy of donor consideration.

You choose to answer Big Brothers Big Sisters' call to "Be a friend. Be a mentor. Just be there." You call the local organization for further information and you are invited to come in and meet representatives, introduce yourself, and complete an application. Because "Bigs" and "Littles" are matched by interests, you decide to create a presentation to introduce you and give information about your interests. Your assignment is to create a PowerPoint slide show about yourself to use in your presentation. You may want to include a slide about a mentor who has positively impacted your life. Forget modesty at this point—toot your own horn!

Your Assignment

- Read the chapter, paying special attention to how to create and enhance a presentation.
- Create a new presentation with a title slide that includes your name. Save the presentation as **chap1_case_introduction_solution**.
- Storyboard a presentation that includes four to six slides that introduce you, your background, and your interests. Include an introduction slide and a summary or conclusion slide as well as your main point slides introducing you.
- Use the storyboard to create a PowerPoint slide show about you.
- Apply a design theme and add a transition to at least one slide.
- Insert at least one clip art image in an appropriate location.
- Display your slide show to at least one class member, or to the entire class if asked by your instructor.
- Print handouts, four slides per page, framed.

Introduction to PowerPoint

This chapter introduces you to PowerPoint 2007, one of the major applications in Microsoft Office 2007. PowerPoint enables you to create a professional presentation without relying on others, and then lets you deliver that presentation in a variety of ways. You can show the presentation from your computer, on the World Wide Web, or create traditional overhead transparencies. You can even use PowerPoint's Package for CD feature to package your presentation with a viewer so those without PowerPoint may still view your presentation.

A PowerPoint presentation consists of a series of slides such as those shown in Figures 1.1–1.6. The various slides contain different elements (such as text, images, and WordArt), yet the presentation has a consistent look with respect to its overall design and color scheme. Creating this type of presentation is relatively easy, and that is the power in PowerPoint. In essence, PowerPoint enables you to concentrate on the content of a presentation without worrying about its appearance. You supply the text and supporting elements and leave the formatting to PowerPoint. If, however, you wish to create your own presentation design, PowerPoint provides you with powerful tools to use in the design process.

Figure 1.1 Title Slide

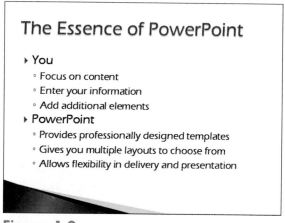

Figure 1.2 Title and Content Slide

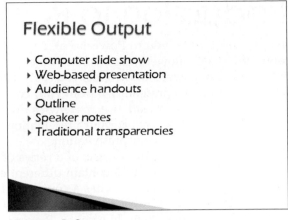

Figure 1.3 Title and Content Slide

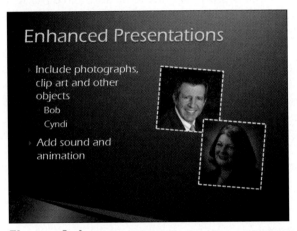

Figure 1.4 Title and Two Content Slides with Images

Figure 1.5 Title and Content Slide

Figure 1.6 Title Slide with WordArt

In addition to helping you create the presentation, PowerPoint provides a variety of ways to deliver it. You can show the presentation on a computer monitor as a slide show or Web presentation, or you can project the slide show onto a screen or a wall for an audience. You can include sound and video in the presentation, provided your system has a sound card and speakers. You can automate the presentation and display it at a convention booth or kiosk. If you cannot show the presentation on a computer with a monitor or projector, you can easily convert it to overhead transparencies or print the presentation in various ways to distribute to your audience.

In this section, you start your exploration of PowerPoint by viewing a previously completed presentation so that you can better appreciate what PowerPoint is all about. You examine the PowerPoint interface and various views to discover the advantages of each view. You modify and save an existing presentation, and then you create your own. Finally, you use Help to obtain assistance within PowerPoint.

Delivery Tips | Reference

Practice the following delivery tips to gain confidence and polish your delivery:

- Look at the audience, not at the screen, as you speak and you will open communication and gain credibility. Use the three-second guide: look into the eyes of a member of the audience for three seconds and then scan the entire audience. Continue doing this throughout your presentation. Use your eye contact to keep members of the audience involved.

- Do not read from a prepared script or your PowerPoint Notes. Know your material thoroughly. Glance at your notes infrequently. Never post a screen full of small text, and then torture your audience by saying "I know you cannot read this so I will..."

- Practice or rehearse your presentation with your PowerPoint at home until you are comfortable with the material and its corresponding slides.

- Speak slowly and clearly and try to vary your delivery. Show emotion or enthusiasm for your topic. If you do not care about your topic, why should the audience?

- Pause to emphasize key points when speaking.

- Speak to the person farthest away from you to be sure the people in the last row can hear you.

- Do not overwhelm your audience with your PowerPoint animations, sounds, and special effects. These features should not overpower you and your message, but should enhance your message.

- Arrive early to set up so you do not keep the audience waiting while you manage equipment. Have a backup in case the equipment does not work: overhead transparencies or handouts work well. Again, know your material well enough that you can present without the slide show if necessary.

- Prepare handouts for your audience so they can relax and participate in your presentation rather than scramble taking notes.

- Thank the audience for their attention and participation. Leave on a positive note.

TIP Polish Your Delivery

The speaker is the most important part of any presentation, and a poor delivery will ruin even the best presentation. Remember that a PowerPoint slide show is a tool to aid YOU in your presentation and that YOU are the key to a good presentation. Do not use a PowerPoint slide show as a crutch for lack of preparation for a presentation. A PowerPoint presentation should not be like "karaoke," where you read your information word for word from the screen!

Identifying PowerPoint User Interface Elements

If you have completed the Exploring Series Office Fundamentals chapter on Office 2007, many of the PowerPoint 2007 interface features will be familiar to you. If this is your first experience with an Office 2007 application, you will quickly feel comfortable in PowerPoint, and because the interface is core to all of the Office 2007 applications, you will quickly be able to apply the knowledge in Word, Excel, Access, and Outlook. In Office 2007, Microsoft organizes features and commands to correspond directly to the common tasks people perform, making it possible for you to find the features you need quickly.

Normal view is the tri-pane default PowerPoint view.

In PowerPoint 2007, you work with two windows: the PowerPoint application window and the document window for the current presentation. The PowerPoint application window contains the Minimize, Maximize (or Restore), and Close buttons. The PowerPoint application window also contains the title bar, which indicates the file name of the document on which you are working and the name of the application (Microsoft PowerPoint). Figure 1.7 shows the default PowerPoint view, the *Normal view*, with three panes that provide maximum flexibility in working with the presentation. The pane on the left side of the screen shows either thumbnails or an outline of the presentation, depending on whether you select the Slides tab or the Outline tab. The Slide pane on the right displays the currently selected slide in your presentation. The final pane, the Notes pane, is located at the bottom of the screen where you enter notes pertaining to the slide or the presentation.

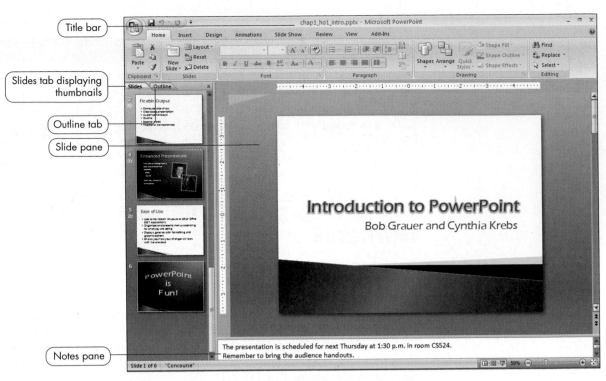

Figure 1.7 The Default PowerPoint View (Normal View)

Refer to Figure 1.8 to see the Microsoft Office Button, hereafter referred to as the Office Button, displayed below the title bar. This button provides you with an easy way to access commands for saving and printing, and includes features for finalizing your work and sharing your work with others. To the right of the Office Button is the Quick Access Toolbar, which gives you quick access to the commands that you may need at any time: Save, Undo, and Redo. You also can add other commands to the Quick Access Toolbar.

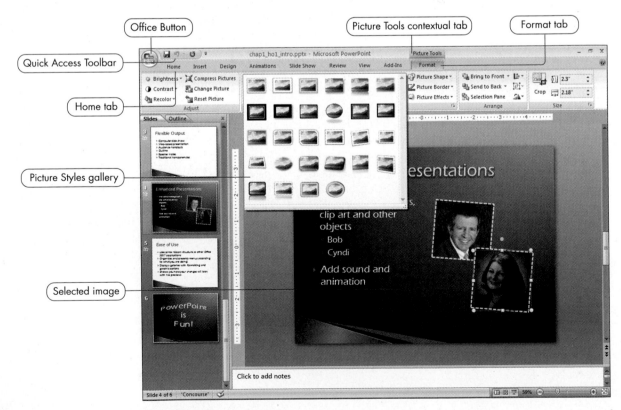

Figure 1.8 PowerPoint's Interface

The **Ribbon** is a command center that organizes commands into groups accessed from tabs.

Beneath the Office Button and the Quick Access Toolbar is the **Ribbon**, a command center that organizes commands into groups. The Ribbon makes it easy for you to find the features you need. Locate the Ribbon in Figure 1.8.

> **TIP** View Hidden Commands
>
> If, when you look at your PowerPoint screen, it does not show all of the commands, your monitor could be set to display at a low resolution. For example, a resolution of 800 by 600 pixels used with small notebooks and older 13" CRT screens will not show all the commands. To see the hidden commands, click the ▶ on the vertical bar on the far right of the Ribbon. The remaining commands will appear. Changing your resolution to 1026 by 768 pixels or a higher resolution will enable all commands to display.

A **tab** sits above the Ribbon and is used to organize or group like features for quick access.

A **tab** sits above the Ribbon and organizes commands by grouping the most commonly used features related to your task for quick access. Once you select a tab based on the task you wish to perform, the commands that relate to one another when working on that task appear together in groups. For example, when you click the Home tab, the core PowerPoint commands appear in groups such as Clipboard, Slides, Font, Paragraph, Drawing, and Editing. PowerPoint has seven tabs: Home, Insert, Design, Animations, Slide Show, Review, and View. You may see an additional tab, Add-Ins, if you have any supplemental programs that add features to Microsoft Office. The author installed a supplemental image-capturing program, so all figures in this text display the Add-Ins tab. Table 1.1 lists each of the tabs, the groups that appear when the tab is selected, and a general description of the available commands.

> **TIP** Minimize the Ribbon
>
> To increase the size of the working area on your screen, you can minimize the Ribbon by clicking any active tab, located above the Ribbon. To restore the Ribbon, click any tab. As an alternative, use the keyboard shortcut by pressing **Ctrl+F1**.

An **object** is any type of information that can be inserted in a slide.

A **contextual tab** is a specialty tab that appears only when certain types of objects are being edited.

(Microsoft . . . "pick and click" formatting . . . gives you results that look good without much design effort.)

A **gallery** displays a set of predefined options that can be clicked to apply to an object.

When you add text, a graphic, a table, a chart, or any other form of information to a slide, you are adding an **object** to the slide. When you select certain types of objects for editing, **contextual tabs** containing commands specific to that object appear. The contextual tabs appear above the Ribbon and, when clicked, open a tab containing multiple tools you need. For example, in Figure 1.8, because the image of Cyndi is selected for editing, the Picture Tools contextual tab displays. Clicking the Picture Tools tab opened the Format tab. The Format tab is organized into groups related to specific tasks (Picture Tools, Picture Styles, Arrange, and Size).

As you examine Figure 1.8, notice the large box that appears on top of the Ribbon, showing a wide variety of styles that could be applied to a picture. This is the Picture Styles gallery, one of many galleries within PowerPoint. A **gallery** provides you with a set of visual options to choose from when working with your presentation. You click an option, and the styles in that option are applied to your object. Microsoft refers to this feature as "pick and click" formatting. "Picking and clicking" gives you results that look good without much design effort.

Table 1.1 Tab, Group, and Description

Tab and Group	Description
Home Clipboard Slides Font Paragraph Drawing Editing	The core PowerPoint tab. Contains basic editing functions such as cut and paste, and finding and replacing text. Includes adding slides and changing slide layout. Formatting using font, paragraph, and drawing tools is available.
Insert Tables Illustrations Links Text Media Clips	Contains all insert functions in one area. Includes ability to create tables and illustrations. Hyperlinks, text boxes, headers and footers, WordArt, and media clips are inserted here.
Design Page Setup Themes Background	Contains all functions associated with slide design including themes and backgrounds. Change page setup and slide orientation here.
Animations Preview Animations Transition To This Slide	Controls all aspects of animation including transitions, advanced options, and customizing.
Slide Show Start Slide Show Set Up Monitors	Includes slide show setup, monitor set up, and timing. Options for starting the slide show available.
Review Proofing Comments Protect	Contains all reviewing tools in PowerPoint, including such things as spelling and the use of comments.
View Presentation Views Show/Hide Zoom Color/Grayscale Window Macros	Contains Presentation Views. Advanced view options include showing or hiding slides, zooming, and available color choices. Set window arrangement here. Enables macro creation.
Add-Ins Custom Toolbars	Displays programs added to system that extend PowerPoint functionality. Does not display if supplemental programs are not installed.

A **ScreenTip** is a small window that describes a command.

Figure 1.9 shows a *ScreenTip,* or small window that appears when the mouse pointer moves over a command. The ScreenTip states the name or more descriptive explanation of a command. Enhanced ScreenTips also contain an icon that you can click to get more assistance from Help. ScreenTips can be invaluable when you need to identify a selected style. In this case, the ScreenTip gives the name of a WordArt choice, Fill–Accent 2, Warm Matte Bevel, and a preview of how it would look if selected. In some instances, an Enhanced ScreenTip provides brief description of the feature and includes a link to a Help topic relating to the command.

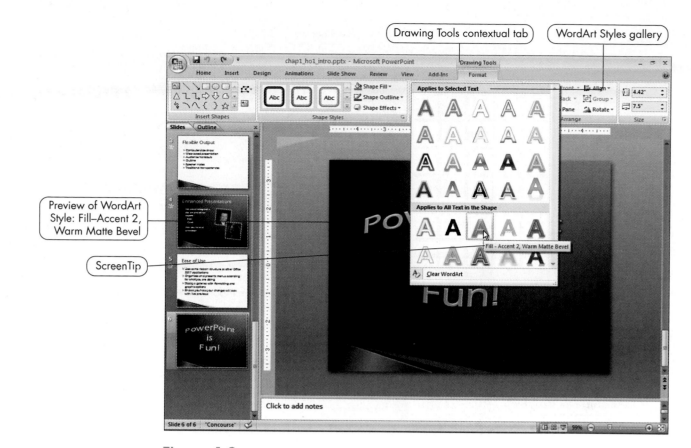

Figure 1.9 WordArt Gallery with ScreenTip

The **Mini toolbar** is a small semitransparent toolbar that appears above selected text (see Figure 1.10) and gives you quick and easy access to the formatting commands commonly applied to text (such as font, font styles, font size, text alignment, text color, indent levels, and bullet features). Because the Mini toolbar appears above the selected text, you do not have to move the mouse pointer up to the Ribbon. When you first select text, the Mini toolbar appears as a semitransparent image, but if you move the mouse pointer over the toolbar, it fades in and becomes active for your use. As the mouse pointer moves away from the toolbar, or if a command is not selected, the Mini toolbar disappears.

Figure 1.10 also shows PowerPoint's unique **status bar**, a bar that contains the slide number, the design theme name, and options that control the view of your presentation: view buttons, the Zoom level button, the Zoom Slider, and the *Fit slide to current window* button. The status bar is located at the bottom of your screen, and can be customized. To customize the status bar, right-click the bar, and then click the options you want displayed from the Customize Status Bar list.

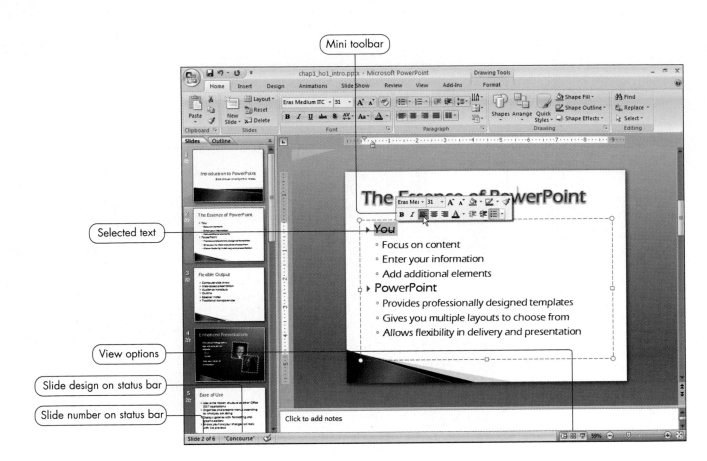

Figure 1.10 Mini Toolbar and Status Bar

Using PowerPoint Views

PowerPoint offers four primary views in which to create, modify, and deliver a presentation: Normal, Slide Sorter, Notes Page, and Slide Show. Each view represents a different way of looking at the presentation and each view has unique capabilities. (You will find some redundancy among the views in that certain tasks can be accomplished from multiple views.) The View tab gives you access to the four primary views, plus three additional views for working with masters. If you prefer, you may use the view buttons on the status bar to switch from one view to another, but only three views are available from the status bar: Normal, Slide Sorter, and Slide Show.

You looked at the default Normal view earlier in the chapter (refer to Figure 1.7), but you will examine it in more detail now and compare it to other PowerPoint views. Knowing the benefits of each view enables to you work more efficiently. Figure 1.11 shows Normal view with the screen divided into three panes: the Outline tab pane showing the text of the presentation, the Slide pane displaying an enlarged view of one slide, and the Notes pane showing a portion of any associated speaker notes for the selected slide. The Outline tab pane provides the fastest way to type or edit text for the presentation. You type directly into the outline pane and move easily from one slide to the next. You also can use the outline pane to move and copy text from one slide to another or to rearrange the order of the slides within a presentation. The outline pane is limited, however, in that it does not show graphic elements that may be present on individual slides. Thus, you may want to switch to the Normal view that shows the Slides tab containing *thumbnail* images (slide miniatures) rather than the outline. In this view, you can change the order of the slides by clicking and dragging a slide to a new position. The Outline and Slides tabs let you switch between the two variations of the Normal view.

A *thumbnail* is a miniature of a slide that appears in the Slides tab.

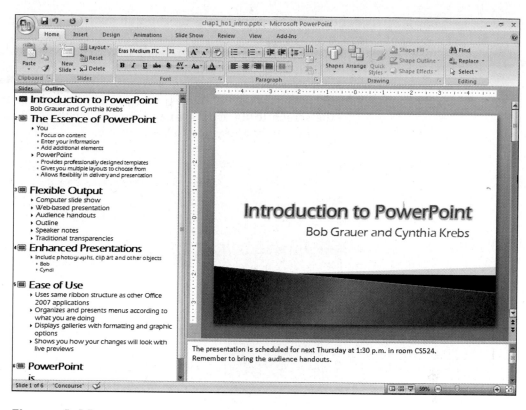

Figure 1.11 Normal View with Outline Tab Selected

The Normal view also provides access to the individual slides and speaker notes, each of which appears in its own pane. The Slide pane is the large pane on the right of the window. The Notes pane displays on the bottom of the window. You can change the size of these panes by dragging the splitter bar (border) that separates one pane from another. Figure 1.12 shows the Slides tab selected, the size of the Slide pane reduced, and the size of the Notes pane enlarged to provide for more space in which to create speaker notes.

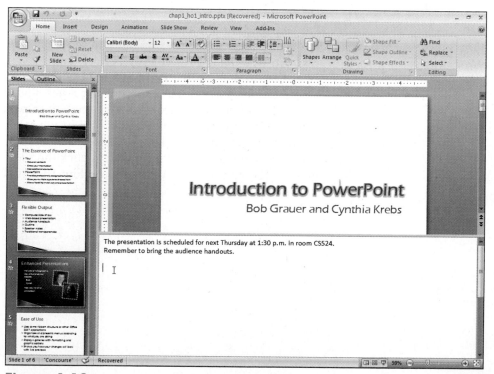

Figure 1.12 Normal View with Resized Panes

The Normal view is probably all that you need, but some designers like to close the left pane completely to see just an individual slide. This variation of the Normal view enlarges the individual slide so you can see more detail. Because the individual slide is where you change or format text, add graphical elements, or apply various animation effects an enlarged view is helpful. Figure 1.13 shows the individual slide in Normal view with the left pane closed. If you close the left pane, you can restore the screen to its usual tri-pane view by clicking the View tab, and then clicking Normal in the Presentation Views group.

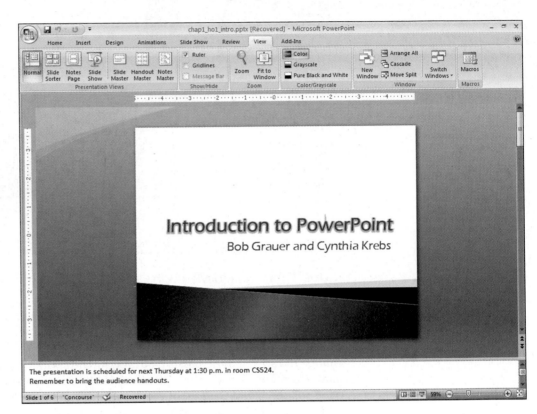

Figure 1.13 Individual Slide View

The **Notes Page view** is used for entering and editing large amounts of text that the speaker can refer to when presenting.

Rather than create speaker notes in the small pane available in the Normal view, you can work in the *Notes Page view*, a view specifically created to enter and edit large amounts of text that the speaker can refer to when presenting. If you have a large amount of technical detail in the speaker notes, you also may want to print audience handouts of this view since each page contains a picture of the slide plus the associated speaker notes. The notes do not appear when the presentation is shown, but are intended to help the speaker remember the key points about each slide. To switch from Normal view to Notes Page view, click the View tab, and then click Notes Page view in the Presentation Views group. Figure 1.14 shows an example of the Notes Page view.

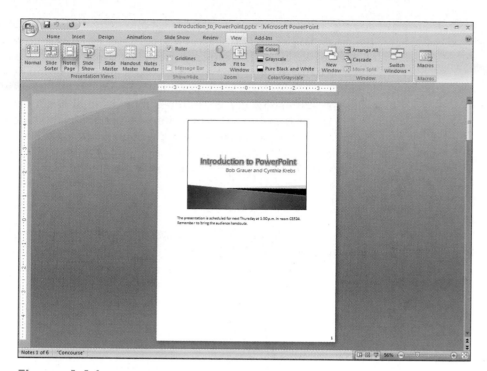

Figure 1.14 Notes Page View

The ***Slide Sorter view*** displays thumbnails of slides.

The ***Slide Sorter view*** enables you to see miniatures of your presentation slides to view multiple slides simultaneously (see Figure 1.15). This view is helpful when you wish to reorder the slides in a presentation. It also provides a convenient way to delete one or more slides. It lets you set transition effects for multiple slides. Any edit that you perform in one view is automatically updated in the other views. If, for example, you change the order of the slides in the Slide Sorter view, the changes automatically are reflected in the outline or thumbnail images within the Normal view. To switch to Slide Sorter view, click the View tab, and then click Slide Sorter in the Presentation Views group. If you are in Slide Sorter view and double-click a thumbnail, PowerPoint returns to the Normal view.

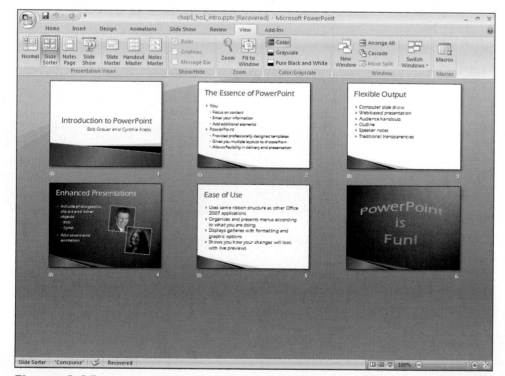

Figure 1.15 Slide Sorter View

The **Slide Show view** displays a full-screen view of a presentation.

The **Slide Show view** is used to deliver the completed presentation full screen to an audience, one slide at a time, as an electronic presentation on the computer (see Figure 1.16). The slide show can be presented manually, where the speaker clicks the mouse to move from one slide to the next, or automatically, where each slide stays on the screen for a predetermined amount of time, after which the next slide appears. A slide show can contain a combination of both methods for advancing. You can insert transition effects to impact the look of how one slide moves to the next. To view the presentation in Slide Show view, click the View tab and then click Slide Show in the Presentation Views group. This step begins the show with Slide 1. To end the slide show, press Escape on the keyboard.

TIP Start the Slide Show

To choose whether you start a slide show from the beginning, Slide 1, or from the current slide, click the Slide Show tab, and then click either From Beginning or From Current Slide in the Start Slide Show group.

Figure 1.16 Slide Show View

Have you been in an audience watching a presenter use PowerPoint to deliver an electronic presentation? Did the presenter look professional at all times? While this is the desired scenario, consider another real-life scenario—the presenter holds a remote in one hand, printed speaker notes in the other hand, and is wearing a watch. The presenter is conscious of the time allotted for the presentation and attempts to look at the watch to see how much time has elapsed. Using the remote, the presenter attempts to slide a long sleeve up and reveal the watch. The remote catches on the printed speaker notes, the notes start to fall, the presenter grabs to catch them . . . and chaos results. Presenter Fumble lives! You can avoid "Presenter Fumble" by using Presenter view.

Presenter view delivers a presentation on two monitors simultaneously. Typically, one monitor is a projector that delivers the full-screen presentation to the audience and one monitor is a laptop or computer at the presenter's station. Having two monitors enables your audience to see your presentation at the same time you are seeing a special view of the presentation that includes the slide, speaker notes, slide thumbnails so you can jump between slides as needed, navigation arrows that advance your slide or return to the previous slide, options to enable a marking on the slide, and a timer that displays the time elapsed since you began. Figure 1.17 shows the audience view on the left side of the figure and the Presenter view on the right side.

> (... avoid "Presenter Fumble" by using Presenter view!)

Presenter view delivers a presentation on two monitors simultaneously.

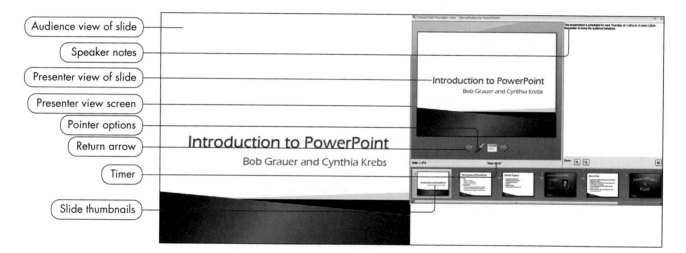

Figure 1.17 Presenter View

In order to use Presenter view, you must use a computer that has multiple monitor capability, and multiple monitor support must be turned on. If you need information about how to enable multiple monitor support, see Microsoft Windows Help. After you enable multiple monitor support, click Show Presenter View in the Monitors group on the Slide Show tab, and then click from Beginning in the Start Slide Show group under the same tab.

Opening and Saving a Slide Show

The Office Button gives you access to an important menu. The available options include the New command so that you can create a new document; in this case, a presentation that is blank or that is based upon a template. You use the Open command to retrieve a presentation saved on a storage device and place it in the RAM memory of your computer so you can work on it. The Print command opens a dialog box so that you may choose print settings and then print. The Close command closes the current presentation but leaves PowerPoint open. To exit PowerPoint, click the X located on the top right of the application window.

While you are working on a previously saved presentation, it is being saved in the temporary memory or RAM memory of your computer. The Save As command copies the presentation that you are working on to the hard drive of your computer or to a storage device such as a flash drive. When you activate the Save As command, the Save As dialog box appears (see Figure 1.18). The dialog box requires you to specify the drive or folder in which to store the presentation, the name of the presentation, and the type of file you wish the presentation to be saved as. All subsequent executions of the Save command save the presentation under the assigned name, replacing the previously saved version with the new version. If you wish to change the name of the presentation, use Save As again. Pressing Ctrl+S also displays the Save As dialog box if it is the first time you are saving the slide show.

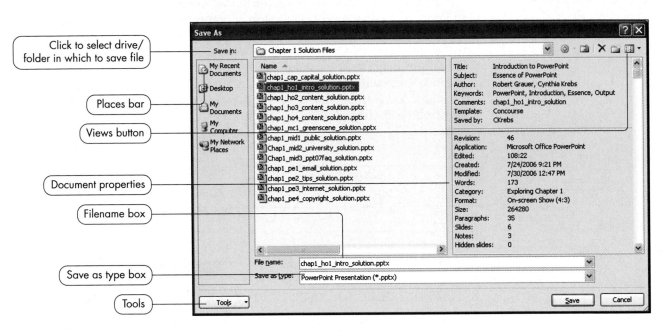

Figure 1.18 Save As Dialog Box

The file name (e.g., chap1_ho1_intro_solution) can contain up to 255 characters including spaces, commas, and/or periods. Periods are discouraged, however, since they are too easily confused with the file extensions explained in the next paragraph. Click the *Save in* drop-down arrow to select the drive and the folder in which the presentation file will be saved.

The file type defaults to a PowerPoint presentation. You can save to other formats including a Web page. When you save a PowerPoint file, it is assigned a .pptx extension. This file type is an XML (eXtensible Markup Language) format. This file format compresses data, which greatly reduces file sizes, thereby saving storage space on your hard drive or storage device. Another benefit of using the XML file format is that it reduces the chance of file corruption and helps you recover corrupted documents. This file format also provides increased security. One caution must be noted, however: Files created in the XML format cannot be opened in earlier versions of Office software unless the Microsoft Compatibility Pack is installed. Your colleagues who share files with you should download the Compatibility Pack on all computers that may be used to open your XML files.

TIP   New Folder Creation

By default, all Office documents are stored in the My Documents folder. It is helpful, however, to create additional folders, especially if you work with a large number of different documents. You can create one folder for school and another for personal work, or you can create different folders for different applications. To create a folder, click the Office Button, select Save As, and then click the Create New Folder button to display the New Folder dialog box. Type the name of the folder, and then click OK to create the folder. The next time you open or save a presentation, use the *Look in* or *Save in* box to navigate to that folder. For this class, you may wish to create a folder with your assignment solutions for each chapter so you can quickly locate them.

The Open command retrieves a copy of an existing presentation into memory, enabling you to work with that presentation. The Open command displays the Open dialog box in which you specify the file name, the drive (and optionally, the folder) that contains the file, and the file type. PowerPoint will then list all files of that type on the designated drive (and folder), enabling you to open the file you want. To aid you in selecting the correct file, click the Views button. The Preview view shows the first slide in a presentation, without having to open the presentation.

TIP   Use the Tools Button for File Management

Both the Open and the Save As dialog boxes contain a Tools button on the bottom left of their dialog boxes. Once you select any existing file and click the Tools button, you can perform basic file management functions. You can delete or rename the file. You also are able to print the file.

Metadata is data that describes other data.

Document properties is the collection of metadata.

The Properties view shows the document **metadata**, or the data that describes the document data. The collection of metadata is referred to as the **document properties**. Author name, keywords, and date created are all examples of metadata displayed in the Properties view. Figure 1.19 shows the Open dialog box in Properties view with the document properties of our sample slideshow displayed.

Click to select drive/ folder from which to open file

Click file name

Views button

Document properties

Tools

Figure 1.19 Open Dialog Box

TIP Sort by Name, Date, or File Size

The files in the Save As and Open dialog boxes can be displayed in ascending or descending sequence by name, size, file type, or date modified. Change to the Details view, then click the heading of the desired column; for example, click the Modified column to list the files according to the date they were last changed. Click the column heading a second time to reverse the sequence—that is, to switch from ascending to descending, and vice versa.

Getting Help

Microsoft Help is designed to give you all the information you need, whether it is locating information about a specific feature, troubleshooting to solve a problem, searching for software updates, finding a template, or receiving additional training. Help is installed on your computer system at the same time your Office software applications are installed. You can use Help online or offline, depending on whether you are connected to the Internet.

To access Help, you click the Microsoft Office PowerPoint Help button located at the top right of the screen below the Close button. Or, if you prefer, you can use the Help keyboard shortcut by pressing F1. The Help window will appear. This window is designed to make Help easier for you to use. You can navigate and locate information by clicking one of the hyperlinked Help topics, or you can enter a topic in the Search box. The bottom portion of the Help Window gives you access to Office Online where you can obtain clip art, download templates or training, or read articles. Clicking the *Get up to speed with Microsoft Office 2007* hyperlink and then reading the resulting Help screen will help you review the information covered thus far.

Hands-On Exercises

1 | Introduction to PowerPoint

Skills covered: 1. Start PowerPoint **2.** Open an Existing Presentation **3.** Type a Speaker's Note **4.** View the Presentation **5.** Save the Presentation with a New Name **6.** Locate Information Using Help

---

Step 1
Start PowerPoint

a. Click **Start** on your Windows taskbar, and then click **All Programs**.

b. Click **Microsoft Office**, and then click **Microsoft Office PowerPoint 2007**.

You should see a blank PowerPoint presentation in Normal view.

Step 2
Open an Existing Presentation

Refer to Figure 1.20 as you complete Step 2.

a. Click the **Office Button** and select **Open**.

The Open dialog box will appear. Do not be concerned that your file list does not match Figure 1.20.

b. Click the **Look in drop-down arrow**, and then click the appropriate drive depending on the storage location of your data.

c. Double-click the **Exploring PowerPoint folder** to make it active.

This is the folder from which you will retrieve files and into which you will save your assignment solutions.

TROUBLESHOOTING: If you do not see an Exploring PowerPoint folder, it is possible that the student files for this text were saved to a different folder for your class. Check with your instructor to find out where to locate your student files.

d. Click the **Views button** repeatedly to cycle through the different views.

As you cycle through the various views, in the Open dialog box observe the differences in each view. Identify a reason you might use each view. Figure 1.20 is displayed in Preview view.

e. Double-click the *chap1_ho1_intro* presentation.

The slide show opens to the *Introduction to PowerPoint* title slide.

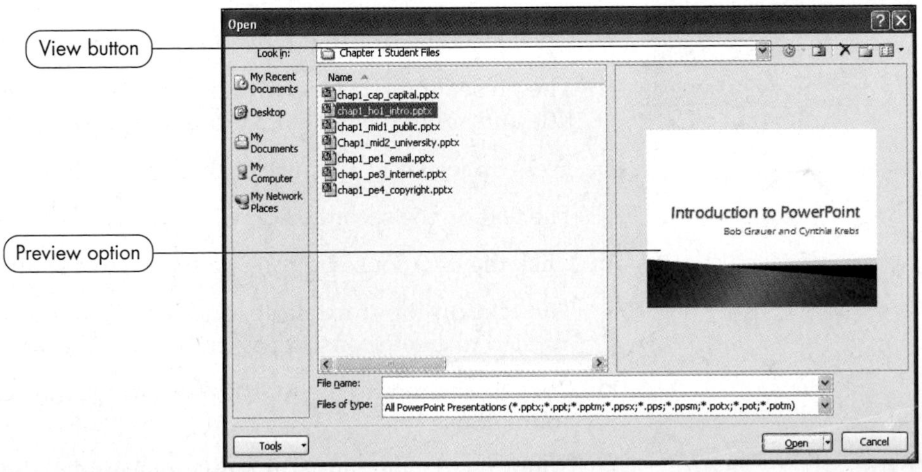

Figure 1.20 Open Dialog Box

Refer to Figure 1.21 as you complete Step 3.

a. Click the **Slide 4 thumbnail** in the Slides tab.

Slide 4 is selected and the slide appears in the Slide pane.

b. Drag the splitter bar between the Slide pane and the Notes pane upward to create more room in the Notes pane area.

c. Type the following information in the Notes pane: **Among the objects that can be inserted into PowerPoint are tables, clip art, diagrams, charts, hyperlinks, text boxes, headers and footers, movies, sound, and objects from other software packages.**

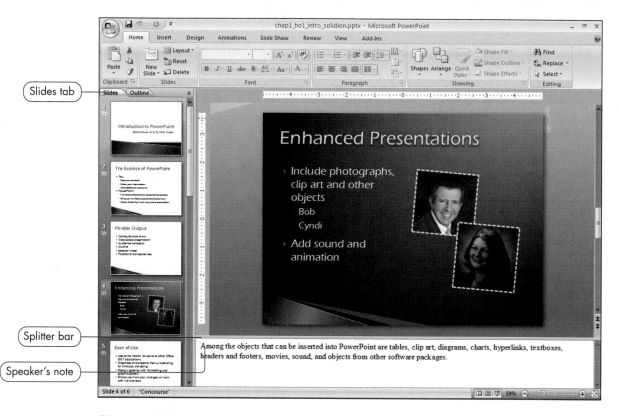

Figure 1.21 Speaker's Note

a. Click **From Beginning** in the Start Slide Show group on the Slide Show tab.

The presentation begins with the title slide, the first slide in all slide shows. The title and subtitle have animations assigned, so they come in automatically.

b. Press **Spacebar** to advance to the second slide.

The text on the second slide wipes down and creates each bullet point.

c. Click the left mouse button to advance to the third slide.

The text on the third slide, and all following slides, has the same animation applied to create consistency in the presentation.

d. Click to advance to the fourth slide, which has sound added to the image animations.

e. Continue to view the show until you come to the end of the presentation.

f. Press **Esc** to return to the PowerPoint Normal view.

Step 5

Save the Presentation with a New Name

Refer to Figure 1.22 as you complete Step 3.

a. Click the **Office Button**, and then select **Save As**.

b. Click the **Save in drop-down arrow**.

c. Click the appropriate drive, depending on where you are storing your data.

d. Double-click the *Exploring PowerPoint* folder to make it the active folder.

If you have created a different folder to store your solutions, change to that folder.

e. Type **chap1_ho1_intro_solution** as the file name for the presentation.

f. Click **Save**.

TIP Change the Default Folder

The default folder is where PowerPoint goes initially to open an existing presentation or to save a new presentation. You may find it useful to change the default folder if you are working on your own computer and not in a classroom lab. Click the Office Button, and then select Application Settings, which enables you to modify your document settings and customize how PowerPoint behaves by default. Click Saving from the frame on the left side. Click in the box that contains the default file location, enter the new drive or the new folder where you wish your files to be saved, and click OK. The next time you open or save a file, PowerPoint will go automatically to that location. This feature may not work in a classroom lab, however, if the lab has a "deep freeze" program to ensure students work from default settings.

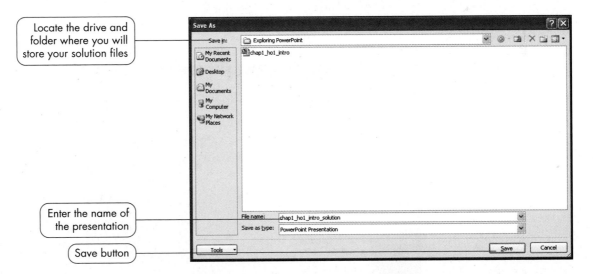

Figure 1.22 Save the Presentation with a New Name

Refer to Figure 1.23 as you complete Step 6.

a. Click **Microsoft Office PowerPoint Help** on the top right side of the screen.

The PowerPoint Help window opens.

> **TROUBLESHOOTING:** If you do not see the same Help viewer, as displayed in Figure 1.23, you may not have an active Internet connection. If you do not have an active Internet connection, the Help feature retrieves the Help information that was installed on your computer. Also, because Help Online is a dynamic feature, Microsoft frequently adds content. Each time you open a Help Online topic, you are asked to give Microsoft feedback on the value of the topic. Due to this feature, topics may be added and links changed.

b. Click the *What's New* hyperlink, and then click the *Use the Ribbon* hyperlink.

c. Scroll to the bottom of the Help window until the *See Also* box is visible. Click *Use the keyboard to work with Ribbon programs*, and then read the article on using access keys with the Ribbon.

d. Close Help, and then press **F1** on the keyboard.

F1 is the shortcut for opening Help.

e. Type **print preview** in the Search box, and then click Search.

f. Click *Print a Help topic* and read the article.

g. Close Help, and then close the *chap1_ho1_intro_solution* presentation.

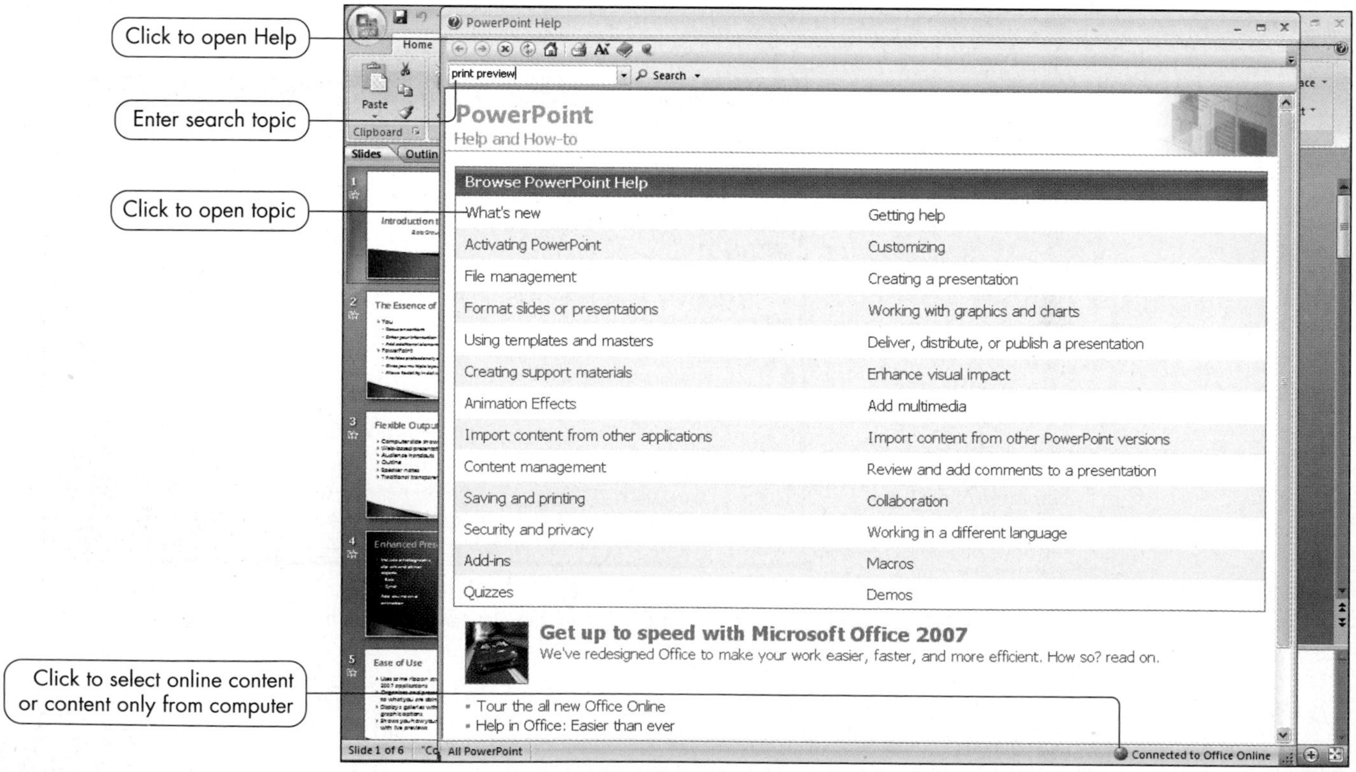

Click to open Help

Enter search topic

Click to open topic

Click to select online content or content only from computer

Figure 1.23 The Help Window

Presentation Creation

You are ready to create your own presentation, a process that requires you to develop its content and apply the formatting through the use of a template or design specification. You can do the steps in either order, but by starting with the content, you can concentrate on your message and the structure of your message without getting distracted by the formatting and design of the presentation.

Before you start the presentation in PowerPoint, you can complete several tasks that could make your presentation more effective and save you time.

Before you start the presentation in PowerPoint, you can complete several tasks that could make your presentation more effective and save you time. While you know the topic you are going to present, the way you present it should be tailored to your audience. Research your audience—determine who makes up your audience, what their needs are, and what their expectations are. By tailoring your presentation to the audience, you will have a much more interesting presentation and an involved audience. After researching your audience, begin brainstorming on how to deliver your information and message to the audience. Sketch out your thoughts to help you organize them.

After you have sketched out your thoughts, enter them into the PowerPoint presentation and apply a theme to give your presentation a polished look. Review the presentation for spelling errors and word choice problems so your presentation is professional.

In this section, you create a visual plan known as a storyboard. You learn how to change layouts, apply design themes, and use the Spell Check and the Thesaurus to review your presentation for errors.

Creating a Storyboard

A **storyboard** is a visual plan that displays the content of each slide in the slideshow.

A **storyboard** is a visual plan for your presentation. It can be a very rough draft you sketch out while brainstorming, or it can be an elaborate plan that includes the text and objects drawn as they would appear on a slide. The complexity of your storyboard is your choice, but the key point is that the storyboard helps you plan the direction of your presentation. Remember the old adage, "If you don't know where you are going, you are going to end up somewhere else!"

A simple PowerPoint storyboard is divided into sections representing individual slides. The first block in the storyboard is used for the title slide. The title slide should have a short title that indicates the purpose of the presentation and introduces the speaker. Try to capture the title in two to five words. The speaker introduction information is usually included in a subtitle and can include the speaker's name and title, the speaker's organization, the organization's logo, and the date of the presentation.

While a title slide may serve as the introduction, having a separate introduction sets a professional tone for the presentation. The introduction should get the audience's attention and convince them your presentation will be worth their time. Creating an agenda showing the topics to be covered in the presentation can serve as an introduction because as you review the agenda with the audience you start them thinking about the topics. Often, presenters use a thought-provoking quotation or question as the introduction, and pause for a short time to give the audience time to think. An image can be particularly moving if it relates to the topic and is displayed in silence for a moment. The presenter may then introduce the idea behind the image or question the audience to extract the meaning of the image from them, thereby inducing the audience to introduce the topic.

Following the title slide and the introduction, you have slides containing the main body of information you want your audience to have. Each key thought deserves a slide, and on that slide, text bullets or other objects should develop that key thought. When preparing these slides, ask yourself what you want your audience to know that they did not know before. Ask yourself what it is you want them to remember. Create the slides to answer these questions and support these main points on the slides with facts, examples, charts or graphs, illustrations, images, or video clips.

Finally, end your presentation with a summary or conclusion. This is your last chance to get your message across to your audience. It should review main points, restate the purpose of the presentation, or invoke a call to action. The summary will solidify your purpose with the audience. Remember the old marketing maxim, "Tell 'em what you're going to tell 'em, tell 'em, then tell 'em what you told 'em,"—or in other words, "Introduction, Body, Conclusion."

After you create the storyboard, review what you wrote. Now is a good time to edit your text. Shorten complete sentences to phrases. As you present, you can expand on the information shown on the slide. The phrases on the slide help your audience organize the information in their minds. Edit phrases to use as bullet points. Review and edit the phrases so they begin with an active voice when possible to involve the user. Active voice uses action verbs—action verbs ACT! Passive verbs can be recognized by the presence of linking verbs (is, am, are, was, were).

TIP   The "7 x 7" Guideline

Keep the information on your slide concise. The slide is merely a tool to help your audience "chuck into memory" the information you give. Your delivery will cover the detail. To help you remember to stay concise, follow the 7 x 7 guideline that suggests you limit the words on a visual to no more than seven words per line and seven lines per slide. This guideline gives you a total of 49 or fewer words per slide. While you may be forced to exceed this guideline on occasion, follow it as often as possible.

After you complete your planning, you are ready to prepare your PowerPoint presentation. Now instead of wasting computer time trying to decide what to say, you spend your computer time entering information, formatting, and designing. Figure 1.24 shows a working copy of a storyboard for planning presentation content. The storyboard is in rough draft form and shows changes made during the review process. The PowerPoint presentation (Figure 1.25) incorporates the changes.

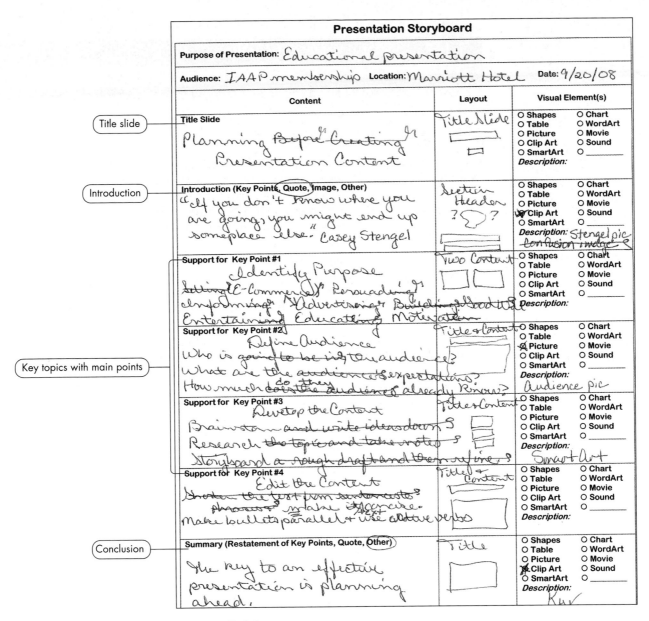

Figure 1.24 Rough Draft Storyboard

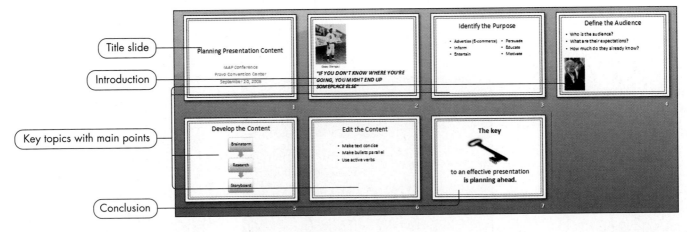

Figure 1.25 Presentation from Storyboard

Using Slide Layouts

When you first begin a new slide show, PowerPoint presents you with a slide for use as a title slide. New slides from that point on are typically created as content slides, consisting of a slide title and a defined area for content. You can enter content in the defined area or add new elements manually. If the slide arrangement does not meet your needs, you can change it by changing the slide layout.

PowerPoint provides a set of predefined slide *layouts* that determine the position of the objects or content on a slide. Slide layouts contain any number and combination of placeholders, and are available each time you click New Slide on the Home tab. When you click New Slide, the gallery of layouts is displayed for you to choose from. All of the layouts except the Blank layout include placeholders. *Placeholders* hold content and determine the position of the objects, or content, on the slide. After you select the layout, you simply click the appropriate placeholder to add the content you desire. Thus, you would click the placeholder for the title and enter the text of the title as indicated. In similar fashion, you click the placeholder for text and enter the associated text. By default, the text appears as bullets. You can change the size and position of the placeholders by moving the placeholders just as you would any object.

> A slide **layout** determines the position of objects containing content on the slide.

> A **placeholder** is a container that holds content and is used in the layout to determine the position of objects on the slide.

Applying Design Themes

PowerPoint enables you to concentrate on the content of a presentation without concern for its appearance. You focus on what you are going to say, and then utilize PowerPoint features to format the presentation attractively. The simplest method to format a slide show is to select a design theme. A design *theme* is a collection of formatting choices that includes colors, fonts, and special theme effects such as shadowing or glows. PowerPoint designers have created beautiful design themes for your use, and the themes are available in other Office applications, which lets you unify all of the documents you create.

When you apply a theme, the formatting implements automatically. To select and apply a theme, click the Design tab and click the More button in the Themes group. From the Themes gallery that appears, choose the theme you like. PowerPoint formats the entire presentation according to the theme you choose. Do not be afraid to apply new themes. As you gain experience with PowerPoint and design, you can rely less on PowerPoint and more on your own creativity for your design. Figures 1.26–1.29 show a title slide with four different themes applied. Note the color, font, and text alignment in each theme.

> A **theme** is a set of design elements that gives the slide show a unified, professional appearance.

Figure 1.26 Opulent Theme

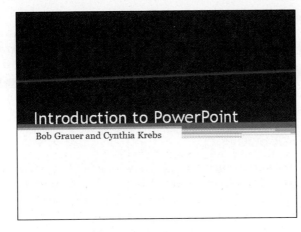

Figure 1.27 Urban Theme

Figure 1.28 Paper Theme

Figure 1.29 Civic Theme

Reviewing the Presentation

After you create the presentation, check for spelling errors and incorrect word usage. This step can be done before or after you apply the design theme, but sometimes applying the theme before checking for spelling errors helps you see errors you did not see before. It gives you a fresh look at the slide, which helps you revisualize what is displaying.

Check Spelling

The first step to checking your spelling is to visually check the slide after you create the text in the placeholders. A red wavy line under a word indicates that a word is misspelled. In the case of a proper name, the word may be spelled correctly but is not in the standard dictionary shared by the software in the Microsoft Office suite. In either event, point to the underlined word and click the right mouse button to display a shortcut menu. Select the appropriate spelling from the list of suggestions. If the word does not appear in the list of suggestions, you can add the word to the *custom dictionary*, a supplemental dictionary Microsoft Office uses to store items such as proper names, acronyms, or specialized words for your business or industry.

A *custom dictionary* is a supplemental dictionary Microsoft Office uses to store items such as proper names, acronyms, or specialized words.

After you complete the presentation and have visually checked each slide, use PowerPoint's Spelling feature to check the entire presentation again. Click the Review tab, and then click Spelling in the Proofing group. If a word does not appear in the dictionary, the Spelling dialog box appears. Use the options on the right side to choose whether you wish to accept the word and resume spell checking, ignore all occurrences of the word, change the word to one of the listed choices, add the word to your custom dictionary, look at other suggested spellings, add the word to AutoCorrect, or close the dialog box.

Finally, display the presentation in Slide Show view and read each word on each slide out loud. Reading the words in the Slide Show view eliminates the distractions in PowerPoint's creation screen and enables you to concentrate fully on the text. Although the Spelling feature is a valuable tool, it does **NOT** catch commonly misused words like to, too, and two, or for, fore, and four. While proofreading three times may seem excessive to you, if you ever flash a misspelled word before an audience in full Slide Show view, you will wish you had taken the time to proofread carefully. Nothing is more embarrassing and can make you seem less professional than a misspelled word enlarged on a big screen for your audience so they cannot miss it.

Use the Thesaurus

As you proofread your presentation, or even while you are creating it, you may notice that you are using one word too often. Perhaps you find a word that does not seem right, but you cannot think of another word. The Thesaurus, which gives you synonyms or words with the same meaning, is ideal to use in these situations. Click the Review tab and click Thesaurus in the Proofing group. The Research task pane appears on the right side of the screen and displays synonyms for the selected word. Point to the desired replacement key, click the drop-down arrow to display a menu, and click Insert to replace the word. Click Undo on the Quick Access Toolbar to return to the original text if you prefer the original word.

TIP The Research Task Pane

Microsoft Office 2007 brings the resources of the Web directly into the application. Click Research in the Proofing group on the Review tab. Type the entry you are searching for, click the down arrow to choose a reference book, and then click the green arrow to initiate the search. You have access to reference, research, business, and financial sites. You even have an online bilingual dictionary. Research has never been easier.

Hands-On Exercises

2 | Creating a Presentation

Skills covered: **1.** Create a New Presentation **2.** Add Slides **3.** Check Spelling and Use the Thesaurus **4.** Modify Text and Layout **5.** Reorder Slides **6.** Apply a Design Theme

Refer to Figure 1.30 as you complete Step 1.

a. Click the **Office Button**, select **New**, and then double-click **Blank Presentation**.

   PowerPoint opens with a new blank presentation.

b. Click inside the placeholder containing the *Click to add title* prompt, and then type the presentation title **Creating Presentation Content**.

c. Click inside the placeholder containing the *Click to add subtitle* prompt and enter your name.

   Type your name as it shows on the class roll. Do not enter a nickname or the words *Your Name*.

d. Click in the Notes pane and type today's date and the name of the course for which you are creating this slide show.

e. Save the presentation as **chap1_ho2_content_solution**.

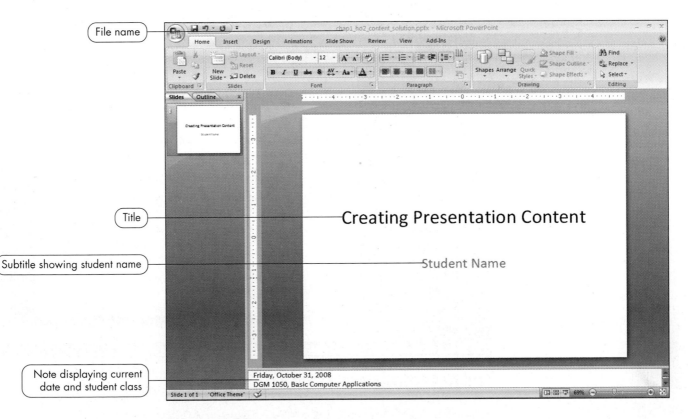

Figure 1.30 Creating Presentation Content Title Slide

Refer to Figure 1.31 as you complete Step 2.

a. Click **New Slide** in the Slides group on the Home tab.

b. Select the **Title and Content** layout from the gallery.

Slide 2 is created with two placeholders: one for the title and one for body content. You can insert an object by clicking on the bar in the center of the content placeholder, or you can enter bullets by typing text in the placeholder.

c. Type **Simplify the Content** in the title placeholder.

d. Click in the content placeholder and type **Use one main concept per slide**, and then press **Enter**.

e. Type **Use the 7 x 7 guideline** and press **Enter** again.

f. Click **Increase List Level** in the Paragraph group on the Home tab.

Clicking Increase List Level creates a new bullet level that you can use for detail related to the main bullet. If you wish to return to the main bullet level, click Decrease List Level.

g. Type **Limit slide to seven or fewer lines** and press **Enter**.

h. Type **Limit lines to seven or fewer words**.

i. Save the *chap1_ho2_content_solution* presentation.

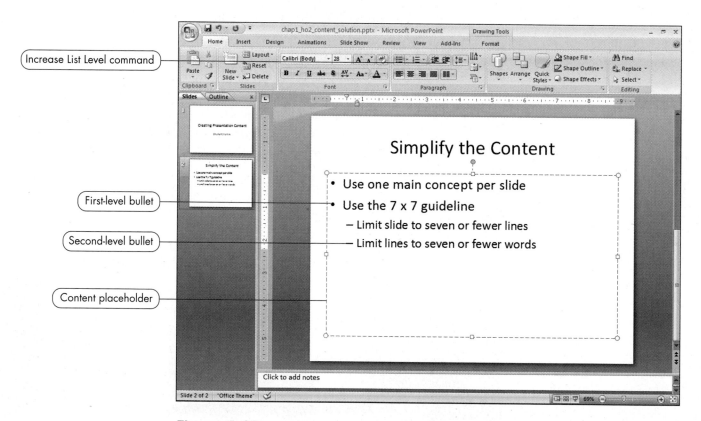

Figure 1.31 New Slide

Refer to Figure 1.32 as you complete Step 3.

a. Use the **New Slide** command to create four more slides with the Title and Content layout.

b. Type the following text in the appropriate slide.

Slide	Slide Title	Level 1 Bullets	Level 2 Bullets
3	Define the Audience	Who is the audience? What are their needs? What are their expectations? How much do they already know? How can you help them understand message?	
4	Develop the Content	Identify purpose Research topic Brainstorm Create storyboard	Title slide Introduction Key points Conclusion
5	Edit the Content	Make text concise Use consistent verb tense Utilize strong active verbs Eliminate excess adverbs and adjectives Use few prepositions	
6		The key to an effective presentation is planning ahead!	

c. Click **Spelling** in the Proofing group on the Review tab.

The result of the spelling check depends on how accurately you entered the text of the presentation. If the spell checker locates a word not in its dictionary, you will be prompted to resume checking, change the word, ignore the word in that occurrence or in all occurrences, or add the word to your dictionary so it is not identified as misspelled in the future. Select one of these options, and then continue checking the presentation for spelling errors, if necessary.

d. Move to **Slide 2** and click anywhere within the word *main*.

e. Click **Thesaurus** in the Proofing group on the Review tab.

The Research task pane opens and displays a list of synonyms from which to choose a replacement word.

f. Point to the word *key*, click the drop-down arrow, and click **Insert**.

The word *main* is replaced with the word *key*.

TROUBLESHOOTING: If you click the replacement word in the Research pane list instead of clicking the drop-down arrow and choosing Insert, the replacement word you clicked will replace the original word in the Search for box, and the Research pane changes to display the synonyms of the replacement word. The word in your presentation will not change.

g. Save the *chap1_ho2_content_solution* presentation.

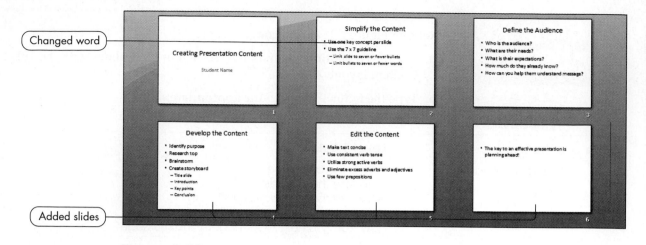

Figure 1.32 Proofed Slide Show

Step 4
Modify Text and Layout

Refer to Figure 1.33 as you complete Step 4.

a. Click the **Slide 6 thumbnail** in the Slide tab pane.

You wish to end the slide show with a statement emphasizing the importance of planning. You created the statement in a content placeholder in a slide using the Title and Content layout. You decide to modify the text and layout of the slide to give the statement more emphasis.

b. Click the **Home tab** and click **Layout** in the Slides group.

c. Click **Title Slide**.

The layout for Slide 6 changes to the Title Slide layout. Layouts can be used on any slide in a slide show if their format meets your needs.

d. Click the border of the Title placeholder, press **Delete** twice on the keyboard, and then drag the Subtitle placeholder containing your text upward until it is slightly above the center of your slide.

The layout in Slide 6 has now been modified.

e. Drag across the text in the subtitle placeholder to select it, and then move your pointer upwards until the Mini toolbar appears.

f. Click **Bold**, and then click **Italic** on the Mini toolbar.

Using the Mini toolbar to modify text is much faster than moving back and forth to the commands in the Font group on the Home tab to make changes.

g. Save the *chap1_ho2_content_solution* presentation.

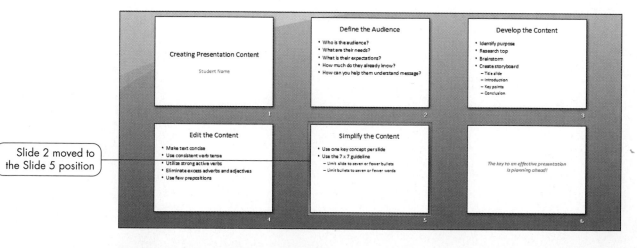

The key to an effective presentation is planning ahead!

Figure 1.33 Slide with Modified Text and Layout

Refer to Figure 1.34 as you complete Step 5.

a. Click the **View tab** and click **Slide Sorter** in the Presentation Views group.

The view changes to thumbnail views of the slides in the slide show with the current slide surrounded by a heavy border to indicate it is selected. Your view may differ from Figure 1.34 depending on what your zoom level is set at. Notice that the slides do not follow logical order. The Slide Sorter view is ideal for checking the logical sequence of slides and for changing slide position if necessary.

b. Select **Slide 2**, and then drag it so that it becomes Slide 5, the slide before the summary slide.

As you drag Slide 2 to the right, the pointer becomes a move cursor and a vertical bar appears to indicate the position of the slide when you drop it. After you drop the slide, all slides renumber.

c. Double-click **Slide 6**.

Double-clicking a slide in the Slide Sorter view returns you to Normal view.

d. Save the *chap1_ho2_content_solution* presentation.

Slide 2 moved to the Slide 5 position

Figure 1.34 Reordered Slide Show

Step 6
Apply a Design Theme

Refer to Figure 1.35 as you complete Step 6.

a. Click the **Design tab** and click the **More button** in the Themes group.

Point at each of the themes that appear in the gallery and note how the theme formatting impacts the text in Slide 6.

b. Click **Urban** to apply the theme to the presentation.

The Urban theme is characterized by a clean, simple background with a business-like color scheme, making it a good choice for this presentation.

c. Drag the Slide 6 Title placeholder down and to the left, and then resize it so that it contains three lines.

When you add the Urban theme, the background of the theme hides the text in the placeholder. You adjust the placeholder location and size to fit the theme.

TROUBLESHOOTING: You may not see the Tittle placeholder on Slide 6. However, click in the middle of the dark gray area of the slide. The sizing handles appear around the placeholder when you click it. Then you can click and drag the placeholder into its new location specified in Step 6c.

d. Save the *chap1_ho2_content_solution* presentation. Close the file and exit PowerPoint if you do not want to continue to the next exercise at this time.

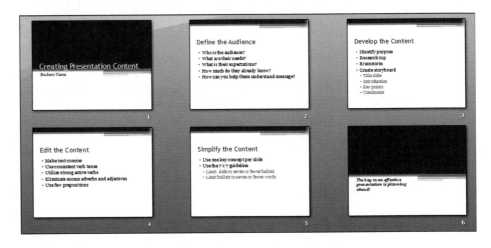

Figure 1.35 Slide Show with Urban Theme Applied

Presentation Development

Thus far, our presentation is strictly text. You can strengthen your slide show by adding objects that relate to the message. PowerPoint enables you to include a variety of visual objects to add impact to your presentation. You can add clip art, images, WordArt, sound, animated clips, or video clips to increase your presentation's impact. You can add tables, charts and graphs, and diagrams to provide more information for the audience. These objects can be created in PowerPoint, or you can insert objects that were created in other applications, such as a chart from Microsoft Excel or a table from Microsoft Word.

> ... clip art, images, WordArt, sound, animated clips, or video clips ... increase your presentation's impact.

In this section, you add a table to organize data in columns and rows. Then you insert clip art objects that relate to your topics. You move and resize the clip art to position it attractively on the slide. Finally, you apply transitions to your slide to control how one slide changes to another, and you apply animations to your text and clip art to help maintain your audience's attention.

Adding a Table

A **table** is an illustration that places information in columns and rows.

A **table** is an illustration that places information in columns and rows. Tables are a great way for you to present related information in an orderly manner. Tables can be simple and include just words or images, or they can be complex and include a great deal of structured numerical data. Because tables organize information for the viewer, they are a great way to augment your presentation.

You can add a table to your presentation by creating it in PowerPoint or by reusing a table created in Word or Excel. In this chapter, you create a basic table in PowerPoint. To create a table, you can select the Title and Content layout and then click the Table icon on the Content bar, or you can select the Title Only layout and click the Insert tab and then click Table in the Tables group. These two options create the table with slightly different sizing, however. Figure 1.36 shows the same data entered into tables created in each of these ways.

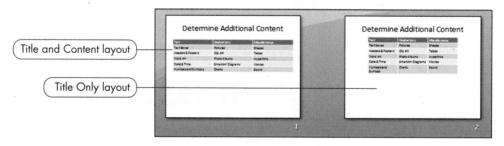

Figure 1.36 Table Layout

Inserting Clip Art

In addition to inserting tables from the Insert tab, you can insert other objects and media in your presentation. From the Illustrations group, click Picture and browse to locate a picture or image that has been saved to a storage device, click Clip Art to insert clip art from the Microsoft Clip Organizer, click Photo Album to create a photo album from images you have saved, click Shape to insert a shape, click SmartArt to insert a diagram, or click Chart to insert a chart.

In this chapter, you concentrate on adding clip art from the Microsoft Clip Organizer, although inserting other types of clips uses the same procedure. The Microsoft Clip Organizer contains a variety of **clips**, or media objects such as clip art, photographs, movies, or sounds, that may be inserted in a presentation. The Microsoft Clip Organizer brings order by cataloging the clips that are available to

A **clip** is any media object that you can insert in a document.

you. Clips installed locally are cataloged in the My Collections folder; clips installed in conjunction with Office are cataloged in the Office Collections folder; and clips downloaded from the Web are cataloged in the Web Collections folder. If you are connected to the Internet, clips located in Microsoft Online also display in the Clip Organizer. You can insert a specific clip into your presentation if you know its location, or you can search for a clip that will enhance your presentation.

To search for a clip, you enter a keyword that describes the clip you are looking for, specify the collections that are to be searched, and indicate the type of clip(s) you are looking for. The results are displayed in the Clip Art task pane, as shown in Figure 1.37. This figure shows clips that were located using the keyword *key*. The example searches all collections for all media types to return the greatest number of potential clips. When you point to a clip displaying in the gallery, the clip's keywords, an indication if the clip is scaleable, the clip's file size, and file format appear. When you see the clip that you want to use, point to the clip, click the drop-down arrow, and then click the Insert command from the resulting menu. You also can click the clip to insert it in the center of the slide, or drag the clip onto the slide.

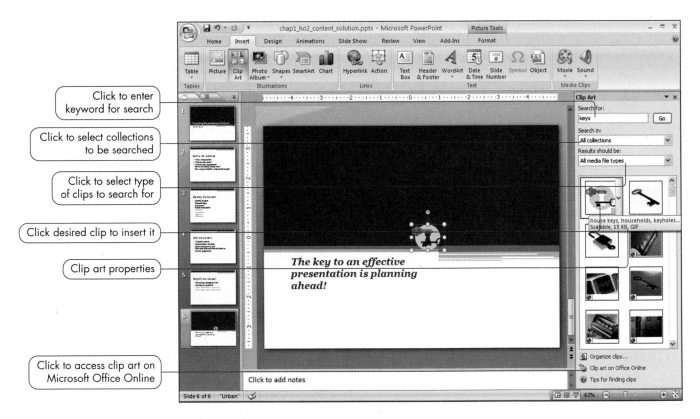

Figure 1.37 Clip Art Task Pane

TIP   Reorganizing Clip Collections

You can access the Microsoft Clip Organizer (to view the various collections) by clicking the Organize clips link at the bottom of the task pane. You also can access the Clip Organizer outside of PowerPoint by clicking the Start button on the task bar, and then clicking All Programs, Microsoft Office, Microsoft Office Tools, and Microsoft Clip Organizer. Once in the Organizer, you can search through the clips in the various collections, reorganize the existing collections, add new collections, and even add new clips (with their associated keywords) to the collections.

Move and Resize Clip Art

Just like any Windows object, clip art can be moved and sized. When you click the clip art, the clip art displays editing handles. Position the mouse pointer inside the boundaries of the handles, and it will change to a four-headed arrow. While the pointer has this shape, you can drag the clip art image to a new location. When you position the mouse pointer on one of the editing handles, a double-headed arrow appears. Use this arrow to resize the image. Dragging one of the corner handles resizes the image and keeps it in proportion. Dragging one of the interior handles distorts the image's width or height. Figure 1.38 shows the clip dragged to a new position.

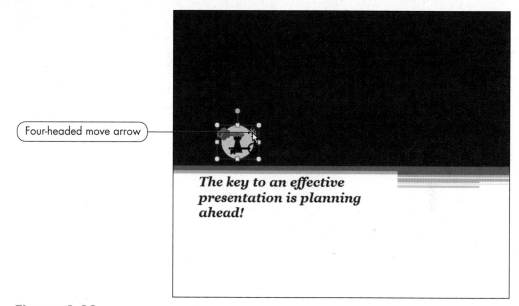

Figure 1.38   Repositioned Clip Art

Using Transitions and Animations

You have successfully created a PowerPoint presentation, but the most important step is yet to come—the delivery of the presentation to an audience. Typically, the slide show is projected on a screen through a projection device. While the slide show is being displayed, the slides change. This process can be enhanced through the use of *transitions*, or movement special effects that take place as you move from slide to slide while in Slide Show view.

> A **transition** is a movement special effect that takes place as one slide replaces another in Slide Show view.

> An **animation** is movement applied to individual elements on a single slide.

While transitions apply to the slide as a whole and control the way a slide moves onto the screen, *animations* are movements that control the entrance, emphasis, path, and/or exit of individual objects on a single slide. Multiple animations can be applied to a single object. Animating objects can help focus the audience's attention on an important point, can control the flow of information on a slide, and can help you keep the audience's attention.

Apply Transitions and Animations

Transition special effects include fades and dissolves, wipes, push and cover, stripes and bars, and random effects. The gallery in Figure 1.39 displays the available transition effects. The Transition Gallery contains 58 transitions. To display the Transitions Gallery, click the More button in the Transitions To This Slide group on the Animations tab. To see the effect of a transition on the slide, point to a transition in the Transitions Gallery to see the Live Preview, which shows how the change will affect the slide show before you select the transition.

Figure 1.39 The Transitions Gallery

After you choose the effect you desire, you can select a sound to play when the transition takes effect and you can select a speed for the transition. If you wish the transition to impact all slides, click Apply to All in the Transition to This Slide group on the Animations tab. Click Preview Slide Show in the Preview group on the Animations tab to move directly to the show and see what you have accomplished. (Transition effects also can be applied from the Slide Sorter view, where you can apply the same transition to multiple slides by selecting the slides prior to applying the effect.)

Another determination you must make is how you want to start the transition process. Do you want to manually click or press a key to advance to the next slide or do you want the slide to automatically advance after a specified number of seconds? The Advance Slide options in the Transition To This Slide group enable you to determine if you want to mouse click to advance or if you want the slide to advance automatically. You set the number of seconds for the slide to display in the same area.

TIP Effectively Adding Media Objects

When you select your transitions, sounds, and animations, remember that a presentation is not a high-speed music video. Too many transition and animation styles are distracting. The audience wonders what is coming next rather than paying attention to your message. Transitions that are too fast or too slow can lose the interest of the audience. Slow transitions will bore your audience while you stand there saying, "The next slide will load soon." Too many sound clips can be annoying. Consider whether you need to have the sound of applause with the transition of every slide. Is a typewriter sound necessary to keep your audience's attention or will it grate on their nerves if it is used on every set. Ask a classmate to review your presentation and let you know if there are annoying or jarring elements.

Animate Objects

An ***animation scheme*** is a built-in, standard animation.

A ***custom animation*** is an animation where the user determines the animation settings.

You can animate objects such as text, clip art, diagrams, charts, sound, and hyperlinks. You can apply a preset ***animation scheme***, which is a built-in, standard animation created by Microsoft to simplify the animation process, or you can apply a ***custom animation*** where you determine the animation effect, the speed for the effect, the properties of the effect, and the way the animation begins. The properties available with animations are determined by the animation type. For example, if you choose a wipe animation effect, you can determine the direction property. If you choose a color wave effect, you can determine the color to be added to the object.

To apply an animation scheme, select the object you want to animate, click the Animations tab, and then click the Animate down arrow in the Animations group. A list of animation schemes opens. If you have text selected, options will appear for you to choose how you wish the text to animate.

To apply a custom animation to an object, select the object that you want to animate, and then click Custom Animation in the Animations group on the Animations tab. In the Custom Animation task pane, click Add Effect. Point to Entrance, Emphasis, Exit, or Motion Paths. Select an effect from the resulting list. Once the effect has been selected, you can determine the start, property, and speed of the transition. In this chapter, you will apply an animation scheme and a basic custom animation.

The slide in Figure 1.40 shows an animation effect added to the title and the subtitle. The title will animate first, because it was selected first. A tag with the number one is attached to the placeholder to show it is first. The subtitle animates next, and a tag with the number 2 is attached to the subtitle placeholder. Examine the Custom Animation task pane and note the effect that was added to the subtitle, the way it will start, the direction and the speed of the animation.

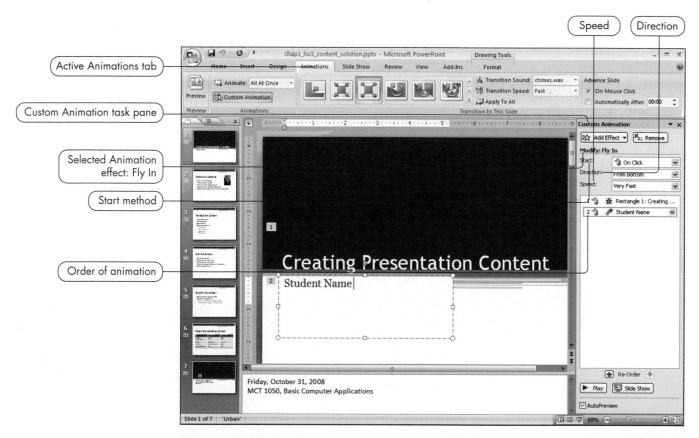

Figure 1.40 The Custom Animation Task Pane

Hands-On Exercises

3 | Strengthening a Presentation

Skills covered: **1.** Add a Table **2.** Insert, Move, and Resize Clip Art **3.** Apply a Transition **4.** Animate Objects

Step 1 **Add a Table**	Refer to Figure 1.41 as you complete Step 1.

a. Open the *chap1_ho2_content_solution* presentation if you closed it after the last exercise, and then save it as **chap1_ho3_content_solution**.

b. Move to **Slide 5**, click the **Home tab**, and click **New Slide** in the Slides group.

c. Click the **Title and Content** layout.

A new slide with the Title and Content layout is inserted after Slide 5.

d. Click inside the title placeholder and type **Determine Additional Content**.

e. Click the **Insert Table icon** on the toolbar in the center of the content placeholder.

The Insert Table dialog box appears for you to enter the number of columns and the number of rows you desire.

f. Type **3** for the number of columns and **6** for the number of rows.

PowerPoint creates the table and positions it on the slide. The first row of the table is formatted differently from the other rows so that it can be used for column headings.

g. Click in the top left cell of the table and type **Text**. Press **Tab** to move to the next cell and type **Illustrations**. Press **Tab**, and then type **Miscellaneous** in the last heading cell.

h. Type the following text in the remaining table cells.

Text Boxes	Pictures	Shapes
Headers & Footers	Clip Art	Tables
WordArt	Photo Albums	Hyperlinks
Date & Time	SmartArt Diagrams	Movies
Symbols	Charts	Sound

i. Save the *chap1_ho3_content_solution* presentation.

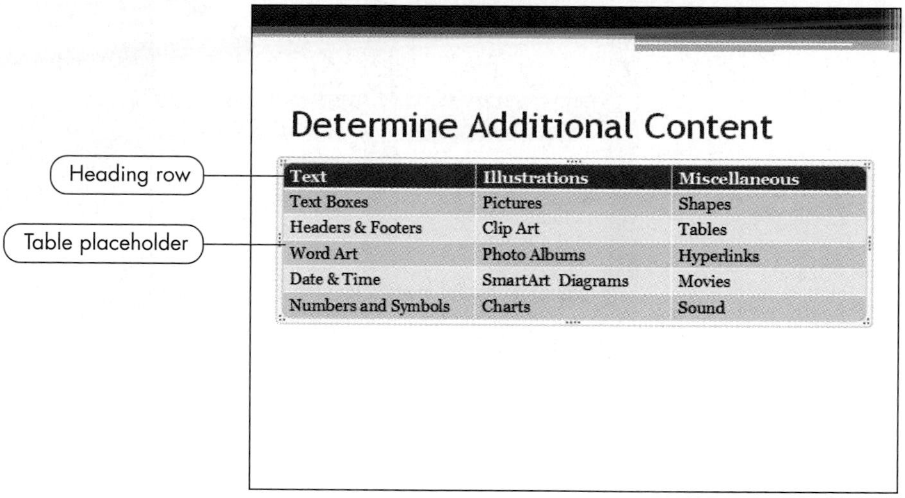

Figure 1.41 PowerPoint Table

Refer to Figure 1.42 as you complete Step 2.

a. Move to **Slide 2**, click the **Insert tab**, and click **Clip Art** in the Illustrations group.

b. Type **groups** in the *Search for* box. Make sure the *Search in* box is set to **All collections**.

c. Click the down arrow next to *Results should be*, deselect all options except Photographs, and then click **Go**.

d. Refer to Figure 1.42 to determine the group image to select, and then click the image to insert it in Slide 2.

   If you cannot locate the image in Figure 1.42, select another group photograph that looks like an audience.

e. Position your pointer in the center of the image and drag the image to the top right of the slide so that the top of the image touches the bars.

f. Position your pointer over the bottom-left sizing handle of the image and drag inward to reduce the size of the photograph.

   The photograph is too large. Not only is it overpowering the text, it is blocking text so that it cannot be read. As you drag the sizing handle inward, all four borders are reduced equally so the photograph no longer touches the bars.

g. If necessary, reposition the clip art image so that it is positioned attractively on the slide.

h. Move to **Slide 7**, change the keyword to **keys**, change the results to show **All media types**, and then click **OK**.

i. Refer to Figure 1.42 to determine the keys clip to select, and then click the image to insert it in Slide 7. Close the Clip Art task pane.

j. Reposition the clip so that it is over the word *key* but do not resize it.

   This clip is an animated move clip. If it is enlarged, the image will become pixelated and unattractive.

k. Save the *chap1_ho3_content_solution* presentation.

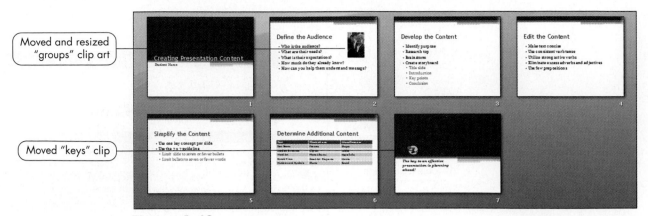

Moved and resized "groups" clip art

Moved "keys" clip

Figure 1.42 Inserted Clip Art

Step 3
Apply a Transition

Refer to Figure 1.43 as you complete Step 3.

a. Click the **Animations tab** and click **More** in the Transitions To This Slide group.

b. Point at several of the transition effects to see how they impact the slide, and then click the **Box Out** wipe transition.

c. Click **Apply To All** in the Transitions To This Slide group on the Animation tab.

The Apply To All will apply the transition set for the current slide to all slides in the slide show.

d. Move to **Slide 1**, click the **Transition Sound down arrow** in the Transitions To This Slide group on the Animations tab, and then click **Chimes**.

The Chimes sound will play as Slide 1 enters. Presenters often use a sound or an audio clip to focus the audience's attention on the screen as the presentation begins.

e. Click **Preview** in the Preview group on the Animations tab.

Because Slide 1 is active, you hear the chimes sound as the Box Out transition occurs.

TROUBLESHOOTING: If you are completing this activity in a classroom lab, you may need to plug in headphones or turn on speakers to hear the sound.

f. Click the **View tab** and click **Slide Sorter** in the Presentation Views group.

Notice the small star beneath each slide. The star indicates a transition has been applied to the slide.

g. Click any of the stars to see a preview of the transition applied to that slide.

h. Save the *chap1_ho3_content_solution* presentation.

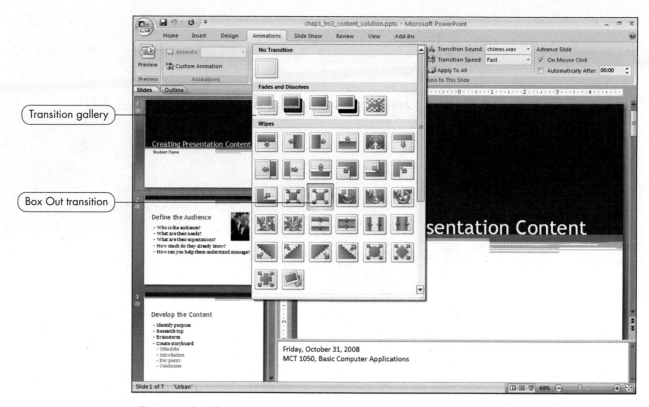

Transition gallery

Box Out transition

Figure 1.43 The Transition Gallery

Step 4	Refer to Figure 1.44 as you complete Step 4.
Animate Objects	**a.** Double-click **Slide 1** to open it in Normal view, and then select the Title placeholder.

b. Click the **Animations tab** and click the **Animate down arrow** in the Animations group.

c. Click **Fade**.

The Fade animation scheme is applied to the Title placeholder. The title placeholder dissolves into the background until it is fully visible.

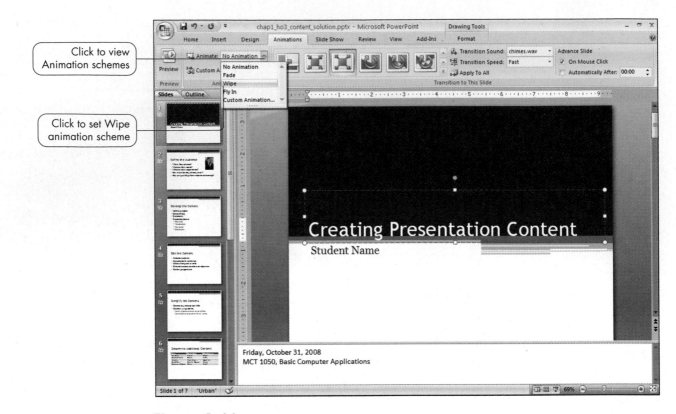

Figure 1.44 Object Animation schemes

d. Select the Subtitle placeholder on Slide 1, and then click the **Animate drop-down arrow** in the Animations group on the Animations tab.

e. Click the **All at once** button located under Fly In.

f. Move to **Slide 2** and select the photograph.

You decide to use a custom animation on the photograph so that you can have more animation choices and can control the speed with which the photograph animates.

g. Click **Custom Animation** in the Animations group on the Animations tab.

The Custom Animation task pane opens, which enables you to add an animation effect to the selected object.

h. Click the **Add Effect button**, point at **Entrance**, and then click **More Effects** from the animation list.

The Add Entrance Effect dialog box appears. The animation effects are separated into categories: Basic, Subtle, Moderate, and Exciting.

i. Scroll down and select **Curve Up** in the Exciting category.

A preview of the Curve Up animation plays, but the dialog box remains open so that you can continue previewing animations until you find the one you like. Experiment with the Entrance Effects so you can see the impact they will have.

j. Select **Boomerang**, and then click **OK**.

k. Click the drop-down arrow for the **Start drop-down arrow**, and then select **After Previous**.

You can choose to start the animation with a mouse click, or by having the animation start automatically. If you wish to begin the animation automatically, you can choose to have it begin at the same time as a previous animation by selecting Start With Previous, or having it begin after a previous animation by selecting Start After Previous.

l. Click the drop-down arrow for the **Speed drop-down arrow**, and then click **Medium**.

m. Save the *chap1_ho3_content_solution* presentation. Close the file and exit PowerPoint if you do not want to continue to the next exercise at this time.

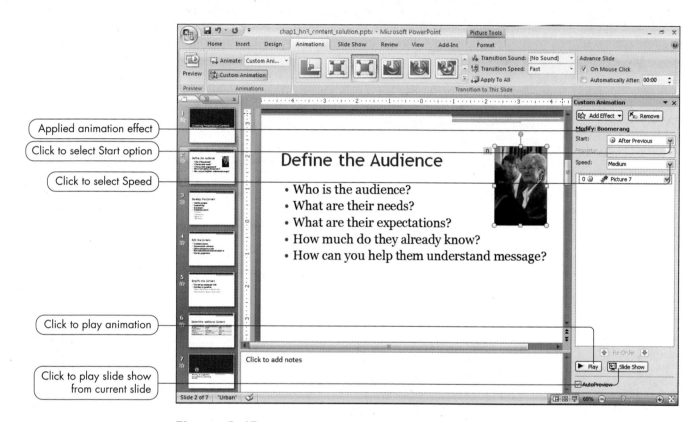

Figure 1.45 Custom Animation Task Pane

Navigation and Printing

In the beginning of this chapter, you opened a slide show and advanced one by one through the slides by clicking the mouse button. This task is possible because PowerPoint is, by default, a linear software tool that advances each slide one after another in a straight line order. Audiences, however, are seldom comfortable with a linear slide show. If they are involved in the presentation, they want to ask questions. As you respond to the questions, you may find yourself needing to jump to a previous slide or needing to move to a future slide. PowerPoint's navigation options enable you to do this maneuver.

(A variety of options are available for audience handouts . . . be aware of the options and choose the one that best suits your audience's needs.)

To help your audience follow your presentation, you can choose to provide them with a handout. You may give it to them at the beginning of your presentation for them to take notes on, or you tell them you will be providing them with notes and let them relax and enjoy your slide show. A variety of options are available for audience handouts. All you need do is be aware of the options and choose the one that best suits your audience's needs.

In this section, you run a slide show and navigate within the show. You will practice a variety of methods for advancing to new slides or returning to previously viewed slides. You will annotate slides during a presentation, and change from screen view to black-screen view. Finally, you print the slide show.

Running and Navigating a Slide Show

PowerPoint provides multiple methods you can use to advance through your slide show. You also can go backwards to a previous slide, if desired. Use Table 1.2 to identify the navigation options, and then experiment with each method for advancing and going backwards. Find the method that you are most comfortable using and stay with that method. That way you will not get confused during the slide show and advance to a new slide before you mean to do so.

Table 1.2 Navigation Options

Navigation Option	Navigation Method
To Advance Through the Slide Show	Press the Spacebar
	Press Page Down
	Press the letter **N** or **n** for next
	Press the right arrow or down arrow
	Press Enter
To Return to a Previous Slide or Animation	Right-click and choose Previous from the Popup menu
	Press the Page Up button
	Press the letter **P** or **p** for previous
	Press the left arrow or up arrow
	Press Backspace
To End the Slide Show	Press Esc on the keyboard
	Press the hyphen key
To Go to a Specific Slide	Type Slide number and press Enter
	Right-click, click Go to Slide, then click the slide desired

Annotate the Slide Show

An ***annotation*** is a note that can be written or drawn on a slide for additional commentary or explanation.

You may find it helpful to add ***annotations***, or notes, to your slides. You can write or draw on your slides during a presentation. To do so, right-click to bring up the shortcut menu, and then click Pointer Options to select your pen type. You can change the color of the pen from the Popup menu, too. To create the annotation, hold down the left mouse button as you write or draw on your slide. To erase what you have drawn, press the letter **E** or **e** on the keyboard. Keep in mind that the mouse was never intended to be an artist's tool. Your drawings or added text will be clumsy efforts at best, unless you use a tablet and pen. The annotations you create are not permanent unless you save the annotations when exiting the slide show and then save the changes upon exiting the file.

Printing with PowerPoint

A printed copy of a PowerPoint slide show is very beneficial. It can be used by the presenter for reference during the presentation. It can be used by the audience for future reference, or as backup during equipment failure. It can even be used by students as a study guide. A printout of a single slide with text on it can be used as a poster or banner.

Print Slides

Use the Print Slides option to print each slide on a full page. One reason to print the slides as full slides is to print the slides for use as a backup. You can print the full slides on overhead transparencies that could be projected with an overhead projector during a presentation. You will be extremely grateful for the backup if your projector bulb blows out or your computer quits working during a presentation. Using the Print Slides option also is valuable if you want to print a single slide that has been formatted as a sign or a card.

If you are printing the slides on transparencies, or on paper smaller than the standard size, be sure to set the slide size and orientation before you print. By default PowerPoint sets the slides for landscape orientation, or printing where the width is greater than the height (11 x 8.5"). If you are going to print on a transparency for an overhead projector, however, you need to set PowerPoint to portrait orientation, or printing where the height is greater than the width (8.5 x 11").

To change your slide orientation, or to set PowerPoint to print for a different size, click the Design tab and click Page Setup in the Page Setup group to open the Page Setup dialog box. Click in the *Slides sized for* list to select the size or type of paper on which you will print. To print overhead transparency, you click Overhead. You also can set the slide orientation in this dialog box. If you wish to create a custom size of paper to print, enter the height and width. Figure 1.46 displays the Page Setup options. Note that the slide show we have been creating has been changed so that it can be printed on overhead transparencies.

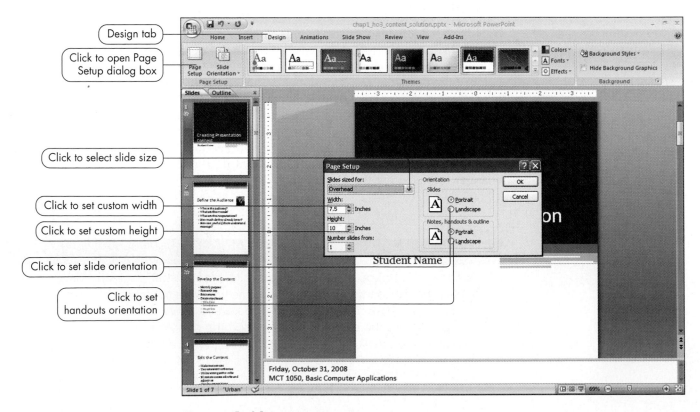

Figure 1.46 Page Setup Options

Once you have determined your page setup, you are ready to print the slides. To print, click the Office Button, select Print, and then select Print in the submenu. The Print dialog box opens so that you can select your printer, your print range, and number of copies—options available to all Office applications. In addition to the standard print options, PowerPoint has many options that tailor the printout to your needs. You can click the *Print what* drop-down arrow and select whether you want to print slides, handouts, notes pages, or outlines.

You can determine the color option with which to print. Selecting Color prints your presentation in color if you have a color printer or grayscale if you are printing on a black-and-white printer. Selecting the Grayscale option prints in shades of gray, but be aware that backgrounds do not print when using the Grayscale option. By not printing the background, you make the text in the printout easier to read and you save a lot of ink or toner. Printing with the Pure Black and White option prints with no gray fills. Try using Microsoft clip art and printing in Pure Black and White to create coloring pages for children.

If you have selected a custom size for your slide show, or if you have set up the slide show so that is it larger than the paper you are printing on, be sure to check the *Scale to fit paper* box. Doing so will ensure that each slide prints on one page. The Frame slides option puts a back border around the slides in the printout, giving the printout a more polished appearance. If you have applied shadows to text or objects, you may want to check the *Print shadows* option so that the shadows print. The final two options, *Print comments and ink markup* and *Print hidden slides*, are only active if you have used these features.

Print Handouts

The principal purpose for printing handouts is to give your audience something they can use to follow during the presentation and give them something on which to take notes. With your handout and their notes, the audience has an excellent resource for the future. Handouts can be printed with one, two, three, four, six, or nine slides per page. Printing three handouts per page is a popular option because it places thumbnails of the slides on the left side of the printout and lines on which the audience can write on the right side of the printout. Figure 1.47 shows the *Print what* option set to Handouts and the Slides per page option set to 3.

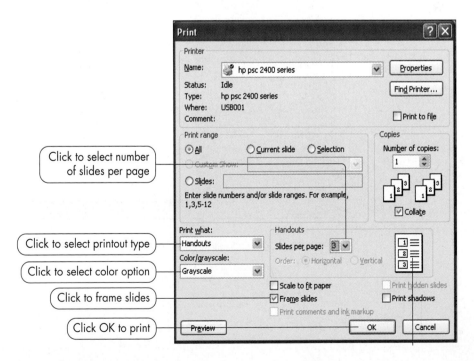

Figure 1.47 Page Setup Options

Print Notes Pages

In the first exercise in this chapter, you created a note in the Notes pane. If you include charts or technical information in your notes, you will want to print the notes for reference. You also may want to print the detailed notes for your audience, especially if your notes contain references. To print your notes, click the Office Button, select Print, select Print from the submenu, and then click Notes Pages in the *Print what* box.

Print Outlines

You may print your presentation as an outline made up of the slide titles and main text from each of your slides. This is a good option if you only want to deal with a few pages instead of a page for each slide as is printed for Notes pages. The outline generally gives you enough detail to keep you on track with your presentation.

You can print the outline following the methods discussed for the other three printout types, but you also can preview it and print from the preview screen. To preview how a printout will look, click the Office Button, and then point to the arrow next to Print. In the list that displays, click Print Preview. Click the arrow next to the *Print what* box, and then click Outline View. If you decide to print, click Print. Figure 1.48 shows the outline for the presentation we have been creating in Print Preview.

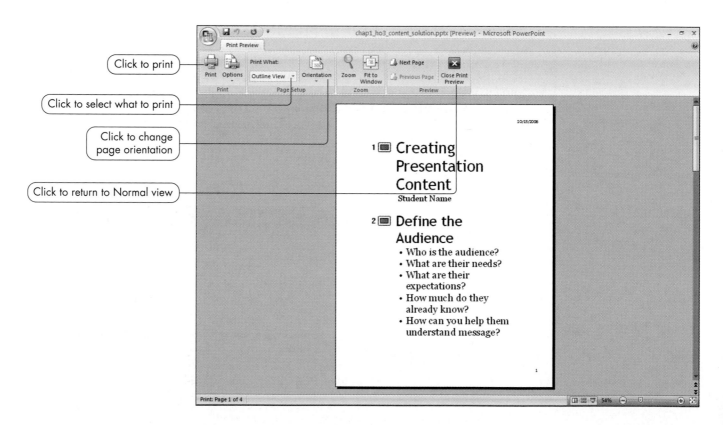

Figure 1.48 Outline View in Print Preview

Hands-On Exercises

4 | Navigating and Printing

Skills covered: 1. Display a Slide Show **2.** Navigate to Specific Slides **3.** Annotate a Slide **4.** Print Audience Handouts

---

Step 1
Display a Slide Show

a. Open the *chap1_ho3_content_solution* presentation if you closed it after the last exercise, and then save it as **chap1_ho4_content_solution**. Type your class under your name in the title placeholder.

b. Click the **Slide Show tab** and click **From Beginning** in the Start Slide Show group.

    Note the transition effect and sound you applied in Hands-On Exercise 3.

c. Press **Spacebar** to animate the title, press **Spacebar** again to animate the subtitle.

    Pressing Spacebar advances to the next animation or the next slide.

d. Click to advance to Slide 2.

    Note that the photograph animation plays automatically.

e. Press **Page Down** to advance to Slide 3.

f. Press **Page Up** to return to Slide 2.

g. Press **Enter** to advance to Slide 3.

h. Press **N** on the keyboard to advance to Slide 4.

i. Press **Backspace** to return to Slide 3.

Step 2
Navigate to Specific Slides

a. Right-click, select **Go to Slide**, and then select **5 Simply the Content**.

    Slide 5 displays.

b. Press the number **3** on the keyboard, and then press **Enter**.

    Slide 3 displays.

c. Press **F1** and read the Slide Show Help menu showing the shortcut tips that are available during the display of a slide show.

d. Close the Help menu.

Step 3
Annotate a Slide

a. Press **Ctrl + P**.

    The mouse pointer becomes a pen.

b. Circle and underline several words on the slide.

c. Press the letter **E**.

    The annotations erase.

d. Press the letter **B**.

    The screen blackens.

e. Press the letter **B** again.

The slide show displays again.

f. Press **Esc** to end the slide show.

Step 4
Print Audience Handouts

a. Click the **Office Button** and select **Print**.

b. Click the **Print what drop-down arrow**, and then click **Handouts**.

c. Specify **4** slides per page, and then click **OK** to print the presentation.

d. Save the *chap1_ho4_content_solution* presentation and close it.

Summary

1. **Identify PowerPoint user interface elements.** PowerPoint features are designed to aid you in creating slide shows in support of presentations you give. Slide shows are electronic presentations that enable you to advance through slides containing content that will help your audience understand your message. PowerPoint 2007 is one of the four main applications in the Office 2007 Suite that uses a new interface designed for easier access to features. PowerPoint has different views, each with unique capabilities. The Normal view is a tri-pane view that displays either thumbnail images or an outline in one pane, the slide in one pane, and a Notes pane. The Slide Sorter view displays thumbnails of multiple slides. The Notes view shows a miniature of the slide and the associated speaker notes. The Slide Show view.

2. **Use PowerPoint views.** PowerPoint contains multiple views to fit the user's needs. The default view is the Normal view—a tri-pane view used predominantly for slideshow creation. The Slide Sorter view enables the user to quickly reorder or delete slides to enhance organization. The Notes Page view displays a thumbnail of the slide and the notes the user has entered for that slide. The Slide Show view displays the slide show in full-screen view for an audience. If a presenter has multiple monitors, the Presenter's view gives the presenter options for greater control of the playback.

3. **Open and save a slide show.** Previously created slide shows can be opened so that they can be modified. After editing, they can be saved with the same file name using the Save feature, or saved with a new file name using the Save As feature. When slide shows are saved, they are assigned an extension of .pptx, indicating they are in XML (eXtensible Markup Language) file format.

4. **Get Help.** PowerPoint's Help can be used to locate information about a specific feature, to troubleshoot, to search for software updates, to find a template, or to locate additional training. Help is available online or offline.

5. **Create a storyboard.** Before creating your slide show you should spend a considerable amount of time analyzing your audience, researching your message, and organizing your ideas. Organize your ideas on a storyboard, and then create your presentation in PowerPoint. After completing the slide show, you should spend a considerable amount of time practicing your presentation so that you are comfortable with your slide content and the technology you will use to present it with.

6. **Use slide layouts.** PowerPoint provides a set of predefined slide layouts that determine the position of the objects or content on a slide. Slide layouts contain any number and combination of placeholders. Placeholders hold content and determine the position of the objects on the slide.

7. **Apply design themes.** PowerPoint themes enable you to focus on the content of a presentation. You create the text and supporting elements, and then you apply a design theme to give the presentation a consistent look. The theme controls the font, background, layout, and colors.

8. **Review the presentation.** To ensure there are no typographical errors or misspelled words in a presentation, use the Check Spelling feature to complete an initial check for errors. You also need to review each slide yourself because the Check Spelling feature does not find all errors. An example of an error that the Check Spelling feature does not find is the misuse of the word "to" or "two" when the correct word is "too." Use the Thesaurus to locate synonyms for overused words in the slide show.

9. **Add a table.** Tables can be created to help organize information needed in the slide show. PowerPoint's table features can be used to specify the number of columns and rows needed in the table. Tables can be inserted from the Content bar in the Content placeholder or through the Insert tab.

10. **Insert clip art.** A variety of clips can be added to slides. Clips are media objects such as clip art, images, movies, and sound. The Microsoft Clip Organizer contains media objects you can insert, or you can locate clips and insert them through the Insert tab. Clips you gather can be added to the Microsoft Clip Organizer to help you locate them more easily.

11. **Use transitions and animations.** Transitions and animations show in Slide Show view. Transitions control the movements of slides as one slide changes to another, while an animation controls the movement of an object on the slide. Both features can aid in keeping the attention of the audience, but animations are especially valuable in directing attention to specific elements you wish to emphasize.

12. Run and navigate a slide show. While displaying the slide show, you need flexibility in moving between slides. Various navigation methods advance the slide show, return to previously viewed slides, or go to specific slides. Slides can be annotated during a presentation to add emphasis or comments to slides.

13. Print with PowerPoint. PowerPoint has four ways to print the slideshow, each with specific benefits. The Slides method of printing prints each slide on a full page. The Handouts method prints miniatures of the slides in 1, 2, 3, 4, 6, or 9 per page format. The Notes Pages method prints each slide on a separate page and is formatted to display a single thumbnail of a slide with its associated notes. The Outline method prints the titles and main points of the presentation in outline format.

Key Terms

Multiple Choice

1. Which of the following methods does not save changes in a PowerPoint presentation?
   (a) Click the Office Button, and then click the Save As command.
   (b) Click the Save button on the Quick Access toolbar.
   (c) Press Ctrl+S.
   (d) Press F1.

2. The Quick Access Toolbar, containing commands you may need at any time regardless of what tab is active, includes which of the following commands?
   (a) Cut and Paste
   (b) Undo and Redo
   (c) Find and Replace
   (d) Spelling and Grammar

3. You have created a very complex table with great detail on a slide. You want to give the audience a printout of the slide showing all the detail so they can review it with you during your presentation. Which of the following print methods would show the necessary detail?
   (a) Audience handout, 4 per page
   (b) Outline
   (c) Notes page
   (d) Full slide

4. While displaying a slide show, which of the following will display a list of shortcuts for navigating?
   (a) F1
   (b) F11
   (c) Ctrl+Enter
   (d) Esc

5. The predefined slide formats in PowerPoint are:
   (a) Layout views
   (b) Slide layouts
   (c) Slide guides
   (d) Slide displays

6. If you need to add an object such as clip art or a picture to a slide, which tab would you select?
   (a) Add-ins
   (b) Design
   (c) Slide
   (d) Insert

7. The Open command:
   (a) Brings a presentation from a storage device into RAM memory
   (b) Removes the presentation from the storage device and brings it into RAM memory
   (c) Stores the presentation in RAM memory to a storage device
   (d) Stores the presentation in RAM memory to a storage device, and then erases the presentation from RAM memory

8. The Save command:
   (a) Brings a presentation from a storage device into RAM memory
   (b) Removes the presentation from the storage device and brings it into RAM memory
   (c) Stores the presentation in RAM memory to a storage device
   (d) Stores the presentation in RAM memory to a storage device, and then erases the presentation from RAM memory

9. Which of the following provides a ghost image of a toolbar for use in formatting selected text?
   (a) Styles command
   (b) Quick Access Toolbar
   (c) Formatting Text gallery
   (d) Mini toolbar

10. Which of the following is a true statement?
    (a) A design theme must be applied before slides are created.
    (b) The design theme can be changed after all of the slides have been created.
    (c) Design themes control fonts and backgrounds but not placeholder location.
    (d) Placeholders positioned by a design theme cannot be moved.

11. Microsoft Clip Organizer searches:
    (a) May be limited to a specific media type
    (b) Locate clips based on keywords
    (c) May be limited to specific collections
    (d) All of the above

12. Which of the following views is best for reordering the slides in a presentation?
    (a) Presenter view
    (b) Slide Show view
    (c) Reorder view
    (d) Slide Sorter view

Multiple Choice

13. Normal view contains which of the following components?

(a) The slide sorter pane, the tabs pane, and the slide pane
(b) The tabs pane, the slide pane, and the slide sorter pane
(c) The tabs pane, the slide pane, and the notes pane
(d) The outline pane, the slide pane, and the tabs pane

14. Which of the following cannot be used to focus audience attention on a specific object on a slide during a slide show?

(a) Apply a transition to the object
(b) Apply an animation to the object
(c) Use the pen tool to circle the object
(d) Put nothing on the slide but the object

15. What is the animation effect that controls how one slide changes to another slide?

(a) Custom animation
(b) Animation scheme
(c) Transition
(d) Advance

The presentation in Figure 1.49 reviews the basics of e-mail and simultaneously provides you with practice opening, modifying, and saving an existing PowerPoint presentation. The presentation contains two slides on computer viruses and reminds you that your computer is at risk whenever you receive an e-mail message with an attachment. Notes containing explanations are included for some slides. You create a summary of what you learn and enter it as a note for the last slide.

a. Click the **Office Button** and select **Open**. Click the **Look in drop-down arrow**, and then locate the drive and folder where your student files are saved. Select the *chap1_pe1_email* presentation, and then click **Open**.

b. Click the **Slide Show tab** and click **From Beginning** in the Start Slide Show group. Read each of the slides by pressing **Spacebar** to advance through the slides. Press **Esc** to exit the Slide Show View.

c. Click in the **Slide 1 title placeholder**, and then replace the words *Student Name* with your name as it appears on the instructor's rolls. Replace *Student Class* with the name of the class you are taking.

d. Click in the **Slide 10 Notes pane**, and then type a short note about what you learned regarding e-mail by reviewing this slide show.

e. Click the **Slide 4 thumbnail** in the Tabs pane to move to Slide 4. Select the sample e-mail address, and then type your e-mail address to replace the sample.

f. Move to **Slide 3** and then click inside the content placeholder. Type **Inbox**, and then press **Enter**. Continue typing the following bullet items: **Outbox**, **Sent items**, **Deleted items**, **Custom folders**.

g. Move to **Slide 8**, select the first protocol, *POP Client – Post Office Protocol Client*, and then move your pointer slightly upward until the Mini toolbar appears. Apply **Bold** and **Italics** to the first protocol. Repeat the process for the second protocol, *IMAP – Internet Message Access Protocol*.

h. Click the **Design tab** and click the **More button** in the Themes group.

i. Click **Technic** to apply the Technic theme to all slides in the slide show.

j. Move to **Slide 1** and adjust the size of the Title placeholder so the complete title fits on one line.

k. Click the **Office Button**, point to **Print**, and then click **Print** in the submenu. Click **Current slide** option in the *Print range* section. Click the **Frame slides check box** to activate it, and then click **OK**. Slide 1 will print for your use as a cover page.

l. Open the Print dialog box again, and then click the **Slides** option in the *Print range* section. Type the slide range **2–10**.

m. Click the **Print what drop-down arrow**, and then select **Handouts**. Click the **Slides per page drop-down arrow** in the *Handouts* section, and then select **3**.

n. Click the **Frame slides check box** to activate it, and then click **OK**. Slides 2–10 will print 3 per page with lines for audience note taking. Staple the cover page to the handouts, and then submit it to your instructor if requested to do so.

o. Click the **Office Button** and select **Save As**. Click the **Save in drop-down arrow** and locate the drive and folder where you are saving your file solutions. Type **chap1_pe1_email_solution** as the file name for the presentation. Click **Save**.

...continued on Next Page

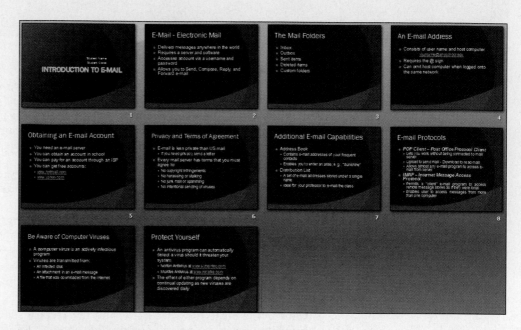

Figure 1.49 Introduction to E-Mail Presentation

2 Successful Presentations

Your employer is a successful author who often presents to various groups. He has been asked by the local International Association of Administrative Professionals (IAAP) to give the group tips for presenting successfully using PowerPoint. He created a storyboard of his presentation and has asked you to create the presentation from the storyboard. Refer to Figure 1.50 as you complete this assignment.

a. Click the **Office Button**, select **New**, click **Blank**, and then click **Create**.

b. Click the **Office Button** and select **Save As**. Click the **Save in drop-down arrow** and locate the drive and folder where you are saving your file solutions. Type **chap1_pe2_tips_solution** as the file name for the presentation. Click **Save**.

c. Click in the **Slide 1 title placeholder**, and then type **Successful Presentations**. Click in the subtitle placeholder and type **Robert Grauer and your name** as it appears on the instructor's rolls.

d. Click the **Home tab**, click the **New Slide down arrow** in the Slides group, and click **Title Only**.

e. Click in the title placeholder and type **Techniques to Consider**.

f. Click **Table** in the Tables group on the Insert tab, and then drag the grid to highlight two columns and five rows.

g. Type the following information in the table cells. Press **Tab** to move from cell to cell.

Feature	Use
Rehearse Timings	Helps you determine the length of your presentation
Header/Footer	Puts information on the top and bottom of slides, notes, and handouts
Hidden Slides	Hides slides until needed
Annotate a Slide	Write on the slide

h. Click the **Home tab**, click the **New Slide down arrow** in the Slides group, and then click **Title and Content**. Type **The Delivery is Up to You**.

i. Click in the content placeholder and type the following bullet text: **Practice makes perfect, Arrive early on the big day, Maintain eye contact, Speak slowly, clearly, and with sufficient volume, Allow time for questions.**

j. Click the **Home tab**, click the **New Slide down arrow** in the Slides group, and then click **Title and Content**. Type **Keep Something in Reserve**.

...continued on Next Page

k. Click in the content placeholder and type the following bullet text: **Create hidden slides to answer difficult questions that might occur, Press Ctrl+S to display hidden slides**.

l. Click the **Home tab**, click **New Slide** in the Slides group, and then click **Title and Content**. Type **Provide Handouts.**

m. Click in the content placeholder and type the following bullet text: **Allows the audience to follow the presentation, Lets the audience take the presentation home**.

n. Click the **Review tab** and click **Spelling** in the Proofing group.

o. Correct any misspelled words Check Spelling locates. Proofread the presentation and correct any misspelled words Check Spelling missed.

p. Click the **Design tab** and click the **More button** in the Themes group.

q. Click **Oriel**.

r. Click the **Slide Show tab** and click **From Beginning** in the Start Slide Show group. Press **Page Down** to advance through the slides.

s. When you reach the end of the slide show, press the number **2**, and then press **Enter** to return to Slide 2. Press **Esc.**

t. Press **Ctrl+S** to save the *chap1_pe2_tips_solution* presentation and close.

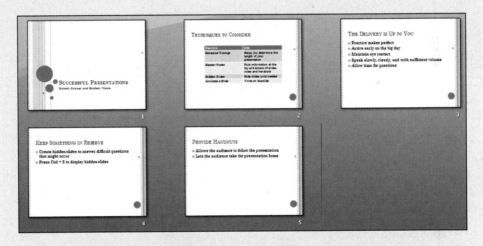

Figure 1.50 Successful Presentations Slide Show

3 Introduction to the Internet

You have been asked to give a presentation covering the basics of the Internet. You created a storyboard and entered the content in a slide show. After viewing the slide show, you realize the slides are text intensive and that transitions and animations would make the show more interesting. You modify the slide show and remove some of the detail from the slides. You put the detail in the Notes pane. You add a transition and apply it to all slides, and you apply custom animations to two images. You print the Notes for you to refer to as you present.

a. Click the **Office Button** and select **Open**. Click the **Look in drop-down arrow**, and then locate the drive and folder where your student files are saved. Click the *chap1_pe3_internet* presentation, and then click **Open**.

b. Click in the **Slide 1** title placeholder and replace the words *Your Name* with your name as it appears on the instructor's rolls. Replace *Your Class* with the name of the class you are taking.

c. Click in the **Slide 2 content placeholder** and modify the text so that it is shortened to brief, easy-to-remember chunks, as displayed in Figure 1.51.

...continued on Next Page

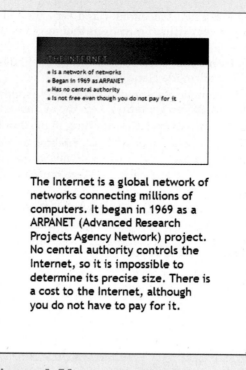

Figure 1.51 Internet Slide 2 Modifications

d. Click the **View tab**. Click **Notes Page** in the Presentation Views group, and then using Figure 1.51 as a guide, enter the notes in the Notes placeholder, which provides the appropriate place for the text omitted in the previous step.

e. Click **Normal** in the Presentation Views group on the View tab, and then move to **Slide 3**. Click in the content placeholder and modify the text so that it is shortened to brief, easy-to-remember chunks, as displayed in Figure 1.52.

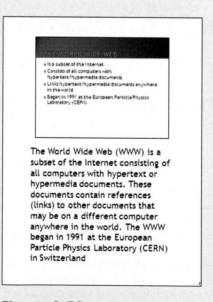

Figure 1.52 Internet Slide 3 Modifications

...continued on Next Page

f. Click the **View tab**, click **Notes Page** in the Presentation Views group, and then using Figure 1.52 as a guide, enter the notes in the Notes placeholder.

g. Click **Normal** in the Presentation Views group, and then click the **Animations tab**. Click the **More button** in the Transition To This Slide group.

h. Click the **Cover Right-Down** option and click **Apply To All**.

i. Move to **Slide 5**, and then click the image of the computer network to select it.

j. Click the down arrow next to **Animate** in the Animations group on the Animations tab and then click **Fly In**. Repeat this process for the image of the modem and telephone.

k. Click the **View tab**, click **Slide Show** in the Presentation Views group, and then advance through the slide show. Press **Esc** to end the slide show after you have viewed the last slide.

l. Click the **Office Button**, select **Print**, and then select **Print Preview**.

m. Select **Notes Pages** from the Print what list, and then press **Page Down** on the keyboard to advance through the slides. If your instructor asks you to print the Notes Pages, click **Print** in the Print group on the Print Preview tab. Click **Close Print Preview** in the Preview group on the Print Preview tab.

n. Click the **Office Button**, and then select **Save As**. Click the **Save in drop-down arrow** and locate the drive and folder where you are saving your file solutions. Type **chap1_pe3_internet_solution** as the file name for the presentation. Click **Save**.

4 Copyright and the Law

The ethics and values class you are taking this semester requires a final presentation to the class. Although a PowerPoint slide show is not required, you feel it will strengthen your presentation. You create a presentation to review basic copyright law and software licensing and add clip art, a transition, and an animation.

a. Click the **Office Button** and select **Open**. Click the **Look in drop-down arrow,** and then locate the drive and folder where your student files are saved. Select the *chap1_pe4_copyright* presentation, and then click **Open**.

b. Click the **Slide Show tab,** and then click **From Beginning** in the Start Slide Show group. Read each of the slides and note the length of some bullets. Press **Esc** to return to Normal view.

c. Click the **Design tab**, click the **More button** in the Themes group, and select the **Flow theme**.

d. Click in the **Slide 1 title placeholder**, if necessary, and then replace the words *Your Name* with your name as it appears on the instructor's rolls. Replace *Your Class* with the name of the class you are taking.

e. Click the **Insert tab** and click **Clip Art** in the Illustrations group. Type **copyright** in the **Search for** box. Select the animated copyright symbol and drag it to the title slide next to your name. Refer to Figure 1.53 to help you identify the copyright logo.

TROUBLESHOOTING: If the animated copyright clip does not appear when you search for the copyright keyword, change the keyword to **law**, and then select an image that relates to the presentation content and uses the same colors.

f. Click the **Animations tab** and click the **More button** in the Transition To This Slide group.

g. Click the **Fade Through Black** option, and then click **Apply To All**.

h. Move to **Slide 6**, and then select the blue object containing text located at the bottom of the slide.

i. Click **Custom Animation** in the Animations group on the Animations tab.

j. Click **Add Effect** in the Custom Animations task pane, click **More Effects** at the bottom of the Entrance group, and then choose **Faded Zoom** from the Subtle category.

k. Click the **Start** drop-down arrow, and then click **After Previous**.

...continued on Next Page

l. Click **Play** at the bottom of the Custom Animation task pane to see the result of your custom animation.

m. Move to the last slide in the slide show, **Slide 9**, click the **Home tab**, and then click **New Slide** in the Slides group.

n. Click **Section Header** from the list of layouts.

o. Click in the title placeholder and type **Individuals who violate copyright law and/or software licensing agreements may be subject to criminal or civil action by the copyright or license owners**. Press **Ctrl + A** to select the text and change the font size to 40 pts.

p. Click the border of the subtitle placeholder and press **Delete**.

q. Drag the title placeholder downward until all of the text is visible and is centered vertically on the slide.

r. Select the text, move your pointer upward until the Mini toolbar appears, and then click the **Center Align** button.

s. Click the **Office Button** and select **Save As**. Click the **Save in drop-down arrow** and locate the drive and folder where you are saving your file solutions. Type **chap1_pe4_copyright_solution** as the file name for the presentation. Click **Save**.

Figure 1.53 Copyright and the Law Presentation

PowerPoint will help you to create an attractive presentation, but the delivery is still up to you. It is easier than you think, and you should not be intimidated at the prospect of facing an audience. You can gain confidence and become an effective speaker by following the basic tenets of good public speaking. Refer to Figure 1.54 as you complete this exercise.

a. Open the *chap1_mid1_public* presentation and save it as **chap1_mid1_public_solution**.

b. Add your name and e-mail address to the title slide. Add your e-mail address to the summary slide as well.

c. Print the notes for the presentation, and then view the slide show while looking at the appropriate notes for each slide. Which slides have notes attached? Are the notes redundant, or do they add something extra? Do you see how the notes help a speaker to deliver an effective presentation?

d. Which slide contains the phrase, "Common sense is not common practice"? In what context is the phrase used within the presentation?

e. Which personality said, "You can observe a lot by watching?" In what context is the phrase used during the presentation?

f. Join a group of three or four students, and then have each person in the group deliver the presentation to his or her group. Were they able to follow the tenets of good public speaking? Share constructive criticism with each of the presenters. Constructive criticism means you identify both positive aspects of their presentations and aspects that could be improved with practice. The goal of constructive criticism is to help one another improve.

g. Summarize your thoughts about this exercise in an e-mail message to your instructor.

h. Save the *chap1_mid1_public_solution* presentation and close.

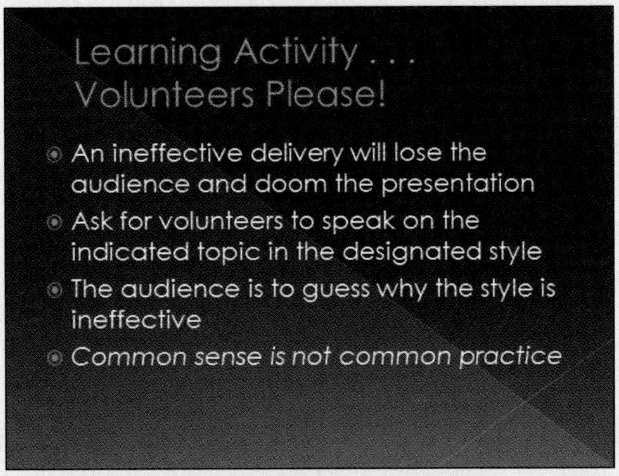

Figure 1.54   Public Speaking 101

...continued on Next Page

The Provost's Office at your university manages policies and practices that affect the academic life of the university as a whole. The new provost, Dr. Richard Shaw, has asked the housing office administrator to meet with him and update him about the purpose and goals of the housing office. As a work-study student employed by the housing office, you have been asked to take the administrator's notes and prepare a presentation for the provost. Refer to Figure 1.55 as you complete this exercise.

a. Open the *chap1_mid2_university* presentation and save it as **chap1_mid2_university_solution**.

b. Add your name and the name of the class you are taking to the title slide.

c. Insert a new slide using the Title and Content layout as the second slide in the presentation. Type **Mission** as the title.

d. Type the mission in the content placeholder: **The mission of the University Housing Office is to provide a total environment that will enrich the educational experience of its residents. It seeks to promote increased interaction between faculty and students through resident masters, special programs, and intramural activities.**

e. Move to the end of the presentation and insert a new slide with the Blank layout. Insert two photograph clips related to college life from the Microsoft Clip Organizer or Office Online.

f. Move to **Slide 4** and create a table using the following information:

Dorm Name	Room Revenue	Meal Revenue	Total Revenue
Ashe Hall	$2,206,010	$1,616,640	$3,822,650
Memorial	$1,282,365	$934,620	$2,216,985
Ungar Hall	$2,235,040	$1,643,584	$3,878,624
Merrick Hall	$1,941,822	$1,494,456	$3,346,278
Fort Towers	$1,360,183	$981,772	$2,341,955
Totals	$9,025,420	$6,581,072	$15,606,492

g. Select the cells containing numbers, and then use the Mini toolbar to right-align the numbers Select the cells containing the column titles, and then use the Mini toolbar to center-align the text..

h. Apply the Cut transition theme to all slides in the slide show.

i. Add the Curve Up custom animation to each of the images on Slide 6. Curve Up is located in the Exciting category of Entrance Effects. Set the animations so that they start automatically after the previous event.

j. Print the handouts, 3 per page, framed.

k. Save the *chap1_mid2_university_solution* presentation and close.

...continued on Next Page

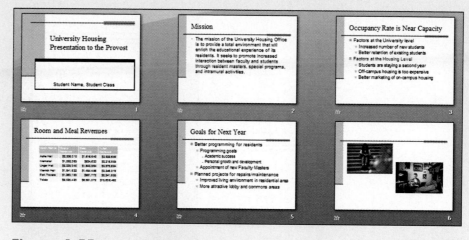

Figure 1.55 University Housing

3 PowerPoint FAQ

As a volunteer in the computer room at the local library, you get a barrage of questions about PowerPoint 2007. To help library personnel and library patrons and to reduce having to repeatedly answer the same questions, you decide to create a PowerPoint FAQ (Frequently Asked Questions) slide show that people can watch when needed. You use Help to help you prepare the FAQ slide show, and as you navigate through Help and read the associated articles, you summarize what you learn in the FAQ slide show. Refer to Figure 1.56 as you complete this exercise.

a. Create a new slide show and save it as **chap1_mid3_ppt07faq_solution**.

b. Type **PowerPoint 2007 Frequently Asked Questions** as the presentation title, and then add your name and the name of the class you are taking to the title slide.

c. Create a new slide for each of the following PowerPoint interfaces using these titles:

- What is the Microsoft Office Button?

- What is the Quick Access Toolbar?

- What is the Ribbon?

- What is a Gallery?

d. Move to **Slide 2** and open Help. Type **Office Button** as the keyword for the search and then conduct the search. When the results page displays, click the link for *What and where is the Microsoft Office Button?*

e. Read the resulting article and close the Help dialog box. In the content placeholder, enter a summary of what you learned. For example, *The Office Button provides access to the basic commands such as open, save, and print, and replaces the File menu.*

f. Use Help to find information about the remaining features, and then enter a summary about each feature in the content placeholder of each slide.

g. Apply the **Origin** design theme to your slide show.

h. Apply the **Fade Smoothly** transition theme to all slides in the slide show.

i. Check the spelling in your presentation, and then proofread carefully to catch any errors that Spelling may have missed.

j. Print the handouts as directed by your instructor.

k. Save the *chap1_mid3_ppt07faq_solution* presentation and close.

...continued on Next Page

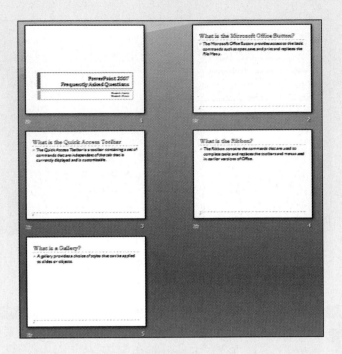

Figure 1.56 FAQ Presentation

Capstone Exercise

Definitely Needlepoint is a successful retail store owned by four close friends. One of them is your mother. The store has been in operation for three years and has increased its revenue and profit each year. The partners are looking to expand their operation by requesting venture capital. They have an important meeting scheduled next week. Help your mother prepare a PowerPoint slide show to help them present their case.

Presentation Setup

You need to open the presentation that you already started, rename the file, and save it. You add your name to the title slide and then you apply a design theme.

a. Locate the file named *chap1_cap_capital*, and then save it as **chap1_cap_capital_solution**.

b. Replace *Your Name* with your name as it appears on your instructor's roll book in the title placeholder of Slide 1.

c. Apply the **Metro** design theme.

Create a Mission Statement Slide

You need to create a slide for the Definitely Needlepoint mission statement. The mission statement created by the four owners clearly reflects their personality and their attitude about their customers. This attitude is a clear factor in the success of the business, so you decide it should be preeminent in the presentation and use it as the introduction slide.

a. Insert a new slide after Slide 1 with the Title Only layout.

b. Type the following mission statement in the title placeholder: **Definitely Needlepoint provides a friendly and intimate setting in which to stitch. Our customers are not just customers, but friends who participate in a variety of social and educational activities that encourage and develop the art of needlepoint**.

c. Select the text, use the Mini toolbar to change the Font size to **28 pts**, and then apply **Italics**.

d. Reposition the placeholder so that the entire statement fits on the slide.

e. Save the *chap1_cap_capital_solution* presentation.

Create Tables

You create tables to show the increase in sales from last year to this year, the sales increase by category, and the sales increase by quarters.

a. Move to **Slide 4**, click the **Insert tab**, and then click **Table** in the Tables group.

b. Create a table with four columns and seven rows. Type the following data in your table:

Category	Last Year	This Year	Increase
Canvases	$75,915	$115,856	$39,941
Fibers	$47,404	$77,038	$29,634
Accessories	$31,590	$38,540	$6,950
Classes	$19,200	$28,200	$9,000
Finishing	$25,755	$46,065	$20,310
Totals	$199,864	$305,699	$105,835

c. Use the Mini toolbar to right-align the numbers and to bold the bottom row of totals.

d. Reposition the table on the slide so that it does not block the title.

e. Move to **Slide 5** and insert a table of six columns and three rows.

f. Type the following data in your table:

Year	Canvases	Fibers	Accessories	Classes	Finishing
Last Year	$75,915	$47,404	$31,590	$19,200	$25,755
This Year	$115,856	$77,038	$38,540	$28,200	$46,065

g. Use the Mini toolbar to change the text font to 16 points, and then right-align the numbers.

h. Reposition the table on the slide so that it does not block the title.

i. Move to **Slide 6** and insert a table of five columns and three rows.

j. Type the following data in your table:

...continued on Next Page

Year	Qtr 1	Qtr 2	Qtr 3	Qtr 4
Last Year	$37,761	$51,710	$52,292	$58,101
This Year	$61,594	$64,497	$67,057	$112,551

k. Spell-check the presentation, check the presentation for errors not caught by spell checking, and then carefully compare the numbers in the tables to your text to check for accuracy.

l. Save the *chap1_cap_capital_solution* presentation.

Insert Clip

Definitely Needlepoint uses a needle and thread as its logo. You decide to use a needle and thread clip on the title slide to continue this identifying image.

a. Move to **Slide 1** and open the Clip Organizer.

b. Type **stitching** in the Search for box and press **Go**.

c. Refer to Figure 1.57 to aid you in locating the needle and thread image.

d. Insert the needle and thread image and position it so that the needle is above the word *Needlepoint* and the tread appears to wrap in and out of the word.

e. Save the *chap1_cap_capital_solution* presentation.

Add Custom Animation

To emphasize the profits that Definitely Needlepoint has made over the last two years, you created two text boxes on Slide 4. You decide to animate these text boxes so that they fly in as you discuss each year. You create custom animations for each box.

a. Move to **Slide 4** and click to select the *Our first year was profitable* text box.

b. Open the Custom Animation task pane and apply a Fly In animation from the Entrance category.

c. Keep the text box selected and click the Add Effect button again. Apply a Fly Out animation from the Exit category. Note the non-printing tags now appear on the text box placeholder indicating the order of the animations.

d. Select the *Our second year was significantly better* text box and then apply a Fly In animation from the Entrance category.

e. Change the Start option to **With Previous**, which will cause this text box to fly in as the other text box flies out.

f. Save the *chap1_cap_capital_solution* presentation.

View and Print the Presentation

You view the presentation to proofread it without the distraction of the PowerPoint creation tools and to check to see if the transitions and animations are applied correctly. When you have proofed the presentation, you print a handout with 4 slides per page to give to the owners so they can see how the presentation is progressing.

a. Click the **Slide Show tab**, and then advance through the presentation. When you get to the table slides, compare the figures with the figures in your text to ensure there are no typographical errors.

b. Exit the slide show and correct any errors.

c. Print handouts in Grayscale, 4 slides per page, and framed.

d. Save the *chap1_cap_capital_solution* presentation and close.

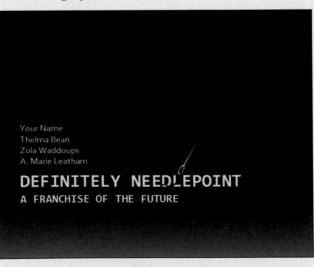

Figure 1.57 Definitely Needlepoint Title Slide

Mini Cases

Green Scene Lawn Service

GENERAL CASE

You create a yard care service to help supplement your income while going to school. You name the yard service "Green Scene." You decide that one way to get your message out to potential customers is to create a presentation about your services and burn it to a CD. You'll deliver the CD to homes around your neighborhood, knowing that by delivering your message in this format, you are most likely to catch the interest of people with technological savvy—those who are busy spending their time in front of a computer instead of doing yard work.

You provide multiple services that customers can choose from. You mow once a week and cut the lawn one-third of its length at a time, you trim and edge along the foundation of the home and any fence lines, and you use a blower to remove the debris left from the trimming. You aerate the lawn in the spring to relieve soil compaction and increase water infiltration. You fertilize using natural-based, granular fertilizers and include lawn, tree, and shrub fertilization. You apply broadleaf weed control and include a surface insect control when this service is ordered. In the spring, you remove winter debris, dethatch the lawn, and restock mulch beds. In the fall, you remove fall leaves and you seed and mulch bare soil patches. Your tree and shrub service includes trimming and removing of trees and shrubs as well as stump removal. You treat the shrubs and trees to protect them from disease.

Create a title slide for your presentation that includes the name of your company and your name. Save your file as **chap1_mc1_greenscene_solution**. Do not worry about burning the presentation to a CD.

Slide 2 should be an introduction slide listing your services:

- Lawn Mowing, Trimming, and Edging
- Aeration, Fertilization, Weed Control
- Spring and Fall Clean-up
- Tree and Shrub Service

Create a slide for each of these topics using the Title and Content layout. The titles for the slides should match the above bullets. Use the case study introductory material to create the content for each slide. Create a summary slide using the Title Slide layout and type **Call today for a free estimate!** in the title placeholder. Include your name and telephone number in the subtitle placeholder. Insert several appropriate clips throughout the presentation, and then resize and position the clips as desired. Apply the design theme of your choice. Reposition placeholders and modify text as desired. Apply a transition of your choice to all slides.

Performance Elements	Exceeds Expectations	Meets Expectations	Below Expectations
Organization	Presentation is easy to follow because information is presented in a logical interesting sequence.	Presentation is generally easy to follow.	Presentation cannot be understood because there is no sequence of information.
Visual aspects	Presentation background, themes, clip art, and animation are appealing and enhance the understanding of presentation purpose and content. There is a consistent visual theme.	Clip art is related to the topic. Animation enhances the presentation.	The background or theme is distracting to the topic. Clip art does not enhance understanding of the content or is unrelated.
Layout	The layout is visually pleasing and contributes to the overall message with appropriate use of headings, subheadings, bullet points, clip art, and white space.	The layout shows some structure, but placement of some headings, subheadings, bullet points, clip art, and/or white space can be improved.	The layout is cluttered and confusing. Placement of headings, subheadings, bullet points, clip art, and/or white space detracts from readability.
Mechanics	Presentation has no errors in spelling, grammar, word usage, or punctuation. No typographical errors present. Bullet points are parallel.	Presentation has no more than one error in spelling, grammar, word usage, or punctuation. Bullet points are inconsistent in no more than one slide.	Presentation readability is impaired due to repeated errors in spelling, grammar, word usage, or punctuation. Most bullet points are not parallel.

The National Debt

The national debt is staggering—more than $8 trillion, or approximately $28,000 for every man, woman, and child in the United States. The annual budget is approximately $2 trillion. Use the Internet to obtain exact figures for the current year, then use this information to create a presentation about the national debt. A good place to start your research is the Web site for the United States Department of the Treasury (http://www.treas.gov) where entering National Debt in the FAQ (Frequently Asked Questions) search box brings up several interesting hyperlinks to information that you can use to develop your presentation.

Do some additional research and obtain the national debt for the years 1945 and 1967. The numbers may surprise you. For example, how does the debt for the current year compare to the debt in 1967 (at the height of the Vietnam War)? To the debt in 1945 (at the end of World War II)? Include your references on a Reference slide at the end of your presentation. Save the presentation as **chap1_mc2_debt_solution**.

Performance Elements	Exceeds Expectations	Meets Expectations	Below Expectations
Organization	Presentation indicates accurate research and significant facts. Evidence exists that information has been evaluated and synthesized showing an understanding of the topic.	Presentation indicates some research has taken place and that information was included in the content.	Presentation demonstrates a lack of research or understanding of the topic. Content misinterpreted or incorrect.
Visual aspects	Presentation background, themes, clip art, and animation are appealing and enhance the understanding of presentation purpose and content. There is a consistent visual theme.	Clip art is related to the topic. Animation is not distracting.	The background or theme is distracting to the topic. Clip art does not enhance understanding of the content or is unrelated.
Layout	The layout is visually pleasing and contributes to the overall message with appropriate use of headings, subheadings, bullet points, clip art, and white space.	The layout shows some structure, but placement of some headings, subheadings, bullet points, clip art, and/or white space can be improved.	The layout is cluttered and confusing. Placement of headings, subheadings, bullet points, clip art, and/or white space detracts from readability.
Mechanics	Presentation has no errors in spelling, grammar, word usage, or punctuation. Bullet points are parallel.	Presentation has no more than one error in spelling, grammar, word usage, or punctuation. Bullet points are inconsistent in one slide.	Presentation readability is impaired due to repeated errors in spelling, grammar, word usage, or punctuation. Most bullet points are not parallel.

Planning for Disaster

This case is perhaps the most important case of this chapter as it deals with the question of backup. Do you have a backup strategy? Do you even know what a backup strategy is? This is a good time to learn, because sooner or later you will need to recover a file. The problem always seems to occur the night before an assignment is due. You accidentally erased a file, are unable to read from a storage device like a flash drive, or worse yet, suffer a hardware failure in which you are unable to access the hard drive. The ultimate disaster is the disappearance of your computer, by theft or natural disaster.

Use the Internet to research ideas for backup strategies. Create a title slide and three or four slides related to a backup strategy or ways to protect files. Include a summary on what you plan to implement in conjunction with your work in this class. Choose the design theme, transition, and animations. Save the new presentation as **chap1_mc3_disaster_solution**.

Performance Elements	Exceeds Expectations	Meets Expectations	Below Expectations
Organization	Presentation indicates accurate research and significant facts. Evidence exists that information has been evaluated and synthesized showing an understanding of the topic.	Presentation indicates some research has taken place and the information was included in the content.	Presentation demonstrates a lack of research or understanding of the topic. Content misinterpreted or incorrect.
Visual aspects	Presentation background, themes, clip art, and animation are appealing and enhance the understanding of presentation purpose and content. There is a consistent visual theme.	Clip art is related to the topic. Animation is not distracting.	The background or theme is distracting to the topic. Clip art does not enhance understanding of the content or is unrelated.
Layout	The layout is visually pleasing and contributes to the overall message with appropriate use of headings, subheadings, bullet points, clip art, and white space.	The layout shows some structure, but placement of some headings, subheadings, bullet points, clip art, and/or white space can be improved.	The layout is cluttered and confusing. Placement of headings, subheadings, bullet points, clip art, and/or white space detracts from readability.
Mechanics	Presentation has no errors in spelling, grammar, word usage, or punctuation. Bullet points are parallel.	Presentation has no more than one error in spelling, grammar, word usage, or punctuation. Bullet points are inconsistent in no more than one slide.	Presentation readability is impaired due to repeated errors in spelling, grammar, word usage, or punctuation. Most bullet points are not parallel.

Presentation Development
Planning and Preparing a Presentation

Objectives

After you read this chapter, you will be able to:

1. Create a presentation using a template **(page 145)**.

2. Modify a template **(page 147)**.

3. Create a presentation in Outline view **(page 155)**.

4. Modify an outline structure **(page 157)**.

5. Print an outline **(page 158)**.

6. Import an outline **(page 163)**.

7. Add existing content to a presentation **(page 164)**.

8. Examine slide show design principles **(page 168)**.

9. Apply and modify a Design Theme **(page 168)**.

10. Insert a header or footer **(page 172)**.

Hands-On Exercises

Exercises	Skills Covered
1. USING A TEMPLATE (page 150) **Open:** New presentation **Insert:** chap2_ho1_photo1.tif **Save as:** chap2_ho1_nature_solution.pptx	• Create a New Presentation Based on an Installed Template • Modify Text in a Placeholder • Add a Slide and Select a Layout • Add a Picture and a Caption • Change a Layout
2. CREATING AND MODIFYING AN OUTLINE (page 159) **Open:** New presentation **Save as:** chap2_ho2_presentations_solution.pptx	• Create a Presentation in Outline View • Enter an Outline • Edit a Presentation • Modify the Outline Structure and Print
3. IMPORTING AN OUTLINE AND REUSING SLIDES (page 166) **Import:** chap2_ho3_success.docx, chap2_ho3_ development.pptx **Save as:** chapt2_ho3_guide_solution.pptx	• Import a Microsoft Word Outline • Reuse Slides from Another Presentation
4. APPLYING AND MODIFYING A DESIGN THEME (page 175) **Open:** chap2_ho3_guide_solution.pptx (from Exercise 3) **Save as:** chap2_ho4_guide_solution.pptx (additional modifications)	• Apply a Theme to a Presentation • Apply a Color Scheme • Add a Font Scheme • Apply a Background Style • Hide Background Graphics on a Slide • Save Current Theme • Create a Slide Footer • Create a Handout Header and Footer

CASE STUDY

Go Back in Time

Dr. Thien Ngo, your professor in world history, has created a very interesting assignment this semester. Each student is to choose a particular voyage, trip, expedition, or journey of interest and create a 10-minute presentation from the perspective of the individual(s) who traveled. You were instructed to create the presentation as an outline in PowerPoint, and to keep it to 6–10 slides. However, Professor Ngo added a twist to the presentation—the audience you are presenting to represents the financial sponsors of your travels (i.e., those who are providing you with whatever provisions you will need to successfully complete your trip). It is up to you to convince them that your idea is worthy of their sponsorship. In addition, you need to request what you will want in return for completing a successful expedition!

Professor Ngo cited several explorers; among them were Lewis and Clark, Amerigo Vespucci, Marco Polo, Queen Hatshepsut, Ferdinand Magellan, Neil Armstrong, Jacques Cousteau, and Christopher Columbus. You can choose from other explorers—it is up to you to determine who you would want to be and what you might like to have discovered!

Your Assignment

- Read the chapter, paying special attention to how to locate and download a template, how to create and modify an outline, and how to apply and modify theme effects in a presentation.
- Locate and download a template from Microsoft Office Online to use for your presentation. Choose a template that enhances the "exploration" theme, such as the Spinning globe template located in the Design slides group, Business category, or the Papyrus extract template, or the Writing on the wall template in the Design slides group Whimsy category. Or, try the Globe on water design in the Presentations group, Design category. Create a title slide with the title **Honoring Our Explorers**, and then enter your choice of explorer as the subtitle. Save the presentation as **chap2_case_explorer_solution**.
- Create an introduction slide indicating to whom the presentation will be given, slides covering main points, and a summary slide reiterating the need for the voyage. Possible slides for main points could cover the current situation, potential reasons or benefits for the voyage, a brief outline of the plan, a list of provisions, the personal qualifications needed for the leaders for this voyage or why you (as that leader) think you have what it takes to make the journey, and what you want in return for your services.
- Modify the theme color scheme or the font scheme, and then save the modified theme.
- Add at least one related clip art image and add animation to at least one slide. Apply a transition to all slides.
- Create a handout with your name in the header, and your instructor's name and your class in the footer.
- Print the Outline View.

Templates

One of the hardest things about creating a presentation is getting started. You may have a general idea of what you want to say, but the words do not come easily to you. You may know what you want to say, but you do not want to spend time designing the look for the slides. Microsoft gives you a potential solution to both of these circumstances by providing templates for your use. Microsoft's templates enable you to create very professional-looking presentations and may include content to help you decide what to say. While previous versions of PowerPoint included an AutoContent Wizard to help you with content development, PowerPoint 2007 incorporates content within some templates to give you more freedom when developing your presentation.

In this section, you learn how to create a presentation using a template. Second, you learn how to modify the template to create a unique appearance.

Creating a Presentation Using a Template

A *template* is a file that incorporates a theme, a layout, and content that can be modified.

A *template* provides for the formatting of design elements like the background, theme, and color scheme, and also font selections for titles and text boxes. Some templates include suggestions for how to modify the template. These suggestions can help you learn to use many of the features in PowerPoint. Content templates include ideas about what you could say to inform your audience about your topic.

> By visiting Microsoft Office Online, you can quickly and easily download. . . professional templates in a variety of categories.

PowerPoint 2007 offers professional built-in templates for you to use, but by visiting Microsoft Office Online, you can quickly and easily download additional templates in a variety of categories. These templates are suitable for virtually every presentation. For example, from the Business and Legal template category at Microsoft Office Online, you can download a template for a bank loan request for a small business, a pre-incorporation agreement for a new business, or a project plan for a new business.

Figure 2.1   Microsoft PowerPoint Templates

Figure 2.1 shows the title slides for featured templates featured on Microsoft Office Online.

Templates are available when you create a new presentation. Click the Office Button and select New. The New Presentation dialog box displays. Template categories display on the left showing the installed templates and links for categories of templates available from Microsoft Office Online. The top center of the dialog box displays the options needed to create a new blank PowerPoint presentation. The left side of the dialog box displays an option to create a new presentation from a blank presentation, from installed templates and from installed themes. Another option enables you to create a presentation from templates you have previously created and saved. Finally, you can create a presentation from an existing presentation. A preview of a selected template is displayed on the far right. Select the Featured category under the Microsoft Office Online section and hyperlinks to check for updates, training, and additional templates appear. Check with your instructor to find out if you are able to download and save Microsoft Office Online Templates in your lab. Figure 2.2 displays the New Presentation dialog box resized to show the entire box. Your dialog box may be different from Figure 2.2 because Microsoft may change its online content.

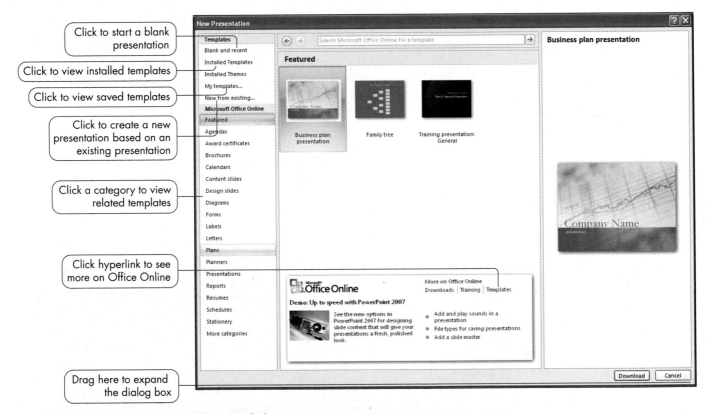

Figure 2.2 New Presentation Dialog Box

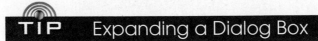

TIP Expanding a Dialog Box

To resize a dialog box to see all available options without having to use the scroll bars, position the pointer on the dots in the bottom-right corner of the dialog box. When the pointer changes to a diagonal two-headed arrow, drag until the full dialog box is visible.

When you select the Installed Templates option in the New Presentation dialog box, the templates installed with PowerPoint 2007 display. Currently, Microsoft includes six templates, but future releases of PowerPoint 2007 may install more. Figure 2.3 shows the Classic Photo Album selected and the preview of the title page for the template.

Modifying a Template

After you download an installed template, you can modify it, perhaps by adding a unifying corporate logo, changing a font style or size, or moving an object on the slide. After you modify the template, you can save it and use it over and over. This feature can save you a tremendous amount of time, as you will not have to redo your modifications the next time you use the template.

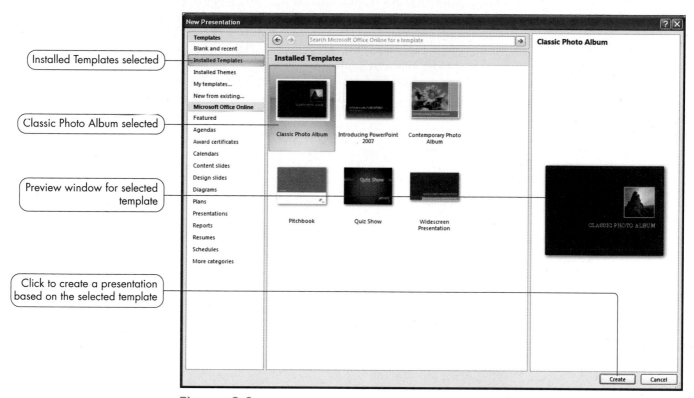

Figure 2.3 PowerPoint Installed Templates

A slide *layout* controls the position of objects containing content on the slide.

A *placeholder* is a container that holds content and is used in the layout to determine the position of objects on the slide.

When you change an object's location on a slide, you are modifying the template *layout* that defines, or controls, the objects on the slide. PowerPoint, as do all Microsoft Office applications, includes standard layouts for your use. The templates you download may have custom layouts unique to that particular template. To modify the location of an object, you must select the *placeholder* containing the object.

Placeholders contain content and are positioned in the layout of a slide. The layout can include any number or combination of placeholders, and every layout can have additional placeholders added to it. You can easily identify placeholders because they are boxes with dotted or hatch-marked borders. In addition to holding text, placeholders can contain elements such as a table, chart, clip art, diagrams, pictures, or media clips. The behavior of the content in a placeholder varies depending on the type of placeholder used. For example, a text placeholder uses internal margins to set the distance between the placeholder borders and the text, while a picture placeholder centers and crops an image that is inserted in it.

A layout may even have no placeholders. PowerPoint also includes a Blank Slide layout with no placeholders so that you can design and create your own layout. If you apply a layout that contains placeholders you do not need, you can delete the placeholder by clicking its border and then pressing Delete. If the placeholder has text, you must delete the text first, and then delete the placeholder.

Sizing handles are small circles or squares that appear at the corner and sides of a selected object.

You can resize a placeholder by clicking on the placeholder to select it, and then pointing at one of the *sizing handles* of the placeholder. When you point at one of the sizing handles, the pointer becomes a two-headed arrow. After your pointer changes into the two-headed arrow, drag the handle until your object is the size you desire. To move a placeholder, select the placeholder and point to any of the placeholder borders. When the pointer becomes a four-headed arrow, drag the placeholder to the location you desire.

You can use text placeholders to quickly change all text contained in the placeholder. First, click to select the placeholder, and then click the border of the placeholder. The border changes from a dashed line to a solid line indicating that all the text is selected. After you select the text, you can change the font, size, case, color, or spacing within the placeholder. Figure 2.4 shows PowerPoint's most commonly used slide layout, the Title and Content layout. This layout has a placeholder for a title and a placeholder that can contain either bulleted text points or graphical objects available from a small icon set. The placeholder has been selected so that any change made to the text format will be applied to all text in the placeholder.

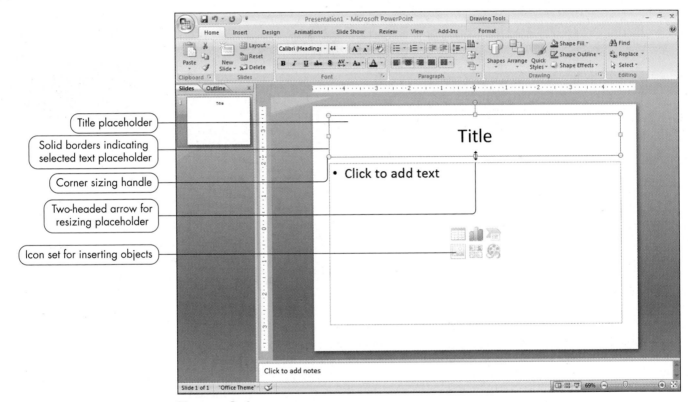

Figure 2.4 Title and Content Layout

Figure 2.5 shows the standard layouts when you open PowerPoint. By default, when you launch PowerPoint, the Home tab is active and displays the Layout command in the Slides group. Clicking Layout brings up the standard layouts for the Office Theme, the default theme. If you cannot determine which layout you need, position the mouse pointer over a layout to show the descriptive name of the layout. The descriptive name indicates the types of placeholders the layout includes.

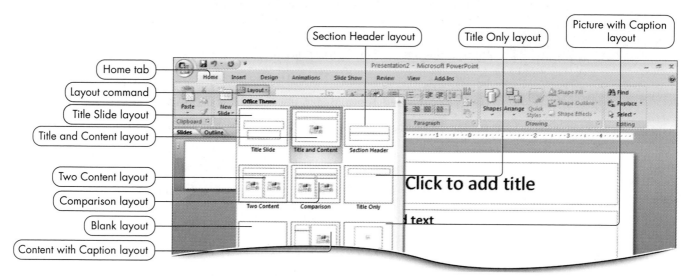

Figure 2.5 Standard Layouts

Hands-On Exercises

1 | Using a Template

Skills covered: 1. Create a New Presentation Based on an Installed Template **2.** Modify Text in a Placeholder **3.** Add a Slide and Select a Layout **4.** Add a Picture and a Caption **5.** Change a Layout

<table>
<tr>
<td>

Step 1

Create a New Presentation Based on an Installed Template

</td>
<td>

Refer to Figure 2.6 as you complete Step 1.

a. Open PowerPoint, click the **Office Button**, and then select **New**.

b. Click **Installed Templates** in the Templates Category.

The New Presentation dialog box changes to display thumbnails of the Installed Templates.

c. Select **Classic Photo Album**, and then click **Create**.

d. Save the presentation as **chap2_ho1_nature_solution**.

</td>
</tr>
</table>

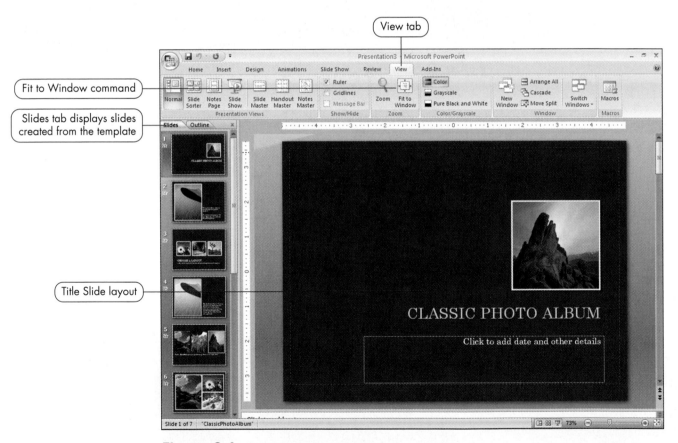

Figure 2.6 The Classic Photo Album Template

Refer to Figure 2.7 as you complete Step 2.

a. Select the text *CLASSIC PHOTO* in the title placeholder, and then type **NATURE**.

The newly entered text replaces the selected text.

b. Replace the subtitle text, *Click to add date and other details*, with **Favorite Pictures 2008!**

c. Click the subtitle placeholder light blue border.

The placeholder's dashed border is replaced with a solid border indicating that all of the content in the placeholder is selected.

d. Click the **Home tab** and click **Italic** and **Shadow** in the Font group.

Italic and shadowing are applied to all text in the placeholder. The shadowing is subtle, but the black shadow helps the white text stand out.

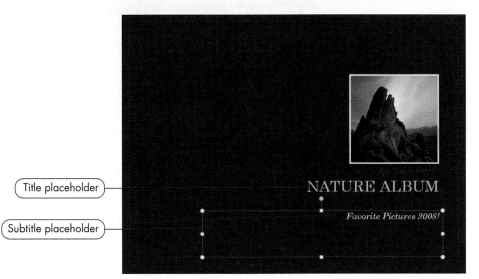

Title placeholder

Subtitle placeholder

Figure 2.7 Modified Text on the Title Page

Refer to Figure 2.8 as you complete Step 3.

a. Click the **Slide 2 thumbnail** displayed in the Slides tab, and then click anywhere in the text to display the placeholder.

b. Click the border of the caption placeholder, and then press **Delete**.

Pressing Delete deletes the text but not the placeholder. Because the placeholder does not print or view, you do not need to worry about it displaying. If, however, you wish to remove the placeholder, you simply click the placeholder border again and press Delete.

c. Click the **Home tab** and click the **New Slide arrow** to display the Classic Photo Album template gallery.

d. Select the **Portrait with Caption** template.

A new slide is created from the template and is inserted after Slide 2.

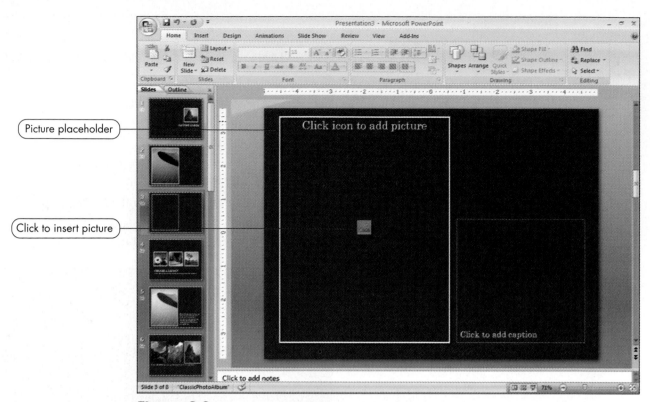

Figure 2.8 The Portrait with Caption Template

Refer to Figure 2.9 as you complete Step 4.

Step 4

Add a Picture and a Caption

a. Click the **Insert Picture button** located in the picture placeholder.

The Insert Picture dialog box displays for your use as you navigate to the location of the files for your textbook.

b. Locate *chap2_ho1_photo1* and click the **Insert button**.

c. Click inside the caption placeholder and type **Each moment of the year has its own beauty.** Press **Enter** twice, and then type **Ralph Waldo Emerson**.

d. Click the border of the caption placeholder to select the text within.

e. Click the **Home tab** and click **Center** in the Paragraph group.

f. Drag the caption placeholder to the left side of the slide, and then drag the picture placeholder to the right side of the slide.

Home tab

Center command

Moved picture placeholder

Centered text within moved placeholder

Views buttons

Each moment of the year has its own beauty.

Ralph Waldo Emerson

Figure 2.9 The Modified Layout

Step 5
Change a Layout

Refer to Figure 2.10 as you complete Step 5.

a. Select **Slide 4**, and then click the **Home tab**, if necessary.

b. Click **Layout** in the Slides group on the Home tab.

c. Click the **2-Up Landscape with Captions** layout to apply it to the slide.

The Classic Photo Album includes a large number of layouts to provide you with a variety of pages in your album.

d. Select the extra photograph and press **Delete**. Select a border surrounding one of the caption placeholders and press **Delete**. Repeat selecting and deleting until the remaining caption placeholders have all been deleted.

When you select a new layout, placeholders may not fit the new layout perfectly. You can move or delete placeholders as necessary.

e. Select the thumbnails for **Slides 5** and **6** in the Slides tab and press **Delete**.

f. Click the **Slide Show tab**, and then click **From Beginning** in the Start Slide Show to view your presentation. Press **Esc** when you are done viewing the presentation.

g. Click **Slide Sorter** in the Slide Show group on the Views buttons area on the status bar to view all the slides showing the wide variety of layouts.

h. Save the *chap2_ho1_nature_solution* presentation and close the file.

Figure 2.10 The Completed Album

Outlines

An ***outline*** is a method of organizing text in a hierarchy to depict relationships.

A ***hierarchy*** denotes levels of importance in a structure.

Creating an *outline* is a method of organizing text using a *hierarchy* with main points and subpoints to denote the levels of importance of the text. An outline is the fastest way to enter or edit text for the presentation. Think of an outline as the road map you use to create your presentation. You created a basic outline when you created a storyboard for your presentation, and now you are ready to input the storyboard information into your presentation. Rather than having to enter the text in each placeholder on each slide separately, a time-consuming process, you type the text directly into an outline.

In this section, you create a presentation in Outline view. After creating the presentation, you modify the outline structure. Finally, you print the outline.

Creating a Presentation in Outline View

Outline view shows the presentation in an outline format with text levels.

To create an outline for your presentation, you must be in Normal view and you need to have the Outline tab selected in the pane that contains the Outline and Slides tabs. This view is considered the *Outline view*. In this view, PowerPoint shows your presentation as an outline made up of the titles and text in each slide. Each slide will display a slide icon and a slide number. The slide title appears next to the slide icon and slide number. Main text on the slide is shown indented under the slide title.

One benefit of working in the Outline view is that you can get a good overview of your presentation. While in this view, you can move easily from one slide to the next. You can copy text from one slide to another and you can rearrange the order of the slides within a presentation. You can change the sequence of the individual bullets (subpoints) in a slide, or move points to another slide. The global overview makes it easy to see relationships between points and determine where information belongs. Figure 2.11 shows a portion of a presentation in Outline view.

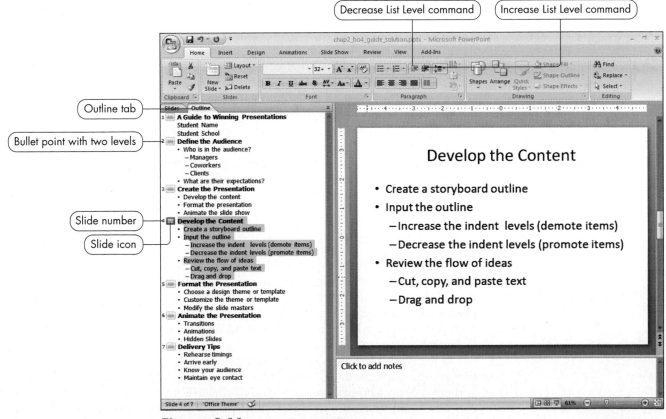

Figure 2.11 The Outline View

> (Remember the lower the level of an item in an outline, the greater the importance of the item.)

While Figure 2.11 shows only two levels of information in the bullet points, PowerPoint 2007 accommodates nine levels of indentation. Previous versions of PowerPoint accommodated only five. Levels make it possible to show hierarchy, or importance, of the data you enter. The main points appear on Level 1. Subsidiary items are indented below the main point to which they apply. Any item can be promoted to a higher level or demoted to a lower level, either before or after the text is entered. This is accomplished clicking Increase List Level or Decrease List Level in the Paragraph group on the Home tab. Consider carefully the number of subsidiary items you add to a main point. Too many levels of hierarchy within a single slide can make the slide difficult to read or understand as the text size automatically re-sizes to a smaller size with each additional level. Remember the lower the level of an item in an outline, the greater the importance of the item. Level 1 items are your main points. Level 9 items would be insignificant in comparison.

TIP   Changing List Levels in an Outline

As a quick keyboard alternative to using Increase and Decrease List Level commands on the Home tab, you can use a keyboard shortcut. Pressing Tab will demote an item or move it to the next level. The result is the same as increasing the indention by clicking Increase List Level. Pressing Shift+Tab promotes an item or moves it back in the list. This action decreases the indention the same as clicking Decrease List Level.

Consider, for example, Slide 4 in Figure 2.11. The title of the slide, *Develop the Content*, appears immediately after the slide number and icon. The first bullet, *Create a storyboard outline*, is indented under the title. The second bullet, *Input the outline*, has two subsidiary bullets at the next level. The next bullet, *Review the flow of ideas*, is moved back to Level 1, and it, too, has two subsidiary bullets.

Enter the Outline

The outline is an ideal way to create and edit the presentation. The insertion point marks the place where new text is entered and is established by clicking anywhere in the outline. (The insertion point automatically is placed at the title of the first slide in a new presentation.) Press Enter after typing the title or after entering the text of a bulleted item, and a new slide or bullet is created, respectively.

When you press Enter, the insertion point stays at the same indentation level as the previous one. You can continue adding more bullet points at the same level by typing the bullet information and then pressing Enter, or you can change the level of the bullet point as described above.

Edit the Outline

Editing is accomplished through the same techniques used in other Windows applications. For example, you can use the Cut, Copy, and Paste commands in the Clipboard group on the Home tab to move and copy selected text. Or, if you prefer, you can simply drag and drop text from one place to another. To locate text you wish to edit, you can click Find or Replace in the Editing group on the Home tab.

Note, too, that you can format text in the outline by using the *select-then-do* approach common to all Office applications; that is, you select the text, then you execute the appropriate command or click the appropriate command. For example, you could select the text, and then apply a new font. The selected text remains highlighted and is affected by all subsequent commands until you click elsewhere in the outline.

Modifying an Outline Structure

Because the Outline view gives you the global picture of your presentation, you can use the view to change the structure of your outline. You can shift bullets or slides around until your outline's structure is refined. To make this process simple, you can collapse or expand your view of the outline contents. A *collapsed outline* view displays only the title of the slides, while the *expanded outline* view displays the title and the content of the slides. You can collapse or expand the content in individual slides or all slides.

Figure 2.12 displays a collapsed view of the outline, which displays only the title of each slide. When a slide is collapsed, a wavy line appears below the slide title letting you know additional levels are collapsed. Positioning the pointer over a slide icon causes it to become a four-headed arrow. To select the slide, click the icon. To move the slide, drag the icon to the desired position.

A *collapsed outline* displays the title of slides only in the Outline view.

An *expanded outline* displays the title and content of slides in the Outline view.

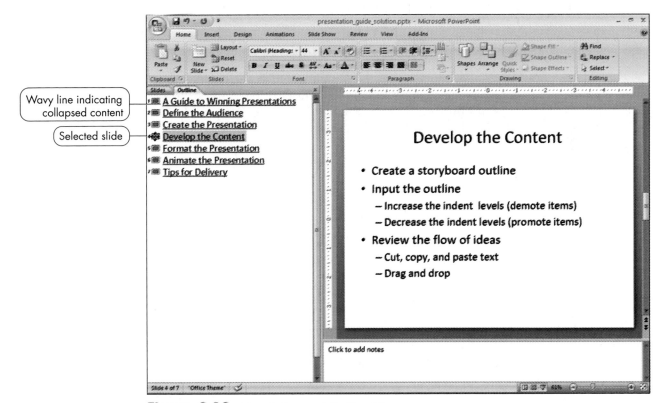

Figure 2.12 The Collapsed Outline View

To collapse a slide, select the text of the slide and right-click. The shortcut menu that appears contains the Collapse command. When you click the Collapse arrow, two new commands appear: Select Collapse or Collapse All. To expand a collapsed slide, select the slide icon and right-click Select Expand or Expand All. See Figure 2.13 for the process involved for collapsing a slide.

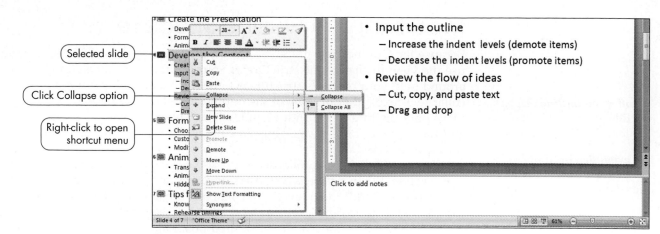

Figure 2.13 Collapse Process

Printing an Outline

You may print the outline in either the expanded or collapsed view. The slide icon and slide number will print with the outline. To print the outline, click the Office Button, point at the arrow next to Print, and select Print, Quick Print, or Print Preview. Figure 2.14 shows the print options.

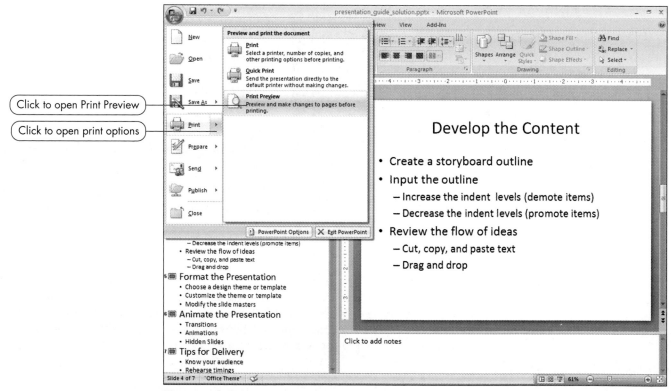

Figure 2.14 Print Options

Hands-On Exercises

2 | Creating and Modifying an Outline

Skills covered: 1. Create a Presentation in Outline View **2.** Enter an Outline **3.** Edit a Presentation **4.** Modify the Outline Structure and Print

Step 1
Create a Presentation in Outline View

Refer to Figure 2.15 as you complete Step 1.

a. Start a new presentation, click the **View tab** and click the **Outline tab** below the Presentation Views group.

b. Click the **Slide 1 icon** on the Outline tab.

c. Type the title of your presentation, **A Guide to Successful Presentations** in the Outline tab pane, and then press **Enter**.

When you pressed Enter, a new slide was created. To change the level from a new slide to a subtitle, you must increase the indent level.

d. Click the **Home tab** and click **Increase List Level** in the Paragraph group.

e. Enter the first line of the subtitle, the words **Presented by**, and then press **Shift+Enter**.

Pressing Shift+Enter moves the insertion point to the next line and keeps the same level.

f. Enter your name in the subtitle.

g. Save the file as **chap2_ho2_presentations_solution**.

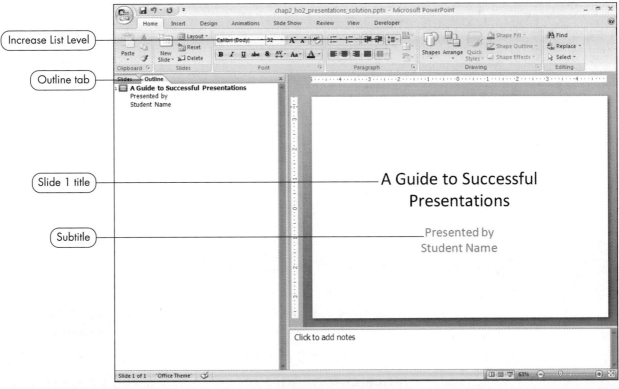

Figure 2.15 Slide 1, Title Slide

Step 2
Enter an Outline

Refer to Figure 2.16 as you complete Step 2.

a. Press **Enter**, and then click **Decrease List Level** in the Paragraph group on the Home tab.

   A new slide, Slide 2, is created.

b. Type the title for Slide 2, **Define the Audience**, and then press **Enter**.

c. Press **Tab** to move to the next level.

   Pressing Tab is a keyboard shortcut that accomplishes the same task as clicking the Increase List Level button.

d. Type **Who is in the audience?**, and then press **Enter**.

e. Press **Tab** to move to the next level and enter the text **Managers**.

   Managers becomes Level 2 text.

f. Press **Enter** and type **Coworkers**.

g. Press **Enter**, and then press **Shift+Tab** twice to return to Level 1 and create Slide 3.

h. Continue entering the text of the outline, and then save the *chap2_ho2_presentations_solution* file. Figure 2.16 contains the text to be typed.

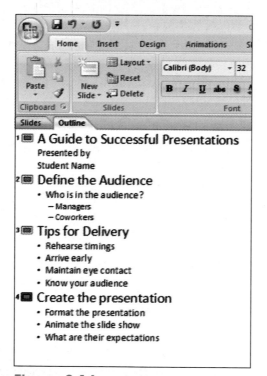

Figure 2.16 Successful Presentations Outline

Step 3
Edit a Presentation

Refer to Figure 2.17 as you complete Step 3.

a. Click at the end of the text *Coworkers* in Slide 2.

   While proofreading your outline, you discover that you did not identify one of your audiences. You need to enter your customers as an audience.

b. Press **Enter** and type **Customers**.

   TROUBLESHOOTING: If your text does not appear in the correct position, check to see if the insertion point was in the wrong location. To enter a blank line for a new bullet, the insertion point must be at the end of an existing bullet point and not at the beginning.

c. Select the text *slide show* in the second bullet point in Slide 4 and replace it with **presentation**.

After replacing the text, you notice that you left off the first step of creating a presentation—developing the content.

d. Click at the end of the title in Slide 4, and then press **Enter**.

e. Press **Tab**, type **Develop the content**, and then press **Enter**.

f. Save the *chap2_ho2_presentations_solution* file.

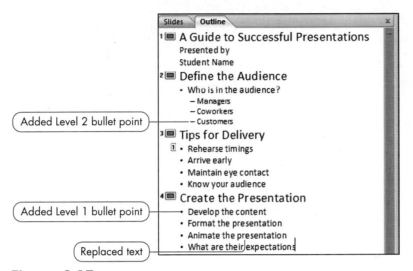

Figure 2.17 The Edited Outline

Step 4
Modify the Outline Structure and Print

Refer to Figure 2.18 as you complete Step 4.

a. Position the pointer over the last bullet in **Slide 4**. When the mouse pointer looks like a four-headed arrow, click to select the text in the bullet point, What are their expectations.

The last bullet in Slide 4 is out of position. It belongs at the end of Slide 2.

b. Right-click and select **Cut**.

c. Click at the end of the last bullet point in **Slide 2** and press **Enter**. Click **Decrease List Level** in the Paragraph group on the Home tab.

d. Right-click and select **Paste**. Then type a question mark at the end of the question you just moved.

In the final review of the presentation, you realize that the slides are out of order. The *Tips for Delivery* slide should be the last slide in the presentation. Collapsing the bullets will make it easy to move the slide.

e. Right-click any bullet point, point at Collapse, and then select **Collapse All**.

f. Click the **Slide 3 icon** to select the collapsed slide.

g. Drag the **Slide 3 icon** below the Slide 4 icon and release.

h. Click the **Office Button**, point at the triangle to the right of the **Print button**, and then select **Print Preview**.

i. Click **Print What** in the Page Setup group on the Print Preview tab, and then select **Outline View**.

j. Click **Orientation** in the Page Setup group on the Print Preview tab, and then select **Landscape**.

k. Click **Close Print Preview** in the Preview group and return to editing the presentation.

l. Select all of the slides in the outline.

m. Right-click, point at the Expand button, and then click **Expand All**.

n. Repeat Steps 4h–j to view the presentation in Print Preview and change the orientation to **Portrait**.

o. Close Print Preview and save the *chap2_ho2_presentations_solution* file. Close the file.

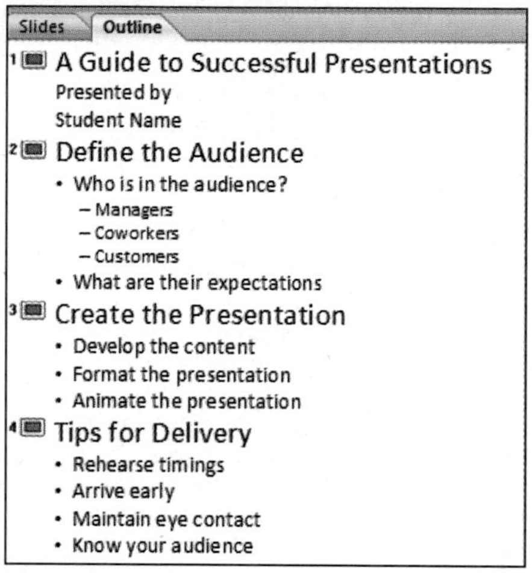

Figure 2.18 The Expanded Outline with Structural Changes

Data Imports

At some time, you may receive an outline created by a colleague using Microsoft Word or another word processing program and you need to create a presentation from that outline. Or perhaps you prefer creating your outlines in a word processing program rather than within PowerPoint. This preference poses no problems as PowerPoint can create slides based on Microsoft Word outlines or outlines saved in a format that PowerPoint recognizes.

Rich Text Format (.rtf) is a file type that retains structure and most text formatting when used to transfer documents between applications or platforms.

PowerPoint recognizes outlines created and saved in a **Rich Text Format (.rtf)**, a file type you can use to transfer text documents with formatting between applications such as any word processing program and PowerPoint, or even between platforms such as Macintosh and IBM. You must save the document in the RTF format with the .rtf extension if you wish to use it in PowerPoint. When you save the document in this format, the extension .rtf is assigned to it. The outline structure and most of the text formatting is retained when you import the outline into PowerPoint.

Plain Text Format (.txt) is a file type that retains only text when used to transfer documents between applications or platforms.

PowerPoint also recognizes outlines created and saved in a **Plain Text format (.txt)**, a file format that retains text only. When .txt outlines are imported, the hierarchical structure is lost and each line of the outline becomes a slide. No text formatting is saved. Another alternative is to import a Web document (.htm), but in this case, all the text from the file appears in one placeholder on one slide.

In this section, you learn how to import an outline into a PowerPoint presentation. You also learn how to add existing content from another presentation into the current presentation.

Importing an Outline

To create a new presentation from an outline created in another format, click the Office Button, and then select Open. When the Open dialog box displays, click All Outlines in the *Files of type* box. Any files in a format PowerPoint recognizes will be listed. Double-click the document you wish to use as the basis for your presentation. Figure 2.19 displays the same outline in three different formats. All three formats appear in the list as they are all formats PowerPoint recognizes.

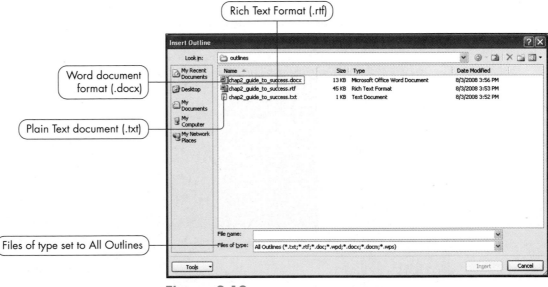

Figure 2.19 Document Formats for Importing

TIP Problems Importing a Word Outline

If you import a Word document you believe is an outline into PowerPoint and after importing, each line becomes a title for a slide, the Word document was created with bullets rather than as an outline. These two features are separate and distinct and do not import in the same manner. You may open the Word document in Word, apply outline formatting, save, and then re-import it, or you may work within the PowerPoint outline and promote and demote text until you obtain the structure you desire.

Adding Existing Content to a Presentation

> With each presentation you create, you create resources for the future.

After you prepare a presentation, you can reuse the content in other presentations. With each presentation you create, you create resources for the future. To obtain the content from other presentations, click New Slide in the Slides group on the Home tab. The bottom of the New Slide gallery contains options for duplicating selected slides, for inserting all the slides from an existing outline, and for reusing slides you select.

When you select the Slides from Outline command, the Insert Outline dialog box displays. By default, only outlines are displayed. You can, however, change the *Files of type* to display other files. Double-click the file you wish to use, and the outline is inserted after the current slide.

For greater flexibility, however, use the Reuse Slides to select the slides you want to use rather than insert all slides. When you select Reuse Slides, a task pane opens on the right side of your window. The Reuse Slides task pane includes a Browse button for locating the file containing the slides you wish to include in your current presentation. When you locate the file and open it, thumbnail images of your slides are displayed in the task pane. Running the pointer over a thumbnail enlarges the image so that text may be read.

At the bottom of the task pane is a check box. By default, when you insert a slide into the presentation, it retains the format of the current presentation. If you wish to keep the format or the original presentation from which you are obtaining the slide, click the *Keep source formatting* check box. Finally, click the thumbnail of your choice to insert it in your presentation after the current slide. The task pane stays open for more selections. The Reuse Slides task pane is shown in Figure 2.20.

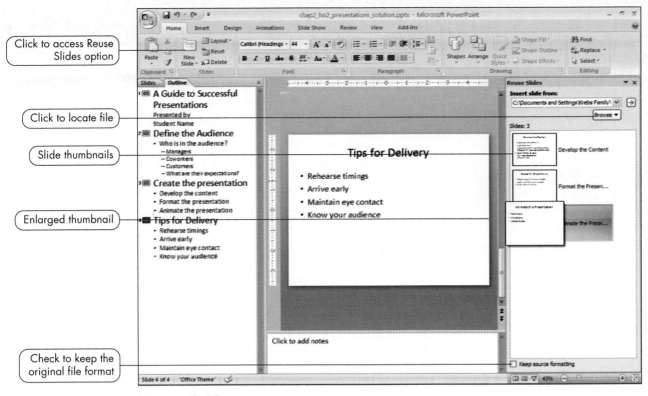

Click to access Reuse Slides option

Click to locate file

Slide thumbnails

Enlarged thumbnail

Check to keep the original file format

Figure 2.20 Reuse Slides Task Pane

Hands-On Exercises

3 | Importing an Outline and Reusing Slides

Skills covered: 1. Import a Microsoft Word Outline **2.** Reuse Slides from Another Presentation

---

Step 1 **Import a Microsoft Word Outline**	Refer to Figure 2.21 as you complete Step 1. **a.** Click the **Office Button**, select **Open**, and then navigate to your classroom file location. **b.** Change the **Files of type** option to show **All Outlines**. **c.** Double-click to open the file *chap2_ho3_success*, a Microsoft Office Word document. The Word outline is opened into PowerPoint and a new presentation based upon the imported document is created. This presentation is similar to the one you created in Hands-On Exercise 1, but some of the content is slightly different. Also, notice that the font is Times New Roman, based on the outline imported into the presentation. **d.** Click the **Outline tab**, and select **Slide 3**, *Create the Presentation*. **e.** Save the file as **chap2_ho3_guide_solution**.

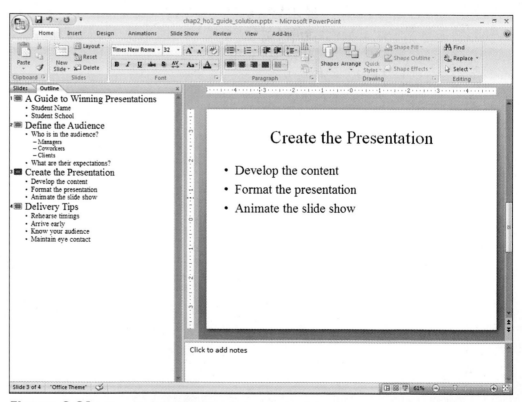

Figure 2.21   New Presentation Based on a Word Outline

Refer to Figure 2.22 as you complete Step 2.

a. Click the **Home tab** and click **New Slide** in the Slides group.

The New Slide gallery appears.

b. Click **Reuse Slides** at the bottom of the gallery.

The Reuse Slides pane appears on the right side of your screen.

c. Click the **Browse button**, click **Browse File**, and locate your student files.

d. Click to select the file *chap2_ho3_development*, and then click **Open**.

> **TROUBLESHOOTING:** If you do not see the *chap2_ho3_development* presentation, change the *Files of type* option to All PowerPoint Presentations.

e. Click each of the sides in the Reuse Slides task pane to insert the slides into the slide show.

f. Close the Reuse Slides task pane.

g. Refer to Figure 2.22. Move slides as needed to obtain the correct structure, if necessary.

Ignore font changes, as we will handle design issues in the next section of this chapter.

h. Save the *chap2_ho3_guide_solution* file and keep it onscreen if you plan to continue to the next hands-on exercise. Close the file and exit PowerPoint if you do not want to continue with the next exercise at this time.

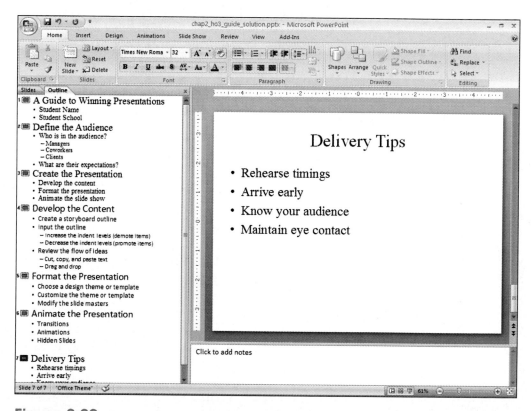

Figure 2.22 Reused Slides Added to Presentation

Design

You should evaluate many aspects when considering the visual design of your presentation.

When you work with the content of a presentation, it can be helpful to work with the blank template, as you did when we worked with the outlines. Working in the blank template lets you concentrate on what you want to say. After you are satisfied with the content, however, you need to consider the visual aspects of the presentation. You should evaluate many aspects when considering the visual design of your presentation. Those aspects include layout, background, typography, color, and animation.

Because the majority of people using PowerPoint are not graphic artists and do not have a strong design background, Microsoft designers created a variety of methods to help users deal with design issues. By now, you should have explored themes and templates that are used to help people create an attractively designed slide show without a background in design.

In this section, you explore additional Microsoft features to aid with design. After you are comfortable using these features, you can modify the design to reflect your own taste. Before doing so, however, you need to examine some basic visual design principles for PowerPoint.

Examining Slide Show Design Principles

Basic design principles are universal. When applied to a project, they can increase its appeal and professionalism. While basic principles are universal, some aspects may be applied in specific ways to the various types of modern communication: communicating through print mediums such as flyers or brochures, through audio mediums such as narrations or music, or through a visual medium such as a slide show. You will focus on a few of the principles that apply to slide shows and examine examples of slides that illustrate the principles.

Remember that these principles are guidelines. You may chose to avoid applying one of these principles, but you should be aware of the principle and why you are not following it. If you are in doubt about your design, ask a classmate or colleague to review the design and make suggestions. Fresh eyes can see things you may not.

Applying and Modifying a Design Theme

You should already have experience applying a theme. You can tweak the theme once it is applied. You can change the colors used in the theme, the fonts used, and effects used. You can even change the background styles. Each of these options is on the Design tab, and each has its own gallery. Figure 2.30 shows the locations for accessing the galleries.

Examples of Designs for Various Audiences | Reference

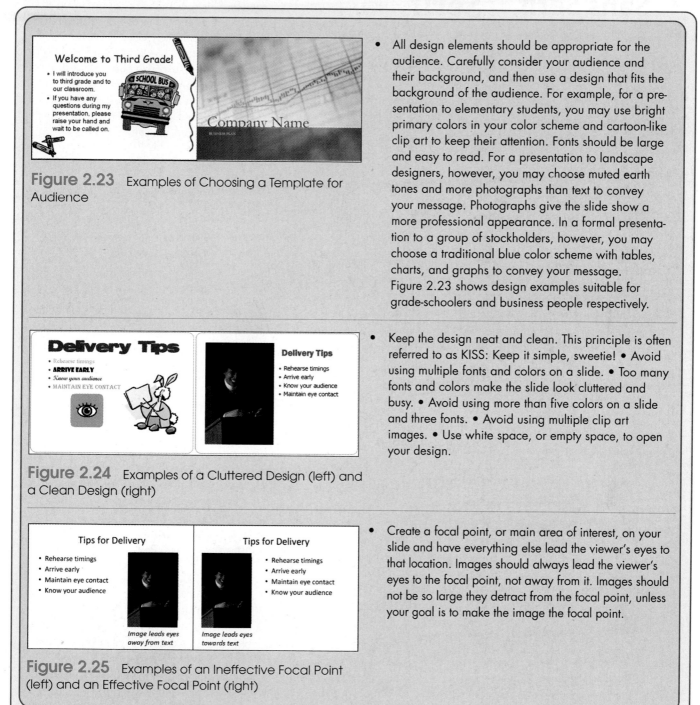

Figure 2.23 Examples of Choosing a Template for Audience

Figure 2.24 Examples of a Cluttered Design (left) and a Clean Design (right)

Figure 2.25 Examples of an Ineffective Focal Point (left) and an Effective Focal Point (right)

- All design elements should be appropriate for the audience. Carefully consider your audience and their background, and then use a design that fits the background of the audience. For example, for a presentation to elementary students, you may use bright primary colors in your color scheme and cartoon-like clip art to keep their attention. Fonts should be large and easy to read. For a presentation to landscape designers, however, you may choose muted earth tones and more photographs than text to convey your message. Photographs give the slide show a more professional appearance. In a formal presentation to a group of stockholders, however, you may choose a traditional blue color scheme with tables, charts, and graphs to convey your message. Figure 2.23 shows design examples suitable for grade-schoolers and business people respectively.

- Keep the design neat and clean. This principle is often referred to as KISS: Keep it simple, sweetie! • Avoid using multiple fonts and colors on a slide. • Too many fonts and colors make the slide look cluttered and busy. • Avoid using more than five colors on a slide and three fonts. • Avoid using multiple clip art images. • Use white space, or empty space, to open your design.

- Create a focal point, or main area of interest, on your slide and have everything else lead the viewer's eyes to that location. Images should always lead the viewer's eyes to the focal point, not away from it. Images should not be so large they detract from the focal point, unless your goal is to make the image the focal point.

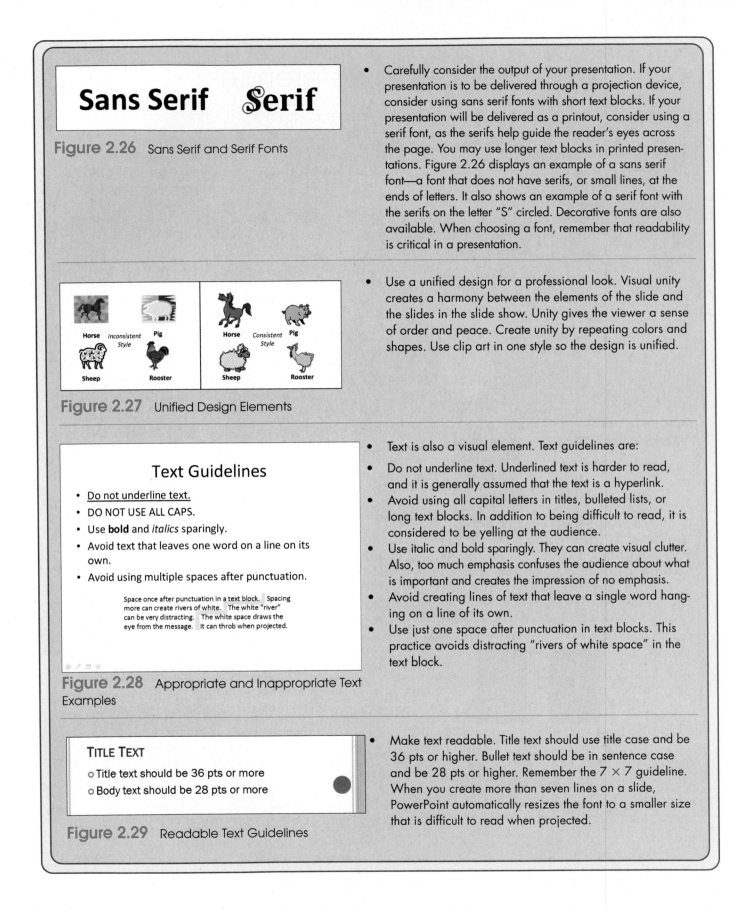

Figure 2.26 Sans Serif and Serif Fonts

Figure 2.27 Unified Design Elements

Figure 2.28 Appropriate and Inappropriate Text Examples

Figure 2.29 Readable Text Guidelines

- Carefully consider the output of your presentation. If your presentation is to be delivered through a projection device, consider using sans serif fonts with short text blocks. If your presentation will be delivered as a printout, consider using a serif font, as the serifs help guide the reader's eyes across the page. You may use longer text blocks in printed presentations. Figure 2.26 displays an example of a sans serif font—a font that does not have serifs, or small lines, at the ends of letters. It also shows an example of a serif font with the serifs on the letter "S" circled. Decorative fonts are also available. When choosing a font, remember that readability is critical in a presentation.

- Use a unified design for a professional look. Visual unity creates a harmony between the elements of the slide and the slides in the slide show. Unity gives the viewer a sense of order and peace. Create unity by repeating colors and shapes. Use clip art in one style so the design is unified.

- Text is also a visual element. Text guidelines are:
- Do not underline text. Underlined text is harder to read, and it is generally assumed that the text is a hyperlink.
- Avoid using all capital letters in titles, bulleted lists, or long text blocks. In addition to being difficult to read, it is considered to be yelling at the audience.
- Use italic and bold sparingly. They can create visual clutter. Also, too much emphasis confuses the audience about what is important and creates the impression of no emphasis.
- Avoid creating lines of text that leave a single word hanging on a line of its own.
- Use just one space after punctuation in text blocks. This practice avoids distracting "rivers of white space" in the text block.

- Make text readable. Title text should use title case and be 36 pts or higher. Bullet text should be in sentence case and be 28 pts or higher. Remember the 7 × 7 guideline. When you create more than seven lines on a slide, PowerPoint automatically resizes the font to a smaller size that is difficult to read when projected.

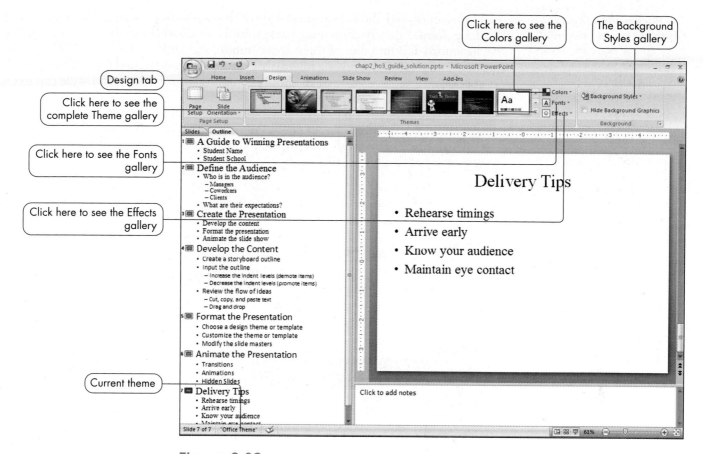

Figure 2.30 Design Galleries

The **Colors gallery** is a gallery with a set of colors for every available theme.

Each PowerPoint theme includes a **Colors gallery**, a gallery that provides a set of colors. Each color in the gallery is assigned to a different element in the theme design. Once the theme is selected, you can click the Colors down arrow to display the Built-In gallery. Clicking one of the color themes applies it to the theme, thereby applying it to the presentation. You can even create your own color theme set by selecting Create New Theme Colors at the bottom of the gallery.

Selecting a font for the title and one for the bullets or body text of your presentation can be difficult. Without a background in typography, it is hard to determine which fonts go together well. The **Fonts gallery** is a gallery that pairs a title font and a body font for your use. Click any of the samples in the Fonts gallery, and the font pair is applied to your theme. You do not need to select the slides because the change applies to all slides.

The **Fonts gallery** contains font sets for title text and body text.

The **Effects gallery** includes a range of effects for shapes used in the presentation.

The **Effects gallery** is a gallery that displays a full range of special effects that can be applied to all shapes in the presentation. This aids you in maintaining the consistency of the look of your presentation. Effects in the gallery include a soft glow, soft edges to the shape, shadows, or a three-dimensional (3-D) look.

You can change the background style of the theme by accessing the **Background Styles gallery**, a gallery containing backgrounds consistent with the color theme. The backgrounds fall into one of three areas: subtle, moderate, or intense. Subtle backgrounds are a solid color, while intense backgrounds are designed with patterns such as checks, stripes, blocks, or dots. Simply changing your background style can liven up a presentation and give it your individual style.

Some of the themes, like Equity, include shapes on their background to create the design. If the background shapes are interfering with other objects on the slide, however, you can click the Hide Background Graphics check box and the background shapes will not display for that slide.

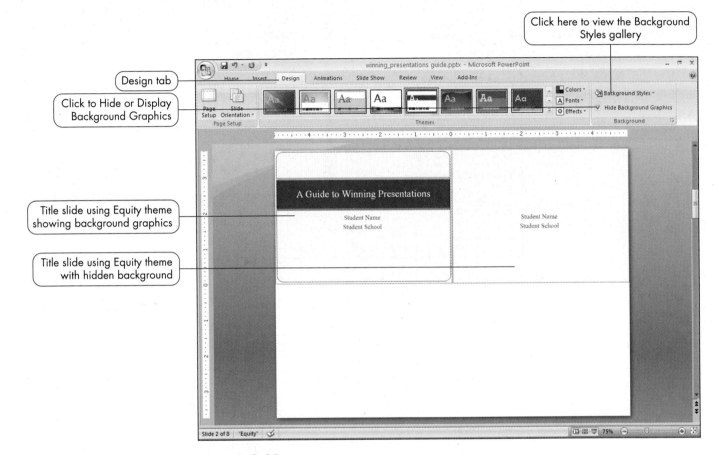

Figure 2.31 Equity Theme

Inserting a Header or Footer

You will find that many times there is information that you want to appear on every slide, handout, or notes page. As a student, your instructor may want your name on every handout you turn in or the date you completed the assignment. Use the Header and Footer feature to do this. A **header** contains information that appears at the top of pages in a handout or on a notes page. A **footer** contains information that appears at the bottom of slides in a presentation or at the bottom of pages in a handout or a notes page.

Common uses of headers and footers are to insert slide numbers, the time and date, a company logo, the presenter's name, or even the presentation's file name. Headers and footers can contain text or graphics. To insert text in a header or footer, you use the Header and footers command. To insert graphics, you modify the header or footer fields in the Slide Master. For now, you will use the Header and footer command. You can use Help to learn how to customize a Slide Master to include a logo graphic in a footer. Figure 2.32 shows an example of a title slide with a footer.

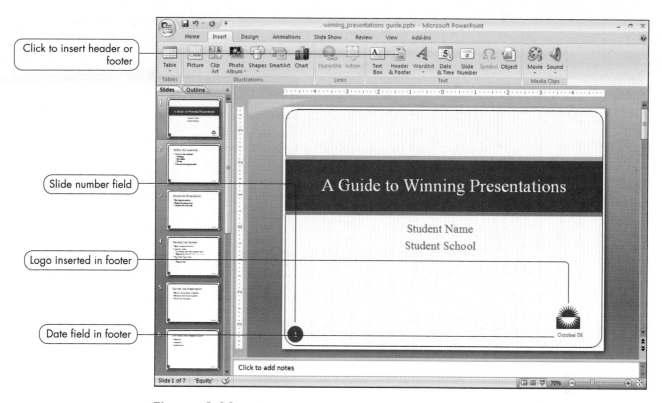

Figure 2.32 Title Slide with Footer

To create a footer for a slide, click the Insert tab, and then click Header & Footer in the Text group. Click the Slide tab when the Header and Footer dialog box displays. Click the Date and time check box in the *Include on slide* section to insert the current date and time. Click *Update automatically* if you wish the date to always be current. Once you select *Update automatically*, you can select the date format you prefer. Alternatively, you can choose the option to enter a fixed date that will not change. You use a fixed date to preserve the original date you created the presentation, which could help you keep track of versions.

A check box also activates the Slide number field. Click the Footer check box to activate the footer field. When you click the check box, the insertion point is placed inside the Footer box, and you can enter any information you desire. The Preview window lets you see the position of these fields. If you do not want the footer to appear on the title slide, click the *Don't show on title slide* check box. The last step is to click Apply to apply the footer to the selected slide or to click Apply All to apply the footer to every slide in the presentation. Figure 2.33 shows the Header and Footer dialog box with the Slide tab selected.

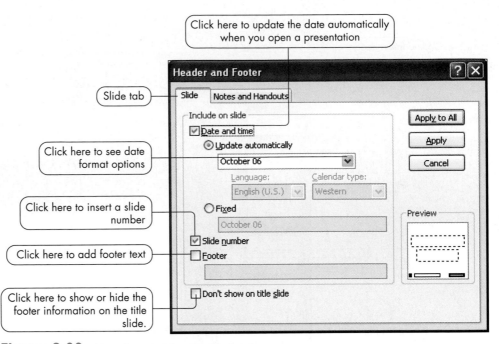

Figure 2.33 Header and Footer Dialog box

The Notes and Handouts tab gives you many of the same options available in the Slides tab. You can add more information in this tab, however, because it gives you an extra field box for information—the Header field. Since this feature is used for printouts, the slides are not numbered, but the pages in the handout are. As you activate the fields, the preview window shows the location of the fields. The Date and Time field is located on the top right of the printout. The Header field is located on the top left. The page number is located on the bottom right, and the Footer field is on the bottom left.

Hands-On Exercises

4 | Applying and Modifying a Design Theme

Skills covered: 1. Apply a Theme to a Presentation **2.** Apply a Color Scheme **3.** Add a Font Scheme **4.** Apply a Background Style **5.** Hide Background Graphics on a Slide **6.** Save Current Theme **7.** Create a Slide Footer **8.** Create a Handout Header and Footer

Step 1
Apply a Theme to a Presentation

Refer to Figure 2.34 as you complete Step 1.

a. Open the *chap2_ho3_guide_solution* file if you closed it after the last hands-on exercise. Save the file as **chap2_ho4_guide_solution**.

b. Click the **Design tab** and click the **More button** in the Themes group.

The Themes gallery opens for you to select from Themes in This Presentation, from the Built-In themes, from Office Online, or enables you to Browse for Themes you have previously created and saved.

c. Click the **Solstice theme**.

The theme is applied to all slides in the presentation.

d. Save the *chap2_ho4_guide_solution* presentation.

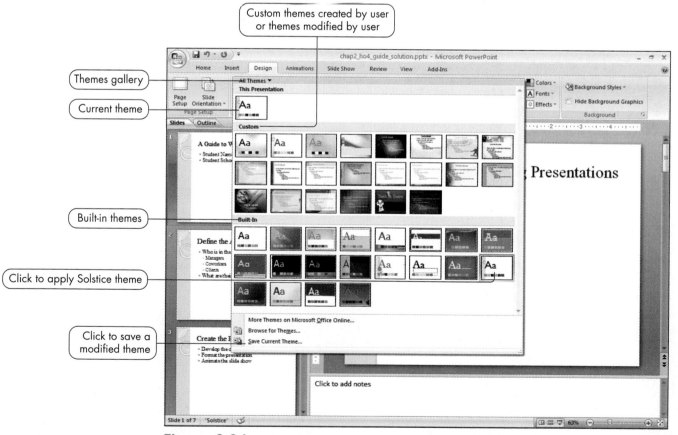

Figure 2.34 Solstice Theme

Step 2
Apply a Color Scheme

Refer to Figure 2.35 as you complete Step 2.

a. With *chap2_ho4_guide_solution* open, point at the Colors button in the Themes group.

Note the ScreenTip that appears showing the currently applied color scheme applied—Solstice.

b. Click **Colors** in the Themes group on the Design tab to see the Built-In gallery.

c. Point to several of the color schemes to see the effects they have on the title slide.

The color scheme is not applied until you click.

d. Click the **Origin color scheme**.

The color scheme is applied to your presentation.

e. Save the *chap2_ho4_guide_solution* presentation.

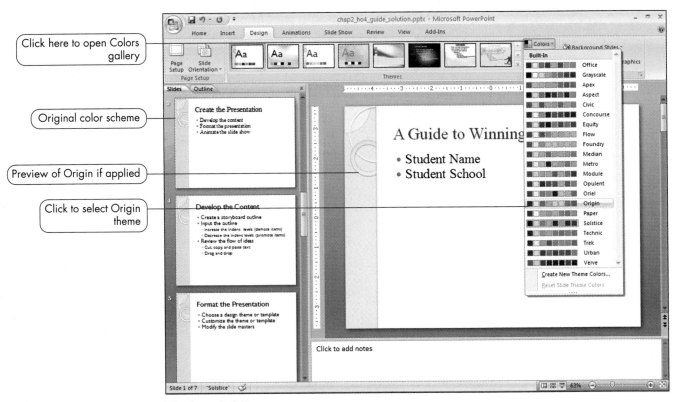

Figure 2.35 Solstice Theme with Origin Color Theme

Step 3
Add a Font Scheme

Refer to Figure 2.36 as you complete Step 3.

a. With *chap2_ho4_guide_solution* open, click the **Outline tab**.

b. Note that Slides 1, 2, 3, and 7 use different fonts than Slides 4, 5, and 6.

Slides 4, 5, and 6 were created by reusing slides from another presentation, causing the font shift. Slides 1, 2, 3, and 7 use a serif font—Times New Roman. Slides 4, 5, and 6 use a sans serif font—Gill Sans.

c. Click the **Design tab** and click **Fonts** in the Themes group.

The Built-In fonts appear in the gallery.

d. Click the **Flow font scheme** to apply it to your presentation.

The Flow font scheme applies the Calibri font to titles and the Constantia font to body text.

TROUBLESHOOTING: If the font scheme does not apply to all slides, select the slide that did not have the scheme applied and then change the title and bullets manually.

e. Save the *chap2_ho4_guide_solution* presentation.

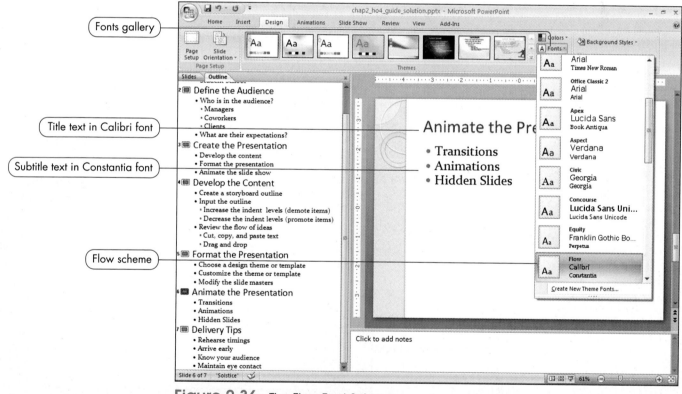

Figure 2.36 The Flow Font Scheme

Step 4
Apply a Background Style

Refer to Figure 2.37 as you complete Step 4.

a. With *chap2_ho4_guide_solution* open, click the **Slides tab**.

Changing to the Slides tab enables you to see the background style you apply on several slides.

b. Click **Background Styles** in the Background group on the Design tab.

c. Point at each of the styles and note the changes to the background graphic on the side of the slide.

> **TIP** Choosing Backgrounds Based on Lighting
>
> A dark background choice is appropriate if you will be giving your presentation in a very light room. If you use a light background in a light room, your audience may not see your text because there would not be enough contrast. If you give your presentation in a dark room, select a light background. A dark background in a dark room gives your audience an invitation to sleep!

d. Click **Style 6**.

e. Save the *chap2_ho4_guide_solution* presentation.

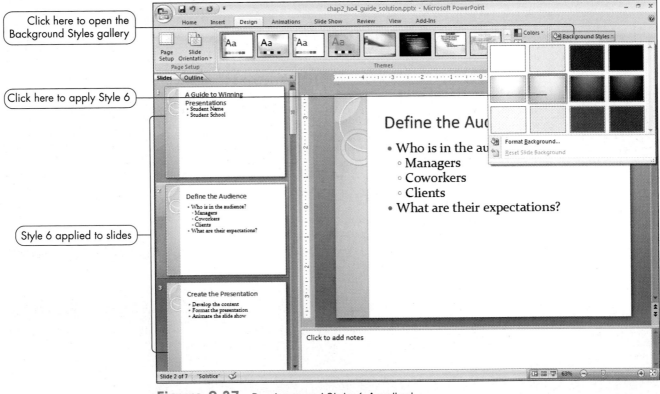

Figure 2.37 Background Style 6 Applied

Refer to Figure 2.38 as you complete Step 5.

a. With *chap2_ho4_guide_solution* open, click to select **Slide 1**, if necessary.

You decide to put a photograph related to presenting on the bottom of the title slide to add color. To keep the slide from being cluttered, you decide to remove the background graphics.

b. Click the **Hide Background Graphics check box** in the Background group on the Design tab.

c. Click the **Insert tab** and click **Clip Art** in the Illustrations group.

d. In the Clip Art task pane, type **presenter** in the **Search for** box.

e. Click the **Results should be arrow**, remove the check marks from all media types except Photographs, and then click **Go**.

f. Click the image of the presenter in the red jacket, drag it to the lower right of your slide, and then close the Clip Art task pane.

The red jacket adds more color to the title slide. Your clip art gallery may have more images if you are connected to Microsoft Online, but you can drag the scroll bar to locate this image. Figure 2.38 indicates the image to click. Because the image is positioned on the lower left, the audience's eyes would flow down to the image after reading the title. The image is looking away, which leads their eyes off the slide—a visual clue that the slide is finished. If the image was placed higher on the slide, you would flip it so that it looks inward to the focal point, the title text. Figure 2.39 displays the completed slide.

g. Click the **Home tab**, click **Layout** in the Slides group, and click **Title Slide**.

The first slide was formatted by the Title and Text layout when you imported the Word outline in Hand-On Exercise 2. You applied Title Slide layout to convert the bullet-list items to a subtitle

h. Save the *chap2_ho4_guide_solution* presentation.

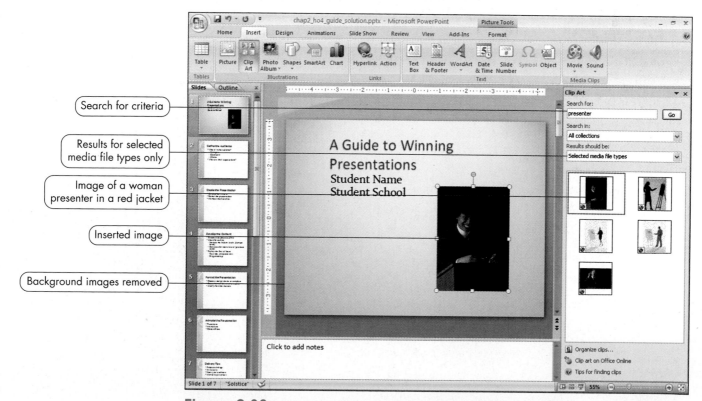

Figure 2.38 Background Image Removed and Clip Art Added

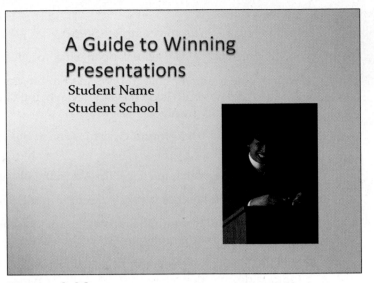

Figure 2.39 Modified Title Slide

Refer to Figure 2.40 as you complete Step 6.

Step 6
Save Current Theme

a. With *chap2_ho4_guide_solution* open, click **More** in the Themes group on the Design tab.

To save time in the future, you save the theme you created when you customized the Solstice theme.

b. Click **Save Current Theme**.

c. Type **presenter_theme** in the **File name** box and click **Save**.

d. Click **More** in the Themes group on the Design tab.

A new theme category has been added to the All Themes gallery—the Custom category.

e. Point at the theme displaying in the Custom category. Note the ScreenTip showing the theme name. This is the presenter_theme you just created.

f. Save the *chap2_ho4_guide_solution* presentation.

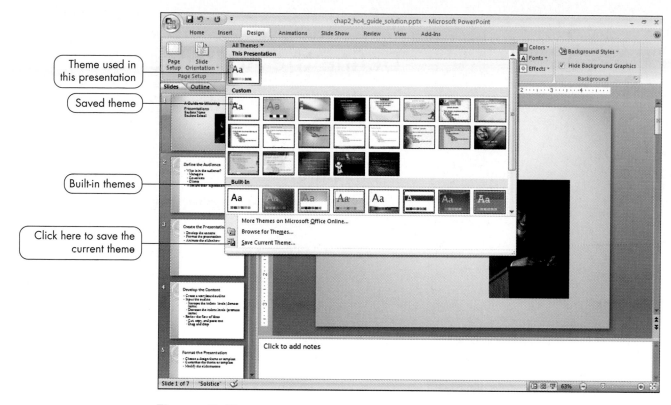

Theme used in this presentation

Saved theme

Built-in themes

Click here to save the current theme

Figure 2.40 All Themes Gallery

Step 7
Create a Slide Footer

Refer to Figure 2.41 as you complete Step 7.

a. With *chap2_ho4_guide_solution* open, click the **Insert tab**, and then click **Header & Footer** in the Text group.

b. In the Header and Footer dialog box, click the **Date and time check box** in the *Include on slide* section.

c. Click **Update automatically**, if it is not already selected.

d. Click the **drop-down arrow** and select the sixth date format in the list.

The sixth date format spells out the month and then includes the year, such as June 08.

e. Click the **Slide number** check box.

f. Click the **Don't show on title slide option check box**.

Clicking this check box adds a check mark hiding the footer on the title slide.

g. Click **Apply to All**.

h. Click the **Slide 1 thumbnail** to display the slide in the Slides pane.

Notice that the footer does not appear on this slide because you selected the option to hide the footer on the title slide.

i. Save the *chap2_ho4_guide_solution* presentation.

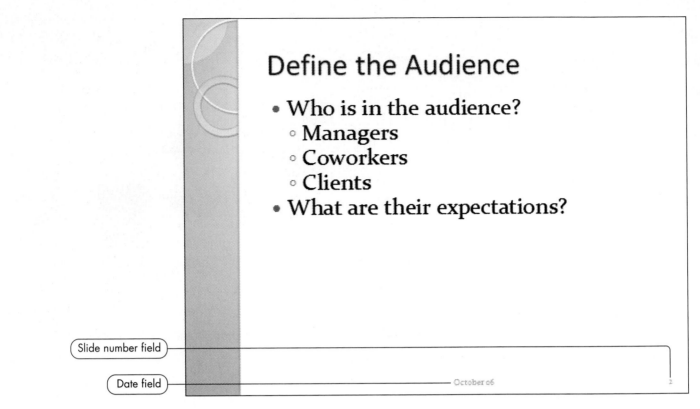

Slide number field

Date field

October o6

Figure 2.41 The Slide Footer

Step 8

Create a Handout Header and Footer

Refer to Figure 2.42 as you complete Step 8.

a. With *chap2_ho4_guide_solution* open, click the **Insert tab**, if necessary, and then click **Header & Footer** in the Text group.

b. Click the **Notes and Handouts tab**.

In the previous exercise, you created a footer that displays when the slide show plays. In this exercise, you create a header and footer that only displays on printouts.

c. Click the **Date and time check box**.

d. Click **Update automatically** if needed.

By selecting the Update automatically option, you ensure that any printouts will display the current date and not the date the presentation originally was created.

e. Click the **drop-down arrow** and select the sixth date format in the list.

f. Click the **Header check box** and enter your name in the text box.

g. Click the **Footer check box** and enter your instructor's name and your class.

Footers often are used for identifying information.

h. Click the **Apply to All button**.

i. Click the **Office Button**, point at the **Print arrow**, and then select **Print Preview**.

j. Change the *Print What* option to **Handouts (4 Slides Per Page)**.

k. Note the placement of the header, date, footer, and slide number. Click **Close Print Preview**.

l. Save the *chap2_ho4_guide_solution* presentation. Close the presentation.

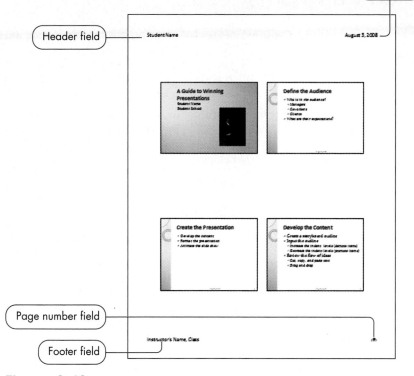

Date field

Header field

Page number field

Footer field

Figure 2.42 Handout Header and Footer

Summary

1. **Create a presentation using a template.** Using a template saves you a great deal of time and enables you to create a more professional presentation. Templates incorporate a theme, a layout, and content that can be modified. You can use templates that are installed when Microsoft Office is installed, or you can download templates from Microsoft Office Online. Microsoft is constantly adding templates to the online site for your use.

2. **Modify a template.** In addition to changing the content of a template, you can modify the structure and design. The structure is modified by changing the layout of a slide. To change the layout, drag placeholders to new locations or resize placeholders. You can even add placeholders so that elements such as logos can be included.

3. **Create a presentation in Outline view.** When you use a storyboard to determine your content, you create a basic outline. Then you can enter your presentation in Outline view, which enables you to concentrate on the content of the presentation. Using Outline view keeps you from getting buried in design issues at the cost of your content. It also saves you time because you can enter the information without having to move from placeholder to placeholder.

4. **Modify an outline structure.** Because the Outline view gives you a global view of the presentation, it helps you see the underlying structure of the presentation. You are able to see where content needs to be strengthened, or where the flow of information needs to be revised. If you find a slide with content that would be presented better in another location in the slide show, you can use the Collapse and Expand features to easily move it. By collapsing the slide content, you can drag it to a new location and then expand it. To move individual bullet points, cut and paste the bullet point or drag-and-drop it.

5. **Print an outline.** When you present, using the outline version of your slide show as a reference is a boon. No matter how well you know your information, it is easy to forget to present some information when facing an audience. While you would print speaker's notes if you have many details, you can print the outline as a quick reference. The outline can be printed in either the collapsed or the expanded form, giving you far fewer pages to shuffle in front of an audience than printing speaker's notes would.

6. **Import an outline.** You do not need to re-enter information from an outline created in Microsoft Word or another word processor. You can use the Open feature to import any outline that has been saved in a format that PowerPoint can read. In addition to a Word outline, you can use the common generic formats Rich Text Format and Plain Text Format.

7. **Add existing content to a presentation.** After you spend time creating the slides in a slide show, you may find that slides in the slide show would be appropriate in another show at a later date. Any slide you create can be reused in another presentation, thereby saving you considerable time and effort. You simply open the Reuse Slides pane, locate the slide show with the slide you need, and then click the thumbnail of the slide to insert a copy of it in the new slide show.

8. **Examine slide show design principles.** With a basic understanding of slide show design principles, you can create presentations that reflect your personality in a professional way. The goal of applying these principles is to create a slide show that focuses the audience on the message of the slide without being distracted by clutter or unreadable text.

9. **Apply and modify a design theme.** PowerPoint provides you with themes to help you create a clean, professional look for your presentation. Once a theme is applied, you can modify the theme by changing the color scheme, the font scheme, the effects scheme, or the background style.

10. **Insert a header or footer.** Identifying information can be included in a header or footer. You may, for example, wish to include the group to whom you are presenting, the location of the presentation, or a copyright notation for original work. You can apply footers to slides, handouts, and Notes pages. Headers may be applied to handouts and Notes pages.

Key Terms

Multiple Choice

1. A file that incorporates a theme, a layout, and content that can be modified is known as a:

   (a) Hierarchy
   (b) Footer
   (c) Speaker note
   (d) Template

2. To create a presentation based on an installed template, click the:

   (a) File tab and then Open
   (b) Office Button and then New
   (c) Insert tab and then Add Template
   (d) Design tab and then New

3. What advantage, if any, is there to collapsing the outline so only the slide titles are visible?

   (a) More slides are displayed at one time, making it easier to rearrange the slides in the presentation.
   (b) Transition and animations can be added.
   (c) Graphical objects become visible.
   (d) All of the above.

4. Which of the following is true?

   (a) Slides cannot be added to a presentation after a template has been chosen.
   (b) The slide layout can be changed before the template has been chosen.
   (c) Placeholders downloaded with a template cannot be modified.
   (d) The slide layout can be changed after the template has been chosen.

5. How do you insert identifying information on every slide in a presentation?

   (a) Click the Design tab and click Events.
   (b) Click the Insert tab and click Headers and Footers.
   (c) Click the View tab and click Headers and Footers.
   (d) Click the Home tab and click Events.

6. Which of the following is true?

   (a) PowerPoint supplies many different templates, but each template has only one color scheme.
   (b) You cannot change the color scheme of a presentation.
   (c) PowerPoint supplies many different templates, and each template in turn has multiple color schemes.
   (d) You cannot change a template once it has been selected.

7. Which of the following is the fastest and most efficient method for reusing a slide layout you have customized in another presentation?

   (a) Open the slide with the customized layout, delete the content, and enter the new information.
   (b) Open the slide with the customized layout and cut and paste the placeholders to a new slide.
   (c) Save the custom slide layout and reuse it in the new presentation.
   (d) Drag the placeholders from one slide to the next.

8. You own a small business and decide to institute an Employee of the Month award program. Which of the following would be the fastest way to create the award certificate with a professional look?

   (a) Access Microsoft Office Online and download an Award certificate template.
   (b) Select a Design Theme, modify the placeholders, and then enter the award text information.
   (c) Open Microsoft Word, insert a table, enter the award text in the table, and then add clip art.
   (d) Enter the text in the title placeholder of a slide, change the font for each line, and drag several clip art images of awards onto the slide.

9. Which of the following moves a bullet point from the first level to the second level in an outline?

   (a) Shift+Tab
   (b) Tab
   (c) Decrease List Level
   (d) Ctrl+Tab

10. The Increase List Level and Decrease List Level commands are available from which tab?

    (a) Home
    (b) Insert
    (c) Design
    (d) Slide Show

11. Which of the following formats cannot be imported to use as an outline for a presentation?

    (a) .docx
    (b) .rtf
    (c) .txt
    (d) .tiff

12. You create a presentation for a local volunteer organization. When you arrive to present at its office, you find the room you are presenting in has many windows. Which of the following procedures should you follow?

    (a) Change the theme of the presentation to a theme with a dark background.

    (b) Change the background style to a dark background.

    (c) Close the blinds to darken the room.

    (d) Any of the above.

13. Which of the following statements is a true text design guideline?

    (a) Title text should be 36 pts or larger.

    (b) Use underlining to emphasize key points.

    (c) Create all titles in ALL CAPS.

    (d) Bold all bullet points.

14. Which of the following is not a field in the Header and Footer dialog box?

    (a) Date and time

    (b) Slide number

    (c) File name

    (d) Footer

15. To add existing content to a presentation, use which of the following features?

    (a) Duplicate Selected Slides

    (b) Slides from Outline

    (c) Reuse Slides

    (d) All of the above

1 Download and Modify a Template

Figure 2.43 displays an Employee of the Year Award for Olsen Cabinets. It was created from a template downloaded from Microsoft Office Online. A small business owner who runs a cabinet shop might use an award program to motivate employees and could create this award quickly by downloading the template and modifying it. Assume you are the owner of Olsen Cabinets and you want to present your employee, Michael Mulhern, with the Employee of the Year Award.

a. Click the **Office Button**, and then select **New**.
b. Click **Award certificates** in the Microsoft Office Online category.
c. Click the **Employee of the year award**, and then click **Download**.
d. Save the file as **chap2_pe1_award_solution**.
e. Drag to select the text *Company Name* and type **OLSEN CABINETS**.
f. Drag to select the text *EMPLOYEE NAME* and type **Michael Mulhern**.
g. Select *Michael Mulhern* and move your pointer slightly upward to activate the Mini toolbar with text options.
h. Click **Bold**, and then click **Italic**.
i. Drag to select the text *Presenter's Name and Title*, and then enter your name and your class.
j. Save the *chap2_pe1_award_solution* file and close it.

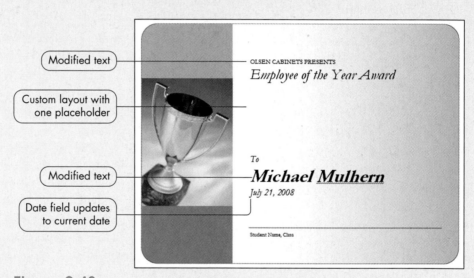

Figure 2.43 Download and Modify a Template

2 Create an Outline

The Wellness Education Center at your school promotes the overall wellness among students and employees. The center provides many services and needs to make the campus community aware of these services. You volunteer to create a presentation that can be shown to campus groups to inform them about the center and its mission. Figure 2.44 shows the outline of the presentation.

a. In a new presentation, click the **View tab**, and then click **Normal** in the Presentation Views group (if necessary).
b. Click the **Outline tab**.
c. Type the title of your presentation, **Wellness Education Center**, and then press **Enter**.
d. Save the file as **chap2_pe2_center_solution**.
e. Click the **Home tab** and click **Increase List Level** in the Paragraph group.
f. Enter the first line of the subtitle, **Dedicated to**.

...continued on Next Page

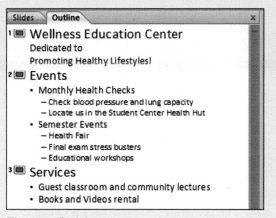

Figure 2.44 Create an Outline

g. Press **Shift+Enter** to move the point of insertion to the next line of the subtitle placeholder.

h. Type the second line of the subtitle, **Promoting Healthy Lifestyles!**

i. Press **Enter**, and then click **Decrease List Level** in the Paragraph group on the Home tab.

j. Type the title **Events**, and then press **Enter**.

k. Press **Tab**, and then type **Monthly Health Checks**.

l. Press **Enter**, and then press **Tab**.

m. Type **Check blood pressure and lung capacity**, and then press **Enter**.

n. Type **Locate us in the Student Center Health Hut**, and then press **Enter**.

o. Press **Shift+Tab**.

p. Continue entering the text of the outline, as shown in Figure 2.44.

q. Save the *chap2_pe2_center_solution* file and keep it onscreen if you plan to continue to the next exercise. Close the file and exit PowerPoint if you do not want to continue to the next exercise at this time.

3 Modify an Outline

The director at the Wellness Education Center reviews your outline. While she is pleased with its development thus far, she would like you to include more information about the Center Services, and she would like the services slide to be the second slide in the presentation. Figure 2.45 shows additional information in the outline.

a. Open the *chap2_pe2_center_solution* presentation if you closed it after the last exercise and save it as **chap2_pe3_center_solution**.

b. Click the **Outline tab**, click at the end of the word *lectures* in Slide 3, and add **including:**

c. Proofread the bullet point you created and note that the word *including* is on a line by itself. To avoid this hanging line, remove the word *Guest* from the bullet and capitalize the word *Classroom*.

d. Position the point of insertion at the end of the line, press **Enter**, and then press **Tab**.

e. Type the following bullet points:

- **Health and Fitness**

- **Alcohol Use and Misuse**

- **Substance/Drug Abuse**

f. Position the pointer over the bullet next to the text *Books and Videos rental* so that the pointer becomes a four-headed arrow, and then click to select the bullet.

g. Replace the existing text by typing **Lending library**.

h. Press **Enter**, and then press **Tab**.

...continued on Next Page

  i. Type the two bullet points for the *Lending library*, as shown in Figure 2.45.

  j. Drag to select all of the text in the outline.

  k. Right-click in the selected area, select **Collapse**, and then select **Collapse All**.

  l. Position the pointer over the slide icon for Slide 3, *Services*, and then drag *Services* above Slide 2.

  m. Click the **Office Button**, point at the arrow to the right of the Print button, and then select **Print Preview**.

  n. Click the **Print What arrow** in the Page Setup group, and select **Outline View**. Print the collapsed outline if directed to do so by your instructor.

  o. Close Print Preview and return to the presentation.

  p. Drag to select all of the slides in the outline, and then right-click the selected area.

  q. Click **Expand**, and then click **Expand All**.

  r. Save the *chap2_pe3_center_solution* file and keep it onscreen if you plan to continue to the next exercise. Close the file and exit PowerPoint if you do not want to continue to the next exercise at this time.

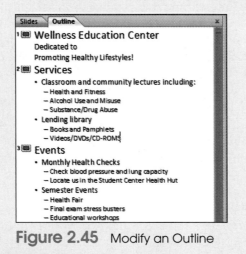

Figure 2.45 Modify an Outline

4 Add Existing Content

While reviewing the Wellness Center presentation, you realize that you do not have an introduction slide or a summary slide. You remember another slide show that has slides that would fit well in this presentation. To save time and maintain consistency, you reuse these slides. Figure 2.46 shows the outline after inserting slides into the presentation.

  a. Open the *chap2_pe3_center_solution* presentation if you closed it after the last exercise, then save it as **chap2_pe4_center_solution**.

  b. Click the **Outline tab**, if necessary, and then click at the end of the word *Lifestyles* in Slide 1.

  c. Click the **Home tab** and click **New Slide** in the Slides group.

  d. Click **Reuse Slides** at the bottom of the gallery.

  e. Click the **Browse button** that appears in the Reuse Slides task pane, click **Browse File**, and then navigate to the location of your student files.

  f. Click to select the file *chap2_pe4_mission*, and then click **Open**.

  g. Click the Mission Statement thumbnail to enter it in your presentation as Slide 2.

  h. Position your point of insertion at the end of your outline, and then click the thumbnail for the remaining slide in the presentation, the slide beginning *We strive. . . .*

  i. Close the Reuse Slides Task Pane.

  j. Save the *chap2_pe4_center_solution* file and keep it onscreen if you plan to continue to the next exercise. Close the file and exit PowerPoint if you do not want to continue to the next exercise at this time.

...continued on Next Page

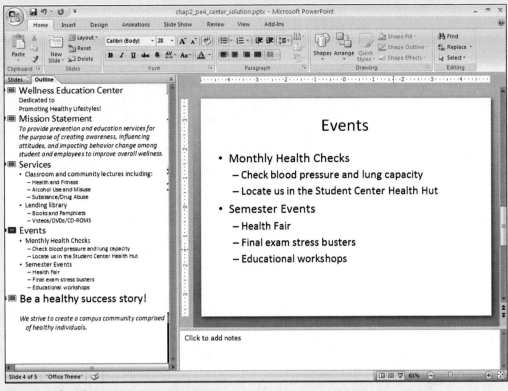

Figure 2.46 Add Existing Content

5 Apply and Modify a Theme

Both you and the director of the Wellness Education Center are satisfied with the content of the presentation, so now you concentrate on the design of the presentation. The director of the center specifies that she would like a calming blue background and a clean look. After you are satisfied with the design, you save it for future presentations you create for the center. Figure 2.47 shows the slide show after changing the theme and background color.

a. Start PowerPoint and open the *chap2_pe4_center_solution* presentation if you closed it after the last exercise, then save it as **chap2_pe5_center_solution**.

b. Click the **Design tab** and click the **More button** in the Themes group on the Design tab.

c. Click the **Trek theme**.

d. Click **Colors** in the Themes group on the Design tab.

e. Click the **Flow color scheme**.

f. Click **Font** in the Themes group on the Design tab.

g. Click the **Opulent font scheme**, which applies the Trebuchet MS font to the title and content placeholders.

h. Click **Background Styles** in the Background group on the Design tab.

i. Click **Style 11**.

j. Click the **More button** in the Themes group on the Design tab.

k. Click **Save Current Theme**.

l. Enter **wellness_theme** in the *File name* box, and then click **Save**.

m. Save the *chap2_pe5_center_solution* file and keep it onscreen if you plan to continue to the next exercise. Close the file and exit PowerPoint if you do not want to continue to the next exercise at this time.

...continued on Next Page

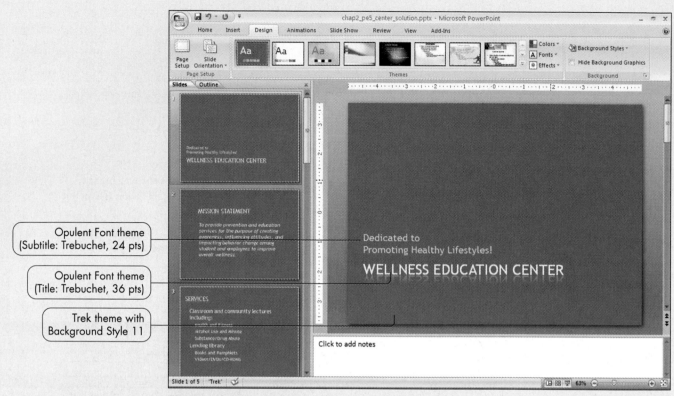

Figure 2.47 Apply and Modify a Theme

6 Create a Header and a Footer

The director of the Wellness Education Center wants to show the presentation to a colleague at a conference she is attending. Because the director does not want to bring a laptop computer on the plane, you prepare a printout using a handout format. You add a header and footer to the presentation with identifying information before printing. Figure 2.48 shows one slide with the header, and Figure 2.49 shows the notes and handouts printout.

a. Open the *chap2_pe5_center_solution* presentation if you closed it after the last exercise, then save it as **chap2_pe6_center_solution**.

b. Click the **Insert tab**, and then click **Header & Footer** in the Text group on the Insert tab.

c. Click the **Slide number check box** to insert a slide number on each slide in the presentation.

d. Click the **Footer check box** and type **Wellness Education Center**.

e. Click the **Don't show on title slide check box**, if necessary. The footer is not necessary on the title slide.

f. Click **Apply to All**. Note that this Microsoft theme moves the footer text to the top of the slide.

g. Click the **Insert tab** and click **Header & Footer** in the Text group.

h. Click the **Notes and Handouts tab**.

i. Click the **Date and time check box**.

j. Click **Update Automatically**, and then click the **drop-down arrow**.

k. Click the sixth date format in the list, which.

l. Click the **Header check box** and then enter your name (your name represents the director's name) in the text box.

m. Click the **Footer check box** and type **Wellness Education Center**.

n. Click **Apply to All**. Note that with this theme, Microsoft has positioned the slide Footer at the top of the slide and not at the bottom as is common. Note also that the

...continued on Next Page

theme has a very slight change in color between the background and the Footer text causing the Footer to be almost hidden.

o. Click the **Office Button**, point at the triangle next to Print, and then select **Print Preview**.

p. Change the **Print What** option to **Handouts** (6 slides per page).

q. Click **Print** if directed to do so by your instructor or click **Close Print Preview**.

r. Save the *chap2_pe6_center_solution* file and close the file.

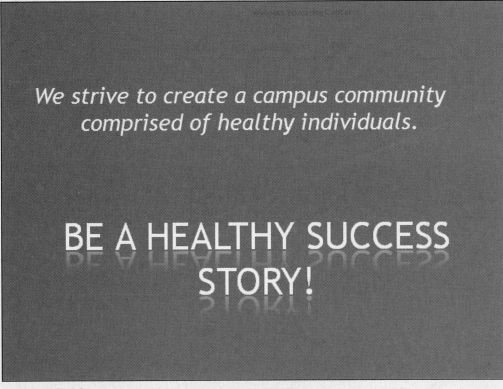

Figure 2.48 Wellness Center Slide with Header & Footer

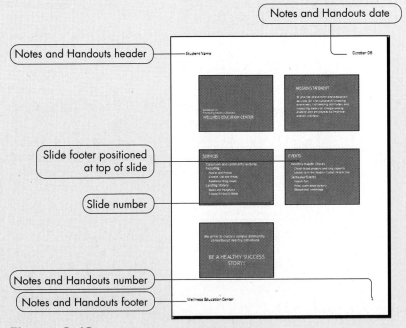

Figure 2.49 Wellness Center Handout

Mid-Level Exercises

1 USDA Food Pyramid

You have been asked to help in a local elementary school. The teacher would like you to teach the children about nutrition and healthy eating. You decide to create a presentation about the U.S. Department of Agriculture (USDA)–recommended food pyramid. (Visit http://www.mypyramid.gov.) You locate a Microsoft Office Online template based on the food pyramid that will help you organize the presentation. Figure 2.50 displays the downloaded template, and Figure 2.51 displays the conclusion slide of your presentation.

a. Download the **Food pyramid presentation**, which is available from Microsoft Office Online. It can be found in the Presentations category, Healthcare subcategory. Immediately save it as **chap2_mid1_pyramid_solution**.

b. Move to **Slide 2** and copy the information on the slide, and then paste it into the notes area. After reading the content tips on the template slides, you think they would make excellent speaker notes for you to refer to when presenting. As you create each new slide in the rest of the exercise, copy the information on the slide and paste it to the notes as you did in this step.

c. Type the following bullet points. The completed slide is displayed in Figure 2.50.

   • **Choosing the right foods helps you feel better**

   • **Eating a good diet keeps you healthier**

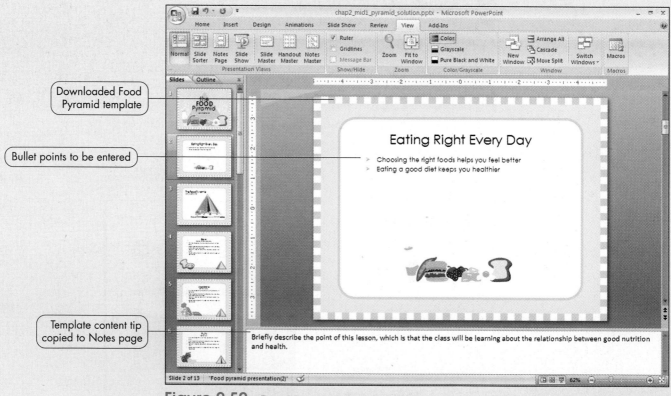

Figure 2.50 Food Pyramid Content Slide

...continued on Next Page

d. Move to **Slide 4** and type the following bullet points.

- **Great grains!**
- **Whole-wheat flour**
- **Cracked wheat**
- **Oatmeal**
- **Whole cornmeal**
- **Brown rice**

e. Make changes to the slides as shown below.

Slide	Level 1 Bullet	Level 2 Bullets
5	Very Cool Veggies!	Broccoli
		Spinach
		Carrots
		Cauliflower
		Mushrooms
		Green beans
6	Fresh Fruit!	Apples
		Bananas
		Grapes
		Peaches
		Oranges
7	Only a Little Oil!	Sunflower oil
		Margarine
		Butter
		Mayonnaise
8	Magnificent Milk!	Milk
		Cheese
		Yogurt
		Pudding
9	Mighty Meats and Beans!	Chicken
		Turkey
		Beef
		Pork
		Fish
		Beans and nuts

10	• Provide bonus calories to give you energy
	• Use for:
	  • Eating more of the food on the list
	  • Eating higher calorie food
	• Eat more than advised and you will gain weight.	

12	Use the MyPyramid Worksheet provided by the USDA.	
13	Follow the Food Pyramid Steps for a healthier you!	

...continued on Next Page

f. Delete **Slide 11**.

g. Change the layout for **Slide 12**, the conclusion, to a Title Slide format.

h. Delete the graphic box with the white background that was left over when you changed the layout.

i. Check the spelling of your presentation and ignore any references to MyPyramid, the USDA worksheet name.

j. Create a handout header with your name and a handout footer with your instructor's name and your class time. Print as required by your instructor.

k. Save the *chap2_mid1_pyramid_solution* file and close the file.

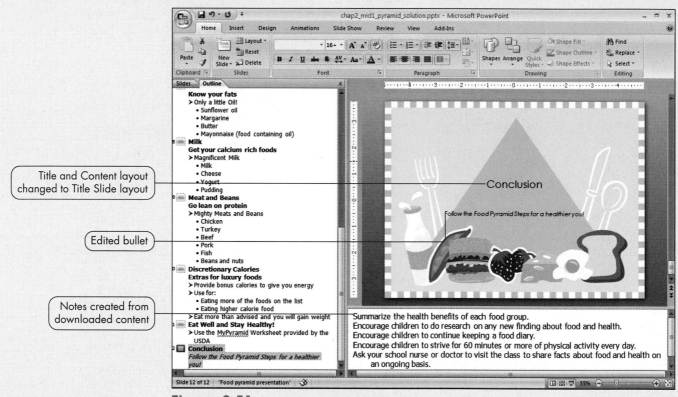

Figure 2.51 Food Pyramid Conclusion

2 Go-Digital

The local senior citizen's center has asked you to speak on photography. The center has many interested seniors—but the center has indicated to you that the seniors are unsure about whether they want information on traditional photography or digital photography. You feel that digital photography would be a good option for amateur photographers, so you decide to slant the presentation in favor of digital photography. Figure 2.52 shows the completed presentation.

a. Save a blank presentation as **chap2_mid2_digital_solution**.

b. Type the title **Go Digital, Get Creative!** so that it is on two lines in the title placeholder. Enter your name in the subtitle placeholder.

...continued on Next Page

c. Use the Outline view to create these slides.

- **Why Go Digital?**
  - **Inexpensive**
  - **Improved pictures**
  - **Instant feedback**
  - **Image sharing**
- **Inexpensive**
  - **No film cost**
  - **Free experimentation**
  - **Cameras in all price ranges**
- **Improved Pictures**
  - **Image editing with software**
    - **Remove red eye**
    - **Improve exposure**
    - **Crop the pictures**
  - **Free experimentation**
    - **Take extra pictures for practice**
    - **Try new camera settings**
- **Instant Feedback**
  - **Viewing screen**
- **Image Sharing**
  - **Traditional**
  - **Web pages/Online photo albums**
  - **E-mail**

d. Review the presentation in Outline view and note that *Free experimentation* appears in two locations, that the Instant feedback slide does not have enough information to be a slide on its own, and that the presentation does not contain a conclusion slide.

e. Move the two bullets under *Free experimentation* on **Slide 4** to the correct location on **Slide 3,** and then delete the *Free experimentation* bullet in **Slide 4**.

f. Move the information in **Slide 5** so that it becomes the first bullet point in Slide 4.

g. Collapse the outline, move the Improved Pictures slide to the **Slide 4** position, and then Expand the outline.

h. Spell-check your presentation.

i. Save the *chap2_mid2_digital_solution* presentation and close the file.

j. Download the **Seasons in sage** design template, which is located on Microsoft Office Online in the Design slides category, Nature Subcategory.

k. Display the Add Slide gallery and click **Slides from Outline**.

l. Browse to where you save your files, change *Files of type* to **All Files**, and then insert your *chap2_mid2_digital_solution* presentation.

m. Drag **Slide 1** so that it becomes the last slide of the presentation, and then type **Go Digital:** in the title placeholder, and **Unleash Your Creativity!** in the subtitle placeholder.

n. Create a handout header with your name, and a handout footer with your instructor's name and your class. Print as required by your instructor.

o. Save the **chap2_mid2_digital_solution** presentation and click **Yes** when asked if you wish to replace the original file. Close the file.

...continued on Next Page

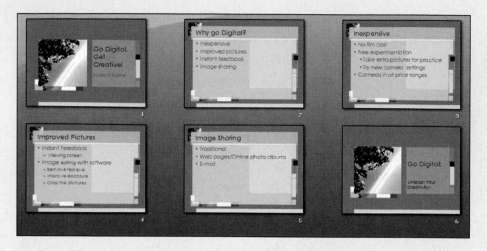

Figure 2.52 Go Digital Presentation with Seasons in Sage Template

3 The Impressionists

The paintings of the Impressionists are some of the most loved paintings in the world. Their paintings may be viewed by going to the Web page of the WebMuseum, Paris (www.ibiblio.org/wm), navigating to the Famous Artworks collections page, and then navigating to the Impressionism page. The museum is maintained by Nicolas Pioch and is not part of any official or supported project. He maintains the site for your pleasure and his. In a continuing project throughout this text, you create an album celebrating the Impressionists and their works. Figure 2.53 shows the completed slide show in the Slide Sorter view.

a. Save a blank presentation as **chap2_mid 3_impressionists_solution**.

b. Type the title **Impressionism**, and then enter your name in the subtitle place holder. Also include the following text in the subtitle placeholder: **All images may be viewed at the WebMuseum**. (You will insert the hyperlink for the WebMuseum in a later project.)

c. Use the Outline view to create these slides.

- **Impressionist Paintings**
  - **Characterized by small brush strokes**
  - **Reproduced the artist's visual impression**
  - **Studied**
    - **Light**
    - **Atmosphere**
    - **Reflections**
    - **Color**
- **Impressionist Artists**
  - **Claude Monet**
  - **Pierre-Auguste Renoir**
  - **Berthe Morisot**
  - **Edgar Degas**

d. Apply the **Flow theme**.

e. Apply the **Metro color theme**.

...continued on Next Page

f. Insert the **Oriel font theme**.

g. Insert the *chap2_mid3_artists* Word outline after the last slide in your presentation.

h. Rearrange the bullets in **Slide 3** so the artists are listed alphabetically by last name.

i. Collapse the outline and move **Slides 4–7** so they are listed alphabetically by last name, and then expand the outline.

j. Create a conclusion slide using the Content with Caption layout.

k. Modify the conclusion slide layout by deleting the text placeholder and moving the title placeholder so that its bottom border is even with the bottom border of the large content placeholder.

l. Leave the audience with one last thought about Impressionism by entering the following text in the title placeholder on the conclusion slide: **Work at the same time on sky, water, branches, ground, keeping everything going on an equal basis . . . Don't be afraid of putting on colour . . . Paint generously and unhesitatingly, for it is best not to lose the first impression. Camille Pissarro.**

m. Italicize the Pissarro name.

n. Spell-check your presentation.

o. Create a handout header with your name and a handout footer with your instructor's name and your class. Print as required by your instructor.

p. Save the *chap2_mid 3_impressionists_solution* presentation and close the file.

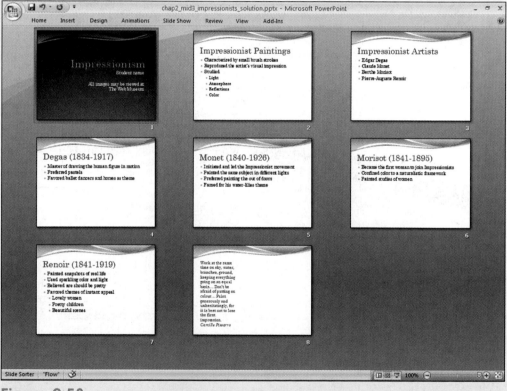

Figure 2.53 Impressionist Presentation in Slide Sorter View

4 Audience Analysis

Your community is experiencing a strong economic growth pattern, and part of this growth is because new business is encouraged and supported. Part of the support structure includes a city-sponsored Small Business Development Center (SBDC). One way the SBDC helps encourage small business owners and future business owners is to provide training on a wide variety of

...continued on Next Page

topics such as developing business plans, refining strategies, and overcoming challenges. A small business owner has requested the next training session cover giving presentations.

The SBDC maintains a list of local speakers, and as a humorous, popular speaker you are invited to address this group. You question the person issuing the invitation about the audience and find out you will be presenting to a small casual group of 8 to 10 men and women over lunch in a very informal room with no windows. You may bring your notebook computer and connect it to the center's projector. When you ask what the audience wants to get from your presentation, the SBDC representative tells you that the attendees want to know how to relax as they present. He adds that since it is a break in the middle of a busy day for them, they will probably be laughing and joking a lot. You decide to begin your presentation by addressing what you believe is the key to being a successful speaker—understanding the audience, but to do it in a humorous way. You want to show them that if a speaker knows his or her material well and analyzes the audience well, the speaker can relax while presenting and still be able to inject personality into the presentation. You also decide to create speaker notes to distribute to the group so that they can see how jotting down ideas of what to say in speaker notes can help them plan what to say to fill in around the bullet points. Figure 2.54 shows the completed slide show in Slide Sorter view.

a. Open *chap2_mid4_audience* and save it as **chap2_mid4_audience_solution**.

b. Read the Note at the bottom of Slide 1 and notice that this is a good location to keep track of when and where a presentation will be given. Move to **Slide 2** and switch to **Outline View**.

c. Click the **Home tab**, click **New Slide**, and then click **Reuse Slides**.

d. Use **Browse** in the Reuse Slides pane and open *chap2_mid4_analysis*.

e. Insert the second slide of the *chap2_mid4_analysis* into the current slideshow, and then close the Reuse Slides task pane.

f. Click the **Home tab**, click **Layout**, and then click **Comparison**.

g. Click the **Home tab**, **New Slide**, and then click **Slides from Outline**.

h. Insert the *chap2_mid4_outline* file.

i. Change the **Layout** of Slide 4 to **Title and Content**.

j. Change the title font on the slides you imported to **Comic Sans Serif** and the bullets to **Calibri**.

k. Change the font color for the titles and bullets you imported to black.

l. Change **Background Styles** to **Style 5**.

m. Create a handout header with your name and a handout footer with your instructor's name and your class. Print as required by your instructor.

n. Save the *chap2_mid 4_audience_solution* presentation and close the file.

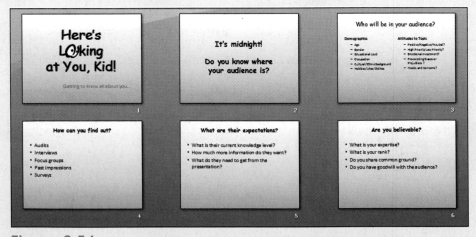

Figure 2.54 Audience Analysis Presentation in Slide Sorter View

Capstone Exercise

Your neighbors in your small southwestern subdivision are concerned about drought, fire danger, and water conservation. You volunteer to gather information about possible solutions and share the information with them at the next neighborhood association meeting. You decide a PowerPoint presentation would be an excellent way to inform them of their options. In this capstone exercise, you concentrate on developing the content. In later chapter capstone exercises, you will enhance the project with illustrations, images, charts, and hyperlinks.

Design Template

You download a Microsoft Office Online template to create the basic design and structure for your presentation, name the presentation, and create the title slide.

a. Download the **Sun spots** design template from Microsoft Office Online, Design slides category, Abstract subcategory.

b. Save the presentation with the file name **chap2_cap_waterwise_solution**.

c. Type **Conserve** as the title on the title slide. Reduce the font size of the title until it fits on one line.

d. Type the subtitle **Waterwise Landscaping**.

Outline and Modifications

Based on the storyboard you created after researching water conservation on the Internet, you create the outline for your presentation. As you create the outline, you also modify the outline structure.

a. Click the **Outline tab**.

b. Type **Waterwise Options** as the title for Slide 2.

c. Enter each of the following as Level 1 bullets for Slide 2: **Zeroscaping, Xeriscaping**.

d. Type **Purpose of Landscaping** as the title for Slide 3.

e. Type each of the following as Level 1 bullets for Slide 3: **Beauty, Utility, Conservation**.

f. Modify the outline structure by reversing Slides 2 and 3.

Imported Outline

You originally started your task intending to hold two information sessions for your neighbors. You began by creating an outline on zeroscaping in Microsoft Word. You determined that using a PowerPoint slide show would let you show images, so you create a slide show on xeriscaping. After going to this work, however, you decide that it is better to make the comparison in one presentation so that

homeowners are more easily able to see the overall picture. You do not want to lose the work you have already done, so you import the zeroscaping outline and reuse the xeriscaping slides.

a. Position the point of insertion at the end of the outline and add a new slide.

b. Use the **Slides from Outline option** to insert the *chap2_cap_zeroscaping* outline.

c. Change the layout of Slide 4 from Title slide to Picture with Caption so that you may insert a picture illustrating zeroscaping later.

d. Position the point of insertion at the end of the outline.

e. Use the appropriate option to reuse slides from *chap2_cap_xeriscaping*.

f. Insert all the slides from *chap2_cap_xeriscaping*.

Design

When you preview the slide show, you note that a lack of contrast makes the text difficult to read. You decide to change the color theme and font scheme to increase the visibility of the text. You realize that you may want to use this changed theme in later presentations, so you save the theme.

a. Change the color theme to **Solstice**.

b. Change the font theme to **Trek**.

TROUBLESHOOTING: If the Picture and Caption layouts in Slides 4 and 8 do not accept the new font change because they were imported, change the caption font to Franklin Gothic Medium, 36 pts.

c. Click the **More button** in the Themes group on the Design tab.

d. Save the current theme as *heat_theme*.

e. Spell-check the presentation.

f. Apply the **Fade Through Black animation scheme** to all slides.

g. Create a handout header with your name and a handout footer with your instructor's name and your class. Print as required by your instructor.

h. Save the *chap2_cap_waterwise_solution* presentation and close the file. Exit PowerPoint if you do not want to continue to the mini cases at this time.

Mini Cases

Use the rubric following the case as a guide to evaluate your work, but keep in mind that your instructor may impose additional grading criteria or use a different standard to judge your work.

Identity Theft

GENERAL CASE

The partially completed *chap2_mc1_identity* presentation is intended to aid you in recognizing the global value of the outline view and how it can be used to modify the structure of a presentation. A combination of slides containing only titles and slides containing content are randomly entered as if they were created from brainstorming. Organize the presentation so there is content under each topic and that the content matches the topic in the slide title. Create an appropriate conclusion. You may add additional slides, if desired. Good resources for your presentation include the Federal Trade Commission Web site (www.consumer.gov/idtheft) and the Social Security Online Electronic Fact Sheet (www.ssa.gov/pubs/idtheft).

Be sure to spell-check and carefully proofread the content of the presentation. Save the presentation as **chap2_mc1_identity_solution**. Locate a template to use for the design and reuse the *chap2_mc1_identity_solution* presentation slides to create a new presentation. Apply a font scheme, color scheme, and background style as desired. You also may modify layouts. Add appropriate clip art to at least two slides. Remember the design guidelines as you insert the clip art. Match the colors of the clips to your background and try to locate clips that are similar—do not apply a cartoon-like clip on one slide and a professional clip on another. Apply a transition to all slides and add a custom animation to the clip art you added. Create a handout header with your name and a handout footer with the file name, your instructor's name, and your class. Print as directed by your instructor. Save the file as **chap2_mc1_identity_solution** and click Yes when asked if you want to save over the original file.

Performance Elements	Exceeds Expectations	Meets Expectations	Below Expectations
Organization	Presentation is easy to follow because information is presented in a logical, interesting sequence.	Presentation is generally easy to follow.	Presentation cannot be understood because there is no sequence of information.
Visual aspects	Presentation background, themes, clip art, and animation are appealing and enhance the understanding of presentation purpose and content.	Clip art is related to topic.	The background, theme, or animation is distracting to the topic.
	There is a consistent visual theme.	Animation is not distracting.	Clip art does not enhance understanding of the content or is unrelated.
Layout	The layout is visually pleasing and contributes to the overall message with appropriate use of headings, subheadings, bullet points, clip art, and white space.	The layout shows some structure, but placement of some headings, subheadings, bullet points, clip art, and/or white space can be improved.	The layout is cluttered and confusing. Placement of headings, subheadings, bullet points, clip art, and/or white spaces detracts from readability.
Mechanics	Presentation has no errors in spelling, grammar, word usage, or punctuation.	Presentation has no more than one error in spelling, grammar, word usage, or punctuation.	Presentation readability is impaired due to repeated errors in spelling, grammar, word usage, or punctuation.
	Bullet points are parallel.	Bullet points are inconsistent in one slide.	Most bullet points are not parallel.

Accuracy Counts

You have a bright, creative, and energetic personality and you are using these talents in college as a senior majoring in Digital Film within the Multimedia Communication Technology Department. You hope to become a producer for a major film company, following the footsteps of your grandfather. This term, you are taking MCT 4000: Administration of Studio Operations. The final project requires every student to create his or her own feature film company and present an overview of the company to the class. The presentation is to be in the form of an employee orientation: It should include the company purpose, the company's history, past and present projects, and a final slide giving the resources you used to create your presentation. Your instructor asks you to write notes for each slide.

The assignment was given at the beginning of the semester with the understanding that it would be developed as the topics were presented. It is now the end of the semester, and you, a creative procrastinator by nature, are in a real bind. You have 24 hours to complete the entire presentation before presenting it to the class. You remember Microsoft Office Online Templates and wonder if it has a template you can use. Using **film** as your keyword, search Microsoft Office Online for templates and then download a template to use in creating your presentation. You will, however, have to research what a feature film company does and add your own content to comply with the case requirements. Add clip art, transitions, and animations as desired. Create a handout header with your name and a handout footer with your instructor's name and your class time. Print as directed by your instructor. Save the presentation as **chap2_mc2_film_solution**.

Performance Elements	Exceeds Expectations	Meets Expectations	Below Expectations
Organization	Presentation indicates accurate research and significant facts. Evidence exists that information has been evaluated and synthesized showing an understanding of the topic.	Presentation indicates some research has taken place and that information was included in the content.	Presentation demonstrates a lack of research or understanding of the topic. Content is misinterpreted or incorrect.
Visual aspects	Presentation background, themes, clip art, and animation are appealing and enhance the understanding of presentation purpose and content.	Clip art is related to the topic.	The background or theme is distracting to the topic.
	There is a consistent visual theme.	Animation is not distracting.	Clip art does not enhance understanding of the content or is unrelated.
Layout	The layout is visually pleasing and contributes to the overall message with appropriate use of headings, subheadings, bullet points, clip art, and white space.	The layout shows some structure, but placement of some headings, subheadings, bullet points, clip art, and/ or white space can be improved.	The layout is cluttered and confusing. Placement of headings, subheadings, bullet points, clip art, and/or white spaces detracts from readability.
Mechanics	Presentation has no errors in spelling, grammar, word usage, or punctuation.	Presentation has no more than one error in spelling, grammar, word usage, or punctuation.	Presentation readability is impaired due to repeated errors in spelling, grammar, word usage, or punctuation.
	Bullet points are parallel.	Bullet points are inconsistent in one slide.	Most bullet points are not parallel.

My State

Your little sister prepared a report on your state for a youth organization merit badge on research, and she is going to present the information to her leader and team members. She spent a lot of time researching the state and created a presentation with the information she wants included. Unfortunately, she is frustrated because the presentation she worked so hard on looks "ugly" to her. She asks you to help her create a presentation that "won't embarrass" her. You sit down with her and show her how to download the presentation for Report on State template from the Microsoft Office Online site, Presentations Category, Academic Subcategory. Save the new presentation as **chap2_mc3_florida_solution**. You reuse her slides saved as *chap2_mc3_florida* to bring them into the new template. From there, you cut and paste the images she gathered into the correct placeholders and move bullet points to the correct slide. Resize placeholders as needed. As you edit the presentation with her, you tell your sister that mixing clip art and pictures is contributing to the cluttered look and ask her what she prefers. She cannot decide, so you use your preference, but be consistent. The template does not have slides for all her information, so you create new slides with appropriate layouts when needed. You remind her that although federal government organizations allow use of their images in an educational setting, your sister should give proper credit if she is going to use their data. Also give credit to the State of Florida's Web site for the information obtained from MyFlorida.com (**http://dhr.dos.state.fl.us/facts/symbols**). Give credit to the U.S. Census Bureau (**www.census.gov**) for the Quick Facts.

You delete any slide for which your sister does not have information. Be sure to spell-check and carefully proofread the content of the presentation as your sister freely admits she "wasn't worried about that stuff." You pick an animation to apply to all slides with her help and resist her pleas to do "something different" on every slide. You explain to her that this is not an MTV music video; rather, it is an informational presentation, and multiple animations are distracting. Create a handout header with your name and a handout footer with your instructor's name and your class time. Print as directed by your instructor.

Performance Elements	Exceeds Expectations	Meets Expectations	Below Expectations.
Organization	Presentation is easy to follow because information is presented in a logical, interesting sequence.	Presentation is generally easy to follow.	Presentation cannot be understood because there is no sequence of information.
Visual aspects	Presentation background, themes, clip art, and animation are appealing and enhance the understanding of presentation purpose and content.	Clip art is related to the topic.	The background or theme is distracting to the topic.
	There is a consistent visual theme.	Animation is not distracting.	Clip art does not enhance understanding of the content or is unrelated.
Layout	The layout is visually pleasing and contributes to the overall message with appropriate use of headings, subheadings, bullet points, clip art, and white space.	The layout shows some structure, but placement of some headings, subheadings, bullet points, clip art, and/or white space can be improved.	The layout is cluttered and confusing. Placement of headings, subheadings, bullet points, clip art, and/or white spaces detracts from readability.
Mechanics	Presentation has no errors in spelling, grammar, word usage, or punctuation.	Presentation has no more than one error in spelling, grammar, word usage, or punctuation.	Presentation readability is impaired due to repeated errors in spelling, grammar, word usage, or punctuation.
	Bullet points are parallel.	Bullet points are inconsistent in one slide.	Most bullet points are not parallel.

Presentation Design
Enhancing with Illustrations

bjectives

After you read this chapter, you will be able to:

1. Create shapes **(page 207)**.

2. Apply Quick Styles and customize shapes **(page 212)**.

3. Create SmartArt **(page 228)**.

4. Modify SmartArt diagrams **(page 231)**.

5. Create WordArt **(page 237)**.

6. Modify WordArt **(page 237)**.

7. Modify objects **(page 244)**.

8. Arrange objects **(page 251)**.

Hands-On Exercises

Exercises	Skills Covered
1. **WORKING WITH SHAPES (page 220)** **Open**: chap3_ho1_shapes.pptx **Save as**: chap3_ho1_shapes_solution.pptx	• Create Basic Shapes • Draw and Format Connector Lines • Modify a Freeform Shape • Apply a Quick Style and Customize Shapes • Change Shape Outlines • Change Outline, Dash, and Arrow Styles • Use Shape Effects
2. **WORKING WITH SMARTART AND WORDART (page 239)** **Open**: chap3_ho2_water.pptx **Save as**: chap3_ho2_water_solution.pptx	• Insert SmartArt • Modify a SmartArt Diagram • Change SmartArt Layout • Create WordArt • Modify WordArt
3. **MODIFYING AND ARRANGING CLIP ART (page 256)** **Open**: chap3_ho2_water_solution.pptx (from Exercise 1) **Save as**: chap3_ho3_cycle_solution.pptx (additional modifications)	• Size and Position Clip Art • Flip Clip Art • Ungroup, Modify, and Regroup Clip Art • Recolor a Picture • Reorder Shapes • Align and Distribute Clip Art

CASE STUDY

The Kelso Performing Arts Center

An appreciation for the arts is essential to the quality of life in any society, but the recent budget shortfall at every level of government has put cultural programs in jeopardy throughout the country. The city of Kelso is no exception, as its residents have tried unsuccessfully for several years to persuade the city council to build a Performing Arts Center. This year, residents have a renewed sense of optimism because the political climate has changed and there is a strong focus on revitalizing the downtown area. In addition, the Kelso family, for whom the city is named, has agreed to donate a prime five-acre site if the council will approve a $30-million bond issue to fund construction.

Kenneth Kelso chairs the Executive Committee of the Kelso Performing Arts Center, a volunteer community board. The Executive Committee proposes organizing the Art Center with committees providing for the following functions: Finance Committee (Investments, Financial Oversite), Program Committee (Grantmaking, Distribution), and Marketing (Public Relations, Fundraising).

You are civic minded and a patron of the arts. Kenneth Kelso is also a close personal friend, and he has asked you to spearhead the effort to secure the funding. You and two colleagues from the Executive Committee are to go before the council on Monday evening to present your case. The Kelso family has worked for several hours to prepare the contents of the presentation, but it is not yet finished. Ken is counting on you to add the finishing touches. He is seeking an eye-catching, attention-grabbing, interest-keeping presentation!

Your Assignment

- Read the chapter, paying special attention to how to create SmartArt, how to change a SmartArt Layout, how to create WordArt, and how to recolor a picture.
- Open the partially completed *chap3_case_arts* presentation and save the presentation as **chap3_case_arts_solution**.
- On Slide 1, convert the title to WordArt by applying a WordArt transformation such as a glow to the text, and then recolor the picture so it matches the red tones of the curtains. Recolor the picture on the last slide so that it matches the picture in the title slide.
- Convert the bullet content in Slide 4 to a horizontal process SmartArt and apply a Quick Style that enhances the process. Change the layout of the Smart Art in Slide 5 to a pyramid layout and apply a Quick Style utilizing the colors of the presentation.
- Use a hierarchy SmartArt to create an organization chart on Slide 6. Refer to the introduction to the case study to determine the content of the chart. The Executive Committee should have the superior level, or top level, as it oversees the committees. The other committees are subordinate to the Executive Committee and as such should occupy the second level. List the functions of the committees on the third level. Apply a Quick Style.
- Create a Notes and Handouts Header and Footer with your name in the header, and your instructor's name and your class in the footer.
- Print handouts, 4 per page, grayscale, framed.

Shapes

Thus far, you have focused on presentations that consisted largely of text. In addition to entering text in presentations, you can use a variety of visual elements to add impact to a presentation. The visual effects in PowerPoint 2007 have been improved over previous versions. New effects such as 3-D, shadow, glow, warp, bevel, and others are accessible through style galleries, making it easy for you to create professional-looking graphics.

. . . you can use a variety of visual elements to add impact to a presentation . . . 3-D, shadow, glow, warp, bevel . . .

A **shape** is a geometric or nongeometric object, such as a rectangle or an arrow.

You can include a **shape**, a geometric or nongeometric object, as a visual element in your presentation, to create an illustration, or to highlight information. For example, after a list of items you could include a quote related to the items and create the quote inside a shape to call attention to it. Shapes also can be used as a design element. You can even combine shapes to create your own complex images or clip art. Figure 3.1 shows three PowerPoint themes utilizing shapes in each of these ways. The Equity theme uses a rectangle shape to draw attention to the information in the title placeholder. The Oriel theme utilizes circles and lines to create an interesting design. The Sunspots theme combines shapes to create a sunburst effect.

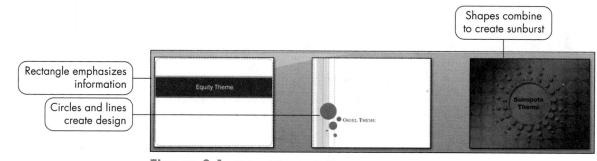

Figure 3.1 Using Shapes in Themes

In this section, you create and modify various shapes and lines. You also learn how to customize shapes and apply special effects to objects. Finally, you learn how to apply and change outline effects.

Creating Shapes

PowerPoint provides tools for creating shapes. You can insert everything from standard geometric shapes like a circle or a square to hearts and stars, equation shapes, and even banners. These are just a few of the multitude of shapes provided. After you create a shape, you can modify it and apply fills and special effects for truly spectacular graphics. To access the Shape Gallery displaying the complete list of shape tools, click the Home tab, and then click Shapes in the Drawing group (see Figure 3.2). The Shape Gallery (see Figure 3.3) displays shapes you have recently used and all shapes available sorted into categories to make the shape you desire easy to find.

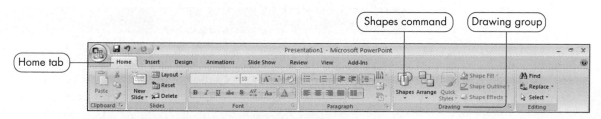

Figure 3.2 Accessing the Shape Gallery

Recently Used Shapes for quick reuse

Click a shape to select it

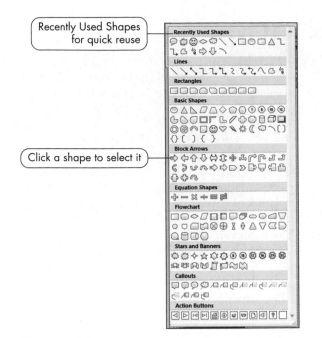

Figure 3.3 The Shape Gallery

TIP   Another Location for Shapes

Shapes are also available in the Illustrations group on the Insert tab so that if the Insert tab is active, you do not have to click the Home tab to get to Shapes in the Drawing group.

The basic procedure for creating a shape is to click the shape you desire in the Shape gallery, and then click in the slide window where you wish to place the shape. The mouse pointer changes to a cross-hair to help you determine the starting and ending points of your shape. Drag the cross-hair until the shape is approximately the size you want and release. You can always resize the shape by dragging the sizing handles that surround the shape after it is created. By default, this feature deactivates after you draw one shape. If you want to add several shapes of the same type on your slide, right-click the shape you want, and then select Lock Drawing Mode. Next, click anywhere on the slide, and then drag to create the first shape. After you create the first shape, click and drag repeatedly to create additional shapes. To release the Lock Drawing Mode, press Esc. If you do not activate the Lock Drawing Mode before creating the first shape, you have to reselect the shape each time you want to use it—a very inefficient process.

TIP   Constrain a Shape

A rectangle can be constrained to form a perfect square, and an oval or ellipse can be constrained to form a perfect circle. To constrain these shapes, press and hold Shift as you drag to create the shape.

Figure 3.4 shows a series of squares created with the Lock Drawing Mode activated, a cloud created using the Cloud shape located in the Basic Shapes category, an explosion created using the Explosion 2 shape located in the Stars and Banners category, and finally a *callout* (a shape that includes a line with a text box that can be used to add notes, often used in cartooning) created using the Oval Callout located in the Callouts category. Notice that the callout shape is selected. The sizing handles display around the callout, and a yellow diamond shows at the bottom on the end-point. This yellow diamond is an *adjustment handle* that you can drag to "reshape the shape" or change the shape. For example, if you select the Smiley Face shape and drag to create it, the shape includes a "smile" (upward curved line) with an adjustment handle attached. Drag the adjustment handle, and the smile becomes a frown (downward curved line). Your Smiley Face becomes a "Frowny Face"! Some shapes have this adjustment handle and some do not.

A *callout* is a shape that includes a line with a text box that you can use to add notes.

An *adjustment handle* is a control in the shape of a yellow diamond that enables you to modify a shape.

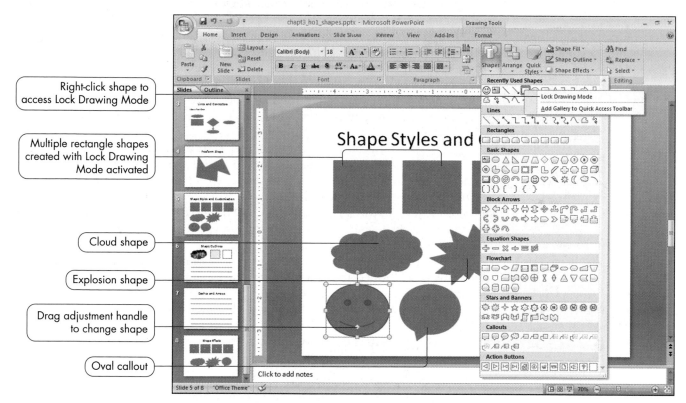

Figure 3.4 Basic Shapes

Draw Lines and Connectors

Lines, as shapes, can be used to point to information, connect shapes on a slide, or divide the slide into sections. Lines also are often used in slide design. Draw a straight line by selecting the line shape, clicking in the slide to begin the line, and then dragging to create the line. Double-click to end the line. To create a curved line, select the Curve line, click the slide where you want to start the curve, and then continue to click and move the mouse to shape the curve the way you want. As you click, you set a point for the curve to bend around. To end the curve, double-click. To draw a shape that looks like it was drawn with a pen or create smooth curves, select the Scribble shape.

TIP Create a Closed Shape

If you click near the line's starting point, the points join and create a closed shape. The advantage of joining the ends of the line and creating a closed shape is that you can include a fill.

A **connector** is a line that is attached to and moves with shapes.

In addition to drawing simple lines for tasks like creating dividing lines and waves, at times, you may need **connectors**, or lines that attach to the shapes you create. That way, when the shapes are rearranged, the connector line moves with it. Three types of connectors are provided: straight, elbow (to create angled lines), and curved.

The first step in working with connectors is to create the shapes you want to connect with lines. After you create the shapes, select the connector line from the Shape Gallery that you wish to use. After you select the connector, red circular dots appear around the shapes if you move your pointer over them. These are the spots where you can attach the connector. You click one of the red dots and drag the line until it connects with the red circle on the next shape. The two shapes are now connected. If you move one of the shapes, the connecting line moves with it. Sometimes when you rearrange the shapes, the connectors may cross shapes and be confusing. If that happens, you can use the yellow adjustment handle to reshape the line. Select the connector line and drag the handle to obtain a clearer path.

A **flowchart** is an illustration showing the sequence of a project or plan.

A **flowchart** is an illustration that shows a sequence to be followed or a plan with steps. For example, you could use a flowchart to illustrate the sequence to be followed in taking a multiple-choice test (1. Read question and possible answers. 2. If you know the answer immediately, select the answer. 3. If you do not know the answer, skip the question and go on to the next question. 4. When finished with new questions, return to any skipped questions.). Connector lines join the shapes in the flowchart.

The typical flowchart sequence includes start and end points shown in an oval shape, steps shown in rectangle shapes, and decisions to be made shown in a diamond shape. Connectors with arrows demonstrate the order in which the sequence should be followed to accomplish the goal. Each shape is labeled to indicate what it represents. It is easy to label the shapes because PowerPoint shapes can contain text. When you select a shape and then type or paste text into it, the text becomes part of the shape and moves with the shape.

A **text box** is an object that enables you to place text anywhere on a slide.

If you need text on a slide (for example, you want to add a quote to a slide but do not want it positioned in the slide content placeholder), you can create a text box. A **text box** is an extremely useful object because it gives you the freedom to create and position text outside of slide content placeholders. Text inside a text box can be formatted just as text in placeholders is formatted. You can even add a border, fill, shadow, or a 3-D effect to the text in a text box. Figure 3.5 displays a basic flowchart created with shapes, connectors, and text boxes.

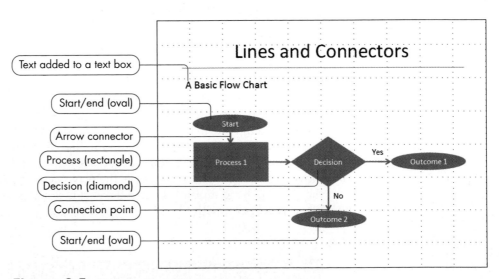

Figure 3.5 A Basic Flowchart

Create and Modify Freeform Shapes

A ***freeform shape*** is a shape that combines both curved and straight lines to create a shape.

When you need a customized shape, you can create a ***freeform shape***, a shape that combines both curved and straight-line segments. Select the Freeform shape in the Lines category of the Shapes Gallery, and then click the slide. Drag to create curves, and click and move the mouse to draw straight lines. Double-click to end the freeform shape. If you click the starting point of the shape, you create a closed shape just as you do with lines.

To modify a freeform shape, select the shape and then under Drawing Tools, click the Format tab. In the Insert Shapes group, click Edit Shape. Finally, select Edit Points. ***Vertexes***, or points where a curve ends or the point where two line segments meet, will appear, and can be moved or deleted to redefine the object's shape. The vertexes appear as black dots. Figure 3.6 shows a freeform with its vertexes displayed. Figure 3.7 shows a selected vertex dragged to a new position. When you release the left mouse button, the freeform will take the new shape.

A ***vertex*** is the point where a curve ends or the point where two line segments meet in a freeform shape.

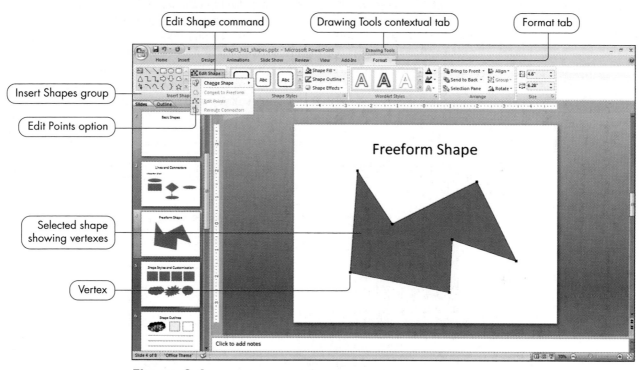

Figure 3.6 Modifying a Freeform Shape

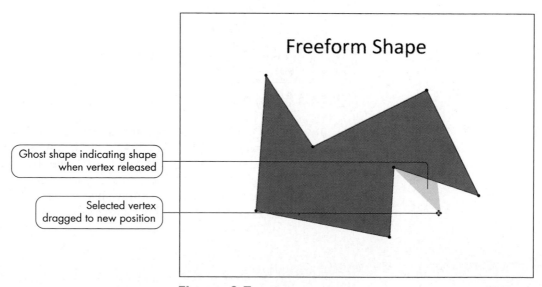

Figure 3.7 Moving a Vertex

Applying Quick Styles and Customizing Shapes

A ***Quick Style*** is a combination of formatting options available that can be applied to a shape or graphic.

After you create a shape, you can add a ***Quick Style*** to it. A Quick Style is a combination of different formats that can be selected from the Quick Style Gallery and applied to a shape or other objects. To see how a Quick Style would look when applied, position your pointer over the Quick Style thumbnail. When you identify the style you desire, click to apply the style. Options in the gallery include edges, shadows, line styles, gradients, and 3-D effects. Figure 3.8 shows the Quick Style gallery and several shapes with a variety of Quick Styles applied to them.

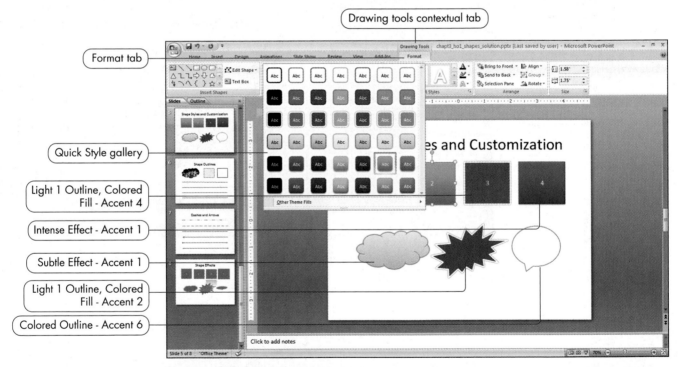

Figure 3.8   Using Quick Styles

To apply a Quick Style to a shape, select the shape. When the Drawing Tools contextual tab appears, click the Format tab. This action provides you with tools to work with as you modify the format of the selected shape. The Shape Styles group includes the More button, which enables you to apply a Quick Style or to manually select the fill and outline of the shape and to apply special effects. When the Quick Style gallery is open, click the Quick Style you wish to apply.

To apply a Quick Style to more than one shape or object at a time, hold down Ctrl and click each object. Each new Ctrl-click adds an object to the selection. Holding down Shift also works. When all objects are selected, choose the style or effect you desire.

A ***selection net*** selects all objects in an area defined by dragging the mouse.

Another method for selecting multiple objects on a slide is to click and drag a *selection net*, or marquee, around all of the objects you wish to select, and then release the mouse button. All objects contained in their entirety in the net, or marquee, will be selected.

Change Shape Fills

A ***fill*** refers to the inside of a shape.

A ***gradient fill*** is a blend of colors and shades.

Rather than apply a Quick Style, you may choose to customize the shape by changing the shape *fill*, or the interior of the shape. You may choose from having a solid color fill, no fill, a picture fill, a *gradient fill* (a blend of one color to another color or one shade to another shade), or a texture fill. To change the fill of a selected object, click Shape Fill in the Shape Styles group on the Format tab. The Shape Fill gallery provides color choices that match the Theme Colors and color choices based on Standard Colors. Figure 3.9 shows the Shape Fill options and a shape filled with Accent 6, Tint 60%.

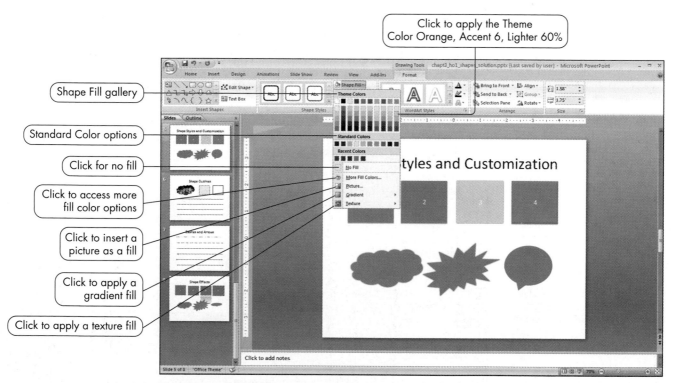

Figure 3.9 Shape Fill Options

If these color choices do not meet your needs, you can always select More Fill Colors to open the Colors dialog box where you can mix colors based on an RGB color model (Red Green Blue) or an HSB color model (Hue Saturation Brightness). The default RGB color model gives each of the colors red, green, and blue a numeric value that ranges from 0 to 255. The combination of these values creates the color assigned to your shape. When all three RGB values are 0, you get black. When all three RGB values are 255, you get white. By using different combinations of numbers between 0 and 255, you can create almost 16 million shades of color.

The Color dialog box also enables you to determine the amount of *transparency*, or visibility, you wish. At 0% transparency, the fill is *opaque*, or solid, while 100% transparency is clear. The Color dialog box enables you to drag a slider to specify the percentage of transparency. Figure 3.10 shows the Color dialog box with the RGB color mode selected, Red assigned a value of 236, Green assigned a value of 32, Blue assigned a value of 148, and a transparency set at 80%.

Transparency refers to how much you can see through a fill.

Opaque refers a solid fill, one without transparency.

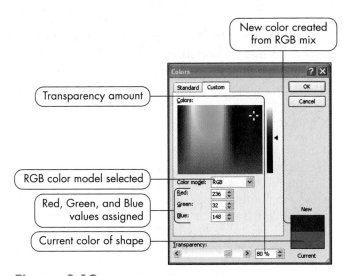

Figure 3.10 The Color Dialog Box

A *picture fill* inserts an image from a file into a shape.

Shapes also may be filled with images using the *picture fill* option. This option enables you to create unusual frames for your pictures and can be a fun way to vary the images in your presentation or create interesting frames for scrap book images. To insert a picture as a fill, click Picture in the Shape Fill gallery accessible from the Format tab under the Drawing Tools contextual tab. Browse to locate the picture that you want to add, and then double-click the picture to insert it. Figure 3.11 shows the cloud shape filled with a casual snapshot taken with a digital camera.

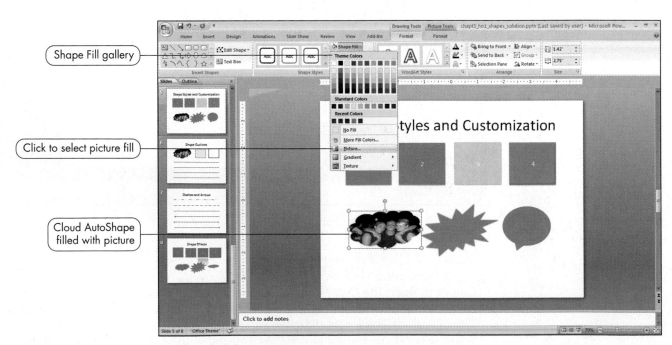

Figure 3.11 Shape Filled with a Picture

Gradient effects make interesting fills for shapes. When Gradient is selected from the Shape Fill gallery, another gallery of options appears, enabling you to select Light and Dark Variations that blend the current color with white or black in linear or radial gradients. Choosing one of these options is a quick and easy way to apply a gradient. To have more control over the gradient and have access to beautiful gradient Presets, click More Gradients at the bottom of the gallery. Figure 3.12 shows the Gradient options with a From Center gradient selected.

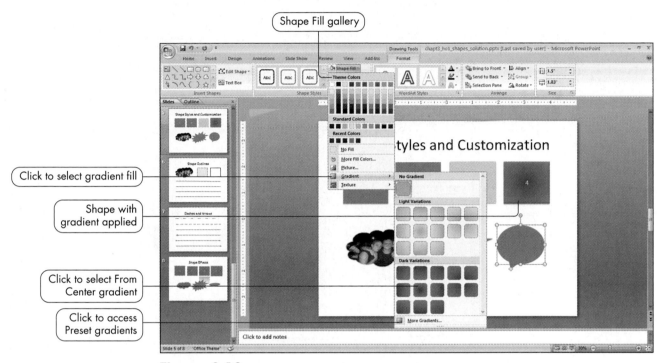

Figure 3.12   Shape Filled with the From Center Gradient Applied

When you select More Gradients, the Format Shape dialog box displays. Clicking the Gradient fill option expands to display many options you can use to customize a fill. The Preset colors gallery gives you a variety of gradients using a multitude of colors to create truly beautiful impressions. You can use other options to select a type of gradient, the direction and angle of the gradient, the number of stops used to add additional colors to a blend, and the rotate gradient option. Figure 3.13 shows the Preset colors gallery.

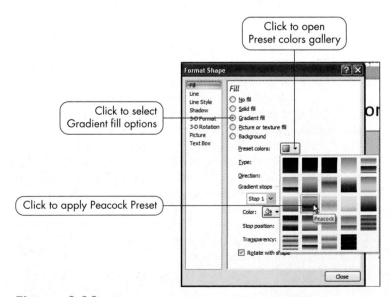

Figure 3.13   PowerPoint's Preset Color Gradients

A *texture fill* inserts a texture such as marble into a shape.

Selecting the Texture option from the Shape Fill Gallery gives you access to common *texture fills* such as canvas, denim, marble, and cork that can be used for the fill of your object. Clicking More Textures at the bottom of the Texture gallery opens the Format Shape dialog box with a multitude of options, including a tiling option. A picture can be stretched to fit the shape, or tiled so the texture is repeated to fill the shape. Tiled textures have seamless edges so that you cannot tell where one tile ends and another begins. See Figure 3.14 for the textures available in the Textures gallery.

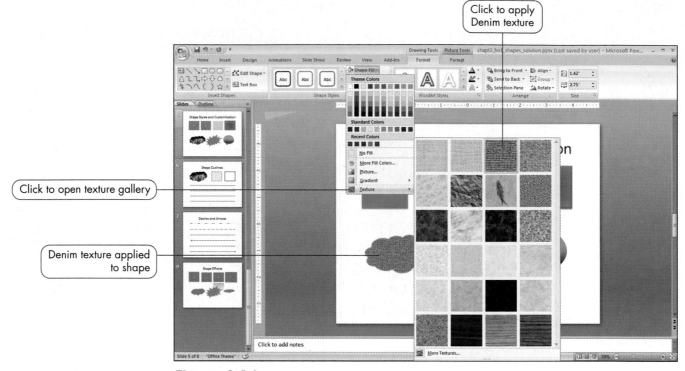

Figure 3.14 Texture Fills

Change Shape Outlines

Line weight is the width or thickness of a line.

By default, shapes have lines forming a border around the shape. You can change the style of this outline by changing its color, style, or ***line weight*** (thickness). This change can be done quickly and easily using the Shape Styles feature you are already familiar with or by customizing using the Shape Outline options available on the Format tab under the Drawing Tools tab. First, select the line, and then open the Shape Outline gallery. The same color options detailed in changing the color of fills are available to change the color of the lines. If you wish to remove an outline, select the No Outline option. In Figure 3.15, the outline surrounding the shape with the picture fill has been removed so that it does not detract from the image.

The width or thickness of a line is measured in points (pts) and is set by using the Weight option available on the Format tab under the Drawing Tools tab. When you select this option, you are given choices of line weights from ¼ pt to 6 pts. One vertical inch contains 72 pts. Therefore, the thickest line you can get is ½" using this option. If you wish to change a line weight to an option not displayed, click More Lines to open the Format Shape dialog box with the Line Style options displayed. This dialog box enables you to change the line weight by selecting a weight using the spin box or by selecting the current weight and then typing in the weight you desire. You can also use the Format Shape dialog box to create Compound type outlines, which combine thick and thin lines. Figure 3.15 displays lines and an outline for a shape in various weights.

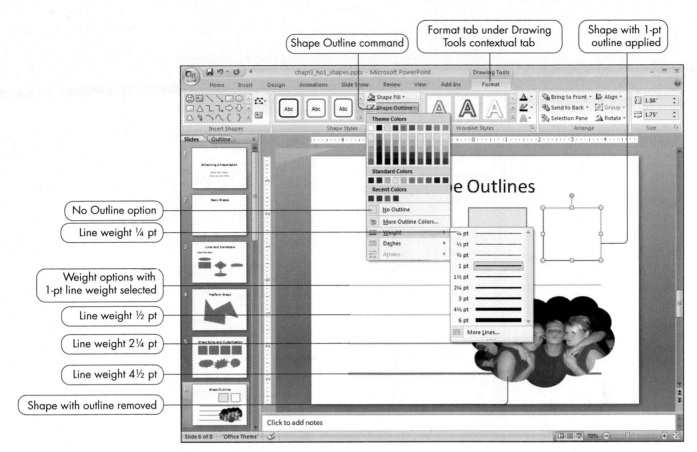

Figure 3.15 Outline Weight Options

For variety, you may wish to change the default solid line to a dashed line. Dashed lines make interesting boxes or borders for shapes and placeholders. PowerPoint lets you apply round dots, square dots, and combinations of short dashes, long dashes, and dots. To make a line dashed, select the line and then under Drawing Tools, on the Format tab, click Shape Outline. Point to the Dashes option, and then click the line style that you want. Figure 3.16 illustrates a variety of dash styles applied to 4½-pt lines.

At times, you may wish to add an arrowhead to the beginning or end of a line to create an arrow that points to critical information on the slide. The Shape Outline feature enables you to create many different styles of arrows using points, circles, and diamonds. Figure 3.16 shows the arrow options as well as 4½-pt lines with arrow styles applied.

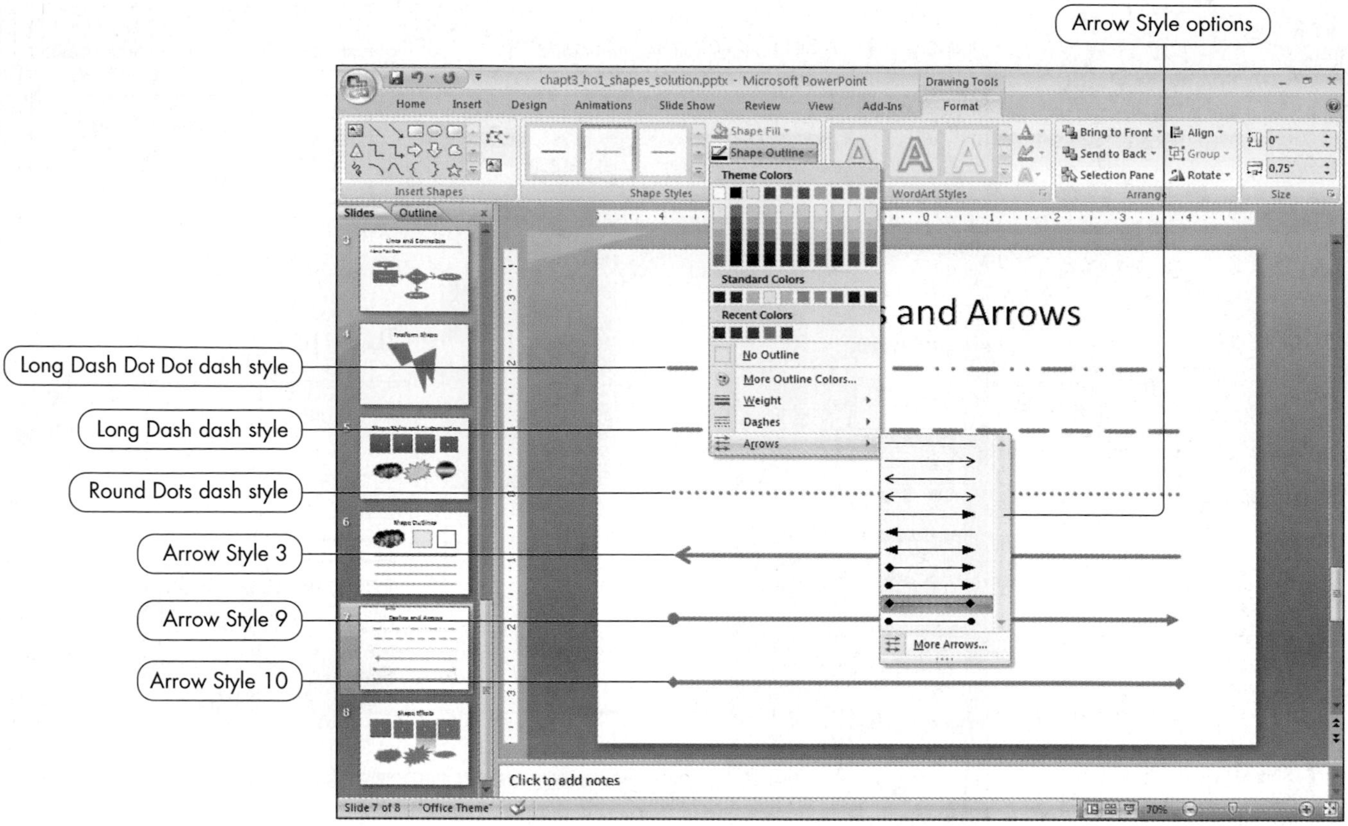

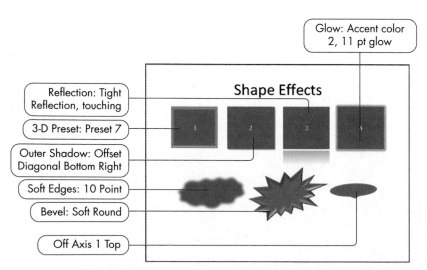

Figure 3.16 Dash and Arrow Outline Styles

Change Shape Effects

> You do not need an expensive, high-powered graphics editor . . . for special effects anymore because PowerPoint 2007 enables you to apply many stunning effects to shapes . . .

You do not need an expensive, high-powered graphics editor such as Adobe Photoshop for special effects anymore because PowerPoint 2007 enables you to apply many stunning effects to shapes: preset three-dimensional effects, shadow effects, reflections, glows, soft edge effects, bevels, and rotations. One of the greatest strengths of PowerPoint 2007 is the ability to update any shape effects you have applied immediately when you choose a new theme. Figure 3.17 shows an example of some of the shape effects available.

Figure 3.17 Shape Effects

To apply effects, click a shape, and then click Shape Effects in the Shape Styles group on the Format tab, under Drawing Tools. Point to Preset effects and select from built-in combinations of effects or select one of the individual options underneath Preset. Or, if you prefer, you can completely customize an effect by clicking 3-D Options at the bottom of the list. For example, if you click 3-D Options at the bottom of the Preset list, you open the Format Shape dialog box with the 3-D Format options available. From there, you can define the bevel, depth, contours, and even the surface of the effect. Figure 3.18 displays the Material options for the surface of a shape.

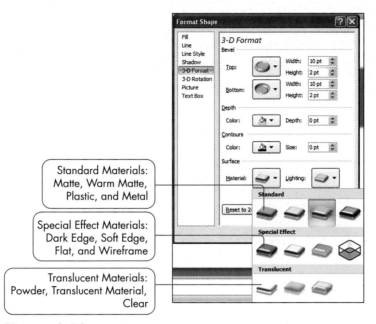

Figure 3.18 3-D Surface Options

Hands-On Exercises

1 | Working with Shapes

Skills covered: 1. Create Basic Shapes **2.** Draw and Format Connector Lines **3.** Modify a Freeform Shape **4.** Apply a Quick Style and Customize Shapes **5.** Change Shape Outlines **6.** Change Outline, Dash, and Arrow Styles **7.** Use Shape Effects

Step 1 **Create Basic Shapes**	Refer to Figure 3.19 as you complete Step 1.

a. Start PowerPoint, open the *chap3_ho1_shapes* presentation, and then immediately save it as **chap3_ho1_shapes_solution**.

b. Move to **Slide 2**, click the **Insert tab**, and then click **Shapes** in the Illustrations group.

c. Right-click the **Rectangle** shape in the Rectangles category, and then select **Lock Drawing Mode**.

The Lock Drawing Mode enables you to stay in a shape creation mode so that you can create additional shapes of the same kind.

d. Hold down **Shift**, position your pointer on the upper-left side of the slide below the title, and then click to create a square. Repeat this process until you have four squares on the slide.

Holding down Shift while clicking constrains your rectangles so they become squares. Do not worry about the size or placement of the squares at this time. You will learn how to resize and place shapes later in this chapter.

e. Click **Shapes** in the Illustrations group on the Insert tab, select **Cloud** from the Basic Shapes category, and then drag a cloud shape beneath the first square.

The Shapes gallery opens when you click Shape and displays the categories and shapes available so that you can locate the Cloud shape.

f. From the Shapes gallery, select **Explosion 2** from the Stars and Banners category, and then drag an explosion shape on the right side of the cloud.

g. From the Shapes gallery, select **Oval Callout** from the Callouts category, and then drag a callout on the right side of the explosion.

h. Save the *chap3_ho1_shapes_solution* presentation.

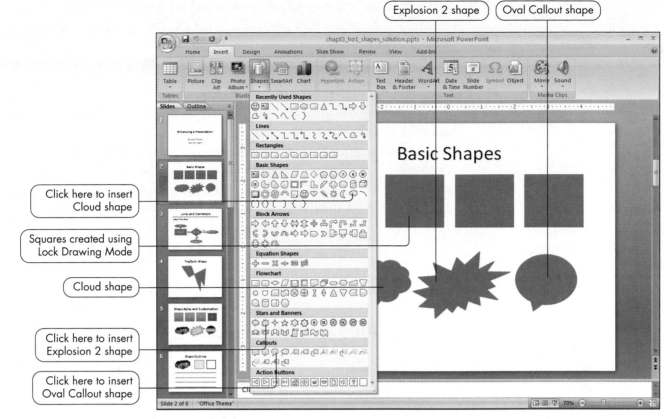

Figure 3.19 Basic Shapes

The following callouts appear in the figure:
- Explosion 2 shape
- Oval Callout shape
- Click here to insert Cloud shape
- Squares created using Lock Drawing Mode
- Cloud shape
- Click here to insert Explosion 2 shape
- Click here to insert Oval Callout shape

Step 2
Draw and Format Connector Lines

Refer to Figure 3.20 as you complete Step 2.

a. With *chap3_ho1_shapes_solution* onscreen, move to **Slide 3**, and then click **Shapes** in the Illustrations group on the Insert tab.

b. Click **Line,** and then drag a horizontal Line separating the slide title, *Lines and Connectors*, from the flowchart.

You create a line to separate the title from the flowchart. Because this line does not touch any shape, you do not need to use a connector line.

c. Select the **Elbow Arrow Connector** in the Lines category, move your pointer over the oval on the left of the slide, and then position the cross-hair on the bottom center red handle.

The shape's connector handles appear when a connector line is selected and an object is pointed at.

d. Drag a connecting line that attaches the red connecting handle on the bottom center of the oval to the top red connecting handle of the rectangle below it.

The arrowhead on the connector does not clearly show because the default line weight is very thin. You will adjust the line weight in step f.

e. Create connecting lines that attach the rectangle to the diamond and the diamond to each of the remaining ovals, as demonstrated in Figure 3.20.

f. Press and hold **Ctrl** and click all four connector lines to select them. Click the **Format tab**, click **Shape Outline** in the Shape Styles group, select **Weight**, and then select **3 pt**.

All four lines are thicker with the 3 pt weight.

g. Select the oval on the top left of the slide and type **Start**.

Selecting a shape and then entering text creates a container for text and the text becomes part of the shape.

h. Select each of the shapes and type the text shown in Figure 3.20.

i. Click **Text Box** in the Text group on the Insert tab.

Clicking Text Box enables you to create text that is not contained in a shape or a placeholder on the slide.

j. Position the pointer above the connector between the decision diamond and the Outcome 1 oval, click, and then type **Yes**.

k. Repeat step h. Position the pointer to the right side of the connector between the decision diamond and the Outcome 1 oval, click, and then type **No**.

l. Save the *chap3_ho1_shapes_solution* presentation.

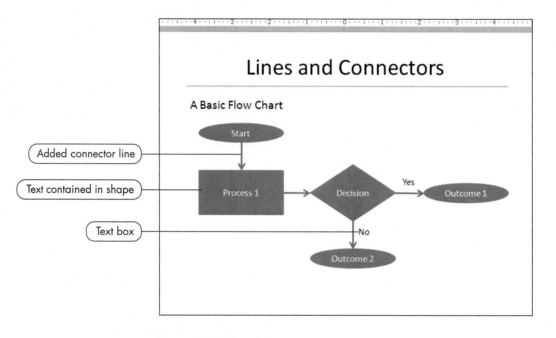

Figure 3.20 A Basic Flowchart

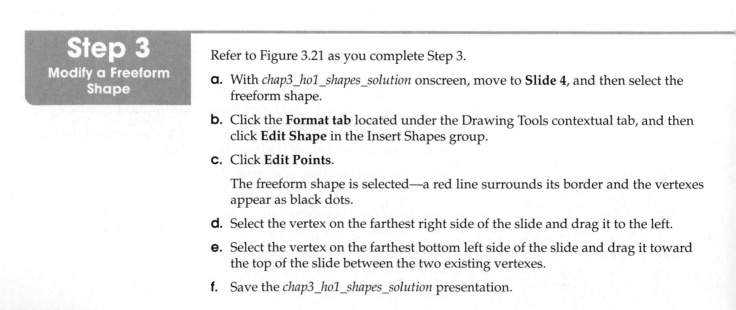

Refer to Figure 3.21 as you complete Step 3.

a. With *chap3_ho1_shapes_solution* onscreen, move to **Slide 4**, and then select the freeform shape.

b. Click the **Format tab** located under the Drawing Tools contextual tab, and then click **Edit Shape** in the Insert Shapes group.

c. Click **Edit Points**.

The freeform shape is selected—a red line surrounds its border and the vertexes appear as black dots.

d. Select the vertex on the farthest right side of the slide and drag it to the left.

e. Select the vertex on the farthest bottom left side of the slide and drag it toward the top of the slide between the two existing vertexes.

f. Save the *chap3_ho1_shapes_solution* presentation.

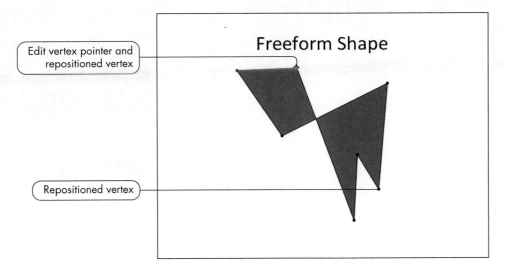

Figure 3.21 Modified Freeform Shape

Refer to Figure 3.22 as you complete Step 4.

a. With *chap3_ho1_shapes_solution* onscreen, move to **Slide 5**, and then select **Rectangle 4**.

b. Click the **Format tab** under the Drawing Tools tab, and then click the **More button** in the Shape Styles group.

c. Move your pointer over the Quick Styles, and then click **Light 1 Outline, Colored Fill – Accent 4** to apply it to Rectangle 4.

d. Click **Rectangle 1**. Press **Ctrl** as you click Rectangles 2 and 3, click the **More button** in the Shape Styles group, and then click **Intense Effect – Accent 1**.

You can apply Quick Styles to more than one shape at a time.

e. Select the cloud shape, click **Shape Fill**, and then select **Picture**.

f. Locate the file *chap3_ho1_friends.jpg*, and then double-click to insert the picture into the shape.

g. Select the explosion shape, click **Shape Fill**, and then select **Texture**.

h. Click **Bouquet**.

i. Select the callout, click **Shape Fill**, select **Gradient**, and then select **More Gradients**.

The Format Shape dialog box opens for your use in customizing a gradient.

j. Click **Gradient fill**, click the **Preset colors drop-down arrow**, click **Rainbow**, and then click **Close**.

k. Save the *chap3_ho1_shapes_solution* presentation.

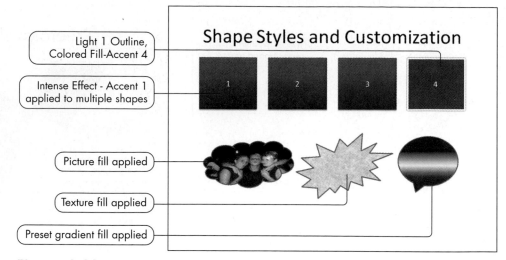

Shape Styles and Customization

Light 1 Outline, Colored Fill-Accent 4

Intense Effect - Accent 1 applied to multiple shapes

Picture fill applied

Texture fill applied

Preset gradient fill applied

Figure 3.22 Quick Styles and Customized Fills

Step 5
Change Shape Outlines

Refer to Figure 3.23 as you complete Step 5.

a. With *chap3_ho1_shapes_solution* onscreen, select **Slide 6**, and then select the cloud shape with the picture fill.

b. Click the **Format tab** under the Drawing Tools tab.

> **TROUBLESHOOTING:** If you see two format tabs (one under Drawing Tools and one under Picture), be sure to select the Format tab under Drawing Tools. The Picture Tools tab appears next to the Drawing Tools tab because of the picture fill.

c. Click **Shape Outline** in the Shape Styles group, and then select **No Outline**.

d. Select the square with the orange tint fill, click **Shape Outline**, and then click **Orange, Accent 6** in the Theme Colors gallery.

e. Select the square with no fill, click **Shape Outline**, and then click **More Outline Colors**.

f. Type **255** in the **Red** box, and then type **0** in the **Green** and **Blue** boxes. Click **OK**.

   This selection creates a pure red outline. Leaving **Transparency** at 0% leaves the outline opaque, or solid.

g. Beginning above and to the left of the top horizontal line, drag a marquee (selection net) around the four horizontal lines.

h. Click the **Format tab**, click **Shape Outline** in the Shape Styles group, select **Weight**, and then click **6 pt**.

i. Save the *chap3_ho1_shapes_solution* presentation.

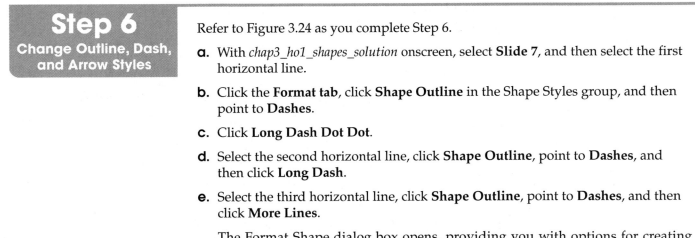

Figure 3.23 Outline Colors and Weights

Step 6	Refer to Figure 3.24 as you complete Step 6.
Change Outline, Dash, and Arrow Styles	

Step 6
Change Outline, Dash, and Arrow Styles

Refer to Figure 3.24 as you complete Step 6.

a. With *chap3_ho1_shapes_solution* onscreen, select **Slide 7**, and then select the first horizontal line.

b. Click the **Format tab**, click **Shape Outline** in the Shape Styles group, and then point to **Dashes**.

c. Click **Long Dash Dot Dot**.

d. Select the second horizontal line, click **Shape Outline**, point to **Dashes**, and then click **Long Dash**.

e. Select the third horizontal line, click **Shape Outline**, point to **Dashes**, and then click **More Lines**.

The Format Shape dialog box opens, providing you with options for creating custom lines including compound line types.

f. Click the **Compound type drop-down arrow**, select the last option on the list, and then click **Close**.

This selection creates a compound line composed of three lines of different weights: one thin line, one thick line, and then one thin line.

g. Select the fourth horizontal line, click **Shape Outline**, point to **Arrows**, and then click **Arrow Style 3**.

h. Select the fifth horizontal line, click **Shape Outline**, point to **Arrows**, and then click **Arrow Style 9**.

i. Select the last horizontal line, click **Shape Outline**, point to **Arrows**, and then click **More Arrows**.

j. Click the **Begin type arrow**, and then click **Stealth Arrow**.

k. Click the **End type arrow**, click **Oval Arrow,** and click Close.

l. Save the *chap3_ho1_shapes_solution* presentation.

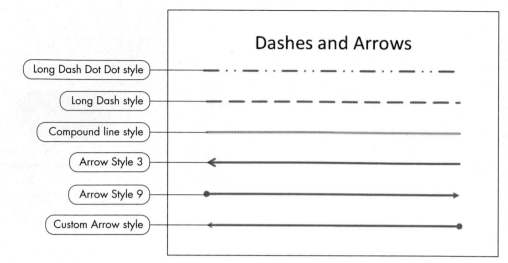

Figure 3.24 Line Dash and Arrow Styles

Step 7
Use Shape Effects

Refer to Figure 3.25 as you complete Step 7.

a. With *chap3_ho1_shapes_solution* onscreen, select **Slide 8**, and then select **Rectangle 1**.

b. Click the **Format tab**, click **Shape Effects** in the Shape Styles group, and then click **Preset**.

c. Click **Preset 7**.

Preset 7 combines a bevel type, a depth, contours, and a surface effect.

d. Select **Rectangle 2**, click **Shape Effects** in the Shape Styles group, click **Shadow**, and then click **Offset Diagonal Bottom Left** in the Outer category.

The Offset Diagonal option applies a 4-pt soft shadow to the rectangle.

e. Select **Rectangle 3**, click **Shape Effects**, click **Reflection**, and then click **Tight Reflection, touching**.

f. Select **Rectangle 4**, click **Shape Effects**, click **Glow**, and then click **Accent color 2, 11 pt glow**.

g. Continue to use the **Shape Effects** options to apply effects to the remaining shapes.

Shape	Effect	Style
Cloud	Soft Edges	10 Point
Explosion	Bevel	Soft Round
Callout	3-D Rotation	Off Axis 1 Top (Parallel category)

h. Save the *chap3_ho1_shapes_solution* presentation and close it.

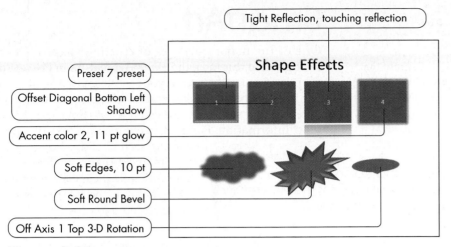

Figure 3.25 Shape Effects

SmartArt

One of the major purposes of creating shapes is to call attention to information. Recognizing this idea, the **SmartArt** feature in PowerPoint enables you to create a diagram and enter the text of your message in one of many existing layouts. The resulting illustration is professional and follows the theme you have selected. You also can take existing slide text and convert it to SmartArt to create a visual representation of your information. Figure 3.26 compares a text-based slide in the common bullet format to a second slide showing the same information converted to a SmartArt diagram. The arrows and colors in the SmartArt diagram make it easy for the viewer to understand the message and remember the cycle. It is especially effective when animation is added to each step.

> The arrows and colors in the SmartArt diagram make it easy for the viewer to understand the message . . .

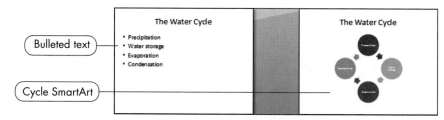

Figure 3.26 A SmartArt Depiction of the Water Cycle

Using the SmartArt feature rather than creating your own shapes is efficient and can even be inspiring when you are at a loss as to how to effectively convey your message. A SmartArt diagram creates a layout for your information, provides a Text pane for quickly entering information, automatically sizes shapes and text, and gives you the ability to switch between layouts, making it easy to choose the most effective layout. Some layouts can be used for any type of information and are designed to be visually attractive, while other layouts are created specifically for a certain type of information. For example, perhaps you have a list of items and you want to present them in an attractive way; you would select a SmartArt graphic that applies special effects but does not imply that steps must be followed in order. If, however, you have a list of steps that must be followed in order, you would select a SmartArt graphic that is numbered as well as having special effects. SmartArt includes more than 80 different layouts.

In this section, you create and modify a SmartArt diagram. Modifications include changing theme colors, using SmartArt Quick Styles, changing the layout, changing the SmartArt type, and converting text to SmartArt.

Creating SmartArt

To create a SmartArt graphic or diagram, you must choose a diagram type. The type you choose should be based on the purpose of your information and the ability of the layout for the SmartArt type to convey your message. The SmartArt gallery has seven different categories of diagrams: lists, processes, cycles, hierarchies, relationships, matrices, and pyramids. Each category includes a description of the type of information appropriate for the layouts in that category. The Reference Table shows the SmartArt categories and their purposes.

SmartArt Diagram | Reference

Icon	Type	Purpose	Sample SmartArt
List	List	Use to show non-sequential information. For example: A list of items to be checked on a roof each year.	Flashing / Shingles / Soffits
Process	Process	Use to show steps in a process or a timeline. For example: The steps to take to wash a car.	Hose > Sponge > Rinse
Cycle	Cycle	Use to show a continual process. For example: The recurring business cycle.	Expansion, Downturn, Recession, Recovery
Hierarchy	Hierarchy	Use to show a decision tree, organization chart, or pedigree. For example: A pedigree chart showing the parents of an individual.	Reed J. Olsen → Ivan Olsen, Gladys Jones
Relationship	Relationship	Use to illustrate connections. For example: The connection between outdoor activities.	Camping, Hiking, Fishing
Matrix	Matrix	Use to show how parts relate to a whole. For example: Keirsey's Temperament Theory involves for personalities.	Rationals, Idealists, Keirsey Temperaments, Artisans, Guardians
Pyramid	Pyramid	Use to show proportional relationships with the largest component on the top or bottom. For example: an ecology chart.	Indirect Consumers, Direct Consumers, Producers

To create a SmartArt diagram, click SmartArt in the Illustrations group on the Insert tab. The Choose a SmartArt Graphic dialog box displays (see Figure 3.27) with three panes. The pane on the left side shows the types of SmartArt diagrams available. Each type of diagram includes subtypes that are displayed in the center pane. Clicking one of the subtypes enlarges it and displays it in the preview pane on the right side. The preview pane describes purposes for which the SmartArt can be used effectively. Some of the descriptions include tips for the type of text to enter.

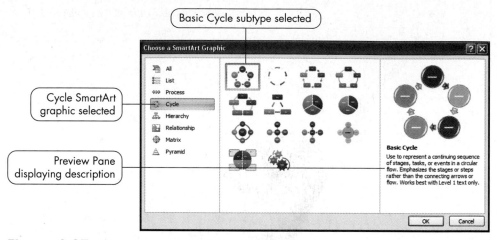

Figure 3.27 The SmartArt Gallery

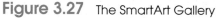

TIP   Text in SmartArt

The amount of text you enter in a SmartArt diagram impacts how many shapes your layout can contain. Keep your text short and limit it to key points to create a visually appealing diagram.

A **Text pane** is a special pane that opens up for text entry when a SmartArt diagram is selected.

Once you click to select the SmartArt diagram type and the subtype you desire, a **Text pane** opens for you to use to enter text. The Text pane works like an outline—enter a line of text, press Enter, and then press Tab or Shift+Tab to increase or decrease the indent level. You do not have to worry about the font size or the position of the text when you use the Text pane. The font size will decrease to fit text inside of the shape or the shape may grow to fit the text. The layout accommodates additional shapes as you enter text—unless the type of shape is designed for a specific number of shapes, such as the Relationship Counterbalance Arrows layout, which is designed to show two opposing ideas. Figure 3.28 shows text entered into the Text pane for a Basic Cycle SmartArt diagram. Because five lines of text were created, five shapes were created.

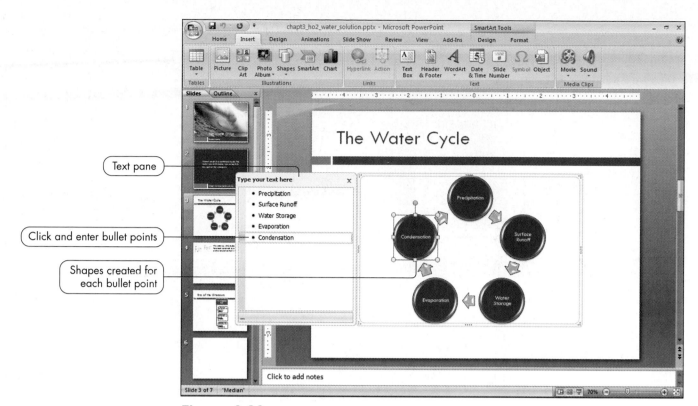

Figure 3.28 The SmartArt Text Pane

Modifying SmartArt Diagrams

Standard editing methods apply to SmartArt diagrams. For example, you can drag a SmartArt diagram by its borders to reposition it. You also can modify SmartArt text in the Text pane just as if it is in a placeholder or you can modify the text in the shape itself. If you need an additional shape, click a shape, and then position your cursor at the beginning of the text where you want to add a shape. Type your text, and then press Enter.

An alternative method for adding shapes is to use the Add Shape command. Click an existing shape in the SmartArt diagram, and then under the SmartArt Tools contextual tab, click the Design tab. Click the Add Shape arrow in the Create Graphic group. Select Add Shape After, Add Shape Before, Add Shape Above, or Add Shape Below.

In addition to these standard methods of modifying, you also can format the SmartArt so that it really stands out. SmartArt diagrams have two galleries you use to change the look of the diagram, both of which are located under the SmartArt Tools contextual tab in the SmartArt Styles group on the Design tab. One gallery changes colors and the other gallery applies a combination of special effects.

Change SmartArt Theme Colors

To change the color scheme of your SmartArt, click the Change Colors command to display the Colors gallery (see Figure 3.29). The gallery contains Primary Theme Colors, Colorful color choices, and color schemes based on Accent colors. Click the color variation that you want and your SmartArt will update.

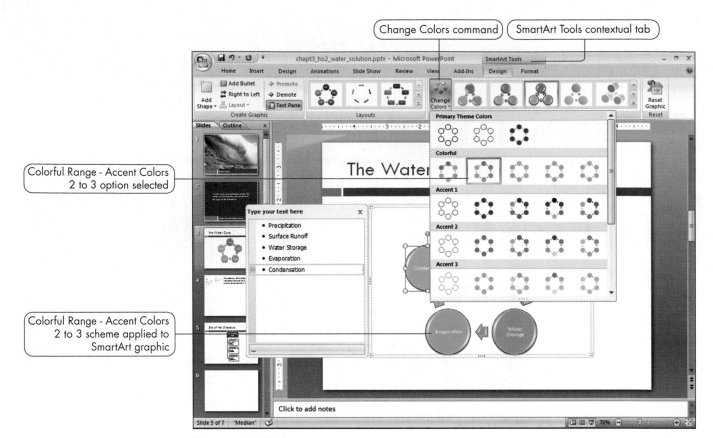

Figure 3.29 The SmartArt Color Options

Use Quick Styles with SmartArt

After creating the diagram, you can adjust the style of the diagram to match previous styles you have used in your presentation or to make the diagram easier to understand. To apply a Quick Style to a SmartArt diagram, click your diagram, and then click the Quick Style that you want from the SmartArt Styles gallery. To see the complete gallery, click the More button located in the SmartArt Styles group on the Design tab. The gallery opens and displays simple combinations of special effects, such as shadows, gradients, and 3-D effects that combine perspectives and surface styles. Figure 3.30 displays the SmartArt Quick Styles gallery.

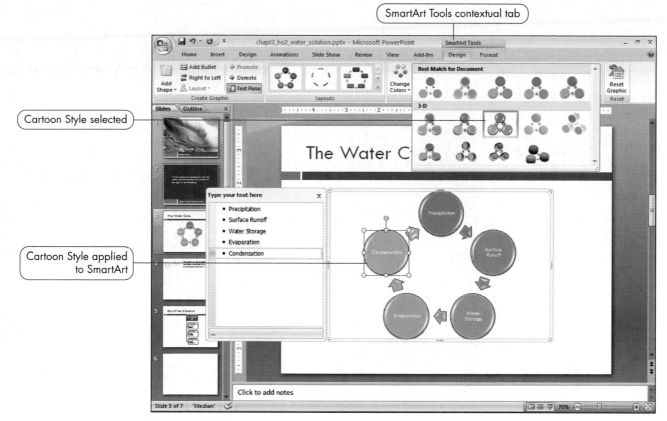

Figure 3.30 The SmartArt Quick Styles Gallery

Change the Layout

After selecting a type of SmartArt diagram, you may find the diagram fits your purpose, but the layout needs tweaking. An example would be a diagram you created that is unreadable due to the amount of text you have entered. Modifying the layout may give you more room for the text. Figure 3.31 shows a Hierarchy diagram displaying the relationship between the Mesozoic Era and its periods, along with the type of animal and dinosaur that lived during the period. In order for the text to fit, PowerPoint reduced the font size to 6 pt. Even projected on a screen, this text would be unreadable for most audience members.

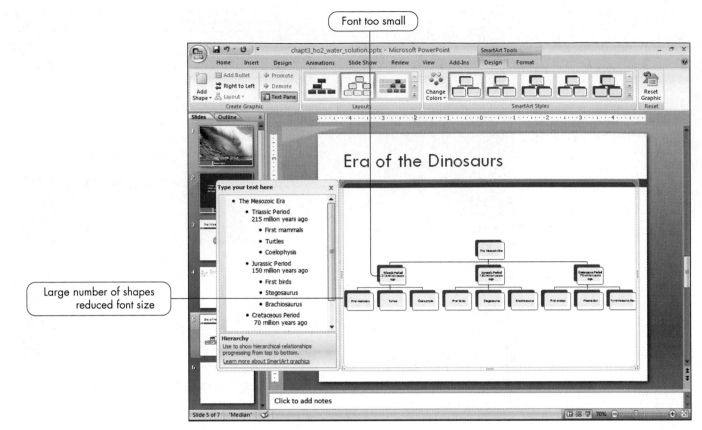

Figure 3.31 Hierarchy 1 SmartArt

By tweaking the layout, you can make the Mesozoic layout much more easily read. First, select the SmartArt diagram, and then click Design under SmartArt Tools. Click the More button in the Layouts group to display the Layouts gallery. Some of the layouts have special effects such as shadowing, some have fill changes, some change the box shape and border, and some change the orientation of the layout from horizontal to vertical. Test the options to determine which one provides for the greatest legibility. Figure 3.32 shows the Mesozoic information in a Hierarchy List diagram that uses a vertical orientation.

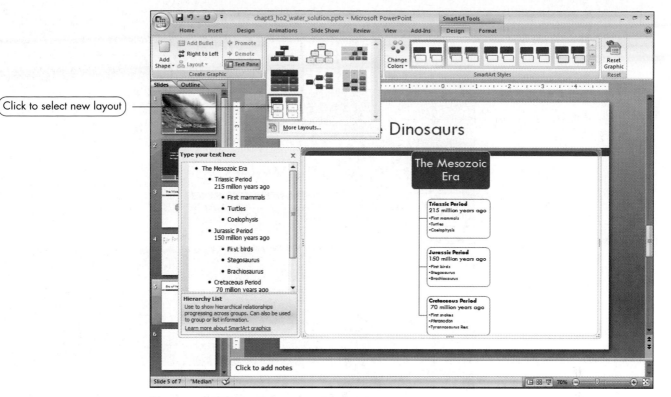

Click to select new layout

Figure 3.32 Hierarchy List SmartArt

Change SmartArt Type

You can switch a SmartArt diagram to another diagram type if you decide another SmartArt layout would better accomplish your goal. Because changing a type is similar to changing the SmartArt layout, the process is the same. To change to another SmartArt diagram, click to select the SmartArt diagram. Click the More button in the Layouts group on the Design tab under SmartArt Tools, and then click More Layouts. The Choose a SmartArt Graphic gallery appears with all the categories and their layouts. Click the type and layout you desire.

Keep in mind that switching diagram types alters the layout, which may impact the audience's perception of your diagram. For example, if you have created a list of nonsequential items, switching to a cycle diagram implies a specific order to the items. Also, if you have customized the shapes, the customizations may not be transferred. Colors, line styles, and fills transfer. Rotation does not. For a complete list of which customizations will transfer and which will not, go to Help and search for *Adding charts, diagrams, or tables*.

Convert Text to a SmartArt Diagram

If you already have created text on a slide and then decide you want a SmartArt diagram, you can convert the existing text into a SmartArt illustration. Select the placeholder containing your text, and then click Convert to SmartArt Graphic in the Paragraph group on the Home tab. When the gallery appears, click the layout for the SmartArt diagram that you want (see Figure 3.33).

(. . . you can convert . . . existing text into a SmartArt illustration.)

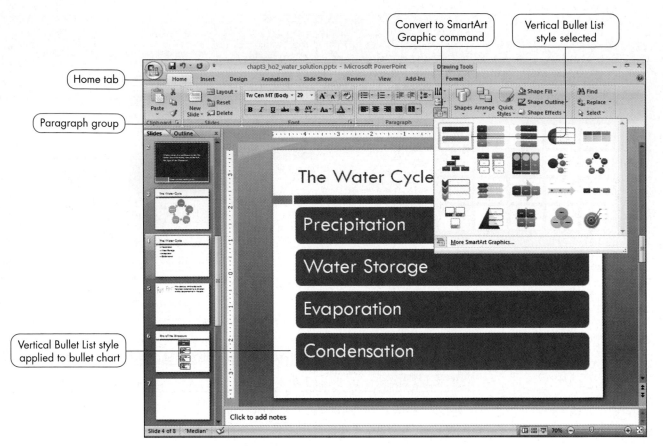

Figure 3.33 Convert to SmartArt Options

TIP Converting Text to SmartArt Using a Shortcut

For a quick method of converting text in a placeholder into SmartArt, right-click text in a placeholder and then select Convert to SmartArt. The Convert SmartArt gallery opens so you can select a SmartArt style.

WordArt

WordArt is text that has a decorative effect applied.

WordArt is text that uses special effects based on styles in the WordArt Gallery for the purpose of calling attention to the text. While at first this may seem like WordArt is the same as SmartArt, there is a major difference. SmartArt emphasizes text by surrounding it with a container that could have special effects applied to the container. In WordArt, however, the special effect applies to the text itself, not a shape surrounding the text. For example, rather than the box surrounding text having a reflection, the text itself would have a reflection. By applying special effects directly to the text, you can create eye-catching text that emphasizes the information for your audience. Imagine text following a curve or shaped as a wave or slanted—the possibilities are endless. In this section, you explore WordArt styles to create and modify a WordArt object.

Creating WordArt

The term **stacked** refers to the vertical alignment of text.

WordArt has a gallery of text styles to choose from as well as options you can use to select individual settings. WordArt text even can be changed from a horizontal alignment to a *stacked* or vertical alignment and can be rotated 90° or 270°. Figure 3.34 shows WordArt text with each of these options applied.

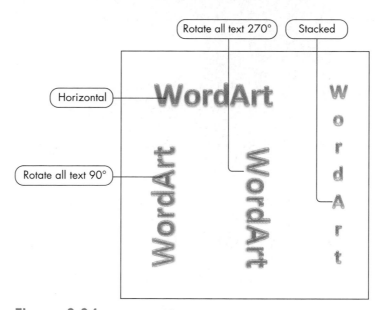

Figure 3.34 WordArt Alignment Options

You can create your text as WordArt or you can convert existing text into WordArt. To create WordArt, click WordArt in the Text group on the Insert tab. When you click WordArt, the WordArt gallery opens with a variety of special effects to choose from. The colors reflected in the gallery match the Theme colors. Click the WordArt style of your choice, and then enter your text in the WordArt placeholder.

Modifying WordArt

You can change the style of your WordArt by clicking a Quick Style located in the WordArt Styles group on the Format tab under the Drawing Tools contextual tab. Or, if you prefer, you can modify the individual elements of the WordArt by changing its fill, outline, or effects by clicking Text Fill, Text Outline, or Text Effects in the WordArt Styles group. WordArt Text Effects has a unique Transform option. Transform can rotate the WordArt text around a path, or add a warp to stretch, angle, or bloat letters. Figure 3.35 displays the WordArt Quick Styles gallery, and Figure 3.36 shows the WordArt Transform options.

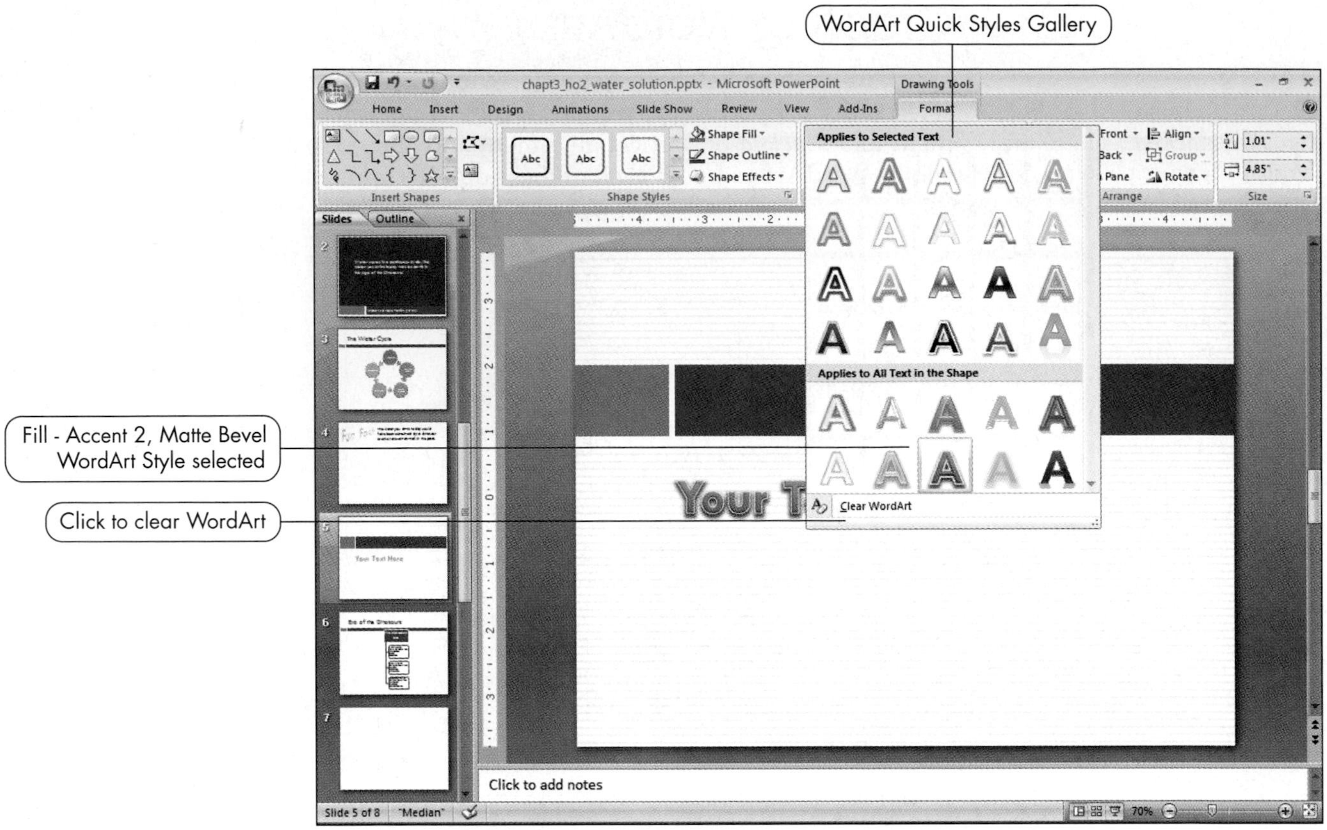

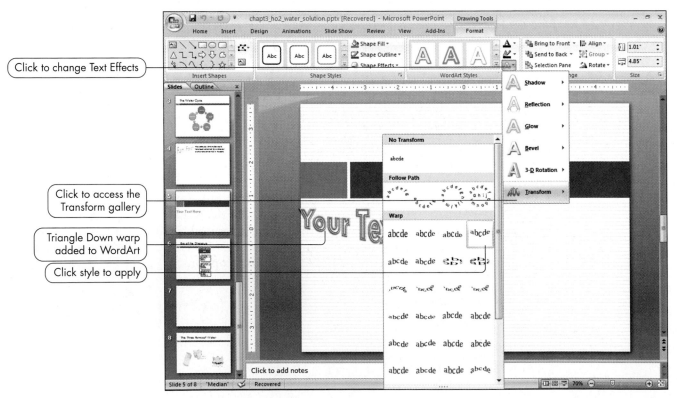

Figure 3.35 Quick Styles Gallery Options

Figure 3.36 Warp Options Available with Transform

Hands-On Exercises

2 | Working with SmartArt and WordArt

Skills covered: 1. Insert SmartArt **2.** Modify a SmartArt Diagram **3.** Change SmartArt Layout **4.** Create WordArt
5. Modify WordArt

Step 1
Insert SmartArt

Refer to Figure 3.37 as you complete Step 1.

a. Open the *chap3_ho2_water* presentation, and then immediately save it as
chap3_ho2_water_solution.

b. Move to **Slide 3**, click the **Insert tab**, and then click **SmartArt** in the Illustrations
group.

c. In the Choose a SmartArt Graphic dialog box, click **Cycle**, click the subtype
Basic Cycle, and then click **OK**.

The Type your text here pane opens, and your pointer is located in the first bullet
location so that you can enter the text for your first cycle shape.

d. Click **Text Pane** in the Create Graphic group.

e. Type **Precipitation**.

The font size for the text reduces so that the text fits inside the shape.

f. Press the down arrow on the keyboard to move to the second bullet and type
Water Storage. Type the two remaining bullet points: **Evaporation** and
Condensation.

g. Press the down arrow on the keyboard to move to the last bullet point and press
Backspace.

The extra shape in the Cycle SmartArt is removed.

h. Click the **X** on the top right of the Type your text here pane to close the pane.

i. Drag to reposition the SmartArt object so that it does not sit on the blue border.

j. Save the *chap3_ho2_water_solution* presentation.

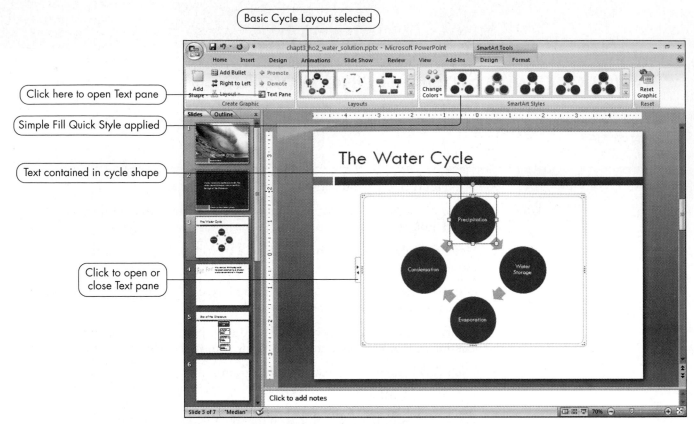

Basic Cycle Layout selected

Click here to open Text pane

Simple Fill Quick Style applied

Text contained in cycle shape

Click to open or close Text pane

Figure 3.37 Basic Cycle SmartArt

Step 2

Modify a SmartArt Diagram

Refer to Figure 3.39 as you complete Step 2.

a. Click the Precipitation shape at the top of the cycle SmartArt, then click the **SmartArt Tools contextual tab** and click the **Design tab** (if necessary).

b. Click **Add Shape** in the Create Graphic group on the Design tab, and then select **Add Shape After**.

Figure 3.38 shows the Add Shape options.

SmartArt Tools

Add Shape command

Add Shape After option

Design tab

Figure 3.38 Add Shape Options

---

c. Type **Surface Runoff** in the new shape.

d. Click a placeholder border to select all the shapes in your SmartArt diagram, and then click **Change Colors** in the Design tab located under the SmartArt Tools contextual tab.

e. Click **Dark 2 Fill** in the Primary Theme Colors category.

f. Click the **More button** in the Smart Art Styles group.

Move your pointer over the styles to see the impact each style has on the text in your SmartArt. Remember—the goal of graphics is to enhance your message, not make it unreadable. Your first priority should always be to make it easy for your audience to understand your message, not to decorate.

g. Click **Cartoon**.

h. Save the *chap3_ho2_water_solution* presentation.

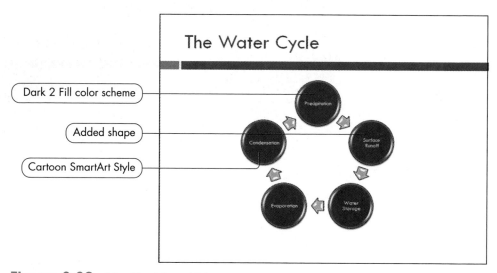

Figure 3.39 Modified SmartArt

Step 3
Change SmartArt Layout

Refer to Figure 3.40 as you complete Step 3.

a. With *chap3_ho2_water_solution* onscreen, move to **Slide 5**.

b. Click to select the SmartArt Hierarchy shape.

c. Click the **Design tab**, which is under SmartArt Tools.

d. Click the **More button** in the Layouts group, and then click **Hierarchy List**.

> **TROUBLESHOOTING:** Your screen may not match Figure 3.40 exactly. The dinosaur names have been added to the author's supplemental dictionary so wavy red lines indicating misspelled words do not appear in Figure 3.40. Your screen may display the wavy red lines.

e. Save the *chap3_ho2_water_solution* presentation.

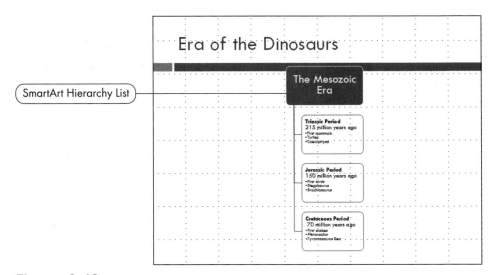

Figure 3.40 Completed SmartArt Diagram

Step 4
Create WordArt

Refer to Figure 3.41 as you complete Step 4.

a. With *chap3_ho2_water_solution* onscreen, move to **Slide 4**.

b. Click the **Insert tab**, and then click **WordArt** in the Text group.

c. Click **Fill – Accent 3, Outline – Text 2**.

d. Type **Fun Fact** in the WordArt placeholder.

e. Save the *chap3_ho2_water_solution* presentation.

WordArt text entered in placeholder

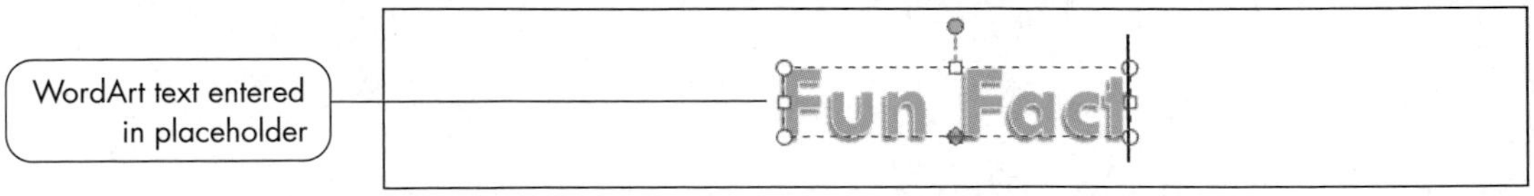

Figure 3.41 WordArt

Refer to Figure 3.42 as you complete Step 5.

a. With *chap3_ho2_water_solution* onscreen, select the WordArt in Slide 4, if necessary, and then click the **Format tab** under **Drawing Tools**.

b. Click **Text Effects** in the WordArt group, and then select **Transform**.

The Transform gallery opens showing Path and Warp options.

c. Select **Cascade Up**, which is located on the bottom row, third from the left.

d. Click in the **Shape Height** box located in the Size group on the far right of the Format tab, type **1.5**, and then press **Enter**.

The height of the WordArt shape adjusts to 1.5".

e. Drag the WordArt to the top left corner of your slide.

f. Click outside of the WordArt shape to deselect the shape.

g. Click the **Insert tab** and click **Text Box** in the Text group.

h. Click to the right of the WordArt, and then type **The water you drink today could have been consumed by a dinosaur or other ancient animal in the past.**

The text box expands to fit the text with the result that the text is contained in one long line that flows off the slide.

i. Change the font size of the text to **28 pt**.

TROUBLESHOOTING: If a text box extends beyond the slide boundaries, you can adjust the placeholder size until it fits on the slide. Drag the right border of the text box until the text box fits on the slide, and then reposition it to the location you desire on the slide.

j. Save the *chap3_ho2_water_solution* presentation.

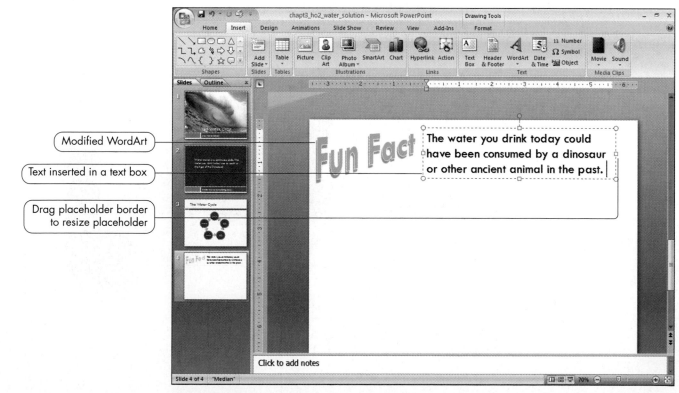

Figure 3.42 Modified WordArt

Object Manipulation

Making slides interesting is one of the goals you have been working toward thus far in this text—making the slides interesting keeps the audience's attention and increases their memory of your message. You have inserted clips, created shapes, added SmartArt, and created WordArt to accomplish this goal. As you add these objects to your slides, however, you will find that often you need to manipulate them. Perhaps you have several shapes created, and you want them to align at their left edges, or you want to arrange them by their center point and then determine the order of the shapes. Perhaps you have inserted a clip art image and the colors used in the clip art do not match the color of the SmartArt on a slide. You may even locate the perfect clip art image—except it is not perfect! It has the images you want but also includes something you do not want. For example, you locate the perfect picnic basket for your Labor Day celebration invitation, but the picnic basket is sitting on a tablecloth. You want to remove the tablecloth from the image and use just the picnic basket.

In this section, you learn how to modify objects. In particular, you isolate objects you need, flip and rotate objects, group and ungroup objects, and recolor clip art. You also learn to determine the order of objects and align objects to each other and to the slide.

Modifying Objects

Examine a clip art object and you will see that the clip art image is made from a series of combined shapes. Modify existing clip art by breaking it apart into its individual shapes and then removing pieces you do not need, capturing just the shapes you need, changing or recoloring shapes, rotating shapes, and combining shapes from several clip art objects to create a new clip art object. It takes a lot of talent to create original clip art by drawing and combining shapes, but it takes only a little imagination to create a picture from existing clip art. Figure 3.43 shows a clip art image available from Microsoft Online by searching for the keyword *picnic*. The clip art was broken apart, the fireworks, flag, fries, and tablecloth removed, the hamburger, hotdogs, and milkshake flipped and resized, and finally the chocolate milkshake recolored so that it became a strawberry milkshake.

Figure 3.43 Modified Clip Art

Resizing objects is the most common modification procedure, and you already have learned to resize an object by dragging a sizing handle. You may need a more precise method of changing size, however. For example, you use PowerPoint to create an advertisement for an automobile trader magazine, and the magazine specifies that the ad must fit in a 2" by 2" space. You must size your photograph exactly to fit the requirement. You can enter an exact height and width measurement for your photographic object or an exact proportion of its original size.

To enter an exact measurement, select the object, and then click Format, which is located under any of the Tools contextual tabs (such as Drawing Tools, SmartArt Tools, Picture Tools, Chart Tools, and so on). The Size group is located at the far right of any of the Format tabs and contains boxes to quickly change the Height and Width. It also contains a Size Dialog Box Launcher that opens the Size and Position dialog box with many more options.

The Size tab in the Size and Position dialog box contains a section for entering exact measurements for Height and Width and a precise Rotation angle, a section for scaling an object based on its original size (note that not all clip art entered from the Clip Organizer is brought in at full size), a section that enables you to *crop* unwanted parts off the image, and a section that restores the object to its original size, which you engage by clicking a Reset button. To keep the original height and width proportions of a clip, make sure the *Lock aspect ratio* check box is selected. *Aspect ratio* refers to the width-to-height ratio of an image. The clip art image in Figure 3.44 was sized to 265% of its original size.

Cropping an image means to reduce its size by removing unwanted portions of an image.

Aspect ratio refers to the ratio of width to height.

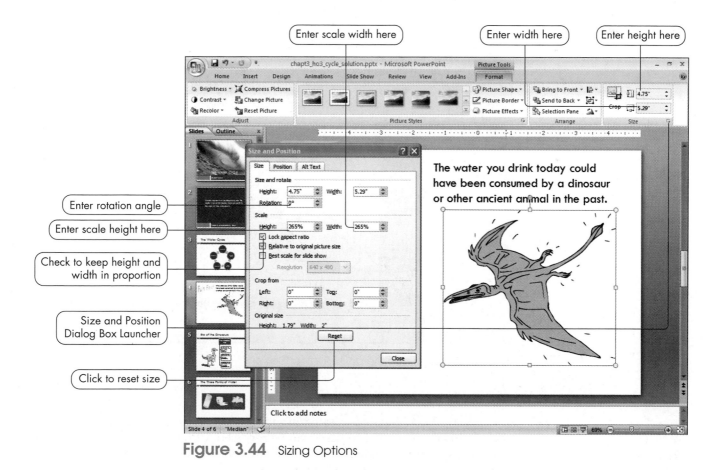

Figure 3.44 Sizing Options

Flip and Rotate

Sometimes, you will find that an object is facing the wrong way. It might be facing off the slide when you need it to face text, or perhaps it is at an angle and you need it to be level. Perhaps you took a photograph with your digital camera sideways to get a full-length view, but when you download the image it is sideways. You can quickly rotate the object left or right 90°, flip it horizontally or vertically, or freely rotate it any number of degrees.

You can freely rotate a selected object by dragging the green rotation handle that appears at the top of the object in the direction that you want to rotate. To constrain the rotation to 15-degree angles, hold down Shift while dragging. To rotate exactly 90° to the left or the right, click Rotate in the Arrange group on the Format tab under the Tools contextual tab.

When you click Rotate, you can choose to flip the object vertically or horizontally so that you can get a mirror-image of an object. If you prefer, you can drag one of the side sizing handles over the opposite side to flip it. If you do not drag far enough, however, you will distort the image. Figure 3.45 shows a clip art image that has been flipped.

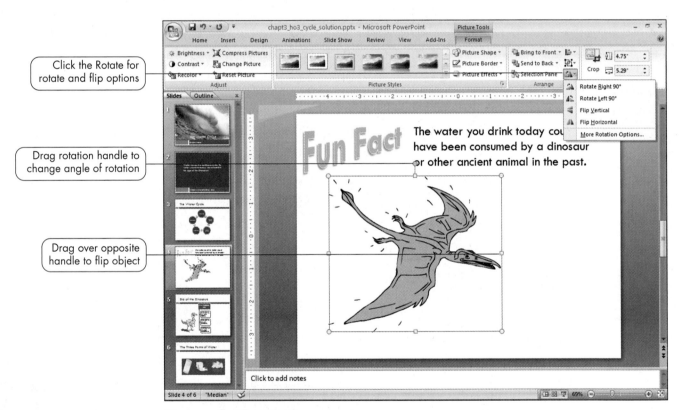

Figure 3.45 Rotating and Flipping Options

Group and Ungroup Objects

A clip art object usually is created in pieces, layered, and then grouped to create the final clip art image. This process can be reversed. Clip art can be ungrouped, or broken apart so the individual pieces can be modified or deleted. *Grouping* enables multiple objects to act or move as though they were a single object, while *ungrouping* lets individual shapes move.

In order for a clip art image to be ungrouped and grouped, it must be created and saved as a vector graphic. *Vector graphics* are created using geometrical formulas to represent images and are created in drawing programs such as Adobe Illustrator and CorelDRAW. The advantage of vector files is that they can be easily edited, can be layered, and use a small amount of storage space. Microsoft's Clip Organizer contains Microsoft Windows Metafile (.wmf) clip art, which are vector graphics.

Grouping is combining two or more objects.

Ungrouping is breaking a combined object into individual objects.

A **vector graphic** is an object-oriented graphic based on geometric formulas.

Clip art inserted from the Clip organizer needs to be converted into a drawing object as the first step of editing. Right-click the clip art image on the slide, and then click Edit Picture. A message appears asking if you want to convert the picture into a drawing object. Click Yes. This action converts and ungroups the clip so individual pieces can be modified. Complex clip art images may have more than one grouping, however. The artist may create an image from individual shapes, group it, layer it on other images, and then group it again. Figure 3.46 is an example of a complex Microsoft Windows Metafile that has multiple groups.

Figure 3.46 Complex Clip Art with Multiple Groups

To continue ungrouping, select the clip, and then click Format under Drawing Tools. The Group option becomes active in the Arrange group. Click Group, and if the clip art image can be broken down further, the Ungroup option is active and Group and Regroup are grayed out. Click Ungroup and each individual shape is surrounded by adjustment handles. Click outside of the clip art borders to deselect the shapes, and then click the individual shape you wish to change. Figure 3.47 shows a clip art graphic that has been repeatedly ungrouped until only individual objects are left.

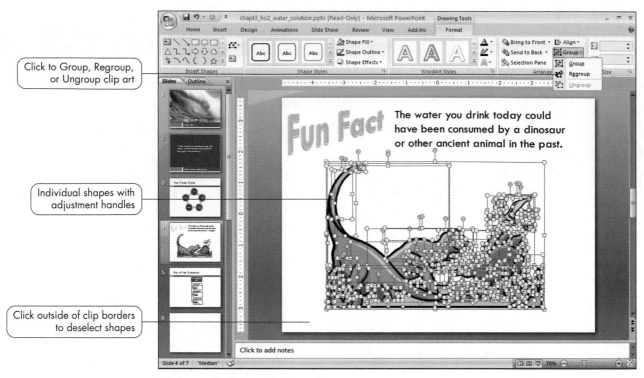

Figure 3.47 Ungrouped Complex Clip Art

When working with the individual shapes of a clip art image, it is helpful to zoom in on the clip art. Zooming helps you make sure you have the correct shape before you make your modifications. Once you select the shape, you can make all the modifications we discussed in the earlier part of this chapter. Figure 3.48 shows a selected shape that has had its fill changed to a theme color. Once you have made all of your needed changes, drag a marquee around all the shapes of the image and Group or Regroup the image. If you do not group the image, you risk moving the individual pieces inadvertently.

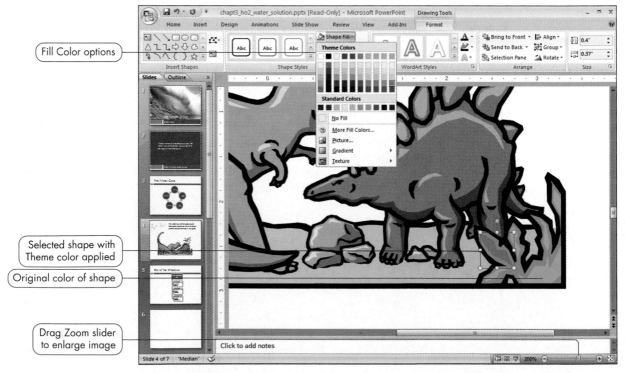

Figure 3.48 Modifying Ungrouped Shapes

Recolor Pictures

The colors in an image can be changed quickly using the Recolor Picture option. This option enables you to match your image to the color scheme of your presentation without taking the time to ungroup the image and change the color of each shape in the image. You can select either a dark or a light variation of your color scheme depending on which fits your color scheme and need.

You also can change the color mode of your picture to Grayscale, Sepia, Washout, or Black and White. Grayscale changes your picture to up to 256 shades of gray. Sepia gives you that popular golden tone often used for an "old-time" photo look. Washout is good for creating watermarks, while Black and White is a way to reduce image colors to straight black and white and simplify an image. Figure 3.49 shows two images from the Clip Organizer that have been changed using the Recolor Picture option.

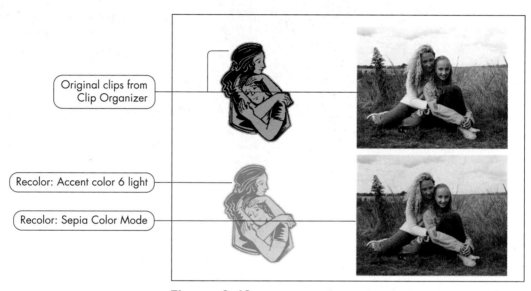

Original clips from Clip Organizer

Recolor: Accent color 6 light

Recolor: Sepia Color Mode

Figure 3.49 Recolored Images

To recolor clip art and pictures, click Recolor in the Picture Tools group on the Format tab. The gallery that opens provides options for Color Modes, and Dark Variations or Light Variations. It also has an option for No Recolor, which allows you to reset the picture to its original color. Click More Variations, and the color gallery opens so you can pick between Theme Colors, Standard Colors, Recent Colors, or More Colors so you can customize the color used. Figure 3.50 shows the recoloring options.

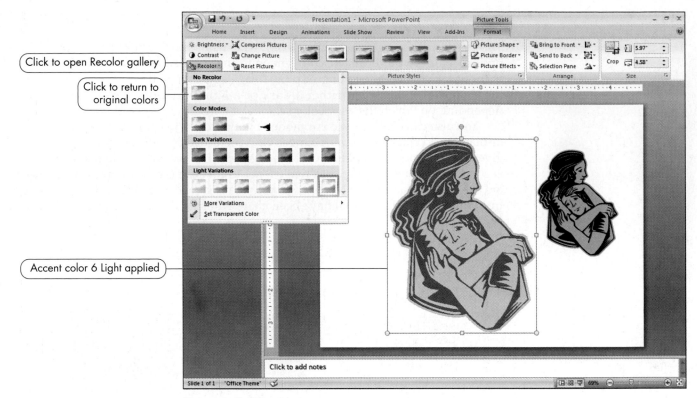

Figure 3.50 Recolored Images

The last option in the Recolor Gallery is the Set Transparent Color control. This feature is extremely valuable for creating a transparent area in most pictures. When you click Set Transparent Color, the pointer changes shape and includes an arrowhead for pointing. Drag the pointer until the arrowhead is pointing directly at the color you wish to make transparent, and then click. The color becomes transparent so that anything underneath shows through. In Figure 3.51, a frame from the Clip Organizer has been placed on top of an image taken with a digital camera. The white background of the frame blocks the image, however. A duplicate of the image and the frame shows the result of using the Set Transparent Color option to make the white background transparent.

Figure 3.51 Set Transparent Color

Pointer changes to this shape

Click to set Transparent Color

Frame clip art layered on top of image

White background made transparent

Arranging Objects

When you have multiple objects such as placeholders, clip art, SmartArt, WordArt, or other objects on the page, it can become challenging to arrange them. Positioning the objects can be time consuming, too. Fortunately, PowerPoint has several features that will help you control the order of the objects, the position of the objects, and how the objects align to each other and the slide. Before using any of these features, however, you must select the object(s). The ***Selection Pane*** is a pane designed to help you select objects. It contains a list of all objects on the slide. You click any object on the list to select it, and once it is selected, you can make the desired change. Click Selection Pane in the Arrange group on the Picture Tools Format tab to open the Selection Pane if an object is selected. If an object is not selected, click the Home tab, and then click Select in the Editing group. Click Selection Pane.

The ***Selection Pane*** is a pane designed to help select objects.

Order Objects

Shapes can be placed under or on top of each other. Think of this idea as layering the objects. For example, the bottom layer of a sandwich is bread. The meat may come next or the tomato. The top layer is more bread. The order of the layers is called the ***stacking order***. PowerPoint puts shapes or other objects in a stacking order as you add them to the slide. The last shape you place on the slide is on top and is the highest in the stacking order. Clip art images are comprised of shapes that have been stacked. Once you ungroup a clip art image and modify it, you may need to change the stacking order. You can open the Selection Pane to see the order in which objects are placed. The topmost object on the list is at the top of the stacking order.

The ***stacking order*** is the order of objects placed on top of each other.

To change the order of a stack of shapes, select one of the shapes, and then click Format under the Drawing Tools contextual tab. The Arrange group that appears on the Format tab includes options for controlling the location of the shape in the stacking order. Clicking the arrow next to Bring to Front opens a submenu that includes the Bring to Front option, which lets you move the shape all the way to the top of the stacking order, and Bring Forward that lets you move the shape up one layer.

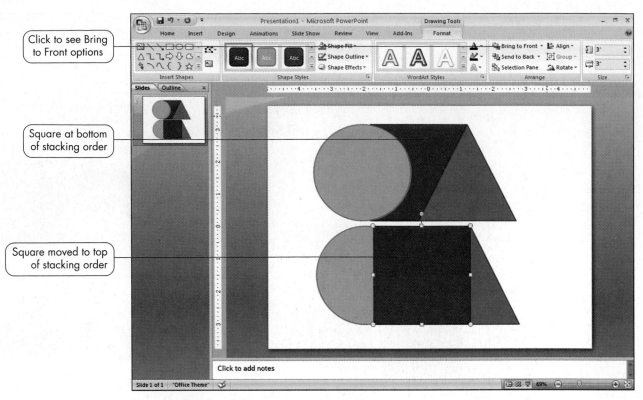

Figure 3.52 Change Stacking Order

TIP Quick Ways to Good Order

You can right-click a shape and select Bring to Front or Send to Back. Using this method, you can still choose whether to move one layer or all layers. You also can open the Selection Pane, select the object, and click Up or Down Re-Order to move the object up the list or down the list.

Similarly, the Send to Back option enables you to move the shape all the way to the bottom of the stacking order or back one layer. Figure 3.52 shows the results of changing a square at the bottom of a stacking order to the top of a stacking order.

Align Objects

Sometimes you need to position objects precisely on the slide. For example, you need a series of boxes aligned at their tops, or you need to adjust the amount of space between the boxes so that they are evenly spaced. PowerPoint has rulers, a grid, and drawing guides that enable you to complete the aligning process quickly.

A ***grid*** is a set of intersecting lines used to align objects.

Underlying each slide is a ***grid*** containing intersecting lines similar to what you would see on traditional graph paper. While normally the grid is nonprinting and nonviewable, you can activate the grid view and use the viewable grid to align your objects and to keep them evenly spaced. When you activate the grid view, the grid still will not be seen when in Slide Show view and cannot be printed. PowerPoint's rulers also can be used to help keep your objects aligned because they enable you to see the exact distance between shapes or to see size. To view the grid and the ruler, click the View tab and click the check boxes for Gridlines or Ruler.

By default, objects snap to the gridlines and measurement lines on the rulers. The Snap to feature forces an object to align with the grid by either the object's center point or the edge of the object, whichever is closest to the gridline. If you prefer, you can change the setting so that objects snap to other objects as well as or instead of the grid. You can also turn the Snap to feature off. To change the grid settings, select an

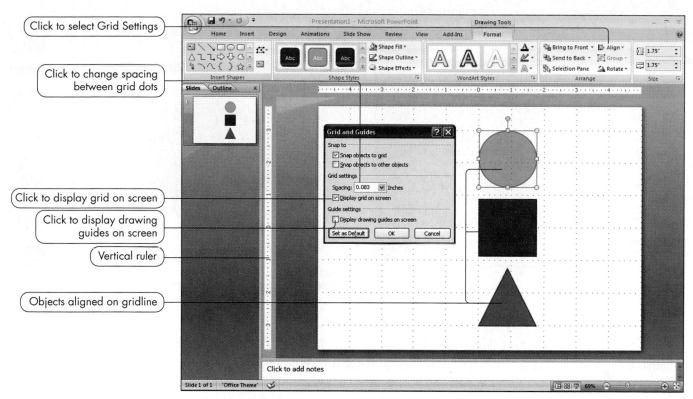

Click to select Grid Settings

Click to change spacing between grid dots

Click to display grid on screen

Click to display drawing guides on screen

Vertical ruler

Objects aligned on gridline

Figure 3.53 Grid and Guide Settings

TIP Overriding Snap-to

To temporarily override the snap-to feature so that you can freely drag an object to any position, press Alt as you drag.

A *guide* is a straight horizontal or vertical line used to align objects.

object, click Align on the Format tab under Drawing Tools, and then click Grid Settings. Figure 3.53 displays the Grid and Guides dialog box options.

Guides are nonprinting vertical or horizontal lines that you can place on a page to help you align objects or determine regions of the slide. For example, you can use guides to mark margins on a page. When you first display the guides, you see two guides that intersect at the center of the slide (the zero setting on both the horizontal and vertical rulers). To move a guide, position your cursor over it and drag. A directional arrow will appear as well as a measurement telling you the distance from the center point you are moving the guide. To create additional guides, press Ctrl+Shift while dragging. To remove guides, drag them off the slide. Refer to Figure 3.53 to see how to display guides. Figure 3.54 displays the default guides and the creation of a new guide.

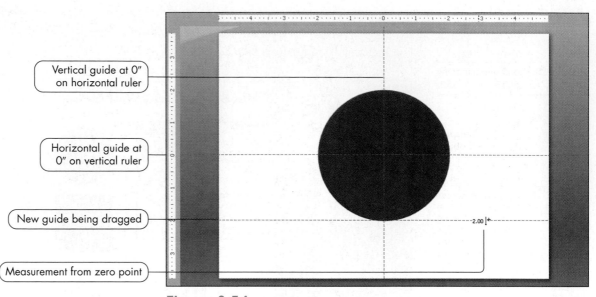

Figure 3.54 Creating a Guide

To **align** is to arrange in a line or so as to be parallel.

The *Align* feature makes it simple to line up shapes and objects in several ways. You can align with other objects by lining up the sides, middles, or top or bottom edges of objects. Or, if you have only one object or group selected, you can align in relation to the entire slide—for example, at the top or left edge of a slide. To align selected objects, click Align on the Format tab under Drawing Tools. When the alignment options display, choose whether you want to align to the slide or to align objects to one another. After you have determined whether you want to align to the slide or to each other, determine how you want to align using the align options.

To **distribute** is to divide or evenly spread over a given area.

The Align feature also includes options to *distribute* selected shapes evenly over a given area. Perhaps you have shapes on the page but one is too close to another, and another is too far away. You want to have an equal amount of space between all the shapes. After selecting the shapes, click Align in the Arrange group on the Format tab under Drawing Tools. Then select Distribute Horizontally or Distribute Vertically. Figure 3.55 shows three shapes that have been aligned at their middles, aligned to the middle of the slide, and distributed horizontally so that the space between them is equidistant.

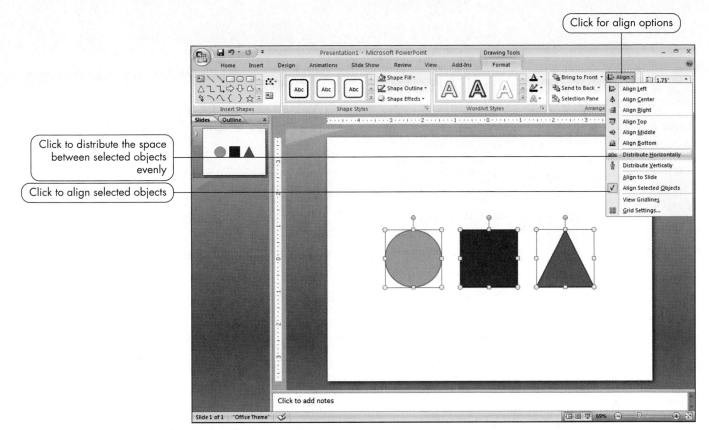

Figure 3.55 Alignment Options

Hands-On Exercises

3 | Modifying and Arranging Clip Art

Skills covered: 1. Size and Position Clip Art **2.** Flip Clip Art **3.** Ungroup, Modify, and Regroup Clip Art **4.** Recolor a Picture **5.** Reorder Shapes **6.** Align and Distribute Clip Art

<table>
<tr>
<td>

Step 1
Size and Position Clip Art

</td>
<td>

Refer to Figure 3.56 as you complete Step 1.

a. Open the *chap3_ho2_water_solution* presentation, and then immediately save it as **chap3_ho3_cycle_solution**.

b. Move to **Slide 4**, click the **Insert tab**, and then click **Clip Art** in the Illustrations group.

c. Type **pterodactyls** in the **Search for** box, and then click **Go**.

Entering the keyword *pterodactyls* narrowed your search more than entering the generic keyword *dinosaurs* would.

d. Click the clip art image containing several dinosaurs, as shown in Figure 3.56, and then close the Clip Art Organizer.

The clip art image is inserted in the center of Slide 4.

e. Click to select the clip art image, if necessary, and then click **Format** under Picture Tools.

f. Click the **Size and Position Dialog Box Launcher** in the Size group.

The Size and Position Dialog Box Launcher has a small arrow on it and is on the far right of the Format tab. When you click it, the Size and Position dialog box appears.

g. Type **4.5** in the **Height** box, and then click in the **Width** box.

The width of the image changes to 6.66, keeping the image in proportion. The proportion is kept because the **Lock aspect ratio** check box is checked.

h. Click the **Position tab**, and then type **1.67"** in the **Horizontal box** in the *Position on slide* section and **2.25"** in the **Vertical box**. Then click **Close**.

i. Save the *chap3_ho3_cycle_solution* presentation.

</td>
</tr>
</table>

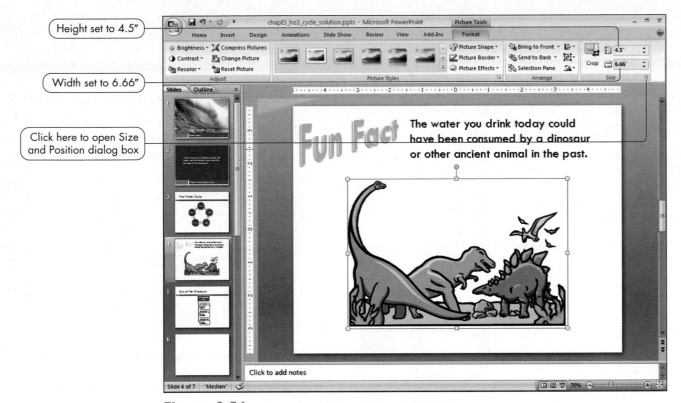

Figure 3.56 Resized and Repositioned Clip Art

Step 2
File Clip Art

Refer to Figure 3.57 as you complete Step 2.

a. With the *chap3_ho3_cycle* presentation open, click the dinosaur clip art.

b. Click **Rotate** in the Arrange group on the Format tab under Picture Tools.

   The rotate and flip options appear.

c. Click **Flip Horizontal**.

d. Click **Rotate** in the Arrange group on the Format tab under Picture Tools, and then click **More Rotation Options**.

e. Type **180** in the **Rotation** box, and then click **Close**.

   The picture rotates upside down.

f. Click **Rotate** in the Arrange group on the Format tab under Picture Tools, and then click **Flip Vertical**.

   The clip art picture appears to be in its original position, but the rotation angle is still set at 180°. You can tell when a picture has been rotated, but not when it has been flipped.

g. Save the *chap3_ho3_cycle_solution* presentation.

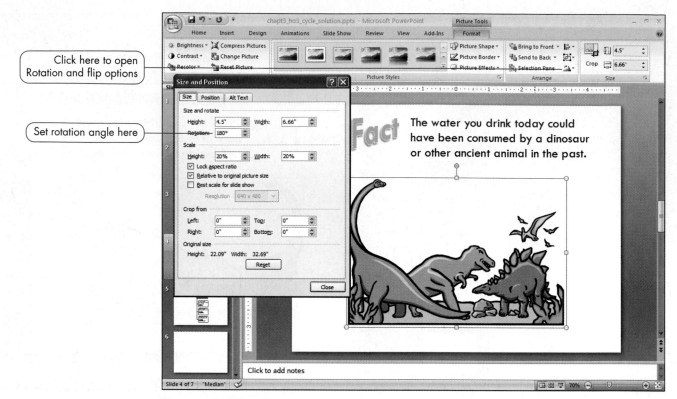

Click here to open Rotation and flip options

Set rotation angle here

Figure 3.57 Flipping and Rotating

Step 3
Ungroup, Modify, and Regroup clip Art

Refer to Figures 3.58 and 3.59 as you complete Step 3.

a. With the *chap3_ho3_cycle_solution* presentation open, right-click on the dinosaur clip art.

b. Select **Edit Picture**, and then click **Yes** when the Microsoft Office PowerPoint information message box appears.

When you click Yes, your picture is turned into a drawing object. After this conversion, you will not be able to use picture tools on the picture, but will be able to use drawing tools. The image has been converted to a drawing object, but it is still grouped. Now you must ungroup the image to modify individual pieces.

c. Select **Format** under Drawing Tools, and then click **Group** in the Arrange group.

d. Select **Ungroup**, and then click outside the clip art border.

When you ungroup the clip art, each shape comprising the image is selected and surrounded with adjustment handles. Clicking outside the border deselects the shapes so that you can select just the one you wish to modify.

e. Drag the **Zoom slider** to **200%**, and then drag the scroll bars to locate the plants in the bottom right of the clip art.

Zooming in makes it easier to select the individual shape you wish to modify.

f. Select one of the bright green shapes in the plant, click **Shape Fill**, and then click **Green, Accent 5, Lighter 60%**.

You wish to change the bright green in the original clip art to a color that matches your theme color.

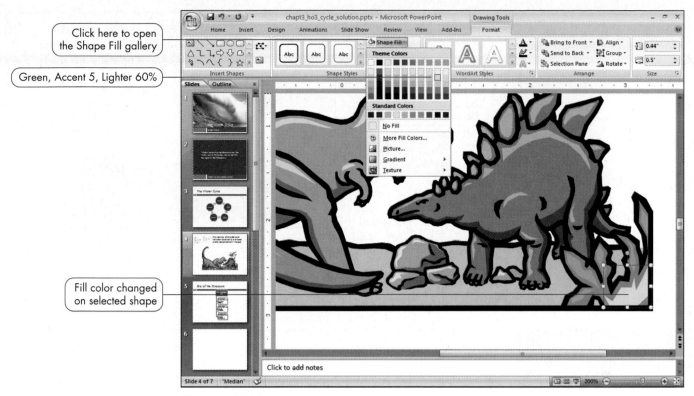

Figure 3.58 Change Fill Color

g. Change the color fill of each of the bright green shapes in the plants on both sides of the clip art to **Green, Accent 5, Lighter 60%**.

You do not have to keep opening the Shape Fill dialog box to apply the color to your shapes. The fill bucket immediately to the left of the Shape Fill command now reflects your color choice. Simply click it to apply the color to selected shapes.

h. Click the **View tab**, and then click **Fit to Window** in the Zoom group.

i. Drag a selection net around the four pterodactyls in the clip art.

Ctrl-clicking the pterodactyls would be time consuming because of the many shapes involved. Dragging a selection net that completely encompasses shapes is a more efficient method for selecting multiple shapes.

j. Drag the pterodactyl shapes up approximately ½" to reposition them.

k. Drag a selection net around all of the shapes making the dinosaur clip art, then click the **Format tab** under Drawing Tools, click **Group**, and then click **Regroup**.

l. Save the *chap3_ho3_cycle_solution* presentation.

Fun Fact The water you drink today could have been consumed by a dinosaur or other ancient animal in the past.

Pterodactyl shapes moved

Plant fills changed to theme color

Figure 3.59 Modified Clip Art

Step 4
Recolor a Picture

Refer to Figure 3.60 as you complete Step 4.

a. Move to **Slide 5** of the *chap3_ho3_cycle_solution* presentation.

b. Click the **Insert tab** and click **Clip Art** in the Illustrations group.

c. Type **coelophysis** in the **Search for** box, and then click **Go**.

d. Drag the thumbnail of the Coelophysis to the bottom left of your slide and release, and then close the Clip Art Organizer.

e. Click **Format** located under Picture Tools.

Because the clip art has not been converted to a drawing object, you can use the picture tools to modify it. Recoloring an image does not require clip art to be ungrouped.

f. Click **Recolor** in the Picture Adjust group.

g. Click **Accent color 1 Light** in the Light Variations category.

The colors in the clip art are recolored to those contained in the color theme.

h. Save the *chap3_ho3_cycle_solution* presentation.

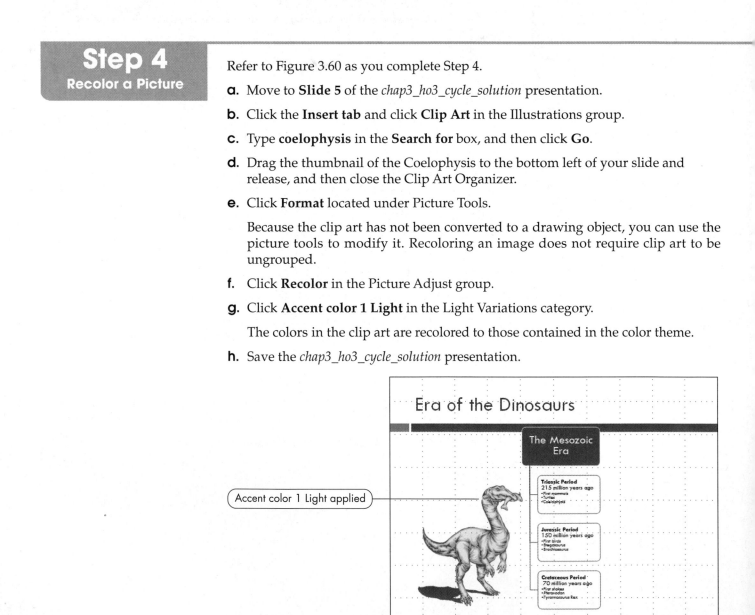

Accent color 1 Light applied

Figure 3.60 Recolored Picture

Refer to Figure 3.62 as you complete Step 5.

a. Move to **Slide 6** of the *chap3_ho3_cycle_solution* presentation.

b. Click the **View tab**, and then click **Ruler** in the Show/Hide group (if necessary).

The horizontal and vertical rulers appear. We will use the rulers to help us create a shape in a specific size.

c. Click the **Insert tab**, click **Shapes** in the Illustrations group, and then click **Rectangle**.

d. Position the cross-hair pointer on the first 4" mark on the horizontal ruler (–4) and the first 1" mark on the vertical ruler.

This is the beginning point for the rectangle we draw. See Figure 3.61 for help identifying the beginning location.

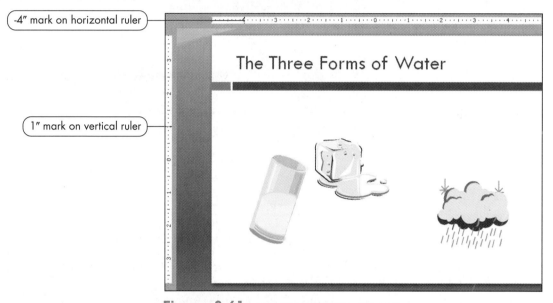

Figure 3.61 Locating Position Using Rulers

e. Drag to the last 4" mark on the horizontal ruler and the last 2" mark on the vertical ruler (–2), and then release.

A large rectangle shape in the theme color is created on top of the clip art on the slide. You will use the rectangle as a background for the clip art. Currently, it is hiding the clip art, however, and must be reordered.

f. Click **Send to Back** in the Arrange group on the Format tab, and then click **Send to Back**.

g. Save the *chap3_ho3_cycle_solution* presentation.

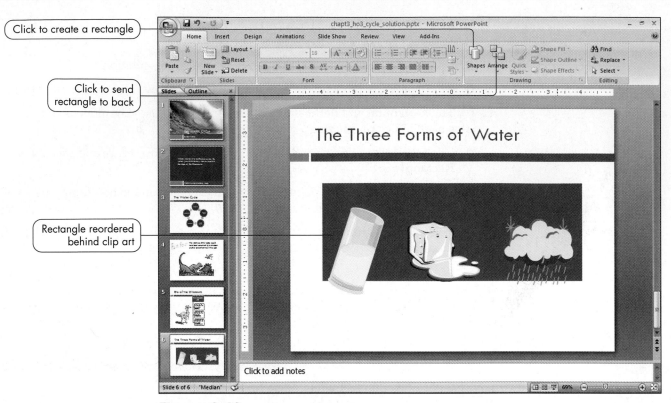

Click to create a rectangle

Click to send rectangle to back

Rectangle reordered behind clip art

Figure 3.62 A Rectangle Background

Step 6
Align and Distribute Clip Art

Refer to Figure 3.63 as you complete Step 6.

a. With the *chap3_ho3_cycle_solution* presentation open, press **Ctrl** as you click each clip art image.

Holding down Ctrl while clicking each clip art image enables you to select all three.

b. Click **Align** in the Arrange group on the Format tab under Drawing Tools.

The align options appear. You need to align the objects by their middles. You do not click center because that would align the objects by their centers and they would appear on top of each other.

c. Click **Align Middle**.

d. Click **Align** and click **Distribute Horizontally**.

PowerPoint adjusts the distances between objects so that they are distributed equally.

e. Click **Group** in the Arrange group on the Format tab under Drawing Tools, and then click **Group**.

The three clip art images are grouped and become a complex picture. Individual handles around the objects are replaced with a single set of handles surrounding all three images.

f. Press **Shift**, and then click the blue rectangle.

Pressing Shift while clicking adds the object to the selection. The rectangle and the clip art group are now both in the selection.

g. Click **Align** in the Arrange group on the Format tab under Drawing Tools, and then click **Align Middle**.

h. Deselect the objects.

i. Create a Notes and Handouts Header and Footer with your name in the header and your instructor's name and your class in the footer.

j. View the presentation and print as directed by your instructor.

k. Save the *chap3_ho3_cycle_solution* presentation and close it.

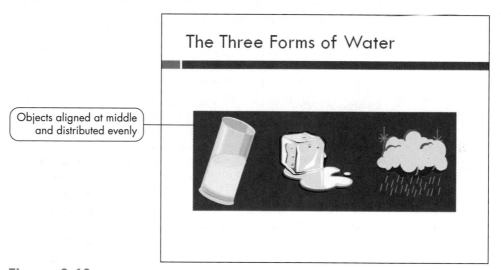

Figure 3.63 The Completed Slide

Summary

1. **Create shapes.** You can use shapes to highlight information, as a design element, or as the basis for creating clip art illustrations. PowerPoint provides tools for creating shapes as well as tools to help size and position shapes.

2. **Apply Quick Styles and customize shapes.** A shape can be customized by changing its default fill to another color, a picture, a gradient, a texture, or no fill. The shape outline color, weight, or dash style can be modified. Special effects such as shadows, reflections, and glows also may be added. Applying a Quick Style enables you to apply preset options. The vertexes of shapes also can be edited to change the form of the shape.

3. **Create SmartArt.** SmartArt graphics are diagrams that present information visually to effectively communicate your message. SmartArt graphics are organized into seven categories: lists, processes, cycles, hierarchies, relationships, matrices, and pyramids. SmartArt diagrams also may be created from existing text.

4. **Modify SmartArt diagrams.** Once created, SmartArt can be modified to include additional shapes or to have shapes deleted, a SmartArt style applied, the color scheme revised, or special effects added. The direction of the SmartArt can be changed. SmartArt can be resized and repositioned.

5. **Create WordArt.** WordArt is text with decorative effects applied in order to draw attention to the text. Select a WordArt style, and then type the text you desire. A Quick Styles gallery provides you with multiple WordArt styles that can be applied to the WordArt text.

6. **Modify WordArt.** WordArt can be modified by transforming the shape of the text and by applying special effects and colors. The shape of the WordArt can be warped and applied to a path. The text created as WordArt can be edited. Among the many special effects available are 3-D presets and rotations.

7. **Modify objects.** Objects may be flipped horizontally or vertically, or they can be rotated by dragging the green rotation handle that appears with selected objects. Vector clip art can be ungrouped so basic shapes can be customized, and then objects can be regrouped so they can be moved as one object. Pictures can be recolored by changing their color mode or by applying a dark or light variation of a theme color or custom color.

8. **Arrange objects.** Objects are stacked in layers. The object at the top of the layer is the one that fully displays, while other objects in the stack may have some portions blocked by other objects. The stacking order of shapes can be reordered so that objects can be seen as desired. Features such as rulers, grids, guides, align, and distribute can be used to arrange objects on a slide and arrange objects in relation to one another.

Key Terms

Multiple Choice

1. Shapes are:

   (a) Images that you create by typing in a key word in the Shape Clip Organizer, and then clicking the shape you desire.

   (b) A collection of graphical shapes, such as lines, arrows, and squares, that you add by using the Shapes gallery.

   (c) A category of clip art that includes pictures with a motor theme.

   (d) Shapes that you create by clicking in the Shape group under Design.

2. You insert a lightning bolt shape on your slide and want to rotate it. You:

   (a) Drag the green handle at the top of the image.

   (b) Drag one of the corner adjustment handles.

   (c) Double-click the lightning bolt and enter the number of degrees you want the shape to rotate.

   (d) Do nothing because Shapes cannot be rotated.

3. The relationship between the height and width of a shape is referred to as:

   (a) Proportion ration

   (b) Rotation aspect

   (c) Size ratio

   (d) Aspect ratio

4. Which of the following is a reason for grouping shapes?

   (a) To be able to individually change each shape individually

   (b) To move or modify the objects as one

   (c) To connect the shapes with connectors

   (d) To create a relationship diagram

5. Which of the following is a reason for ungrouping a clip art object?

   (a) To be able to individually change shapes used to create the composite image

   (b) To move the objects as one

   (c) To add text on top of the group

   (d) To resize the group as one piece

6. Which of the following features would you use on an ungrouped clip art image after completing your modifications?

   (a) Connector lines

   (b) Combine

   (c) Regroup

   (d) Join together

7. You have inserted a clip art image of the ocean with a palm tree on the right side of the beach. If you flip the image vertically, what would the resulting image look like?

   (a) The image would show right side up, but the palm tree would be on the left side.

   (b) The image would be upside down with the palm tree pointing down.

   (c) The image would be rotated 90 degrees, and the palm tree would be on the bottom.

   (d) The image would be rotated 270 degrees, and the palm tree would be at the top.

8. Which of the following might be a reason for changing the stacking order of shapes?

   (a) To show a relationship by placing shapes in front of or behind each other

   (b) To hide something on a shape

   (c) To uncover something hidden by another shape

   (d) All of the above

9. You stack three shapes on top of each other on a slide by inserting a large square on the page, then a small circle, and then a large triangle. Which shape will be on the top of the stacking order?

   (a) The square because you added it first

   (b) The circle because curves show above angles

   (c) The triangle because it was added last

   (d) The circle because it is small and would be hidden by the triangle

10. In the above example, how would you move the triangle to the bottom of the stacking order?

    (a) In the Arrange group, click Align, and then Align bottom.

    (b) In the Design group, click Shape Fill, and then Move Backward.

    (c) In the Arrange group, click Send to Back, and then Send Backward.

    (d) In the Arrange group, click Send to Back, and then Send to Back.

11. A Microsoft Windows Metafile (.wmf) is a vector object created by:

    (a) Rastors

    (b) Bits

    (c) Mathematical formulas

    (d) Pixels

Multiple Choice

12. Which of the following features does not help with arranging objects on a slide?

    (a) Cascade
    (b) Rulers
    (c) Grid
    (d) Guides

13. Which of the following is not available from the SmartArt gallery?

    (a) Periodic table
    (b) Pyramid diagram
    (c) Process graphic
    (d) Matrix block

14. Which of the following SmartArt graphics displays objects in a continual process?

    (a) Hierarchy
    (b) Cycle
    (c) List
    (d) Relationship

15. You are trying to align a shape directly on top of another, but it always jumps above or below where you need to place it. What feature should you deactivate in order to accomplish this task?

    (a) Align to
    (b) Snap to
    (c) AutoAlign
    (d) Line Snap

1 Create and Modify Shapes

Your *sensei* (teacher) has asked for your aid in creating a narrated slide show on Judo that prospective students can view in a small room—a special place reserved for visitors when they first visit the *dojo* (training hall). You want to introduce visitors to the wisdom of Judo in a strong, visual way, but you want the slide show to demonstrate the principles of simplicity. To follow the principle of simplicity, you wish to avoid bullet points and text. You want the show to have empty space and a tranquil feel. Figure 3.64 displays the third slide in a slide show on Judo that uses shapes, SmartArt, and modified clip art.

a. Open the *chap3_pe1_judo* file and save it as **chap3_pe1_judo_solution**.
b. Move to **Slide 3**, click the **Insert tab**, and then click **Shapes** in the Illustrations group to open the Shapes gallery.
c. Right-click the **Rounded Rectangle** shape, and then select the **Lock Drawing Mode**.
d. Position the pointer on the slide and drag to create a long rounded rectangle. Repeat this process so you have two rounded rectangles on the slide.
e. Select the rounded rectangle on the left and type **Maximum Efficiency**.
f. Select the rounded rectangle on the right and type **Mutual Welfare and Benefit**.
g. Select the **Elbow Double-Arrow Connector** in the Lines grouping of the Shapes gallery, move your pointer over the rounded rectangle on the left, and then position the cross-hair on the right center red handle.
h. Drag a connecting line that attaches the right, center, red connecting handle on the left rounded rectangle to the right, center, red connecting handle on the right rounded rectangle.
i. With the connector selected, click **Shape Outline** in the Shape Styles group on the Format tab, and then click **Red, Accent 1** under Theme Colors.
j. Click **Shape Outline**, click **Weight**, and then click **1½ pt**.
k. Click the left rounded rectangle, and then press **Ctrl** as you click the right rounded rectangle.
l. Click **Shape Fill**, click **More Fill Colors**, and then set the **Transparency** to 20%.
m. With both shapes still selected, change the **Height** of the shapes to 3" and the **Width** to **1.5"** by clicking the spin boxes in the Size group located on the Format tab under **Drawing Tools**.
n. Save the *chap3_pe1_judo_solution* file and keep it onscreen if you plan to continue to the next exercise. Close the file and exit PowerPoint if you do not want to continue to the next exercise at this time.

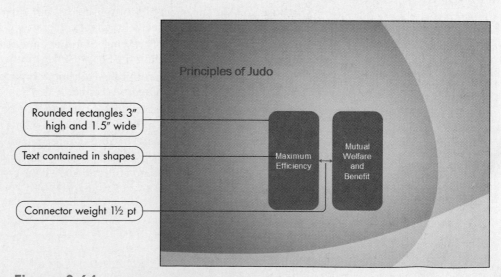

Figure 3.64 Use Shapes for Illustrations

...continued on Next Page

You decide to create a slide showing the techniques used in Judo. Because Judo is a form of wrestling that emphasizes throws and pins, you create a Hierarchy SmartArt diagram to show the relationship between techniques. Figure 3.65 shows the SmartArt diagram after creation and modification.

a. Open the *chap3_pe1_judo_solution* file if you closed it after the last exercise and save it as **chap3_pe2_judo_solution**, and then move to **Slide 4**.

b. Click the **Home tab**, click **New Slide**, and then click **Blank**.

c. Click the **Insert tab**, click **Smart Art**, in the Illustrations group, and then click **Hierarchy** in the Choose a SmartArt Graphic dialog box.

d. Click the subtype **Hierarchy**, and then click **OK**.

e. Type **Judo Techniques** in the first level bullet of the Text pane.

f. Type the following Level 2 and Level 3 bullets in the Text pane:

- **Throwing (Nage)**
  - **Standing (Tachi)**
  - **Sacrifice (Sutemi)**

- **Grappling (Katame)**
  - **Holding (Osae Komi)**
  - **Choking (Shime)**
  - **Joint Locking (Kansetsu)**

- **Striking (Atemi)**
  - **Arm (Ude Ate)**
  - **Leg (Ashi Ate)**

- **Forms (Kata)**

g. Click the **More button** in the Layouts group on the Design tab under the SmartArt Tools contextual tab, and then click **Horizontal Labeled Hierarchy**.

h. Click **Format** under the SmartArt Tools contextual tab.

i. Click the **arrow** in the Size group, and then type **7** in the **Height** and **Width** boxes.

j. Drag the SmartArt to the left and up so that it fits on the slide.

k. Click the **Design tab**, and then click **Change Colors** in the Quick Styles group.

l. Click **Colorful Range – Accent Colors 5 to 6**.

Because you like the effect of multiple colors, but wish to highlight the relationship between techniques, you decide to change the individual fill colors of the shapes.

m. Press **Ctrl** as you click the Throwing, Standing, and Sacrifice boxes, and then click the **Format tab**, click **Shape Fill** in the Shape Styles group, and click **Red Accent 1**.

n. Press **Ctrl** as you click the Grappling, Holding, Choking, and Joint Locking boxes, click **Shape Fill**, and then click **Green Accent 5**.

o. Press **Ctrl** as you click the Striking, Arm, and Leg boxes, click **Shape Fill**, and then click **Orange Accent 6**.

p. Click **Design** under the SmartArt Tools contextual tab, and then click **Right to Left** in the Create Graphic group.

q. Save the *chap3_pe2_judo_solution* file and keep it onscreen if you plan to continue to the next exercise. Close the file and exit PowerPoint if you do not want to continue to the next exercise at this time.

...continued on Next Page

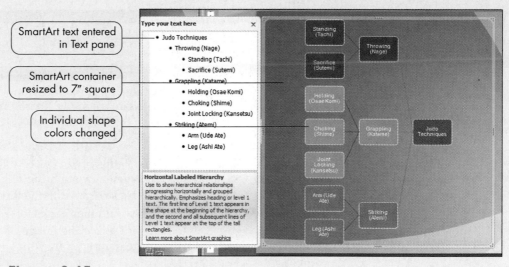

Figure 3.65 Create SmartArt

3 Convert Text to SmartArt

A Venn diagram is designed to show interconnected relationships. Using a SmartArt Venn graphic on the second slide of the slide show would emphasize how the three areas of Judo overlap to create a way of life. Figure 3.66 shows the text after it has been converted to SmartArt.

a. Open the *chap3_pe2_judo_solution* file if you closed it after the last exercise and save it as **chap3_pe3_judo_solution**, then move to **Slide 2**.

b. Click the placeholder containing the bullet points, and then click the **Home tab**.

c. Click **Convert to SmartArt Graphic** in the Paragraph group.

d. Click **Basic Venn**.

e. Click **Change Colors** in the Quick Styles group in the Design tab under SmartArt Tools.

f. Click **Colorful Range – Accent Colors 5 to 6**.

g. **Ctrl-click** each of the circles, and then click the **Format tab**.

h. Click **Text Fill** in the WordArt Styles group, and then click **White, Background 1**, which is the first option on the top row.

i. Save the *chap3_pe3_judo_solution* file and keep it onscreen if you plan to continue to the next exercise. Close the file and exit PowerPoint if you do not want to continue to the next exercise at this time.

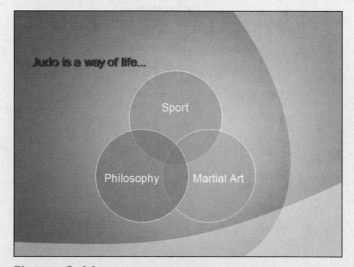

Figure 3.66 Venn Diagram

...continued on Next Page

The *judogi* is the traditional uniform used for Judo practice and competition. It is constructed of heavy-weight cotton and has heavy stitching for durability. You want to show a *judogi* being worn to show its flexibility. You found a clip art image in the Microsoft Clip Organizer, but it includes faces that you feel give a cartoony feel to the clip art. You decide to use the clip art, but want to modify it. Figure 3.67 shows the modified clip art.

a. Open the *chap3_pe3_judo_solution* file if you closed it after the last exercise and save it as **chap3_pe4_judo_solution**, then move to **Slide 4**.

b. Click the **Insert tab**, and then click **Clip Art** in the Illustrations group.

c. Type **judo** in the **Search for** box, and then click **Go**.

d. Refer to Figure 3.67 to help you locate the image of two fighting men in *judogi* uniforms, and then click the image to insert it on your slide. Close the Microsoft Clip Art Organizer.

e. Drag the **Zoom slider** in the bottom right side of your screen to **300%**.

f. Drag the scroll bars until you can see the faces on the fighters, right-click, and then click **Edit Picture**.

g. Click **Yes** to convert the picture into a drawing object.

h. Click the **Format tab** under **Drawing Tools**, and then click **Group** in the Arrange group.

i. Click **Ungroup**, and then click off the image to deselect the shapes.

j. **Ctrl-click** to select the lines and shapes that were used to create the eyebrows, eyes, and mouths on the two fighters, and then press **Delete**. Also delete the nose of the fighter on the right.

k. Click to select the purple shape composing the fighter on the left's hair, click **Format**, **Shape Fill**, and then click **Red, Accent 1, Darker 50%**.

l. Change the color of the two purple shapes composing the fighter on the right's hair to the same color as you changed the fighter's hair on the left.

m. Click the **View tab**, **Fit to Window**. If necessary, drag your scroll bars until the slide is visible.

n. Drag a selection net around all the shapes composing the clip art image, and click **Format, Group**, and then click **Regroup**.

o. Save the *chap3_pe4_judo_solution* file and keep it onscreen if you plan to continue to the next exercise.

Figure 3.67 Modified Clip Art

...continued on Next Page

You locate a picture in the Clip Art Organizer that you would like to add to the title slide. It does not match the theme color scheme, however. You use PowerPoint's Recolor feature to change the Color Mode of the image. Refer to Figure 3.68 when completing this exercise.

a. Open the *chap3_pe4_judo_solution* file if you closed it after the last exercise and save it as **chap3_pe5_judo_solution**, then move to Slide 1.

b. Click the **Insert tab** and click **Clip Art** in the Illustrations group.

c. Type **judo** in the **Search for** box, if necessary, and click **Go**.

d. Drag either the gold male or the gold female figure onto the slide, and then close the Clip Organizer.

e. Click the **Format tab** and click **Recolor** in the Picture Tools group.

f. Click **Grayscale**.

g. Type **3** in the **Height** box in the Size group on the Format tab.

h. Drag the clip art picture to the right side of the screen to maintain the asymmetrical design of the title slide.

i. Save the *chap3_pe5_judo_solution* file and keep it onscreen if you plan to continue to the next exercise.

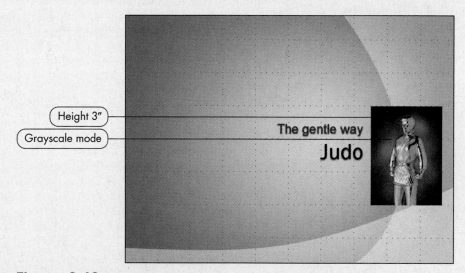

Figure 3.68 Recolored Clip Art

...continued on Next Page

When you viewed the judo clip art in the Clip Art Organizer, you liked the three clip art images with a stained glass effect. You decide that you will add them to your slide show after the slide on techniques because they show two kicks and a throw. Refer to Figure 3.69 as you complete this exercise.

a. Open the *chap3_pe5_judo_solution* file if you closed it after the last exercise and save it as **chap3_pe6_judo_solution**, then move to **Slide 5** and click the **Home tab**.

b. Click **New Slide** in the Slides group, and then click **Blank**.

c. Click the **Insert tab**, and then click **Clip Art** in the Illustrations group.

d. Type **judo** in the **Search for** box, if necessary, and click **Go.**

e. Drag the three stained glass judo pictures onto the slide.

f. Click the **View tab** and click **Gridlines**.

g. Click the clip art picture of the man kicking, and then drag it until its top left corner is aligned with the -4" mark on the horizontal ruler and the zero point on the vertical ruler. The border of the clip art picture will snap in place when released, so the image itself will look like it is slightly under the gridlines.

h. Press **Ctrl** as you click the picture of the woman kicking so that it is included in the selection with the man.

i. Click **Align** on the Format tab under Picture Tools, and then click **Align Left**.

j. If the picture of the woman is blocking the picture of the man, press **Shift** and drag upward until the picture of the man is no longer blocked.

k. Drag the last picture of the two men so it aligns on a grid point between the two previously positioned pictures.

l. Create a Notes and Handouts header and footer with the date and your name in the header and your instructor's name and your class in the footer.

m. View the slide show and print as directed by your instructor.

n. Save the *chap3_pe6_judo_solution* file and close the file.

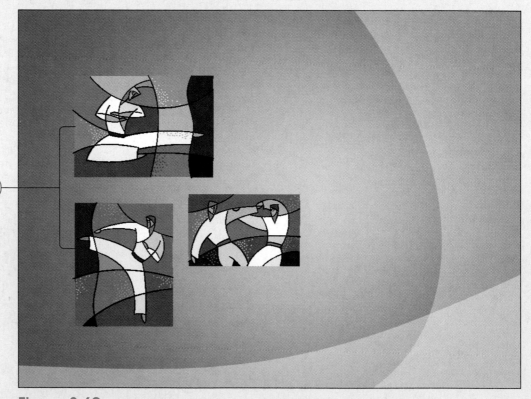

Left edges aligned

Figure 3.69 Clip Art Aligned

You have been asked to help train the employees of a new company who seem to be having difficulty with organizing and completing company projects. Because it is a small family-owned company, many of the employees are family members who are enthusiastic and have great ideas, but who need help seeing the process a project must go through before it is complete. You start the training by reviewing the Project Management Life Cycle at the next employee meeting. Use PowerPoint's SmartArt and Shapes as needed to prepare the illustrations for this presentation. Apply Quick Styles and make customizations to create a professional look for your presentation. The partial presentation is shown in Figure 3.70.

a. Open the *chap3_mid1_projmgt* file and immediately save it as **chap3_mid1_projmgt_solution**.

b. Move to **Slide 2** and insert a **Process SmartArt** diagram using the **Vertical Process** style.

c. Type the following points in the Text pane, and then close the Text pane.

  • **Project Initiation**

  • **Project Planning**

  • **Project Execution**

  • **Project Completion**

  • **Review and Evaluation**

d. Apply SmartArt Subtle Effect to the SmartArt.

Refer to Figure 3.70 to complete the following steps.

e. Create two rounded rectangles to the right of the SmartArt to demonstrate the cyclical nature of project execution. Apply **Moderate Effect – Accent 1** to the rectangles, and then apply Shape Fill color **Brown, Accent 3, Darker 25%**.

f. Type **Monitor** in one rounded rectangle shape, and then type **Adjust** in the other. Change the font color to black.

g. Change the Shape Fill color of the Project Execution shape to **Brown, Accent 3, Darker 25%**.

h. Create arrows between the three rounded rectangles to indicate the cycle. Change their weight to ¾ pt.

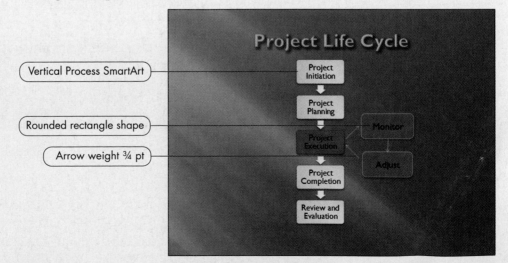

Figure 3.70 SmartArt Diagram of Project Life Cycle

...continued on Next Page

i. Move to **Slide 3** and create four shapes with the following specifications:

Shape	Fill	Position	Dimensions	Text
Rectangle 1	Subtle Effect, Accent 1	From Top Left Corner: Horizontal: 3.25" Vertical: 1.33"	Height: 3" Width: 2.17"	Project Initiation
Rectangle 2	Moderate Effect, Accent 3	From Top Left Corner: Horizontal: 1.58" Vertical: 3.83"	Height: 1.42" Width: 2.5"	Determine Project Purpose and Scope
Rectangle 3	Moderate Effect, Accent 3	From Top Left Corner: Horizontal: 4.58" Vertical: 3.83"	Height: 1.42" Width: 2.5"	Determine Boundaries
Up Arrow Callout	Moderate Effect, Accent 6	From Top Left Corner: Horizontal: 5.17" Vertical: 5.25"	Height: .92" Width: 3"	Conduct Feasibility Study

j. Move to **Slide 4** and create a **List SmartArt diagram** using the **Horizontal Bullet List style**.

k. Type the following in the Text pane:

- **Time**
  - **People**
  - **Facilities**
  - **Materials**
  - **Equipment**

l. Copy the text you entered and then paste it into the Text pane two times. Edit the first-level bullets so they read: **Time, Cost, Resources**.

m. Apply **Simple Fill** SmartArt style.

n. Create a Notes and Handouts Header and Footer with the date and your name in the header and your instructor's name and your class in the footer. Print as required by your teacher.

o. Save the *chap3_mid1_projmgt_solution* file and close the file.

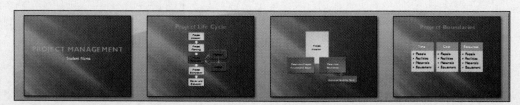

Figure 3.71 The Partially Completed Project Management Slide Show

...continued on Next Page

In this exercise, you practice your clip art modification and alignment skills. Being able to quickly modify clip art to fit your theme and topic is an essential skill for a PowerPoint professional to have, and the more you practice modifying clip art, the faster you will become at it. You need to be able to ungroup or disassemble clip art, delete unwanted objects, change shape colors, reposition shapes, and then regroup the shapes so they form one coherent image. You do not have to be an artist to have fun manipulating clip art. In this exercise, you manipulate a classic clip art cartoon that has been around almost as long as the microcomputer. While it serves as a humorous, fun image representing frustration on which to practice your object manipulation skills, remember that any image used in a slide show created with a message (not for practice) needs to relate to the topic. As to hitting a computer with a sledge hammer when frustrated? Don't! Violence against the computer is never a computer problem solution and is very expensive! Refer to Figure 3.72 as you complete this exercise.

a. Open the *chap3_mid2_artist* file and immediately save it as **chap3_mid2_artist_solution**.

b. Use the Slides tab to duplicate Slide 2.

c. Ungroup the Duck clip art in the new Slide 3 and convert it to a drawing object. Because this is a complex clip art image made up of a group containing the duck and a group containing the computer and computer stand, you will need to ungroup again.

d. Drag the duck group to the upper left of the slide and make a copy of the group. Drag the new duck group to the right side of the screen. Flip the new group horizontally.

e. Turn on the view of the grid and drag each of the duck groups and the base of the computer table so they snap to the same grid location.

f. Change the slide title to **Flip Horizontally**.

g. Duplicate Slide 3.

h. In the new Slide 4, ungroup the original duck group until it is in individual pieces, and then change the duck's jacket to green. Change the slide title to **Change Color**.

i. Duplicate Slide 2 and drag it until it becomes Slide 4 (the Change Color slide becomes Slide 5), and then change the name to *Resize*. Place the duck on top of the computer table and change the size of the computer so that it is 4" by 4".

j. Add a sixth slide. Copy and paste one of the left facing ducks onto it. Search the Clip Organizer for the cartoon clip of the mother kangaroo and insert it in Slide 6. Ungroup the duck. Delete all shapes except for the ones used to create the duck head. Change the line weight for the head and beak to 2½ pts. Group the head shapes, flip horizontally, and then tuck the head slightly above the babies in the mother kangaroo's pouch.

k. Move to the title slide and delete the title and the slide title placeholder. Create a WordArt title using **Fill – Accent 3, Powder Bevel** as the WordArt Style. Type **Clip Art Artistry** in the WordArt placeholder.

l. Modify the WordArt size to 1.5" height and 6" width.

m. Position the bottom edge of the WordArt placeholder so it aligns with the zero point on the vertical ruler. Drag the left edge of the placeholder so it aligns with the 2" mark on the horizontal ruler.

n. Create a Notes and Handouts Header and Footer with the date and your name in the header and your instructor's name and your class in the footer. Print as required by your teacher.

o. Save the *chap3_mid2_artist_solution* presentation and close the file.

...continued on Next Page

Figure 3.72 Fun with Clip Art

3 SmartArt Ideas

The SmartArt Graphic gallery displays the categories of SmartArt diagrams available, the subtypes, and tips for the uses of the diagram. Some of the descriptions may seem difficult to understand if you do not have a great deal of experience with the various types of diagrams. To help you see an example of the type of information appropriate for each type of diagram, you create a slide show of "SmartArt ideas." You also will work extensively with sizing, placement, and fills and will be proficient with these tools by the end of the exercise. Refer to Figure 3.73 while completing this exercise.

a. Open the *chap3_mid3_smartart* file and save it as **chap3_mid3_smartart_solution**.

b. On **Slide 2**, create a **Vertical Box List** SmartArt Graphic. Apply **Subtle Effect** SmartArt Style. Type the following list items:

- **List**
- **Process**
- **Cycle**
- **Hierarchy**
- **Relationship**
- **Matrix**
- **Pyramid**

c. Size the SmartArt to 7" wide, and then align it to the center of the page. Align the bottom border of the Smart Art with the last row of the gridline.

d. Move to **Slide 3**, and then create an **Upward Arrow** SmartArt graphic. Apply the **Simple Fill** SmartArt Style, and then type the following process steps:

- **Initiation and Development**
- **Institutional Review**
- **Campus Community Review**
- **Preparation for Trustees**
- **Trustees Approval**

...continued on Next Page

e. Change the height of the SmartArt to 6.27" and the width to 10". Drag the Process arrow so it fits on the slide.

f. Move to **Slide 4**, and then create a **Basic Radial** SmartArt diagram. Apply the **Subtle Effect** SmartArt Style.

g. Type **Residential College** as the center hub, and then type **Build Community**, **Promote Personal Growth**, and **Support Academic Success** as the spokes around the hub.

h. Set the height of the Smart Art to 5.5" and the width to 6.67", and then center the SmartArt on the slide.

i. Move to **Slide 5**, and then create a **Horizontal Hierarchy** SmartArt. Apply the **Subtle Effect** SmartArt Style.

j. Leave the first- and second-level bullets blank in the Text pane, and then type the following in the third-level bullets: **Jones Paint & Glass**, **Quality Cleaners**, **Ames Automotive**, and **Smith Real Estate**. These are the teams in a tournament, and it is unknown who will move forward.

k. Use the Right to Left option in the Create Graphic group to change the orientation of the diagram. Drag the borders of the SmartArt graphic until it fits the page and the text is large enough to read.

l. Move to **Slide 6** and insert a **Basic Venn** SmartArt graphic. Type the following in the Text pane: *Anesthesiology*, *Nurses*, and *Surgeon*.

m. Format the *Anesthesiology* shape using the right-click shortcut menu. Apply a picture fill using **doctors** as the Clip Art search keyword and include content from Office Online. Locate an appropriate photograph, and then click OK and Close.

n. Format the *Anesthesiology* shape with the **Fill – Text 2, Outline – Background 2** WordArt Style—the glow around the letter helps the text visibility.

o. Repeat Steps m and n to insert photographs in the remaining two shapes and to make the text visible. Use the grid to center the Venn diagram in the available space.

p. Move to **Slide 7**, create a **Basic Matrix** SmartArt graphic, apply the **Subtle Effect** SmartArt Style, and type the following text in the Text pane:

- **Urgent & Important**

- **Not Urgent & Important**

- **Urgent & Not Important**

- **Not Urgent and Not Important**

q. Move to **Slide 8**, create a **Basic Pyramid** SmartArt graphic, apply the **Subtle Effect** SmartArt Style, and type the following text in the Text pane:

- (Press **Enter** here so nothing appears in the top of the pyramid. If you type the necessary text in the SmartArt, the text size reduces until it is virtually unreadable. You will add the text for this box in a text box in a later step.)

- **Esteem**

- **Belonging and Love**

- **Safety**

- **Biological Needs**

r. Create a text box in the top shape of the pyramid and type **Self Actualization**. Drag into position. (Creating this text in the Text pane would have reduced the size of the font so that it would be close to unreadable.) Drag the border of the pyramid to enlarge it.

...continued on Next Page

s. Create a Notes and Handouts header and footer with the date and your name in the header and your instructor's name and your class in the footer. Print as required by your instructor.

t. Save the *chap3_mid3_smartart_solution* file and close the file.

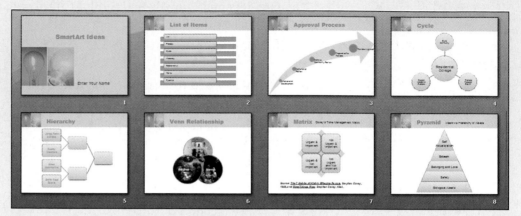

Figure 3.73 SmartArt Ideas

4 Greeting Cards

Between nieces, nephews, friend's children, and neighbor's children, you give a lot of children's birthday cards. You know that PowerPoint can be used for many types of documents in addition to slide shows. For example, you can create single sheet signs and multisheet posters. Knowing this feature, you decide to create your own card template that you can use in PowerPoint to quickly create a birthday card. After you create and save the card template, you create a birthday card for your niece who turns 1 year old next week. Refer to Figure 3.74 as you create the template and Figure 3.75 as you create the card.

a. Open a blank slide show and immediately save it as **chap3_mid4_cardtemplate_solution**.

b. Select portrait orientation.

c. Display the guide.

d. Create a text box and type **Front of Card**. Flip the text box vertically. Drag the text box to the top left quadrant of the card. This location will serve as a reminder that when the card is folded after printing, the top of the page becomes the bottom.

e. Duplicate the text box. Drag the duplicate to the top right quadrant of the card and edit the text to read **Back of Card**.

f. Drag a selection net around the two text boxes and make a duplicate. Flip the duplicate selection vertically, and then drag the duplicate selection to the bottom quadrants of the card.

g. Edit the text on the bottom left quadrant to read **Left Inside of Card**. Edit the text on the bottom right quadrant to read **Right Inside of Card**.

h. Select the text boxes on the left side of the card (*Front of Card* and *Left Inside of Card*), and then align them at their center.

i. Select the text boxes on the right side of the card (*Back of Card* and *Right Inside of Card*), and then align them at their center.

j. Select the text boxes in the top quadrant of the card (*Front of Card* and *Back of Card*), and align them at their top.

...continued on Next Page

k. Select the text boxes in the bottom quadrant of the card (*Left Inside of Card* and *Right Inside of Card*), and then align them at their bottom.

l. Save the file as a PowerPoint Template with **chap3_mid4_cardtemplate_solution** as the file name.

m. Print the template and fold it to check the text rotation. Close the file.

n. Create a new PowerPoint Presentation based on the card template you created.

o. Locate the clip art image of a "1" candle, birthday balloons, and birthday bear. Insert the picture on the slide. Size the image so it fits in a quadrant, and then vertically flip the image. Drag the clip art image to the Front of Card quadrant and position it evenly between margins. Remember—pressing Alt while dragging temporarily releases the grid so you can move the object freely.

p. Select the Back of Card text and type **Created by**, and then enter your name.

q. Delete the text box that reads *Left Inside of Card*. Edit the *Right Inside of Card* text to read **Happy First Birthday Sweet Niece!**

r. Print as required by your instructor.

s. Save the card as **chap3_mid4_card_solution** and close the file.

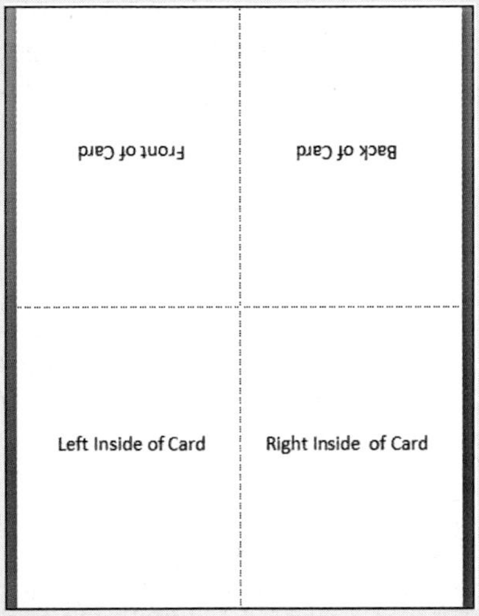

Figure 3.74 Birthday Card Template

Figure 3.75 Birthday Card

Capstone Exercise

In Chapter 2, you began a presentation on Waterwise landscaping for your neighbors in your southwestern subdivision. Previously, you concentrated on the content of the presentation, but now you are anxious to include visual elements. You also have additional information that would take a lot of text explanation, but can be presented in a much simpler and easier-to-remember format if you incorporate shapes. In this capstone exercise, you will continue working on the Waterwise landscaping presentation and utilize the features you have learned in this chapter to create a new slide and revise previously created slides.

Create a "Fire Aware" Landscape

Rather than create lengthy bulleted text to explain the concept of creating zones to protect a home from fire, you decide to create a landscape using shapes and indicate the depth of the zones on the landscape. You use a combination of oval shapes, text boxes, and clip art to create the landscape.

a. Open the *chap3_cap_xeriscape* file and immediately save it as **chap3_cap_xeriscape_solution**.

b. Move to **Slide 12** and create an oval on the slide.

c. Change the Shape Fill to a custom RGB color, Red:51, Green:102, and Blue:0, and a Transparency of 50%. Remove the outline from the shape.

d. Change the oval size to height 1.67" and width 6".

e. Make a copy of the oval. Change the second oval size to height 2.92" and width 8.08". Make another copy of the oval and change the third oval size to height 4" and width 10".

f. Select all three ovals and Align Center. Group the three ovals so they will move as one, and then position the group at horizontal position: 0" from top left corner and vertical position: 1" from top left corner.

g. Insert a text box, type **Zone 1**, and then drag it to the bottom center of the small oval. Apply the **Fill – White, Outline – Accent 1** WordArt Style to the text. Make two copies of the text box and edit them to read *Zone 2* and *Zone 3*. Drag Zone 2 to the bottom center of the medium sized oval and Zone 3 to the bottom center of the large oval.

h. Locate and insert a clip art image of a house, and position it in the center of Zone 1. Size it appropriately.

i. Create arrows to indicate the depth of the zones, and label the arrows using text boxes. Zone 1's arrow should be labeled 30', and Zones 2 and 3 should be labeled 10'. Refer to Figure 3.76 for placement of arrows and labels. Set the weight for the arrows at 1 pt. Set arrow color and text color to white.

j. Locate and insert a clip art image of a tree. Duplicate it multiple times and position a few trees in Zone 2, and more trees in Zone 3. Size trees toward the top of the slide smaller than trees nearer the bottom of the zones. Refer to Figure 3.76, but your tree and tree placement can vary.

"Fire Aware" Landscaping

Figure 3.76 Completed "Fire Aware" Landscaping

Convert Text to SmartArt

Now you need to go through the slide show and convert some bulleted lists to SmartArt graphics. In particular, you will convert bulleted lists to Basic Venn, Converging Arrows, and Continuous Arrow Process SmartArt graphics.

a. Move to **Slide 2**, and then convert the bulleted text to a **Basic Venn** SmartArt graphic. Refer to Figure 3.77. Apply Quick Style 3-D Style 2.

b. Move to **Slide 3**, select the Waterwise bulleted text, and convert it to a **Converging Arrow** SmartArt graphic. Resize the graphic so that the arrows almost touch to show the convergence of the methods around the theme of conserving water. Position the SmartArt in the middle of the horizontal space for Waterwise Options, and then apply the **Polished** SmartArt Style.

c. Select the Wildfire Aware bulleted text and convert it to a **Continuous Arrow Process** SmartArt graphic to indicate that the creation of defensible landscaping leads to zones. Apply the **Polished** SmartArt Style, and change the text color for each text block in the arrow to white. Refer to Figure 3.77.

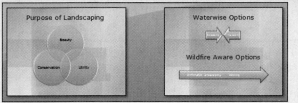

Figure 3.77 SmartArt Used to Relieve Bullet Boredom

Create SmartArt

You now need to insert a title slide, insert a text box, and create a SmartArt graphic in the form of a list.

a. Move to **Slide 12**, add a new slide with a Title Only layout, and then type **Principles for Waterwise Landscaping** as the title. Change the title font size to 32 pt and stretch the placeholder so the title displays on one line.

b. Insert a text box and type **Tips from the Office of Community Services, Fort Lewis College** inside. Center the text box under the title. Refer to Figure 3.78.

c. Create a **Vertical Block List** SmartArt to show the steps, or workflow, in the wise water landscaping process. Type the following in the Text pane. The principle number should be at Level 1, and the principle should be at Level 2.

- **1 Develop Landscape Plan**
- **2 Condition Your Soil**
- **3 Limit Lawn Size**
- **4 Irrigate Efficiently**
- **5 Use Appropriate Plants**
- **6 Apply Mulches**
- **7 Maintain**

Figure 3.78 SmartArt Showing a Workflow

Convert Text to WordArt

The last graphic you want to insert is a WordArt object. After inserting the WordArt, you will apply an animation scheme and then create a Notes and Handouts header and footer.

a. Move to **Slide 1** and select the title.

b. Apply the **Gradient Fill – Accent 6, Inner Shadow** WordArt Style to the title.

c. Apply a Transform Text Effect to the title using the Chevron Up warp style.

d. Apply the **Fill – Accent 3, Outline Text 2** WordArt Style to the Subtitle.

Figure 3.79 WordArt Title and Subtitle

e. Apply the Fly In animation scheme to the title, and then apply the Fade animation scheme to the subtitle.

f. Create a Notes and Handouts Header and Footer with your name in the header and your instructor's name and your class in the footer. Print as required by your teacher.

g. Save the *chap3_cap_xeriscape_solution* file and close the file.

Use the rubric following the case as a guide to evaluate your work, but keep in mind that your instructor may impose additional grading criteria or use a different standard to judge your work.

Institutional Policies and Procedures Approval Process

GENERAL CASE

The president of your college has asked you to create a one-page document that shows the process that a policy or procedure must go through in order to be adopted by the college. The process involves five stages with multiple steps to be taken in each stage. You realize that this process is best shown as a flowchart. You decide to create the flowchart in PowerPoint rather than a word processor because of the convenience of grids and guides for placement and the ease of creating shapes. You decide to use shapes instead of SmartArt so that it is easier to adjust the shapes to fit on the page. Because your output will be a printed page and a Web page, you can use smaller fonts than you could use for a presentation. Save your file as **chap3_mc1_flowchart_solution**. Figure 3.80 shows one possible solution to this task. The information you need is in the following table.

Stage 1	Stage 2	Stage 3	Stage 4	Stage 5
Initiation and Development	Institutional Entity Review	Campus Community Review	Procedures Approval	Policy Approval
Origination	Steward	President's Council Approval for Review	President's Council Final Approval	Board of Trustees Reviews Policy
President's Council Sponsorship	Dean's Council	Posted on Intranet for Review	Procedures Approved	Policies Approved
Policy Steward Assigned	Faculty Senate		Web Manager Notifies Campus Community	Web Manager Notifies Campus Community
Policy/Procedure Development	PACE			Forward Policy to Board of Regents When Required
	Student Council			
	Others as Needed			

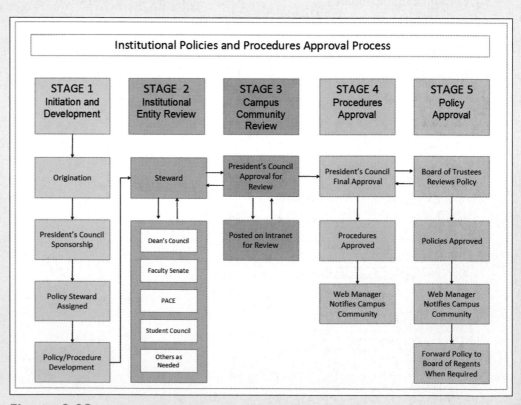

Figure 3.80 Sample Solution to Mini Case 1

Performance Elements	Exceeds Expectations	Meets Expectations	Below Expectations
Organization	Flowchart stages can be easily identified. Steps in each stage are easily identified so process is understood.	Flowchart identifies steps to be followed.	Flowchart cannot be understood because there is no sequence of information.
Visual aspects	Flowchart shapes, fills, outlines, and text are appealing and enhance understanding of the stages in flowchart process. There is a consistent visual theme.	Flowchart shapes relate to purpose and content. Text is readable.	The fills, outlines, or shapes are distracting and do not enhance understanding of the process and stages in the process.
Layout	The layout is visually pleasing and contributes to understanding the stages in the process. White space aids in separating stages in the process. Arrows indicate steps to be followed.	The layout shows some structure, but placement of some shapes, arrows, and/or white space can be improved.	The layout is cluttered and confusing. Placement of shapes, arrows, and/or white space detracts from understanding. Understanding of the process is lost.
Mechanics	Presentation has no errors in spelling, grammar, word usage, or punctuation. No typographical errors present.	Presentation has no more than one error in spelling, grammar, word usage, or punctuation.	Presentation readability is impaired due to repeated errors in spelling, grammar, word usage, or punctuation. Multiple typographical errors.

To PowerPoint or Not to PowerPoint: That Is the Question

RESEARCH CASE

This textbook has endeavored to show you the benefits of creating PowerPoint slide shows for use in presentations—but do not take the author's word for it. You need to see what industry or business professionals have to say about PowerPoint. Referring to professional Web sites can provide you with a wealth of tips and ideas for creating slide shows that move your work above the ordinary, but they also can make you aware of the dangers of relying too heavily on the software. Visit the locations shown in the table below, and then read the articles. Some locations are favorable to PowerPoint and electronic presentations, and some articles are not. Some locations are simply Web sites to aid you in your quest for PowerPoint knowledge. If a Web site is no longer active, remember that the Internet is dynamic and changes constantly. Then move on to the next article. After visiting these sites, search the Internet for articles relating to PowerPoint tips and tricks and read at least two more articles. See if you can locate an article asking if an inadvertent error in the creation of a PowerPoint presentation may have contributed to the space shuttle Columbia disaster.

Create a slide show highlighting what you learn from this experience. Your slide show might include a slide highlighting pros for using PowerPoint, a slide indicating cautions for using PowerPoint, and a slide with Tips and Tricks. Create a slide illustrating a tip you learned in your travels through the wealth of sites on PowerPoint usage. Save the presentation as **chap3_mc2_powerpoint_solution**.

Professional Web Sites to Visit

Article Title	Author	Web Site
Presentation Zen	Garr Reynolds	http://presentationzen.blogs.com/presentationzen/2005/09/whats_good_powe.html
Beyond Bullets: Zen and the Art of PowerPoint	Cliff Atkinson	http://www.beyondbullets.com/2005/01/story.html
Deadly Sins of Modern PowerPoint Usage	Rick Altman	http://www.altman.com/editorial/archive/04mar.htm
The Gettysburg Powerpoint Presentation, 11/19/1863	Peter Norvig	http://www.norvig.com/Gettysburg/index.htm
Ask the PowerPoint experts	Microsoft Office Online	http://office.microsoft.com/en-gb/assistance/ha011082211033.aspx
Microsoft PowerPoint	Indezine, complied by Geetesh Bajaj	http://www.indezine.com/products/powerpoint/index.html

Performance Elements	Exceeds Expectations	Meets Expectations	Below Expectations
Organization	Presentation indicates accurate research and significant facts. Evidence exists that information has been evaluated and synthesized showing an understanding of the topic.	Presentation indicates some research has taken place and that information was included in the content.	Presentation demonstrates a lack of research or understanding of the topic.
Visual aspects	Presentation background, themes, clip art, and animation are appealing and enhance the understanding of presentation purpose and content. There is aconsistent visual theme.	Clip art is related to the topic. Animation is not distracting.	The background or theme is distracting to the topic. Images do not enhance understanding of the content or are unrelated.
Layout	The layout is visually pleasing and contributes to the overall message with appropriate use of headings, subheadings, bullet points, clip art, and white space.	The layout shows some structure, but placement of some headings, subheadings, bullet points, clip art, and/or white space can be improved.	The layout is cluttered and confusing. Placement of headings, subheadings, bullet points, images, and/or white space detracts from readability.
Mechanics	Presentation has no errors in spelling, grammar, word usage, or punctuation. Bullet points are parallel.	Presentation has no more than one error in spelling, grammar, word usage, or punctuation. Bullet points are inconsistent in one slide.	Presentation readability is impaired due to repeated errors in spelling, grammar, word usage, or punctuation. Most bullet points are not parallel.

Seating Chart Blues

A colleague with some knowledge of PowerPoint downloaded a Microsoft Online template for seating charts. She tried to position the shapes representing student desks on her slide in the approximate positions of desks in her classrooms, but because she does not fully understand grouping and ungrouping, she is frustrated with the process. She has grouped and ungrouped odd combinations of shapes. You offer to help her revise her seating chart. Open the *chap3_mc3_seat* file and save it as **chap3_mc3_seat_solution**. Revise the seating chart based on the position of desks in your computer lab. Create a shape and label for printer location or download a printer clip art image and position it to indicate printer location.

Performance Elements	Exceeds Expectations	Meets Expectations	Below Expectations
Organization	Placement of desk shapes reflects the arrangement of school computer laboratory. Printer table shape is in correct location.	Placement of desk shapes indicates arrangement of school computer laboratory.	Desk shapes do not indicate the arrangement of school computer laboratory. Printer location is incorrect or is missing.
Visual aspects	Any changes to shapes, fills, outlines, and text are appealing and enhance understanding of the classroom arrangement. There is a consistent visual theme.	Text is readable. Shape size is appropriate.	The fills, outlines, or shapes are distracting or unappealing and do not enhance understanding of the classroom arrangement.
Layout	The layout is visually pleasing and contributes to immediate understanding of desk and printer arrangement. White space indicates rows or walking space.	Layout contributes to understanding of the class room setup.	The layout is cluttered and confusing. Placement of desks and printer is incorrect, or desks are layered on top of each other, creating an impossible situation for classroom use.
Mechanics	Any added text has no errors in spelling, grammar, word usage, or punctuation. No typographical errors present.	Seating Chart has no more than one error in spelling, grammar, word usage, or punctuation.	Any added text has impaired readability due to repeated errors in spelling, grammar, word usage, or punctuation. Multiple typographical errors.

PowerPoint Multimedia Tools

Enhancing with Multimedia

bjectives

After you read this chapter, you will be able to:

1. Insert and modify a picture **(page 291)**.

2. Use the Internet as a resource **(page 297)**.

3. Create a Photo Album **(page 309)**.

4. Set Photo Album options **(page 309)**.

5. Insert movies **(page 314)**.

6. Set movie options **(page 316)**.

7. Add sound **(page 322)**.

8. Record and play narration **(page 324)**.

Hands-On Exercises

Exercises	Skills Covered
1. **USING PICTURES** (page 302) **Open:** chap4_ho1_memories.pptx **Save as:** chap4_ho1_memories_solution.pptx	• Insert Pictures • Apply and Modify a Picture Style • Adjust Brightness and Contrast • Crop and Compress • Create a Background from a Picture • Insert a Picture from the Internet
2. **CREATING A PHOTO ALBUM** (page 311) **Open:** none **Save as:** chap4_ho2_album_solution.pptx, chap4_ho3_album2_solution.pptx, and chap4_ho2_album3_solution.pptx	• Select and Order Pictures • Adjust Contrast and Brightness • Set Picture Layout • Select Frame Shape • Edit Album Settings • Apply a Design Theme
3. **INSERTING A MOVIE** (page 318) **Open:** chap4_ho1_memories _solution.pptx (from Exercise 1) **Save as:** chap4_ho3_memories_solution.pptx (additional modifications)	• Insert a Movie from the Clip Organizer • Insert a Movie from a File • Set Movie Options
4. **ADDING SOUND** (page 327) **Open:** chap4_ho3_memories_solution.pptx (from Exercise 3) **Save as:** chap4_ho4_memories_solution.pptx (additional modifications)	• Add Sound from a File • Change Sound Settings • Insert Sound from the Clip Organizer • Add Narration

CASE STUDY

Forensics Geology Class Album

The college you attend has a strong criminal justice program culminating in a bachelor of arts degree. Graduates of the program are trained for criminal justice opportunities in law enforcement, the Drug Enforcement Agency (DEA), the Federal Bureau of Investigation (FBI), the Bureau of Alcohol, Tobacco, Firearms, and Explosives (ATF), corrections, security, investigations, immigration, and border patrol. You are newly employed in the Criminal Justice department as an aide to Professor Taume Park. She teaches a forensics geology class that provides a survey of the uses of geology in solving crime. Her class emphasizes actual criminal cases, and her students complete hands-on laboratory activities to develop their critical observation skills. During the class, the students are divided into teams and assigned one of four possible presentations: identifying mineral pigments related to art forgery and cosmetics; examining and recognizing imitation amber and other gems; studying environmental pollution; or reviewing crimes in archeology.

Professor Park takes pictures of her students on the first day of class. She brings you the memory card with the pictures of her students and asks you to print each picture. She explains to you that she writes each student's name on his or her picture to help her put the right name with the right face. With your knowledge of PowerPoint, you decide to prepare an album for Professor Park that she can copy for her students. You decide to include identifying class information, a picture of Professor Park, and a picture of her lab assistant, Katreena Castillo, on the title page of the album. Because Professor Park took the pictures of the students quickly in a poorly lit classroom with a white board behind the students, you use the album tools to improve the contrast and brightness of some pictures. You use the captions feature of the album options to add the students' names for a more professional look.

Your Assignment

- Read the chapter, paying special attention to information that explains image brightness and contrast and explains how to use PowerPoint's Photo Album feature.
- Insert all the images in the *chap4_case_images* folder except for the Professor Taume Park image and the Katreena Castillo_Lab Assistant to create a Photo Album.
- Lay out the album with four pictures per page and include captions below all pictures, thereby including the student name under the associated picture.
- Preview each picture in the album and decrease the brightness of any pictures that are especially light. Change the contrast on images that appear dim or washed out.
- Frame the pictures with the Frame shape of your choice.
- Apply the theme of your choice in either the Photo Album dialog box or in the album after it has been created.
- Include **Forensics Geology** in the title placeholder of the Title Slide. In the subtitle placeholder enter the following on separate lines: **9 a.m. MWF**, **Fall Semester**, and **your name**. Also include the pictures of Professor Park and Assistant Castillo, appropriately sized. Use a text box to insert their names beneath their pictures.
- Create a slide footer with your name, your instructor's name, and your class. Do not include the footer on the title page.
- Print the handouts, four slides per page, framed.
- Save the presentation as **chap4_case_forensics_solution**.

Pictures

Multimedia is multiple forms of media such as text, graphics, sound, animation, and video that are used to entertain or inform a user. You can utilize any of these types of media in PowerPoint by placing the multimedia object on a slide. You already have placed text and graphics in presentations, and you have applied animations to objects and transitions to slides. In this chapter, you expand your experience with multimedia by inserting pictures, sound, and video in slides.

Multimedia graphics include clip art, diagrams and illustrations, pictures or photographs, scanned images, and other categories. You have worked extensively with clip art, diagrams, illustrations, and pictures from the Clip Art Organizer. In this section you concentrate on pictures. Pictures are one of the most popular aspects of multimedia added to PowerPoint presentations. Mark Jaremko, senior program manager in the Microsoft PowerPoint OfficeArt group, posted in the MSDN PowerPoint & OfficeArt Team Blog on June 22, 2006 ". . . Pictures are found in over 57% of all office documents, it's our single biggest graphic type and deserves some special attention."

Pictures are bitmap images that computers can read and interpret to create a photorealistic image. Unlike clip art vector images that are created by mathematical statements, *bitmap images* are created by bits or pixels placed in a grid or map. Think of vector images as connect-the-dots and bitmap images as paint-by-number, and you begin to see the difference in the methods of representation.

In a bitmap image, each pixel in the image contains information about the color to be displayed. A bitmap image is required to have the realism necessary for a photograph. Each type of image has its own advantage. Vector graphics can be sized easily and still retain their clarity but are not photorealistic. Bitmap images represent a much more complex range of colors and shades, but can become pixelated (get the "jaggies") when they are enlarged. Figure 4.1 displays a pumpkin created as a vector image and one created as a bitmap image. Note the differences in realism. The boxes show a portion of the images enlarged. Note the pixelation in the enlarged portion of the bitmap image.

Figure 4.1 Types of Graphics

To display a photograph in a slide, you must save it in a computer bitmap format. You can accomplish this task by scanning and saving a photograph or piece of artwork, by downloading images from a digital camera, by downloading a previously created bitmap image from the Microsoft Clip Organizer or the Internet, or by creating an image in a graphics-editing software package like Photoshop. Table 4.1 displays the common types of graphic file formats that you can add to a PowerPoint slide.

Table 4.1 Types of Graphic File Formats Supported by PowerPoint 2007

File Format	Extension	Description
Computer Graphics Metafile	.cgm	Older format originally used for clip art libraries. Often used for complex engineering drawings.
Enhanced Windows Metafile	.emf	A Windows 32-bit file format.
Graphics Interchange Format	.gif	Limited to 256 colors. Effective for scanned images such as illustrations rather than for color photographs. Good for line drawings and black and white images. Supports transparent backgrounds.
Joint Photographic Experts Group	.jpg, .jpeg	Supports 16 million colors and is optimized for photographs and complex graphics. Format of choice for most photographs on the Web.
Macintosh PICT	PICT	Holds both vector and bitmap images. PICT supports 8 colors; PICT2 supports 16 million colors.
Microsoft Windows Metafile	.wmf	A Windows 16-bit file format.
Portable Network Graphics	.png	Supports 16 million colors. Approved as a standard by the World Wide Web Consortium (W3C). Intended to replace .gif format.
Tagged Image File Format	.tif, .tiff	Best file format for storing bitmapped images on personal computers. Can be any resolution. Lossless image storage creates large file sizes. Not widely supported by Web browsers.
Vector Markup Language	.vml	An XML format for vector graphics that can be embedded in Web pages in place of bitmapped .gif and .jpeg images.
Windows Bitmap (Device Independent Bitmap)	bmp, .dib, .rle	A representation consisting of dots. The value of each dot is stored in one or more bits of data. Uncompressed and creates large file size.

In this section, you insert pictures (bitmap images) into a slide without using a content placeholder and then insert pictures using content placeholders. You apply a Picture Style and modify its effects. You use picture tools to adjust the brightness and contrast of a picture. You crop a picture and compress all the images in the slide show. You also create a background for a slide from a picture. Finally, you learn about using the Internet as a resource for images and review the Fair Use guidelines relating to student use of media downloaded from the Internet. You download a picture from the Internet and insert the picture into a slide show.

TIP   Scanning Images

In PowerPoint 2007, if you wish to add images from a scanner or digital camera, you must first download the images to your hard drive or storage device. Once the images are downloaded, click the Insert tab, click Picture in the Illustrations group, navigate to where you stored the image, select the image, and then click Insert. As an alternative, you can scan and download images directly to your Clip Organizer. Put your image on the scanner glass and open the Clip Organizer by clicking Organizing clips at the bottom of the Clip Art task pane. Click File, point to Add Clips to Organizer, and then click From Scanner or Camera. When the Insert Picture from Scanner or Camera dialog box opens, select your scanner from the Device box. Click Insert. The clip you scan appears in My Collections, not on your slide. You would then need to insert the scanned image as you do any other image from the Clip Organizer.

Inserting and Modifying a Picture

You can use several methods to insert an image on a page. To add a picture using a placeholder, select a layout with a placeholder that includes an Insert Picture button (see Figure 4.2). Click the Insert Picture button and the Insert Picture dialog box opens. Navigate to the location of your picture files, and then click the bitmap picture you want to use. Click the Insert button and the picture is inserted in the placeholder. When you insert a picture in this manner, however, the picture is centered within the placeholder frame and cropped as needed. This effect can cause unexpected results and can be startling if tops of heads are cropped off. If this situation occurs, simply undo and enlarge the placeholder, and then repeat the steps for inserting an image.

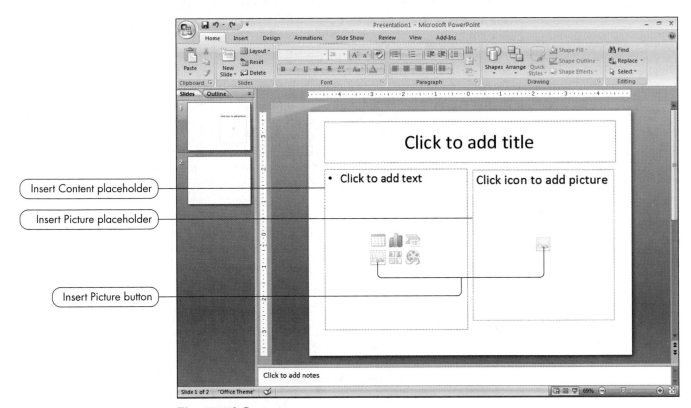

Figure 4.2 Insert Picture Using Placeholders

Another method for inserting an image is to click Picture on the Insert tab. The advantage of this method is that your image comes in at full size rather than centered and cropped in a placeholder. You can then resize the image to fit the desired area. The disadvantage is you spend time resizing and positioning the image. To insert a picture using this method, click Picture in the Illustrations group on the Insert tab. Navigate to the location of your picture files, and then click the bitmap picture you want to use. Click the Insert button and the picture is inserted in the slide.

> **TIP** **Adding Images Using Windows Explorer**
>
> If you are adding multiple images to a slide show, you can speed up the process by opening Windows Explorer and navigating to the folder where the images are located. Position the Windows Explorer window on top of your slide show, and then drag the images from the Explorer window onto the slides of your choice.

Use Picture Tools

Once you bring a picture into a slide, PowerPoint provides powerful tools that you can use to adjust the image. Some tools are designed to correct problems with a picture; others are designed to let you add stylized effects. The Picture Tools are available when you have the picture selected in the slide and you have clicked the Format tab beneath the Picture Tools contextual tab (see Figure 4.3).

Figure 4.3 The Picture Tools

Brightness refers to the lightness or darkness of a picture.

The *brightness* (lightness or darkness) of a picture is often a matter of individual preference. You might need to change the brightness of your picture for reasons other than preference, however. For example, sometimes printing a picture requires different brightness than is needed when projecting an image. This situation occurs because during printing the ink may spread when placed on the page, making the picture darker. Or, you might decide you want a picture as a background and reduce the lightness so that text will show on the background. The Brightness control in the Picture Tools group on the Format tab enables you to adjust the brightness of your picture to your preference. You can increase or decrease the brightness in 10% increments. For increments other than 10%, click the Picture Corrections Options button, which gives you access to sliders that can be used to adjust the brightness at any increment up to 100%. Figure 4.4 shows a picture of a couple adjusted for an increase in brightness of 10%.

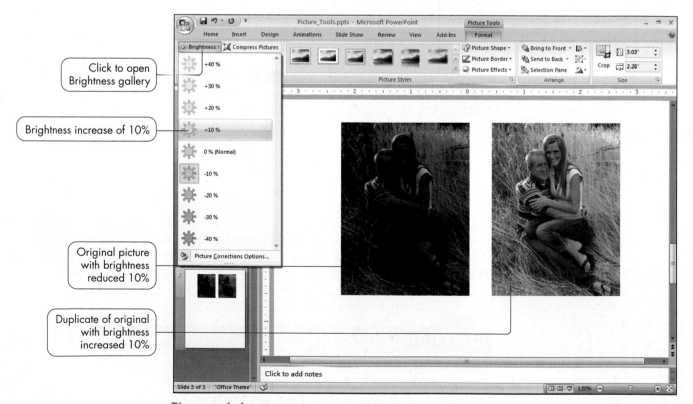

Figure 4.4 The Brightness Control

Contrast refers to the difference between the darkest and lightest areas of a picture.

Contrast refers to the difference between the darkest area (black level) and lightest area (white level). If the contrast is not set correctly, your picture can look washed out or muddy. Too much contrast and the light portion of your image will appear to explode off the screen or page. Once again, your setting may vary depending on whether you are going to project the image or print it. Projecting impacts an image due to the light in the room. Setting the contrast adjustment in a very light room will make the image seem to need a greater contrast than setting the adjustment in a darker room. Try to set your control in the lighting that will appear when you display the presentation. Figure 4.5 shows an image adjusted for an increase in contrast of 30%. While the original actually has a good contrast setting, it appears washed out next to the image with the contrast increase. The image with the contrast increase, however, has blown out the pale blue color of the bride-to-be's shirt and would appear to throb or glow if projected.

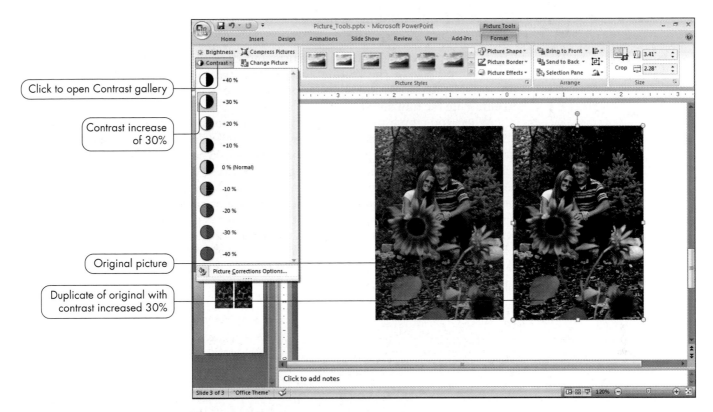

Figure 4.5 The Contrast Control

When you add pictures to your PowerPoint presentation, especially high-resolution pictures downloaded from a digital camera, the presentation file size dramatically increases. It may increase to the point that the presentation becomes slow to load and sluggish to play. The increase in the file size depends on the resolution of the pictures you add. Use the Crop tool and the Compress Picture feature to eliminate a large part of this problem.

Cropping is the process of eliminating unwanted portions of an image.

Cropping the picture using the Crop tool lets you eliminate unwanted portions of an image, thereby focusing the viewer's attention to what it is you want him or her to see. Remember, though, that if you crop an image and try to enlarge the resulting picture, pixilation may occur that reduces the quality of the image. Figure 4.6 shows a picture that was cropped to focus attention on the young couple. The result was enlarged to an acceptable level. Further enlargement would cause unacceptable image degradation.

Original picture

Cropped and compressed image

Figure 4.6 Use Crop to Focus Attention

To crop a picture, select the picture and click Crop in the Size group on the Format tab beneath the Picture Tools contextual tab. Cropping handles appear around the picture. Position the cropping tool over a center handle and drag inward to eliminate the unwanted portion of the image.

When you crop a picture, the part that was cropped out does not display in the slide, but it is not removed from the presentation file. This result is in case you decide at a later date to reset the picture to its original state. When you resize an image, the resolution containing the detail of an image is retained so the file size is not reduced. The Compress Pictures option can help you manage large image files by permanently deleting the cropped areas of the selected picture or all pictures in the slide show. It also changes the resolution to a default of 220 pixels per inch (ppi), which ensures you will obtain a good quality printout. If you know, however, that you will only be displaying the slide show on screen, you can click the Options button and change your target output to 150 ppi. If you plan on e-mailing the slide show, you should change the target output to 96 ppi. Figure 4.7 shows the Compression Settings options.

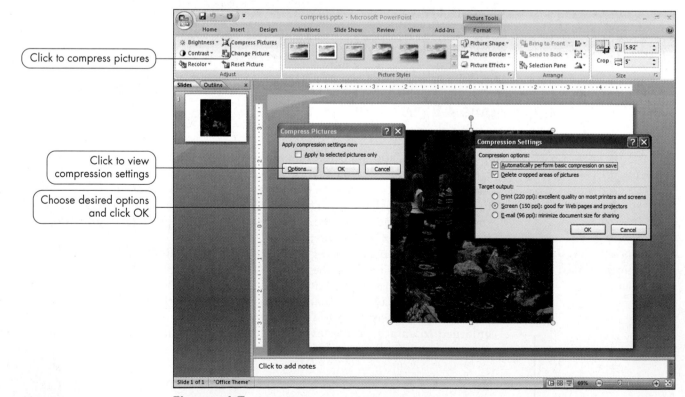

Click to compress pictures

Click to view compression settings

Choose desired options and click OK

Figure 4.7 Picture Compression Options

Apply Picture Styles

> Many . . . effects are possible with Picture Styles, and when you consider that each of these effects can be modified, your creative opportunities are endless!

The Picture Styles in PowerPoint 2007 are absolutely awesome. With the new Picture Styles, you can surround your picture with attractive white frames, soften the edges of pictures, add soft shadows to the edges of pictures, apply 3-D effects to pictures, and add glossy reflections below your pictures. Many other effects are possible with Picture Styles, and when you consider that each of these effects can be modified, your creative opportunities are endless! Figure 4.8 shows a few of the possibilities.

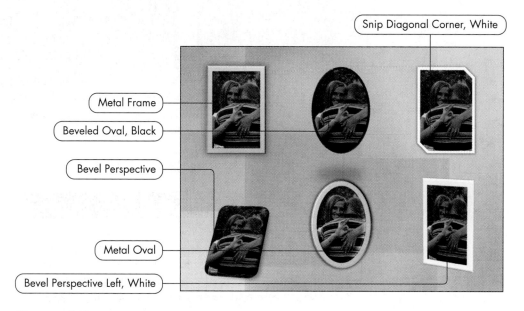

Figure 4.8 Picture Style Applications

To apply a Picture Style, select a picture and click a gallery image displayed in the Pictures Styles group on the Format tab beneath the Picture Tools contextual tab. To see more styles, click the More button. To change the shape of the picture into any of the basic shapes available in PowerPoint, click Picture Shape in the Picture Styles group. Picture Border in the Picture Styles group enables you to select your border color, weight, or dash style. You can select from Presets, Shadow, Reflection, Glow, Soft Edges, and 3-D Rotation effects from the Picture Effects option.

Create a Background from a Picture

Pictures can make appealing backgrounds if they are transparent enough that text can be read on top of them. Picture backgrounds personalize your presentation. To use a photograph as a background, use the Background command. Using the Insert Picture option involves more time because when the picture is inserted it must be resized, its transparency must be adjusted, and the order of the objects on the screen has to be changed because the photograph blocks the placeholders (see Figure 4.9).

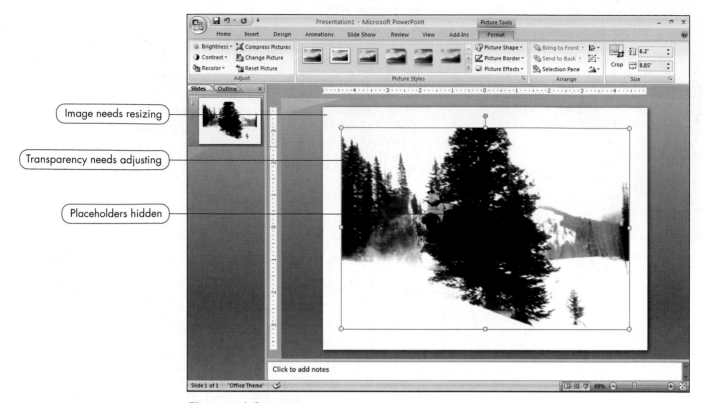

Figure 4.9 Background from Insert Picture Option

To create a background from a picture using the Background command, click the Design tab, and then click Background Styles in the Background group. When the gallery appears, click Format Background at the bottom of the gallery. The Format Background dialog box opens with option buttons for the various fills available for backgrounds. Click Picture or Texture fill and the dialog box changes to include a File button. Click the File button and navigate to the location where your picture is stored. Click the picture file, and then click Insert. The dialog box also includes options for moving the picture by offsetting it to the left or right or the top or bottom, and for adjusting the transparency amount. Figure 4.10 shows the same picture as Figure 4.9 inserted as a background and with a transparency adjustment.

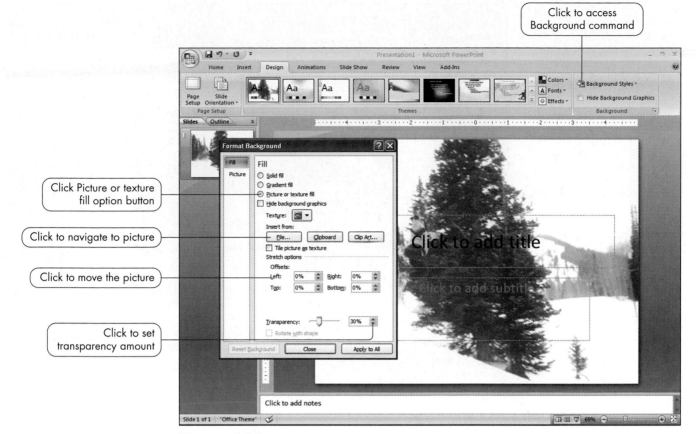

Figure 4.10 Background from Background Styles Option

Using the Internet as a Resource

The Internet and the World Wide Web are thoroughly integrated into PowerPoint, as they are throughout the Microsoft Office Suite. PowerPoint integrates with the Internet in three important ways. First, you can download resources from any Web page for inclusion in a PowerPoint presentation. Second, you can insert hyperlinks into a PowerPoint presentation, and then click those links to display the associated Web page in your Web browser. Finally, you can convert any PowerPoint presentation into a Web page. In this chapter, you will use the Internet as a resource for pictures.

Figure 4.11 illustrates how resources from the Internet can be used to enhance a PowerPoint presentation. The slide displays a photograph that was downloaded from Image*After (www.imageafter.com), a site that maintains a large, online, free photo collection that allows for free downloading of images for personal or commercial use. The photograph is displayed as an object and is typical of how most people use photographs downloaded from the Web in a presentation. To give credit to the download source, even though the site permits use, the Web site address has been entered in a text box.

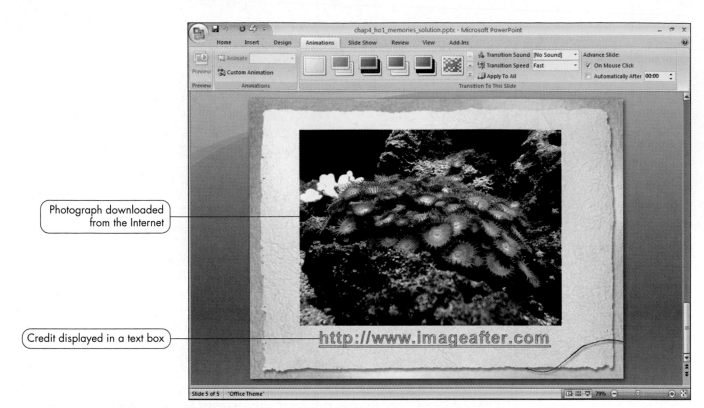

Photograph downloaded from the Internet

Credit displayed in a text box

Figure 4.11 Downloaded Picture

Regardless of how you choose to use a photograph, your first task is to access the Web and locate the required image (e.g., an underwater image). After this step is done, right-click the photograph to display a shortcut menu, and then select Save Picture As to download the file to your hard drive. As an alternative, when you right-click the photograph, you can click the Copy button to copy the picture into the Clipboard memory.

In PowerPoint, you use the Insert Picture command in the Illustrations group on the Insert tab to insert the picture if you have downloaded it. If you copied the picture, you paste it onto your slide. You also can use the Insert Hyperlink command in the Links group on the Insert tab to insert a hyperlink to the resource Web site. You then can click the hyperlink during the slide show, and provided you have an Internet connection, your Web browser will display the associated page.

Microsoft makes the Internet readily accessible to you through its Research service. Click Research in the Proofing group on the Review tab and the Research task pane opens on the right side of your screen. Enter a keyword in the Search for box, and then select the type of reference you wish to search. All Reference Books is the default for searching, but because the dictionary and thesaurus do not include images, you will speed the search process by narrowing the resources you wish to search. The Encarta Encyclopedia is a good resource that includes images. Figure 4.12 displays the Research task pane set to search for information about Cancun (Mexico).

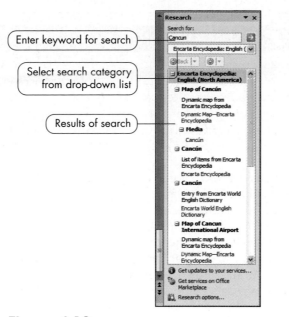

Enter keyword for search

Select search category from drop-down list

Results of search

Figure 4.12 Research Pane

Click a link in the results area of the Research pane, and a Web browser window opens. The Research task pane is displayed on the left side of your screen, and the article is displayed on the right. While most of the information you find using this method is free, some Web providers require a fee. If, however, the content is fee-based, a premium content icon appears by the link. You are not charged for clicking a premium content link, but you will be charged if you use the information. If you locate an image in a free area, you can download it by right-clicking the image and copying it or by downloading it as described previously.

Copyright Protection

Copyright is the legal protection afforded to a written or artistic work.

A *copyright* provides legal protection to a written or artistic work, including literary, dramatic, musical, and artistic works such as poetry, novels, movies, songs, computer software, and architecture. It gives the author of a work the exclusive right to the use and duplication of that work. A copyright does not, however, protect facts, ideas, systems, or methods of operation, although it may protect the way these things are expressed.

(Anything on the Internet should be considered copyrighted unless the site specifically says it is in the public domain . . .)

The owner of the copyright may sell or give up a portion of his or her rights; for example, an author may give distribution rights to a publisher and/or grant movie rights to a studio. *Infringement of a copyright* occurs any time a right held by the copyright owner is violated without permission of the owner. Anything on the Internet should be considered copyrighted unless the site specifically says it is in the *public domain,* in which case, the author is giving everyone the right to freely reproduce and distribute the material, thereby making the work owned by the public at large. A work also may enter the public domain when the copyright of the work has expired. Does copyright protection prevent you from quoting a document found on the Web in a research paper? Does copyright protection imply that you cannot download an image for inclusion in a slide show? (Facts themselves are not covered by copyright, so you can use statistical data without fear of infringement. Images are protected unless the owner gives his or her permission for downloading.)

Infringement of copyright occurs when a right of the copyright owner is violated.

Public domain is when the rights to a literary work or property are owned by the public at large.

TIP   Using Microsoft Media Elements

Photos, clip art, fonts, sounds, and movies available from Microsoft are part of Microsoft's Media Elements and are protected. To see what uses of Media Elements are prohibited, access Help, select the link for Working with graphics and charts, and then click Adding pictures, shapes, WordArt, or clip art. Select the *What uses of photos, clip art, and font images are prohibited* link and review the list of prohibited uses.

The answer to what you can use from the Web depends on many things, including the amount of the information you reference, as well as the intended use of that information. It is considered fair use, and thus, not an infringement of copyright, to use a portion of a work for educational, nonprofit purposes, or for the purpose of critical review for commentary. In other words, you can use a quote, facts, or other information from the Web in an educational setting, but you should cite the original work in your footnotes, or resource, or bibliography slide. The Reference table on the next page presents guidelines students and teachers can use to help determine what multimedia can used in an educational project based on the Fair Use Guidelines for Educational Multimedia created in 1996. These guidelines were created by a group of publishers, authors, and educators who gathered to interpret the Copyright Act of 1976 as it applies to educational and scholarly uses of multimedia. You should note, however, that while these guidelines are part of the Congressional Record, they are not law. They can, however, help you determine when you can use multimedia materials under Fair Use principles in a non-commercial educational use.

Multimedia Copyright Guidelines for Students and Teachers | Reference

The following guidelines are based on Section 107 of the U.S. Copyright Act of 1976 and the Proposal for Fair Use Guidelines for Educational Multimedia (1996), which sets forth fair use factors for multimedia projects. These guidelines cover the use of multimedia based on Time, Portion, and Copying and Distribution Limitations. For the complete text of the guidelines, see www.uspto.gov/web/offices/dcom/lia/confu/indexx.htm.

General Guidelines

- Student projects for specific courses may be displayed and kept in personal portfolios as examples of their academic work.
- Students in specific courses may use multimedia in projects with proper credit and citations. Full bibliographic information must be used when available.
- Students and teachers must display copyright notice if copyright ownership information is shown on the original source. Copyright may be shown in a sources or bibliographic section unless the presentation is being used for distance learning. In distance learning situations, copyright must appear on the screen when the image is viewed.
- Teachers may use media for face-to-face curriculum-based instruction, for directed self-study, in demonstrations on how to create multimedia productions, for presentations at conferences, and for distance learning. Teachers may also retain projects in their personal portfolio for personal use such as job interviews or tenure review.
- Teachers may use multimedia projects for educational purposes for up to two years, after which permission of the copyright holder is required.
- Students and teachers do not need to write for permission to use media if it falls under multimedia guidelines unless there is a possibility that the project could be broadly distributed at a later date.

Text Guidelines

- Up to 10 percent of a copyrighted work may be used, or up to 1000 words, whichever is less.
- Up to 250 words of a poem, but no more than five poems (or excerpts) from different poets or an anthology. No more than three poems (or excerpts) from a single poet.

Illustrations

- A photograph or illustration may be used in its entirety.
- Up to 15 images, but no more than 15 images from a collection.
- No more than 5 images of an artist's or photographer's work.

Motion Media

- Up to 10 percent of a copyrighted work or 3 minutes, whichever is less.
- Clip cannot be altered in any way.

Music and Sound

- Up to 10 percent of a copyrighted musical composition, not to exceed 30 seconds.
- Up to 10 percent of a sound recording, not to exceed 30 seconds.
- Alterations cannot change the basic melody or fundamental character of the work.

Distribution Limitations

- Multimedia projects should not be posted to unsecured web sites.
- No more than two copies of the original may be made, only one of which may be placed on reserve for instructional purposes.
- A copy of a project may be made for backup purposes, but may be used only when the original has been lost, damaged, or stolen.
- If more than one person created a project, each person may keep only one copy.

Hands-On Exercises

1 | Using Pictures

Skills covered: 1. Insert Pictures **2.** Apply and Modify a Picture Style **3.** Adjust Brightness and Contrast **4.** Crop and Compress **5.** Create a Background from a Picture **6.** Insert a Picture from the Internet

| **Step 1**
Insert Pictures | Refer to Figure 4.13 as you complete Step 1. |

a. Open the *chap4_ho1_memories* presentation and then save it as the **chap4_ho1_memories_solution** presentation.

You decide to create a memories presentation for your sister, who was recently married. You include engagement pictures, a wedding picture, and a picture to remind her of scuba diving on her honeymoon.

b. With the title slide selected, click the **Insert tab**, and click **Picture** in the Illustrations group.

Because the Title Slide layout does not include a placeholder for content, you add a picture using the Insert Picture from File feature. The Insert Picture dialog box appears.

c. Navigate to the location of your student files and open the *chap4_ho1_memories_images* folder. Click the *chap4_ho1_1memories.jpg* file to select it, and then click **Insert**.

d. Click the **Size Dialog Box Launcher** to open the Size and Position dialog box, click in the **Height** box in the *Scale* section, and then type **38**. Click in the **Width** box in the *Scale* section and it will change to 38% automatically.

By default, the picture was sized to fit the slide and centered on the slide. You need to adjust the size and the position of the picture. Because you are adjusting both settings, it is fastest to enter the information in the dialog box. Typing 38 in the Height box automatically sets the scale for Width to 38% because the Lock aspect ratio is checked.

e. Click the **Position tab** in the still open Size and Position dialog box, and then set the **Horizontal Position on slide** options to **5"** from the **Top Left Corner**. Set the **Vertical Position on slide** options to **.3"** from the **Top Left Corner**. Click **Close**. Send the photo to the back so that the photographer credit displays.

f. Move to **Slide 2**, and then click the **Add Picture button** in the large content placeholder on the left side of the screen. Open the *chap4_ho1_memories_images* folder. Click the *chap4_ho1_2memories.jpg* file to select it, and then click **Insert**.

g. Use the **Add Picture buttons** in the two small content placeholders on the right side of the screen to insert *chap4_ho1_3memories.jpg* and *chap4_ho1_4memories.jpg* into your presentation.

Note that in all three cases, the images were resized to fit within the existing placeholders. While they have a "smaller" appearance, the file size is exactly the same. The resolution has not changed, and the actual image size is intact.

h. Create a Notes and Handouts Header and Footer with the date and your name in the header and your instructor's name and your class in the footer.

i. Click **Save**.

Figure 4.13 Inserted Pictures

Refer to Figure 4.14 as you complete Step 2.

a. Move to **Slide 1**, select the picture of the young couple, and then click the **Format tab** beneath the Picture Tools contextual tab.

b. Click the **More button** in the Picture Styles group on the Format tab.

The Picture Styles gallery opens showing styles using a variety of borders, shadow effects, 3-D effects, reflection effects, and more. Move your mouse over the styles and watch how each style impacts the image. Some of the styles involve extensive changes so expect a slowdown as the preview is created.

c. Select **Simple Frame, White**.

This style applies a white border around the image, which sets the edges of the picture nicely.

d. Click **Picture Border** in the Picture Styles group on the Format tab, and then click **Indigo, Accent 4** in the Theme Colors section.

e. Click **Picture Effects** in the Picture Styles group on the Format tab, click **Bevel**, and then click **Relaxed Inset**.

The Bevel effect applied to the outer edges of the picture make the border look as if it is raised and more like a picture frame.

f. Click **Save**.

Figure 4.14 Picture Style Applied

Refer to Figure 4.15 as you complete Step 3.

a. Move to **Slide 3** and use the **Add Picture buttons** in the content placeholders to insert *chap4_ho1_5memories.jpg* and *chap4_ho1_6memories.jpg* into your presentation.

The two images were taken in different lighting conditions. You decide to adjust the brightness and contrast of one of the images to match the other. You could darken the image on the right to maintain a romantic evening mood or you could brighten and adjust the contrast of the image on the left to show the color and detail in the image. You decide to work with the image on the left.

b. Select the image on the left, and then click **Brightness** in the Adjust group on the Format tab beneath the Picture Tools contextual tab. Click **+10%**.

The image became brighter but is muddy-looking. There needs to be greater contrast to bring out the detail.

c. Click **Contrast** in the Adjust group on the Format tab beneath the Picture Tools context tab. Click **+10%**.

d. Click **Save**.

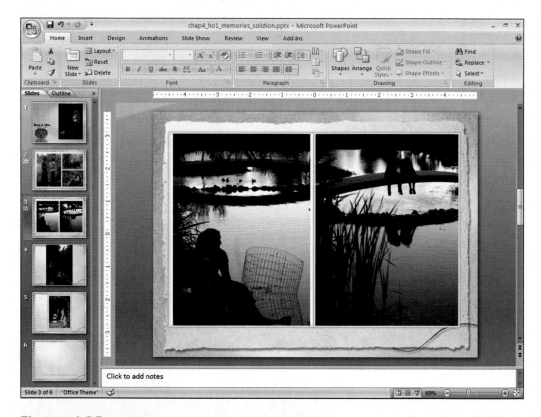

Figure 4.15 Brightness and Contrast Increases

Step 4
Crop and Compress

Refer to Figure 4.16 as you complete Step 4.

a. Move to **Slide 4** and examine the picture.

The picture was inserted using the Insert Picture command, which centers it on the slide. You decide you want to focus attention on the couple by cropping the picture, but do not want to delete the wild flowers growing by the path. You decide to crop the image from the top and bottom.

b. If necessary, click the **View tab** and click **Ruler** in the Show/Hide group.

Activating the ruler will make it easier for you to determine the area to crop.

c. Select the picture and click the **Format tab** beneath the Picture Tools contextual tab.

d. Click **Crop** in the Size group on the Format tab.

e. Position the Crop tool over the top, center cropping handle, and drag inward until the guiding line on the vertical ruler reaches the +2" mark.

f. Position the Crop tool over the bottom, center cropping handle, and drag inward until the guiding line on the vertical ruler reaches the -2.5" mark.

The resulting size of the image is almost a perfect 5" square.

g. Click the **Crop** tool again to toggle it off.

The image has been resized on screen, but the file size has not been reduced. You need to compress the image to remove the unwanted portions and to lower the resolution.

h. Click **Compress Pictures** in the Adjust group on the Format tab, and then click **Options.**

Do not check the Apply to selected pictures only option. You need to compress all the pictures you have used in the presentation to reduce the presentation file size.

TROUBLESHOOTING: If you checked the selected pictures only option, press Cancel in the Compression Settings dialog box. You will be returned to the Compress Pictures dialog box, where you can deselect the option and click Options once again.

i. Click **Screen** in the *Target output* section.

j. Click **OK**, and then click **OK** in the Compress Pictures dialog box.

Figure 4.16 Cropped and Compressed Picture

<table>
<tr>
<td>

Step 5

Create a Background from a Picture

</td>
<td>

Refer to Figure 4.17 as you complete Step 5.

a. Move to **Slide 5** and click the **Design tab**.

The bride selected summer flowers as the wedding theme, so you decide to insert a photo of the flowers in her bouquet as a background for her bridal picture.

b. Click **Background Styles** in the Background group, and then click **Format Background** at the bottom of the gallery.

c. In the Format Background dialog box, check **Hide background graphics**.

d. Click **Picture or texture fill**, click **File**, select *chap4_ho1_7memories.tif*, and then click **Insert**. Click **Close**.

TROUBLESHOOTING: If the bouquet is not displayed, it may be blocked by the background graphics. Check **Hide Background Graphics** in the Background group on the Design tab.

e. Click **Save**.

</td>
</tr>
</table>

Figure 4.17 Background from a Picture

Refer to Figure 4.18 as you complete Step 6.

a. Move to **Slide 6** and note the hyperlink to Image*After (imageafter.com).

Slide 6 has a hyperlink to *Image*After*, a Web site that provides pictures free for personal or commercial use. The young couple went scuba diving in Cancun, Mexico, during their honeymoon so you want to insert a picture of an underwater scene to round off your slide show.

b. Right-click, and then select **Open Hyperlink** to launch the Web site in your default browser.

TROUBLESHOOTING: If you are not connected to the Internet, the hyperlink will not work. Connect to the Internet, and then repeat Step b.

The Image*After Web site displays the nature-underwater group and shows thumbnails of images pertaining to underwater views.

c. Point to the scissors showing on each of the images to display the image's file name until you locate *dark scene 1,* which may also be found under the file name *water plant fish under water dark rock-images,* without clicking, to each thumbnail to see a bigger image. Try to find the same image that is shown in Figure 4.18. If you do not see that image, find another image that is very similar.

d. Click the thumbnail to bring up a larger image. Right-click the image, select **Copy**, and then close the Web browser.

e. Right-click in **Slide 6**, and then select **Paste**.

Notice that because you are pasting the image instead of inserting it through the Insert Picture feature, the picture is not centered on the page.

f. Drag the picture into the approximate center of the page. Depending on the size of the image you insert, you may need to adjust the image size prior to moving it to the center.

g. Click **Save**, and then close the presentation.

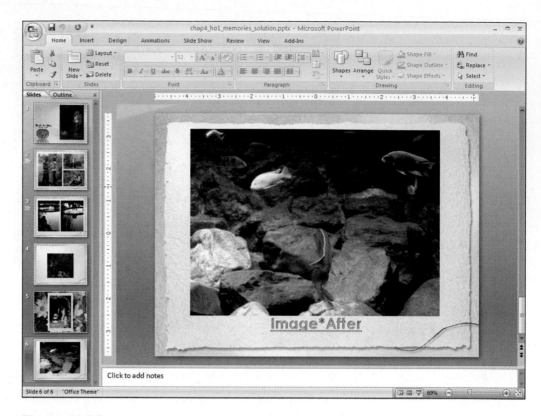

Figure 4.18 Inserted Picture from the Internet

Photo Albums

In the previous section, you created a personalized photo album containing saved photographs. While the customized product was personalized and contained images of various sizes, it was time consuming to create. PowerPoint has a Photo Album feature designed to speed this process. The feature takes the images you select and arranges them on album pages based on selections you make, saving considerable effort.

In this section, you use the Photo Album feature to create an album and use the feature settings to customize your album.

Creating a Photo Album

A *photo album* is a presentation containing multiple pictures organized into album pages.

A Microsoft PowerPoint *Photo Album* is a presentation that contains multiple pictures that are imported and formatted through the Photo Album feature. Because each picture does not have to be formatted individually, you save a considerable amount of time. The photo album in Figure 4.19 contains the same images used in the first hands-on exercise. This time, however, it took less than two minutes to create the album and assign a background. Because a four-per-page layout was selected, portrait images were reduced to fit the size of the placeholder. This setting drastically reduced the size of some images, although it does create an interesting asymmetrical design on the page.

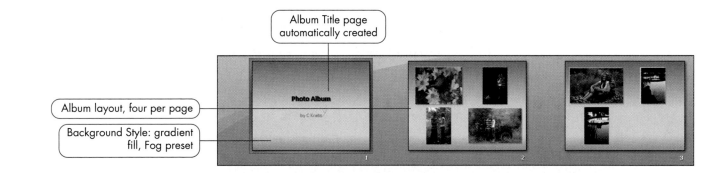

Figure 4.19 PowerPoint Photo Album

To create a photo album, click Photo Album in the Illustrations group on the Insert tab. The Photo Album dialog box opens. If you click the Photo Album arrow instead, you may choose between creating a new album or editing a previously created album. Click the File/Disk button in the Album Content area and navigate to the location of your photographs. Select the photographs you wish to include in your album—do not worry about the order of the photographs you select. You can change the order later. Once an album has been created, you can edit the album settings by clicking the Photo Album arrow in the Illustrations group on the Insert tab, and then clicking Edit Photo Album.

Setting Photo Album Options

After importing the photographs of your choice, they will appear in a list in the dialog box. Click the name of a picture and a preview of the picture will display. This preview will help you determine the order of photographs in the album. Use the move up arrow and the move down arrow to reposition a selected photograph. You can use Ctrl or Shift to select more than one image. You can delete any unwanted photographs by clicking the Remove button.

If you have downloaded photographs from a digital camera, you may need to rotate some of the images. Rotate buttons are included in the dialog box to accomplish this task. Contrast and brightness controls also are included so you can fine-tune your pictures within the Photo Album dialog box. You can even change the pictures to black and white. The Album Content area includes an option to insert a New Text Box so that area in the album is reserved for a text placeholder. The text placeholder is the same size as the placeholders for pictures. The Caption option in the Album Content area will not become available until you select the layout of your album. When you select the layout, the Captions below ALL pictures option is activated. Checking this box displays the file name of the picture as a caption below the picture in the album. Figure 4.20 shows the location of these tools.

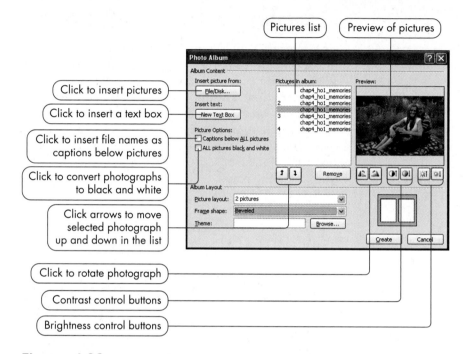

Figure 4.20 PowerPoint Photo Album Dialog Box

The Album Layout area of the Photo Album dialog box gives you your greatest opportunity for personalizing the album. First, you get to select the layout for your album page. You can select from the following options: fitting a single picture on a page; one, two, or four pictures on a page; or one, two, or four pictures per page with each page including a title placeholder. When you fit a single picture per page, the image is maximized on the page. Add automatic transitions and loop the presentation, and you have a beautiful presentation for a family gathering or special event. Why not create an album of favorite family photographs through the years, burn it to a CD, and mail a copy to each family member as a holiday greeting?

> ... create an album of favorite family photographs ... and mail a copy to each family member as a holiday greeting.

You can select from a variety of frame shapes in the Album Layout area. Options include rectangles, rounded rectangles, simple black or white frames, a compound black frame, a center shadow rectangle, or Soft Edge Rectangle. For a nostalgic "old-time" feeling picture, insert a picture into a photo album, select the black and white option, and then select Simple Frame, White to create the album. Finally, change the background to a parchment theme.

You can apply a theme for the background of your album while in the Photo Album dialog box. If you are in a networked lab situation, however, it may be difficult to navigate to the location where themes are stored. If this is the case, create the album, and then in the main PowerPoint window, click the Design tab and click the More button in the Themes group. Select your theme from the gallery.

Hands-On Exercises

2 | Creating a Photo Album

Skills covered: 1. Select and Order Pictures **2.** Adjust Contrast and Brightness **3.** Set Picture Layout **4.** Select Frame Shape **5.** Edit Album Settings **6.** Apply a Design Theme

Select and Order Pictures

Refer to Figure 4.21 as you complete Step 1.

a. Click the **Insert tab**, then click **Photo Album** in the Illustrations group.

The Photo Album dialog box opens.

b. Click **File/Disk** and navigate to the location of your student files. Open the *chap4_ho1_memories_images* folder.

c. Press **Control+A** to select all pictures in the folder, and then click **Insert**.

The list of pictures displays in the Pictures in album box.

d. Use the **Move up arrow** to reposition *chap4_ho1_2memories.jpeg* so that it is the first picture in the list.

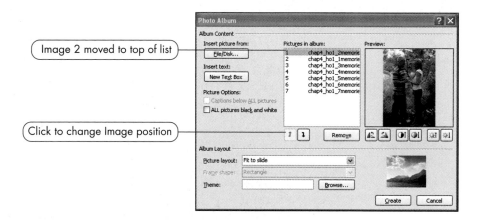

Figure 4.21 Repositioning Images in the Photo Album

Step 2

Adjust Contrast and Brightness

a. Select *chap4_ho1_5memories.jpg* in the Pictures in Album list.

This image needs editing because it is too dark to see detail.

b. Click the **Increase Contrast** button four times.

c. Click the **Increase Brightness** button six times.

Color now may be seen in the Preview window. If you had changed brightness only, the image would be washed out.

d. Select *chap4_ho1_6memories.jpg* in the list of pictures.

e. Click the **Increase Contrast** button four times and the **Increase Brightness** button six times.

Step 3
Set Picture Layout

a. Click the **Picture Layout drop-down arrow** in the *Album Layout* section of the Photo Album dialog box.

b. Click each of the layouts and view the layout in the Album Layout preview window on the right.

c. Click **4 pictures**.

Clicking *4 pictures* will create an album of three pages—a title page, a page with four pictures, and a page with three pictures.

Step 4
Select Frame Shape

Refer to Figure 4.22 as you complete Step 4.

a. Click the **Frame shape drop-down arrow** in the *Album Layout* section.

b. Click each of the frames and view the preview window on the right.

c. Click **Simple Frame, White**, and then click **Create**.

The album is created, but because portrait and landscape pictures are included on the same page and because portrait pictures are squeezed into small placeholders, the appearance of the album is not the best it can be.

d. Save the **chap4_ho2_album_solution** presentation.

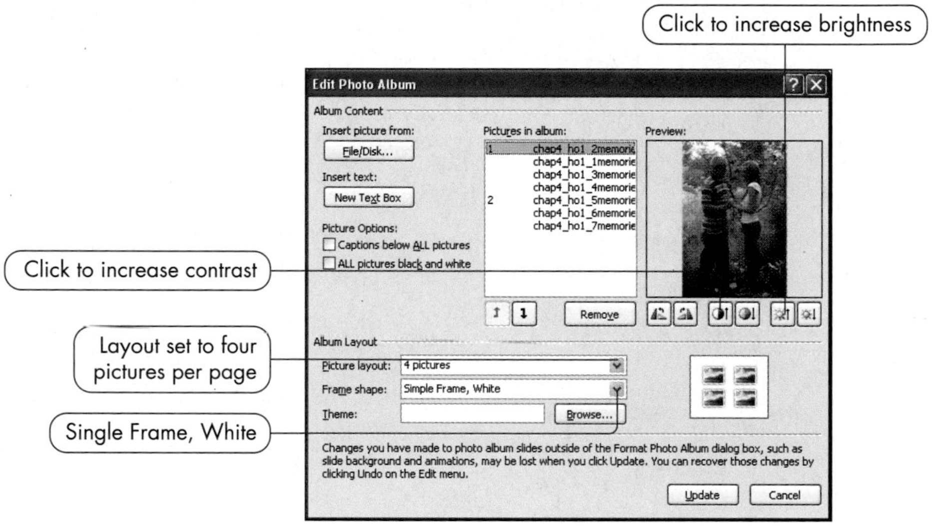

Figure 4.22 Album Setup

Step 5
Edit Album Settings

Refer to Figure 4.23 as you complete Step 5.

a. Click the **Photo Album down arrow** in the Illustrations group, and then click **Edit Photo Album**.

The Photo Album dialog box opens displaying the current settings, which you may now change. Note that the picture list has changed to indicate which pictures appear on which slide and that because you only have three images on Slide 2, a text box has been added.

b. Select the picture of the bouquet, *chap4_ho1_7memories.jpeg*, in the pictures list and click the **Remove button**. Also remove the text box.

c. Click the **Picture layout drop-down arrow,** and then click **2 pictures**.

d. Click the **Frame shape drop-down arrow** and select **Center Shadow Rectangle**.

e. Click **Update**.

f. Save as **chap4_ho2_album2_solution**.

The pictures now appear two per page, and the landscaped pictures are on separate pages from the portrait pictures.

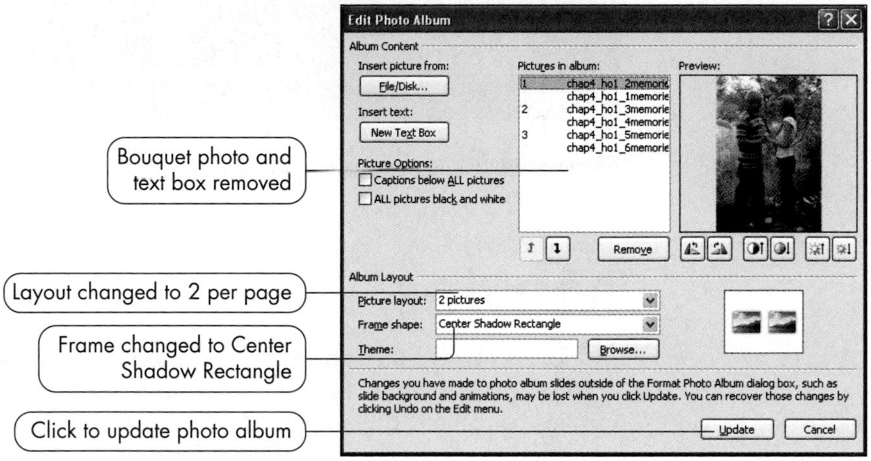

Figure 4.23 Updated Album

Step 6
Apply a Design Theme

Refer to Figure 4.24 as you complete Step 6.

a. Click the **Design tab**, and then click the **More button** in the Themes group.

While you could have selected a Theme in the Photo Album dialog box, you would have needed to navigate to wherever Themes are saved on your system. This step can be quite complicated in a networked laboratory.

b. Click **Paper** to apply the theme to the presentation.

The Paper theme is characterized by a torn parchment look that goes well with the idea of memories.

c. Click **Background Styles** in the Background group on the Design tab, and then click **Style 9**.

d. Create a Notes and Handouts Header and Footer with your name in the header and your instructor's name and your class in the footer.

e. Save as **chap4_ho2_album3_solution**. Close the file and exit PowerPoint if you do not want to continue to the next exercise at this time.

Figure 4.24 Completed Photo Album

Movies

Motion is always fascinating to an audience. Just as the animation effects we have applied to a single image used motion to direct the audience's focus to the image, movies command the audience's attention to multiple moving images. *Movies* can be added to your presentation as video clips or as animated GIF files containing multiple images that stream to create an animation effect. While animated GIF files technically are not movies, Microsoft includes them in the Clip Organizer as movies because the animations use motion to tell a story. In this section, you will learn the types of video clips that PowerPoint supports, examine the options available when using video, and add an animated movie clip from the Clip Organizer to our memories presentation.

Movies are video files, or GIF files containing multiple images that stream to produce an animation.

Inserting Movies

Movies are the most memorable multimedia event that you can add to your presentation. With a movie clip added to your project, you can greatly enhance and reinforce your story, and your audience can retain more of what they see. For example, a movie clip of hurricane powered water surging over levee walls and the walls collapsing beneath the pressure would stir the emotion of a viewer far more than a table listing the number of gallons of water a levee is designed to withstand. Anytime you can engage a viewer's emotions, they will remember your message.

Table 4.2 displays the common types of movie file formats you can use with PowerPoint. The different file formats use different types of *codec* (coder/decoder) software that uses an algorithm to compress or code the movie and then to decompress or decode the movie for playback. Movie playback places a tremendous demand on your computer system in terms of processing speed and memory. Using a codec reduces that demand. In order for your video file to be viewed correctly, the video player needs to have the right software installed. Because of this, even though your file extension is the same as one listed in Table 4.2 or in Help, it may not play correctly if the correct version of the codec is not installed.

A *Codec* (coder/decoder) is a digital video compression scheme used to compress a video and decompress for playback.

Table 4.2 Types of Video File Formats Supported by PowerPoint 2007

File Format	Extension	Description
Movie file	.mpg or .mpeg	**Moving Picture Experts Group** Evolving set of standards for video and audio compression developed by the Moving Picture Experts Group. Designed specifically for use with Video-CD and CD-i media.
Windows Media file	.asf	**Advanced Streaming Format** Stores synchronized multimedia data. Used to stream audio and video content, images, and script commands over a network.
Windows Media Video file	.wmv	**Windows Media Video** Compresses audio and video by using Windows Media Video compressed format. Requires a minimal amount of storage space on your computer's hard drive.
Windows Video file	.avi	**Audio Video Interleave** Stores sound and moving pictures in Microsoft Resource Interchange File Format (RIFF) format. Common format because audio or video content that is compressed can be stored in an .avi file.

TIP Inserting a QuickTime Movie

PowerPoint 2007 does not support insertion of an Apple QuickTime movie (.mov) file. You can, however, create a hyperlink to the QuickTime movie on a PowerPoint slide. Then, while you are presenting, you can click the hyperlink and QuickTime for Windows will start and automatically play the movie. When the movie is finished, you close the QuickTime window, which will return you to your slide show.

An **embedded object** is an object from an external source stored within a presentation.

A **linked object** is an object stored outside the presentation in its own file.

When you add video to your presentation, the video is linked to the presentation rather than embedded. The essential difference in embedding and linking objects is that an *embedded object* is placed into the presentation, whereas a *linked object* is stored in its own file and the presentation is one of many potential documents that are linked to that object. The advantage of linking over embedding is that the presentation is updated automatically if the original object is changed. One caution for using linked movies—because the movie is not part of the presentation, if you move the presentation, you must make sure you move a copy of the movie, too. If you change the location of the movie, you must make sure to change the link in the presentation.

To insert a movie, click the Insert tab and click the Movie down arrow in the Media Clips group. Then select Movie from File or Movie from Clip Organizer (if you click the Movie button instead of the down arrow, you go directly to the Insert Movie dialog box). When you select Movie from File, the Insert Movie dialog box displays so that you may browse to locate your file (see Figure 4.25). Locate your file and click OK. A dialog box opens to ask you how you want the movie to play inside your presentation. The movie can play automatically when the slide is displayed or it can play when you click the mouse. You can change the settings so the movie plays after a specific time delay.

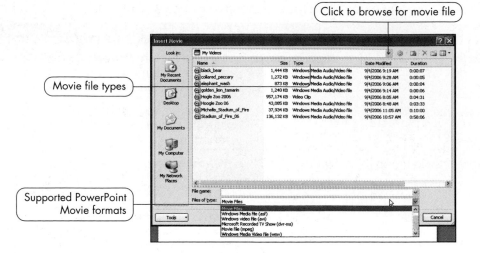

Figure 4.25 Insert Movie Dialog Box

When you click the Movie from Clip Organizer option, the Clip Organizer opens. Just as you did with clip art, you enter a keyword, indicate the type of clip you are looking for—in this case, Movie—and then click Go. The results are displayed in the Clip Art task pane, as shown in Figure 4.26. You can identify movie clips by the animation icon on the bottom right of the clip. The icon shows a yellow star.

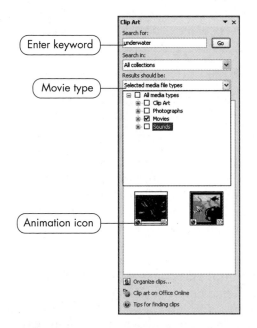

Figure 4.26 Movie from Clip Organizer

Setting Movie Options

After you insert a movie using the Movie from File option, a new contextual tab displays—Movie Tools. The Options tab beneath Movie Tools provides access to the options that enable you to preview the movie, control how your movie starts, display or hide the movie icon, play the movie full screen or not, loop the movie so it starts over after playing, and to rewind the movie after playing. Also, if your movie includes sound, the volume can be controlled through Movie Options. Figure 4.27 displays the Movie Tools and Options.

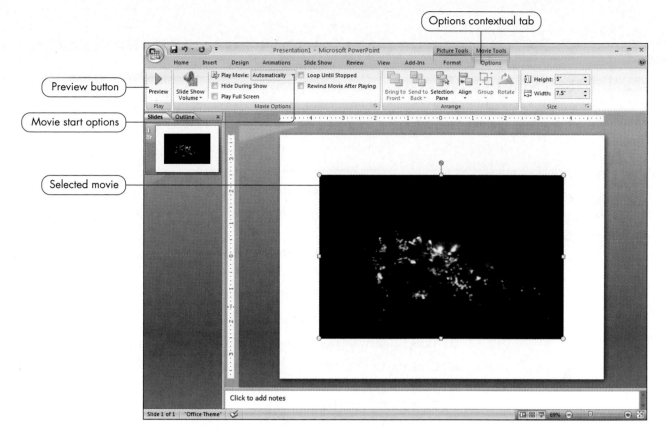

Options contextual tab

Preview button

Movie start options

Selected movie

Figure 4.27 Movie Options

You may resize your movie by changing its viewing resolution. To do so, click the Size Dialog Box Launcher in the Size group on the Options tab beneath Movie Tools. The Size and Position dialog opens (see Figure 4.28). By default, the movie is sized relative to its original picture size, but you may check Best scale for slide show, which enables you to select the desired resolution. The greater the resolution, the smaller the image size and the clearer the image. For example, a resolution of 640 x 480 fills more of the screen than a resolution of 1024 x 768, but is not as clear.

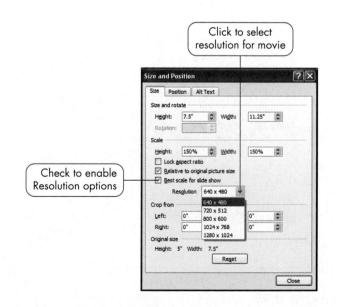

Click to select resolution for movie

Check to enable Resolution options

Figure 4.28 Size and Position Dialog Box

Hands-On Exercises

3 | Inserting a Movie

Skills covered: 1. Insert a Movie from the Clip Organizer **2.** Insert a Movie from a File **3.** Set Movie Options

---

Step 1
Insert a Movie from the Clip Organizer

Refer to Figure 4.29 as you complete Step 1.

a. Open the *chap4_ho1_memories_solution* presentation, and then save as **chap4_ho3_memories_solution**.

b. Move to **Slide 6**, click the **Insert tab**, and then click the **Movie down arrow** in the Media Clips group.

c. Click **Movie from Clip Organizer**.

The Microsoft Clip Organizer opens.

d. Type **underwater** as the keyword for your search, and then click **Go**.

e. Click the image of the scuba diver's head watching fish swim to insert it in your slide. Close the Clip Organizer. Select the option to have the clip start automatically.

TROUBLESHOOTING: If you do not have a direct connection to the Internet, PowerPoint will not be able to download images from Microsoft Office Online. You will not see the image of the scuba diver watching fish swim. In that case, use **fish** as your keyword and insert a fish movie into the slide.

f. Drag the movie to the lower-right corner of your slide.

Clips are centered on the slide by default.

g. Save the presentation.

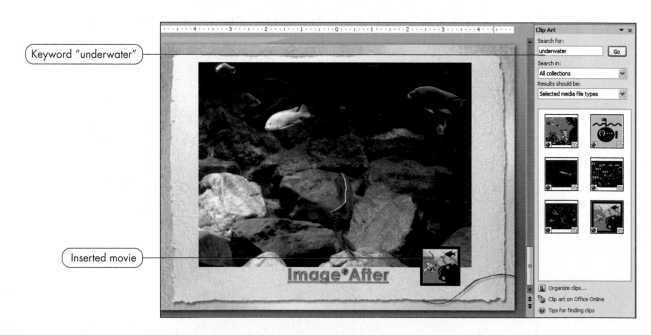

Figure 4.29 Movie from Clip Organizer

Refer to Figure 4.30 as you complete Step 2.

a. Click the **Home tab** and click the **New Slide down arrow** in the Slides group.

b. Click the **Blank** layout.

A new blank slide (Slide 7) is created and should be positioned after Slide 6. If your new slide is in a different position, drag the slide thumbnail to the end of the slides in the Slides tab.

c. Click the **Insert tab** and click the **Movie down arrow** in the Media Clips group.

The groom took digital video of the fireworks they watched on their honeymoon. You decide to add the fireworks video as the finale of your presentation.

d. Click **Movie from File**, and then navigate to the location of your student files.

e. Click *chap4_ho3_fireworks04.wmv*, and then click **OK**.

f. When the dialog box displays asking you how you want the movie to start in the slide, click **Automatically**.

g. If necessary, reposition the movie image so that it is positioned attractively on the slide.

h. Save the *chap4_ho3_memories_solution* presentation.

Figure 4.30 Inserted Windows Media Video File

a. If necessary, select the movie object, and then click the **Options tab** beneath the Movie Tools contextual tab.

b. Check the **Play Full Screen** option.

Enlarging the movie to play full screen causes some pixelation, but as the video is already somewhat blurry due to the speed of the fireworks, the pixelation is acceptable.

c. Check the **Rewind** option.

After a movie plays, the last frame stays on the screen. Clicking Rewind rewinds the movie so that the first frame displays on the screen when the movie is over.

d. Click **Preview**.

The movie plays on the slide for you to preview.

e. Click the **Slide Show tab** and click **From Beginning** in the Start Slide Show group.

Advance through the slide show. Note the movie changes to full screen when playing the movie but returns to its original size and first frame when it is finished playing. The Preview option did not display the options, but the options display during the slide show.

f. Save the *chap4_ho3_memories_solution* presentation. Keep the slide show open for the next hands-on exercise.

Sound

Sound can be the perfect finishing touch to a presentation or it can be an irritating interruption. Sounds can draw on common elements of any language or culture—

$$\left(\begin{array}{c} \text{Harnessing the emotional impact of} \\ \text{sound in your presentation can trans-} \\ \text{form your presentation from "good"} \\ \text{to "extraordinary."} \end{array} \right)$$

screams, laughs, sobs, etc. Sound can spice up your presentation, provide listening pleasure in the background, set the mood for your message, or serve as a wake-up call for the audience. People respond emotionally to sound. Harnessing the emotional impact of sound in your presentation can transform your presentation from "good" to "extraordinary." On the other hand, use sound incorrectly and you can destroy your presentation and leave the audience with a headache and confused. Just keep in mind the guideline emphasized throughout this text—any added object must enhance your message, even when used for emphasis or effect—and you will not go wrong.

Your computer needs a sound card and speakers to play sound. In a classroom or computer laboratory, however, you will need a headset or headphones for playback so that you do not disturb other students. You can play sounds and music files stored on a hard drive, flash drive, or any other storage device. You also can locate and play sounds and music stored in the Clip Organizer. If you have a CD that has an audio track you wish to play, you can direct PowerPoint to locate the audio track and play it. You can also record your own sounds, music, or narration to play from PowerPoint. Table 4.3 lists the types of Audio file formats supported by PowerPoint 2007.

Table 4.3 Types of Audio File Formats Supported by PowerPoint 2007

File Format	Extension	Description
AIFF Audio file	.aiff	**Audio Interchange File Format** Waveform files stored in 8-bit monaural (mono or one channel) format. Not compressed. Can result in large files. Originally used on Apple and Silicon Graphics (SGI) computers.
AU Audio file	.au	**UNIX Audio** Typically used to create sound files for UNIX computers or the Web.
MIDI file	.mid or .midi	**Musical Instrument Digital Interface** Standard format for interchange of musical information between musical instruments, synthesizers, and computers.
MP3 Audio file	.mp3	**MPEG Audio Layer 3** Sound file that has been compressed by using the MPEG Audio Layer 3 codec (developed by the Fraunhofer Institute).
Windows Audio file	.wav	**Wave Form** Stores sounds as waveforms. Depending on various factors, one minute of sound can occupy as little as 644 kilobytes or as much as 27 megabytes of storage.
Windows Media Audio file	.wma	**Windows Media Audio** Sound format used to distribute recorded music, usually over the Internet. Compressed using the Microsoft Windows Media Audio codec (developed by Microsoft).

In this section, you review the methods for inserting sound and tips for each method. You insert sound from the Clip Organizer and learn how to determine the number of times a sound clip plays, the number of slides through which the sound plays, and the method for launching the sound. Finally, you record a short narration for a presentation.

Adding Sound

To insert sound from a file, click the Insert tab, and then click Sound in the Media Clips group. If you want to choose between inserting sound from a file, inserting sound from the Clip Organizer, playing a CD audio track, or recording sound, click the Sound drop-down arrow and make your selection from the resulting list. When you select Sound from File, the Insert Sound dialog box displays. Navigate to the file location, select the file, and click OK. A dialog box displays, asking you how you want the sound to start in the slide show, automatically or on a mouse click. After you select how you want the sound to start, the box disappears and a small speaker icon representing the file appears in the center of the slide. The appearance of the Sound icon will change depending on options you select. A number next to the icon indicates that the sound is part of an animation sequence while a hand next to the icon indicates that the sound will start with a click.

To insert sound from the Clip Organizer, click the Insert tab, and then click the Sound down arrow in the Media Clips group. Select Sound from the Clip Organizer and the Clip Organizer task pane opens. Just as you have done when searching for pictures and movies, you insert a keyword for your search and click Go. You can point at one of the sound clips in the results pane, and a tip appears showing keywords, file size, and the sound format of the clip. To hear a preview of the clip, click the blue bar that appears on the right side of the clip when your mouse hovers over it, and then click Preview/Properties. The Preview/Properties dialog box opens, playing the sound clip and providing you with valuable information about the clip. If you prefer, you can insert the sound clip in the slide show. Once the clip is in the slide show, you can click the Preview button in the Play group on the Options tab beneath the Sound Tools to hear it. Right-click the sound icon and you can choose Preview.

Do you have the perfect music for your presentation but it is on a CD? Do the lyrics of a song on a CD support your theme? Would the song be good background music for a slide? Do you want to welcome the audience with music as they enter the room? For all of these reasons and more, PowerPoint enables you to play sound from a CD. You can determine which track on the CD to play and whether you want the entire track to play or just a portion.

To add sound from a CD, put the CD in the CD drive of your computer, and then move to the slide from which you want the sound to play. Click the Insert tab, and then click the arrow under Sound in the Media Clips group. Click Play CD Audio Track and the Insert CD Audio dialog box displays. Enter the starting and ending track numbers in the Start at track and End at track boxes under Clip Selection (see Figure 4.31). If you are playing only one track, the starting and ending number will be the same. If you want the sound to repeat, check the Loop until stopped option. When you click OK, you will be prompted to select whether you want the CD to play automatically or whether you want to click a CD icon to start the sound.

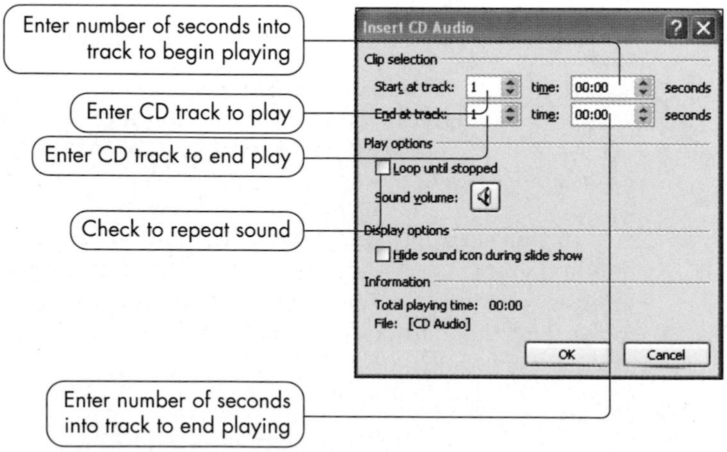

Figure 4.31 CD Audio Options

To record comments on individual slides, move to the slide in which you wish to add the comment. Click the Insert tab, click the arrow under Sound in the Media Clips group, and then click Record Sound. Click Record and start speaking (see Figure 4.32). When you stop speaking, click Stop to end the recording. Click the Play button to check the recording and continue recording until you are satisfied with the comment. In the Name box, type a name for the comment, and then click OK. A sound icon will appear on your slide.

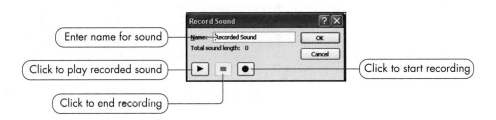

Figure 4.32 Record Sound Dialog Box

TIP   Storing Sounds

Sounds that are less than 100 kb and .wav sounds are embedded in a slide show. All other sounds are linked. This link can cause problems if you take your presentation to another computer but do not take the sound files, too. One way to prevent this problem is to create a folder for your presentation. Then save the slide show, all sound files, and any other linked files like movie files to the folder for storage. Before displaying the slide show in a presentation, test it to make sure all links are working. If not, redo the links using the resource files in your folder.

Changing Sound Settings

Although only two options for starting appear in the dialog box, you have other options available through the Custom Animation task pane. You can have the sound start after a delay or you can have the sound set up to play as part of an animation sequence. To set up for delay before the sound starts, select the sound icon, and then click the Animations tab. Click Custom Animation in the Animations group. The Custom Animation task pane displays and the selected sound will appear in the list. Click the arrow on the right side of the selected sound and click Effect Options. The Play Sound dialog box opens.

The Play Sound dialog box includes three tabs: Effect, Timings, and Sound Settings. In the Effect tab (see Figure 4.33), you can determine the start and stop settings for your sound. The Timings tab (see Figure 4.34) enables you to set the number of times a sound clip will repeat. The Sound Settings tab (see Figure 4.35) enables you to change the sound volume and hide the sound icon and displays information about the length of the sound clip and the sound location.

Figure 4.33 Effect Tab Settings

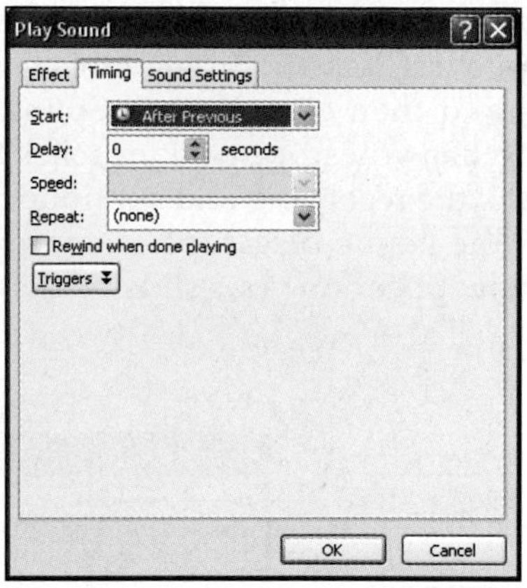

Figure 4.34 Timing Tab Settings

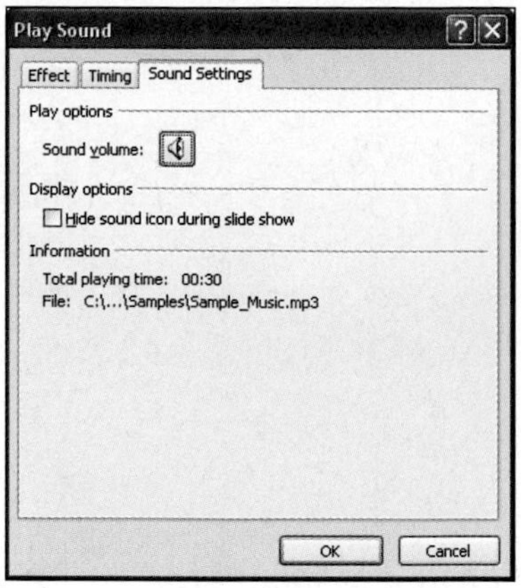

Figure 4.35 Sound Settings Tab

Play a Sound over Multiple Slides

By default, a sound plays until it ends or until the next mouse click. If you are playing background music, this default means the music ends when you click to advance to the next slide. If you would like the sound to continue as you click through slides, open the Custom Animation list, and then select the sound in the list. Click the arrow to the right of the sound, and then click Effect Options. The Play Sound dialog box appears with the Effects tab active. In the Stop Playing area of the Effects tab, click the option for After. Then you simply enter the number of slides you want the sound to play through. If you do not know how long the slide show will be, just enter 99! If the background music stops before you get to the last slide, you can use the Loop Until Stopped feature to keep the sound repeating. Click Loop Until Stopped in the Sound Options group on the Options tab beneath Sound Tools.

Recording and Playing Narration

Narration is spoken commentary that is added to a project.

Sometimes, you may find it helpful to add recorded *narration*, or spoken commentary, to your slide show. One example of a need for recorded narration is when you want to create a self-running presentation, such as a presentation displaying in a kiosk at the mall. Another example would be if you are trying to create an association between words and an image on the screen, such as in a presentation to a group trying to learn a new language or for young children expanding their vocabulary. Rather than adding a narration prior to a presentation, however, you might want to create the narration during the presentation. For example, recording during a meeting would create an archive of the meeting.

You have the choice of either embedding a narration in a slide show or linking the narration to a slide show. Embedding the narration makes for a large file size and may slow down the slide show, but you will be assured that the narration travels with the slide show. If you decide to link the narration so the narrated file is smaller and plays faster, make sure the narration is stored in a location where it can travel with or be accessed with the presentation—preferably in a folder containing the slide show and all its resources.

Before creating the narration, keep in mind the following:

- Your computer will need a sound card, speakers, and a microphone.
- Long narrations should be linked to the presentation rather than embedded.
- Comments on selected slides may be recorded rather than a narration of the entire presentation, which creates smaller file size.
- Voice narration takes precedence over any other sounds during playback.
- PowerPoint records the amount of time it takes you to narrate each slide, and if you save the slide timings, you can use them to create an automatic slide show.
- When you record your presentation, you run through the presentation and record on each slide. You can pause and resume recording during the process.

To record the narration, click the Slide Show tab, and then click Record Narration in the Set Up group (see Figure 4.36). Before recording, you need to set the microphone level to ensure that the narration can be heard. Click the Set Microphone Level button on the Record Narration dialog box. You will be asked to read a sentence to ensure the microphone is working and the volume is appropriate. When you have completed this process, click OK.

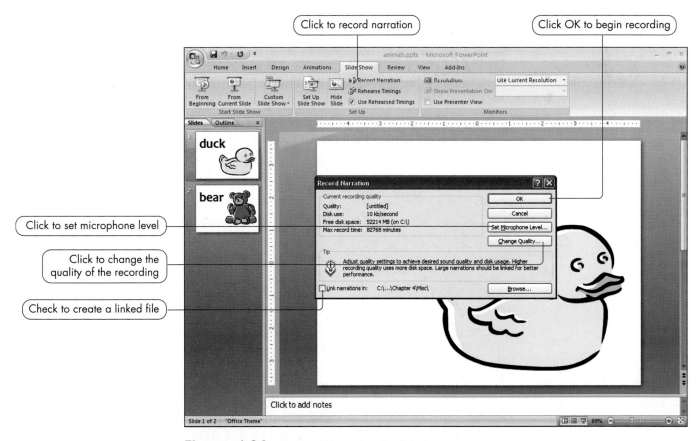

Figure 4.36 Record Narration Dialog Box

If you plan on a long narration, be sure to click the option to link the narration rather than embed the narration in the slide show. You can then navigate to the folder you wish to save the linked file in. Once again, if you have linked files in your slide show, you should create a folder for your presentation and save the slide show plus any linked files inside the folder. That way if you move the presentation to another computer, you bring all the resources with you when you copy the folder.

When you click OK at the top of the Record Narration dialog box, you enter the slide show mode and you can begin. Narrate the first slide, click to advance to the next slide, narrate, and continue advancing and narrating through the show until you reach the end. To pause during the narration and then resume again, right-click the slide, and then click either Pause Narration or Resume Narration on the shortcut menu.

When you exit the slide show, you will be asked if you want to save the show timings. PowerPoint not only recorded your voice, it recorded the amount of time you stayed on each slide. If you were creating the slide show to be self-running, you would save the timings; otherwise, there is no need to save. After making your selection, you are returned to Normal view. A sound icon appears in the lower right of the slides you narrated. View the slide show and you will hear your narrations.

To create an archive of a presentation in a meeting during which you capture your own comments and the comments of your audience, you can turn on narration before you begin your presentation.

TIP   Create Notes of Your Narration

A transcript of your narration should be available for those in your audience who are hearing impaired, or for those who receive a copy of your self-running slide show but do not have a sound card in their computer. Providing the transcript lets these audiences gain from your presentation, too. Putting the transcript in the PowerPoint's Notes feature and printing the Notes accomplishes this task nicely.

Hands-On Exercises

 4 | Adding Sound

Skills covered: 1. Add Sound from a File **2.** Change Sound Settings **3.** Insert Sound from the Clip Organizer **4.** Add Narration

---

Step 1 Add Sound from a File	**a.** Open the *chap4_ho3_memories_solution* presentation if you closed it after the last exercise, and then save it as the **chap4_ho4_memories_solution** presentation. **b.** On Slide 1, click the **Insert tab** and click the **Sound down arrow** in the Media Clips group. **c.** Click **Sound from File**. The Insert Sound dialog box opens. **d.** Navigate to the location of your student files, click *Beethoven's Symphony No. 9*, and then click **OK**. **e.** When asked how you want the sound to start, click **Automatically**. The sound icon is displayed in the center of the slide. **f.** Drag the slide icon to the bottom right. **g.** Save the *chap4_ho4_memories_solution* presentation.

Step 2 Change Sound Settings	Refer to Figure 4.37 as you complete Step 2. **a.** Click the **Slide Show tab**, and then click **From Beginning** in the Start Slide Show group. Advance through the slides, and then end the slide show. Note that the sound clip on Slide 1 discontinues playing as soon as you click to advance to the next slide. You will change the sound settings so the sound clip plays through several slides. **b.** Select the sound icon on Slide 1. **c.** Click the **Animations tab** and click **Custom Animation** in the Animations group. **d.** Click the **drop-down arrow** on the right side of the sound in the animation list, and then click **Effect Options**. **e.** In the Stop Playing section of the Effect tab, type **4** in the After box, and then click **OK**. **f.** Save the *chap4_ho4_memories_solution* presentation. **g.** Play the slide show and note the music plays through the fourth slide.

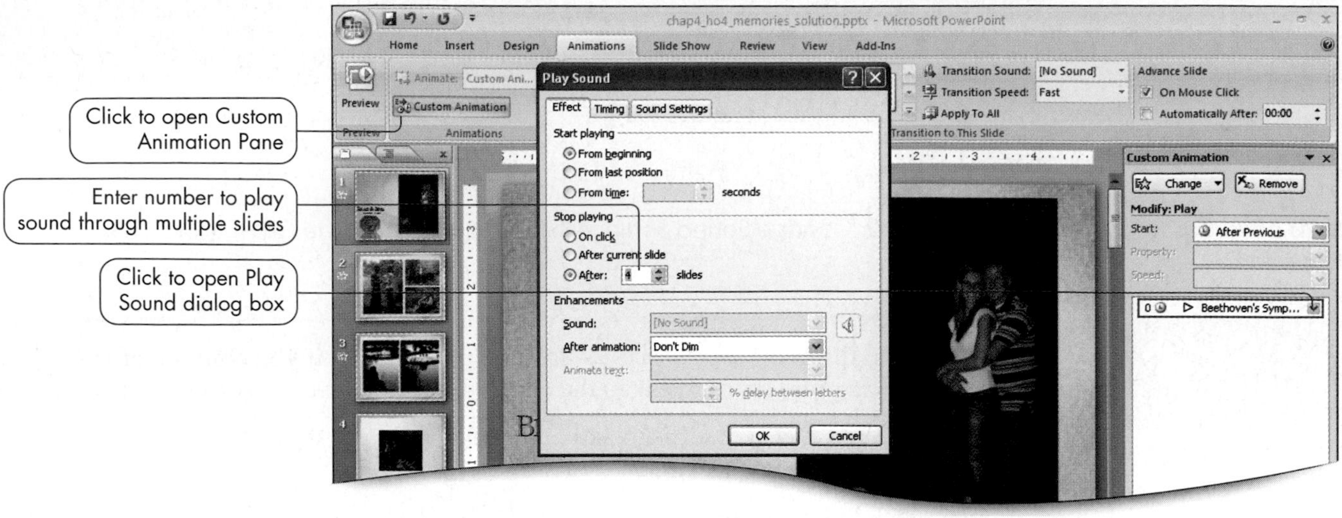

Click to open Custom Animation Pane

Enter number to play sound through multiple slides

Click to open Play Sound dialog box

Figure 4.37 Play Sound Options

Step 3
Insert Sound from the Clip Organizer

a. Move to **Slide 5**.

b. Click the **Insert tab**, and then click the **Sound down arrow** in the Media Clips group.

c. Click **Sound from Clip Organizer**, and then type the keyword **wedding**.

d. Insert the resulting clip, Here Comes the Bride, into Slide 5 and have it start automatically.

e. Select the sound icon and drag it to the lower-right side of the screen so that it does not display during the slide show.

f. Right click the sound icon and click **Preview**.

g. Save the *chap4_ho4_memories_solution* presentation.

Step 4
Add Narration

a. Move to **Slide 1** and click the **Slide Show tab**.

b. Click **Record Narration**, and then click **OK**.

TROUBLESHOOTING: You will not be able to complete this step without a microphone, speakers, and a sound card.

c. When the slide show displays Slide 1, read the text on Slide 1.

d. Press **Spacebar** to advance to the next slide, and then press **Escape** to exit the slide show.

e. Click **Don't Save** so that slide timings are not saved with the slide show.

f. Click **From Beginning** in the Start Slide Show group so that you can hear the narration and the sounds you have added.

g. Save the *chap4_ho4_memories_solution* presentation.

Summary

1. **Insert and modify a picture.** Pictures are very popular for enhancing slide shows. Pictures are in a bitmap format and are realistic portrayals of what we see. They can be inserted using the Insert Picture option, which centers the image on the slide, or by using placeholders that center and crop the image inside the placeholder. The brightness and contrast of pictures can be adjusted and the picture cropped to eliminate unwanted areas. Because bitmap images can be large files, images should be compressed.

2. **Use the Internet as a resource.** The Internet can be extremely valuable when searching for information for a presentation. Although students and teachers have rights under the Fair Use Act, care should be taken to honor all copyrights. Before inserting any information or clips into your slide show, research the copyright ownership. To be safe, contact the Web site owner and request permission to use the material. Any information used should be credited and include hyperlinks when possible, although attribution does not relieve you of the requirement to honor copyright.

3. **Create a Photo Album.** When you have multiple images to be inserted, using the Photo Album feature enables you to quickly insert the images into a slide show. After identifying the images you wish to use, you can rearrange the order of the pictures in the album. You also can choose among layouts for the best appearance.

4. **Utilize Photo Album options.** Album options for contrast and brightness enable you to make image changes without having to leave the album settings dialog box. In addition to adjusting contrast and brightness, you can change the pictures to black and white. Filenames can be turned into captions for the pictures. Frame shape can be selected and a theme applied to complete the album appearance.

5. **Insert movies.** Movies can be powerful tools when inserted into a slide show. PowerPoint plays two types of movies: digital videos and small animated clips stored in the Clip Organizer.

6. **Set movie options.** Movies can be played full screen, looped until stopped, and rewound to the first frame of the movie upon completion of the movie. You can change the movie size by changing the resolution of the movie, but pixelation can occur.

7. **Add sound.** Sound effects and music catch audience attention and add excitement to a presentation. Take care when adding sound that the sound enhances your message rather than detracts from it. All sound files except WAV files under 100 kilobytes are linked to the presentation rather than embedded. Because they are linked, you should take care to copy and move the sound files when you copy and move the presentation.

8. **Record and play narration.** You can narrate a slide show for use in a self-running presentation, or you can turn on narration during a meeting to create an archive of comments made during the presentation.

Key Terms

Multiple Choice

1. Which of the following file formats is best for photographs?

   (a) Vector

   (b) Line

   (c) Bitmap

   (d) Illustration

2. Which of the following is not a Windows graphics file format?

   (a) PICT

   (b) .jpg

   (c) .tif

   (d) .gif

3. Which of these is a feature that can be used to identify a photograph on a slide?

   (a) Frames

   (b) Captions

   (c) Labels

   (d) Full slide

4. All of the following are forms of multimedia except:

   (a) Placeholders

   (b) Video clips

   (c) Text

   (d) Sound clips

5. Which of the following file formats supports 16 million colors, is optimized for photographs and complex graphics, and is the format of choice for most photographs on the Web?

   (a) .bmp

   (b) .jpg

   (c) .gif

   (d) .tiff

6. Which procedure would you follow to change the resolution of a movie clip?

   (a) Click the Set Resolution button in the Movie Options group on the Options tab beneath the Movie Tools contextual tab.

   (b) Click the Movie Options Dialog Box Launcher in the Movie Options group on the Options tab beneath the Movie Tools contextual tab.

   (c) Click the Resolution button in the Arrange group on the Options tab beneath the Movie Tools contextual tab.

   (d) Click the Size and Position Dialog Box Launcher in the Size group on the Options tab beneath the Movie Tools contextual tab.

7. Which of the following Picture Tools would help you adjust a scanned photograph that appears muddy and does not show much difference between the light and dark areas of the image?

   (a) Brightness

   (b) Contrast

   (c) Recolor

   (d) Compress Pictures

8. Which of the following is permitted for a student project in a class?

   (a) The educational project is produced for a specific class and then retained in a personal portfolio for display in a job interview.

   (b) Only a portion of copyrighted material was used, and the portion was determined by the type of media used.

   (c) The student received permission to use copyrighted material to be distributed to classmates in the project.

   (d) All of the above uses are permitted.

9. The Photo Album dialog box enables you to make all but this edit to pictures:

   (a) Rotate

   (b) Crop

   (c) Brightness

   (d) Contrast

10. Which of the following are included in the Clip Organizer?

    (a) Windows Video Files (.avi)

    (b) Moving Picture Experts Group Movies (.mpg or .mpeg)

    (c) Animated GIF Files (.gif)

    (d) Windows Media Video files (.wmv)

11. Which of the following statements is not true?

    (a) Objects linked to a PowerPoint slide show automatically move with the slide show when its location is changed.

    (b) Embedded objects become part of a slide show.

    (c) A linked object in a slide show updates when the original object is changed.

    (d) Embedded objects do not update when the originals are changed.

Multiple Choice Continued

12. Which of the following sound formats may be embedded in a slide show?

    (a) Windows Audio File (.wav)

    (b) MIDI file (.mid or .midi)

    (c) MP3 Audio file (.mp3)

    (d) Windows Media Audio file (.wma)

13. All of the following can be used to play to a sound clip for preview except:

    (a) Click the blue bar on the right side of the clip in the Clip Organizer, and then click Preview/Properties.

    (b) Select the clip on the slide, and then click the Preview button in the Play group on the Options tab beneath Sound Tools.

    (c) Click the clip on the slide.

    (d) Right-click the sound icon and click Preview.

14. Which of the following options for inserting sound is available under the Slide Show tab rather than the Insert tab?

    (a) Record Sound

    (b) Sound from a File

    (c) Play CD Audio Track

    (d) Record Narration

15. Which of the following is a true statement regarding recording a narration?

    (a) Long narrations should be embedded in the slide show.

    (b) CD Audio takes precedence over voice narration on playback.

    (c) The slide timings are recorded with the voice narration for use in a self-running presentation.

    (d) It is not possible to pause the recording during a voice narration.

1 Adding Pictures Using Placeholders

The presentation in Figure 4.38 covers the birth and first year in the life of your niece. You were invited to her first birthday party and decided to put the presentation together as a gift for the baby. The presentation is based on the Contemporary template, so you review your skills in using a template at the same time you practice inserting pictures in Picture placeholders. You also rotate a picture.

a. Open the *chap4_pe1_birthday* presentation, and then save it as **chap4_pe1_birthday_ solution**.

b. On **Slide 1**, click the **Add Picture** button.

c. Navigate to the location of your student files and open the *chap4_pe1_birthday_images* folder. Click the *chap4_pe1_birthday1.jpg* file to select it, and then click **Insert**.

d. Select the text in the orange content placeholder and type **My First Year!** Click in the green placeholder and type **Happy Birthday from Uncle/Aunt and your first name**.

e. Move to **Slide 2**. Click the **Add Picture button** in the left placeholder. In the *chap4_pe1_birthday_images* folder, select and examine the *chap4_pe1_birthday2* picture.

f. Click **Insert**, and then examine the image in Slide 2 and note the cropping.

g. Insert *chap4_pe1_birthday3* in the center placeholder of Slide 2, and then insert *chap4_pe1_birthday4* in the right placeholder, noting the changes that take place as the images are centered and cropped in the placeholders.

h. Select the picture in the center placeholder and click the **Format tab** under the Picture Tools contextual tab.

i. Click **Rotate** in the Arrange group, and then click **Rotate Right 90°**.

j. Select the text *Choose a Page Layout*, and then type **July 30, 2008**. Select the text *click the placeholders to add your own pictures and captions*, and then type **My life as a newborn— sleep, yawn, and cry!** Select the text in the green placeholder and delete.

k. Move to **Slide 3** and read the text in the placeholder. Select the first caption text and type **Proud Papa**, and then select the second caption text and type **Loving Mama**.

l. Click the **Add Picture button** and insert *chap4_pe1_birthday5*.

m. Save the *chap4_pe1_birthday_solution* presentation.

Figure 4.38 Birthday Presentation with Added Pictures

...continued on Next Page

You locate pictures of your niece at the Fourth of July Baby Contest. You decide to add them to your birthday presentation. One of the pictures of your niece is of her on the judging table and has a lot of distracting images, so you decide to crop the picture to focus attention to her. After cropping, you need to compress the picture to save file space. Because you plan on showing the presentation to your family at the birthday party and also on printing the presentation and putting it in a scrapbook for the baby, you compress and save one version at a resolution appropriate for printing, and then you compress and save another version at a resolution for viewing on the screen. Refer to Figure 4.39 as you complete this activity.

a. Save the *chap4_pe1_birthday_solution* presentation as **chap4_pe2_birthday_solution**.

b. Move to **Slide 4**, click the **Home tab**, and click the **New Slide** down arrow. Click **Portrait with Caption**.

c. Replace the text in the content placeholder by typing **Baby Contest** on the first line and **July 4, 2009** on the second line.

d. Click the **Add Picture button** and examine the landscape oriented picture *chap4_pe1_birthday6*. Click **Insert** and note that the picture is forced into the portrait-oriented placeholder and that considerable cropping took place to make this possible.

e. Click the **Insert tab** and click **Picture** in the Illustrations group. Click *chap4_pe2_birthday7* and click **Insert**.

f. Click the **View tab** and click **Ruler** in the Show/Hide group, if necessary.

g. Select the picture, click the **Format tab** beneath the Picture Tools contextual tab, and then click **Crop** in the Size group on the Format tab.

h. Position the Crop tool over the top center cropping handle and drag inward until the guiding line on the vertical ruler reaches the +1" mark.

i. Position the Crop tool over the right center cropping handle and drag inward until the guiding line on the horizontal ruler reaches the +2" mark.

j. Position the Crop tool over the left center cropping handle and drag inward until the guiding line on the horizontal ruler reaches the −1" mark.

k. Click the **Crop** tool again to toggle it off.

l. Click the **Size Dialog Box Launcher** to open the Size and Position dialog box, and then click the **Position tab**.

m. Set the **Horizontal Position on the slide** option to 6" from the **Top Left Corner**. Set the **Vertical Position on slide** option to 3.5" from the **Top Left Corner**. Click **Close**.

n. Click **Compress Pictures** in the Adjust group on the Format tab, and then click **Options**.

o. Click **Print** in the Target Output area, click **OK**, and then click **OK** in the Compress Pictures dialog box.

p. Click the **Office Button**, select **Save As**, and save the presentation as **chap4_pe2_birthdayprint_solution**.

q. Click **Compress Pictures** in the Picture Tools group on the Format tab, and then click **Options**.

r. Click **Screen** in the Target Output area, and then click **OK** in the Compress Pictures dialog box.

s. Click the **Office Button**, select **Save As**, and save the presentation as **chap4_pe2_birthday_solution**. Click **Yes** when asked if you want to replace the previous file.

...continued on Next Page

Baby Contest
July 4, 2009

Figure 4.39 Inserted Pictures and Cropping

3 Create a Border and Apply Picture Styles

You notice that the picture you inserted does not have a border as does the picture inserted through the placeholder. You decide to add a border similar to the one on the other picture on the page. Then you decide to apply Picture Quick Styles as frames to other images in the show to add some fun variety. Refer to Figure 4.40 as you complete this activity.

a. Save the *chap4_pe2_birthday_solution* presentation as **chap4_pe3_birthday_solution**.

b. In **Slide 5**, select the small cropped picture on the right, and then click the **Format tab** beneath the Picture Tools contextual tab.

c. Click **Picture Border** in the Picture Styles group, and then click **White, Background1**.

d. Click **Picture Border** again, and then click **Weight**. Click **3 pt**.

e. Click **Picture Effects**, and then click **Shadow**. Click **Offset Center** in the Outer Shadow area.

f. Click **Picture Effects**, click **Shadow**, and then click **Shadows Options** at the bottom of the list.

g. Set the **Size** to **100%**, **Blur** to **5**, and the **Distance** to 2, and then click **Close**. Deselect the picture.

h. Move to **Slide 4**, select the picture on the left, and then click the **Format** tab beneath the Picture Tools contextual tab.

i. Click **More** in the Picture Styles group.

j. Apply **Rotated, White**.

k. Select the picture in the center, click **More** in the Picture Styles group, and then click **Relaxed Perspective, White**.

l. Select the picture on the right, click **More** in the Picture Styles group, and then click **Bevel Perspective Left, White**.

m. Select the picture on the left and click the right arrow on the keyboard to shift it to the right until it fits on the slide. Select the image on the right and move it closer to the center so that the pictures in the grouping all touch.

n. Select the picture in the middle, click **Arrange** in the Drawing Group, and then click **Bring to Front**.

o. Select the caption text, and then type **Look at me grow!** Click **Center align** on the Mini toolbar.

p. Save the *chap4_pe3_birthday_solution* presentation.

...continued on Next Page

Figure 4.40 Using Picture Styles

4 Adjust Brightness and Contrast

When playing the slide show to see how it presents at this point, you notice that on the last slide, the slide showing a series of images of your niece playing with a flower, one of the photos has very dark areas because of the shadowing on a bright summer day. You decide to see if you can improve the picture using PowerPoint's Picture Tools. Refer to Figure 4.41 as you complete this activity.

    a. Save the *chap4_pe3_birthday_solution* presentation as **chap4_pe4_birthday_solution.**

    b. Move to **Slide 6** and select the picture of the child standing up in the lower-left corner.

    c. Click **Format** beneath the Picture Tools contextual tab.

    d. Click **Brightness** in the Picture Tools group and click +20%.

    e. Click **Contrast** in the Picture Tools group and click +20%.

    f. Save the *chap4_pe4_birthday_solution* presentation.

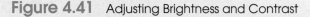

Figure 4.41 Adjusting Brightness and Contrast

5 Inserting a Movie

You decide a movie clip of your brother holding your niece on the day of her birth would enhance the presentation you are creating for your niece and the family. While the first frame of the video is all that will print in the scrapbook, the presentation will play the video because it is in Windows Media Audio/Video file format, a format PowerPoint supports. Refer to Figure 4.42 as you complete this activity.

    a. Save the *chap4_pe4_birthday_solution* presentation as **chap4_pe5_birthday_solution**.

    b. Move to **Slide 3**, and then click the **Home tab**.

    c. Click the **New Slide down arrow** in the Slides group, and then click the **Blank** layout.

...continued on Next Page

d. Click **Movie** in the **Media Clips** group on the Insert tab, click *chap4_pe5_birth.wmv*, and click **OK**.

e. Click to play the movie **Automatically**.

f. Select the movie object, and then click the **Options tab** beneath the Movie Tools contextual tab. Click **Preview** in the Play group to view the movie clip.

g. Check **Play Full Screen** in the Movie Options group.

h. Click the **Slide Show tab** and click **From Current Slide** in the Start Slide Show group.

i. Save the *chap4_pe5_birthday_solution* presentation.

Figure 4.42 Inserted Movie Clip

6 Inserting Sound

You decide to add sound to the last slide in the slide show as a finale. You use Microsoft Office Online as an Internet resource to locate happy music that you can insert in your final slide. Refer to Figure 4.43 as you complete this activity.

a. Save the *chap4_pe5_birthday_solution* presentation as **chap4_pe6_birthday_solution**.

b. Move to **Slide 7**.

c. Click the **Insert tab**, click the **Sound** down arrow in the Media Clips group, and then click **Sound from Clip Organizer**.

d. Click **ClipArt from Office Online** located at the bottom of the Clip Organizer pane.

e. Enter **happy** in the Search box.

f. Click the **Search drop-down arrow** and click **Sounds**.

g. Click **Next** to move to the second page of results and locate the Humoresque sound clip.

h. Click the **Click to copy this item to your clipboard button** beneath the Humoresque sound, and then close Microsoft Office Online to return to your slide show.

i. Right-click in Slide 7 and click **Paste**.

j. Click to play the sound **Automatically**.

k. Click the **Options tab** beneath the Sound Tools contextual tab.

l. Check **Hide During Show** in the Sound Options group on the Options tab.

m. Check **Loop Until Stopped** in the Sound Options group on the Options tab.

n. Click **Preview** in the Play group.

o. Create a Notes and Handouts Header and Footer with the date and your name in the header and your instructor's name and your class in the footer.

p. Save the *chap4_pe6_birthday_solution* presentation and close the file.

...continued on Next Page

Figure 4.43 Inserted Sound Clip

7 Creating an Album

Your parents bought a small car for you to drive while going to school. While stopped at a street-light waiting to turn right, someone driving an SUV and talking on a cell phone drives into the back of your car. A police report is filed, and the insurance companies are contacted, but you decide to use your digital camera to take pictures to keep a record of the damage. Your father wants to see the damage to the car so you think of the perfect way to show him—you quickly create an album to use as a professional record that is suitable for sending by e-mail. Refer to Figure 4.44 as you complete this activity.

a. Click the **Insert tab**, click the **Photo Album** down arrow in the Illustrations group, and then click **New Photo Album**.

b. Click **File/Disk** and navigate to the location of your student files. Open the *chap4_pe7_accident_images* folder.

c. Click one of the files, and then press **Control+A** to select all pictures in the folder. Click **Insert**.

d. Click the drop-down arrow for **Picture Layout** in the Album Layout section.

e. Click **4 pictures**.

f. Click the down arrow for **Frame Shape** in the Album Layout section, and then click **Rounded Rectangle**.

g. Click **Create**.

h. Move to the title slide and change the *Photo Album* text to **Accident Record**.

i. Change your name to the date of the accident, **September 7, 2008**.

j. Select one of the images in your album, click **Compress Pictures** in the Picture Tools group on the Format tab, and then click **Options**.

k. Click **E-mail** in the Target Output area, click **OK**, and click **OK**.

l. Create a Notes and Handouts Header and Footer with the date and your name in the header and your instructor's name and your class in the footer.

m. Save the album as **chap4_pe7_accident_solution**.

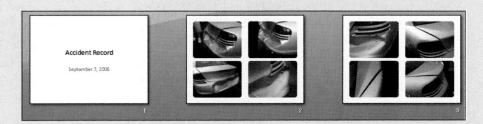

Figure 4.44 Accident Record

You have enjoyed a number of years as a motorcyclist, but now decide that you would like to sell your motorcycle and purchase a car. You added a specialized carbon fiber exhaust system to your motorcycle, have kept the bike in perfect condition, and customized the paint job. Using PowerPoint, you create a flyer advertising the motorcycle that you can reproduce and hang on bulletin boards at the college, local grocery stores, auto shops, and more. Figure 4.45 shows the completed flyer.

a. Open a blank presentation and save it as **chap4_mid1_motorcycle_solution**.

b. Change the layout to a blank layout so you have more freedom in designing your advertisement.

c. Change your slide orientation to Portrait as you will be printing a single slide to use as a flyer.

d. Search the Clip Organizer for the *For Sale* sign shown in Figure 4.45. Insert it, and then change the scale to 47% of its original size. Position the sign horizontally at 0" from the Top Left Corner. Position it vertically at .33" from the Top Left Corner.

e. Create a WordArt using Style 20, and then type **1995 Motorcycle**. Change the WordArt Text Fill to Text/Background 2. Change the Height to .8" and the Width to 3.3". Position the WordArt horizontally at 3.25" from the Top Left Corner. Position it vertically at .42" from the Top Left Corner.

f. Create a text box and type the following information inside it:

   Year: 1995
   Miles: 22,145
   Engine cc: 600
   Type: Street
   Exterior: Black
   Title: Clear

g. Position the text box horizontally at .5" from the Top Left Corner. Position it vertically at 2.17" from the Top Left Corner.

h. Insert *chap4_mid1_motorcycle1* and scale it to 60% of its original size. Drag the image so that it is to the right of the text box and beneath the WordArt.

i. Insert *chap4_mid1_motorcycle2*. Crop the photograph to get rid of unnecessary parking space area and focus in on the motorcycle. After cropping, position the text box horizontally at 0" from the Top Left Corner. Position it vertically at 4.5" from the Top Left Corner.

j. Create a text box and type **Call 555-1212**. Apply WordArt Style 20 to the text, and then apply a black Text Fill—Text/Background 2. Drag it so it is approximately centered under the photograph above.

k. Insert *chap4_mid1_motorcycle3* and scale it to 30% of its original size. Position the photograph horizontally at 2.94" from the Top Left Corner. Position it vertically at 5.25" from the Top Left Corner.

l. Insert *chap4_mid1_motorcycle4* and scale it to 30% of its original size. Position the photograph horizontally at 5.3" from the Top Left Corner. Position it vertically at 5.25" from the Top Left Corner.

m. Create a text box and type **Custom Paint**. Apply WordArt Style 20 to the text, and then apply a black Text Fill—Text/Background 2. Drag it so it is approximately centered under the two photographs above.

...continued on Next Page

n. Insert *chap4_mid1_motorcycle5* and scale it to 75% of its original size. Position the photograph horizontally at 3.12" from the Top Left Corner. Position it vertically at 7.38" from the Top Left Corner.

o. Create a text box and type **Carbon Fiber Exhaust**. Apply WordArt Style 20 to the text, and then apply a black Text Fill—Text/Background 2. Position the text box horizontally at .42" from the Top Left Corner. Position it vertically at 8.67" from the Top Left Corner.

p. Insert an arrow that starts at the *Specialized Exhaust* and points to the exhaust pipe of the motorcycle. Change the weight of the arrow to 3 pt. Change the outline color to Accent 2.

q. Compress the photographs on the flyer using the default setting.

r. Create a Notes and Handouts Header and Footer with the date and your name in the header and your instructor's name and your class in the footer.

s. Save the *chap4_mid1_motorcycle_solution* flyer and close it.

Figure 4.45 Motorcycle Sales Flyer

2 Impressionist Paintings

In this exercise, you will use the Internet as a source for obtaining images of paintings by some of the masters of the Impressionist style of painting. The paintings in Figure 4.46 may be viewed at the Web Museum (www.ibiblio.org/wm), a Web museum that is maintained by Nicolas Pioch for academic and educational use. Follow the link to Explore the Web Museum unique Famous Artworks collections to the Famous Artworks exhibition page. Locate and click the Impressionism Theme (or search for Impressionist paintings or painter's names) and search for the paintings used in this assignment.

a. Open the *chap4_mid2_paintings* presentation and save it as **chap4_mid2_paintings_ solution**.

b. When you locate a painting, click the thumbnail image to enlarge the painting, then right-click the painting and save the image to a new folder you create on your storage

...continued on Next Page

device named **Impressionist Paintings**. If necessary, change the name of the file to include the artist and the name of the painting. Repeat this process until you have saved each of the images of the paintings shown in Figure 4.46.

c. The painting in Slide 2 is an excellent example of the guiding principles in the Impressionist movement. It was painted by Claude Monet, and its title is *Impression: soleil levant*.

d. The painting in Slide 4 is a Degas painting, *Ballet Rehearsal*.

e. The painting in Slide 5 is a Monet painting, *Waterlilies, Green Reflection, Left Part*.

f. The painting in Slide 6 is a Morisot painting, *The Artist's Sister at a Window*.

g. The painting in Slide 7 is a Renoir painting, *On the Terrace*.

h. The painting in Slide 8 is a Pissarro painting, *Peasant Girl Drinking her Coffee*.

i. Insert Alfred Sisley's *Autumn: Banks of the Seine near Bougival* as the background of the title slide.

j. Now that you have gathered your resources, return to your slide show and insert each of the images on the appropriate artist's slide. Resize the images as needed, and then position the images attractively on the page. You do not need to compress the images as they are already at a low resolution.

k. Insert the upbeat song *Fur Elise* from the Clip Organizer in Slide 1. Hide the Sound icon during play and loop the song. Set the song animation so it plays continuously and does not stop with the next mouse click.

l. Save the *chap4_mid2_paintings_solution* presentation and close it.

Figure 4.46 Impressionism Presentation

3 A Visit to the Zoo

As a first-grade teacher, you enjoy taking your class on field trips. Each year, you take your students and parent helpers to the local zoo. The zoo has an excellent education program and is very supportive. The day your class visits, a zookeeper takes your students to specific animals and gives presentations on the animal, its habitat, its diet, and other fun facts. The keeper also teaches the children the difference between skin, fur, feathers, and scales. Because the zookeeper likes to keep the children involved by asking them questions they know the answers to now and then, the keeper asks you to teach the students about animal facts before the visit. You prepare a presentation about the coverings of some of the animals you took pictures of during last year's visit to the zoo. Refer to Figure 4.48 as you complete this activity.

a. Create a New Photo Album using the zoo photographs located in the *chap4_mid3_zoo_images* folder in your student files.

...continued on Next Page

b. Use a layout of 4 pictures per album page.

c. Because you want to include the type of covering for each animal on each slide, you must include a text box for each type of animal. Insert a text box for each animal type and use the Move Up and Move Down arrows to position the boxes for each album page (see Figure 4.47).

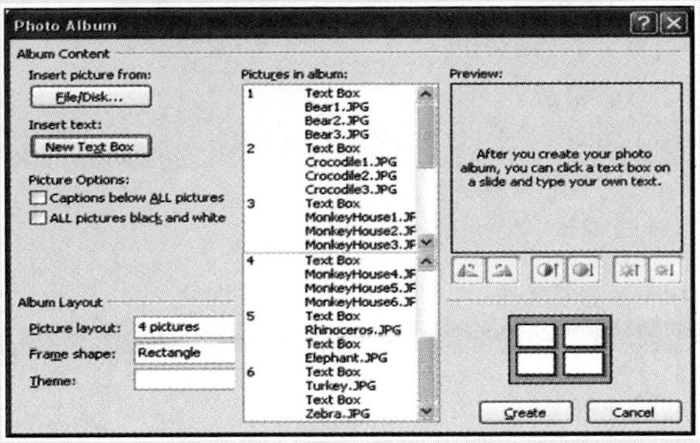

Figure 4.47

d. Use Rectangle Frames.

e. Apply the Trek theme.

f. Enter the following in the appropriate slides:

- **Black Bears are covered with fur.**

- **Crocodiles are covered with scales.**

- **Monkeys are covered with hair.**

- **Monkeys eat fruit, leaves, nuts, berries, eggs, and insects.**

- **A Rhinoceros is covered with grey skin.**

- **Elephants are covered with extremely tough skin.**

- **Turkeys are covered with feathers.**

- **Zebras are covered with striped hair.**

g. Compress the pictures for screen use.

h. Change the subtitle on Slide 1 to **Animals and Their Coverings**, and then change the title to **OUR ZOO VISIT!**

i. Record a narration for the slide show by reading the text on each slide. Do not save the slide timings.

TROUBLESHOOTING: If you do not have a microphone, you will not be able to record the narration. In that case, skip the narration recording and insert a sound from the Clip Organizer in each slide.

j. Insert the movie *chap4_mid3_zoo* in Slide 1 and have the movie start with a click.

k. Reposition the subtitle and title on Slide 1 so that they are not blocked by the movie.

l. Check the spelling in your presentation, and then proofread carefully to catch any errors that Spell Checking may have missed.

m. Create a Notes and Handouts Header and Footer with the date and your name in the header and your instructor's name and your class in the footer.

n. Save the **chap4_mid3_zoo_solution** presentation and close it.

...continued on Next Page

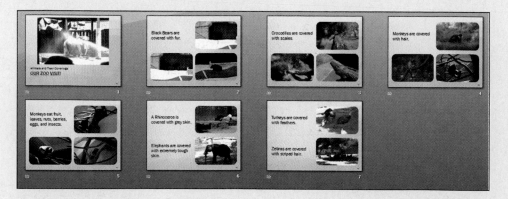

Figure 4.48 Zoo Presentation

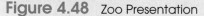

4 ESL Tutor

As a tutor of ESL (English as a Second Language) students, you would like to introduce the students to the English names of common musical instruments. Your slide presentation will feature one instrument per slide, with narration of the name of the instrument and a sound button that will play the instrument's sound. The photographs and sounds of the instruments are available from Microsoft Office Online. This exercise requires a computer with a sound card, speakers or headphones, and a microphone. Refer to Figure 4.49 for an example slide.

a. Open the *chap4_mid4_esl* presentation and save it as **chap4_mid4_esl_solution**.

b. Move to **Slide 2**.

c. Use the Clip Organizer to access the Microsoft Office Online Web site.

d. Narrow your search to Photographs, and then search for a photograph of a violin.

e. Mark a photograph of a violin named *j0382780.jpg* for download, by clicking in the checkbox.

f. Change the search filter to sounds. The word *violin* should remain in the Search box. Listen to the violin sounds by clicking on the icons. Find the *Happy Violins* and mark it for download.

g. Continue by marking the following photographs and sounds for download:

Search Word	Photograph Name	Sound Name
Drums	j0402397.jpg	Drum Clash 2
Flute	j0385372.jpg	Single Flute
Harps	j0175036.jpg	Harp Up
Cymbals	j0382767.jpg	Cymbals Tag
Horn	j0315705.jpg	Short Horn Part 5

h. Click **Download Now** to download the selected clips to the Clip Organizer. Close Microsoft Office Online.

i. Use the Clip Organizer to locate the violin photograph you downloaded, and then insert the image on Slide 2.

j. Decrease the height of the violin photograph to 4.5 inches. Center the violin photograph under the title.

...continued on Next Page

k. Apply the picture style Perspective Shadow, White to the violin photograph.

l. Insert the Happy Violins sound. Set the sound to start When Clicked. Move the icon from the middle of the photograph to the lower-right side of the slide.

m. Repeat Steps k–m for each remaining instrument slide using the appropriate photograph and sound clip for each slide.

n. Compress all of pictures to Screen Target Output.

o. Move to **Slide 1**. Click the **Slide Show tab** and select **Record Narration**.

p. Click the **Set Microphone Level** button and check the sound by speaking a few words into the microphone. Move the slider to adjust the level to green. Click **OK**.

q. When the full-screen slide appears, slowly and carefully read the first slide out loud into the microphone. Click to advance to the next slide.

r. Read the instrument name slowly and clearly twice. Click to advance to the next slide. Repeat this action for each slide. At the End of the slide show screen, click to exit.

s. Do not save the slide timings.

t. Create a Notes and Handouts Header and Footer with the date and your name in the header and your instructor's name and your class in the footer.

u. View the slide show and test each sound button. Save *chap4_mid4_esl_solution* and close the file.

Figure 4.49   ESL Presentation

5 Birth Announcement

A close friend and her husband recently had a new baby. The father is an extremely accomplished athlete and is currently attending the university on a football scholarship. He is delighted with his "future running back." Sherry, the talented mother of your friend created handmade birth announcements that also served as an invitation to an "end zone celebration"—a luau for family and friends to meet the new baby. You attended the celebration of life and took pictures with your digital camera. You decide to record the event by putting the photographs in a PowerPoint album, print the album on heavy specialty paper, and then bind the album for the baby's first scrapbook. After viewing it, your friend's husband asks you for a copy so he can e-mail the presentation to family members who live in Tonga and were not able to attend the celebration. You modified Microsoft's Contemporary Photo Album template to resemble the invitation your friend's mother created. In this activity, you will create the content, insert the photographs, and use Microsoft's picture tools to finish the project. Refer to Figure 4.50 as you complete this activity.

...continued on Next Page

a. Open the *chap4_mid5_announcement* presentation, and then save it as **chap4_mid5_announcement_solution**.

b. Move to **Slide 1**, modify the Title placeholder to read **IT's A BOY!**, and then center-align the text.

c. Search the Clip Organizer for the old leather football shown in Figure 4.50. Insert it, and then change the scale to 200% of its original size. Position the image horizontally at 1.83″ from the Top Left Corner. Position it vertically at .13″ from the Top Left Corner. Use the Set Transparent Color tool on the white background of the football so that the background shows through.

d. Move to **Slide 2** and insert *chap4_mid5_announcement1.jpg* in the picture placeholder. Enter the following text in the text placeholder, pressing Enter after each comma: **Casanova Hamani, August 22, 2008, 4:45 p.m., 6 lbs 2 oz, 19.5″**. Center-align the text and change the line spacing to **2**. Change the font for the baby's first and middle names to 28 pts.

e. Move to **Slide 3** and search the Clip Organizer using **background** as the keyword and locate the grass and leaf background. Insert the image, and then set the image width to 10″ and the height to 5.25″. Position the background horizontally at 0″ from the Top Left Corner. Position it vertically at 1″ from the Top Left Corner.

f. Use the Crop tool to remove the leaf from the background, and then arrange the background so it is aligned in the center of the slide.

g. Create a rectangle 5″ wide by 4″ high and apply the Intense Effect–Accent 1 Shape Style. Change the shape fill color to the Dark Blue, Text 2, Darker 50% theme color.

h. Type the following information inside it, breaking lines where appropriate: **Our future running back scored his touchdown August 22, 2008! Come join his fans in an End Zone Celebration Luau. Huddle up: August 29, 2008, 5 p.m. Dave and Alison's home.**

i. Position the rectangle horizontally at 2.5″ from the Top Left Corner. Position it vertically at 1.67″ from the Top Left Corner.

j. Move to **Slide 4**. Insert *chap4_mid5_announcement2*, *chap4_mid5_announcement3*, and *chap4_mid5_announcement4* in the placeholders. Apply the Metal Oval picture style to the images of the mother and father and apply the Metal Rounded Rectangle to the image of the baby. Replace the text in the text placeholders. Type **Mother: Alison, Baby: Casanova, Father: Dave** in their respective placeholders. Center-align the text in the placeholders.

k. In **Slide 5**, starting in the top left and continuing in a clockwise order, insert *chap4_mid5_announcement5*, *chap4_mid5_announcement6*, *chap4_mid5_announcement7*, and *chap4_mid5_announcement8*. Select the image of Grandma and Grandpa and increase the contrast 20%.

l. In **Slide 6**, starting in the top left and continuing in a clockwise order, insert *chap4_mid5_announcement9*, *chap4_mid5_announcement10*, *chap4_mid5_announcement11*, *chap4_mid5_announcement12*, and *chap4_mid5_announcement13*. Select the image of the grandfather and uncle and decrease the brightness by 10%.

m. Compress the images at print quality.

n. In **Slide 6**, create a WordArt using the Fill–Accent 2, Warm Matte Bevel style. Enter the text **End Zone Luau**. Apply the Double Wave 2 transform special effect. Change the text direction to Rotate all text 270°. Drag the WordArt to the right into the area not covered by text.

o. Create a Notes and Handouts Header and Footer with the date and your name in the header and your instructor's name and your class in the footer.

p. Save the *chap4_mid5_announcement_solution* file.

q. Compress the images at E-mail quality.

r. Save the presentation as **chap4_mid5_announcement2_solution** and close it.

...continued on Next Page

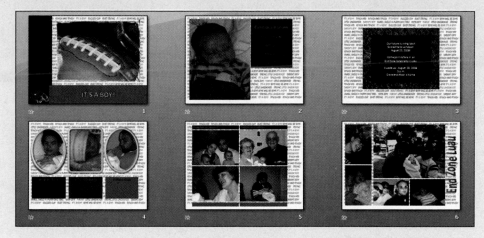

Figure 4.50 Announcement Presentation

Capstone Exercise

In Chapter 2 and Chapter 3, you developed a presentation on Waterwise Landscaping for your neighbors in your southwestern subdivision. While on a drive with your family, you saw several excellent examples of zeroscaping and captured the images on your digital camera. You are anxious to add these examples to the Waterwise presentation you have been creating. You also have been in communication with a company that you found on the Web that specializes in xeriscaping. The company, XericUtah (xericutah.com), has given you permission to use images from its Web site showing its work and demonstrating how beautiful xeriscaping can be. In this capstone exercise, you will complete the Waterwise landscaping presentation.

Insert Pictures

You need to open the presentation that you already started, rename the file, and save. You insert pictures, crop, size, and then position the images.

a. Locate the file named *chap4_cap_landscape*, and then save it as **chap4_cap_landscape_solution**.

b. Create a Notes and Handouts Header and Footer with the date and your name in the header and your instructor's name and your class in the footer.

c. Move to **Slide 4**, and then click the **Add Picture** button in the large content placeholder. Navigate to the location of your student files and open the *chap4_cap_landscape_images* folder. Insert the *chap4_cap_1landscape.jpg* file.

d. Move to **Slide 5**. To create room for pictures, drag the right side of the text placeholder to the 1" position on the horizontal ruler.

e. Insert the *chap4_cap_2landscape.jpg* file.

f. Select the picture and activate the Crop tool.

g. Crop the green power pole from the picture (crop the left side of the image to the –3" mark on the horizontal ruler).

h. Change the width of the picture to **3"** and let the height adjust automatically.

i. Set the horizontal position to **6"** from the **Top Left Corner** and the vertical position to **4.67"** from the **Top Left Corner**.

j. Insert the *chap4_cap_3landscape.jpg* file in Slide 5.

k. Change the width of the image to **3"**. Let the height adjust automatically.

l. Set the horizontal position to **6"** from the **Top Left Corner** and the vertical position on slide options to **1.83"** from the **Top Left Corner**.

m. Save the *chap4_cap_landscape_solution* presentation.

Apply and Modify a Picture Style

After displaying the slide show, you decide that the pictures you inserted in Slide 5 would stand out better if they had a frame. You decide to frame the pictures by applying a Picture Style and then modifying the style.

a. On **Slide 5**, select the top picture and apply the Beveled Oval, Black picture style.

b. Apply the Picture Effect **Preset 7**.

c. Use the Format Painter to copy the effects applied to the top photograph to the bottom photograph.

d. Save the *chap4_cap_landscape_solution* presentation.

Adjust Brightness and Contrast and Compress

You insert another example of zeroscaping in your slide show, but notice it seems faded and washed out. You use the Picture Tools to adjust the brightness and contrast tools to adjust the image. After making the changes, you apply an onscreen compression to all photographs.

a. Move to **Slide 7**, and then insert *chap4_cap_4landscape.jpg*.

b. Decrease the image brightness to **–20%**.

c. Increase the image contrast to **+20%**.

d. Scale the height of the image to **40%**.

e. Drag the image to the bottom center of the slide.

f. Compress the images for screen output.

g. Save the *chap4_cap_landscape_solution* presentation.

Create a Background from a Picture

The title slide of your slide show is rather bland, so you determine to add a picture as a background.

a. Move to **Slide 1** and click the **Design tab**.

b. Access the Format Background options so that you can select a picture fill.

c. Insert *chap_cap_5landscape.jpg*.

d. Save the *chap4_cap_landscape_solution* presentation.

Use the Internet as a Resource

For examples of xeriscaping, you turn to the Internet and use XericUtah (*xericutah.com*) as your resource. Xeric's "goal is to create beautiful, drought-tolerant landscapes that conserve water, bring wildlife to our gardens, and breed aesthetically pleasing landscapes that appeal to all walks of life." Ryan Phillips of XericUtah has given you permission to include photos from the Web site in your presentation.

a. Connect to the Internet and go to xericutah.com. Click the link to jump to the *about us* page. Save the picture on the right side of the Web site as *xericutah1.jpg*.

b. Insert the *xericutah.1.jpg* file in the placeholder on Slide 8.

c. Move to **Slide 9** and then return to the XericUtah Web site. Navigate to the *portfolio showcase* page.

d. Click the first image on Row 1 of the portfolio pieces, and then position your pointer over the enlarged image on the right side of the screen. Right-click and click **Copy**. Return to the slide show and right-click, and then click **Paste**. Drag the image to the lower-left side of the slide.

e. Copy the enlargement of the third image on Row 2 of the portfolio pieces, paste it in Slide 9, and then position it in the lower middle of the slide.

f. Copy the second image on Row 3 of the portfolio pieces, and then paste it in Slide 9. Drag the image to the lower-right side of the slide.

g. Select the three images, scale them to 50%, align them at their bottom, and distribute them horizontally.

h. Move to **Slide 10**, and then return to the XericUtah Web site. Navigate to the *xeric plants* page and copy the image of the flowers on the left side of the screen.

i. Paste the image onto Slide 10 and drag the picture to the lower bottom of the slide.

j. Duplicate the image, and then flip the duplicate horizontally.

k. Drag the image so the groups of white flowers overlap and the two images appear to be one, and then align their bottoms.

l. Group the two images of white flowers so they become one large bar across the bottom of the slide. Size the group to 10".

m. Search the Clip Organizer using the keyword **Petals**, and locate the image of the yellow flower. (See Figure 4.51 to help select the correct flower.) Insert the clip on Slide 11.

n. Size the image to 4" x 4", and then drag the image to the lower part of the slide in approximately the center.

o. Save the *chap4_cap_landscape_solution* presentation.

Insert a Movie

You need to create a Resource page for your presentation. Not only will this give credit to your sources, it will give your viewers the Web sites to visit for more information later. Please remember that giving credit to your source **does not** mean you are released from copyright require-ments. After creating the page, you insert an animated movie clip from the Clip Organizer to recapture the attention of the audience if it is lagging. You select a clip that relates to planting.

a. Insert a slide after Slide 13 using the **Title and Content** layout.

b. Type **Resources** in the Title placeholder.

c. Click in the Content Placeholder, and then type **Office of Community Services**, press **Shift+Enter**, and type **Fort Lewis College** (*http://ocs.fortlewis.edu/waterwise*).

d. Press **Enter** twice, and then type XericUtah Landscape Design (*http://xericutah.com*).

e. Search the Clip Organizer for a movie using **digging** as the keyword for your search.

f. Insert the image of the man and woman planting a tree by the title.

g. Save the *chap4_cap_landscape_solution* presentation.

Insert Sound

Your presentation is almost done, but you decide that a soft background music clip that plays continuously on Slide 1 while your neighbors enter the presentation room would help set the mood. You use the Clip Organizer to locate a soft sound clip and then you modify it to play continuously in Slide 1 and discontinue playing when you click to advance to Slide 2.

a. Search the Clip Organizer using the keyword **soft** and locate the sound clip *Soweto Underscore*.

b. Insert *Soweto Underscore* into Slide 1 and have it start automatically.

c. Set the sound options to hide the sound icon during the show.

d. Activate the **Loop Until Stopped** sound option.

e. Save the *chap4_cap_landscape_solution* presentation.

Add a Transition and Animations

To add interest to your slide show, you decide to add a transition to advance from one slide to another. To relieve you of having to constantly click to have slide objects appear, you decide to add animations. While serving as a reminder of a skill previously learned, this step completes the basic process for preparing a slide show for a presentation: create content, select design options, add objects that enhance your message, and finally add a transition and animations.

a. In Slide 1, select the **Fade Through Black** transition and apply to all slides.

b. Select the SmartArt graphic on Slide 2, and then set the animation to **Fade, One by one**.

c. Select the SmartArt graphic on Slide 3, and then set the animation to **Fly In, One by one**.

d. Select the bottom SmartArt graphic on Slide 3, and then set the animation to **Fly In, By level one by one**.

e. Select the SmartArt graphic on Slide 13 and set the animation to **Wipe, By level at once**.

f. Save the *chap4_cap_landscape_solution* presentation and close it.

Figure 4.51 Waterwise Presentation

Create a Photo Album

After you make your presentation to your neighbors, they are intrigued by the idea of xeriscaping but would like copies of your images to review at home. You determine the quickest way to provide them with all your images, not just those used in the presentation, is to prepare a photo album and then print copies.

a. Create a New Photo Album using the images in the *chap4_cap_landscape_images* folder.

b. Select *chap4_cap_4landscape.jpg* in the list of pictures.

c. Click the **Increase Contrast** button two times.

d. Click the **Decrease Brightness** button two times.

e. Select *4 pictures* for your album layout.

f. Use Rounded Rectangle for the **Frame Shape**.

g. Apply the **Apex** theme to the presentation.

h. Apply **Background Style 5**.

i. Enter your name as the subtitle on Slide 1. Apply the **Wipe, All at once** animation.

j. Create a Notes and Handouts Header and Footer with your name in the header and your instructor's name and your class in the footer.

k. Save the album as **chap4_cap_landscape2_solution** and close it.

Figure 4.52 Waterwise Album

Mini Cases

Use the rubric following the case as a guide to evaluate your work, but keep in mind that your instructor may impose additional grading criteria or use a different standard to judge your work.

Lately, you have noticed one of your friends or coworkers seems a little "down." You decide that a quick multimedia PowerPoint slide show will show that you care. Collect photographs, animations, and sounds from Internet resources (remember the copyright information). The solution to this problem is a three-to-five-slide presentation that shows you are thinking about your friend. Include at least two photographs, one movie animation, and one sound. Save your file as **chap4_mc1_greeting_solution**. Figure 4.53 shows one possible solution to this task.

Figure 4.53 Sample Solution to Mini Case 1

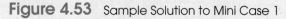

Performance Elements	Exceeds Expectations	Meets Expectations	Below Expectations
Organization	Slides follow a logical sequence with the multimedia supporting the message.	Presentation is easy to follow.	The multimedia elements are not put in a logical order and appear to be haphazardly placed.
Visual aspects	The multimedia elements are appealing and enhance the presentation. They are consistent and blend in with the message.	Clip art is related to the topic. Animation enhances the presentation.	The multimedia does not enhance the message. The theme of the multimedia is confusing. Sounds are not well controlled.
Layout	The layout is visually pleasing and contributes to understanding the greeting. The layout is cohesive.	The layout shows structure and multimedia elements enhance the presentation.	The layout is cluttered and confusing. Understanding of the message is lost.
Mechanics	Presentation has no errors in spelling, grammar, word usage, or punctuation. No typographical errors present. A well-organized resource page shows Internet sites used.	Presentation has no more than one error in spelling, grammar, word usage, or punctuation.	Presentation readability is impaired due to repeated errors in spelling, grammar, word usage, or punctuation. Multiple typographical errors. No resource page was included.

Your presentation on digital photography to the senior citizens group was so successful you have been invited back to speak about etiquette on the Internet. A surprising number of senior citizens are sending and receiving e-mail. Since this activity is new to these people, they want to make sure that they don't offend anyone. To prepare for your presentation, you complete Internet research on netiquette. Since you know how to add multimedia to presentations, include at least one movie animation. Collect images of computer users, especially older people, to add interest to your slides. Save your file as **chap4_mc2_netiquette_solution**. Figure 4.54 shows one possible solution to this task.

Figure 4.54 Sample Solution to Mini Case 2

Performance Elements	Exceeds Expectations	Meets Expectations	Below Expectations
Organization	Slides follow a logical sequence with the multimedia supporting the message.	Presentation indicates some research has taken place and that information was included in the content.	The multimedia elements are not placed in a logical order. The message is lost because the multimedia is distracting.
Visual aspects	The multimedia elements are appealing and enhance the presentation. They are consistent and blend in with the message. Text is easy to read.	The multimedia elements are consistent with the message.	The multimedia does not enhance the message. The theme of the multimedia is confusing. Text is difficult to read due to size or color.
Layout	The layout is visually pleasing and contributes to understanding the topic. White space, photographs, and the movie are cohesive.	The layout shows some structure, but placement of some headings, subheadings, bullet points, multimedia elements, and/or white space can be improved.	The layout is cluttered and confusing. The multimedia elements detract from understanding.
Mechanics	Presentation has no errors in spelling, grammar, word usage, or punctuation. No typographical errors present. Sources of research are shown on an ending slide.	Presentation has no more than one error in spelling, grammar, word usage, or punctuation. Bullet points are inconsistent in one slide.	Presentation readability is impaired due to repeated errors in spelling, grammar, word usage, or punctuation. Multiple typographical errors. No resource page is included.

On weekends, you volunteer at the local humane society. You walk the dogs and play with the cats. One day when you arrived, you noticed the manager struggling with PowerPoint. The manager was trying to create a slide show that would showcase animals in positive ways to play during the annual humane society fundraiser. You offer to complete the task for the manager because you know that a PowerPoint presentation is the solution. Download photographs from Microsoft Office Online and create a 10- to 15-slide photo presentation. Include enhancements such as framing and themes to make the presentation professional looking. Save the new presentation as **chap4_mc3_humane_solution**. Figure 4.55 shows one possible solution to this task.

Figure 4.55 Sample Presentation for Mini Case 3

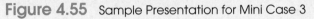

Performance Elements	Exceeds Expectations	Meets Expectations	Below Expectations
Organization	Sufficient number of photographs and slides to make the photo album interesting. Sequence of the photos leads from one type of animal to another with smooth transitions between slides.	A variety of animals are represented in the photographs.	Fewer than 10 photographs in the photo album. Photographs are not sequenced in a logical way.
Visual aspects	There is a consistent visual theme. The contrast and brightness of the photographs is pleasing. Frame shapes enhance the photographs.	Text is readable. Frame shapes used.	The visual theme is not apparent. No frame shapes were used to enhance the photographs. Appealing photographs were not included.
Layout	The layout is visually pleasing and draws attention to the animals. Captions are added to increase the appeal of the animals.	Layout of photographs displays photographs adequately.	The layout is cluttered and confusing. Captions are not included.
Mechanics	Any added text has no errors in spelling, grammar, word usage, or punctuation. No typographical errors present. Sources of photographs recognized on a well-organized resource page.	Added text has no more than one error in spelling, grammar, word usage, or punctuation.	Any added text has impaired readability due to repeated errors in spelling, grammar, word usage, or punctuation. Multiple typographical errors. Sources of photographs not included.

Charts and Graphs

Working with Text and Statistical Charts and Graphs

Objectives

After you read this chapter, you will be able to:

1. Create a poster or a banner **(page 358)**.
2. Create and insert a table **(page 359)**.
3. Design a table **(page 361)**.
4. Apply a table style **(page 369)**.
5. Change table layout **(page 372)**.
6. Share information between applications **(page 375)**.
7. Identify chart types and elements **(page 383)**.
8. Create and insert a chart **(page 388)**.
9. Change a chart type **(page 395)**.
10. Change the chart layout **(page 395)**.
11. Format chart elements **(page 396)**.

Hands-On Exercises

Exercises	Skills Covered
1. **CREATING TEXT-BASED CHARTS** (page 363) **Open:** chap5_ho1_poster.pptx **Save as:** chap5_ho1_poster_solution.pptx **Open:** chap5_ho1_antioxidants.pptx **Save as:** chap5_ho1_antioxidants_solution.pptx	• Create a Poster • Print the Scaled Poster • Insert a Table • Enter and Format Table Data • Draw and Format a Table
2. **MODIFYING TABLES** (page 378) **Open:** chap5_ho2_antioxidants2.pptx **Insert:** chap5_ho2_cranberries.jpg and chap5_ho2_fruits.jpg **Save as:** chap5_ho2_antioxidants2_solution.pptx	• Apply Table Styles • Change Table Layouts • Change Cell Fills • Link an Excel Table
3. **CREATING BASIC CHARTS** (page 391) **Open:** chap5_ho3_foundation.pptx **Save as:** chap5_ho3_foundation_solution.pptx	• Create a Column Chart • Edit Chart Data • Switch the Row and Column Data • Create a Pie Chart
4. **MODIFYING CHARTS** (page 397) **Open:** chap5_ho4_foundation2.pptx **Save as:** chap5_ho4_foundation2_solution.pptx	• Change Chart Type and Subtype • Modify a Line Chart • Modify a Bar Chart • Modify a Pie Chart

CASE STUDY

Game World

Dave Moles and Cathi Profitko started Game World five years ago. Their vision was, and still is, to create a chain of stores that offers its customers a complete collection of video games for sale, trade, or rent. The two friends struggled initially until they realized that they should focus on the three top players in the market: PlayStation, Xbox, and Nintendo. Sales and profits have climbed steadily ever since. Last year, they broke through the $1-million barrier as they recorded a 50% increase in sales over the previous year.

Dave and Cathi have already rejected several offers to sell their growing business and are looking to expand. They have demonstrated that their concept is successful and are seeking to franchise their operation, but they will need a substantial amount of

cash to do so. Thus, they have decided to seek venture capital. One potential source has asked that they create a PowerPoint presentation for their initial meeting that provides a comparison of quarterly revenues between this year and last year. The budding entrepreneurs have asked you to create the presentation and provided some content in the form of an Excel workbook with financial data, as well as a partially completed presentation. This is an excellent opportunity—you love video games and you have the chance to get in on the ground floor.

Your Assignment

- Read the chapter, paying special attention to how to link worksheets and charts from an Excel workbook into a PowerPoint presentation, how to create a chart from an Excel worksheet, and how to animate charts.
- Open the partially completed *chap5_case_gameworld* presentation and save the presentation as **chap5_case_gameworld_solution**.
- Open the *chap5_case_gameworld* Excel workbook. This workbook contains four worksheets, so be sure to link the correct worksheet to the appropriate slide in the presentation.
- In Excel, copy the worksheet data from the *This Year* and the *Last Year* worksheets and then paste the data into the appropriate placeholders in Slide 4 of the presentation.
- Use the data in the Year-to-Year Comparison worksheet to create a Clustered Column chart that compares the sales of the game systems from last year to this year. Copy the resulting chart and paste it into Slide 5 of the presentation.
- Copy the Comparison Chart from Excel, and then paste the chart in Slide 6 of the presentation.
- Format the charts as desired, but be sure to size the charts so that they fit on the presentation slides.
- Insert at least one appropriate clip art image on Slide 1 or Slide 2 for interest.
- Animate the charts using an animation that directs your eyes to the chart but is not distracting.
- Create a Notes and Handouts header and footer with your name in the header, and your instructor's name and your class in the footer.
- Print handouts, four per page, grayscale, framed.

Text-Based Charts

(. . . organize the information in a way that makes it clear and easy to read.)

A **chart** is a visual display of information.

A **text-based chart** is a chart based on text that is arranged to illustrate a relationship between words, numbers, and/or graphics.

In today's electronic environment, information is readily and quickly available, which makes it easy to feel overwhelmed. One way you can prevent feeling overwhelmed with information overload is to organize the information in a way that makes it clear and easy to read. Organizing and displaying information within a **chart** is a process that has been used successfully through the years. With software packages such as Excel and PowerPoint, this has become easier to do. Charts can be based on text or statistics.

A **text-based chart** is used to convey a relationship between words, numbers, and/or graphics rather than being based on statistics. Tables, diagrams, posters, and banners are popular examples of text-based charts. Though text can communicate a message by its appearance (typeface, color, size, style, contrast), it can also communicate a message by how it is positioned or arranged. Therefore, when you design a text-based chart you need to carefully plan how the information is arranged within the chart and fully utilize the formatting tools.

The following figures show examples of common text-based charts. Figure 5.1 shows a banner that has been printed locally on vinyl for durability. Figure 5.2 shows a poster advertising an event that was uploaded to an online printing service that printed multiple copies of the poster and mounted it on foam. The posters appeared on two college campuses, where they were displayed on easels.

Figure 5.1 Eye-Catching Vinyl Banner

Figure 5.2 Event Advertisement Poster Mounted on Foam

A **cell** is the intersection of a horizontal row and a vertical column in a table.

Figure 5.3 shows a PowerPoint table template illustrating a classic example of a relationship between numbers. This example, a simple multiplication table, is used to teach multiplication in an elementary school classroom. The table shows the product derived when a number in the column heading is multiplied by a number in the row heading. Notice that the first *cell* (an intersection of a row which runs horizontally and column which runs vertically) shows the multiplication operator. Figure 5.4 shows another PowerPoint table template. This example illustrates a more complex relationship—the process steps for sales to consumers. Text color and size along with cell shading and arrow graphics are used to guide the viewer through the process. Figure 5.5 displays an attention-grabbing banner announcing a football game designed to be hung over the doors to a school gym. The poster in Figure 5.6 is a standard size for uploading to an online printing service: 17" by 22". After you upload your file to the printing service, the service can print large quantities and send them to you via any number of delivery options so that you can distribute the poster to your campus or your community.

In this section, you learn how to create a poster and a banner. You also learn how to create and insert a table in a slide. Finally, you learn how to design a table to effectively communicate and organize your ideas.

Multiplication Table

Column

Multiplication operator

Row

Product

x	0	1	2	3	4	5	6	7	8	9	10	11	12
0	0	0	0	0	0	0	0	0	0	0	0	0	0
1	0	1	2	3	4	5	6	7	8	9	10	11	12
2	0	2	4	6	8	10	12	14	16	18	20	22	24
3	0	3	6	9	12	15	18	21	24	27	30	33	36
4	0	4	8	12	16	20	24	28	32	36	40	44	48
5	0	5	10	15	20	25	30	35	40	45	50	55	60
6	0	6	12	18	24	30	36	42	48	54	60	66	72
7	0	7	14	21	28	35	42	49	56	63	70	77	84
8	0	8	16	24	32	40	48	56	64	72	80	88	96
9	0	9	18	27	36	45	54	63	72	81	90	99	108
10	0	10	20	30	40	50	60	70	80	90	100	110	120
11	0	11	22	33	44	55	66	77	88	99	110	121	132
12	0	12	24	36	48	60	72	84	96	108	120	132	144

Figure 5.3   Table Illustrating a Relationship Between Numbers

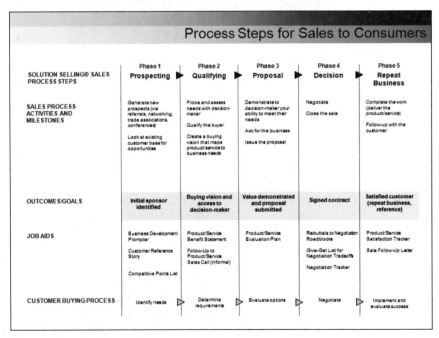

Process Steps for Sales to Consumers

	Phase 1 Prospecting	Phase 2 Qualifying	Phase 3 Proposal	Phase 4 Decision	Phase 5 Repeat Business
SOLUTION SELLING® SALES PROCESS STEPS					
SALES PROCESS ACTIVITIES AND MILESTONES	Generate new prospects (via referrals, networking, trade associations, conferences) Look at existing customer base for opportunities	Probe and assess needs with decision-maker Qualify the buyer Create a buying vision that maps product/service to business needs	Demonstrate to decision-maker your ability to meet their needs Ask for the business Issue the proposal	Negotiate Close the sale	Complete the work (deliver the product/service) Follow-up with the customer
OUTCOMES/GOALS	Initial sponsor identified	Buying vision and access to decision-maker	Value demonstrated and proposal submitted	Signed contract	Satisfied customer (repeat business, reference)
JOB AIDS	Business Development Prompter Customer Reference Story Competitive Points List	Product/Service Benefit Statement Follow-Up to Product/Service Sales Call (informal)	Product/Service Evaluation Plan	Rebuttals to Negotiation Roadblocks Give-Get List for Negotiation Tradeoffs Negotiation Tracker	Product/Service Satisfaction Tracker Sale Follow-Up Letter
CUSTOMER BUYING PROCESS	Identify needs	Determine requirements	Evaluate options	Negotiate	Implement and evaluate success

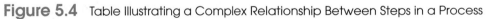

Figure 5.4   Table Illustrating a Complex Relationship Between Steps in a Process

Figure 5.5   Banner Created in PowerPoint

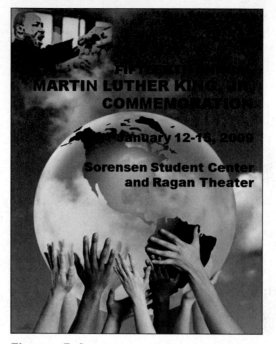

Figure 5.6   Poster Created in PowerPoint

Creating a Poster or a Banner

Creating a poster or banner is done on a single slide. An important part of planning for a poster or banner is to consider how you will output the slide because this often determines how you format the single slide. You must consider the printer when determining margins. Also, when you print wide-format banners or posters, your printer may not support large-size sheets of paper. If your printer does not support banner- or poster-sized paper, you can take your banner or poster file to a local printer. As an alternative, submit your file to an online printing service by e-mail or by uploading your file to the service's Web site.

You use the page setup feature to design the size of your poster or banner. Using the page setup feature you can create documents that range from wide-format text-based documents such as posters and banners to small banners that appear at the top of Web pages. To use the page setup feature, click the Design tab and then click Page Setup. When the Page Setup dialog box displays, click the Slides sized for down arrow and scroll to locate the size you desire. Note that the Banner option in the Slides sized for area is designed for a Web page banner. To create a wide-format banner or a poster, click the custom option. Figure 5.7 shows the setup for the poster in Figure 5.6. Once you have set your page size, you design and print the slide.

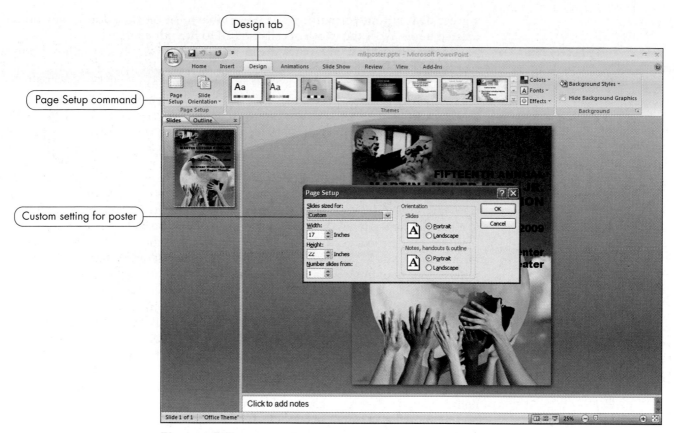

Figure 5.7 The Page Setup Dialog Box

Creating and Inserting a Table

(... the interface for Word tables and PowerPoint tables is almost identical, which reduces your learning curve!)

As you discovered earlier, tables organize information into a highly structured grid composed of columns that run vertically and rows that run horizontally. Information is stored in the cell created from the intersection of the column and row. This makes it easier to identify and locate information and makes it easy to compare numbers in the table. Because tables are such a common tool in information presentation, they can be created in PowerPoint, Word, or Excel. In fact, if you create a table in Word, you will find that the interface for Word tables and PowerPoint tables is almost identical, which reduces your learning curve! What an advantage for you! If you prefer, you can create your table in Word or Excel and then paste it into a PowerPoint slide. You will not even have to adjust the table's formatting after adding it to PowerPoint.

To create a PowerPoint table, you specify a size for the table in a dialog box or draw a custom table. Next, you modify the table structure as desired, and finally add a format to the table to make information easier to understand. Just as with other PowerPoint charts such as SmartArt diagrams, you can quickly apply formatting by applying a Quick Style. New to PowerPoint 2007 is the ability to apply special effects such as shadows, reflections, glow, soft edges, 3-D rotations, and transformations to a table. PowerPoint 2007 enables the insertion of up to 75 rows and columns, up from 25 rows and columns in the previous version. One of the best changes to the table feature in PowerPoint 2007, however, is that a table is sized by fitting its width now. In the past, PowerPoint users were often frustrated because a table inserted on a slide was maximized to fit a set area depending on the number of rows. Users often spent a great deal of time formatting to fix the table to fit on the slide if they added or deleted a row. Now the width of cells is used to fit your content.

To quickly insert a table, click the Insert tab, click Table in the Tables group, and then drag to select the number of columns and rows you desire. As an alternative, you can click the Insert tab, click Table in the Tables group, click Insert Table, enter the number of columns and rows you want, and then click OK. The table is inserted into your slide in a style the corresponds to your theme—you no longer have to format the table unless you so desire. This is new to PowerPoint 2007. Once you create the table structure, you add text to the table cells by clicking within a cell and entering your text.

If your table design requires multiple cell heights and widths or diagonal borders, drawing your table using the Pencil tool may save you time. Click the Insert tab, click Table in the Tables group, and then click Draw Table. The pointer changes to a pencil pointer, which you drag to define the table boundary. Once the outer table boundary is defined, click Draw Table in the Draw Borders group on the Design tab located under the Table Tools contextual tab. The pencil once again becomes a pencil pointer that you drag to draw the column and row borders inside the table. You do not need to be exacting when drawing because the Layout tab includes buttons that will distribute space equally between selected columns or between selected rows. To erase a cell border or table boundary, you click the Eraser button in the Draw Borders group on the Design tab and then drag the eraser pointer that appears across the border between the two cells you wish to join or the boundary you wish to delete. When you finish drawing your table, press Esc. Figure 5.8 shows the steps you would follow to create a table with two columns and two rows, one of which is split diagonally. Though this same table could be created by merging table cells and changing a border, drawing the table is more efficient.

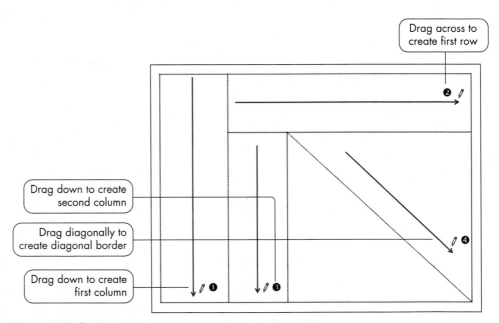

Figure 5.8 Using the Pencil Tool to Create Inside Borders

Designing a Table

Think carefully about the structure of a table when designing it to maximize the impact of the data. Tables should convey essential facts that supplement the message of your presentation, but should omit distracting details. The table should be easy to understand and should be consistent with other tables in the presentation. The table should follow the style of the presentation, which PowerPoint 2007 makes easy.

A table needs a title to communicate the purpose of the table. Keep the title short but ensure that it gives enough information to accurately identify the table purpose. A subtitle can be used to give further information about the title but should be in a smaller font size. The top row of the table body usually contains *column headings* to identify the contents of the columns. Column headings should be distinguishable from cell contents. Set your column headings off by using color, bold, italics, and/or a larger font than you use in table body cells. Make sure that your column headings are not a larger font size than your title and subtitle.

A *column heading* is the text in the top row of the table that identifies the contents of the column.

The table *stub* is the left column of a table that identifies the data in each row.

The left column of a table, or the *stub*, contains the information that identifies the data in each row. You can set off your stub with bolding, font size or color, or indention if you having subheadings in the stub. The last row of a table can be a note or source information. Use a smaller font size for the note or source, but make sure it is still large enough to be readable.

Table data should be simplified when possible yet still convey your message. For example, rather than listing the top 20 antioxidants in your presentation, list the top 5. You can provide the audience with a printed Word table if you want them to have a list of all 20. Do not include all 20 on the slide and then read the slide to the audience because the font is too small. Another way you can simplify the data is to shorten numbers by rounding them to whole numbers. An alternative to this is showing numbers with a designation stating that the number is in thousands or millions. How you align the data in a cell depends on the type of data the cell contains. Numbers should be aligned at the right if they do not have a decimal point, or aligned on the decimal point if they do. Text in the left column should be left-aligned but may be left-aligned or centered in other columns.

You can use table boundaries and cell borders to help clarify the information. Typically, horizontal borders are used to set off the title and subtitle from the headings and to set off headings from the table body. Vertical borders help define your columns. Figure 5.9 shows a basic table structure with the table elements identified. Bolding is used to set off the table title and column headings. Font size varies depending on the table element, but the note or source information row uses the smallest font size. One of the columns is shaded in blue and one of the rows is shaded in pale pink to help you identify the differences. This is for illustration purposes only—this is not a table style. The intersection of the column and row, the cell, is shaded in purple. The table is boxed, or surrounded by borders, and borders surround each cell. A heavier border is used to set the title information off from the column headings and the column headings off from the body of the table, and to set off the note information.

Table Title		
Subtitle		
Stub Heading	**Column Heading**	**Column Heading**
Stub (Row Heading)	cell	
Stub (Row Heading)		
Stub (Row Heading)		
Stub (Row Heading)		
Note or Source Information		

Figure 5.9 Table Elements

The formatting of table elements is no longer as rigid as in years past unless you are preparing a table to adhere to specific guidelines such as the APA (American Psychological Association) style. If this is the case, be sure to check a style guide for the style you are required to use and format the table per the guidelines. Otherwise, you can use type size, type style (bold, italics), alignment, or color to distinguish the table elements from one another. Remember the overriding principle in PowerPoint design at all times, however—design with a purpose, do not decorate!

Hands-On Exercises

1 | Creating Text-Based Charts

Skills covered: 1. Create a Poster **2.** Print the Scaled Poster **3.** Insert a Table **4.** Enter and Format Table Data **5.** Draw and Format a Table

Step 1
Create a Poster

a. Open the *chap5_ho1_poster* presentation and save it as **chap5_ho1_poster_solution**.

The title slide for the presentation opens. You revise the title slide to create a poster to place outside the room door identifying your session and topic.

b. Click the **Design tab**, and then click **Page Setup** in the Page Setup group to open the Page Setup dialog box.

c. Select the existing number for Width and change it to **17**.

d. Select the existing number for Height and change it to **22**.

The Slides sized for box changes to Custom and the Orientation changes to Portrait because the height of the slide is now greater than its width.

e. Select the placeholder that contains the session information. Delete the dash and press **Enter**.

The placeholder sizes changed when you changed the paper size. Because the session information no longer fits on one line, you split it into two lines.

f. Press the **up arrow** on the keyboard three times so that the placeholder information does not appear on the photograph of the blackberries.

g. Save the *chap5_ho1_poster_solution* presentation.

Step 2
Print the Scaled Poster

Refer to Figure 5.10 as you complete Step 2.

a. With the *chap5_ho1_poster_solution* presentation onscreen, click the **Office Button**, and then select **Print**.

b. Click the **Scale to fit paper** option box when the Print dialog box appears, and then click **OK**.

The poster will now print at the size of paper in your printer.

TROUBLESHOOTING: If only the center portion of the poster prints, check the Scale to fit paper option box to ensure that a green check appears in the option box.

c. Save and close the *chap5_ho1_poster_solution* file.

Figure 5.10 Session Poster

<table>
<tr>
<td>**Step 3**
Insert a Table</td>
<td>

Refer to Figure 5.11 as you complete Step 3.

a. Open the *chap5_ho1_antioxidants* file, and then immediately save it as **chap5_ho1_antioxidants_solution**.

b. Move to **Slide 7**, click the **Insert tab**, and then click **Table** in the Tables group.

c. Drag to create a **2-column × 7-row** table.

A table is created based on the Medium Style 2 – Accent 1 style, which is the default for the template selected for this activity.

d. Click outside of the table to the left of the first cell in the first row to select the entire first row.

e. Click the **Layout tab** underneath the Table Tools contextual tab, and then click **Merge Cells** in the Merge group.

The selected cells merge into one cell for the table title. The table style includes a dark fill and a white font color so the table title will be emphasized.

f. Type **Top Five Foods Rich in Antioxidants** in the title row.

g. Save the *chap5_ho1_antioxidants_solution* presentation.

</td>
</tr>
</table>

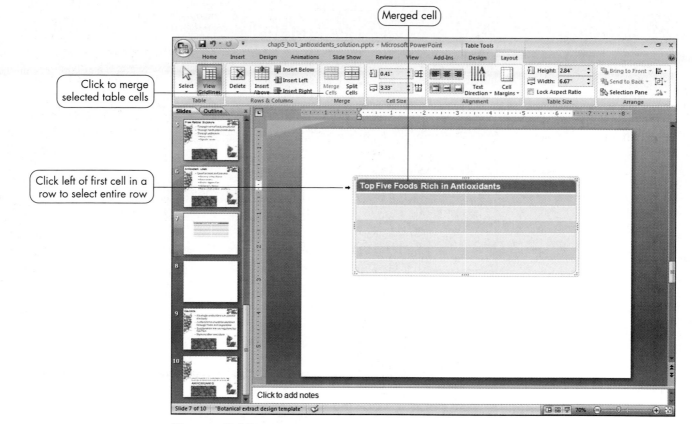

Figure 5.11 Initial Table Structure

Refer to Figure 5.12 as you complete Step 4.

a. With the *chap5_ho1_antioxidants_solution* presentation onscreen, select the text *Top Five Foods Rich in Antioxidants* in the title row.

b. Click the **Font Size arrow on the Mini toolbar**, click **24**, click **Bold**, and click **Center**.

   The table title is set off even further from the body of the table by increasing the font size, bolding, and center alignment.

c. Click in the first cell of the second row and type **Food**. Press **Tab** to move to the next cell in the row and type **Antioxidants mmol/serving**. Select the second row.

d. Click the **Font Size arrow** on the Home tab, click **20**, and then click **Bold**. Click **Center** in the Paragraph group.

   The column heading for the second column word wraps to fit in the cell.

e. Click the **Layout tab**, and then click **Align Bottom** in the Alignment group.

   Headings containing multiple lines are generally aligned at the bottom.

f. Enter the remaining data as displayed in Figure 5.12.

g. Select the text in the second column, and then click **Center** in the Alignment group on the Layout tab.

   Because the numbers in the second column are not used in calculations, they can be centered rather than right-aligned.

h. Save the *chap5_ho1_antioxidants_solution* presentation.

Table Tools contextual tab

Layout tab

Click to center-align text

Click to align selected text at bottom

Top Five Foods Rich in Antioxidants

Food	Antioxidants mmol/serving
Blackberries	5.746
Walnuts	3.721
Strawberries	3.584
Artichokes, prepared	3.559
Cranberries	3.125

Terminology:
mmol (abbreviation for millimole)
mole is a measure of substance

Figure 5.12 The Top Five Foods Rich in Antioxidants Table

Step 5
Draw and Format a Table

Refer to Figure 5.13 as you complete Step 5.

a. With the *chap5_ho1_antioxidants_solution* presentation onscreen, click **View** and then activate the **Ruler** in the Show/Hide group (if necessary).

b. Move to **Slide 7**, click the **Insert tab**, click **Table** in the Tables group, and then click **Draw Table**.

The pointer changes to a pencil shape.

c. Using the ruler as a guide, draw a table starting at -4" horizontal and 2.5" vertical and ending at 4" and -2.5" vertical.

The outer boundaries of the table are created.

d. Click **Draw Table** in the Draw Borders group on the Design tab.

e. Beginning at approximately 1" on the horizontal ruler, drag the pencil pointer down to create a column boundary. Release the mouse button as soon as you see the complete boundary appear.

Note that the ruler has changed the way it measures. The inches are now measured from the top left edge of the table.

TROUBLESHOOTING: If a new table is created in this step, you may have dragged the pencil pointer horizontally before dragging it vertically. Click **Undo** on the Quick Access Toolbar, and then select **Draw Table** in the Draw Borders group on the Design tab if you clicked outside the table. Drag straight down and release when you see the complete boundary.

f. Drag a row border beginning from the column border to the right boundary of the table approximately one-half inch from the top boundary (see Figure 5.13).

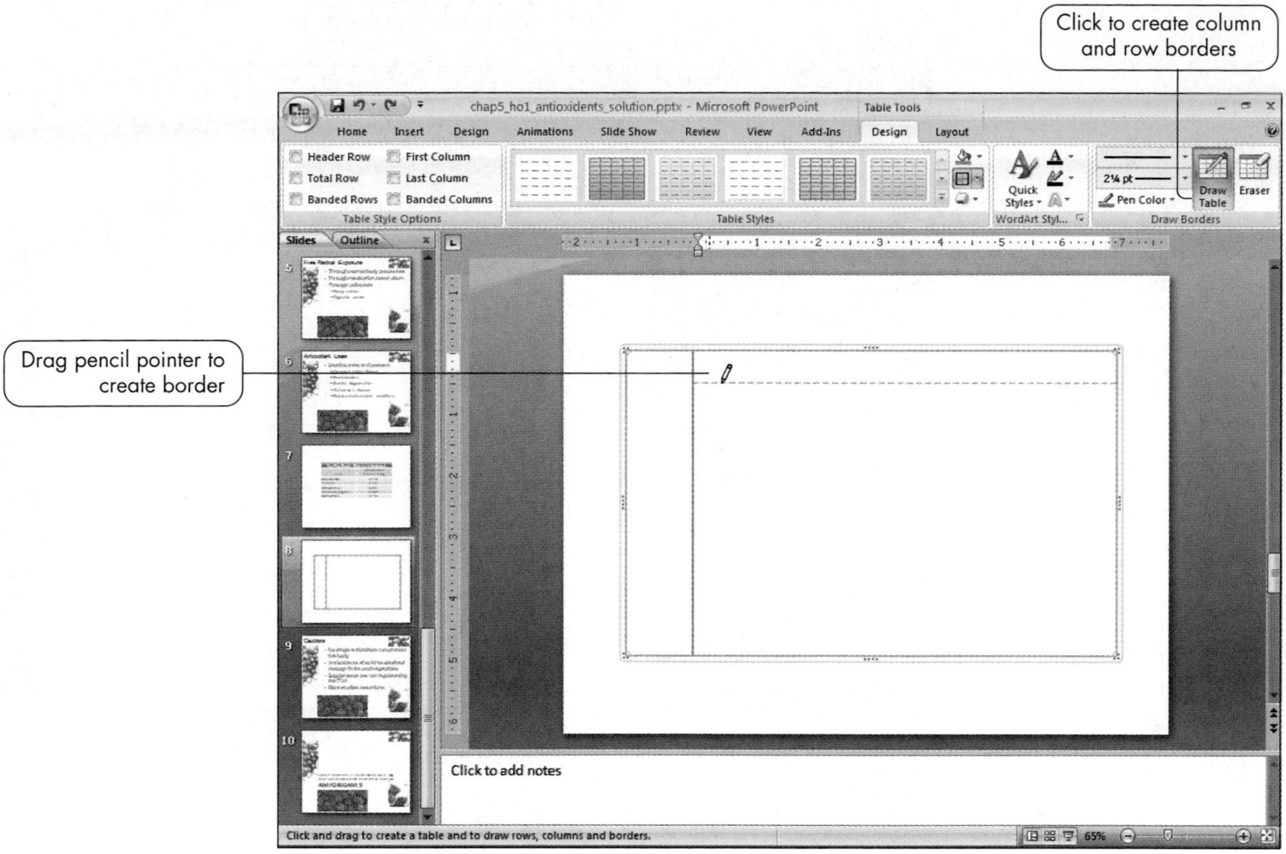

Figure 5.13 Create a Row Border

g. Drag three more row borders (see Figure 5.14).

Do not worry if the rows are not exactly the same height at this time.

h. Split the top row of the table into two cells by dragging a border through the row.

i. Press **Esc** to deactivate the table-drawing mode.

j. Select the two cells in the top row, click the **Layout tab**, and then click **Distribute Columns** in the Cell Size group.

The Distribute Columns feature distributes the width of selected columns so that the space is distributed equally within the selected area.

k. Select the four rows that were created by drawing the three borders.

l. Click the **Layout tab**, and then click **Distribute Rows** in the Cell Size group.

The Distribute Rows feature distributes the height of selected rows so that the space is distributed equally within the selected area.

m. Save the *chap5_ho1_antioxidants_solution* presentation and keep it onscreen if you plan to continue to the next hands-on exercise. Close the file and exit PowerPoint if you do not want to continue with the next exercise at this time.

The basic table structure has been completed by using the Draw Table feature and the table layout options.

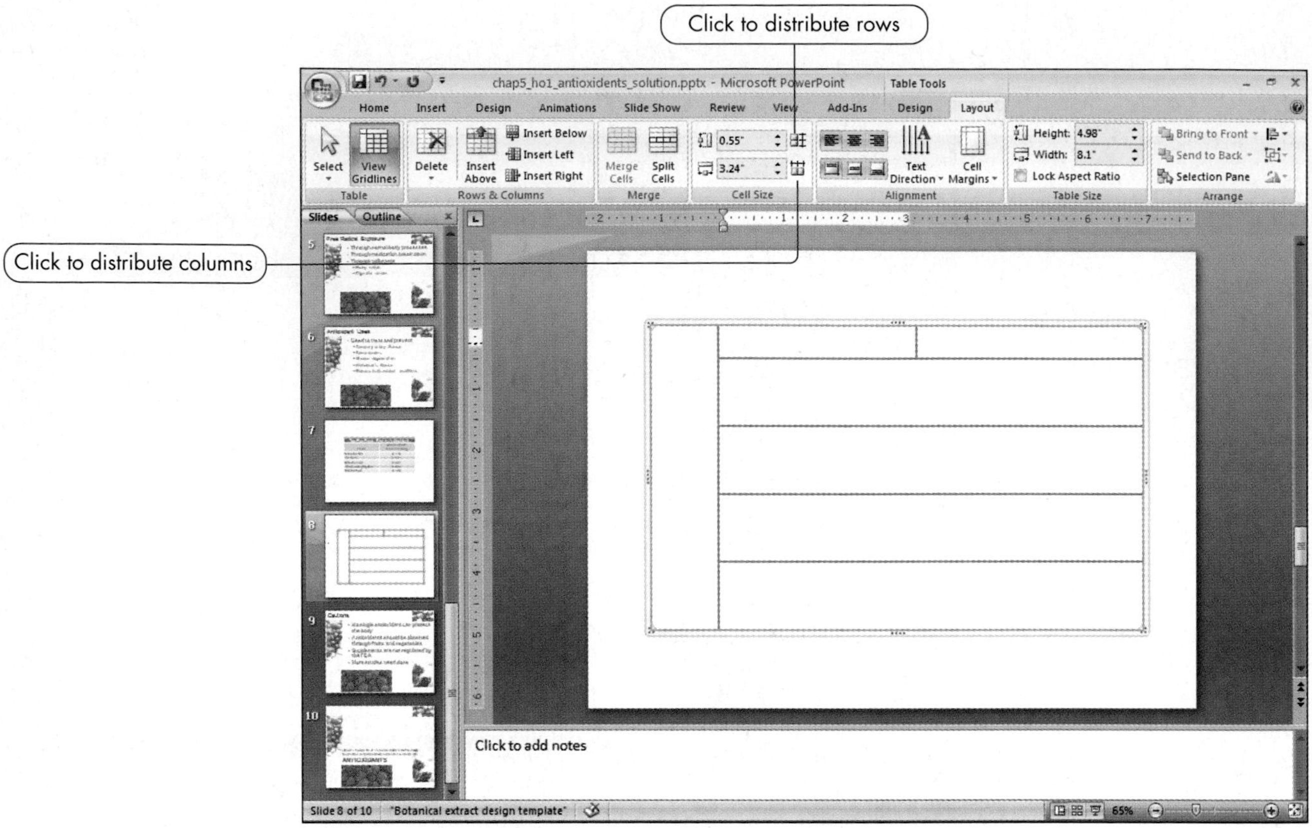

Figure 5.14   Table Structure Created by Drawing

Table Modification

Whether enhancing a table by design changes or modifying its structure by layout changes, the Table Tools contextual tabs give you the power to accomplish your task!

After you create a table, you may wish to enhance it by changing its appearance. The look of the table can be quickly changed using the tools available in the Design tab in the Table Tools contextual tab.

You may also find that you need to modify the structure of the table, a process that can be accomplished using the tools available in the Layout tab in the Table Tools contextual tab. Most likely, you find yourself taking advantage of both tabs, as you did in the previous hands-on activity. Whether enhancing a table by design changes or modifying its structure by layout changes, the Table Tools contextual tabs give you the power to accomplish your task!

In this section, you learn how to apply a table style. Specifically, you learn how to set a background fill, change table borders, and apply a table effect. In addition, you learn how to change table layout. Specifically, you insert and delete columns and rows; change row height, column width, and table size; and adjust text within cells, rows, and columns. Finally, you learn how to share information between applications.

Applying a Table Style

To change the appearance of a table, you can format cells yourself. You may prefer to use the Table Style Options group in the Design tab of the Table Tools contextual tab to change options individually. The quickest way, however, is to apply a table style. A *table style* is a Quick Style provided by PowerPoint that provides a combination of formatting choices based on the theme of the presentation. Whether you choose to format the individual style options yourself or apply a full table style, you should understand the seven different types of formatting available to you. A PowerPoint table consists of the following styles:

A ***table style*** is a combination of formatting choices available to you that are based on the theme of the presentation.

- Table formatting, which includes a background fill
- Header Row formatting, which is the row used for the table title
- Total Row formatting, which is the last row in the table and used to show column totals
- First Column formatting, which makes it easy to set the stub off from other columns
- Last Column formatting, which can be used to set off figures
- Banded Row formatting, which is used to format even rows differently than odd rows
- Banded Column formatting, which is used to format even columns differently than odd columns

To apply a style to an individual option, simply click the option box in front of the style name in the Table Style Options group on the Design tab. To apply a table style that impacts all of the formatting options based on the theme of your presentation, click the More button in the Table Styles group. This brings up the Quick Styles gallery, which displays the Best Match for the Document at the top of the gallery along with Light, Medium, and Dark styles. Note that at the bottom of the Quick Styles gallery there is an option to clear the table of all styles. It does not remove attributes you have applied, however. Figure 5.15 shows the Table Style Options group and the Table Quick Styles gallery.

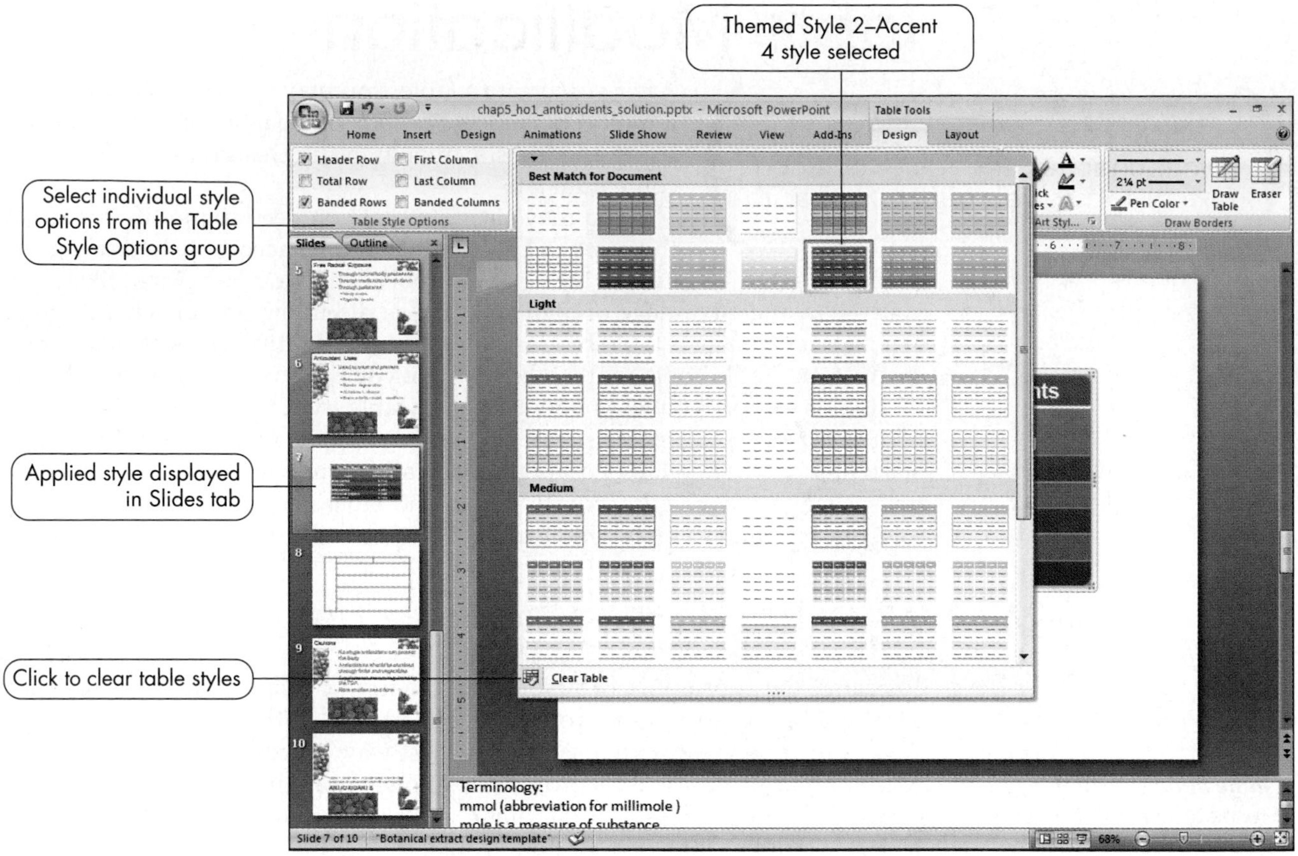

Figure 5.15 The Table Quick Styles Gallery

Set a Background Fill

Though header and total row styles, first and last column styles, and banded rows and banded column styles are easily formatted in the Table Style Options group on the Design tab, the background fill style is changed using the Shading button. Select the cells in which you wish the background change, click the Design tab under Table Tools, click the Shading button, and then point to the fill option you desire. You may choose from the following:

- Color
- Picture
- Gradient
- Texture
- Table Background

Another way to change these attributes is to right-click in the cell or selected cells where you desire the background change, and then click Format Shape. The main advantage of using the right-click method is the Format Shape dialog box appears. This dialog box enables you to choose multiple options including transparency and tiling or repeating stretch options. For example, to change the background of a table cell, click Format Shape, and then click Fill in the left pane. Click Picture or texture fill in the right pane, and then click File. Navigate to locate the picture file you want to insert, click the file name, and then click Insert. You can also insert a clip art image by clicking the Clip Art button rather than the Picture or texture fill. Click Close. Figure 5.16 has an added row above the title, which uses a fruits and vegetables picture from Microsoft's Clip Organizer as a background fill. It also displays the Format Shape dialog box options.

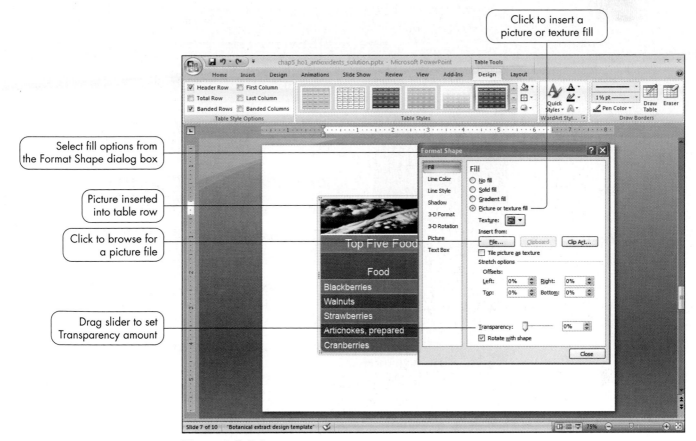

Figure 5.16 The Format Shape Dialog Box

Change Table Borders

Change border style, weight, and color by using the pen options located in the Draw Borders group on the Design tab. The Pen Style option changes the style of the line used to draw borders and includes options for dotted and dashed lines. The Pen Weight option changes the width of the border, and the Pen Color option changes the color of the border.

After selecting the style, weight, and color of a border, you click the border you want to change with the pencil pointer. You may also drag to create additional borders with the pencil pointer. If you have multiple borders to change, however, it is faster to use the Borders button in the Table Styles group on the Design tab. Select the cell or cells you want to impact, or select the entire table. You can choose to have no border; all cells bordered; only outside borders; only inside borders; just a top, bottom, left, or right border; inside horizontal or vertical borders; or diagonal down or up borders.

Apply a Table Effect

New to PowerPoint 2007 is the ability to apply special effects to a cell, selected cells, or a table. The effects enable you to apply a 3-D bevel to selected cells, apply a soft shadow, or apply a reflection. To apply one of the effects, click the Effects button in the Table Styles group on the Design Tab. Three effects options appear: Cell Bevel, Shadow, and Reflection. Clicking one of these options will open that effect's gallery. As with other galleries, you can preview the effects on the selected cells or table to see if you like the impact of the effects. The gallery also includes a No effect option that removes a previously applied effect. Figure 5.17 shows four tables: the original table with the default style settings, a table with the Riblet bevel effect applied to all cells, a table with the Perspective Diagonal Upper Left shadow effect, and a table showing a Half Reflection, touching reflection style.

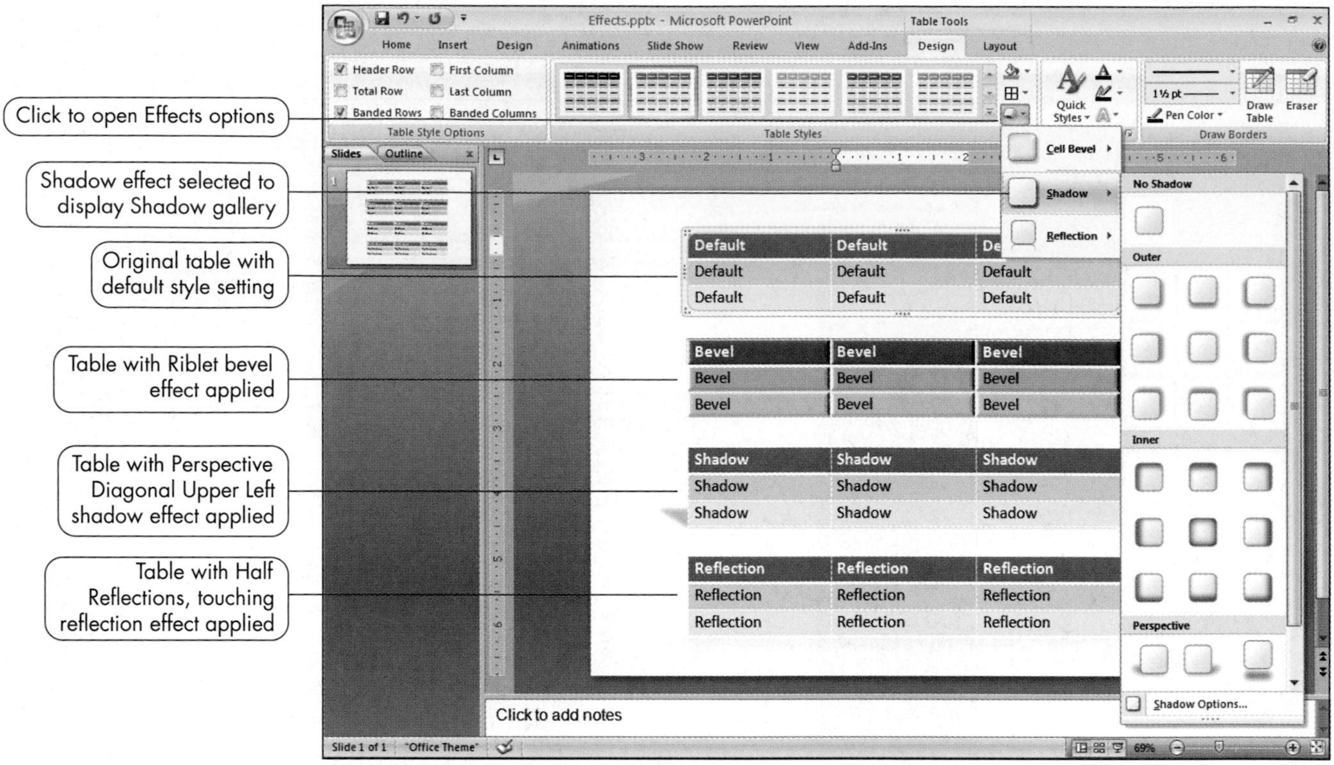

Figure 5.17 Table Special Effect Styles

Labels (left side of figure):
- Click to open Effects options
- Shadow effect selected to display Shadow gallery
- Original table with default style setting
- Table with Riblet bevel effect applied
- Table with Perspective Diagonal Upper Left shadow effect applied
- Table with Half Reflections, touching reflection effect applied

Changing Table Layout

After creating your table, or even while creating it, you may want to change the layout or structure of the table. The tools you need to accomplish this change are contained on the Layout tab under Table Tools. You insert or delete columns and rows, merge or split cells, change the size of cells or the table, and adjust the height of a row or the width of a column. In addition to changing the alignment of text as you did in the previous section, you can change the direction of the text.

To aid you in modifying a table, the Layout tab includes a button you can use to quickly select a table, a column, or a row. Click your pointer inside a cell in the row or column you wish to select, click Select in the Table group on the Layout tab, and then select from Select Table, Select Column, or Select Row. Also included in the Table group on the Layout tab is View Gridlines. This is a toggle button that you use to show or hide the table gridlines.

Insert and Delete Columns and Rows

After creating a table, or even while creating it, you may realize that you need to add a row or a column. If you want the new row to appear at the bottom of a table, click in the last cell of the table and press **Tab**. To control where the row appears, however, click in a cell next to where you want the new row, and then click the Insert Above or Insert Below button in the Row and Columns group on the Layout tab. The process is similar for inserting a column to the left or right of an existing column: Click in a cell next to where you want the new column, and then click the Insert Left or Insert Right button in the Row and Columns group on the Layout tab. As an alternative to using the Layout tab, you can right-click in selected cells, point at Insert, and then click one of the insert column or insert row options that appear.

To delete selected columns and rows, click Delete in the Rows and Columns group on the Layout tab, and then click Delete Columns or Delete Rows. You may also right-click in selected cells, and then click Delete Rows or Delete Columns. Figure 5.18 displays the table from Figure 5.16 after modifications. The top row with the picture fill has been deleted. A column was added to the left of the Food column and a Microsoft Office clip art image inserted in each of the resulting cells. Finally, a row was added to the bottom of the table so source information could be included.

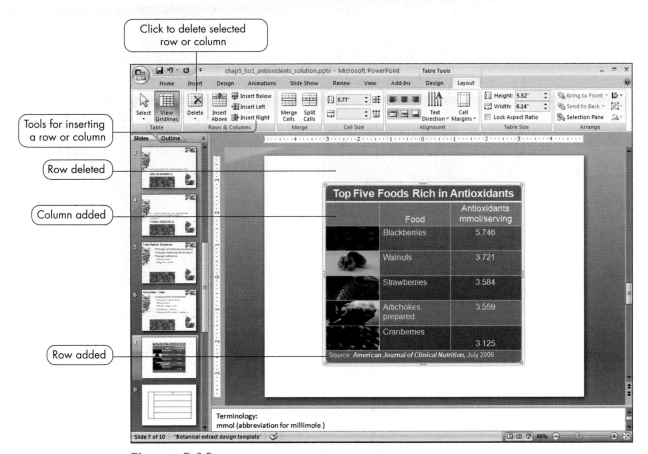

Figure 5.18 Antioxidant Table with Modified Layout

Change Row Height, Column Width, and Table Size

To accommodate your information or to call attention to a row or cell, you can change the row height or column width. For example, title rows are often taller than the rows containing body cells. To quickly adjust row height or column width, position the pointer over the border of a row or column you want to adjust until the pointer changes into a resizing pointer, then drag the border to adjust the row or column to the desired height or width. For a more exacting change, use the Table Row Height or Table Column Width features in the Cell Size group on the Layout tab. You can adjust the size by the spin boxes or by entering an exact size in the box.

You can resize the table manually by dragging a corner or middle resizing handle. Dragging the top or bottom middle handles will change the table height, whereas dragging the left or right middle handles will change the table width. Dragging a corner handle proportionally resizes the table. To set a specific size for the table, specify Height or Width in the Table Size group of the Layout tab.

Figure 5.19 shows the table from Figure 5.18 resized to a height of 6" and a width of 7". The top row of the table has been resized to 1" and the text alignment changed to Center Vertically using the Alignment group on the Layout tab.

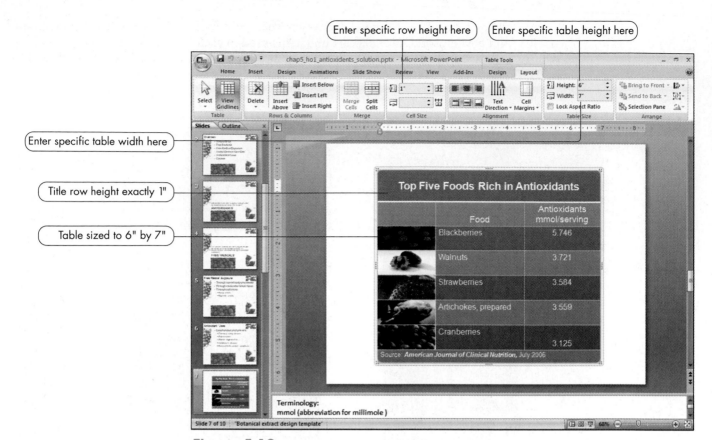

Figure 5.19 Resized Antioxidant Table

Align Text Within Cells, Rows, and Columns

The Alignment group on the Layout tab includes features that not only align the contents of a cell horizontally and vertically, but also change the direction of the text by rotating it or changing its orientation. You can even change the margins inside the cell! First, you select the text you want to align in a single cell, row, or column. Then, to align text, click one of the alignment buttons in the Alignment group on the Layout tab. To align text horizontally, select Align Left, Center, or Align Right. To align vertically, select Align Top, Center Vertically, or Align Bottom.

When you want to change the direction of the text within a cell, row, or column, click the Text Direction button, and then select from the options. To rotate the text, choose Rotate all text 90 degrees (text faces away from page) or choose Rotate all text 270 degrees (text faces inward to the page). To change the text orientation from horizontal to vertical, select Stacked. Internal margins can be changed from a default of .5" for top and bottom margins and 1" for left and right margins to no margins, narrow margins, and wide margins. To customize the margin settings, click Custom Margins in the Cell Margin gallery, where you can set each margin individually. Figure 5.20 shows a table with text rotated 270 degrees within a column and a column with the text aligned at the bottom.

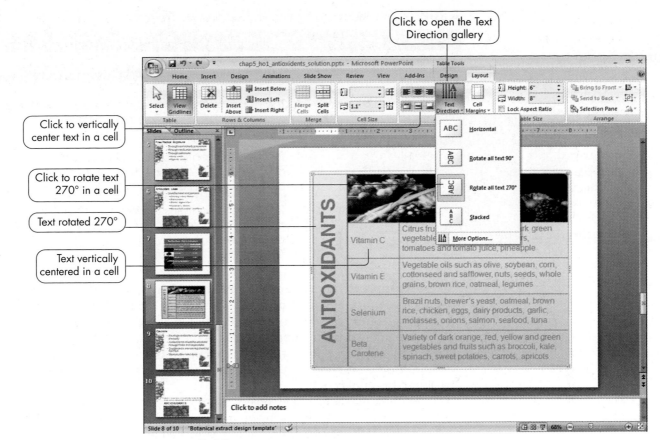

Figure 5.20 Rotated Text Within a Column

Sharing Information Between Applications

PowerPoint's table feature handles simple tables well, but if your table is complicated or needs periodic updating you can create it in Word. If, however, it requires calculations, you should create it in Excel to take advantage of Excel's powerful data features. After you create the table, you can embed the Word table or Excel worksheet in a presentation slide as an object. An alternative to embedding would be to link the slide to the Word table or Excel worksheet. *Object linking and embedding (OLE)* lets you insert an object created in one application into a document created in another application.

Linking an object differs from embedding an object, however, and it is important that you understand these differences to select the process that best meets your needs. To understand the differences, you need to understand four key terms used in the object linking and embedding process.

Object linking and embedding (OLE) is inserting an object created in one application into a document created in another application.

Table 5.1 Object Linking and Embedding Key Terms

Key Term	Definition
Source application	The application you used to create the original object, such as Word or Excel.
Destination application	The application that created the document into which the object is being inserted, such as PowerPoint.
Source file	The file that contains the table or data that is used to create a linked or embedded object, such as a Word document or an Excel worksheet.
Destination file	The file that contains the inserted object, such as a PowerPoint presentation with an Excel worksheet embedded in it.

A **source application** is the application used to create the original object.

A **destination application** is the application that created the document into which the object is being inserted.

A **source file** is the file that contains the table or data that is used to create a linked or embedded object.

A **destination file** is the file that contains the inserted object.

A **linked object** is a representation of data stored in the source file.

An **embedded object** is an object that has the contents of a source file inserted in it.

For example, if you create a table in Excel and transfer it into a PowerPoint slide, Excel is the source application and PowerPoint is the destination application. The table is the source file object within Excel. Once you insert the table object into PowerPoint, the PowerPoint presentation is the destination file. The simplest way to transfer the table object, or any object, is to copy it in the source application and then paste it into PowerPoint, or the destination application. This embeds the copied object into the application.

If you link the table, or any object, into PowerPoint the information is stored in the source file and updated when you modify it in the source file. When you double-click the object, the source application is launched and you are actually editing the source object. The **linked object** is only a picture or representation of the data stored in the source file. The changes you make in the source file display in PowerPoint. The representation in PowerPoint is only a shortcut to the source file so that changes to the file reflect in your presentation. The advantage of linking is a smaller file size because PowerPoint stores only the data needed to display the information.

An **embedded object**, however, maintains a direct connection to the application in which it was created. Instead of just inserting a representation of the object, you insert a copy of the object. Double-clicking the embedded object will open the tools from the source program for you to use in editing the object. You are still in PowerPoint. In the case of a table created in Excel and embedded in PowerPoint, when you double-click the object the Excel Ribbon replaces the PowerPoint Ribbon. You then edit the table using Excel tools. Keep in mind, however, that this increases your presentation file size because PowerPoint now stores the data plus the information that connects the data to the original application. Figure 5.21 shows a PowerPoint presentation with an embedded table. When the table was double-clicked, the Excel Ribbon replaced the PowerPoint Ribbon, but the title bar shows that you are still working within PowerPoint. It is important to note that if you edit the embedded table, the source document is **not** changed.

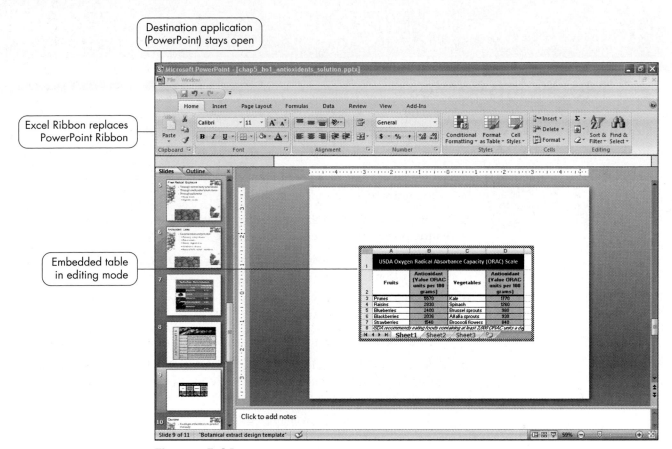

Figure 5.21 Excel Table Embedded in Presentation Slide

To link or embed an object, click the Insert tab, and then click the Insert Object button. If you wish to create a new object and then insert it, click the Create new option, and then click the type of object you want to insert. Click OK and use the source application to create the object. When you are done creating the object, click outside of the object to return to PowerPoint. If you want to insert a previously created file, click the Create from file option. Click browse, and then navigate to locate the file containing the object you want to insert. To link the object, activate the Link check box. To embed the object, clear the Link check box (if necessary).

If you have the original source document open, you can copy the object and then paste it into your PowerPoint slide. Pasting an object embeds it. If you wish to link the file instead of embedding it, you can use the Paste Special command. To use the Paste Special command, copy the object in the source application, move to your presentation slide, click Home, click the Paste button arrow, and then click Paste Special. Then click Paste link, click the object type you desire, and finally, click OK.

Hands-On Exercises

2 | Modifying Tables

Skills covered: 1. Apply Table Styles **2.** Change Table Layouts **3.** Change Cell Fills **4.** Link an Excel Table

---

Step 1
Apply Table Styles

Refer to Figure 5.22 as you complete Step 1.

a. Open the *chap5_ho2_antioxidant2* presentation if you closed it after the last hands-on exercise. Save it as **chap5_ho2_antioxidants2_solution**.

b. Move to **Slide 7** and select the table. Click the **Design tab**, and then click the **More** button in the Table Styles group.

c. Select the **Themed Style 2 – Accent 4** in the second row, fifth column of the Best Match for Document category.

Themed Style 2 – Accent 4 includes a Header Row style and Banded Rows.

d. Move to **Slide 8** and select the table. Click **More** in the Table Styles group on the Layout tab, and then click **Themed Style 1 – Accent 4** in the first row, fifth column of the Best Match for Document category.

e. Save the *chap5_ho2_antioxidants2_solution* presentation.

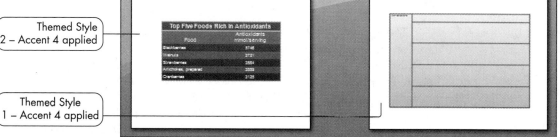

Themed Style
2 – Accent 4 applied

Themed Style
1 – Accent 4 applied

Figure 5.22 Table Styles Applied

Step 2
Change Table Layouts

Refer to Figures 5.23 and 5.24 as you complete Step 2.

a. With the *chap5_ho2_antioxidants2_solution* presentation open, click in Column 1 of the table in Slide 8, and then click the **Layout tab**. Click the **Text Direction button** in the Alignment group, and then click **Rotate all text 270°**.

b. Select the *Antioxidants* text in Column 1, and then use the Mini toolbar to change the font size to **44 points** and the alignment to **Center**.

c. Click the **Design tab**, and then click the option for **First Column** in the Table Style Options group.

d. Click the **Layout tab**, and then click **Center Vertically** in the Alignment group.

e. Click inside the first row, and then change the **Table Row Height** option in the Cell Size group of the Layout tab to **1.5"**.

f. Select the text in the **Height** box in the Table Size group on the Layout tab and type **6.06"**.

g. Select the text in the **Width** box in the Table Size group on the Layout tab and type **8"**.

h. Drag the table to the approximate vertical and horizontal center of the slide.

i. Move to **Slide 7**, position the pointer in the last cell of the table, and press **Tab**.

j. Position the pointer in the first column, click the **Layout tab**, and then click **Insert Left**.

k. Select the cells in the newly created last row, and then click **Merge Cells** in the Merge group.

l. Type **Source:** *American Journal of Clinical Nutrition,* **July 2006**. Select the text and use the Mini toolbar to change the font size to **14 points**.

m. Select the cells in the top row, and then click **Merge Cells** in the Merge group.

n. With your pointer inside the top row, change the **Table Row Height** option in the Cell Size group of the Layout tab to **1"**. Set the alignment for the top row to **Center Vertically** in the Alignment group.

o. Select the cells in the first column and change the **Table Column Width** to **1.8"**.

p. Select the cells in the second and third columns and change the **Table Column Width** to **2.8"**.

q. Select the table body cells (rows 2–7), then change the **Table Row Height** option in the Cell Size group of the Layout tab to **.75"**. Set the alignment to **Center Vertically** in the Alignment group.

r. Drag the table to the approximate vertical and horizontal center of the slide.

s. Save the *chap5_ho2_antioxidants2_solution* presentation.

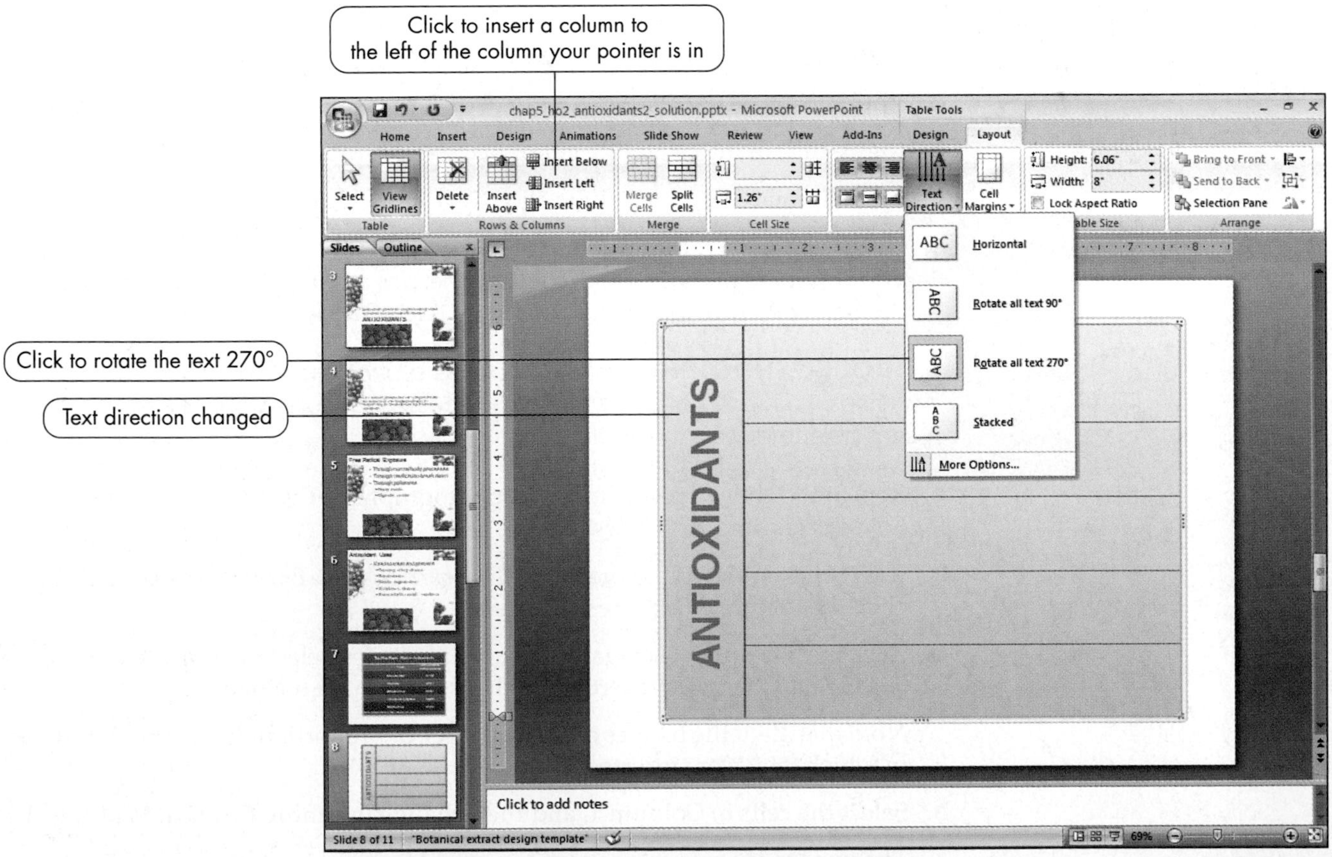

Figure 5.23 Antioxidant Table Structure Modified

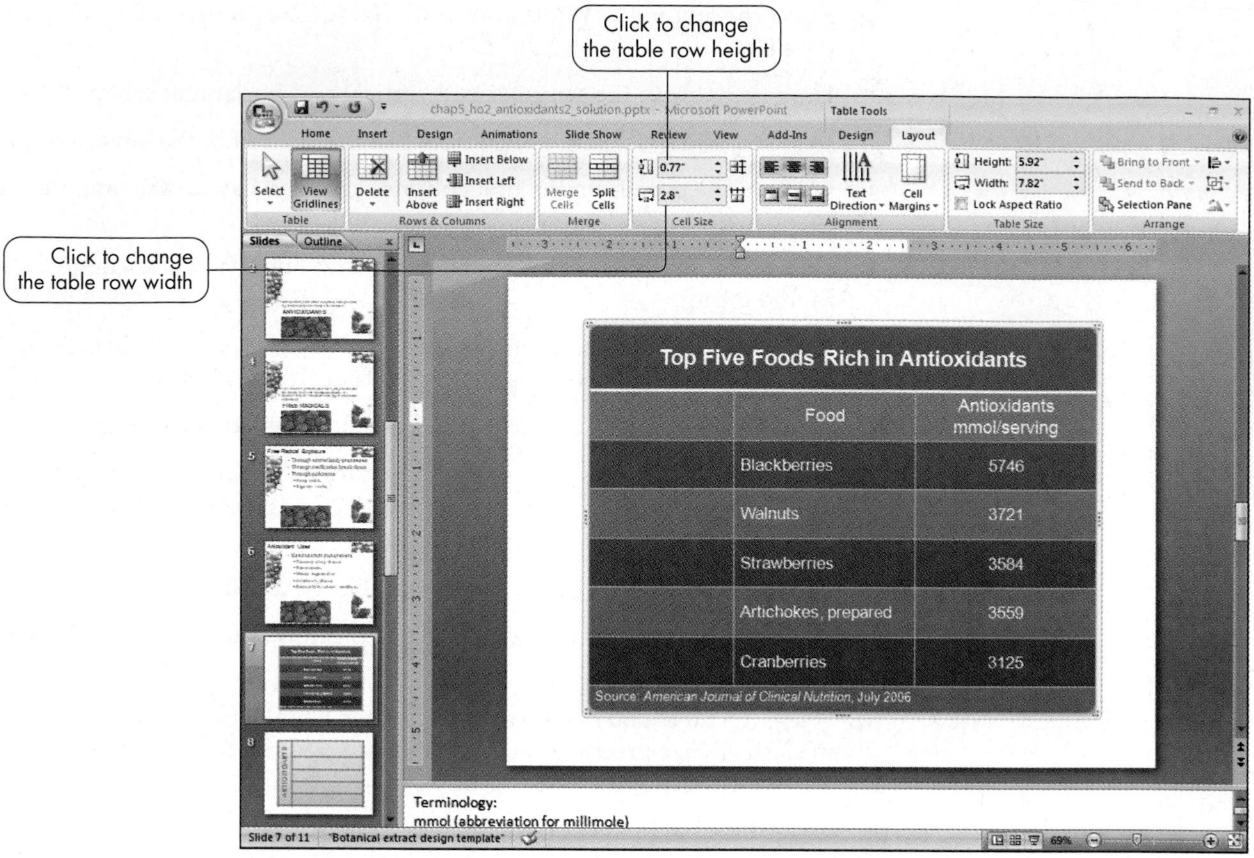

Figure 5.24 Top Five Foods Table Structure Modified

Step 3
Change Cell Fills

Refer to Figure 5.25 as you complete Step 3, instructions i–m.

a. With the *chap5_ho2_antioxidants2_solution* presentation open, move to **Slide 7**.

b. Right-click in the cell to the left of *Blackberries*.

c. Click **Format Shape**, and then click the **Picture or texture fill** option.

d. Click the **Clip Art button**, type **blackberries** in the Search text box, and click **Go**. Select the photograph of the blackberries and raspberries that appears in the **Select Picture** dialog box, and then click **OK**.

TROUBLESHOOTING: If you do not see a photograph of blackberries and raspberries, you may not have Internet access. Substitute a clip art image if you are not able to access the Internet.

e. Repeat the above process to insert photographs in the cells for *Walnuts*, *Strawberries*, and *Artichokes*.

f. Right-click in the cell to the left of *Cranberries*, click **Format Shape**, and then click the **Picture or texture fill** option.

g. Click the **File button**, navigate to your student files, select the *chap5_ho2_ cranberries .jpg* file, and then click **Insert**. Close the Format Shape dialog box.

Note that all of the images are slightly out of proportion due to the size of the cell in which they were inserted.

h. Select the cells in Column 1, and then change the **Table Column Width** to **1.2"**.

The images are now in proportion.

i. Move to **Slide 8** and position your pointer in the first row of the table.

j. Right-click, click **Format Shape**, and then click the **Picture or texture fill** option.

k. Click the **File button**, navigate to your student files, select the *chap5_ho2_fruits .jpg* file, and then click **Insert**. Close the Format Shape dialog box.

This is a Microsoft clip art image that has been resized to fit the row.

l. Enter the remaining data as shown in Figure 5.25, creating cells as necessary.

m. Save the *chap5_ho2_antioxidants2_solution* presentation.

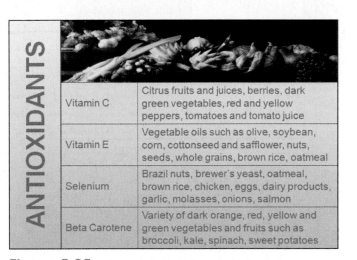

Figure 5.25 Completed Antioxidants Table

<table>
<tr><td>

Step 4

Link an Excel Table

</td><td>

Refer to Figure 5.26 as you complete Step 4.

a. With the *chap5_ho2_antioxidants2_solution* presentation onscreen, move to Slide 9.

b. Click the **Insert tab**, and then click **Object** in the Text group.

c. Click the **Create from file** option, and then click the **Browse** button.

d. Locate and select the *chap5_ho2_oracscale.xlsx* file, and then click **OK**.

e. In the Insert Object dialog box, clink the **Link** option, and then click **OK**.

A representation of the table is inserted into your presentation. Because of this, the **Format tab** on the Drawing Tools contextual tab becomes active.

f. Set the **Shape Height** to **4"**.

g. Double-click the table object.

The source application, Microsoft Excel, opens for editing.

h. In Excel, select the column headings, and then click the **Home tab**. Change the **Font Color** to **Automatic**. Close Excel.

Note the column headings in the linked table are now changed to reflect the editing you performed in Excel.

</td></tr>
</table>

i. Save the *chap5_ho2_antioxidants2_solution* presentation and keep it onscreen if you plan to continue to the next hands-on exercise. Close the file and exit PowerPoint if you do not want to continue with the next exercise at this time.

USDA Oxygen Radical Absorbance Capacity (ORAC) Scale			
Fruits	Antioxidant (Value ORAC units per 100 grams)	Vegetables	Antioxidant (Value ORAC units per 100 grams)
Prunes	5570	Kale	1770
Raisins	2830	Spinach	1260
Blueberries	2400	Brussel sprouts	980
Blackberries	2036	Alfalfa sprouts	930
Strawberries	1540	Broccoli flowers	840
USDA recommends eating foods containing at least 3,000 ORAC units a day.			

Figure 5.26 Linked Excel Table

Statistical Charts and Graphs

(Statistical charts and graphs . . . communicate numerical relationships more effectively than using just words . . .)

Statistical charts and graphs are valuable tools in today's world. They help you communicate numerical relationships more effectively than using just words to describe them. You are able to emphasize and organize the information in a way that conveys your message effectively. A chart or graph can compare data and show trends or patterns. Summarizing information in a chart or graph helps your audience understand and retain your message.

In this section, you identify chart types and elements. Then you learn how to create and insert a chart in a slide.

Identifying Chart Types and Elements

Microsoft Office 2007 makes it easy to create charts and to professionally format them. You can even save your chart as a template so you can apply the same formatting to new charts of the same type. When you create a chart using PowerPoint 2007, you enter the information in an Excel workbook. The Excel worksheet you used to create the chart is then embedded in your PowerPoint presentation.

A **graph** displays a relationship between two sets of numbers plotted as a point with coordinates on a grid.

A **column chart** shows data changes over a period of time or comparisons among items.

A **line chart** displays data over time.

A **pie chart** shows proportions to a whole as slices in a circular pie.

A **bar chart** shows comparisons between items.

An **area chart** emphasizes the magnitude of change over time.

An **XY (scatter) chart** shows distributions, groupings, or patterns.

A **stock chart** shows fluctuations or the range of change between the high and low values of a subject over time.

A **surface chart** is used to plot a surface using two sets of data.

A **doughnut chart** shows proportions to a whole and can contain more than one data series.

A **bubble chart** shows relationships using three values.

A **radar chart** compares the aggregate values of three or more variables represented on axes starting from the same point.

> ### TIP Linking a PowerPoint Chart and an Excel Worksheet
>
> To create a smaller presentation file, link the Excel worksheet used to create your chart instead of embedding it. To link the worksheet (which saves it as a separate file instead of as part of the PowerPoint file), copy the chart from Excel, and then paste it into your presentation.

Whereas the term *chart* refers to a visual display of information such as posters, banners, tables, maps, lists, diagrams, and others, the term *graph* is specific to a chart that displays a relationship between two sets of numbers plotted as a data point with coordinates on a grid. These two terms have become synonymous and are used interchangeably now. Microsoft Office applications use the term *chart* to describe the charts and graphs provided for your use.

Before beginning to create your chart, you think about the information you are presenting and ask yourself what message you want to convey using a chart. Are you representing changes over time? Are you comparing or summarizing data? Are you representing a single series or multiple series? What type of chart will your audience understand quickly? How sophisticated is your audience in reading charts?

Select Basic Chart Types

Each of the basic chart types answers these questions and each has appropriate uses. Choose the type that portrays your message most effectively. The chart should be clear and easy to read, and should present enough detail to provide your audience with an understanding of your message without overwhelming people with detail. Generally audiences can easily understand the common charts such as pie charts, line charts, and column and bar charts because they are used frequently on the Internet and in newspapers and magazines. Sophisticated audiences or experts are familiar with the specialty charts and graphs like XY (scatter) charts, bubble charts, and radar charts.

Office 2007 includes a wide variety of charts: *column chart, line chart, pie chart, bar chart, area chart, XY (scatter) chart, stock chart, surface chart, doughnut chart, bubble chart*, and *radar chart*. The most common purpose of each of these charts is listed in the following Reference Table. For greater detail, including chart subtype information, enter *chart types* in the Search box for PowerPoint Help, and then click the hyperlink for *Available chart types*.

Chart Purposes | Reference

Type	Purpose and Series Type	Sample SmartArt
Pie Chart	**Purpose**: Use to show proportions of a whole. Slices are proportioned to show the relative size of each piece. Information is arranged in one column or row only to create a pie chart. **Series Type**: Single-series	
Doughnut Chart	**Purpose**: Use to show the relationship of parts to a whole like a pie chart, but can contain more than one data series. The pie contains a hole in the center. Information is arranged in columns or rows only to create a doughnut chart. **Series Type**: Multi-series	
Column Chart	**Purpose**: Use to show data changes over a period of time or comparisons among items. Information is arranged in columns or rows and is used to plot the chart using a horizontal and a vertical axis. Categories are typically organized along the horizontal axis and values along the vertical axis. The information is displayed in vertical columns. Shapes other than vertical bars can be used for the columns, including 3-D bars, cylinders, cones, and pyramids. **Series Type**: Single- or multi-series	
Line Chart	**Purpose**: Use to display data over time. Ideal for showing trends over equal time intervals such as months, quarters, or years. Information is arranged in columns or rows on a worksheet and set against a common scale. Category information is distributed evenly along the horizontal axis, and all value information is distributed evenly along the vertical axis. The information is displayed as individual points linked by lines. **Series Type**: Single- or multi-series	
Bar Chart	**Purpose**: Use to show comparisons between items. Chart is created using information that is arranged in columns or rows on a worksheet the same as in a column chart, but the bars stretch horizontally instead of vertically. **Series Type**: Single- or multi-series	
Area Chart	**Purpose**: Use to emphasize the magnitude of change over time. Draws attention to the total value across a trend. Basically, a line graph with the area below the plotted lines filled in. Information is arranged in columns or rows on a worksheet. **Series Type**: Single- or multi-series	

| --- | --- | --- |
XY (scatter) Chart	**Purpose**: Scatter charts show the relationships among the numeric values in several data series, or plot two groups of numbers as one series of xy coordinates. This shows distributions, groupings, or patterns. A scatter chart plots two variables, one of which is plotted on the horizontal (X) scale and one of which is plotted on the vertical (Y) scale. **Series Type**: Single- or multi-series	
Stock Chart	**Purpose**: Use to show fluctuations or the range of change between the high and low values of a subject over time. Commonly used to show fluctuation of stock prices, but can be used for fluctuations in temperature or scientific data. Data must be arranged in columns or rows in a specific order on the worksheet. To create a simple high-low-close stock chart, data must be arranged with High, Low, and Close entered as column headings, in that order. **Series Type**: Single- or multi-series	
Surface Chart	**Purpose**: Use to plot a surface using two sets of data. Colors indicate areas that are in the same range of values. Information is arranged in columns or rows on a worksheet. This is similar to a line graph but with a dimensional effect added. **Series Type**: Single- or multi-series	
Bubble Chart	**Purpose**: Use to show relationships like an XY (scatter) chart, but uses three values instead of two. The third value determines the size of the bubble. Bubble charts should not be used to show absolute quantities, as the scales are relative. Information is arranged in columns on the worksheet so that X values are listed in the first column and corresponding Y values and bubble size values are listed in adjacent columns. **Series Type**: Single- or multi-series	
Radar Chart	**Purpose**: Use to compare the aggregate values of three or more variables represented on axes starting from the same point, like the spokes on a wheel. Allows you to use multiple criteria. Information is arranged in columns or rows on a worksheet. **Series Type**: Multi-series	

Identify Chart Elements

A **data point** is a numeric value used in plotting data on a chart.

A **data series** contains the data points representing a set of related numbers.

A **single-series** chart contains only one set of data points.

A **multi-series** chart contains data points for two or more sets of data.

A **label** identifies information in a chart.

A **leader** is a connecting line between labels and pie slices.

An **exploded pie chart** separates one or more slices of the pie chart for emphasis.

The **chart area** is the chart and all its elements.

The **plot area** is the area representing the data in a chart.

When you enter the data for your table in an Excel workbook, the cells that contain numeric values are **data points**. A **data series** contains the data points representing a set of related numbers. The data series can be **single-series** (representing only one set of data) or **multi-series** (representing data for two or more sets of data). If you plot the profits for a store in Destin, Florida, you would be plotting a single-series chart. If you plot the profits for stores in Destin, Fort Walton Beach, and Pensacola, Florida, you would be plotting a multi-series chart.

A pie chart is an example of a single-series chart. Because a pie chart shows the proportional relationship of each segment to the whole, the whole is displayed as a circle. A fill may be applied to each segment, or slice, or applied to the entire pie. A **label** identifies the slices in the pie. The slices can be labeled with the series name, category name, value, and/or percentage. The labels can be centered, positioned at the inside end of a slice, positioned at the outside end of the slice, or in "Best Fit," which is based on the amount of text inside the label. **Leaders** are lines used to connect the label to the slice of pie. Though it is preferable to have the labels within a pie slice, often they do not fit and leaders become necessary to avoid possible confusion. **Exploded pie charts** emphasize data by separating or "exploding" a slice or slices from the pie. Figure 5.27 shows a pie chart with a single series—the assets of a charitable foundation. The chart includes a title and labels indicating the category names and the percentages each slice of the pie contributes to the total. The Trusts slice is exploded for emphasis. The **chart area** (the chart and all of its elements) is bounded by the placeholder borders, whereas the **plot area** (the area representing the data) is defined by a bounding box comprised of single lines. A doughnut chart includes the same elements as the pie chart, but the doughnut chart is a multi-series chart and stacks the pies inside one another. The center of a doughnut chart is hollowed out.

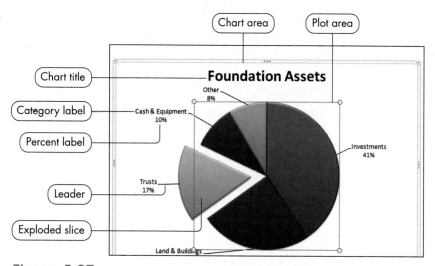

Figure 5.27 Basic Elements of a Pie Chart

The *x-axis* is the horizontal category axis.

The *y-axis* is the vertical value axis.

The *z-axis* is the axis used to plot the depth of a chart.

Chart *gridlines* are horizontal and vertical lines that extend from the horizontal and vertical axes of a chart to make the data in the chart easier to read.

Tick marks are short lines on axes that mark the category and value divisions.

A *data marker* is a graphical representation of a data point, such as a bar, circle, or slice.

A *legend* is a key that displays identifying information about the data series connected to the data series name.

The remaining chart types available in Office 2007 are plotted on a coordinate system and may be single-series or multi-series charts. The chart is created by plotting data points between two reference lines, or scales, called axes. The *x-axis* is the horizontal axis and usually contains the category information, such as products, companies, or intervals of time. The *y-axis* is the vertical axis and usually contains the values or amounts. Three-dimensional charts have a third axis, the *z-axis*, used to plot the depth of a chart. Note that pie and doughnut charts do not have an axis and a radar chart does not have an x-axis, only a y- or value axis. Axes can be given titles to describe what the data represent. *Gridlines*, lines that extend from the horizontal or vertical axes, can be displayed to make the chart data easier to read and understand. *Tick marks* are short lines on the axes that mark the category and value divisions. Data points plotted on the chart are indicated by *data markers*, or graphical representations such as bars, dots, or slices that can be enhanced with lines, filled areas, or pictures. To help identify the data series, a *legend* assigns a format or color to each data series and then displays that information with the data series name.

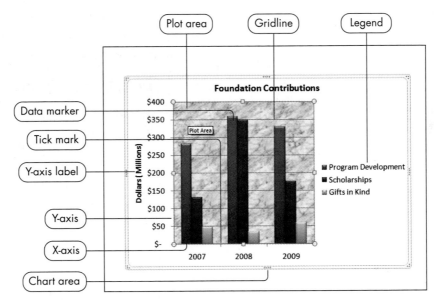

Figure 5.28 Basic Elements of a Column Chart

Creating and Inserting a Chart

Begin the process of creating a chart by clicking the Chart icon in a content placeholder or by clicking the Insert tab, and then clicking Chart in the Illustrations group. The Insert Chart dialog box displays with two panes. The left pane contains the chart type and the right pane contains chart styles, or subtypes of the select chart. Figure 5.29 displays the default chart type, a Column chart, in the left pane and the default chart style, Clustered Column, in the right pane.

TIP Set Chart Type and Style Defaults

If you find that you constantly use the same Chart type and style, use the Set as Default Chart button so that it will be used when creating a new chart.

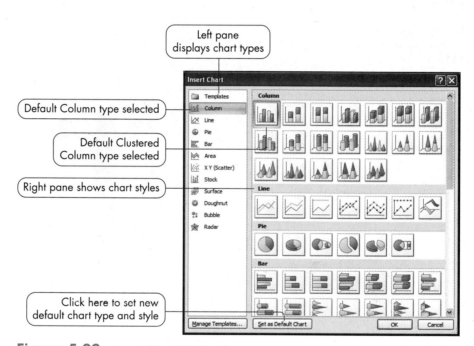

Figure 5.29 Insert Chart Dialog Box

After selecting your chart type and style, click OK. Microsoft Excel opens a worksheet containing sample data. PowerPoint now contains a chart based on the sample data. Replace the sample data with your own data and the PowerPoint chart updates to reflect your information. The Excel worksheet contains a grid of rows and columns. When you type in a cell, it replaces the sample data and your data point is created in your chart. When you enter your data, you might need to change the column widths to fit the data. If you see ##### in a cell, it means there is not enough room in the cell to display the data. To increase the width of the column, position the pointer on the line to the right of the column heading and then double-click to adjust the column width automatically. When you finish entering your data, click Close in Excel and view your chart embedded in PowerPoint.

If you close Excel, and then need to edit the data the chart is based upon, click the Design tab under the Chart Tools contextual tab, and then click the Edit Data button in the Data group. The Excel worksheet reopens so you can edit your data. When you are done editing, click the Close button on the Excel worksheet to return to PowerPoint. Figure 5.30 shows an Excel Worksheet and Figure 5.31 shows the associated chart created in PowerPoint.

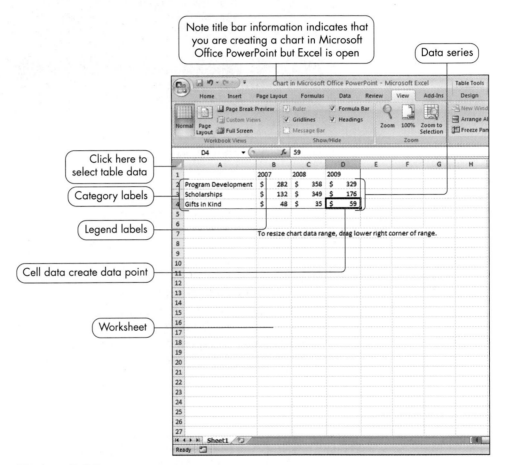

Figure 5.30 Excel Worksheet

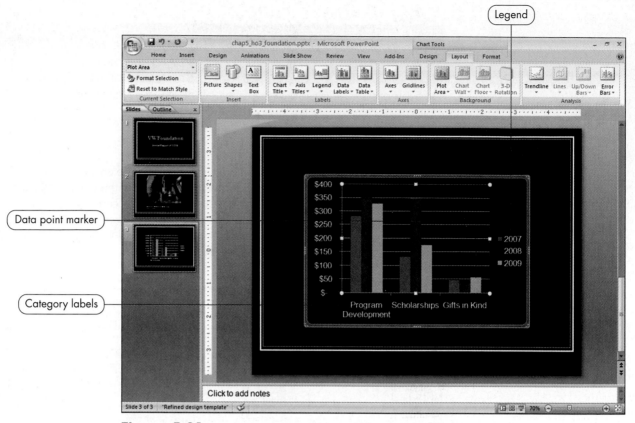

Figure 5.31   PowerPoint Chart Based on Excel Worksheet

By default, the chart is plotted based on the series data displayed in the columns of the worksheet and the column headings displayed in the legend. Because of this, the chart in Figure 5.31 emphasizes the changes in each category over the three-year period. If you want to emphasize the changes by year rather than by category, you can click the Switch Row/Column button in the Data group on the Design contextual tab in PowerPoint.

The chart shown above (Figure 5.31) is at its most basic level. You can modify and format the chart to ensure that your chart conveys your message. For example, without a descriptive title or labels it is impossible to tell the purpose of the chart or what the amounts represent. In the following hands-on exercise, you create a basic pie chart and column chart, and then in the next section, you explore modifications and formatting changes that complete your chart.

3 | Creating Basic Charts

Skills covered: 1. Create a Column Chart **2.** Edit Chart Data **3.** Switch the Row and Column Data **4.** Create a Pie Chart

<table>
<tr><td>Step 1
Create a Column Chart</td><td>

Refer to Figure 5.33 as you complete Step 1.

a. Open the *chap5_ho3_foundation* presentation, and then immediately save it as **chap5_ho3_foundation_solution**.

b. Move to **Slide 3**, click the **Insert tab**, and then click **Chart** in the **Illustrations** group.

c. Click **OK** in the Insert Chart dialog box.

By accepting the defaults, you are creating a Clustered Column Chart.

d. Click the **Heading** button in the upper-left corner of the worksheet to select the sample data, and then press **Delete** on your keyboard.

e. Enter the data in Figure 5.32 in your worksheet.

</td></tr>
</table>

	A	B	C	D
1		2007	2008	2009
2	Program Development	$ 282	$ 358	$ 329
3	Scholarships	$ 132	$ 349	$ 176
4	Gifts in Kind	$ 48	$ 35	$ 59

Figure 5.32 Worksheet Data

f. Click **Close** on the Excel worksheet and return to PowerPoint.

g. Save the *chap5_ho3_foundation_solution* presentation.

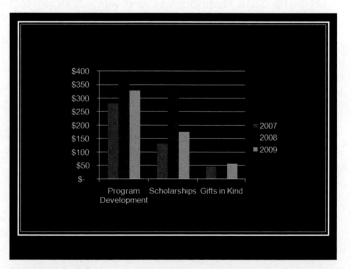

Figure 5.33 Foundation Clustered Column Chart

Refer to Figure 5.34 as you complete Step 2.

a. With the *chap5_ho3_foundation_solution* presentation onscreen, click to select the chart (if necessary).

b. Click the **Design tab**, and then click **Edit Data** in the Data group.

Excel opens, displaying your chart data.

c. Click in **cell C3** and type **249**.

d. Position the pointer in Row 4 and right-click. Point to **Insert**, and then click **Table Rows Above**.

A new row is created.

e. Type **Merit Grants**, press **Tab** and type **$85**, press **Tab** and type **$67**, and press **Tab** and type **$125**.

f. Click **Close** on the Excel worksheet and return to PowerPoint.

Because an additional data series has been added, the category labels have changed from a horizontal orientation to an angled orientation.

g. Save the *chap5_ho3_foundation_solution* presentation.

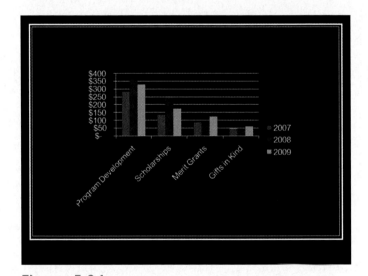

Figure 5.34 Foundation Chart with Additional Category

Refer to Figure 5.35 as you complete Step 3.

a. With the *chap5_ho3_foundation_solution* presentation open, select the chart (if necessary).

b. Click **Select Data** in the Data group on the Design tab.

The Select Data Source dialog box opens. The Legend Entries (Series) pane shows the years and the Horizontal (Category) Axis Labels display the donation categories.

c. Click the **Switch Row/Column** button.

The Legend Entries (Series) now display the donation categories and the Horizontal (Category) Axis Labels now display the years.

d. Click **Close** on the Excel Worksheet.

e. Save the *chap5_ho3_foundation_solution* presentation.

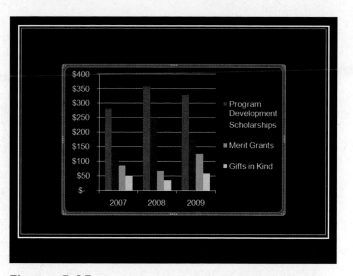

Figure 5.35 Foundation Chart Emphasizing Changes Over Time

Step 4
Create a Pie Chart

Refer to Figure 5.37 as you complete Step 4.

a. With the *chap5_ho3_foundation_solution* presentation open and Slide 3 selected, click the **Home tab**, and then click **New Slide** in the Slides group. Select **Blank**.

b. Click the **Insert tab**, and then click **Chart** in the **Illustrations** group.

c. Click **Pie** in the Chart pane, and then click **OK**.

d. Refer to Figure 5.36 and enter the data for your pie chart.

   Because a pie chart is a single-series chart, only one series is entered.

	A	B
1		Foundation Assets
2	Investments	14,230,723
3	Land & Buildings	8,588,521
4	Trusts	5,849,484
5	Cash & Equipment	3,374,373
6	Other	2,982,196

Figure 5.36 Foundation Pie Chart Worksheet

e. Click **Close** on the Excel worksheet.

   A basic pie chart is displayed in PowerPoint.

f. Save the *chap5_ho3_foundation_solution* presentation and keep it onscreen if you plan to continue to the next hands-on exercise. Close the file and exit PowerPoint if you do not want to continue with the next exercise at this time.

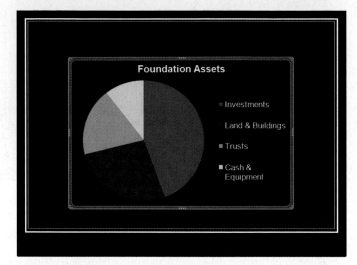

Figure 5.37 Basic Pie Chart

Chart Modification

After you enter the data and close the Excel window, you can modify and format the chart to ensure that your message is conveyed. Adding a chart title or subtitle axes titles, data labels, or a legend can help clarify your message, but you must take care not to clutter the chart. Remember the KISS principle and balance your need for clarity with the need for simplicity. This can be a challenge, so ask a classmate or coworker to review your table and explain to you what they feel your message is.

Review your chart data to see if the numbers can be shortened by showing them as thousands or millions. If you shorten the numbers that show on the value axis (y-axis) you must include an axis label identifying the axis as "in thousands" or "in millions." If you want your audience to see the actual data upon which the chart is based, you can show the data table with or without a legend.

In this section, you learn how to change a chart type, change a chart layout, and format chart elements.

Changing a Chart Type

After creating your chart, you can experiment with other chart types to see which chart type conveys your message most effectively. For example, you may find that due to the number of bars created by your data your column chart is cluttered and difficult to read. Changing the chart type to a line chart, however, shows the same information in a clean, easy-to-understand format.

Rather than changing your chart type, however, a chart subtype change may emphasize the point you are seeking. Each of the 11 chart types available includes subtypes or variations. Changing the subtype can give the chart a totally different look or can change the purpose of the chart dramatically. The variations include changing from 2-D formatting to 3-D formatting, stacking the data, changing the marker shape, and exploding slices, to name a few.

To change the chart type or subtype, click the Design tab, and click Change Chart Type in the Type group. From the Change Chart Type dialog box, select the chart type you want from the left task pane or the chart subtype from the right task pane.

Changing the Chart Layout

Each chart type has predefined layouts that you can quickly apply to your chart. Though you can change each element of the layout individually by manually selecting a style for the individual elements, using a predefined layout keeps your charts consistent and maintains a professional feel to your presentation. To apply one of the predefined layouts, select your chart, then click the Design tab under the Chart Tools contextual tab. Choose from one of the layouts displayed in the Chart Layout group, or click the More button to display the Chart Layout gallery. Click a gallery layout to apply it to your chart.

To change the layout manually, click the Layout tab under the Chart Tools contextual tab. Choose which element of the layout you want to change by clicking the Chart Elements arrow in the Current Selection group, and then clicking the element you wish to change from the list that appears. For example, the numbers on the value axis (y-axis) have been simplified in the chart you created in Hands-On Exercise 3. To be accurate, the y-axis needs a label identifying that the information is actually in millions. Select Vertical (Value) Axis in the Current Selection group on the Layout tab. After choosing this option, the axis is selected and you click Axis Titles in the Labels group of the Layout tab. Select Primary Vertical Axis Title, and then select Rotated Title. A text box appears for the label. You would then enter the text "in millions" in the text box.

A chart layout generally includes a title, axis titles, and a legend. You can modify each of these elements manually by clicking the associated button in the Labels group on the Layout tab. You can also attach data labels and choose the label location in the Labels group. Instead of attaching labels, however, you may choose to display the data table.

PowerPoint determines the measurement or increments on the chart's y-axis automatically by the data you enter in the worksheet. You can change the measurement used, but be careful when changing the measurements of the axes. Changing the y-axis measurement to a smaller increment can exaggerate the data peaks and valleys displayed in the chart. Changing the measurements to larger increments can flatten or smooth out the data peaks and valleys. To change the chart axis, click the Layout tab, and then click Axis in the Axis group. Select the layout you wish to change and make your desired changes.

Formatting Chart Elements

To change chart elements such as the fill of a bar in a bar chart, select the element by either clicking it or by choosing the element from the list available when you click the Chart Elements arrow in the Current Selection group on the Format tab. You can change shape fills, outline styles, and shape effects on the chart objects just as you changed shapes in SmartArt. After selecting the element choose Shape Fill, Shape Outline, or Shape Effects from the Shape Styles group on the Format tab.

To choose multiple changes, however, click Format Selection in the current Selection group on the Format tab. This brings up the Format dialog box for whichever element you have selected. Depending on that element, you can change the fill, border color, border styles, shadow, and 3-D format simply by clicking on your choice in the left pane and then selecting from available options in the right pane. Figure 5.38 shows the Program Development data series selected and the Format Data Series dialog box open. Series Options has been selected in the left pane and the Series Overlap adjusted in the right pane. The overlap has been set to just over 50% so the data columns overlap one another by 50%.

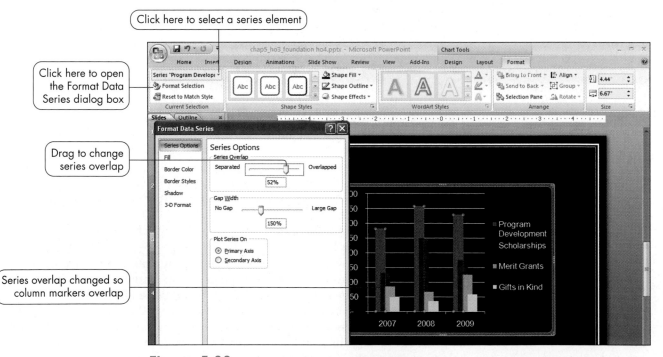

Figure 5.38 Format Data Series Dialog Box

Hands-On Exercises

4 | Modifying Charts

Skills covered: 1. Change Chart Type and Subtype **2.** Modify a Line Chart **3.** Modify a Bar Chart **4.** Modify a Pie Chart

Step 1 Change Chart Type and Subtype

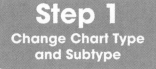

Refer to Figure 5.39 as you complete Step 1.

a. Open the *chap5_ho4_foundation2* presentation, and then immediately save it as **chap5_ho4_foundation2_solution**.

b. Move to **Slide 5** and select the chart.

   The chart on Slide 5 contains data covering the total amount awarded by the foundation over the past 10 years. Because the chart covers a 10-year period, a line chart would be a more appropriate chart type. That would eliminate the clumsiness of 10 bars in the chart and make the chart easier to read.

c. Click the **Design tab**, and then click **Change Chart Type** in the Type group.

d. Select **Line** as the chart type.

e. Change the line subtype from **Line with Markers** to **Line**, and then click **OK**.

   Because this is a single-series chart, markers are unnecessary.

f. Save the *chap5_ho4_foundation2_solution* presentation.

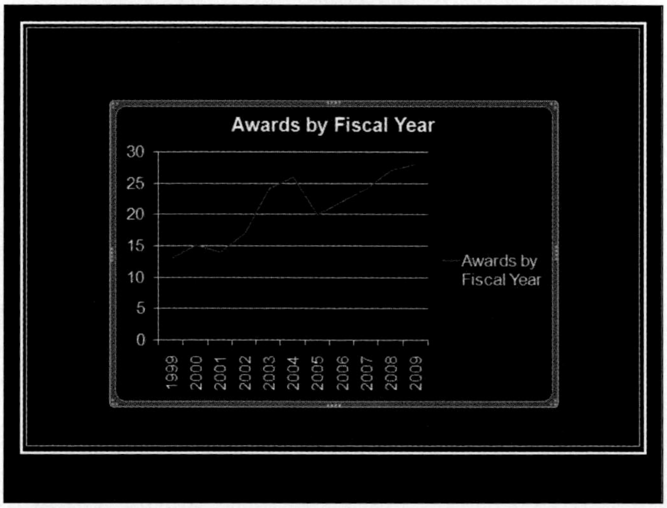

Figure 5.39 Bar Chart Changed to Line Chart

Step 2 Modify a Line Chart

Refer to Figure 5.40 as you complete Step 2.

a. With the *chap5_ho4_foundation2_solution* presentation open, click to select the chart (if necessary).

b. Click to select **Layout 6** in the **Chart Layouts** group on the Design tab.

   Layout 6 rotates the category axis labels and creates axis title text boxes.

c. Enter **(in millions)** in the y-axis title box. Select the x-axis title box and press **Delete**.

The years are self-explanatory and do not require a title.

d. Click **Style 4** in the Chart Styles group on the Design tab.

Normally, you would want to avoid using a red line in a single-series line chart because of the association red has with loss in the business world. In this case, however, red is an integral part of the Microsoft template and stands out more than the default blue.

e. Click the **Layout tab**, and then click **Legend** in the Labels group. Click **None**.

Single-series charts do not need a legend to identify series. Legends are only necessary in multi-series charts.

f. Click the **Format tab**, click the **Chart Elements arrow**, and then select **Vertical (Value) Axis**.

g. Click **Format Selection** in the Current Selection group on the Format tab.

h. Click **Number** in the left pane, and then click **Currency** in the right pane.

i. Change the number of decimal places from 2 to **0**. Click **Close**.

j. Save the *chap5_ho4_foundation2_solution* presentation.

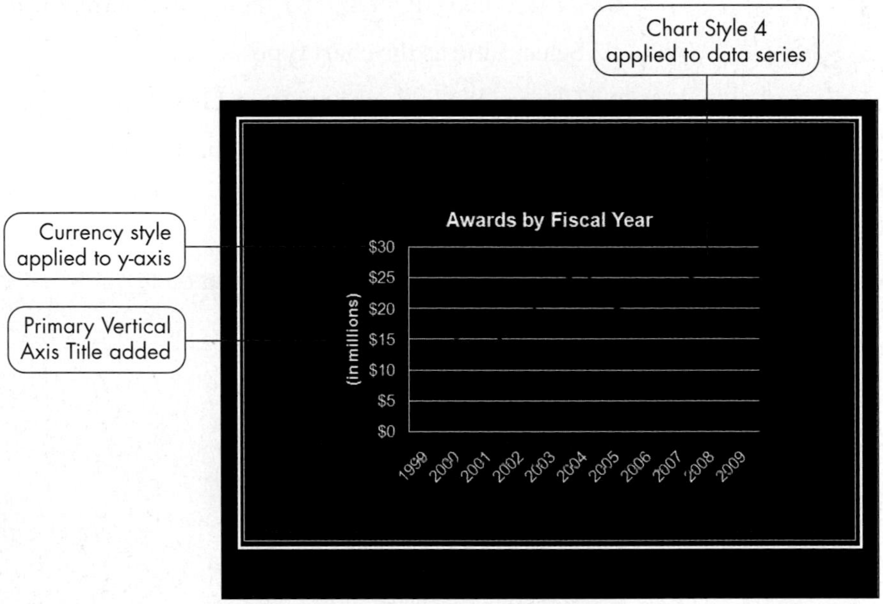

Figure 5.40 Modified Line Chart

Step 3
Modify a Bar Chart

Refer to Figure 5.41 as you complete Step 3.

a. With the *chap5_ho4_foundation2_solution* presentation open, select the chart.

b. Click the **Layout tab**, and then click **Chart Title** in the Labels group.

c. Click the **Above Chart** option.

d. Type **FOUNDATION CONTRIBUTIONS**.

e. Click **Axis Titles** in the Labels group on the Layout tab, and then select **Primary Vertical Axis Title**.

f. Select **Rotated Title**, and then enter **(in dollars)** in the Axis Title text box.

g. Click **Legend** in the Labels group on the Layout tab, and then click **Show Legend at Bottom**.

h. Click the **Format tab**, click inside the **Shape Height** box in the Size group, and then type **5**.

i. Click **Align** in the Arrange group, and then click **Align Middle**.

j. Save the *chap5_ho4_foundation2_solution* presentation.

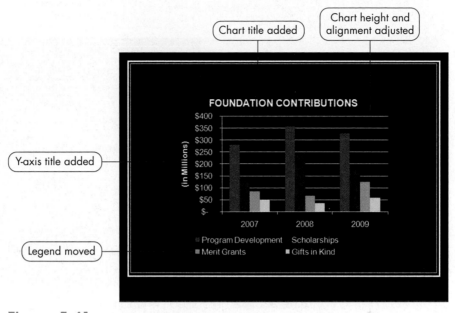

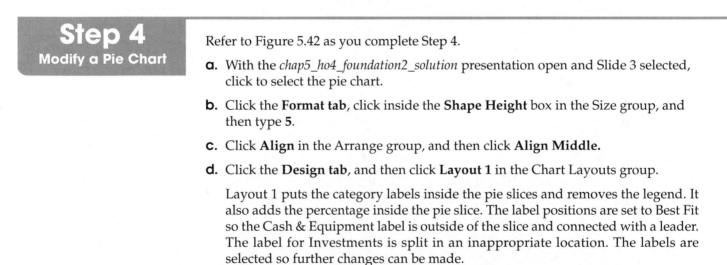

Figure 5.41 Modified Bar Chart

Step 4
Modify a Pie Chart

Refer to Figure 5.42 as you complete Step 4.

a. With the *chap5_ho4_foundation2_solution* presentation open and Slide 3 selected, click to select the pie chart.

b. Click the **Format tab**, click inside the **Shape Height** box in the Size group, and then type **5**.

c. Click **Align** in the Arrange group, and then click **Align Middle.**

d. Click the **Design tab**, and then click **Layout 1** in the Chart Layouts group.

Layout 1 puts the category labels inside the pie slices and removes the legend. It also adds the percentage inside the pie slice. The label positions are set to Best Fit so the Cash & Equipment label is outside of the slice and connected with a leader. The label for Investments is split in an inappropriate location. The labels are selected so further changes can be made.

e. Click the **Home tab**, and then click the **Font Size arrow**. Choose **16**.

The labels are resized.

TROUBLESHOOTING: If only the Investments label is resized, you may have clicked that label a second time, which deselects all labels and selects just the label clicked. If this happens, click anywhere away from a label to deselect and then click any label again. All labels should be selected. Repeat Step e.

f. Click the *Cash & Equipment* label.

g. Drag the label down and to the left (see Figure 5.42).

h. Save the *chap5_ho4_foundation2_solution* presentation and close it.

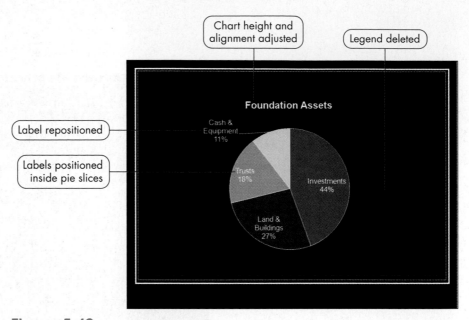

Figure 5.42 Modified Pie Chart

Summary

1. **Create a poster or a banner.** Text-based charts convey a relationship between words, numbers, and/or graphics. Posters and banners are specialized text-based charts. Poster and banner files can be uploaded to an online printing service or delivered to a local printing company to be printed on special-sized paper.

2. **Create and insert a table.** Tables are text-based charts that organize information, making it possible to see relationships between words, numbers, and/or graphics more easily. Tables can be inserted by specifying the number of columns and rows needed or by drawing the table.

3. **Design a table.** Carefully planned tables make it easy for a viewer to understand the table message. The table title clearly identifies the purpose of the table, and a subtitle can provide even more clarification. Column headings and row (stub) headings identify the information in the body of the table. Each of these elements can be formatted to improve the appearance of the table.

4. **Apply a table style.** A table style is a combination of formatting options that can be used to automatically format a table. Table styles are used to emphasize the first row that can contain the column headings (Header Row), the last row (Total Row) that can contain totals, alternating rows (Banded Rows), the first and last columns (First Column and Last Column), or alternating columns (Banded Column). You can select each option you desire, or choose from a gallery of styles to apply.

5. **Change table layout.** Table layout can be modified by the addition of columns and rows, merging or splitting cells, changing cell size or alignment, or by changing row height or column width. The table can also be arranged from front to back, aligned with other objects on the slide, or rotated.

6. **Share information between applications.** Tables created in Word or Excel can be embedded in or linked to a PowerPoint presentation. Embedding creates a larger file than linking because linking places a copy of the table into the presentation and all editing takes place in the source application. Other objects, such as charts, can also be linked or embedded in a presentation.

7. **Identify chart types and elements.** Charts and graphs are graphical representations of data. They are an integral part of today's world, and a basic understanding of their purpose is essential. An understanding of each of the elements used to create a chart contributes to a general understanding of charts. Elements in various chart types include the chart area, plot area, axes, labels, legend, gridlines, tick marks, and data series.

8. **Create and insert a chart.** PowerPoint charts are based on Excel worksheets. Information is entered into a worksheet, and then plotted to create the PowerPoint presentation.

9. **Change a chart type.** Each chart type organizes and emphasizes data differently. Pie charts show proportions of a whole. Line charts show changes over time or demonstrate a trend. Bar charts show comparisons between two or more items. Column charts can show a comparison of two or more items or show changes over time. Specialty charts such as XY (scatter) charts and radar charts meet specific needs and generally take longer to interpret the information.

10. **Change the chart layout.** PowerPoint provides Chart Layout styles that determine the placement of chart elements, but you can edit the layout manually by choosing from chart title and axis title options, legend options, data label options, data table options, and axes and gridline options. You can also set backgrounds in chart elements.

11. **Format chart elements.** The shape style (fill, outline, and effects) can be changed for individual chart elements. You can also use the Format Selection option to impact a current selection, which enables you to choose from fill, border color, border styles, shadow, and 3-D format options.

Key Terms

Multiple Choice

1. Which of the following is not a text-based chart?

   (a) A SmartArt Pyramid List diagram

   (b) A table showing an itinerary for a trip to New York City

   (c) A clip art image of a house that is for sale

   (d) A banner advertising an outdoor automobile show

2. The graphical representation you would use to communicate a relationship between numerical data is:

   (a) A photograph

   (b) A statistical chart or graph

   (c) A SmartArt diagram

   (d) A text-based chart

3. A table stub is:

   (a) The title that appears at the top of a table describing the table contents

   (b) The subtitle that appears beneath the title and gives detail related to the table contents

   (c) The column heading

   (d) The row heading

4. Which of the following will not insert a row in a table?

   (a) Clicking the Insert tab and then clicking Table Row Above or Table Row Below

   (b) Pressing tab in the last cell of the table

   (c) Right-clicking in a cell, pointing to Insert, and clicking Insert Rows Above or Insert Rows Below

   (d) Clicking the Layout tab under the Table Tools contextual tab, and then clicking Insert Above or Insert Below in the Rows & Columns group

5. The maximum size for a PowerPoint table is:

   (a) 10×10

   (b) 25×25

   (c) 50×50

   (d) 75×75

6. Which of the following text alignments is not available when changing text direction in a table cell?

   (a) Rotate all text 90°

   (b) Rotate all text 270°

   (c) Flip text vertically

   (d) Stacked

7. Table effects include all but the following:

   (a) Cell Bevel

   (b) Shadow

   (c) Reflection

   (d) Glow

8. A PowerPoint slide displaying a table object that is a copy or representation of a file stored in Excel displays what type of object?

   (a) An embedded object

   (b) A linked object

   (c) A pasted object

   (d) An outsourced object

9. Which of the following is not a true statement regarding creating charts for display in a PowerPoint presentation?

   (a) When you create a chart in PowerPoint, you use an Excel worksheet to enter the data you wish to plot.

   (b) When you create a chart in PowerPoint, you use a Word table to enter the data you wish to plot.

   (c) You can create a chart by clicking the chart icon in a content placeholder.

   (d) You can paste a copy of an Excel chart into a PowerPoint slide by using the Paste Special command.

10. Which of the following chart types is limited to a single series?

    (a) Area

    (b) Column or Bar

    (c) Pie

    (d) Column

11. The purpose of a legend is to:

    (a) Identify the type of information defined by the x-axis.

    (b) Identify the type of information defined by the y-axis.

    (c) Identify the chart type.

    (d) Identify what marker colors and patterns represent.

12. To represent the portion of time you spend studying versus the time you spend in other activities in a day, which chart should you use to show the proportion relative to a 24-hour time period?

    (a) Pie

    (b) Radar

    (c) Line

    (d) Column

13. Which of the following processes would you follow to explode a slice of a Pie chart for emphasis?

    (a) Double-click the slice.

    (b) Right-click the slice and select Explode.

    (c) Select the slice and then drag it outward from the pie center.

    (d) Select the slice and then select Emphasize.

14. To show the enrollment growth of students enrolled at your college over the past 20 years, the best choice for your chart type would be:

    (a) Pie

    (b) Bar

    (c) Line

    (d) Column

15. To compare the sales of three sales representatives for the past two years, the best choice for your chart type would be:

    (a) Pie

    (b) Bar

    (c) Line

    (d) Doughnut

16. Which of the following chart types typically does not use a legend?

    (a) Pie

    (b) Bar

    (c) Line

    (d) Column

17. Which of the following enables you to edit the data used to plot your chart?

    (a) Click the Layout tab, and then click Plot Area in the Background group.

    (b) Click the Design tab, and then click Edit Data in the Data group.

    (c) Double-click the chart area.

    (d) Click the Design tab, and then click Select Data in the Data group.

1 Create a Poster

In your role as your school's student council publicity chairperson for special events, you are responsible for designing a poster to advertise the school's 15th annual Martin Luther King, Jr., Commemoration. The poster will be stapled to bulletin boards all over campus and placed in stores a month before the commemoration. The student council wants the poster to be simple but eye-catching, so you decide to include the event's Web site address rather than event detail. Interested parties can go to the Web site for a detailed program listing. The detailed listing will be published in the school newspaper and community newspaper closer to the event. Once the poster is designed you plan to take the file to the school's print shop for reproduction, but before doing so you need a copy for the council to review. You print a copy scaled to fit a standard 8.5" by 11" page for their review. Refer to Figure 5.43 as you complete this exercise.

a. Begin a new presentation and save it as **chap5_pe1_mlk_solution**.
b. Click the **Design tab**, and then click **Page Setup** in the Page Setup group to open the Page Setup dialog box.
c. Select the existing number for Width and change it to **17**.
d. Select the existing number for Height and change it to **22**. Note that the Slides sized for box now displays **Custom** as its paper size and the Orientation is now set to **Portrait**. Click **OK**.
e. Open the Clip Organizer and search for photographs using the keyword **diversity**.
f. From the results, insert the globe photograph that is in portrait orientation (see Figure 5.43).
g. Click the **Size and Position Dialog Box Launcher** in the Size group on the far right of the **Format tab**.
   The Size and Position dialog box opens with the Size tab active.
h. Click in the **Height** box and type **22**.
i. Click in the **Width** box and type **17**.
   Because Lock aspect ratio is checked, the width changes to 17.04. This small amount of overage will not impact the poster.
j. Click the **Position tab**, and then type **0** for the horizontal position and **0** for the vertical position. Close the Size and Position dialog box and the Clip Organizer.
k. Click the **Insert tab**, and then click **Picture** in the Illustrations group. Locate *chap5_pe1_mlkimage.png* and insert it into your poster. Drag the image to the upper left so it aligns with the top and left sides of the slide.
l. Insert a text box, change the font to **Arial Black 72 pt** and type the following:

   • FIFTEENTH ANNUAL

   • MARTIN LUTHER KING, JR.

   • COMMEMORATION

   • January 12–15, 2009

   • Sorensen Student Center and Ragan Theater

   • www.mlk.sorensen.edu

m. Open the Print dialog box. Make sure the green check appears next to **Scale to fit paper** and click **OK**.
   Your poster will print on the size of paper loaded in your printer. Because desktop printers have a nonprintable region your poster will probably have a white border surrounding it.

...continued on Next Page

n. Create a Notes and Handouts header with your name and a footer with your instructor's name and your class.

o. Save the *chap5_pe1_mlk_solution* file and close the file.

Figure 5.43 Scaled Commemoration Poster

2 Insert and Modify a Table

You have been working on a presentation for the Housing Office at your university. Initially, you were asked to create a presentation to update the university provost on the purpose and goals of the Housing Office. The Housing Office director has asked you to insert a table showing the room type and meal plan and the costs of these options. Refer to Figure 5.44 as you complete this exercise.

a. Open the *chap5_pe2_housing* presentation, save it as **chap5_pe2_housing_solution**, and then move to Slide 3.

b. Click the **Home tab** (if necessary), click **Add Slide**, and then click **Blank**.

c. Click the **Insert tab**, and then click **Table** in the Tables group.

d. Drag to create a **2**-column × **5**-row table.

e. Click outside of the table to the left of the first cell in the first row to select the entire first row.

f. Click the **Layout tab** underneath the Table Tools contextual tab, and then click **Merge Cells** in the Merge group. Type **University Housing**.

g. Click the **Row Height** box in the Cell Size group on the Layout tab and type **1**.

h. Click **Center Vertically** in the Alignment group on the Layout tab.

i. Click the **Design tab**, and then click **More** in the Table Styles group. Click Themed Style 1 – Accent 4. Modify the Style by deselecting the **Banded Rows** option in the Table Style Options group on the Design tab.

j. Select the title text in Row 1. On the Mini toolbar, click the **Font Size arrow**, click **32**, and click **Center**.

k. Click in the first cell of the second row and type **Room Type**. Press **Tab** to move to the next cell in the row and type **Charge**. Select the second row.

l. Click the **Shading arrow** in the Table Styles group on the Layout tab, and then select **Aqua, Background 1, Darker 10%**.

m. Click the **Home tab**, click the **Font Size arrow**, select **20**, and then click **Bold**. Click **Center** in the Paragraph group on the Home tab.

n. Click in the first cell of Row 2 and type **Double Room**. Press **Tab** and type **$2,290**.

...continued on Next Page

o. Click in the first cell of the third row and type **Meal Plan**. Press **Tab** to move to the next cell in the row and type **Charge**. Select the third row.

p. Click the **Font Size arrow** on the Home tab, click **20**, and then click **Bold**. Click **Center** in the Paragraph group.

q. Click the **Shading arrow** in the Table Styles group on the Layout tab, and then select **Aqua, Background 1, Darker 10%**.

r. Click in the first cell of the fourth row and type **5-Day Plan**. Press **Tab** to move to the next cell in the row and type **$1,684**.

s. Press **Tab** to create a new row, then type **7-Day Plan**. Press **Tab** and type **$2,034**.

t. Position your pointer in the first cell of the third row. Click the **Layout tab**, and then click **Insert Below** in the Rows & Columns group.

u. Type **Single Room** in the first cell of the new row, press **Tab**, and then type **$3,050**.

v. Select the last column in the table and click **Center** in the Alignment group on the Layout tab.

w. Create a Notes and Handouts header with your name and a footer with your instructor's name and your class.

x. Save the *chap5_pe2_housing_solution* presentation and keep it onscreen if you plan to continue to the next exercise. Close the file and exit PowerPoint if you do not want to continue to the next exercise at this time.

University Housing	
Room Type	Charge
Double Room	$2,290
Single Room	$3,050
Meal Plan	Charge
5-Day Plan	$1,684
7-Day Plan	$2,034

Figure 5.44 Modified Housing Table

3 Create and Modify Charts

Continue creating the housing presentation by adding charts to the presentation. The director has asked you to create a Stacked Cylinder chart based on the revenues of three campus dorms that are being considered for remodeling. Refer to Figure 5.46 as you complete this exercise.

a. Open the *chap5_pe2_housing_solution* presentation if you closed it after the last exercise, save it as **chap5_pe3_housing_solution**, then move to Slide 5.

b. Click the **Insert tab**, and then click **Chart** in the Illustrations group.

c. Click **Go** to accept the default Clustered Column chart.

d. Refer to Figure 5.45 and enter the information on the Excel worksheet.

	A	B	C
1	Dorm Name	Room Revenue	Meal Revenue
2	Ashe Hall	$2,206,010	$1,616,640
3	Memorial	$1,282,365	$934,620
4	Ungar Hall	$2,235,040	$1,643,584

Figure 5.45 Housing Chart Worksheet

e. Click the **Close** button on the Excel Worksheet.

f. Click **Switch Row/Column** in the **Data** group on the Design tab to compare the revenue brought in by each dormitory by year.

g. Click **Change Chart Type** in the Type group on the Design tab.

...continued on Next Page

h. Click the **Stacked Cylinder** subtype of Column charts, and then click **OK**.

i. Save the *chap5_pe3_housing_solution* presentation and keep it onscreen if you plan to continue to the next exercise. Close the file and exit PowerPoint if you do not want to continue to the next exercise at this time.

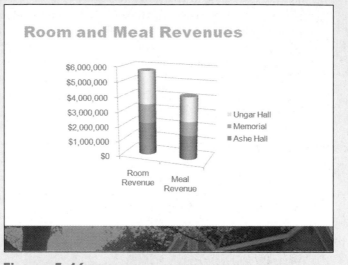

Figure 5.46 Stacked Cylinder Chart

4 Link an Excel Worksheet

You continue preparing the University Housing presentation for the provost of your university. You recall that you have an Excel worksheet showing the total room and meal revenue for each of the campus dorms, so you decide to include it as part of your presentation by linking the worksheet as an object in your presentation. After linking it and examining the data, you realize the data for one of the dorms is incorrect and needs editing. Refer to Figure 5.47 as you complete this exercise.

a. Open the *chap5_pe3_housing_solution* presentation if you closed it after the last exercise, save it as **chap5_pe4_housing_solution**, then move to Slide 5. Click **New Slide** in the Slides group on the Home tab. Click **Blank**.

b. Click the **Insert tab**, and then click **Object** on the Text tab.

c. Click the **Create from file** option, and then click **Browse**. Locate the *chap5_pe4_housing.xlsx* file and click **OK**.

d. Check the **Link** option, and then click **OK**.

e. Click the **Format tab**, and then click the **Shape Height** box and type **3**.

f. Click the **Align arrow** in the Arrange group on the Format tab, and then click **Align Center**. Click the **Align arrow** again, and then click **Align Middle**.

g. Double-click the table to launch Excel and open the source file. Change the meal revenue for Memorial to **$834,620**. Note that the linked table in the presentation immediately updated. Click the **Close** button in Excel.

h. Save the *chap5_pe4_housing_solution* file. Close the file.

Dorm Name	Room Revenue	Meal Revenue	Total Revenue
Ashe Hall	$2,206,010	$1,616,640	$3,822,650
Memorial	$1,282,365	$934,620	$2,216,985
Ungar Hall	$2,235,040	$1,643,584	$3,878,624
Merrick Hall	$1,941,822	$1,494,456	$3,346,278
Fort Towers	$1,360,183	$981,772	$2,341,955
Totals	$9,025,420	$6,581,072	$15,606,492

Figure 5.47 Linked Worksheet

Mid-Level Exercises

1 Request for Venture Capital

You put together a presentation for a successful retail store owned by three close friends, one of whom is your mother. They wish to expand their operation by requesting venture capital. Instead of using PowerPoint tables in the presentation as before, you decide to link the worksheet that contains sales data for last year to the presentation.

a. Open the *chap5_mid1_needlepoint* presentation and immediately save it as **chap5_mid1_ needlepoint_solution**.

b. Open the *chap5_mid1_needlepoint* workbook.

c. In the open workbook, move to the worksheet containing the sales data for the previous year and copy. Switch to PowerPoint and paste the data in Slide 4. Change the table size by locking the Aspect Ratio and changing the table height to 1.75". Drag the linked worksheet to the left of the text *Our first year was profitable*.

d. Repeat the above process to link the worksheet containing the sales data for the current year to the same slide. Drag the linked worksheet to the right of the text *Our second year was significantly better*.

e. Link the *Increase by Category* Excel chart to Slide 5 in the presentation. Size the chart height to 5.5". Align the table at the center and in the middle.

f. Link the *Increase by Quarter* Excel chart to Slide 6 in the presentation. Size the chart height to 5.5". Align the table at the center and in the middle.

g. Create a Notes and Handouts header with your name and a footer with your instructor's name and your class.

h. Save the *chap5_mid1_needlepoint_solution* presentation. Close the file and exit PowerPoint if you do not want to continue to the next exercise at this time.

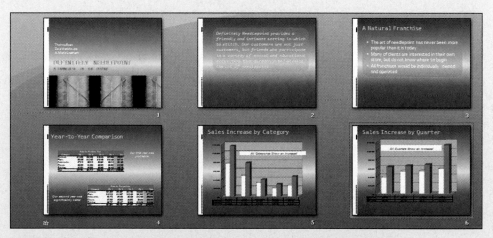

Figure 5.48 The Partially Completed Needlepoint Presentation

2 Savings Charts

No matter what age you are—a student, a recent college graduate, a newlywed, a new parent, or a retiree—you will want to create a savings account for some kind of goal. Whether your goal is saving for a wedding, retirement, or just creating an emergency fund, you will want to put time to work for you. One way to accomplish this is to determine the amount you need, and then break it

...continued on Next Page

down into regular contributions necessary to reach your goal amount. A key idea to remember is that the more time you give your money to grow, the less money you have to invest. In this exercise, you begin a presentation on savings by creating several charts.

a. Create a new presentation based on the *Essence of time design template* available from Microsoft Office Online, Design slides category, Business subcategory. Save the presentation as **chap5_mid2_savings_solution**.

b. Create a title slide with **Putting Time to Work** as the title and **Saving for the Future** as the subtitle.

c. Add a new slide using the Content with Caption layout.

d. Add the title **Time Means Everything**. Remove bolding and increase the font size to **32 pts**.

e. Enter the text displayed in Figure 5.49.

Figure 5.49 Text for Caption Placeholder

f. Click the Insert Chart icon in the right content placeholder.

g. Clear the sample data in the Excel worksheet, and then enter the following information:

	Time Period
5-year	286.44
10-year	122.50
15-year	69.37

h. Change the chart style to Style 17.

i. Change the chart layout by removing the chart title and turning off the legend.

j. Enter a Primary Horizontal Axis Title that reads **Required Period of Time**.

k. Change the Primary Vertical Axis options for numbers to Currency with 0 decimal places.

l. Do not display Primary Horizontal Gridlines.

m. Display data labels at Outside End. Change the Data Label Options for numbers to Currency with 2 decimal places.

n. Create a new text box positioned beneath the x-axis label and type **Goal: $20,000**. Change the font to **Impact 32 pts**.

...continued on Next Page

o. Create a Notes and Handouts header and footer with the date and your name in the header and your instructor's name and your class in the footer. Print as required by your teacher.

p. Save the *chap5_mid2_savings_solution* presentation and close the file.

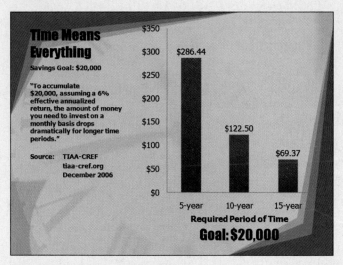

Figure 5.50 Savings Column Chart

3 PowerPoint Chart Reference

To help you understand each of the 11 chart types and to give you practice creating charts, create a slide show illustrating each of the chart types. The charts you create will use the data for a fictional kayak company, but the slides will provide the purpose for the chart you create. Slide 2 of your slide show provides a Quick Chart Reference table summarizing tips to help you determine which of the most common chart types you can select to deliver your message. Refer to Figure 5.61 while completing this exercise.

a. Open the *chap5_mid3_charts* file and immediately save it as **chap5_mid3_ charts_ solution**.

b. On Slide 3, create a Clustered Column chart. Use the data shown in Figure 5.51 to create the worksheet.

	A	B	C
1		2008	2009
2	Flatwater	$ 3.5	$ 4.8
3	Touring	$ 1.8	$ 2.4
4	Sea	$ 1.9	$ 2.1
5	Sit-on-top	$ 4.5	$ 3.6
6	Accessories	$ 1.8	$ 1.0
7			

Figure 5.51 Data for a Clustered Column Chart

c. Format the y-axis so that it is in currency format, add a y-axis title **(in hundreds of thousands)**, and reformat the title so it is not bolded and the font size is **14 pts**.

d. Move to Slide 4, and then create a Line chart. Use the data shown in Figure 5.52 to create the worksheet.

...continued on Next Page

	A	B	C	D	E
1		2006	2007	2008	2009
2	Flatwater	$ 1.5	$ 2.7	$ 3.5	$ 4.8
3	Touring	$ 2.9	$ 3.2	$ 1.8	$ 2.4
4	Sea	$ 1.5	$ 2.3	$ 1.9	$ 2.1
5	Sit-on-top	$ 3.5	$ 4.0	$ 4.5	$ 3.6
6	Accessories	$ 0.9	$ 1.5	$ 1.8	$ 1.0

Figure 5.52 Data for a Line Chart

e. Add a y-axis title **(in thousands)** and reformat the y-axis title so it is not bolded and the font size is **14 pts**.

f. Move to Slide 4, and then create a Pie chart. Use the data shown in Figure 5.53 to create the worksheet.

	A	B
1		Sales
2	Drifter	6.2
3	Platypus	4.1
4	Bass	3.3
5	Minnow	1.6

Figure 5.53 Data for a Pie Chart

g. Change the title to **2009 Flatwater Kayak Sales**. Apply Layout 1, and then drag any labels appearing outside of the pie onto their slices. The text *Minnow* will slightly overlap the *Drifter* slice but not enough to cause confusion.

h. Copy the column chart on Slide 3. Move to Slide 6 and delete the content placeholder. Paste the copied column chart in Slide 6. Edit the chart type to the default bar chart type (Clustered Bar). Bar and column charts are interchangeable but often comparisons are more easily seen in bar charts. Edit the chart so that **(in hundreds of thousands)** appears beneath the values. Reformat the y-axis title so it is not rotated, not bolded, and the font size is **14 pts**.

i. Move to Slide 7 and create an Area chart. Use the data shown in Figure 5.54 to create the worksheet.

	A	B	C
1		Oyster Tour	Eco Tour
2	1/5/2009	6	2
3	1/12/2009	5	3
4	1/19/2009	6	1
5	1/26/2009	3	3
6	2/2/2009	6	4

Figure 5.54 Data for Area Chart

j. Move to Slide 8 and create an XY (Scatter) chart for the Kayak Eco Tour. The XY (Scatter) chart will reveal the relationship between the number of tours and the average temperature for the four months of the second quarter of 2009. Use the data shown in Figure 5.55 to create the worksheet.

...continued on Next Page

	A	B
1	X-Values	Y-Values
2	22	3
3	19	1
4	36	4
5	50	9
6	66	10
7	75	15
8	91	13
9	104	8
10	88	9
11	76	16
12	54	10
13	35	5

Figure 5.55 Data for XY (Scatter) Chart

k. Add a Primary Vertical Axis Title in the Rotated Title style that reads **Number of Tours**. Add a Primary Horizontal Axis Title in the Title Below Axis style that reads **Average Temperature**. Remove the legend and the chart title.

l. Move to Slide 9 and insert a Stock chart to show the Open, High, Low, and Close range for a five-day interval. Use the data shown in Figure 5.56 to create the worksheet.

	A	B	C	D	E
1		Open	High	Low	Close
2	6/5/2009	34	48	22	40
3	6/6/2009	18	37	18	23
4	6/7/2009	28	47	24	45
5	6/8/2009	40	54	33	43
6	6/9/2009	24	30	15	18

Figure 5.56 Data for Stock Chart Displaying Fluctuations for a Five-Day Period

m. Change the Chart Style to Style 3.

n. Move to Slide 10 and create a Surface chart to plot a surface using two sets of data. Use the data shown in Figure 5.57 to create the worksheet.

	A	B	C	D	E	F	G
1		0	20	40	60	80	100
2	20	0	0	0	0	0	0
3	40	0	10	10	10	2	10
4	60	0	10	25	30	30	10
5	80	0	10	25	30	30	25
6	100	0	10	10	25	25	10

Figure 5.57 Data for Surface Chart

o. Move to Slide 11 and create a Doughnut chart to show the percentage of sales for each style of kayak for each of three years. Use the data shown in Figure 5.58 to create the worksheet.

	A	B	C
1	Number of tours	Income	Market Share %
2	82	$ 62,450	15
3	20	$ 22,100	8
4	54	$ 59,870	10

Figure 5.58 Data for Doughnut Chart

p. Select the data and then switch the Row/Column designation so that the legend displays the years. Change the Chart Layout to Layout 6. Select the labels for each series and change the font size to 12 pts. Remove the chart title.

...continued on Next Page

q. Move to Slide 12 and create a Bubble chart. Use the data shown in Figure 5.59 to create the worksheet.

	A	B	C
1	Number of tours	Income	Market Share %
2	82	$ 62,450	15
3	20	$ 22,100	8
4	54	$ 59,870	10

Figure 5.59 Data for Bubble Chart

r. Remove the legend and the chart title.

s. Move to Slide 13 and create a Radar chart to compare features of two Flatwater kayaks. A radar chart identifies the item with the most perfect shape, which means it would be the item that met the predetermined qualities best. Use the data shown in Figure 5.60 to create the worksheet.

	A	B	C
1		Drifter	Minnow
2	Ease of Use	5	4
3	Safety	4	3
4	Design	5	2
5	Stability	4	5
6	Cargo Capacity	3	5

Figure 5.60 Data for Radar Chart

t. Create a Notes and Handouts header and footer with the date and your name in the header, and your instructor's name and your class in the footer. Print as required by your instructor.

u. Save the *chap5_mid3_charts_solution* presentation and close the file.

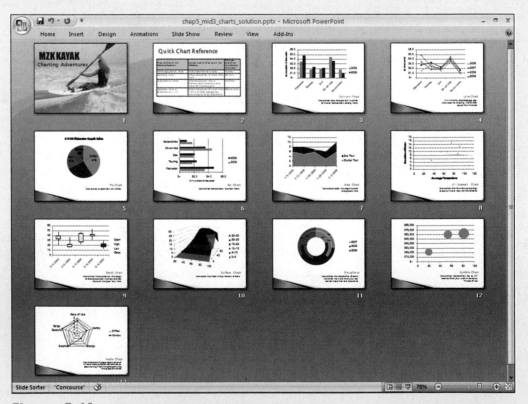

Figure 5.61 Charts Reference Slide Show

...continued on Next Page

Rather than create a series of pie charts on different slides showing the contribution of music categories to the sales of your music store for the past three years, you decide to create a doughnut chart. Using a doughnut chart enables you to compare the percentages on one slide instead of flipping back and forth between slides. Each ring in the doughnut chart represents the sales for a single year, and each ring shows the proportion of total sales for which each category of music is responsible.

a. Open a blank slide show and immediately save it as **chap5_mid4_music_solution**.

b. Change the slide layout from Title to Blank.

c. Change the slide design background to a picture fill by inserting the picture from Clip Art rather than File. Use amplifiers as the key term and include content from Office Online. Set the transparency for the background fill to 10%.

d. Insert a chart using the default Doughnut chart type. In Excel, enter the following data, and then close Excel.

	2007	2008	2009
Rock	35	40	48
Hip Hop	35	27	30
Reggae	5	18	12
R&B	25	15	10

e. Change the height of the chart to 6" and center and middle-align the chart.

f. Change the size of the doughnut hole by selecting a series and choosing Format Selection. Set the Doughnut Hole Size to 10%.

g. Change the chart style to Style 26.

h. Show percentage data labels.

i. Change the legend to the bottom of the chart and apply a white fill and a border using Red Accent 2.

j. Insert a left arrow shape with a White, Background 1 fill and a Red Accent 2 outline. Type 2007 within the arrow. Change the font color to Black and the font size to 14 pt. Slightly rotate the arrow.

k. Duplicate the arrow twice and change the years to 2008 and 2009. Drag the arrow point to the proper ring.

l. Save the *chap5_mid4_music_solution* presentation and close the file.

...continued on Next Page

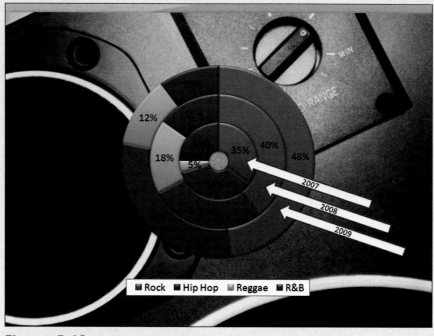

Figure 5.62 Music Sales Doughnut Chart

5 Wages Presentation

A minimum wage is the lowest hourly, daily, or monthly wage that employers may legally pay to employees or workers, and it affects most private and public employment. A minimum wage was first created in the United States in 1912 by the state of Massachusetts. The federal government first set a minimum wage in 1938, with subsequent amendments defining who is covered by the minimum age requirement. The current minimum wage (March 2006) is $5.15 per hour. Youths under 20 years of age, however, may be paid a minimum wage of $4.25 an hour during the first 90 consecutive calendar days of employment. In this exercise, you begin a slide show on the minimum wage for a presentation to the Chamber of Commerce monthly employer's luncheon. Refer to Figure 5.64 when completing this exercise.

    a. Open the *chap5_mid5_wages.pptx* presentation, and then save it as **chap5_mid5_ wages _solution.pptx**.

    b. Open the *chap5_mid5_minwage.xlsx* file in Excel.

    c. Select cells A1 through E14 in the worksheet and copy the data.

    d. Move back to the PowerPoint presentation, select Slide 5, and then paste the data.

    e. Double-click in any cell of the embedded table and note that whereas you can edit the cell in PowerPoint, you do not link back to Excel for modification of the original cell. Using this method creates a smaller file but does not maintain the link.

    f. Use the Insert tab to insert an object on the slide. Have the object created from an existing file. Browse to locate the *chap5_mid5_minwage.xlsx* file and insert it into the slide show.

    g. Double-click in any cell of the table and note that you are returned to Excel to make modifications. The advantage of this is that the information is updated in both locations using this method. Be cautious, however, because if you move or delete the original Excel file, the link to the PowerPoint slide is broken and the table will not display.

...continued on Next Page

h. Change the object height to 5" and the object width to 6.94".

i. Create a new slide using the Blank layout.

j. Create a Line chart using the Line with Markers subtype. Use the data shown in Figure 5.63 to create the worksheet.

	A	B
1		Minumum Wage
2	1938	0.25
3	1945	0.4
4	1950	0.75
5	1961	1.15
6	1968	1.6
7	1976	2.3
8	1990	3.8
9	1997	5.15

Figure 5.63 Data for Minimum Wage Line Chart

k. Delete the legend.

l. Change the Primary Vertical Axis options to the Currency Number style.

m. Display Data Labels to the right of the data points. Change the Data Label options to the Currency Number style. Apply bold to the labels.

n. Change the Chart Style to Style 27.

o. Change the Plot Area options to include a picture fill using clip art. Search for dollars. Select the photograph of dollar bills (see Figure 5.64), and then change the transparency amount to 60%.

p. Save the *chap5_mid5_wage_solution* powerpoint and close the file.

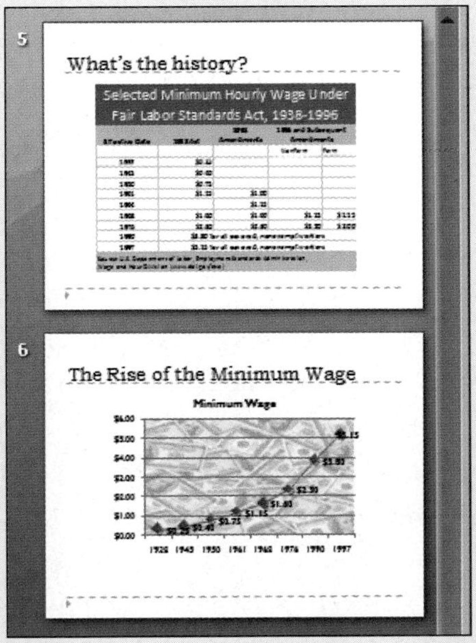

Figure 5.64 Minimum Wage Slide

Capstone Exercise

A Kiss of Chocolate, a spa and lounge dedicated to the appreciation of chocolate and its benefits, has operated successfully for five years. The operation has been so successful the owners opened two additional locations during the five years. They are now considering further expansion through franchising. They are meeting with officers of a franchising corporation that offers strategic corporate, management, and marketing services for franchisers. In this initial meeting, the franchising representatives have asked for an overview of the services and products of A Kiss of Chocolate, sales for this year and last year, a year-to-year comparison, and charts showing the increase. The owners of A Kiss of Chocolate ask for your help in preparing the presentation for the meeting.

Create a Poster

The owners of A Kiss of Chocolate have reserved a meeting room at a local conference center for the initial meeting. To help people recognize the room they want a large, foam-backed poster on an easel next to the conference room door. They ask you to prepare the poster, and then they will have a local company print and mount it.

a. Open *chap5_cap_chocolateposter*, and then immediately save it as **chap5_cap_chocolateposter_solution**.

b. Change the width of the page to 17 and the height of the page to 22 in the Page Setup dialog box.

c. Type **Gardenia Room, 9 a.m.** in a new text box.

d. Use the Format Painter to copy the formatting in the subtitle *A Chocolate Decadence Spa and Lounge* to the new text box.

e. Position the new text box at 1" horizontal and 20" vertical positions from the Top Left Corner.

f. Create a Notes and Handouts header with your name and a footer with your instructor's name and your class.

g. Print a copy of the poster as a handout, one per page, using the Scale to fit paper option.

h. Save and close the *chap5_cap_chocolateposter* presentation.

Create a Day Spa Packages Table

You have created the first four slides of the A Kiss of Chocolate slide show including an introduction to the spa,

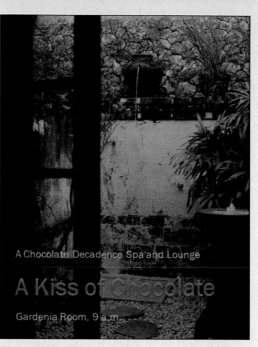

Figure 5.65 A Kiss of Chocolate Poster

products available for sale in the gift store, services available in the spa, and chocolate desserts and drinks available in the lounge. Now you create a table showing the packages available in the Day Spa.

a. Open *chap5_cap_chocolatespa* and save it as **chap5_cap_chocolatespa_solution**.

b. Create a new slide using the Title and Content layout following Slide 4.

c. Type the title **Day Spa Packages**.

d. Create a 4-column × 5-row table.

e. Type the following column headings: **Package**, **Length**, **Cost**, **Services**.

f. Fill in the table using the following information (the table will exceed the slide, but you will format the table to fit in the next Capstone exercise):

A Kiss of Chocolate	1.5 hours	$160	Spa Rain Shower, Full-Body Mint-Chocolate Exfoliation, 45-Minute Peppermint-Chocolate Massage
A Chocolate Hug	1.5 hours	$160	Hot Stone Treatment with Warm Raspberry-Chocolate Oil, Hydrating Body Wrap, 45-Minute Peppermint-Chocolate Massage
The Chocolate Dip	2 hours	$175	Mint-Chocolate Soufflé Body Mask, Full-Body Mint-Chocolate Exfoliation, Hydrating Body Wrap, Raspberry-Chocolate Shower
Chocolate Decadence	3 hours	$300	Hot Stone Treatment with Warm Raspberry-Chocolate Oil, Raspberry-Chocolate Shower, Full-Body Mint-Chocolate Exfoliation, Mint-Chocolate Soufflé Body Mask, 50-Minute Peppermint-Chocolate Massage

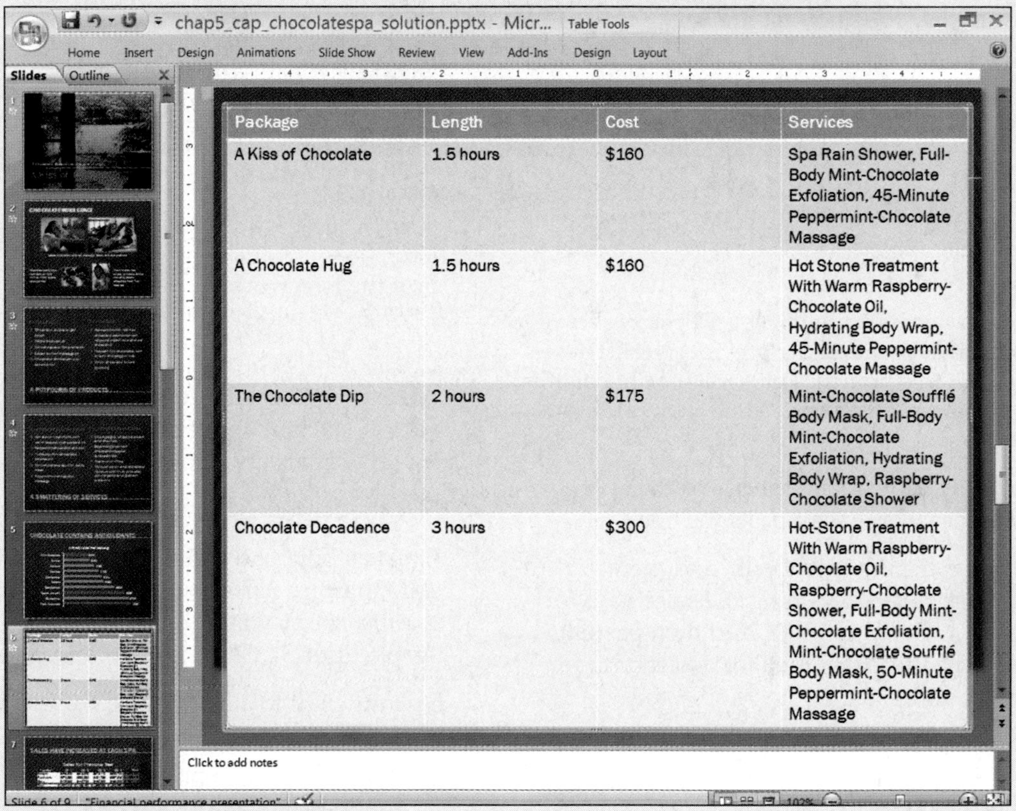

Figure 5.66 Day Spa Packages Table

Modify Table Structure and Format Table

You need to modify the table structure so the table fits on the slide. You also format the table to get the appearance you want. You size the table and apply a Table Style.

a. Change the table structure by dragging the first three column borders until they closely fit the column headings (refer to Figure 5.67).

b. Set the table size to a height of 5.01" and a width of 9".

c. Apply the Light Style 2 – Accent 1 Table Style.

d. Center-align the second column.

DAY SPA PACKAGES

Package	Length	Cost	Services
A Kiss of Chocolate	1.5 hours	$160	Spa Rain Shower, Full-Body Mint-Chocolate Exfoliation, 45-Minute Peppermint-Chocolate Massage
A Chocolate Hug	1.5 hours	$160	Hot Stone Treatment With Warm Raspberry-Chocolate Oil, Hydrating Body Wrap, 45-Minute Peppermint-Chocolate Massage
The Chocolate Dip	2 hours	$175	Mint-Chocolate Soufflé Body Mask, Full-Body Mint-Chocolate Exfoliation, Hydrating Body Wrap, Raspberry-Chocolate Shower
Chocolate Decadence	3 hours	$300	Hot-Stone Treatment With Warm Raspberry-Chocolate Oil, Raspberry-Chocolate Shower, Full-Body Mint-Chocolate Exfoliation, Mint-Chocolate Soufflé Body Mask, 50-Minute Peppermint-Chocolate Massage

Figure 5.67 Formatted Day Spa Packages Table

Link Excel Tables and Charts

A Kiss of Chocolate owners have tables and charts showing sales figures for this year and the previous year. These figures show that all three branches of A Kiss of Chocolate have increased revenue and profit each year, and the charts emphasize the data.

a. Create a Title Only slide after Slide 5, and then type **Sales Have Increased at Each Spa** as the title.

b. Open the *chap5_cap_sales* workbook, and then move to the worksheet containing the sales data for the previous year. Copy the data, and then paste it into Slide 6. Copy and paste the worksheet data for the current year and paste it into Slide 6, too.

c. Size the two worksheets in Slide 6 to a height of 2.06" and a width of 8".

d. Create a Title Only slide after Slide 6, and then type **All Stores Show an Increase** as the title. Link the *Increase by Store* Excel chart to the new slide. Apply Style 34 Chart Style to the chart.

e. Size the chart to a height of 4.5" and a width of 7.5".

f. Create a Title Only slide after Slide 7, and then type **All Quarters Show an Increase** as the title. Link the *Increase by Quarter* Excel chart to the new slide. Apply Style 34 Chart Style to the chart.

g. Size the chart to a height of 4.5" and a width of 7.5".

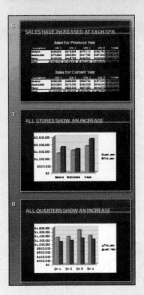

Figure 5.68 Slides Containing Linked Excel Worksheets and Charts

Create a Bar Chart

Because you serve dark and milk chocolate desserts and drinks in the Chocolate Lounge, you decide to add a slide to support the idea that chocolate intake may be healthy. You create a bar chart to show the amount of antioxidants in a serving of chocolate in comparison to other foods that contain antioxidants.

a. Create a Title Only slide after Slide 4, and then type **Chocolate Contains Antioxidants** as the title.

b. Create a bar chart using the default type, Clustered Bar. Enter the following data in the Excel worksheet:

	ORAC Units Per Serving
Dark Chocolate	9080
Blueberries	8708
Cocoa (natural)	8260
Raspberries	6895
Pecans	5382
Cranberries	5201
Cherries	4705
Walnuts	4062
Prunes	3431
Milk Chocolate	3200

c. Size the chart to a height of 5" and a width of 8".

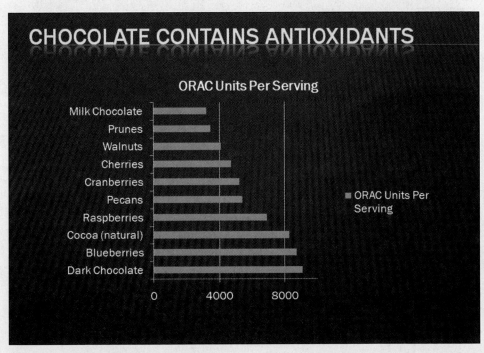

Figure 5.69 Antioxidant Bar Chart

Capstone

Modify and Format a Bar Chart

Whereas the basic bar chart would convey your message, you decide to modify and format the bar chart to improve the appearance.

a. The legend is unnecessary in a single-series chart if the chart title is displayed. Remove the legend.

b. Apply Chart Style 18 to the chart.

c. Do not display the Primary Horizontal Axis.

d. Display Data Labels on the outside end of the bars.

e. Do not display Primary Vertical Gridlines.

f. Format the filling for *Milk Chocolate, Cocoa (natural)* and *Dark Chocolate* to a solid fill using Brown, Accent 2 for the fill color. Apply an Accent color 1, 8 pt glow shape effect to each of the bars.

g. Create a Notes and Handouts header with your name and a footer with your instructor's name and your class.

h. Save the *chap5_cap_chocolatespa_solution* presentation and close the file.

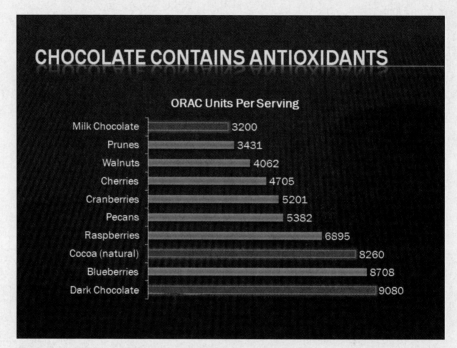

Figure 5.70 Modified Antioxidant Bar Chart

Mini

Use the rubric following the case as a guide to evaluate your work, but keep in mind that your instructor may impose additional grading criteria or use a different standard to judge your work.

Conference Poster with Charts

GENERAL CASE

✓

Conduct an Internet search for online printing services and note the procedures for submitting a poster for printing. What are the standard sizes for posters? What color options are available? What paper types can you select? Are paper coatings available? What is the minimum quantity of posters that can be ordered? What file formats will the printing service accept, and what proofing options are available? What delivery options are available?

In this project, you will create a poster to be presented at a business education conference. The poster will present the research conducted by a team of business educators related to skills required in the business office. Create a new presentation based on the *Medical poster with graphics* template available from the Microsoft Office Online section of the New Presentation dialog box, More categories, Posters subcategory. Note that this poster is 56 inches wide and 40 inches high. If asked to print this poster by your instructor, be sure the *Scale to fit paper option* is selected in the Print dialog box. Complete the poster using the files and instructions listed in the following table. Figure 5.71 shows the completed scaled-down poster. Save the file as **chap5_mc1_poster_solution**.

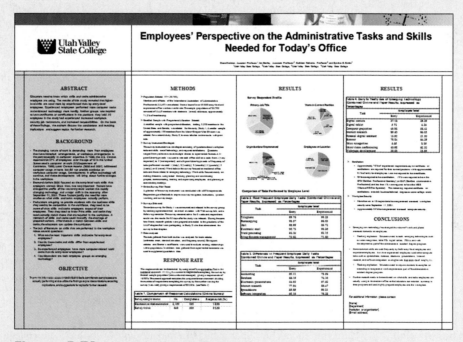

Figure 5.71 Completed Scaled-Down Poster

Poster Elements	Instructions
Logo	Insert: *chap5_mc1_posterlogo.tif*
Poster title	Enter: **Employees' Perspective on the Administrative Tasks and Skills Needed for Today's Office**
Names, titles, and affiliation of contributors	Enter: **Diane Hartman, Assistant Professor, Utah Valley State College** **Jan Bentley, Associate Professor, Utah Valley State College** **Kathleen Richards, Professor, Utah Valley State College** **Cynthia Krebs, Professor, Utah Valley State College**
Abstract	Insert the text from: *chap5_mc1_posterabstract.docx*.
Background	Insert the text from: *chap5_mc1_posterbackground.docx*. In the poster, change the bullets appearing next to the four questions at the end of the background to a numbered list and adjust the indention so that the questions are indented a half inch.
Objective	Enter: **To provide information about what skills and tasks administrative employees are actually performing and to utilize the findings to provide conclusions, teaching implications, and suggestions for topics for further research.**
Methods	Delete the existing headings and text in the Methods column. Copy the text box saved in *chap5_mc1_postermethods.docx* and paste it in the Methods column. Insert Table 1, a comparison of response calculations for the online survey, as an object from the Excel workbook *chap5_mc1_postermethods.xlsx*. Position it at the bottom of the Methods column.

Results	Add the title **Survey Respondent Profile**, and then delete the existing text in the placeholder. Resize the placeholder to fit the title. Create four pie charts using the Job Title, Years, Organizations, and Employees worksheets from the workbook *chap5_mc1_postermethods.xlsx*. Add chart titles and then format the pie charts to include data labels and percentages in the pie slices. Copy the charts from the associated data sheet and paste them in the poster in the first Results column. Format titles and labels as necessary. Apply the Chart Style of your choice.
	Add a text box below the pie charts and add a new title, **Comparison of Tasks Performed by Employee Level**. Insert Table 2, Table 5, and Table 4 from the Excel workbook *chap5_mc1_postermethods.xlsx*. Position these tables beneath the pie charts and in the results columns.
	Enter the following key points after the last table:
	• **Certification**
	    • **Approximately 72% of experienced respondents say no certificates or certifications are required for their current positions, while approximately 91% of entry-level employees were not required to have certificates.**
	    • **Of those required to have certification, 15% were required to have the CPS (Certified Professional Secretary) or CAP (Certified Administrative Professional) and less than 1% were required to have the MOS (Microsoft Office Specialist). The remaining required certificates or certifications included business/technical degrees or some college credit.**
	• **Workplace Security**
	    • **More than 6 in 10 respondents have experienced increased workplace security since September 11, 2001.**
	    • **Approximately 54% have experienced increased computer security.**

Conclusions	Delete the existing headings and text in the Conclusion area. Insert the text saved in *chap5_mc1_posterconclusions.docx* in the area.
Additional Information	Use your name, the department your major is housed within, your college or university, and your e-mail address.

Performance Elements	Exceeds Expectations	Meets Expectations	Below Expectations
Organization	All elements of the poster are present and clearly identifiable.	All elements of the poster are present, but headings are not present or not easily identifiable.	One or more elements of the poster is missing or identifying headings are missing.
Visual aspects	The poster has a consistent visual theme. Chart styles relate to the template theme. Fonts are large enough to read easily.	Fonts are too small in size, making text difficult to read, or fonts are so large that elements are too close in the poster. Charts are created correctly but the style does not match the template.	Text is unreadable. Tables and/or pie chart styles are distracting.
Layout	The layout is visually pleasing and contributes to immediate understanding of poster. White space clearly delineates the columns.	The layout shows some structure, but placement of some poster elements is misleading or incorrect.	The layout is cluttered and confusing. Elements are layered on top of each other.
Mechanics	Any added text has no errors in spelling, grammar, word usage, or punctuation. No typographical errors present.	Any added text has no more than two errors in spelling, grammar, word usage, or punctuation.	Any added text has impaired readability due to repeated errors in spelling, grammar, word usage, or punctuation. Multiple typographical errors.

Snowboarding, Skiing, and Snowfall

RESEARCH CASE

You decide to get away next week and indulge in your favorite sports—snowboarding and skiing. You research current daily snowfall and the price of a lift ticket at your favorite snowboarding locations. Because you are also studying charting in your Basic Computer Applications class you decide to practice your charting skills by creating a line graph showing the new snowfall for the past seven days at four of your favorite locations. You also create a bar chart showing the price of full-day lift tickets for a minimum of three resorts. You may choose to add additional slides, if desired.

Visit any site on the Internet you choose to gather the data you need to complete the charts. Create a presentation and save it as **chap5_mc2_snowboarding_solution**. Enter the data for each of the charts in worksheets and then format the charts in an attractive, easy-to-read format. Display the data table with your chart so your instructor can see the data you used as the basis for your chart. Apply appropriate titles and labels as needed to ensure that your chart is easily and accurately understood.

Performance Elements	Exceeds Expectations	Meets Expectations	Below Expectations
Organization	Information is easy to understand because it is presented in a logical, interesting sequence.	Presentation is generally easy to follow.	Presentation cannot be understood because there is no sequence of information.
Visual aspects	Presentation background, clip art, and animations enhance the understanding of the presentation. The presentation has a consistent visual theme.	Clip art relates to the topic; chart colors and effects match the overall presentation color scheme. Animation enhances the presentation.	The background or theme is distracting to the topic. Clip art does not enhance understanding of the content.
Layout	The layout is visually pleasing and contributes to the overall message with appropriate headings, bullet points, clip art, and white space. Requested chart types are used.	The layout shows some structure, but placement of some headings, subheadings, bullet points, clip art, and/or white space can be improved. Charts are not the requested type but convey the message.	The layout is cluttered and confusing. Placement of headings, subheadings, bullet points, clip art, and/or white space detracts from the readability. Charts use an incorrect format for the data and message being conveyed.
Mechanics	Any added text has no errors in spelling, grammar, word usage, or punctuation. No typographical errors present.	Any added text has no more than two errors in spelling, grammar, word usage, or punctuation.	Any added text has impaired readability due to repeated errors in spelling, grammar, word usage, or punctuation. Multiple typographical errors.

Chart Improvements

DISASTER RECOVERY

The presentation *chap5_mc3_disaster* includes four charts that confuse the message they are supposed to deliver. In some cases, the wrong chart type has been applied, and in others the formatting of the chart is distracting. In the Notes window of each slide, design tips are given that you can read to help you identify the errors in the chart. Open the *chap5_mc3_disaster* file and immediately save it as **chap5_mc3_disaster_solution**. Read the notes associated with each slide and then edit the chart on the slide so it incorporates the tips. Make all modifications necessary to create a professional, easy-to-understand chart. Even if you do not complete this exercise, you should read the design tips in this slide show.

Performance Elements	Exceeds Expectations	Meets Expectations	Below Expectations
Organization	Presentation indicates accurate research and significant facts. Evidence exists that information has been evaluated and synthesized, showing an understanding of the topic.	Presentation indicates some research has taken place and that information was included in the content.	Presentation demonstrates a lack of research or understanding of the topic.
Visual aspects	Presentation background, themes, clip art, and animation are appealing and enhance the understanding of presentation purpose and content. The presentation has a consistent visual theme.	Some of the clip art or shapes seem to be unrelated to the presentation purpose and content and do not enhance the overall concepts. Images are too large/small in size. Animation is distracting.	The background or theme is distracting to the topic. Images do not enhance understanding of the content or are unrelated.
Layout	The layout is visually pleasing and contributes to the overall message with appropriate use of headings, subheadings, bullet points, clip art, and white space.	The layout shows some structure, but placement of some headings, subheadings, bullet points, images, and/or white space is distracting.	The layout is cluttered and confusing. Placement of headings, subheadings, bullet points, images, and/or white space detracts from readability.
Mechanics	Presentation has no errors in spelling, grammar, word usage, or punctuation. Bullet points are parallel.	Presentation has no more than two errors in spelling, grammar, word usage, or punctuation. Bullet points are inconsistent in several slides.	Presentation readability is impaired due to repeated errors in spelling, grammar, word usage, or punctuation. Most bullet points are not parallel.

Presentation Customization

Customizing the Slideshow

bjectives

After you read this chapter, you will be able to:

1. Modify handout and notes masters **(page 429)**.
2. Create and modify slide masters **(page 433)**.
3. Customize a color scheme **(page 445)**.
4. Create a custom template **(page 449)**.
5. Apply a custom animation **(page 451)**.
6. Create a custom slide show **(page 463)**.
7. Run and navigate a custom slide show **(page 465)**.
8. Designate and display hidden slides **(page 465)**.

Hands-On Exercises

Exercises	Skills Covered
1. WORKING WITH MASTERS (page 438) **Open:** chap6_ho1_game.pptx **Save as:** chap6_ho1_flashcard_solution.pptx and chap6_ho1_game_notes_solution.pptx **Open:** none **Save as:** chap6_ho1_master_solution.pptx and chap6_ho1_master_template.potx	• Modify Handouts • Modify Notes Pages • Modify Slide Master Fonts • Modify a Title Slide Layout • Modify Slide Layouts • Save Masters
2. CUSTOMIZING TEMPLATES (page 458) **Open:** chap6_ho1_master_template.potx (from Exercise 1) **Save as:** chap6_ho2_master_template.potx	• Modify a Color Scheme • Create a Custom Template • Apply Custom Animations • Play Animations
3. CREATING A CUSTOM SLIDE SHOW (page 467) **Open:** chap6_ho3_powerful.pptx **Save as:** chap6_ho3_powerful_solution.pptx **Open:** chap6_ho3_hidden.pptx **Save as:** chap6_ho3_hidden_solution.pptx	• Create a Custom Slide Show • Display and Print a Custom Slide Show • Hide Slides • Display Hidden Slides • Print Hidden Slides

CASE STUDY
Club Travel

Club Travel is a travel agency that has been owned by your family for the past 50 years. The majority of the business comes from clubs and other small organizations wishing to arrange for travel for 10–30 people. Club Travel is responsible for 6 million miles of travel in the past two years, with customers visiting exotic places such as Bora Bora, New Zealand, Greenland, and Madagascar. Travel to destinations in the United States represents one-third of the revenue of the agency. The company prides itself in providing luxury accommodations, limousine transportation, and gourmet dining at every stop for the travelers.

This year, you are joining the firm as a marketing specialist. Your skills in PowerPoint will be used to create sales presentations that can be tailored for the individual groups.

Sales representatives make presentations at club meetings to highlight the benefits of using the services of Club Travel. You quickly realize that creating a presentation for each group would be time-consuming. Creating just one presentation for all groups would not permit customization. Instead, you will create the structure of a presentation with slide masters and templates, which will later be filled with the customized information for the traveling organization. The template will reflect the forest green and light yellow color scheme currently used on promotional materials, as well as the logo. Custom animation will be added to select elements in the presentation to add interest. Additional customization will be accommodated with custom slide shows and the use of hidden slides.

Your Assignment

- Read the chapter, paying attention to how to create a slide master and custom slide shows.
- Modify the master title and text styles on the slide master. Use Lucida Sans for the font in both cases, in an appropriate font size.
- Create a title slide layout, with placeholders for the name of the club and the travel location its members are interested in visiting.
- Create a slide layout, with placeholders for photographs and a title.
- Create another slide layout, with placeholders for a title and bullets. Select arrow bullets to suggest movement.
- Create a template on the slide master, using the company logo, file *club_travel_logo.gif*, on the title slide layout and the company colors of forest green and soft yellow throughout the presentation. Put your name in the footer, in a small font at the bottom of the title slide layout, followed by the words **Marketing Specialist**.
- Save the template as **chap6_case_solution.potx**.
- Import the outline *chap6_case_outline* to the slide view of the template. Select the appropriate layouts for the content of each slide. Locate photographs of mountain retreats and seaside fun, using the Internet, and place them in the appropriate layouts.
- Animate the title on the final slide so that it glows and then fades.
- Create a custom show from the *chap6_case_solution.pptx* presentation. This show should feature slides 1–3, 9–12, and 14–15. Name the custom show Seaside Fun Custom Show.
- Save the presentation as **chap6_case_solution.pptx**.
- If your instructor wishes, display the presentation and the custom presentation to a class member.
- Customize the handouts by putting your name in the header, and your instructor's name and your class in the footer. Include the company logo at the top of the page. Print handouts (nine slides to a page) of the custom show.

Master Basics

Customize a PowerPoint presentation, and you will be putting your unique creative ideas to work. Although you want to customize your presentation, you still want a consistent look throughout the presentation. **Masters** permit formatting of layouts, background designs, and color combinations for presentations, handouts, and notes pages, giving the presentation a consistent appearance. By changing the masters, you make selections that affect the entire slide show and the supporting materials. This is much more efficient than changing each slide in the presentation. The design elements you already know about, such as themes and placeholders, can be applied to each type of master. Masters give consistency to your presentations, notes, and handouts. Slide masters can be reused in other presentations.

In this section, you learn how to modify handout and notes masters. Specifically, you learn how to display or hide elements and how to customize placeholders. Then you learn how to create and modify slide masters.

TIP   The Template

Modifications to masters can be made at any time as you create the slide show, but it is best to make your selections on a blank presentation. This gives you a clean workspace, which enables you to concentrate on what is important to the design of your slide show, handouts, and notes. After opening PowerPoint, click the Office Button, click New, and double-click Blank Presentation.

Modifying Handout and Notes Masters

You have used the Print dialog box to print handouts and notes pages of your presentation. The handouts printout displays thumbnails of the slides. You can distribute the handouts to your audience so that they can take notes during your presentation. The notes pages printout displays one slide and the respective speaker notes on a sheet of paper. As the speaker, you can refer to these printed notes during your presentation. Although you know how to print handouts and notes, you might want to customize these types of printouts.

Customize the Handout Master

The **handout master** contains the design information for audience handout pages. The handout master controls the orientation of the page, the number of slides per page, and the placement of elements such as the header, footer, date, and page number on the page. To modify the handout master, click the View tab, and then click Handout Master in the Presentation Views group. Click Handout Orientation in the Page Setup group to change the orientation of the handouts from portrait to landscape. Portrait orientation is the layout of the page that is longer than it is wide, like the portrait of a person. Landscape orientation is the layout of the page that is wider than it is long, resembling a landscape.

You may select the number of slides you want to appear on the handouts. Click Slides Per Page in the Page Setup group. As shown in Figure 6.1, your choices include one to four, six, or nine slides per page. The presentation outline can also be printed as a handout.

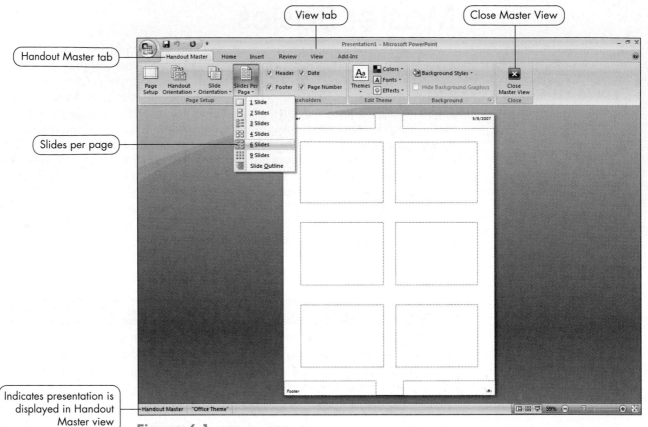

Figure 6.1 Handout Master

On the handout master, you specify whether the elements of a header, date, footer, or page number will appear. Click the check box in the Placeholders group to select the elements you want. You may omit any of these elements from the master by removing the check. Initially, the placeholders for the header and date are at the top of the page. The footer and the page number are at the bottom of the page. You can move or resize each placeholder element on the page. Click the placeholder and drag it to a new location. Drag the handles on the placeholder to change the size. The date placeholder has been moved to the bottom of the page and resized in Figure 6.2.

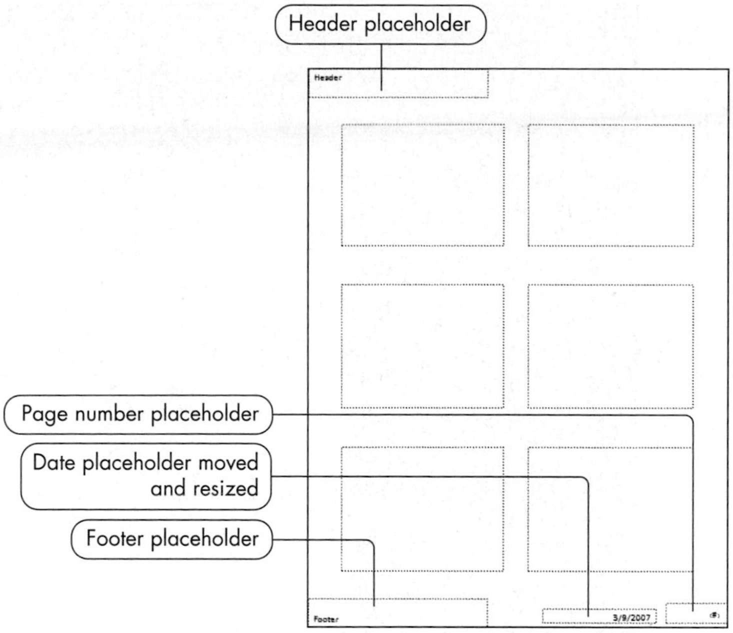
Header placeholder
Header
Page number placeholder
Date placeholder moved and resized
Footer placeholder
Footer
3/9/2007

Figure 6.2 Handout Master View

You can modify the handout master even further using the options on the Home and Insert tabs. If you want to have the company logo on each handout page, click the Insert tab, and then Clip Art in the Illustrations group to search for the logo file. Figure 6.3 shows a simple WordArt element on a handout master. Because every option on the Home and Insert tab is available to you, remember that your selections should support the message you are presenting to your audience via the handouts. Keep in mind that the handouts are to supplement your presentation. People will often take notes on the handouts that you give them, and later file the handouts for future reference or use them for a follow-up discussion with you. Audience members appreciate handouts that are easy to read. Remember the KISS principle and "Keep It Simple, Sweetie." To return to the Slide Show view, click the Close Master View on the Handout Master tab.

> . . . the handouts are to supplement your presentation. People will often take notes on the handouts that you give them, and later file the handouts for future reference or use them for a follow-up discussion with you. Audience members appreciate handouts that are easy to read.

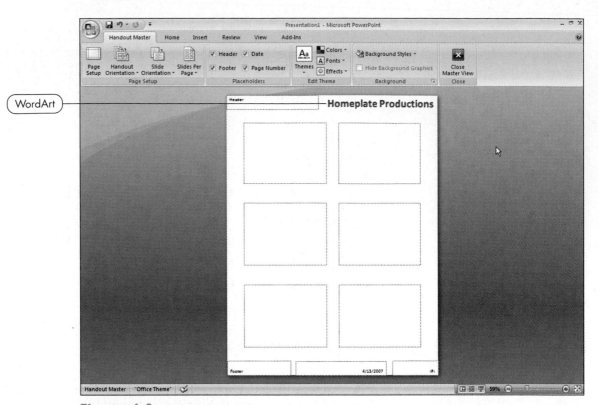

Figure 6.3 Handout Master with WordArt

Customize the Notes Master

The **notes master** contains design information for speaker's notes. The speaker, to prepare for and deliver the presentation, uses notes pages that contain a representation of the slide and the speaker's notes for that slide. Occasionally, notes pages will be distributed to an audience. A business executive might pass out copies of speaker's notes so that other people in the office can comment on an important speech prior to delivery. The notes are typed below the slide in the Normal view. Just as you can specify the elements on the handout master, you may do the same with the notes master. Click the View tab, and then click Notes Master in the Presentations group. To select the slide orientation on the notes master, click Notes Page Orientation in the Page Setup group.

The placeholders for the notes master include the same elements as the handouts master with the addition of the Slide Image and the Body options shown in Figure 6.4. A check in the Slide Image check box shows the placeholder for a small version of the slide. A check in the Body check box shows the placeholder for the notes. The placeholder for the body can be resized. Click the body placeholder and drag the handles to the desired shape. If the notes exceed the space allowed by the body placeholder, some of the notes will be lost, so avoid making the body placeholder too small. After you make your selections, click Close Notes Master View.

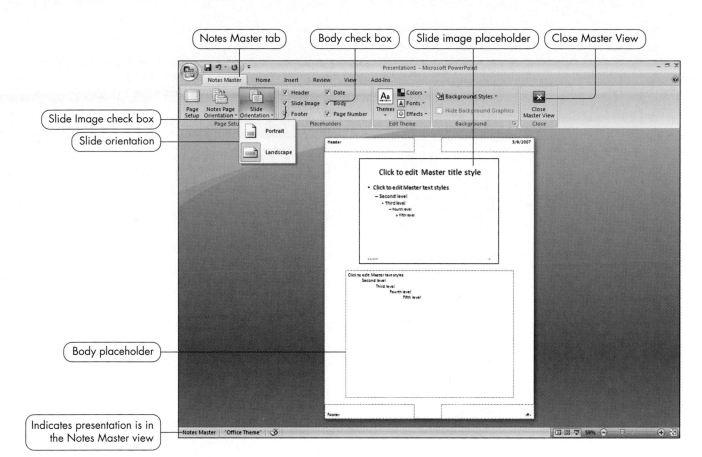

Figure 6.4 Notes Master View

> **TIP   Notes Master Options**
>
> You can use the formatting options on the Home tab and the Insert tab to modify the notes master. Click the Home tab, select the text in the Body placeholder, and use the options in the Font group to make the text larger or bolder. The larger font makes the notes easier to read as you make the presentation. Remember that more is not better in this case. Avoid adding extras such as clip art, which can clutter the notes and make them harder to read.

Creating and Modifying Slide Masters

The *slide master* contains design information for the slides in a presentation.

Just as the handout master and the notes master contain design information, the *slide master* contains layout and formatting information for the slides in a presentation. As you modify the slide master, you will concentrate on font choices and the underlying template that supplies consistent color and graphic elements to your slide show. Within the slide master, slide layouts are created for title and content slides. Placeholders designate the location of text, graphics, and other objects on slides. The slide master is saved as part of a template and can be applied to other slide presentations.

(The slide master, Title Slide Layout, and other slide layouts are all adjustable.)

To open the Slide Master view, click the View tab, and then click Slide Master in the Presentation Views group. Figure 6.5 shows the slide master view. The slide master is the larger, top slide shown in the slide thumbnail pane. The Title Slide Layout is the second slide in the slide thumbnail pane. The following ten slide thumbnails represent the default slide layouts provided for a blank presentation by Office 2007. The slide master, Title Slide Layout, and other slide layouts are all adjustable.

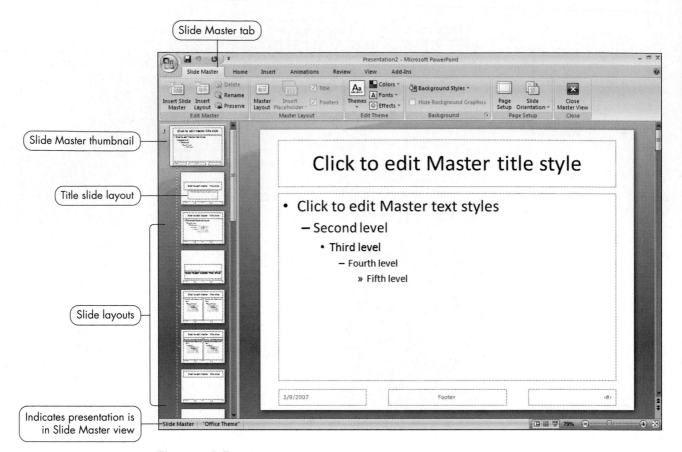

Figure 6.5 Slide Master View

The slide master is best used for setting the fonts and color scheme for the entire slide show. To set the fonts and color scheme, click the slide master thumbnail in the slide thumbnail pane. As shown in Figure 6.5, the slide master contains placeholders for title style, text styles, a date, a footer, and a page number. Double-click the text in the Master title style placeholder and use the Mini toolbar to apply a different font, size, alignment, or color to the title style that will be used throughout the slide show. Double-click the text in the Master text styles placeholder and modify the font appearance. You can adjust each level differently. Remember to keep it simple. Consistency helps you make your point more effectively.

Font adjustments are also made to the footer, date, and page number on the slide master. Double-click the text in any of these placeholders and make modifications using the Font group on the Home tab or on the Mini toolbar. The footer, date, and page number are supporters of the message and should be kept discreet.

You can move and size the placeholders on the slide master. Click and drag your selection to a new location to move it. To size a placeholder, click and drag the handles in or out. The modifications in position and size will be reflected on the slide layouts. This may conflict with some of the slide layout placeholders. The placeholders can be moved on the slide layouts as needed.

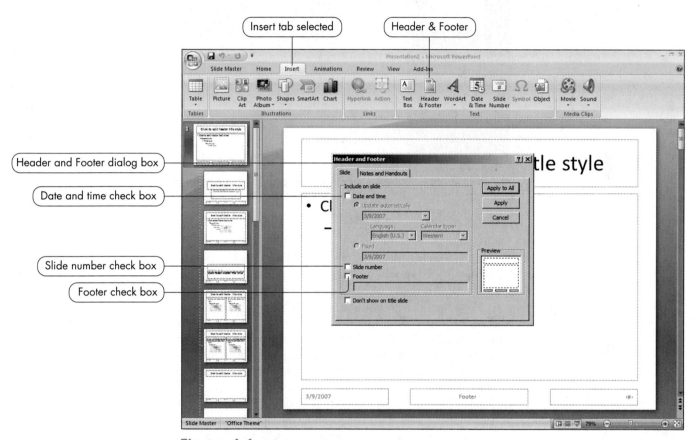

Figure 6.6   Header and Footer Modifications

The blank slide master provides a title slide layout and ten slide layouts. Templates often contain more slide layouts. Each slide layout contains different elements such as text, clip art, pictures, media, and tables.

If you only want a small number of layouts, delete the extras. Click the slide layout thumbnail you wish to delete and click Delete in the Edit Master group. If you want to add a slide layout, click Insert Layout in the Edit Master group. You should rename added slide layouts so that they are easy to recognize as you build the presentation. Click the added slide layout thumbnail and click Rename in the Edit Master group. Type a new name for the layout in the Rename Layout dialog box, as shown in Figure 6.7.

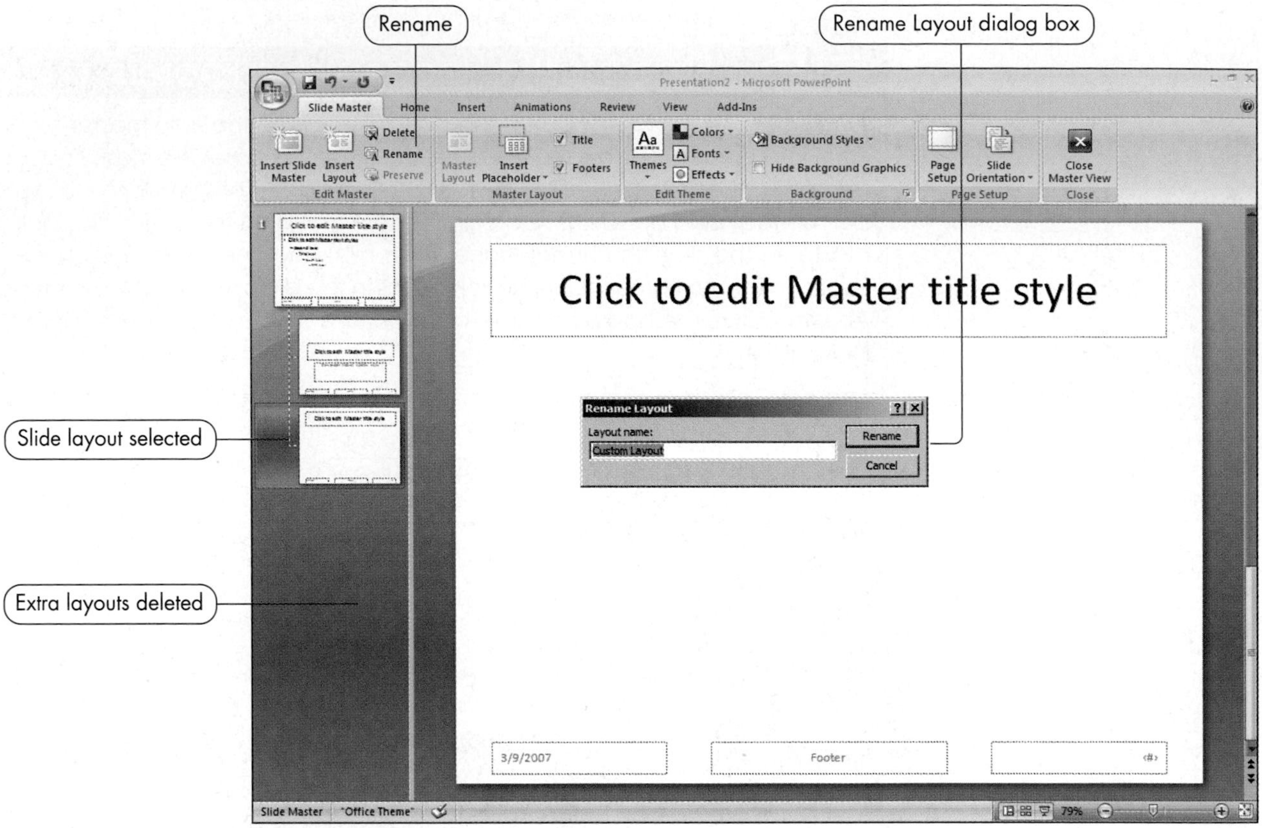

Figure 6.7 Slide Layout Renaming

The placeholders can be added, removed, and sized as needed. To add a place-holder, click the Insert Placeholder arrow in the Master Layout group. Figure 6.8 shows the choices you can make. Select the element type from the gallery. The cursor will become a crosshair that you drag diagonally to create the placeholder. Using the Content placeholder enables you to select any type of content. The Text placeholder accepts text. The rest of the placeholders are obvious in their purpose. Once you select a type of placeholder, you can continue adding this type by clicking Insert Placeholder. To change the type, click the Insert Placeholder arrow and make a selection from the list.

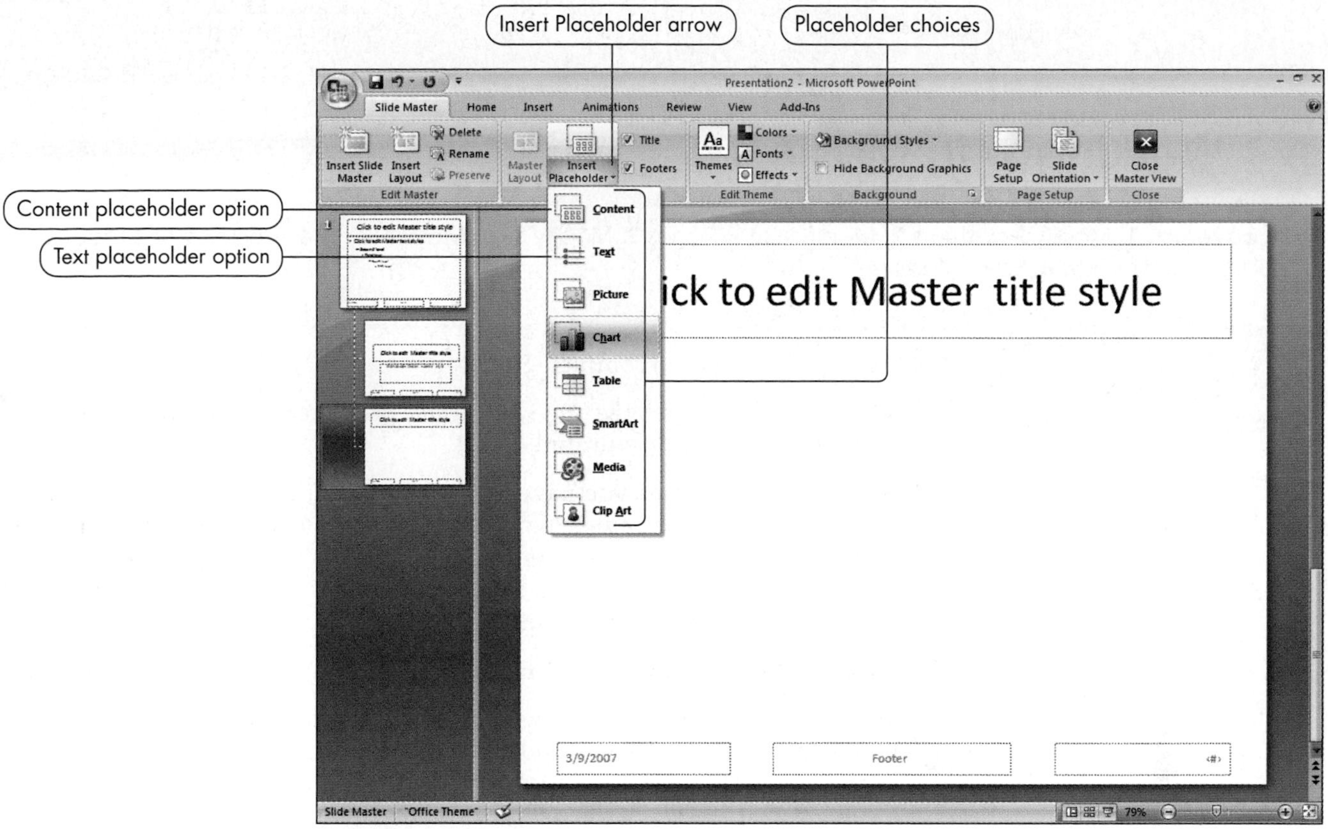

Figure 6.8 Layout Placeholders

You may access the tabs and add elements such as graphics, WordArt, shapes, sound, and animations to slide layouts. Elements added on a slide layout, such as a bullet list layout, will appear on every slide in the presentation that uses that layout.

The title placeholder is omitted from the slide layout when you click the check box in the Master Layout group to remove the check. The same applies to the footers. If you remove the footer from a slide layout, you are removing the date, page number, and footer text box. You may decide to delete individual placeholders from the footer on the slide layouts. Click the placeholder that you want to remove and press Delete on the keyboard.

> **TIP Remove Placeholders**
>
> The Delete command in the Edit Master group on the Slide Master tab deletes the entire slide layout. If you want to remove placeholders from a slide layout, click the placeholder and press Delete.

After you modify any of the masters, you save the file as a presentation template. PowerPoint saves the templates with an extension of .potx. Saving the presentation file after you have modified the handout master or Notes master will retain the changes in the file.

Hands-On Exercises

1 | Working with Masters

Skills covered: 1. Modify Handouts **2.** Modify Notes Pages **3.** Modify Slide Master Fonts **4.** Modify a Title Slide Layout **5.** Modify Slide Layouts **6.** Save Masters

Step 1 Modify Handouts	Refer to Figure 6.9 as you complete Step 1.

a. Start PowerPoint, open the *chap6_ho1_game* presentation, and then save it as the **chap6_ho1_flashcard_solution**.

As a first grade teacher, you have noticed that games are very engaging to your students. You decide to create flash cards for them to take home and play with their parents. You will use PowerPoint to create a handout master of the game. You will print the handouts and copy them back to back so that the answers will be on the back of the appropriate questions.

b. Click the **View tab** and click **Handout Master** in the Presentation Views group.

The Handout Master tab displays so that you can change the page setup, select placeholders, edit the theme, and change the background of the handouts.

c. Click **Slides Per Page** in the Page Setup group. Click **4 Slides**.

d. Uncheck the **Header check box** in the Placeholders group. Uncheck the **Page Number check box** in the Placeholders group.

e. Click the **Date placeholder** and drag it to the former position of the page number on the bottom right of the handout master.

TROUBLESHOOTING: If you have trouble moving the placeholder into the correct position, use the arrow keys to help you align it.

f. Click the **Footer placeholder**. Type your name, your instructor's name, and your class.

g. Click the **Home tab** and click **Center** in the Paragraph group. Select **Arial** font and **12** font size.

h. Click the **Date placeholder** and select **Arial** font and **12** font size.

i. Click **Center** in the Paragraph group. Click **Align Text** in the Paragraph group and select **Bottom.**

j. Click the **Insert tab** and click **Header & Footer** in the Text group. Click the **Notes and Handouts tab**. Click the **Date and time check box**. Click the **Fixed** option. In the Fixed box, type **today's date**, and then click **Apply to All**.

k. Click the **Handout Master tab** and click **Close Master View**.

l. Click the **Office Button**, position the mouse over **Print**, and select **Print Preview**.

m. Click the **Print What down arrow** in the Page Setup group and select **Handouts (4 Slides Per Page)**.

The handouts contain your name and class information, and the date and page at the bottom of the page.

n. Click **Close Print Preview** on the Print Preview tab. Click **Save**.

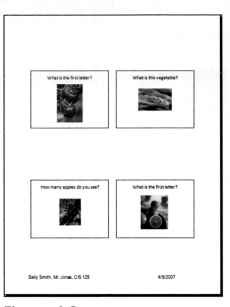

Figure 6.9 Handout Page

Step 2
Modify Notes Pages

Refer to Figure 6.10 as you complete Step 2.

a. Save the *chap6_ho1_flashcard_solution* file you created in the last step as **chap6_ho1_game_notes_solution**.

b. Click the **View tab** and click **Notes Master** in the Presentation Views group.

After creating the flash cards, you decide to share the notes you placed on the presentation with the parents so that they would have some ideas for additional questions to ask their children while they play the game.

c. Remove the checks for the **Date**, **Page Number**, and **Footer check boxes** in the Placeholders group.

d. Select the **Header placeholder** and drag the right selection handle to the **right** until the header fits across the top of the page. Type your name followed by **First Grade**. Press **Enter** and type **Please use these notes as you play the game with your child.**

e. Click the **Insert tab** and click **Header & Footer** in the Text group. Click the **Header check box** in the Header and Footer dialog box, and then click **Apply to All**.

f. Click the border of the **Master text styles placeholder** (the bottom placeholder). Click the **Home tab**. Increase the font size to **16.**

g. Click the **Notes Master tab** and click **Close Master View**.

h. Click the **Office Button**, mouse over **Print**, and select **Print Preview**.

i. Click the **Print What down arrow** in the Page Setup group and select **Notes Pages**.

j. Verify that the notes are in large text and that the header information is correct. Click **Close Print Preview**.

TROUBLESHOOTING: At times, you need to look at the fine details in a preview. Use Zoom to increase the size of the notes page as needed.

k. Use the Print Options to **print one page** of the notes pages.

l. Save and close the *chap6_ho1_game_notes_solution* file.

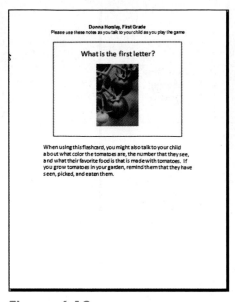

Figure 6.10 Speaker's Notes Page

Refer to Figure 6.11 as you complete Step 3.

a. Click the **Office Button** and select **New**. Double-click **Blank Presentation**. Save the presentation as **chap6_ho1_master_solution**.

b. Click the **View tab**, and then click **Slide Master** in the Presentation Views group.

c. Click the slide master thumbnail in the slide thumbnail pane.

As you prepare to teach your classes, you have been making game presentations to show pictures, ask questions, and give feedback. Creating a slide master will keep your favorite fonts on the slides and make the job of preparing the presentations just a little quicker.

d. Select the text in the **Master title style placeholder**. Refer to Figure 6.11 for an example. From the Mini toolbar, select **Arial Black Rounded MT Bold** and change the font color to **Red**.

e. Select the text in the **Master text styles placeholder**, click the **Home tab**, and select **Arial** from the Font group.

TROUBLESHOOTING: When fonts are applied on the slide master, you will see all of the fonts change to the selected font on the slide thumbnails. If this does not happen, you should make sure that you have the slide master thumbnail selected rather than another layout slide. Refer to Figure 6.11 for an example.

f. Click the **Slide Master tab**.

g. Save the file.

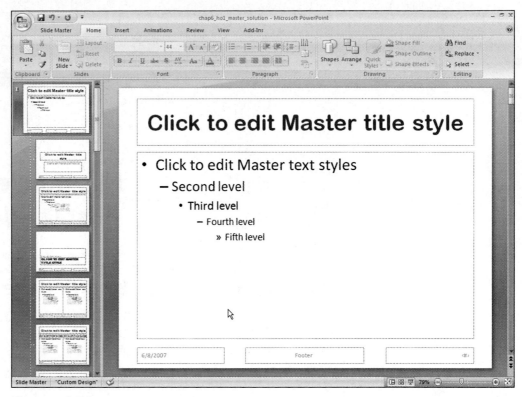

Figure 6.11 Master Slide

Refer to Figure 6.12 as you complete Step 4.

a. Click the **Title Slide Layout** in the slide thumbnail pane.

b. Click the **Master subtitle style placeholder**. Press **Delete**.

c. Click the **Footers check box** in the Master Layout group to remove the footers from the Title Slide Layout.

d. Select the text in the **Master title style placeholder** and type **Click to enter the name of the lesson**.

e. Click the border of the **Master title style placeholder** and move the placeholder to the bottom third of the slide.

f. Click the **Insert tab**, and then click **WordArt** in the Text group. Click the **Fill-Accent 2, Matte Bevel** at the bottom center of the gallery.

g. Type the proper prefix for you (Mr., Mrs., Ms., etc.) along with your last name. Press **Enter** and type **First Grade**.

TROUBLESHOOTING: If your text is appearing in the middle of the words Your Text Here, highlight the words and begin typing again.

h. Click the **border** of the WordArt placeholder and drag the WordArt to the upper center of the page.

i. Click the **Slide Master tab**.

j. Save the file.

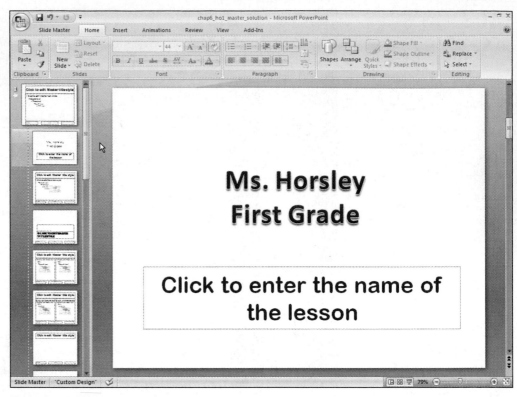

Figure 6.12 Title Slide Layout

Refer to Figure 6.13 as you complete Step 5.

a. Click the **Title and Content Layout** in the slide thumbnail pane. **Scroll** to the bottom of the pane, press **Shift**, and click the **last slide layout** thumbnail. Click **Delete** in the Edit Master group.

You decide to start with new slide layouts so you can place elements where you want them. You have two layouts in mind. One will contain the question and show a picture. The other will contain clip art with text below the graphic. You will create the question layout first and copy it, making changes for the second layout.

b. Click **Insert Layout** on the Edit Masters group.

c. Click the **Custom Layout Layout** on the slide thumbnail pane. Click **Rename** in the Edit Master group, type **Question Layout**, and click **Rename**.

d. Click the **Date placeholder** and press **Delete**. Click the **Footer placeholder** and press **Delete**.

e. Select the text in the **Master title style placeholder** and type **Click to edit the question**.

f. Click the **Insert Placeholder down arrow** in the Master Layout group. Select **Picture**. Drag a box that fills most of the slide.

g. Click in front of the word **Picture** and type **Insert a picture here**.

TROUBLESHOOTING: If the Picture placeholder is not centered on the slide, click the placeholder and move it into the correct position.

h. Click the **Page number placeholder**. Click the **Insert tab**, and then click **Slide Number** in the Text group. Click the **Slide number check box** and click **Apply to All**.

i. Click the **Slide Master tab**.

j. Click the **Question Layout** in the slide thumbnail pane. Right-click and select **Copy** from the shortcut menu.

k. Click in a blank area of the slide thumbnail pane. Right-click and select **Paste** from the shortcut menu.

l. Click the **second slide layout** that you just pasted and rename the layout **Answer Layout**.

m. Select the text in the **Master title style placeholder** and type **Click to edit the answer**.

n. Select the **Picture placeholder** and press **Delete**. Click **Insert Placeholder** in the Master Layout group and select **Clip Art**. Drag a placeholder for clip art in the center of the slide.

o. Click in front of the word **Clip Art** and type **Insert clip art here**.

p. Click **Close Master View**.

q. Save the file.

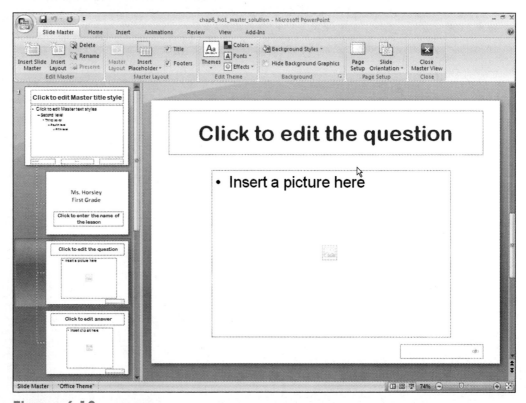

Figure 6.13 Slide Layout

Step 6
Save Masters

Refer to Figure 6.14 as you complete these steps.

a. Click the **Office Button** and position the mouse over **Save As**.

b. Select **Other Formats**.

c. Click **PowerPoint Template** in the Save as type box.

TROUBLESHOOTING: If you save the file as a regular presentation by mistake, open the file in PowerPoint and use Save As to save it as a template.

d. Save the *chap6_ho1_master_template* template and keep it onscreen if you plan to continue to the next hands-on exercise. Close the file and exit PowerPoint if you do not want to continue with the next exercise at this time.

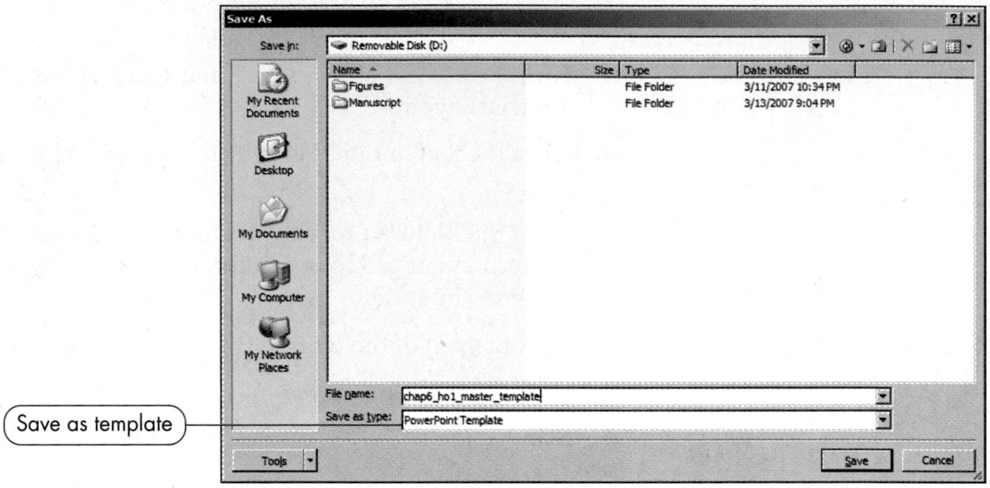

Save as template

Figure 6.14 Save As Dialog Box

Custom Templates

Custom templates are composed of many parts. You can decide to modify only the masters and call that a custom template or you can add more to the template to make it uniquely yours. Mixing your own colors to create custom colors adds a creative touch to templates. Custom backgrounds can be made that take your presentations beyond solid colors or photograph backgrounds. You can even create custom animations that are applied to the template. Create a custom template and you build a new theme complete with your own layouts, colors, backgrounds, and animations.

Custom templates have advantages beyond showcasing your creativity. Custom templates can save you time as you put together slide shows. Use your custom template as your beginning place for your presentations and you will not have to worry about colors, placeholders, backgrounds, and animation. Those decisions will already be made.

In this section, you will create custom colors, backgrounds, and animations. As you work through the exercises think about the possibilities. Your company logo could be a part of the background you use. Your favorite team colors can be represented on your slides. Tasks that you repeat over and over can be streamlined.

Customizing a Color Scheme

Color selection can make or break a presentation. Consider your audience and the message of your presentation as you select colors. Look at things around you to come up with color combinations. Other PowerPoint presentations that you may see, magazines, Web sites, and other graphically designed materials will give you a good idea of what colors work well together.

Select Appropriate Colors

(Consider your audience and the message of your presentation as you select colors.)

One of the main goals for your slides is for them to be readable by the audience. Certain color combinations work well together and other combinations are hard to read when they are placed together. Look for combinations that provide high contrast. Think of your favorite team colors and you are probably thinking about high-contrast color combinations. If black-and-white printouts are made for the audience, then the choice of colors for the text should provide even more contrast so the handouts are legible. Generally, the slides will be easiest to read when a dark text is placed on a lighter background. You see many presentations where the background is dark and the text is light. This is where you need to consider your audience. Some members of your audience may have problems reading light text on a dark background.

Colors convey meanings to your audience. Write the word "hot" in blue letters and your audience will be confused. Write "hot" in red or orange and the audience will grasp what you are trying to say. Certain colors evoke feelings. Blue, green, and violet are cool, relaxing colors. Yellow, orange, and red are invigorating, warm, action colors. If your presentation is long, using a warm color will quickly wear your audience out. The reference table shows common colors, associations people make with the colors, and emotions that are linked with the colors.

Color Associations | Reference

Colors can be used to attract the attention of the audience. They have a powerful effect on emotions. Colors are associated with different things. Color plays a significant role in audience response. Use this chart to select colors that support the message of your presentations. Use color wisely!

Color	Associations	Emotions	Use
Red	Danger, blood, strength, courage, fire, energy	Love, power, passion, rage, excitement, aggressive, determination, decision-maker, romance, longing	Make a point or gain attention. Stimulate people into making quick decisions.
Orange	Fall, warmth, fun, joy, energy, creativity, tropics, heat, citrus fruit	Pleasure, excitement, strength, ambition, endurance, domination, happiness, enthusiasm, playfulness, determination, success, stimulation	Emphasize happiness and enjoyment. Stimulate thought. For high visibility. Highlight important elements.
Yellow	Sunshine, bright, warnings	Cheerful, joy, happiness, warmth, optimism, intellect, energy, honor, loyalty, cowardice, lighthearted, jealousy	Gain a positive response. Gain attention.
Green	Nature, calm, refreshing, money, growth, fertility	Tranquility, growth, safety, harmony, freshness, healing, restive, stability, hope, endurance, envy, jealousy	Present a new idea. Suggest safety. Promote "green" products.
Blue	Sea, sky, peace, calm, cold, impersonal, intellect, masculine, expertise, integrity	Truth, dignity, trust, wisdom, loyalty, harmony, stability, confidence, calming, tranquility, sincerity, healing, understanding, melancholy, belonging	Build trust and strength. Promote cleanliness. Suggest precision. Suppress diet.
Violet	Wealth, royalty, sophistication, intelligence, spirituality, wisdom, dignity, magic, feminine	Power, stability, luxury, extravagance, creativity, frustration, gloom, sadness	Gain respect and attention. Promote children's products.
Black	Formal, mystery, death, evil, power, elegant, prestigious, conservative, the unknown	Authority, boldness, seriousness, negativity, strength, seductive, evil	Emphasis. Contrast with bright colors.
White	Snow, cleanliness, safety, simplicity, youth, light, purity, virginity	Perfection, distinction, enlightenment, positive, successful, faith	Emphasis. Suggest simplicity. Promoting medical products.
Gray	Neutral, science, architecture, commerce, cold	Easy-going, original, practical, earnest metals	Complement other colors. Unify colors. Bring focus to other colors.
Brown	Earth, richness, masculine, harvest, fall	Conservative, steady, dependable, serious, stability	Build trust.

Design a Color Scheme

A **color scheme** consists of the color combinations for the text, lines, background, and graphics in a presentation.

Color schemes are a combination of 12 colors used for the text, lines, background, and graphics in a presentation. Until now, you have relied on the color schemes in Office 2007 to add interest to your presentation. You have probably noticed that the color schemes may not include color combinations that are used by your school, business, or other organization. You are not limited to the color schemes that are available in Office 2007. You can create your own schemes!

As you focus your attention on creating your own color schemes in PowerPoint, you will have 16 million colors from which to choose. You may change any of the colors in the theme to customize it to your needs. Avoid making each of the 12 colors completely different. Choose one color family, use different shades of the colors in the family, and add two or three accent colors. Select colors that work well together. Keep your color scheme consistent throughout your presentation. Use light and dark shades of the same color within your color scheme for a unified, professional appearance.

A **hyperlink** links to other places in the presentation, Web sites, or other documents.

Color schemes become part of the template design theme. As you complete this section, you will apply color schemes to the master slide. Click the View tab, the slide master, and then the master slide thumbnail. Click the Colors down arrow in the Edit Theme group to show the Built-In theme colors. Click on Create New Theme Colors at the bottom of the list. Figure 6.15 shows the theme color elements you may customize. These elements include four text and background combinations, six accent colors, and two hyperlink colors. *Hyperlinks* are text links to other places in the PowerPoint document, Web sites, or other documents or presentations. The hyperlink color selection enables you to specify one color for an unvisited link and another for a visited hyperlink. The sample box, on the right slide of the Colors dialog box, provides a preview of the color selections on slides. Click the arrow of the element that you want to change. Click More Colors at the bottom of the Theme Colors menu to customize the color scheme.

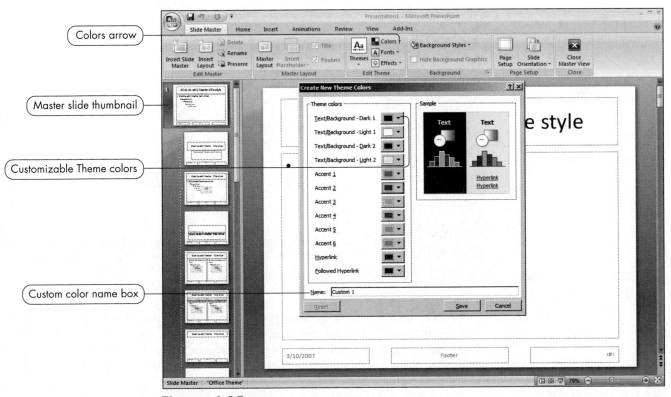

Figure 6.15 Theme Color Elements

RGB is a numeric system for identifying the color resulting from the combination of red, green, and blue light.

HSL is a color model in which the numeric system refers to hue, saturation, and luminosity of a color.

The Colors dialog box offers two options for selecting colors. The Standard tab contains 127 colors and 14 shades of white to black. The Custom tab enables you to make selections based on the **RGB** color model where numbers are assigned to red, green, or blue. A zero for each of the colors represents black. The number 255 for each of the colors in the model represents white. The RGB model allows 16 million colors. Using this system you can match any color where you know the three RGB numbers. A similar color model, **HSL**, balances hue, saturation, and luminosity to produce a color. The numbers for black and white are represented the same way as in the RGB model.

Figure 6.16 shows the Custom Colors tab dialog box. Drag the crosshairs in the Color box to the color family you wish to use, for instance green. The slider to the right of the Color box is used to select the shade of that color. If you know the RGB number, you may use the spin box to increase or decrease the number or you may type the number into the boxes for each of the colors. The Sample box shows the current color and the color you have selected for the new color. After selecting the color, click OK to place that color into the theme. As you make changes to the theme element colors, the Sample box gives you an idea of how your color scheme will look on the slide.

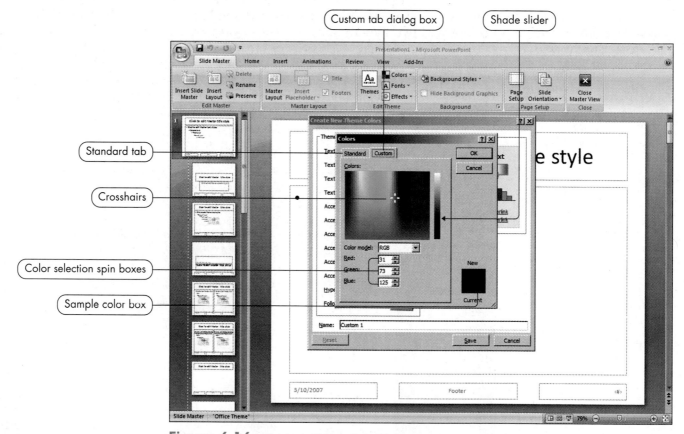

Figure 6.16 Custom Colors Tab Dialog Box

After making your selections, type a name for the new color theme in the Name box. Click Save. This color theme is saved on the hard drive of the computer in the Document Themes folder. Your instructor may ask you to include identifying information in the color theme name so that you can find it later. Click Close Master View in the Close group.

You may wonder why four different theme color elements exist for Text and Background, as shown in Figure 6.15. Once you return to the Normal view, you might decide to change the background. Click the Design tab and click the Background Styles in the Background group. The four color selections in the gallery relate to the four Text/Background color element selections you made. If you wish to limit the color choices for the background to just one, set all of the Text/Background color elements to the same RGB numbers.

You can edit color schemes if you change your mind. Right-click the custom color scheme you created and click on Edit in the shortcut menu. Make the changes to the color elements and click Save. Color schemes can be deleted if they are no longer needed. Right-click on the custom color scheme you wish to delete and click Delete on the shortcut menu.

Color schemes do not have to be developed in a template, but if they are, the template retains the color scheme. The color schemes are saved as a part of the template file with the extension of potx.

Creating a Custom Template

As you know, templates are reusable. Building a professional template with customization gives you the opportunity to base your presentations on common color schemes and layouts. As you have seen, templates provide you with many creative options.

You can create a template for award certificates, advertisements, party invitations, work schedules, and timelines. It makes quick work of creating these documents when you pull up a template in PowerPoint, type just a few lines of text in placeholders, and print the document.

You can apply graphics, such as logos, slogans, photographs, WordArt, and shapes, to the slide master layouts to create a consistent look for presentations. You have selected templates and themes to apply to slides based on their visual appeal and how they relate to your message and audience. Now you will create and place the elements in the background of your template for a truly custom presentation.

Backgrounds may be built on previously developed templates where you have made color and layout decisions, or on a blank presentation. The previously developed template often contains slide layouts and a color theme. If you start from a blank presentation, you can later modify slide masters, slide layouts, and color themes.

In custom templates, the slide master and slide layouts contain the elements that will appear in the background of your presentation. If you add the elements to the slide master, all of the slides will contain the same elements. You have the option to add elements to each of the layouts in your template so that slides based on the layouts have different backgrounds. As you create special backgrounds for the layouts, remember that the audience is expecting slides to relate to each other. Drastically changing colors between layouts is confusing. Consistency in feel and look is a key in designing backgrounds for layouts.

With a presentation open in PowerPoint, click View, and then click Slide Master in the Presentation Views group. Click the slide master thumbnail at the top of the slides thumbnail pane. Click the Home or Insert tab to use the tools. For instance, if you want to add a logo to the slide master, click the Insert tab. Click Picture in the Illustrations group. Navigate to the logo file, click on it, and click Insert. The Picture Tools on the Format tab are available for you to modify the logo as needed. Remember that if the slide master thumbnail is selected, this image will appear on every slide layout in the same position.

Your intention might be to have the logo appear prominently displayed on the title slide and in a smaller version on the other layouts. Click the title layout thumbnail in the slides thumbnail pane and use the Insert tab to place the logo. Once you are satisfied with the title layout, click the slide layout thumbnail and place the logo again using the Insert tab. Insert the logo on each slide layout in the Slides thumbnail pane. Figure 6.17 shows the logo placed on the title slide and each of the slide layouts.

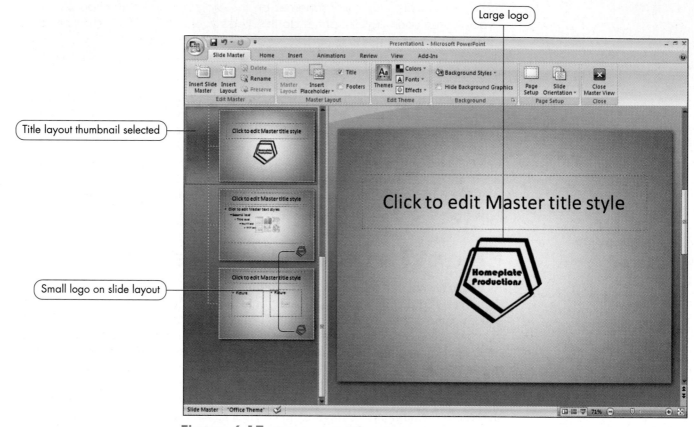

Figure 6.17 Title Layout Slide with Logo

Think about the possibilities of adding other objects to your slides. Would a series of squares dress up your layout and make your slides more interesting? Is a washout effect photograph an appropriate image for the background? Could a corner be shaded and contain a logo? Figure 6.18 shows some possibilities for custom slide templates.

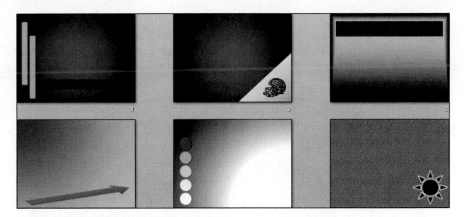

Figure 6.18 Custom Slide Templates

When you finish the design of the templates on the slide masters, click the Slide Master tab and click Close Master View. Save the file as a template. As you create a new presentation, click New, then click My Templates, and select the template you will use as the basis for your presentation.

Applying a Custom Animation

Just about anything can be animated on a slide. Typical elements for animation are text, clip art, SmartArt, and WordArt. Animations can be added to placeholders on the slide master, and then everything in that placeholder will be animated on all slides that use the layout. Because the KISS principle applies to animations, too, adding animation to the placeholder should be avoided.

Animation adds movement to text and other objects in presentations. Used correctly, animation supports the message of the slide and adds interest. Used incorrectly, animation is distracting to the audience.

$\Big($ Used correctly, animation supports the message of the slide . . . $\Big)$

With a presentation open, select the slide you wish to animate. Click the text or object you want to animate, and then click the Animations tab. Click Custom Animation in the Animations group. The Custom Animation pane, as shown in Figure 6.19, appears on the right side of the window.

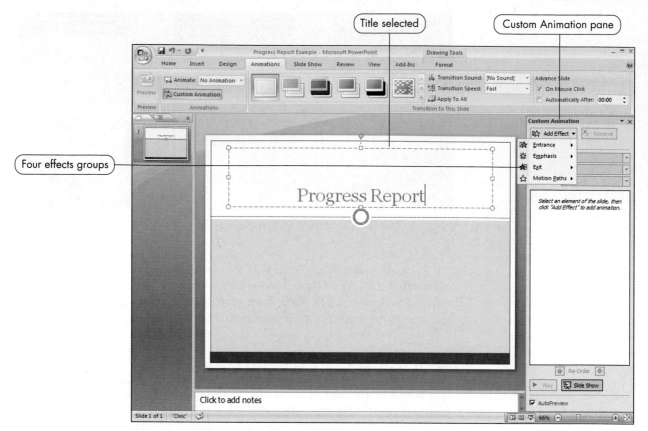

Figure 6.19 Custom Animation Effects

Add an Animation Effect

As Figure 6.19 shows, four groups of effects with which to animate your slides are available. Each effect contains many actions from which to select. The entrance effect causes the object to enter the slide. The emphasis effect causes the text or object on the slide to change. The exit effect causes text or objects to leave the slide. Motion paths make objects move in a defined way. More than one effect can be applied to text or objects, so you could have the company logo fly into the slide as it loads, grow and shrink, move from the left to the right on the slide, and then exit by flying off the slide. You can control the timing of the effect as well as the trigger that causes the animation to start. Obviously, this is a complex set of animations that may not be necessary, but it shows the power of the animation effects.

To apply an animation, click the Add Effect down arrow and select an effect. A menu of options appears so that you may select the best effect to fit your needs. Figure 6.20 shows the actions available when the Entrance effect is selected. Click More Effects and options for Basic, Subtle, Moderate, and Exciting actions appear, as Figure 6.21 shows. When you click an action, a preview on the slide shows the effect on the selected object. Click OK and the action will be applied to the object.

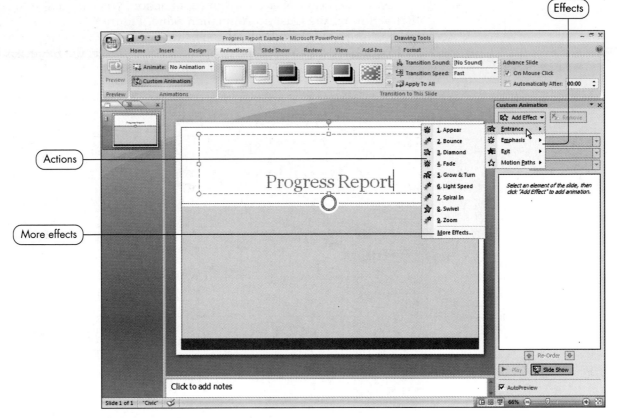

Figure 6.20 Custom Effect Actions

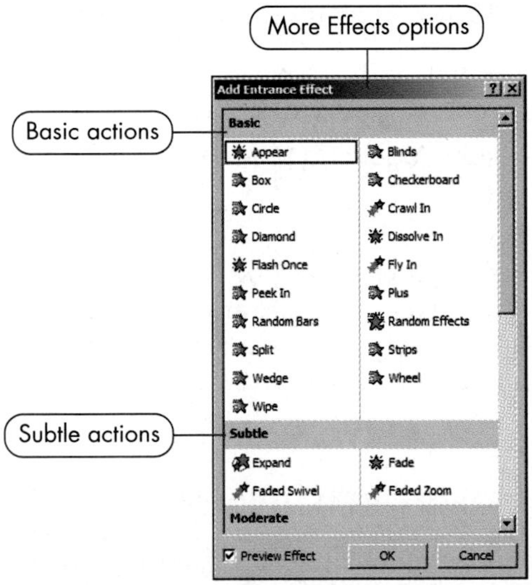

Figure 6.21 Custom Actions Menu

TIP   Actions List

The actions list may obscure your view of the selected object. Drag the Add Entrance Effect title bar to move the list out of the way.

Once the text or object is assigned an action, you can modify the properties of that action on the Custom Animation pane. Figure 6.22 shows the modification options for Speed. Modifications can be made for the Start trigger. Different animations will have different property options. For instance, the Emphasis options have properties of size, font, or style to be applied to text and objects.

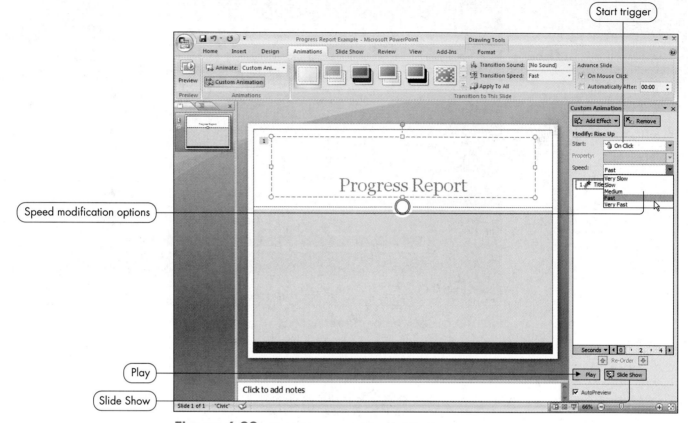

Figure 6.22 Start Trigger and Speed Options

Animation sequences should be checked as you create them to make sure they respond in the way you expect. At any time, click Play at the bottom of the Custom Animation pane to see the animation of the text and objects on the screen. A Slide Show button offers you the opportunity to see the animation occur with the slide filling the screen.

Create a Motion Path Animation

Motion path animation is a little different from other effects. With the object selected, click Add Effect, and click Motion Paths. If you select any of the top six options, the object will move from its current position to the new position in the direction you selected. Figure 6.23 shows the motion path, with a green arrowhead at the beginning of the path and a red arrowhead at the end. Choose More Motion Paths from the menu and a wide variety of shapes appear for your selection. The most interesting motion path might be the Draw Custom Path option shown in Figure 6.24. Select one of these options and a pencil appears. Drag the pencil around the slide to record a motion path. When you release the mouse button, a preview of the motion is shown. Figure 6.25 shows the Custom Path drawn on a slide.

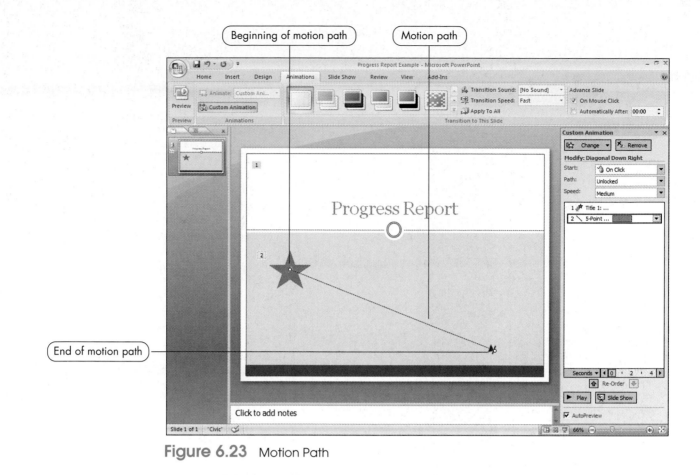

Figure 6.23 Motion Path

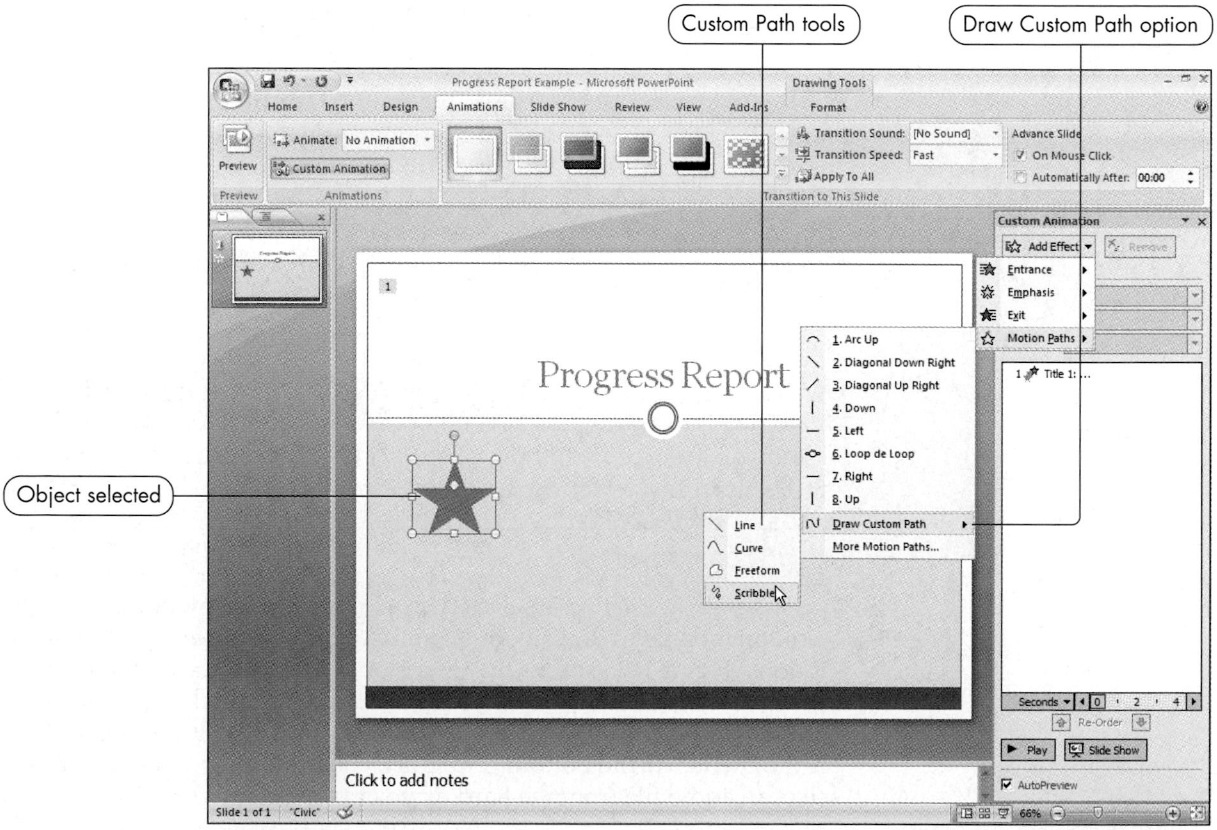

Figure 6.24 Draw Motion Path

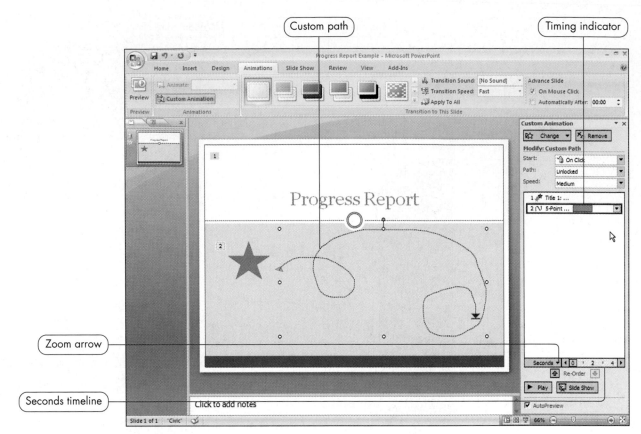

Figure 6.25 Custom Motion Path

Set the Timing of an Animation

As you look at Figure 6.25, notice the orange bar next to the selected effect in the Custom Animation pane. This is the timing indicator. A Seconds timeline at the bottom of the pane gives you an idea of how long the animation will last. If you want to increase or shorten the length of time for an animation, you drag the end of the orange bar with the double-line, double-headed arrow. The timeline contains a feature for zooming so that you can see more or fewer seconds. Click the arrow next to Seconds and select whether you want to zoom in or out.

TIP   Seconds Timeline

If the timeline does not show at the bottom of the Custom Animation pane, click the arrow next to a selected animation and click Show Advanced Timeline.

When an animation is selected on the Custom Animation pane, the arrow next to the animation gives you an opportunity to modify the action even more. Click Effect Options. Figure 6.26 shows the Effect tab that enables you to change the Settings or add Enhancements. Sound-effect enhancements can be set up to play as the object animates during the slide show. Click the Sound down arrow and 20 sounds appear on the menu. At the bottom of the list, the option for Other Sound enables you to select an audio file from the hard drive or other storage device.

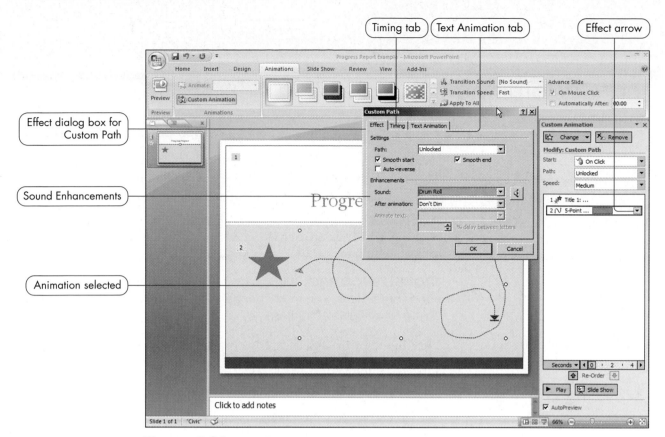

Figure 6.26 Effect Tab

The Timing tab, available when you click the Effects Option, enables you to fine-tune the timing of the events in the animation. You can set delays, speed, repeats, triggers, and other start effects. The Text Animation tab groups the text so that paragraphs animate as one.

Apply Multiple Animations

Objects on the slide can be assigned multiple animations. For example, the star shown in Figure 6.26 could follow the custom motion path and then shrink and grow. If more than one object on your slide is animated, you can change the order in which the animations will occur. Click on the animation you wish to move, and then click the Reorder arrow up or arrow down at the bottom of the Custom Animation pane. If you decide that you no longer want a particular animation to occur, click the animation you wish to remove, and then click Remove at the top of the pane.

Hands-On Exercises

2 | Customizing Templates

Skills covered: 1. Modify a Color Scheme **2.** Create a Custom Template **3.** Apply Custom Animations **4.** Play Animations

<table>
<tr><td>**Step 1**
Modify a Color Scheme</td><td>

Refer to Figure 6.27 as you complete Step 1.

a. Start PowerPoint, open the *chap6_ho1_master_template* template if you closed it after the last hands-on exercise, and save it as a template named **chap6_ho2_master_template**.

TROUBLESHOOTING: If you saved and closed the template in the previous hands-on exercise, you must change the Files of type setting in the Open dialog box to PowerPoint Templates.

b. Click the **View tab** and click **Slide Master** in the Presentation Views group.

c. Click the **Colors arrow** in the Edit Theme group.

d. Select **Create New Theme Colors**.

The Create New Theme Colors dialog box opens so that you can select a theme color.

e. Select **Text/Background – Dark 1**, and then select **More Colors**.

f. Click the **Custom tab** in the Colors dialog box, replace the numeric values in the Red color box with **0**, the Green color box with **50**, and the Blue color box with **155**. This produces a royal blue color. Click **OK**.

g. Click **Text/Background – Light 1**, and then select **More Colors**. Click the **Custom tab** in the Colors dialog box, replace the RGB numbers with **220**, **215**, and **255**, respectively. This creates a light blue color. Click **OK**.

h. Continue this process, altering **Text/Background – Dark 2** and **Text/Background – Light 2** as follows:

</td></tr>
</table>

	Red	Green	Blue	Resulting Color
Dark 2	0	25	80	Dark navy blue
Light 2	240	240	125	Pale yellow

i. Click in the Name box and type **Game Colors**. Click **Save**.

j. To see the color scheme, click **Background Styles** in the Background group. Select the **yellow Style 2 color** at the top of the second column.

Notice that as you move your mouse over the color choices, the selection is previewed on the slides. The background color choices are based on the four Text/Background settings you made in the previous steps.

k. Click **Close Master View** and save the *chap6_ho2_master_template* file as a **Presentation Template**.

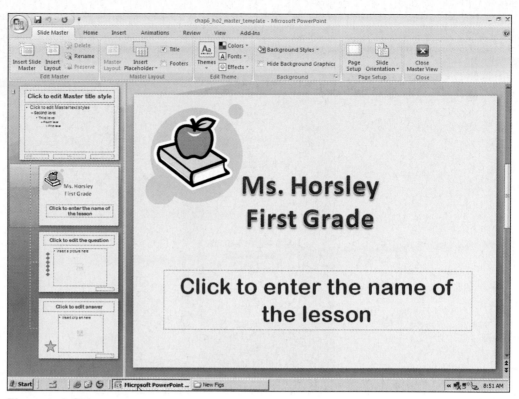

Figure 6.27 Modified Color Scheme

Step 2
Create a Custom Template

Refer to Figure 6.28 as you complete Step 2.

a. Click the **View tab** and click **Slide Master**.

b. Select the **Title Slide Layout** in the slide thumbnail pane.

   You have decided to dress up the presentation template for the first grade game with some appropriate graphics.

c. Click the **Insert tab** and click **Clip Art** in the Illustrations group. Type **school** in the Search for box in the Clip Art pane. Select clip art of an apple on books or one with a similar theme. Insert the clip art. Refer to Figure 6.28 and make adjustments to the size and position of the clip art on the title slide layout.

d. Click on the **Question Layout thumbnail**, and then click **Shapes** in the Illustrations group on the Insert tab. Draw six diamonds on the left side of the picture placeholder.

   TROUBLESHOOTING: Copy the first diamond you draw to ensure that all of the shapes are the same size. Use Align in the Arrange group to format the diamonds into an aligned row that is distributed vertically.

e. Click the **Answer Layout thumbnail** and draw a **star** on the lower-left side of the slide. Change the fill color of the star to **orange** using Standard Colors.

f. Click **Close Master View**.

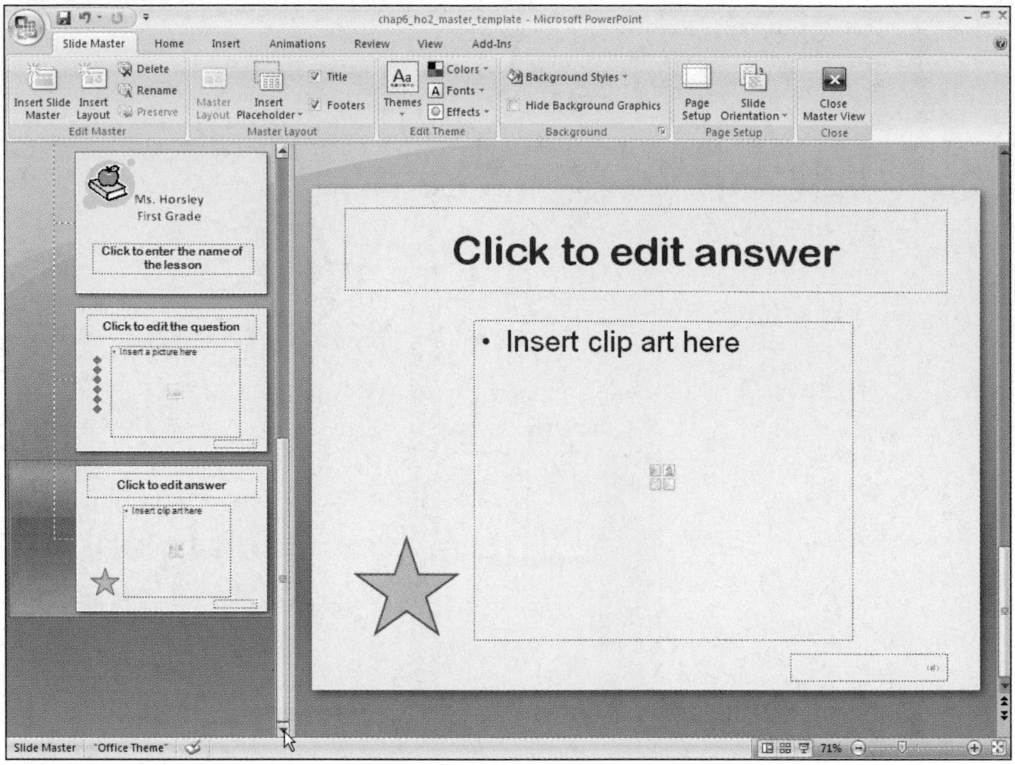

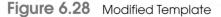

Figure 6.28 Modified Template

Step 3
Apply Custom Animations

Refer to Figure 6.29 as you complete Step 3.

a. Click the **View tab** and click **Slide Master.**

Knowing the students in your first grade class enjoy action, you decide to animate the title and star on the Answer slide layout. By animating the elements on the template, you will not have to apply the animation on each slide.

b. Select the **Answer Layout thumbnail**.

c. Click the **title placeholder** and click the **Animations tab**. Click **Custom Animation.**

You decide to use a motion path to add interest to the title placeholder.

d. Click **Add Effect** in the Custom Animation pane. Click **Motion Paths** and select **More Motion Paths.**

e. Click **Loop de Loop** from the Special group. Click **OK.**

f. Click the **Start arrow** and select **With Previous.**

g. Click the **star** graphic.

You decide that a random effect will be more interesting than the same effect over and over.

h. Click **Add Effect** in the Custom Animation pane. Click **Entrance**, click **More Effects**, and select **Random Effects** from the Basic Choices. Click OK.

i. Click the **Start arrow** and select **With Previous.**

j. Click **Add Effects** again. Click **Emphasis**, click **More Effects**, and click **Spin** from the Basic Choices. Click **OK.**

k. Select the **Spin effect**, if it is not selected, and click the **arrow** for the **Start** and click **After Previous**. Use the arrow for **Amount** and select **Two Spins**.

TROUBLESHOOTING: If you are confused about the effects you have set, click on one and the name below Add Effect in the Custom Animation pane will display the name of the effect.

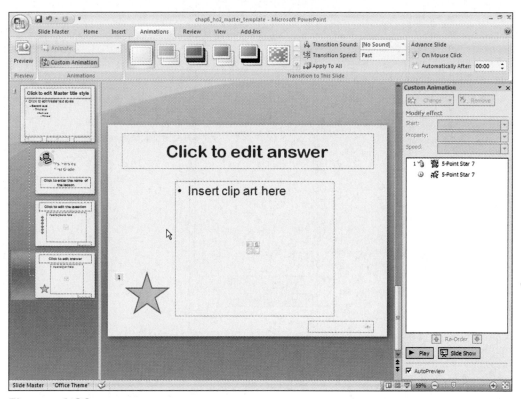

Figure 6.29 Custom Animation

Step 4
Play Animations

Refer to Figure 6.30 as you complete Step 4.

a. Click **Play** at the bottom of the Custom Animation pane to view the effects you have set. Play it more than once to get an idea of how the random effects will look.

b. Click the **Slide Master tab** and click **Close Master View**.

c. Save the *chap6_ho2_master_template* file as a template file. Close the file. Exit PowerPoint if you do not want to continue with the next exercise at this time.

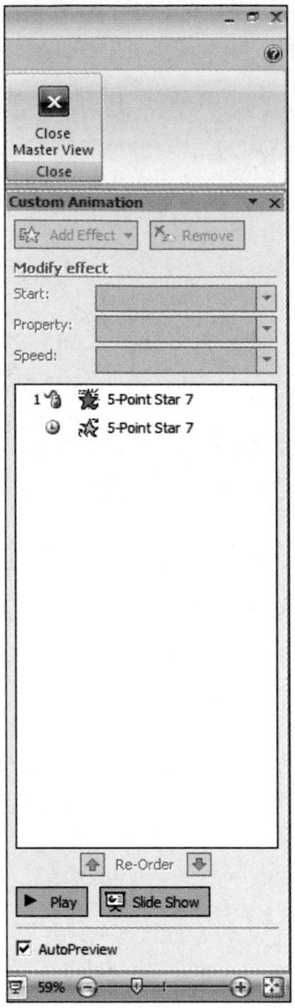

Figure 6.30 Custom Animation on Slide Layout

Custom Shows

A *custom show* is a grouped subsets of the slides in a presentation.

Custom shows are composed of a subset of slides assembled for a presentation. Often, a single slide show can be used for a number of different presentations. For instance, you may plan for a 40-minute presentation, only to find out at the last minute that your time has been cut to 25 minutes. Rather than show all of the slides in the presentation, breezing by the less important ones, you create a custom show and select only the most important slides. In another instance, you have multiple custom slide shows defined in a presentation that are linked so that the presentation pulls slides from each. You may give a presentation to the school board that contains information about a new program proposal, use a link during the presentation to show slides from a custom show about the effects the program will have on students, and use another link to show a custom show regarding the budget. Custom shows save you time and allow you to focus your presentations to your audience.

> Rather than show all of the slides in the presentation, breezing by the less important ones, you create a custom show and select only the most important slides.

An alternative to creating a custom show is to hide slides. In this case, you designate slides within the show as hidden. As you give your presentation, you can reveal the slides within the sequence or not. You will experiment with hiding slides and revealing them as you display a slide show. In this section, you will learn how to create multiple custom shows from a single presentation. In addition, you run and navigate a custom slide show. Finally, you designate and display hidden slides.

Creating a Custom Slide Show

A *basic custom show* is a single presentation file, from which you can create separate presentations.

In *basic custom shows*, you select slides from one presentation, grouping them together into another presentation. If your original presentation contains 10 slides, you might designate the first, third, eighth, and tenth slides for a custom show. The original presentation will contain all of the slides needed in the custom show.

Open the presentation in which you want to create the basic custom show. Click the Slide Show tab. Click Custom Slide Show in the Start Slide Show group. Click Custom Shows if a submenu appears. Click New. As shown in Figure 6.31, a dialog box accepts a custom Slide show name. Type a name for the new show. The slides in the original presentation are listed in the left box and identified by the slide number and the title of the slide. Click the slide that will appear in the custom show, and then click Add. The slide moves to the Slides in custom show box, and it is numbered based on its position in the new show.

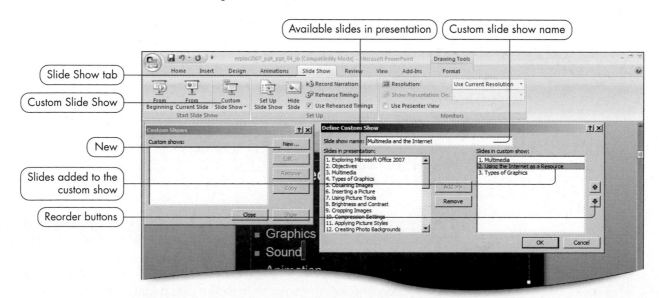

Figure 6.31 Custom Show Dialog Box Settings

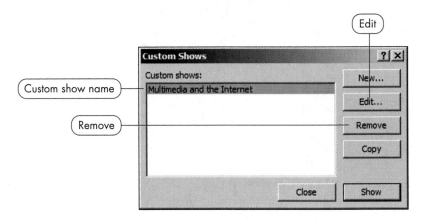
As you add slides to the custom show, the reorder buttons become active. Select the title of a slide to move in the custom show box and click the reorder buttons to move the slide up or down in the new presentation. When you are satisfied with the slide selections and order, click OK. The name of the new show will appear in the Custom Shows dialog box, as shown in Figure 6.32. Later, if the show needs to be updated, select the custom show name and click Edit. If the show is no longer needed, click the custom show name and click Remove. Click Close to return to the full presentation file.

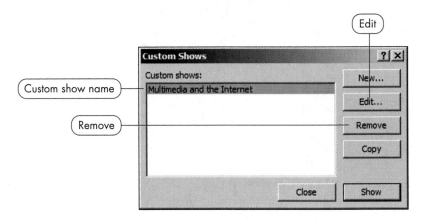

Figure 6.32 Custom Show Dialog Box

A ***hyperlinked custom show*** begins with a main custom show and use hyperlinks to link between other shows.

Hyperlinked custom shows connect a main custom show to other custom shows using hyperlinks. You might be giving a presentation to a group of potential students who are exploring college degrees. One slide in your presentation could have links to parts of your slide show that discuss individual degrees. After you quickly poll your audience, you find that everyone is interested in hearing you talk about the nursing degree, while half are interested in the business degree, and only one or two people want to hear about the other degree programs. As you present the hyperlinked show, you can decide whether to branch to the supporting shows containing other degree program information or not. All of the slides must be in the same presentation. This presentation is then divided into custom shows. A hyperlinked custom show might include 10 slides from the main presentation, 3 slides from another part of the show, and 5 slides from yet another.

Create the main custom slide show as previously described by opening the presentation and selecting the slides that will be in the main show. Name this custom show with a unique name, such as "Business_Proposal_HL," so that you will be able to identify it later as the show that contains the hyperlinks. Create the supporting custom slide shows, as described, by selecting slides from the presentation and naming each with a different name.

After you create all of the custom shows, click the Home tab to return to the original presentation. Use the slide thumbnail pane to select the slide in the main custom slide show that will contain the hyperlinks. Select the text or other object that you will click to start the supporting slides. Click the Insert tab, and then click Hyperlinks in the Links group. In the Edit Hyperlink dialog box, as shown in Figure 6.33, click Place in This Document. Scroll to the bottom of the slide list, where the Custom Show list begins, and click the name of the support slide show. A preview of the first slide in that show will appear in the Preview box. Click in the Show and Return check box so that the supporting slide show will return to the main show after all of the slides have been shown. Repeat these steps to set up the remaining hyperlinks.

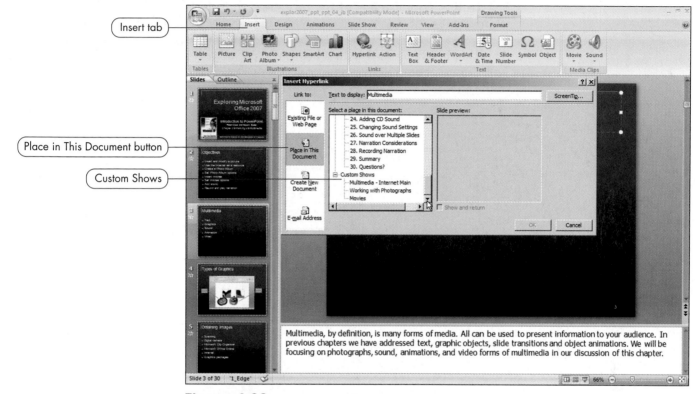

Figure 6.33 Hyperlink Dialog Box

Running and Navigating a Custom Slide Show

The presentation file must be saved so that the custom show remains a subset of it. To show the basic custom slide show, open the presentation and click the Slide Show tab. Click Custom Slide Show, and then click the name of the custom show you wish to present. The show will begin without further selections.

To show the hyperlinked presentation, open the presentation, click the Slide Show tab, and then click Custom Slide Show. Select the name of the main custom slide show and the custom presentation will begin. When a slide is reached that contains a hyperlink, click on the hyperlink and continue through the supporting slides. Advance through all of the supporting slides and return to the main custom slide. Select another hyperlink if one appears on this slide or continue displaying the slides in the main custom slide show.

Designating and Displaying Hidden Slides

Although custom shows fit many needs, in some cases, you would rather simply skip slides in the main presentation but show them if the audience requests additional information. Hiding slides within the sequence of the presentation depends on

> Hiding slides within the sequence of the presentation depends on your ability to guess what your audience might ask.

your ability to guess what your audience might ask. For example, a presentation on budgeting might include slides that speak of the budgeting process as a concept. Your audience might ask to see some actual numbers plugged into a budget. If you anticipate this question, you can create a slide with this information and hide it within the presentation. During the presentation, if no one asks to see numbers in a budget, you can continue through your slide show. If someone says, "Show me how this would look," you can show the hidden slide. Once the answer has been given, you continue through your slide show. The next time you make a presentation with this slide show, the slide will again be hidden.

In the Normal view of the presentation, select the slide to hide in the slide thumbnail pane. Click the Slide Show tab, and then click Hide Slide in the Set Up group. As shown in Figure 6.34, the slide number is in a square with a slash to indicate that it is hidden. The thumbnail will also appear grayed out. If you later change your mind about hiding a slide, select it on the slide thumbnail pane and click Hide Slide again.

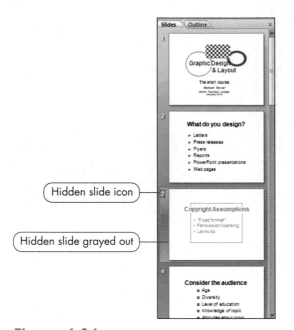

Hidden slide icon

Hidden slide grayed out

Figure 6.34 Hidden Slide

During the presentation, when you arrive at the location of the hidden slide, you reveal the slide by pressing H or by right-clicking and selecting the hidden slide from the Go to Slide list. Hidden slides on this list have the slide number in parentheses. An advantage of using the Go to Slide option is that you can go to any hidden slide, not just the next one in the sequence.

As you print your slide presentation, you may decide to print the hidden slides or not. The Print dialog box contains a check box to designate whether to print the hidden slides. If you print the hidden slides on handouts, the audience will be able to see what it missed! It is also a good idea to print the hidden slides on the notes pages for the presenter. This way, as the speech is being delivered, the presenter will be reminded of the hidden slide and its content.

Hands-On Exercises

3 | Creating a Custom Slide Show

Skills covered: 1. Create a Custom Slide Show **2.** Display and Print a Custom Slide Show **3.** Hide Slides **4.** Display Hidden Slides **5.** Print Hidden Slides

---

<table>
<tr><td>

Step 1

Create a Custom Slide Show

</td><td>

Refer to Figure 6.35 as you complete Step 1.

a. Start PowerPoint if you closed it after the last hands-on exercise, then open the *chap6_ho3_powerful* file and save it as **chap6_ho3_powerful_solution**.

In your Speech class, you were asked to create a presentation on giving presentations. At the last minute, your instructor shortened the amount of time for the presentation. You create a custom show to show only slides with the most important information.

b. Click the **Slide Show tab**.

c. Click **Custom Slide Show**, and then click **Custom Shows**.

d. Click **New**.

e. Type **Custom Powerful Presentations** in the Name box.

f. Select slides **1, 2, 3, 4**, and **15**. Click **Add**.

TROUBLESHOOTING: If you select the wrong slide, click the name of the slide on the right side of the Define Custom Show dialog box and then click Remove.

g. Click **OK**, and then click **Close**.

</td></tr>
</table>

Figure 6.35 Define Custom Show Dialog Box

<table>
<tr><td>

Step 2

Display and Print a Custom Slide Show

</td><td>

Refer to Figure 6.36 as you complete Step 2.

a. Click **Custom Slide Show** on the Slide Show tab, select **Custom Powerful Presentations** from the Custom Show dialog box, and review the slides.

TROUBLESHOOTING: If the slides you see during your review are not the ones you expect, you can return to Custom Slide Show on the Slide Show tab, right-click on the custom show name, and select Edit. Slides can then be transferred from the right or left side of the Define Custom Show dialog box as needed.

b. Click the **Office Button**, position the mouse over **Print**, and select **Print** to open the Print dialog box.

c. Select the **Custom Show** and use the drop-down arrow to select **Custom Powerful Presentations**.

</td></tr>
</table>

d. Change the Print what option to **Handouts** with **6 Slides per page**.

e. Save the *chap6_ho3_powerful solution* file. Close the file.

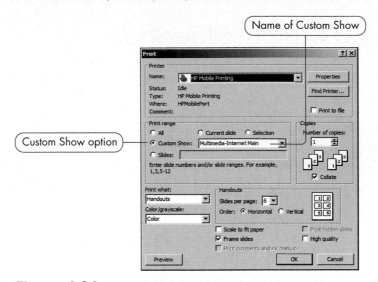

Figure 6.36 Print Dialog Box

Step 3
Hide Slides

Refer to Figure 6.37 as you complete Step 3.

a. Open the *chap6_ho3_ hidden* file, and then save it as **chap6_ho3_hidden_solution**.

You decide to hide the fifth, sixth, and seventh slides in the presentation.

b. Click the **slide 5 thumbnail** in the slide thumbnail pane to select it.

c. Click the **Slide Show tab**, and then click **Hide Slide** in the Set Up group.

Look at the slide thumbnail pane. A square with a slash appears around the number for the slide. The slide is also grayed out.

d. Click the **slide 6 thumbnail** and **hide** the slide. Repeat to **hide slide 7**.

TROUBLESHOOTING: If you hide a slide by mistake, select the slide, then click Hide Slide in the Set Up group on the Slide Show tab.

Figure 6.37 Hidden Slide View

Refer to Figure 6.38 as you complete Step 4.

a. Click **From Beginning** in the Start Slide Show group. Press **Enter** to advance through the slide show. At the end of the show, press **Esc** to return to the Normal view.

Notice that the hidden slides did not appear in the show.

b. Once again, click **From Beginning** in the Start Slide Show group. Press **Enter** to advance through the slide show. After you display the fourth slide, press **H**.

c. Press **Enter** to continue to the next slide. Right-click and select **Go to Slide**. Click **(7) How do you get to Broadway?** Finish displaying the rest of the slides.

TROUBLESHOOTING: Using the Go to Slide option during a presentation allows you to move to any hidden slide in the show. Hidden slides are designated by parentheses on the Go to Slide list.

d. Press **Esc** to return to the Normal view.

After experimenting with both ways to reveal hidden slides, you can decide which fits your presentation style better.

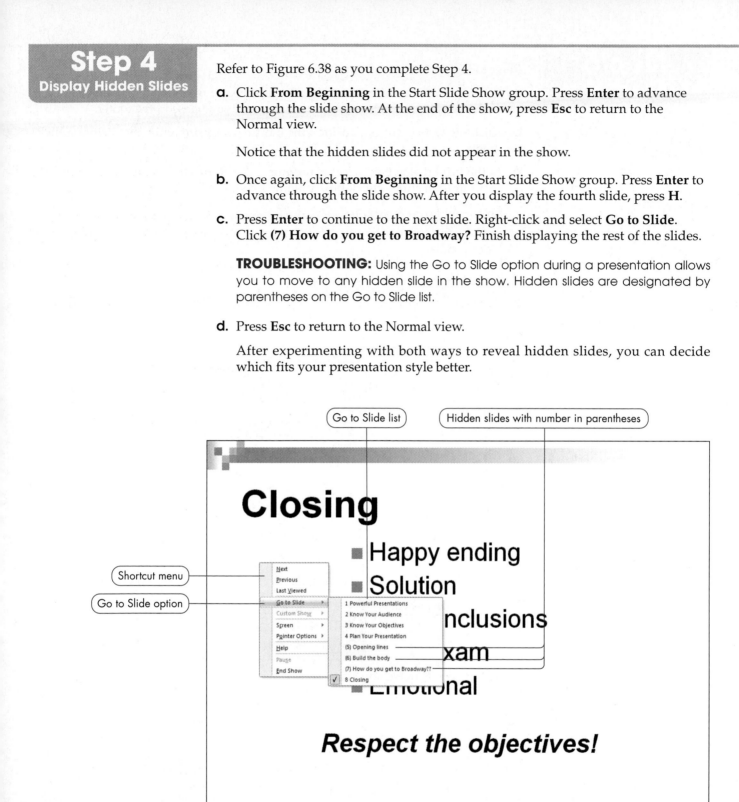

Figure 6.38 Hidden Slide View

Step 5
Print Hidden Slides

Refer to Figure 6.39 as you complete Step 5.

a. Create a **Notes and Handouts Header and Footer** with the date and your name in the header and your instructor's name and your class in the footer.

b. Click the **Office Button**, position the mouse over **Print** and select **Print** on the menu.

c. In the Print dialog box, select **Handouts** and **4 Slides per page**. Confirm that the **Print hidden slides check box** contains a check.

> **TROUBLESHOOTING:** When you designate that the hidden slides are to be printed, they will be printed as part of the whole group. You cannot just print the hidden slides.

d. Press **OK** to print the handouts.

e. Save the *chap6_ho3_hidden_solution* presentation. Close the presentation. Exit PowerPoint.

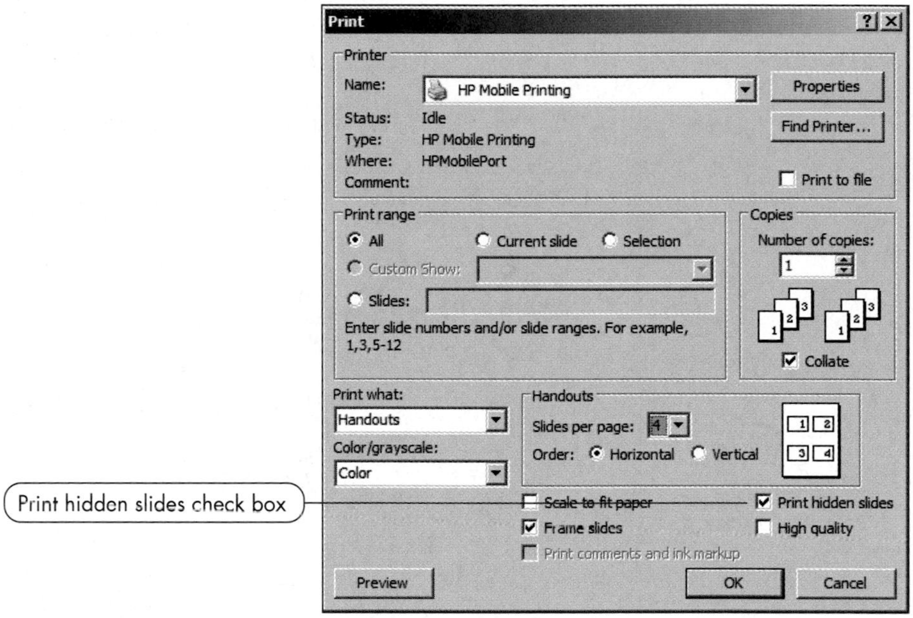

Figure 6.39 Print Hidden Slides

Summary

1. **Modify handout and note masters.** Handouts and notes pages are often controlled as masters. Modifications in the placement of the content, headers, and footers become part of a template and can be reused.

2. **Create and modify slide masters.** Slide masters provide a high level of customization to presentations. Slide masters control the fonts, layouts, color schemes, and backgrounds of presentation templates. Title slide layouts and slide layouts are individually customizable.

3. **Customize a color scheme.** Color schemes may be modified to fit specific color requirements, such as school or company standard colors. The color model RGB enables the creation of over 16 million colors. Twelve colors in each color scheme can be customized.

4. **Create a custom template.** Custom templates are a combination of slide masters, color schemes, and customized backgrounds. Modified backgrounds can be created for each slide layout, using the color scheme developed for the presentation.

5. **Apply a custom animation.** Objects such as text, graphics, WordArt, and SmartArt can have custom animations applied. Each object can be assigned more than one animation sequence. Typically, the animation is controlled for effect, action, and speed.

6. **Create a custom slide show.** A custom slide show is a subset of a larger presentation. It is used to focus the audience on particular slides within the presentation without revealing the less important ones. Basic custom slide shows contain any number of slides from the original presentation and the slides can be reordered within the basic custom slide show. Hyperlinked custom slide shows link between one slide in a presentation and a custom slide show within the presentation.

7. **Run and navigate a custom slide show.** To display a basic custom slide show, the original presentation is opened and the custom show selected from the Slide Show tab. To display a hyperlinked custom slide show, the original presentation is opened and displayed until a hyperlink is encountered. At that point, the speaker can decide to use the hyperlinked custom slide show and click on the link or continue on in the original presentation.

8. **Designate and display hidden slides.** Hidden slides allow for a different level of customization. Slides within the sequence of the presentation are hidden. The speaker can show the hidden slide by pressing H when the slide is reached in the sequence or by using the Go To menu. Hidden slides may be printed on the handouts and notes pages if desired.

Key Terms

Basic custom show 463
Color scheme 447
Custom show 463
Handout master 429

HSL 448
Hyperlinked custom show 464
Hyperlink 447
Master 429

Notes master 432
RGB .448
Slide master 433

Multiple Choice

1. The slide master is used to control:

   (a) The font and color scheme

   (b) The font, font size, color scheme, and background style

   (c) Layout of the slide

   (d) Number of placeholders on a slide

2. Changes to the title placeholder on the slide master determine:

   (a) The font and size of the title on the slide master only

   (b) The placement of the title on the slide layouts

   (c) The exact text that will appear on the slide

   (d) The font and size of the title text on all slide layouts

3. Text keyed into the footer on the slide master:

   (a) Automatically appears on all slides in the presentation

   (b) Must be added to the slides using the Header and Footer commands

   (c) Only appears on the title slide

   (d) Must be in boldface in order to appear

4. The page orientation of handout masters can be:

   (a) Landscape or portrait

   (b) Only portrait

   (c) Only landscape

   (d) Eight slides per page

5. By default, notes masters contain:

   (a) Two slides per page

   (b) Only the slide and note text

   (c) The header, date, slide, note text, footer, and page number

   (d) Placeholders for content

6. The title slide layout title placeholder may be:

   (a) Filled with the text that will appear as the title for every slide in the presentation

   (b) Filled with a color

   (c) Blank

   (d) Moved to a new location on the slide layout or deleted from the layout

7. Slide layouts may only contain:

   (a) One type of placeholder

   (b) Multiple placeholders of the same type

   (c) A title, content placeholder, headers, and footers

   (d) Four placeholders

8. Color schemes are:

   (a) Fifteen colors selected from 255

   (b) Based only on standard colors

   (c) Permanent and cannot be changed after they are applied to a presentation

   (d) Twelve colors selected from 16 million

9. Custom templates:

   (a) Can only be used in the presentation on which they are based

   (b) Are previewed prior to printing

   (c) Are created from existing presentations

   (d) Are created by modifying slide masters, color schemes, and backgrounds

10. Basic custom slide shows are:

    (a) Multiple subsets of a single presentation

    (b) Multiple presentations copied from one presentation

    (c) Linked from one presentation to another

    (d) Shells for building presentations

11. Basic custom slide shows cannot contain:

    (a) Slides that are not a part of the original presentation

    (b) Hidden slides

    (c) Some of the same slides used in other basic custom presentations based on the same original presentation

    (d) More than 25 slides

12. Custom animation:

    (a) Can only be used on basic custom slide shows

    (b) Includes effects that can be timed and triggered individually

    (c) Only appears on the title slide

    (d) Can only be set for one object on a slide

Multiple Choice Continued

13. Motion path animations:

(a) Apply only to graphic objects
(b) Cannot be combined with other animations
(c) Can be set for movement of the object along a custom path
(d) Confuse the audience

14. Which of the following rules does not apply to sound animations:

(a) Limit the sounds throughout the presentation.
(b) Use sound only in support of your message.
(c) Sounds must be a part of the Entrance effect of an object.
(d) Check the sound levels before the presentation to insure that the audience will be able to hear the effects.

15. Hidden slides:

(a) Cannot be combined with animations
(b) Are revealed by pressing H
(c) Can be set while the presentation is being made by pressing H to hide the next slide in the sequence if you don't want to show it
(d) Confuse the audience

Your manager prepared a presentation discussing the positive features of building a home using the services of Sunshine Buildings. You have been asked to modify the handouts so that the print-outs will have two slides per page and contain the date for Wednesday of next week, the company name, and a page number. The manager would also like to have the notes pages printed in an easy-to-read font, so you decide to modify the Notes master. The date will remain at the top of the page and the page number will be at the bottom. The headers placeholders will be deleted. Figure 6.40 shows a handout and Figure 6.41 shows a sample note page. Proceed as follows:

a. Open PowerPoint if you closed it after the last exercise and open the *chap6_pe1_sunshine* presentation. Save it as **chap6_pe1_building_solution**.

b. Click the **View tab** and click **Handout Master**.

c. Click **Slides Per Page** in the Page Setup group. Click **2 Slides**.

d. Uncheck the **Footer check box** on the Placeholders group.

e. Click on the **Date placeholder** and drag it to the former position of the Footer placeholder.

f. Click the **Header placeholder** and drag the handles so that the placeholder is as wide as the page and the bottom of the placeholder is at the top of the first slide.

g. Double-click the word **Header** in the Header placeholder. Type **Sunshine Buildings**. Press **Enter** and type your name, your instructor's name, and your class.

h. Click the **Home tab** and click **Center** in the Paragraph group. Select **Arial Black** font and **16** font size.

i. Click the **Date placeholder** and select the **Arial** font and **10** font size.

j. Select **Align Text Left** in the Font group. Click **Align text** in the Paragraph group and select **Bottom**.

k. Click the **Insert tab** and click **Header & Footer** in the Text group. Click the **Date and Time check box** and click the **Fixed** option. In the Fixed box, type **Wednesday**, followed by the **month and day** of Wednesday of next week, then click **Apply to All**.

l. Click the **Home tab**.

m. Click the **Page number placeholder** and select **Arial** font and **10** font size.

n. Click the **Handout Master tab** and click **Close Master View**.

o. Click the **Office Button** and click **Print Preview** from the Print option.

p. Click **Handouts 2 Slides per Page** in the Page Setup group and confirm that you have completed all of the requested settings. The handouts contain the name of the company centered at the head of the document. The date and page number are at the bottom of the page.

q. Click the **View tab** and click **Notes Master** in the Presentation Views group.

r. Remove the check for the **Header** in the Placeholders group.

s. Click the **Insert tab** and click **Header & Footer** in the Text group. Click the **Footer check box** in the dialog box. Click in the Footer box and type your name, your instructor's name, and your class, then click **Apply to All**.

t. Click the border of the Master text styles. Click the **Home tab**. Increase the font size to **16**.

u. Click the **Notes Master tab** and click **Close Master View**.

v. Click the **Office Button** and click **Print Preview** from the **Print** option.

w. Click **Notes Pages** in the Page Setup group.

x. Verify that the notes are in large text and that the page number and footer information are at the bottom of the page. Close the **Print Preview**.

y. Save and close the file. Exit PowerPoint if you do not want to continue with the next exercise at this time.

...continued on Next Page

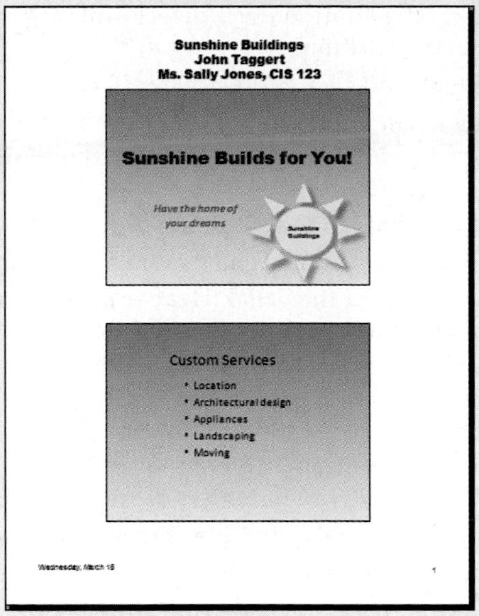

Figure 6.40   Handout Master Example

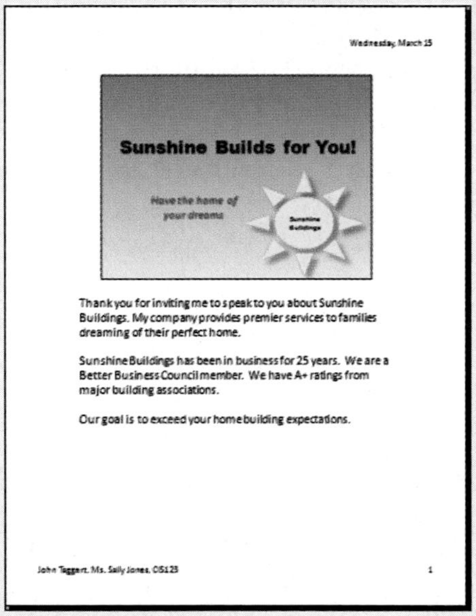

Figure 6.41   Notes Master Example

2 Working with Slide Masters

As the administrative clerk for the mayor of the city, you are responsible for preparing a PowerPoint presentation for every city council meeting. This slide show is the agenda for the meeting. The presentation contains a title slide listing the date of the meeting, location, the city's name, and the mayor's name. Each agenda item is listed on a single slide with the name of the person responsible for the discussion of this item. A third type of slide contains additional resources related to the agenda item, such as text, graphics, or SmartArt. You will create a slide master template so that the structure of the presentation is prepared. All you will have to do prior to the meeting is to put the information in the presentation using the template. Refer to Figure 6.42 for the slide master layouts.

...continued on Next Page

a. Open a blank presentation in PowerPoint and save it as a template named **chap6_pe2_mayor_solution**.

b. Click the **View tab** and click **Slide Master** in the Presentation Views group.

c. Select the **Slide master** in the slide layout thumbnail pane.

d. Click the **title placeholder**, and then click the **Home tab**. Select the font **Franklin Gothic Demi**. Select **Italic**.

e. Click the **text placeholder** and select the font **Franklin Gothic Book**.

f. Click the **Footer placeholder** and enter your name, your instructor's name, and your class.

g. Click the **Insert tab**, and then click **Header and Footer** in the Text group. Check **Date and Time** (update automatically), **Footer**, and **Slide Number**. Click **Apply to All**.

h. Select the **title slide layout** in the slide thumbnail pane. Click the **Insert tab** and **WordArt**. Select the third option down on the left, **Fill White Gradient Outline, Accent 1**, and type the **name of your town or city** followed by the words **City Council**. Move the WordArt to a position above the title placeholder.

i. Select the **Title** text and type **Enter the presiding person's name**.

j. Select the **Subtitle** text and type **Enter the meeting location**.

k. Select the **slide layouts** below the title slide layout and click **Delete**.

l. Click **Insert Layout** twice. Click the **first slide layout** and click **Rename**. Name the layout **Agenda Item**. Click the **second slide layout** and click **Rename**. Name the layout **Supporting Material**.

m. Select the **Agenda Item layout**. Click **Insert Placeholder**, select **Text**, and drag a placeholder that fills the open portion of the slide. Click the **title placeholder** and type **Click to Insert Agenda Title**.

n. Select the **Supporting Material layout**. Click **Insert Placeholder**, select **Content**, and drag a placeholder that fills the open portion of the slide. Click the title placeholder and type **Click to Insert Title**.

o. Save the *chap6_pe2_mayor_solution* template. Close the file and exit PowerPoint if you do not want to continue with the next exercise at this time.

Figure 6.42 Slide Master Setup

...continued on Next Page

The local historical society has elected you as the planner for the annual picnic. You decide to create a custom slide show color scheme and template for presentations you will make throughout the year leading up to the Fourth of July event. Figure 6.43 shows the customized color scheme and WordArt element. Figure 6.44 shows elements added to the content slide to customize the template.

a. Open the *chap6_pe3_july4* template and save it as a template named **chap6_pe3_july4_solution**.

b. Click the **View tab** and click **Slide Master** in the Presentation Views group.

c. Select the **slide master** from the slide thumbnail pane. Click the **Colors** arrow in the Edit Theme group.

d. Click **Create New Theme Colors**. Set the colors as detailed in the table:

Text/Background Dark 1	Red = 34, Green = 27, Blue = 127
Text/Background Light 1	Red = 255, Green = 255, Blue = 255
Text/Background Dark 2	Red = 250, Green = 20, Blue = 0
Text/Background Light 2	Red = 215, Green = 215, Blue = 250
Accent 1	Red = 27, Green = 27, Blue = 229
Accent 2	Red = 14, Green = 4, Blue = 160
Accent 3	Red = 113, Green = 107, Blue = 241
Accent 4	Red = 163, Green = 133, Blue = 247
Accent 5	Use Recent Colors—Dark Blue
Accent 6	Use Recent Colors—Blue

e. Click the **Name** box and enter **July 4**. Click **Save**.

f. Click **Background Styles** and select **Style 12**.

g. Select the **title slide layout** in the thumbnail slide pane. Click the **Insert** tab, and then click **WordArt**. Select **Fill Text2, Outline Background 2**, which is red. Type **July 4, 2008**, press Enter, and type **Picnic in the Park**.

h. Select the **content slide layout** in the thumbnail slide pane. Click the **Insert** tab, and then click **Shapes**. Select the **Rounded Rectangle** shape and draw a rectangle between the title placeholder and the content placeholder. Refer to Figure 6.44 for placement of the shape. Use the Drawing Tools Format tab to **Fill** the rectangle with the color **red**. Set the **Shape Effect** to **Offset Bottom Shadow**.

i. Click **Shapes** and select the **Star** shape. Draw a star at the bottom of the slide. Set the **Fill** to the color **white** and the **Shape Effect** to **Cool Slant Bevel**. Copy the star and paste it four times. Arrange the stars at the bottom of the slide as shown in Figure 6.44.

j. Click the **Slide Master tab** and click **Close Slide Master**.

k. Save the template and exit PowerPoint if you do not wish to continue with the next exercise.

...continued on Next Page

Figure 6.43   Color Scheme Setup with Title Slide WordArt

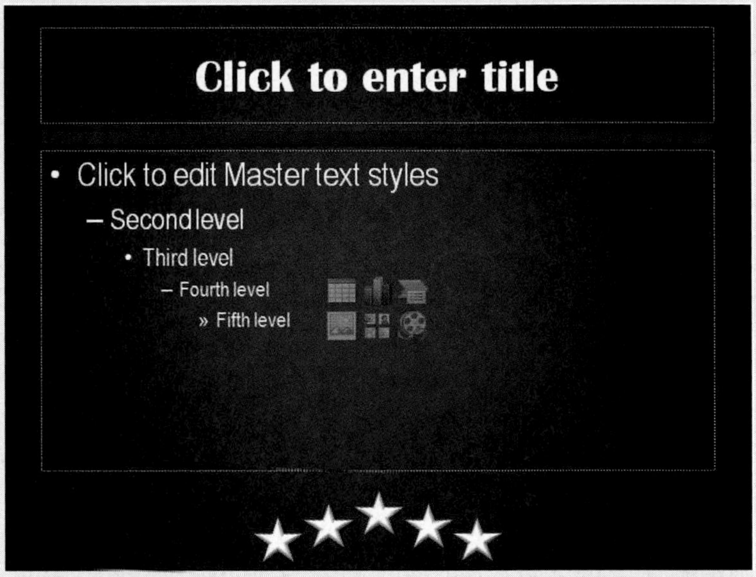

Figure 6.44   Custom Template Setup

4 Customizing Animations

Your job as a park ranger at the Mill Run Preserve takes you to schools and club meetings. Normally, you take a bird or other animal with you to discuss preserving wildlife. Recently, programs have been introduced at the Preserve that are designed for family adventures. Each time you make a visit to talk to groups, you now include the upcoming programs in your presentation. Animation and sounds add to the slides. Figure 6.45 shows the animation effects on the Hoots and Hollers slide.

a. Open the *chap6_pe4_park* file and save it as a file named **chap6_pe4_park_solution**.

b. Click the **second slide** in the slide thumbnail pane, click the **Animation tab**, and select **Custom Animation**.

c. Click the top-left owl photograph. Click **Add Effect**, select **Entrance**, and then click **More Effects**. Click **Fade** and **OK**. Click the **Start** arrow and select **With previous**. Click **Speed** and change it to **Very Slow**.

...continued on Next Page

d. Click on the owl photograph on the right. Click **Add Effect**, select **Entrance**, and then click **More Effects**. Click **Grow and Turn**. Click the **Start** arrow and select **After Previous**. Click **Speed** and change it to **Slow**.

e. Click the bottom left owl photograph. Click **Add Effect**, select **Entrance**, and then click **More Effects**. Click **Zoom**. Click the Start arrow and select **After Previous**. Click **Speed** and change it to **Slow**. Click the arrow next to the effect and select **Effect Options**. Click the **Sound** arrow and scroll down to **Other Sound**. Navigate to the **Owl.wav** file and select it. Click **OK**.

f. Click the third slide in the slide thumbnail pane. Select the large frog photograph. Click **Add Effect**, select **Entrance**, and then click **More Effects**. Click **Bounce**. Click the **Start** arrow and select **With Previous**. Click the arrow next to the effect and select **Effect Options**. Click the **Sound** arrow and scroll down to **Other Sound**. Navigate to the **Frogs.wav** file and select it. Click **OK**.

g. Select the small frog photograph. Click **Add Effect**, select **Entrance**, and then click **More Effects**. Click **Swivel**. Click the **Start** arrow and select **After Previous**. Click **Speed** and change it to **Slow**.

h. Select the fourth slide in the slide thumbnail pane. Click on the photograph of the nest. Click **Add Effect**, select **Motion Paths**, and then select **Left**. Click the **Start** arrow and select **With Previous**. Click **Speed**, and then select **Medium**. Click the arrow next to the effect and select **Effect Options**. Click the **Sound** arrow and scroll down to **Other Sound**. Navigate to the **Chicks.wav** file and select it. Click **OK**.

i. Click on the photograph of the bird chicks. Click **Add Effect**, select **Entrance**, and then click **More Effects**. Click **Fade**. Click the **Start** arrow and select **After Previous**. If you cannot see the Seconds Timeline, click the arrow next to the effect and select Show Advanced Timeline. **Scroll** the timeline until you can see the end of the time for the effect. Drag the **orange bar** until the effect is **6 seconds** long.

j. Click the title slide in the slide thumbnail pane. Select the ranger's name and replace it with your own.

k. Save the file and exit PowerPoint if you do not want to continue with the next exercise at this time.

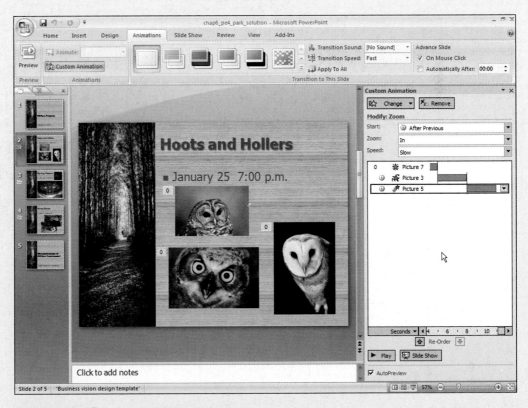

Figure 6.45 Custom Animation Setup

...continued on Next Page

This week, you will meet with two potential customers. The presentation has been created using the most recent photographs and information about estates that you have available. Each customer in the presentation has a title slide with his or her name. All the estate offerings are in the presentation. You create custom shows for each customer, highlighting the estates that fit their needs. You hide slides with the cost information on each estate, to show only if the customer expresses an interest in the property. Figure 6.46 shows the entire slide show with the hidden slides.

a. Open the *chap6_pe5_realestate* file and save it as a file named **chap6_pe5_realestate_ solution**.

b. Click the **Slide Show tab**, and then click **Custom Slide Show**. Click **Custom Shows** from the menu.

c. Click **New** and name the show **Roberts**.

d. Select slides **1, 3, 4, 5, 9, 10, 11**, and **18**. Click **Add**, and then click **OK**.

e. Click **New** and name the show **Lewis**.

f. Select slides **2** and **6–18**. Click **Add**, and then click **OK**.

g. Press **Ctrl** and select **slides 5, 8, 11, 14**, and **17**, in the slide thumbnail pane. Click **Hide Slide**.

h. Click the **Insert tab**, and then click **Header and Footer**. Change the footer to include your name, your instructor's name, and your class.

i. Click the **Slide Show tab**. Click **Custom Slide Show** and display the **Roberts** presentation. When complete, view the **Lewis** presentation. Remember to use H to display the hidden slides with cost information.

j. Save the *chap6_pe5_realestate_solution* file and close it.

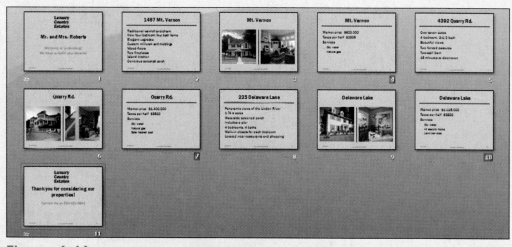

Figure 6.46 Roberts Custom Slide Show

The invitation to your next family reunion requests that each family provide a picture labeled with the names of the people in the picture from left to right, recent family information and accomplishments, and the connection of that family to your great-great-grandfather. As organizer of this reunion, you decide to create a presentation from these materials. You modify the slide masters so that you may quickly update the presentation. You plan three slide layouts for each family. The first layout shows a picture of the family, with a title of their family name, and a caption naming the people in the photograph. The second layout has a title and text placeholders for the family information and accomplishments. The third layout features SmartArt that shows the relationship of the family to the patriarch. You also create a unique color scheme for the presentation. The slide master view is shown in Figure 6.47.

a. Begin with a **New Blank** presentation and save it as a template called **chap6_mid1_reunion_solution**.

b. On the slide master, change the title placeholder font to **Cooper Black**, size 40. Change the text placeholder font to **Lucida Sans**.

c. On the title slide layout, move the title placeholder to the top of the slide. Select the text in the title placeholder and type **Family Name Here**.

d. Resize the subtitle text placeholder to be large enough for one line of text. Highlight the text in the subtitle placeholder and change the font size to **20**. Select the text in the subtitle placeholder and type **Family Member Names**.

e. Add a **Picture placeholder** in the middle of the slide.

f. Remove the date and page number placeholders from the title slide layout. Replace the text in the footer placeholder with your family name and the words **Reunion 2007**. Use the Header and Footer dialog box on the Insert tab to **apply the footer** to the title slide layout only.

g. Delete all other slide layouts. Insert a new slide layout. Rename the slide layout **Family Information**.

h. On the Family Information slide layout, select the text in the title placeholder and type **Family Name Here**.

i. Remove all footers from the Family Information slide layout. Add a placeholder to the slide layout for **text** that fills the blank space of the slide.

j. Copy the Family Information slide and paste it on the slide thumbnail pane. Rename the slide layout **Family Relationship**.

k. Remove the title and text placeholders on the Family Relationship slide layout. Insert a **SmartArt** placeholder that fills the blank space of the slide.

l. On the slide master, create a new color scheme. Name the color scheme **Reunion** and modify the color scheme in the following way:

Element	Red	Green	Blue
Text/Background—Dark 1	35	140	110
Text/Background—Light 1	250	250	175
Text/Background—Dark 2	25	20	65
Text/Background—Light 2	145	200	215

...continued on Next Page

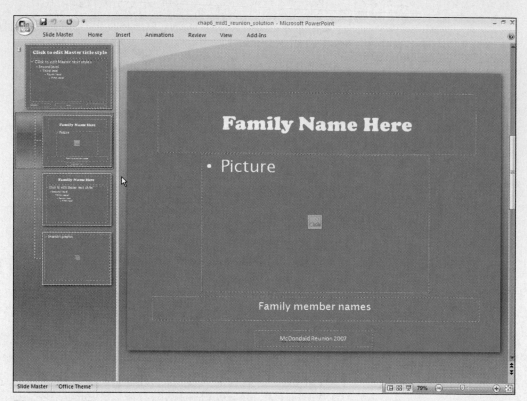

Figure 6.47 Family Reunion Template

m. Change the background style to Style 4.

n. Save the *chap6_mid1_reunion_solution* template and close the file.

2 PTA Fundraising

The PTA at the elementary school has regular meetings, where discussions focus on plans for fundraising throughout the year. At the beginning of the year, all of the plans are put into a PowerPoint presentation. Two slides cover the plans for each fundraising project. The slides contain the project description, dates, and committee assignments. At the end of the presentation, one slide details the budget for all of the fundraising activities. You create two custom shows that contain the title slide, the slides pertaining to the most recent project and the next project, and the budget slide. For fun, you animate the title on the title slide. You hide the budget slide in the presentation. Figure 6.48 shows the slides in the custom show and the hidden budget slide.

a. Open the *chap6_mid2_fundraising* presentation and save it as **chap6_mid2_fundraising_ solution**.

b. On the title slide of the presentation, animate the title with an entrance effect of **Fly In** that starts with previous, which causes the effect to begin when the slide loads.

c. Add a second animation to the title for emphasis with the effect of **Wave** after the previous effect plays at a **medium speed**.

d. Add a third animation to the title for an exit effect of **Faded Swivel**. Modify the timeline for the third animation so that it takes **4 seconds** for the animation to play.

e. Add an animation to the subtitle to **Grow with Color** at a **medium speed** after the previous effect has played. Change the color of that effect to **yellow**.

...continued on Next Page

f. Create a custom show called **Fall Projects**.

g. Add slides **1–5** and slide **8**.

h. Create a custom show called **Winter Projects**.

i. Add slides **1** and **4–8**.

j. Hide slide **8**.

k. Display the Fall Projects custom show. Show the hidden slide.

l. Display the Winter Projects custom show. Show the hidden slide.

m. Display the entire presentation. Show the hidden slide.

n. Save the file and close it.

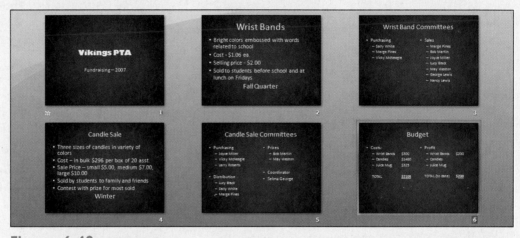

Figure 6.48 PTA Fall Projects Custom Slide Show

3 Psychology Lecture Presentation

Your psychology instructor has asked you to assist her in creating presentations for her PSY 150 course. After your discussions with her, you create a custom template with slide masters, handout masters, and Notes masters. The slide masters are shown in Figure 6.49.

a. Open a **New Blank** presentation and save it as a template called **chap6_mid3_psychology_solution**.

b. On the slide master, change the title placeholder font to **Verdana**, size **40**. Change the text placeholder font to **Verdana**, size **28**. Change the bullet style to **Filled Square Bullets**.

c. In the footer of the slide master, type the name of the course, **Psychology in the 21st Century**. Insert the **footer** accepting the Date and Time (automatically update), Slide number, and footer and apply to all slides.

d. On the title slide layout, select the text in the title placeholder and type **Chapter Title Here**. Select the text in the subtitle placeholder and type **Chapter Number Here**. Delete the slide number placeholder. Insert clip art appropriate for a psychology course above the title placeholder.

e. Delete all other slide layouts. Insert three new slide layouts. Rename one slide layout **Text Layout**. Rename the next slide layout **Photograph Layout**. Rename the last slide layout **Media Layout**.

...continued on Next Page

f. **Add** and **modify** the following placeholders to the slide layouts:

Slide Layout	Placeholder Type	Additional Modifications
Text layout	Text	Type **Concept Title** in the title placeholder. Draw a Rounded Rectangle between the title and the text placeholder. Select colors for the fill and outline that work well with the clip art used.
Photograph layout	Picture	Move title placeholder to just above the footer. Type **Photograph Title** in the title placeholder.
Media layout	Media	Remove the title placeholder.

g. On the handout master, allow three slides per page. Type **Psychology in the 21st Century** in the header placeholder. Change the size of the text in the header placeholder to **16**. In the footer, type your name, your instructor's name, and your class name.

h. On the Notes master, remove the date header and footer. Type **PSY 150** in the header and resize the header to fit across the page. Center the text in the header and change the size to **20**.

i. Save the *chap6_mid3_psychology_solution* template and close it.

Figure 6.49 Psychology Lecture Template

...continued on Next Page

4 Tabby Cat Gallery

As an owner/manager of the Tabby Cat Gallery, you decide to create a personalized work schedule for each employee every week. You prepare a custom template with a layout that includes days of the week and placeholders for the times the employee will work. You include a placeholder for the employee name. Because this is an art gallery, you add an appropriate graphic to the template. Figure 6.50 shows the template work schedule.

a. Begin with a **New Blank** presentation and save it as a template called **chap6_mid4_gallery_solution**.

b. On the slide master, change the title placeholder font to **Brush Script MT**.

c. On the title slide master, replace the text in the title placeholder with **Employee Name Here**. Move the placeholder to the top of the slide. Reduce the size of the subtitle placeholder so that it will hold one line of text. Replace the text in the subtitle placeholder with **Enter Week Here**.

d. On the title slide master, add a **text placeholder** so that it fills about two-thirds of the right of the slide. Change the text font to **Arial**, size **28**. Remove the text placeholders for level 2–level 5. Remove the **bullets** from the text placeholder. Type **Work hours here**.

e. On the left side of the title slide master, add a text placeholder. Repeat the changes for the font, size, placeholders, and bullets used above. Type **Work days here** and right-justify the text.

f. In the footer placeholder on the title slide layout, type the name of the gallery. Insert the footer and apply it. **Delete** the date and page number placeholders.

g. On the title slide layout, insert an appropriate clip art image. Resize the title placeholder if necessary.

h. **Delete** all other slide layouts.

i. Save the *chap6_mid4_gallery_solution* template and close it.

Figure 6.50 Employee Work Schedule Template

Capstone

As a volunteer docent at the Bayside Park Conservatory, you learned about plants and their care. You have specialized knowledge of exotic plants and roses. You have studied both in courses you have taken at the community college. The volunteer supervisor recently observed you as you led a group through the conservatory. She approached you about your willingness to serve as a speaker at various gardening guild meetings throughout the state. You have agreed to this exciting opportunity. In this capstone exercise, you will create a custom presentation demonstrating the skills learned in this chapter.

Slide Master Setup

You create slide masters for the presentation. You modify the fonts and placeholders. You alter the title slide layout. You insert two slide layouts that you customize. Figure 6.51 shows the slide master setup.

a. Begin with a new blank presentation and save it as a template called **chap6_cap_gardening_solution**.

b. Move to the **Slide Master View**.

c. On the **master slide**, select the text in the **title placeholder**. Using the Mini toolbar, change the font to **Eras Bold ITC**. Italicize the title text.

d. Change the text in the **text placeholder** to **Eras Demi ITC**.

e. Change the text in the footer placeholder to the Web address **www.bayparkconservatory.org**.

f. Apply the **footer** to all slides.

g. Change the text in the **title placeholder** to **Place title here**.

h. Change the text in the **subtitle placeholder** to **Place docent name and e-mail address here**.

i. Delete the other slide layouts and **insert two** new slide layouts.

j. Select the first slide layout and rename it **Information Layout**.

k. Replace the text in the title placeholder with **Title here**.

l. Fill the blank portion of the slide layout with a **text** placeholder.

m. Select the second slide layout and rename it **Photograph Layout**.

n. Replace the text in the title placeholder with **Plant name here**.

o. Fill the blank portion of the slide layout with a **picture** placeholder.

p. Delete the bullet from the picture placeholder and replace the word Picture with **Place photograph here**.

q. Close the Master.

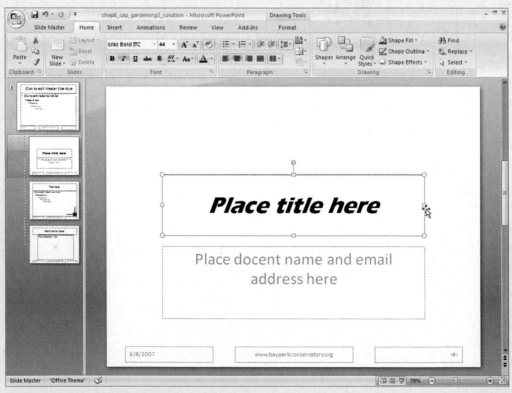

Figure 6.51 Gardening Slide Masters

Handout Master Setup

The handout master is modified to contain important information. You alter the number of slides per page. You apply the logo to the master. You modify the content of the header and footer. The handout layout is shown in Figure 6.52.

a. Move to the **Handout Master View**. Set the slides per page to **6**.

b. Select the **Header** text and enter **Bay Park Conservatory**, followed by your name. Change the font to **Eras Demi ITC**, size **14**.

c. Replace the Footer text with the Web address **www.bayparkconservatory.org**.

d. Close the Master View.

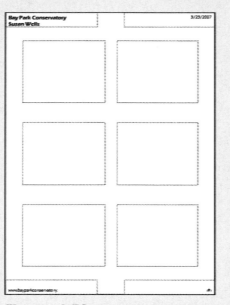

Figure 6.52 Gardening Handout Masters

Custom Color Scheme

You need to create a unique color scheme that will complement the colors of the plants you will show. You apply the color scheme to the master slide and set the background style. Figure 6.53 shows the color scheme added to the slide master.

a. Move to the **Slide Master View**.

b. Select the **slide master** and create a new color theme, called Gardening Colors, as follows:

c. Apply the **Background Style 2**.

d. Close Master View.

Element	Red	Green	Blue
Text/Background—Dark 1	35	70	45
Text/Background—Light 1	215	250	200
Text/Background—Dark 2	0	95	105
Text/Background—Light 2	250	250	210

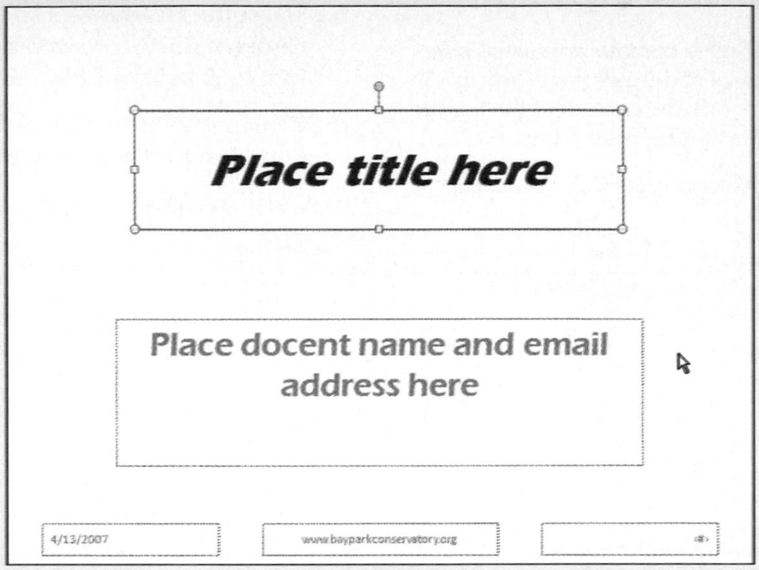

Figure 6.53 Gardening Color Scheme

On the custom template, you add graphic objects to enhance the layouts. On the title slide, you insert the logo. On the Information Layout, you add some shapes. You repeat the shapes on the Photograph Layout. Figure 6.54 shows the title slide with the custom template layout.

a.   Move to the **Slide Master View**.

b.   Insert the *baypark.gif* file onto the **title slide layout**. Move the image to the top left of the slide. Resize and move the title placeholder to the right of the logo.

c.   Select the **Information layout**. At the right bottom of the text placeholder, draw a small square. Fill it with Dark Green, Text 1, Lighter 40%, outlined in Dark Green, Text 1, Darker 50%. Draw two lines that intersect in the middle of the square using Dark Green, Text 1, Darker 50%.

d.   Select the **Photograph layout**. Between the title placeholder and the picture placeholder, draw a line with a fill of Dark Green, Text 1, Lighter 40%.

e.   Close the Master View.

Figure 6.54 Gardening Custom Template

Custom Animation Setup

On the custom template, you add a custom animation to the title slide layout. You add effects that are subtle but add interest. The title slide with animations is shown in Figure 6.55.

a. Move to the **Slide Master View**.

b. Select the **title layout placeholder**.

c. Apply the Entrance animation effect of **Fade** to start with the previous action.

d. Apply the Emphasis animation effect of **Shimmer**, to occur after the previous action at a fast speed.

e. Select the **subtitle placeholder** and apply an Entrance effect of **Crawl In** after the previous effect and at a very slow speed.

f. Close the Master View.

g. Save the *chap6_cap_gardening_solution* template and close it.

Figure 6.55 Gardening Animations

Custom Show Setup and Display

You create two slide shows using a single presentation. Both will contain the title slide, the information about the conservatory, and slides specific to the slide show. One slide will be hidden in each presentation. Figure 6.56 shows the complete slide show.

a. Open the *chap6_cap_gardening2* presentation and save it as **chap6_cap_gardening2_solution**.

b. Create a custom show named **Rose Presentation**, with slides **1, 3–7**, and **14–18**.

c. Create a custom show named **Exotic Plant Presentation**, with slides **2** and **8–15**.

d. Hide slide **14**.

e. Display the entire presentation.

f. Display the Rose Presentation. Display the hidden slide.

g. Display the Exotic Plant Presentation.

h. Save the *chap6_cap_gardening2_solution* template and close it.

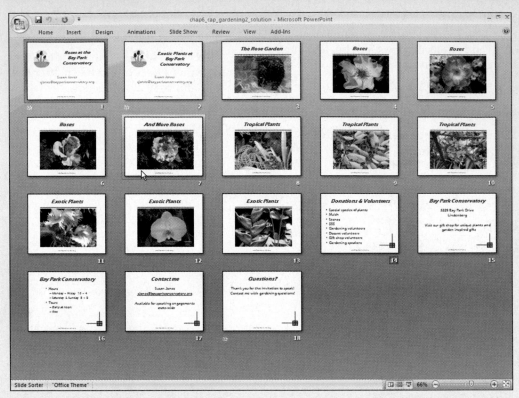

Figure 6.56 Gardening Slide Show

Mini Cases

Use the rubric following the case as a guide to evaluate your work, but keep in mind that your instructor may impose additional grading criteria or use a different standard to judge your work.

Franklin Food Advertisements

GENERAL CASE

The Franklin Food Company operates small grocery stores in communities with populations of fewer than 3,000 people. The same products are advertised for each of the stores in the local papers. Each week, you are asked to create a new advertisement. Some of the information remains fairly stable from week to week. The store name and logo appear in the same place on every advertisement. Photographs of food products along with sale prices are changed each week. Three food products are featured every week. To streamline your work, create a custom template with placeholders and a custom color scheme based on the company colors. Include at least two graphic elements in your layout. Save your file as a template called **chap6_mc1_food_solution**. Use the template to prepare a store ad for the week. Save your file as **chap6_mc1_food2_solution**.

Performance Elements	Exceeds Expectations	Meets Expectations	Below Expectations
Organization	Placeholders for the store name and logo are named appropriately. Placeholders for products are creatively arranged.	Placeholders for the store name and logo are on the layout, but are not named. Placeholders for products are arranged in a grid format.	There are not enough placeholders for all of the elements. The placeholders overlap or appear to be haphazardly arranged. The placeholders are not named.
Visual aspects	The placeholders for the store name and logo are logically placed. Graphic elements fit the purpose of the advertisement. There is a consistent visual theme.	Placeholders for store name and logo are not logically placed. Some of the graphic elements are inconsistent in form and theme.	The placeholders for the products are too large/small in size. The graphic elements do not relate to the purpose of the advertisement.
Layout	The layout is visually pleasing. White space aids in reading the advertisement.	The layout shows some structure, but lack of white space makes the advertisement difficult to read.	The layout is cluttered and confusing. Readers do not understand the advertisement.
Mechanics	Presentation has no errors in spelling, grammar, word usage, or punctuation. No typographical errors present.	Presentation has no more than two errors in spelling, grammar, word usage, or punctuation.	Presentation readability is impaired due to repeated errors in spelling, grammar, word usage, or punctuation. Multiple typographical errors.

Colds, Flu, or Worse

RESEARCH CASE

As a nurse practitioner with the Lindenberg Health Department, you spend a few hours each week talking to small groups. One week, you might talk to an elementary school class, and the next week, you may be presenting to senior citizens. Popular topics in the winter are colds, flu, bronchitis, and pneumonia. Most groups request information on the symptoms of these illnesses and ways to prevent getting them. After your research, you develop a presentation that contains information that will be useful to all of these groups. Use your knowledge of slide masters to create appropriate layouts. Use custom animation on your slides. Include at least five graphics that are appropriate to the topic. You realize that elementary school students probably aren't interested in bronchitis and pneumonia, so create a custom slide show on colds and flu just for these students. Save the new presentation as **chap6_mc2_nurse_solution**.

Performance Elements	Exceeds Expectations	Meets Expectations	Below Expectations
Organization	Presentation indicates accurate research and significant facts. Evidence exists that information has been evaluated and synthesized, showing an understanding of the topic.	Presentation indicates some research has taken place and that information was included in the content.	Presentation demonstrates a lack of research or understanding of the topic.
Visual aspects	Presentation background, themes, clip art, and animation are appealing and enhance the understanding of presentation purpose and content. There is a consistent visual theme.	Some of the clip art or shapes seem to be unrelated to the presentation purpose and content and do not enhance the overall concepts. Images are too large/small in size. Animation is distracting.	The background or theme is distracting to the topic. Images do not enhance understanding of the content or are unrelated.
Layout	The layout is visually pleasing and contributes to the overall message with appropriate use of headings, subheadings, bullet points, clip art, and white space. The custom show contains slides that focus on the topics for elementary students.	The layout shows some structure, but placement of some headings, subheadings, bullet points, images, and/or white space is distracting. The custom show does not include all of the information on the elementary school topics.	The layout is cluttered and confusing. Placement of headings, subheadings, bullet points, images, and/or white space detracts from readability. A custom show was not created.
Mechanics	Presentation has no errors in spelling, grammar, word usage, or punctuation. Bullet points are parallel.	Presentation has no more than two errors in spelling, grammar, word usage, or punctuation. Bullet points are inconsistent in several slides.	Presentation readability is impaired due to repeated errors in spelling, grammar, word usage, or punctuation. Most bullet points are not parallel.

Animation Gone Haywire

DISASTER RECOVERY

Your fourteen-year-old brother has been working on a presentation that will be shown during Science Fair judging. Once he discovered the animations in PowerPoint, he loaded every slide and every element with multiple animations and sounds. His presentation is a mixed-up jumble of words and graphics flying all over the screen. Although he likes all of the action, you offer him your advice. You explain that the judges will be adults who will find all of the movement and sound distracting to his message. After much discussion, your brother finally sees your point and agrees with you. You offer to help him sort out the mess, and you both sit down on a Saturday afternoon to work together on the presentation. You also offer to help him with his spelling and grammar. Open the file *chap6_mc3_animation* and make adjustments to the animations. Save the file as **chap6_mc3_animation_solution**.

Performance Elements	Exceeds Expectations	Meets Expectations	Below Expectations
Visual aspects	Each slide contains an effective animation.	Each slide contains two animations.	Each slide contains elements with multiple animations applied.
Audio aspects	Sounds are appropriate to the message of the slide when used.	Every slide contains an appropriate sound effect.	Sounds occur on entry and exit of all slides.
Mechanics	Text has no errors in spelling, grammar, word usage, or punctuation. No typographical errors present.	Text has no more than two errors in spelling, grammar, word usage, or punctuation.	Text has impaired readability due to repeated errors in spelling, grammar, word usage, or punctuation. Multiple typographical errors.

Web Presentations

Adding Interactivity and Using Web Features

bjectives

After you read this chapter, you will be able to:

1. Insert and use hyperlinks **(page 496)**.

2. Add action buttons **(page 500)**.

3. Use a trigger **(page 504)**.

4. Save a presentation as a single file Web page **(page 516)**.

5. Save a presentation as a Web page **(page 517)**.

6. Preview a Web page **(page 518)**.

7. Publish a Web page **(page 523)**.

8. Set Web page options **(page 524)**.

Hands-On Exercises

Exercises	Skills Covered
1. USING HYPERLINKS AND ACTION BUTTONS (page 507) **Open:** chap7_ho1_review.pptx **Attach:** chap7_ho1_applause.wav, chap7_ho1_incorrect.wav, chap7_ho1_sorry.wav, chap7_ho1_tryagain.wav, and chap7_ho1_reference.docx **Save as:** chap7_ho1_review_solution.pptx	• Insert and Edit an E-Mail Hyperlink • Assign an Action to a Clip Art Object • Create and Edit Sound Action Buttons • Create Action Buttons for Navigation on a Slide Master • Create a Trigger • Create a Hyperlink to an Existing File • Test Hyperlinks and Action Buttons
2. SAVING WEB PAGES (page 519) **Open:** chap7_ho1_review_solution.pptx **Save as:** chap7_ho2_review_solution.mht and chap7_ho2_review_solution.htm	• Save a Presentation as a Single File Web Page • Save a Presentation as a Web Page • Preview a Web Page
3. PUBLISHING A WEB PAGE (page 526) **Open:** chap7_ho1_review_solution.pptx (from Exercise 1) **Save as:** chap7_ho3_review_revised.pptx and chap7_ho3_review_revised.htm	• Set Web Options • Publish the Web Page

CASE STUDY

Get Up & Go

The alarm rings and you struggle to get out of bed. If you are typical of your generation, you may begin your day with some type of hot drink, such as hot chocolate, coffee, or tea, none of which offers significant nutritional value. There should be a better choice, and the food products company where you are interning this summer is planning to introduce an alternative beverage. The product is named **Get Up & Go**, and it is slated for introduction into the college market next fall. The company believes that there is a large potential demand for a beverage that contains a significant portion of the daily recommended nutritional requirement as recommended by the FDA (Food and Drug Administration).

Marketing personnel often conduct focus groups in which a group of people are questioned about their attitude towards products, services, and concepts. The **Get Up & Go** marketing department has conducted a series of focus groups to determine consumer preferences for the precise formulation of the new drink. The study also sought to determine

whether consumers would be inclined to give up their morning coffee in favor of the new drink. These sessions are over, and it is your task to complete a PowerPoint presentation that shows the results. The presentation is to be posted to the company's internal Web site for others to view. This is an ideal assignment for you because you are an avid hot chocolate drinker, and you have wanted to complete a project that reviews many of the skills you have learned in Office 2007. Your internship is paid, and you get college credit upon completing the presentation.

Your Assignment

- Read the chapter, paying special attention to how to create hyperlinks and action buttons. Review how to save the presentation as a Web page.
- Use shapes, clip art, and/or WordArt to create a logo for *Get Up & Go*.
- Select a theme for the presentation, and then edit the master so that the slides incorporate the logo you designed. Make any other desired modifications to the logo.
- The presentation is confidential, and this should be indicated at the bottom of each slide in the Slide footer.
- To bring the information into your custom-designed presentation, use the Reuse Slides feature to insert all of the slides from the *chap7_case_getup&go.pptx* presentation. Edit as necessary to obtain a professional look in your slide show.
- Edit the *Focus Group Design* slide to create a hyperlink of the text *Click here to see results*. The link should take you to the *Formulation Preferences* slide.
- Hide the *Formulation Preferences* slide so that it can only be viewed by activating the hyperlink. Create a "return" action button on this slide that will take you to the *Study Design* slide.
- Edit the hyperlink to the Recommended Dietary Allowance (RDA) guidelines in the *Study Design* slide to include a ScreenTip that reads **Click here to view RDA Guidelines**.
- Animate the slide show as you desire, and include limited sound effects if desired.
- Save the slide show as **chap7_case_getup&go_solution**.
- Create a Notes and Handouts header with your name and a footer with your instructor's name and your class. Print Handouts, four slides per page, framed.
- Save the presentation as a Web page, but you are not required to post the presentation to a Web server unless requested to do so by your instructor.

Hyperlinks and Action Buttons

A *linear presentation* progresses sequentially starting with the first slide and ending with the last slide.

Interactivity is the ability to branch or interact based upon decisions made by a viewer or audience.

A *non-linear presentation* progresses based upon choices made by the viewer that affect which slide comes next.

A typical PowerPoint presentation is a *linear presentation*. In a linear presentation, the viewer or audience progresses sequentially through slides starting with the first slide and advancing in a straight-line fashion until the last slide is reached—much like watching a film where the final ending is set. In a linear PowerPoint presentation, each slide is designed to move one right after another until the conclusion. If you add *interactivity*, or the ability to branch to another area based upon decisions made by a viewer or audience, you create a *non-linear presentation*. Adding interactivity involves your audience in your presentation, helps retain their attention, and captures their interest. In addition to this, the ability to customize your presentation to allows you to focus your message on the needs or interests of the audience. The flexibility and spontaneity of a non-linear presentation typically free you to become more conversational with the audience, which leads to even more interaction.

When you are displaying the slide show and position the mouse pointer over a hyperlink, the mouse pointer becomes a hand pointer. If the hyperlink is attached to

(Adding interactivity involves your audience in your presentation, helps retain their attention, and captures their interest.)

text, the text color will be different from regular text and the text will be underlined. Click the hyperlink and you jump to a new location. The first time you click the hyperlink, the color of the hyperlink changes so that you know the link has been previously accessed. The color of the unused link and the used link is set by the theme you have applied to your slide show.

One common way you can add interactivity to your slide show is to create hyperlinks for navigation. To use interactivity for navigation, you create buttons or text that can be used to branch to another slide. This allows you, as a presenter, to tailor your presentation to the needs of the audience based on the audience's questions. If a single viewer is navigating through the slide show, the viewer can choose his/her own route through the presentation and visit the slides desired to gain more information in areas of interest. The viewer can also advance through the presentation at a comfortable pace and review as needed.

Another common use of interactivity in a PowerPoint presentation, especially in an educational environment, is as a quiz to test and review knowledge. A slide can present a question and a selection of answers. When the viewer chooses an answer, a feedback slide appears letting the viewer know if the answer is correct or incorrect. If the viewer's choice is correct, the show moves forward to the next question. If the viewer's choice is incorrect, the show moves the student back to re-answer the question. The movement between slides is not one-way, but non-linear because the path through the show is determined by the viewer's interaction with it. Figure 7.1 demonstrates the sequential progression through a linear slide show and the multiple paths that could be available with a non-linear slide show. In the non-linear slide show, Slide 1 could include a menu option enabling the viewer to choose any of the remaining five slides, and the remaining slides could be designed to allow the viewer to navigate back to the first slide or other related slides.

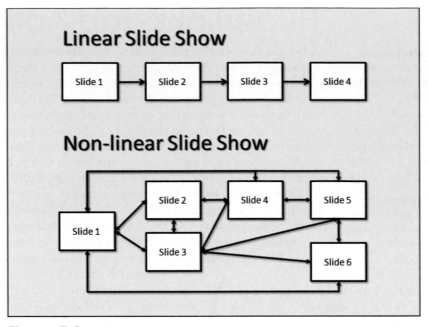

Figure 7.1 Linear Versus Non-Linear Navigation Options in a Slide Show

In this section, you add interactivity to a slide show by adding hyperlinks, action buttons, and a trigger. Interactivity can be added to a slide show through the use of hyperlinks, action buttons, and triggers.

Inserting and Using Hyperlinks

You have previously used the Internet to complete exercises in this text and you hyperlinked between two custom shows in Chapter 6, so you are familiar with using a hyperlink, a connection between two locations. PowerPoint enables you to attach a hyperlink to any selected object such as text, shapes, images, charts, and even SmartArt or WordArt. The hyperlink enables you to jump to almost any type of location. Select the type of location to which you want to move by using the buttons on the left side of the dialog box. You can link to:

- A Web page or a file on the Web
- A slide in a different presentation or an existing file
- A slide in the open presentation
- A new file
- An e-mail address

Regardless of the location to which you want to move, the process for inserting a hyperlink is basically the same. First, you select the object you want the link attached to, you click the Insert tab, and then you click Hyperlink in the Links group. The Insert Hyperlink dialog box appears in which you select the location you wish to link to. The remaining options vary depending on the location you select.

TIP Using Other Methods to Insert Hyperlinks

Instead of using the Ribbon to attach a hyperlink, you can use the keyboard short-cut Ctrl+K to open the Insert Hyperlink dialog box. You can also right-click the selected object and choose Hyperlink from the shortcut menu.

Link to a Web Page or an Existing File

When you open the Insert Hyperlink dialog box, the Link to Existing File or Web page is selected by default. If you selected text before opening the dialog box, the text appears in the Text to display box at the top of the dialog box. If you did not select text, you may enter the text you wish to be displayed on your slide in this box.

A ***Uniform Resource Locator (URL)*** is the address of resources on the Web.

At the bottom of the dialog box is an address box where you enter the ***Uniform Resource Locator (URL)***, or Web address, of the Web page you wish to link to. If you know the address, you can type the URL in the box. If you do not know the URL, you can find it in one of several ways. If you visited the page recently, you can simply click on it from the list of URLs shown. You can also click the Browsed Pages button. This will show a list of the places you have recently visited on the Web. If the URL does not show up, you can click the Browse the Web button which opens your browser. You can then browse for the Web page. When you locate the page, press Alt+Tab to switch back to PowerPoint. The URL will appear in the Address box. If you prefer, you can copy the URL from the Web page address box, close the browser, and then paste the URL in the dialog box.

Figure 7.2 shows the Balancing image slide, one of Microsoft's Content slides. Text identifying the location of the balancing rocks is selected so that a link to a Web site giving information about the rocks can be attached. The Insert Hyperlink dialog box is open, showing the selected text in the Text to display box. Recently browsed Web pages are shown in the list, and the hyperlink to the desired Web site is shown in the address box.

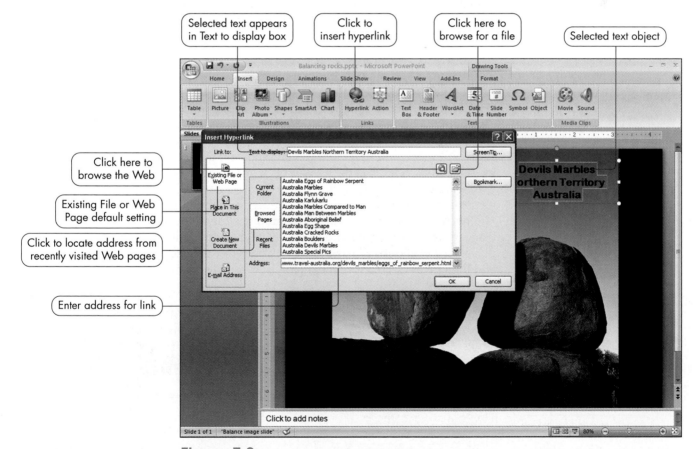

Figure 7.2 Insert Hyperlink Dialog Box

If you want to link to another document stored on your computer or a network, you can use this same method. Instead of selecting Browsed Pages in the Insert Dialog box, click either Current Folder or Recent Files to navigate to the file location. Select the file and create the link. If you know the path name and file name, you can type it in the dialog box instead of browsing to locate the file. When you click the link during your presentation, the application in which the file was created opens and your file displays.

TIP   Linking Picture Files

What if you have a company logo that you want to use in all presentations you create? Every time you insert the logo in a presentation, the picture file is embedded in a presentation. The same picture is embedded multiple times, wasting space on your storage drive. Rather than embed the picture, you can create a picture link to keep your PowerPoint file sizes much smaller. To create the link, click the Insert tab, and then click Picture in the Illustrations group. Browse for the picture you want; when you locate it, instead of clicking Insert, click the list arrow next to Insert, and then click Link to File. PowerPoint inserts a link to your picture instead of embedding the picture file in your slide show. The link stores the entire path to the file, the location of the picture, and the picture size. An added bonus is that if you ever have to change the logo, you replace the old logo file with the new logo file in the same location. When a presentation is opened with the linked picture path, the new logo appears, so you don't have to replace the logo over and over.

Link to a Slide in the Open Presentation

The ability to link to another slide in the presentation gives you many options for displaying your content. One example is a menu displaying topics that you or your viewer can click. After your choice on the menu, the presentation branches to the slide exploring content related to your choice. The last slide of each topic area could include a link that takes the viewer back to the menu slide. Creating links also gives you flexibility when presenting because you can use links to branch to the slides that focus on your audience's anticipated questions or comments.

To create a link that branches to another slide in the slide show, you would select Place in This Document from the Insert Hyperlink dialog box. PowerPoint then displays a list of slides in the slide show. You select the slide to which you wish to link, and then press OK to close the dialog box (see Figure 7.3).

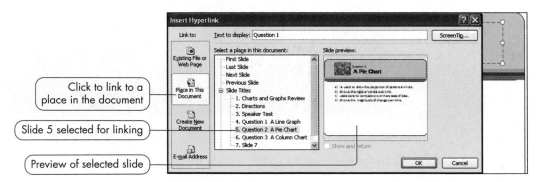

Figure 7.3 Link to a Place in the Document

Link to a New Document

Clicking the Create New Document option lets you create a hyperlink and a new PowerPoint presentation at the same time. This option enables you to enter a file name for the new presentation and designate the location for the new presentation. In addition to that, you can specify if you want to open the new presentation immediately for editing or you can choose to edit later. Regardless of which option you choose, the link is created immediately. Figure 7.4 shows the options for creating a new presentation with the file name *Using Interactivity* and opening it for immediate editing.

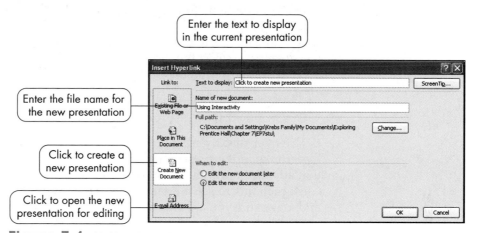

Figure 7.4 Linking to a New Presentation

Link to an E-Mail Address

You can add an e-mail link to a slide if you select the E-mail Address option in the Insert Hyperlink dialog box. This allows your viewer to contact you for more information and is especially helpful if you post your presentation on the Web. To create the link, click the E-mail Address button, and then type the address in the Address box. A shortcut to doing this, however, is simply to type your e-mail address directly on the slide (see Figure 7.5). PowerPoint will automatically format it as a link for you.

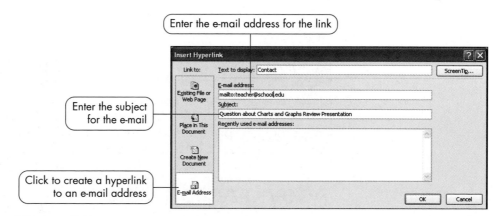

Figure 7.5 Creating an E-Mail Link

Add a ScreenTip

To help a viewer determine whether or not to click a hyperlink, you can insert a ScreenTip that will display when the viewer points to the hyperlink. The ScreenTip should provide information about the link. The text you enter in the ScreenTip will appear below the link. You can add a ScreenTip to any of the hyperlink locations discussed above. To add the ScreenTip, click the ScreenTip button in the Insert Hyperlink dialog box. PowerPoint displays the Set Hyperlink ScreenTip dialog box. Type the text you want to display in the box.

An excellent use of ScreenTips is to define technical or new terms in a presentation. When you or your viewer rolls the mouse over the term, a ScreenTip will appear with the definition. To use a ScreenTip in this manner, create and select a text box with the new word inside it, or select text in the body of information on your slide, click the Insert tab, and then click Hyperlink in the Links group. Link to Place in This Document and select the slide you are currently in. Finally, click the ScreenTip button and type in the definition for the word you selected.

Check and Modify or Remove a Hyperlink

Before ever displaying a presentation to an audience, be sure to check each of the hyperlinks in the presentation. View your presentation and test each hyperlink as you advance through the show. Check to see if the ScreenTips you entered display. Click each link to see if it takes you to the proper location. Close the linked location and make sure you are returned to the presentation. If you find a hyperlink that does not link properly, stop the slide show immediately and fix that link. This ensures that you do not forget to fix the link that does not work. Edit the nonworking link and then repeat the testing process until you have tested every link.

You can quickly edit your hyperlinks in the Edit Hyperlink dialog box. Select the object with the hyperlink attached, and then click the Hyperlink button in the Links group on the Insert tab. You may also press Ctrl+K or right-click on the selected object and click Edit Hyperlink. Once the Edit Hyperlink dialog box opens, you can modify the existing hyperlink.

To remove the hyperlink, click Remove Link in the Edit Hyperlink dialog box. As an alternative, right-click the selected object, and then click Remove Hyperlink from the shortcut menu. If you delete the object to which a hyperlink is attached, the hyperlink is also deleted. The keyboard shortcut for removing a selected hyperlink is Ctrl+Shift+F9.

TIP Attaching Hyperlinks to All Slides

If you want the same hyperlink or group of hyperlinks to appear on every slide in a presentation, attach the hyperlink to an object on the slide master. Make sure you attach it to the primary master (the top slide master).

Adding Action Buttons

An ***action button*** is a ready-made button designed to serve as an icon to which an action can be assigned.

You may prefer to add interactivity by using ***action buttons***, buttons that Microsoft designed to serve as icons that can be clicked to initiate an action. Action buttons can contain shapes such as arrows and symbols. Not only can action buttons hyperlink to another location, they can display information, movies, documents, sound, and the Help feature. Action buttons are excellent tools for navigating a slide show and are especially useful if you want to create a presentation for a *kiosk*, an interactive computer terminal available for public use. Campuses and malls frequently have kiosks available for use. An interactive slide show is perfect for a kiosk display.

A ***kiosk*** is an interactive computer terminal available for public use.

Table 7.1 lists the 12 different ready-made buttons that PowerPoint includes in the Shapes gallery.

Table 7.1   PowerPoint Ready-Made Action Buttons

Action Button Icon	Action Button	Default Button Behavior
◁	Back or Previous	Moves to previous slide
▷	Forward or Next	Moves to next slide
◁	Beginning	Moves to first slide in the slide show
▷	End	Moves to the last slide in the slide show
⌂	Home	Moves to the first slide of the slide show by default, but can be set to go to any slide
ⓘ	Information	Can be set to move to any slide in the slide show, a custom show, a URL, another presentation or another file in order to reveal information
↩	Return	Returns to previous slide view regardless of the location in the slide show
🎞	Movie	Can be set to play a movie file
🗋	Document	Can be set to load a document in the application that was used to create it
🔊	Sound	Can be set to play a sound when clicked
?	Help	Can be set to open the Help feature or a Help document
☐	Custom	Can be set to move to a slide in the slide show, a custom show, a URL, another PowerPoint presentation, a file, or a program; or to run a macro, add an action to an object, or play a sound

To insert an action button, click the Home or Insert tab, click the Shapes button, and then click the action button you want from the bottom of the Shapes gallery. Figure 7.6 shows the open shapes gallery with the action button designed to return to the beginning of a slide show selected.

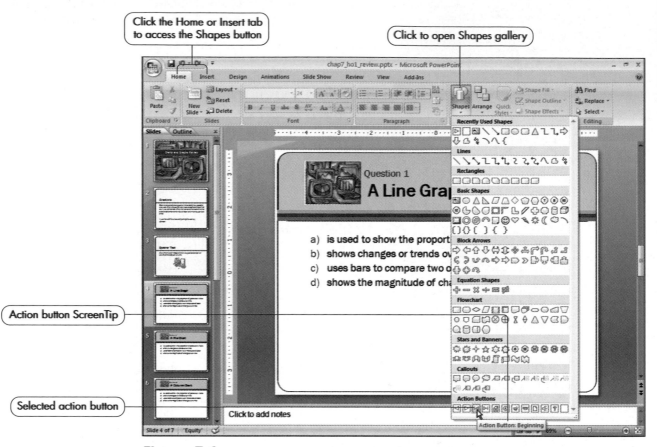

Figure 7.6   Action Buttons Displayed in Shapes Gallery

TIP   Attaching Actions to Objects

You do not have to create an action button to use actions. Select any object **except a SmartArt object**, and then click Actions in the Links group on the Insert tab. The Action Settings dialog box opens so that you can select the type of action and how you want the action to be initiated. Action settings give your presentation life! Know, however, that you cannot assign an action to a SmartArt object at this time.

After you select the desired action button from the gallery, drag it onto the slide to create the button. Release the mouse button when the action button is the size you desire. When you release the mouse button, the Action Settings dialog box opens. The Action Settings dialog box enables you to select the action you desire and the way you initiate the action. You can initiate the action by clicking on the button, or by moving the mouse over the button. Regardless of which of these two methods of initiation you select, the action options are the same.

You can choose to have the action button hyperlink to various locations in the slide show, a Custom Show, a URL, other PowerPoint presentations, or another file. To hyperlink to a specific slide in the slide show, click Slide . . . , and then select the slide you desire from the resulting list. To have the action button link to a specific program, click Run program, and then browse to locate the program you wish to open.

You can also program the action button to run a macro or to add an action to an object. Figure 7.7 shows the settings for an action button that returns to the previous slide.

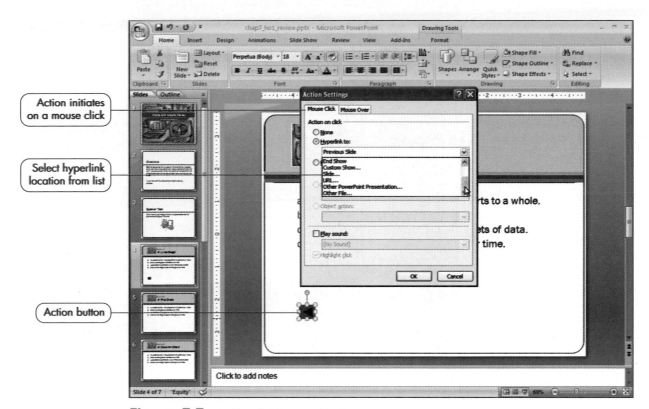

Figure 7.7 Action Setting Dialog Box

TIP   Returning to the Last Slide Viewed

The Return action button returns you to the last slide you viewed, regardless of its location in the presentation. The Previous button takes you to the slide preceding the slide you are currently viewing.

Any object on a slide may be turned into an action button. You are not restricted to using the action buttons at the bottom of the Shapes gallery. For example, you can select a clip art object and then apply an action to the image. To add an action to a selected object, click the Insert tab, and then click the Action button in the Links group. The Action Settings dialog box opens, and you can select whether you want the action to activate by a mouse click or a mouse over. Finally, select the action you wish to assign to the object. Figure 7.8 shows a selected rounded rectangle shape. The Action Settings options are set to initiate the hyperlink to the Phase 2 Violence slide upon a mouse over.

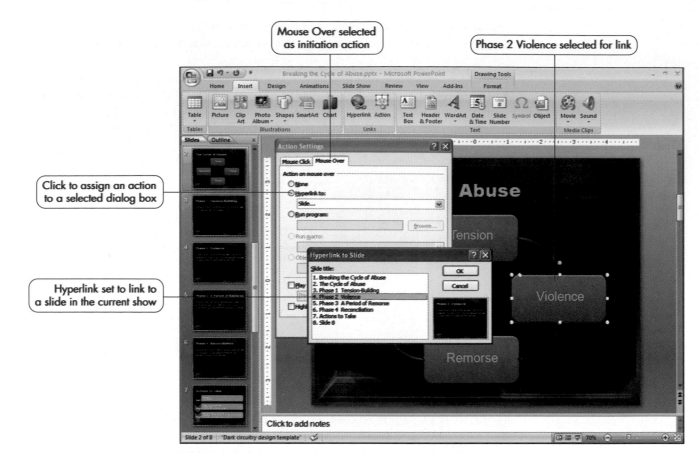

Figure 7.8 Action Setting for a Selected Object

Add Sound to an Object

Sound can be added to a hyperlink attached to an object. Click the Insert tab, and then click the Action button in the Links group. Select either the Mouse Click or Mouse Over tab, and then select the Play Sound checkbox. Click the Play Sound list arrow, and then click the sound you want to play when the object is clicked during the show. To assign a custom sound, you can scroll to the bottom of the Play Sound list, click Other Sound, browse for the sound, and then select it.

PowerPoint has a pre-made action button for sound that you can use to insert a sound in your slide show. Click the Insert tab, and then click Shapes in the Illustrations group. Click the Sound Action Button at the bottom of the list in the Action Buttons category. Drag to create the sound action button, and then click the Play Sound list arrow. Select the sound you want, and then click OK.

Using a Trigger

A ***trigger*** is an animation that sets off an action when you click the associated object.

Another way to introduce interactivity into your presentation is through the use of triggers. A ***trigger*** is an animation attached to an object that sets off an action when clicked. For example, you can create an object that, when clicked, is an animation trigger that plays a sound or a movie. You can even set up a trigger to make text or images appear. This is an excellent way to create pop-up windows in your presentation. This adds interactivity to your presentation because the viewer chooses whether or not to click the object setting off the trigger. Remember these two key points about triggers: A trigger cannot be set up without using animation, and a trigger must be acted upon—clicked or moused over—for the action to take place.

To set up a trigger, select the object to which you wish to apply the trigger, click the Animations tab, and then click Custom Animation in the Animations group. Click the Add Effect button in the Custom Animation task pane, and then apply the animation of your choice. The object will be selected in the Custom Animation list. Click the arrow and select Timing. The Appear dialog box, which includes the Triggers button, will display. Click the Triggers button. By default, the trigger animates as part of a click sequence—the method you have been using for animations to this point. Click Start effect on click, and then drop down the list of objects that can be used for the trigger. Select the object you want to click on, and then click OK. Figure 7.9 displays a selected option that has had an Appear animation applied and has a trigger set.

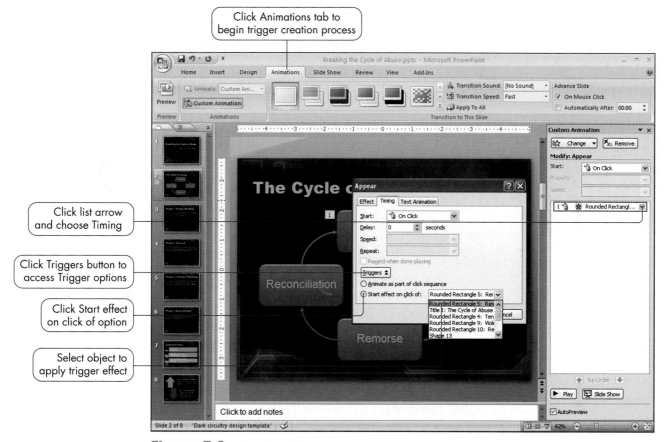

Figure 7.9 Create a Trigger

In Hands-On Exercise 1, you add interactivity to the beginning slides of a presentation designed to help students review charts and graphs using a quiz format. More questions can be added later, if desired. You want the viewer to be able to read a question and select an answer to the question from a list of choices (multiple-choice format). If the viewer answers correctly, you want the viewer to hear applause. If the viewer chooses incorrectly, you want the viewer to hear feedback that indicates an incorrect choice was made. You want the viewer to be able to navigate through the slide show using action buttons. You also want the viewer to be able to open a Charts and Graphs Reference Table in Microsoft Word before beginning the presentation and to open a Charts and Graphs Assignment after completing the presentation.

TIP Using Games for Quizzes

Microsoft includes a QuizShow template in the Installed Templates category. You can use this template to create quizzes and review exercises. It includes question layouts such as Simple Question and Answer, True or False, Multiple Choice, and Item Match Up. You can also go to the Internet and use a search engine to search for "PowerPoint Games." Games in popular game show formats are freely available from many sites.

Just as in any presentation, remember the old adage "If you don't know where you are going, you will end up somewhere else." Create a storyboard to plan out what slides you will need for the quiz and the interactive elements required by your plan. A storyboard for a standard quiz presentation would probably contain the following elements:

- Title Slide (let the viewer know what the test covers)
- Introduction (define the test boundaries or summarize the test content)
- Directions (let the viewer know how to take the test)
- Question Slides (include the answers on the same slide)
- Feedback Slides (create a "correct" feedback slide and an "incorrect" answer slide)
- Ending Slide (let the viewer know that the quiz is over)

In the above presentation roadmap, the answers to the questions would link to the feedback slides and the "correct" feedback slide would link to the next question. The "incorrect" feedback slide would link to the same-question slide so the viewer could try again. The plan for your quiz varies from this standard format. Rather than link to feedback slides, you will create action buttons next to the answer that a student clicks to hear audio responses to his or her choice. The format has been changed to give you practice in creating sound action buttons and navigation action buttons. In addition to this, you will create an e-mail hyperlink and a hyperlink to an existing file. The storyboard for your quiz would look something like Table 7.2.

Table 7.2 Hands-On Exercise 1 Storyboard

Slide	Content	Interactive Element
1	Title Slide	None
2	Directions	Existing file hyperlink E-mail hyperlink
3	Speaker Test	Clip art object with sound action attached
4	Question One	Four sound action buttons, one for each answer Four navigation buttons: Beginning, Back, Forward, End
5	Question Two	Four sound action buttons, one for each answer Four navigation buttons: Beginning, Back, Forward, End
6	Ending Slide	Existing file hyperlink

Hands-On Exercises

1 | Using Hyperlinks and Action Buttons

Skills covered: 1. Insert and Edit an E-Mail Hyperlink **2.** Assign an Action to a Clip Art Object **3.** Create and Edit Sound Action Buttons **4.** Create Action Buttons for Navigation on a Slide Master **5.** Create a Trigger **6.** Create a Hyperlink to an Existing File **7.** Test Hyperlinks and Action Buttons

---

Step 1
Insert and Edit an E-Mail Hyperlink

Refer to Figure 7.10 as you complete Step 1.

a. Open the *chap7_ho1_review* presentation, and then save it as **chap7_ho1_review_ solution** presentation.

b. Move to Slide 2, position your mouse pointer after the colon following *contact:* at the bottom of the screen, and enter your e-mail address.

Because PowerPoint recognizes the format of an e-mail address, it creates an automatic hyperlink to your e-mail. Point at your e-mail address and you will see the ScreenTip display the e-mail tag *mailto:* and your e-mail address.

c. Right-click your e-mail address and click **Edit Hyperlink**. Enter **Charts and Graphs Review Question** in the Subject box, and then click **OK**.

d. Create a Notes and Handouts header and footer with the date and your name in the header and your instructor's name and your class in the footer.

e. Save the *chap7_ho1_review_solution* presentation.

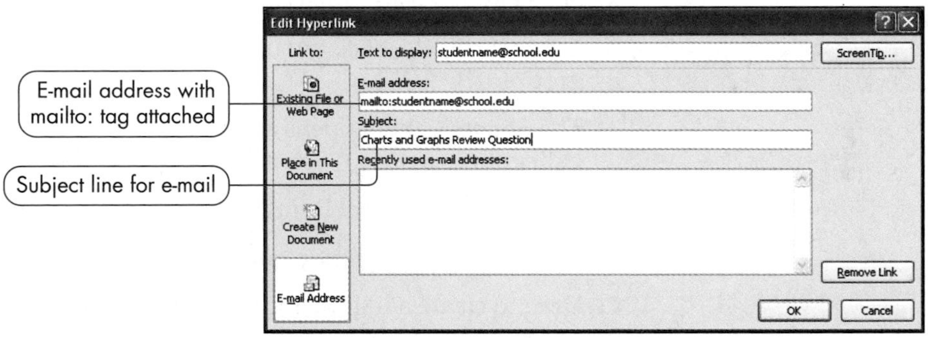

Figure 7.10 E-Mail Hyperlink

Step 2
Assign an Action to a Clip Art Object

Refer to Figure 7.11 as you complete Step 2.

a. Move to Slide 3, select the picture of the speakers, and then click the **Insert tab**.

b. Click **Action** in the Links group on the Insert tab.

The Action Settings dialog box opens so that you can assign an action to the selected clip art image.

c. Click the **Mouse Over** tab.

By selecting the Mouse Over tab, you assign any applied actions to occur when the mouse moves over the selected object.

d. Check **Play Sound**, and then click the list arrow.

Microsoft installs a variety of sounds you can attach to objects, or you can select the Other Sound option and browse to locate a sound you have saved.

e. Click **Voltage**, and then click **OK**.

f. Save the *chap7_ho1_review_solution* presentation.

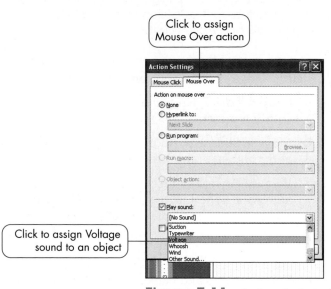

Figure 7.11 Action Assigned to a Clip Art Object

Step 3
Create and Edit Sound Action Buttons

Refer to Figure 7.12 as you complete Step 3.

a. Move to Slide 4, click the **Insert tab,** and then click **Shapes** in the Illustrations group.

The Shapes gallery opens and the action buttons display at the bottom of the gallery.

b. Click **Action Button: Sound**.

The Shapes gallery closes and the mouse pointer becomes a crosshair pointer.

c. Drag to create a button approximately ⅓″ x ⅓″.

Do not worry about position or size at this time. You will adjust both in a later step.

d. Click the arrow in the Play sound list box and then click Other Sound.

e. Locate and select the *chap7_ho1_incorrect.wav* file, and then click **OK**.

The sound file is assigned to the action button. Because this is not the correct answer, the viewer will hear *Incorrect* when the button is clicked.

f. Click **OK**.

The action button now has sound attached to it. The sound will play when the button is clicked while playing the slide show.

g. Click the **Format tab**, and then click the **arrow** in the Size group to open the Size and Position dialog box.

h. Set the **Height** to **.33″** and the **Width** to **.33″**.

i. Click the Position tab and set the **Horizontal** position to **.5"** and the **Vertical** position to **2.5"**. Click **Close**.

j. With the sound action button still selected, press **Ctrl+D** three times.

Three duplicates of the original sound action button are created. It is easier to edit the duplicates than to recreate the button because the duplicates are already sized. The last duplicate created is now selected so you can edit it first.

k. Click the **Format tab**, and then click the **arrow** in the Size group to open the Size and Position dialog box. Click the Position tab and set the **Horizontal** position to **.5"** and the **Vertical** position to **3.9"**. Click **Close**.

l. Right-click the selected button and click **Hyperlink**. Click the drop-down arrow in the Play sound list box and then click Other Sound. Locate and select the *chap7_ho1_tryagain.wav* file, and then click **Close**.

The sound action button has been edited to play a different sound file. Because this is not the correct answer, the viewer will hear *Try Again* when the button is pressed.

m. Click the third sound action button from the top (the second duplicated button). Click the **Format tab**, and then click the **arrow** in the Size group to open the Size and Position dialog box. Click the Position tab and set the **Horizontal** position to **.5"** and the **Vertical** position to **3.43"**. Click **Close**.

n. Right-click the selected button and click **Hyperlink**. Click the arrow in the Play sound list box, and then click Other Sound. Locate and select the *chap7_ho1_sorry.wav* file, and then click **OK**.

Once again, the sound action button has been edited to play a different sound file. Because this is not the correct answer, the viewer will hear *Sorry* when the button is pressed.

o. Click the second sound action button from the top (the first duplicated button). Click the **Format tab**, and then click the **arrow** in the Size group to open the Size and Position dialog box. Click the Position tab and set the **Horizontal** position to **.5"** and the **Vertical** position to **2.97"**. Click **Close**.

p. Right-click the selected button and click **Hyperlink**. Click the arrow in the Play sound list box, and then click Other Sound. Locate and select the *chap7_ho1_applause.wav* file, and then click **OK**.

This is the correct answer, so the viewer will hear applause when the button is pressed.

q. Select the four sound action buttons and press **Ctrl + C** to copy them. Move to Slide 5 and press **Ctrl+V** to paste them into the slide.

Because the answers to the questions change, you cannot put the answers on a slide master. Therefore, it is fastest to copy, paste, and edit the buttons.

r. Select the top sound action button (the sound action button for Answer a), right-click, and then click **Hyperlink**. Click the arrow in the Play sound list box, and then click Other Sound. Locate and select the *chap7_ho1_applause.wav* file, and then click **OK**.

This is the correct answer, so the viewer will hear applause when the button is pressed.

s. Select the second sound action button (the sound action button for Answer b), right-click, and then click **Hyperlink**. Click the arrow in the Play sound list box, and then click Other Sound. Locate and select the *chap7_ho1_incorrect.wav* file, and then click **OK**.

This is an incorrect answer, so the viewer will hear *Incorrect* when the button is pressed.

t. Save the *chap7_ho1_review_solution* presentation.

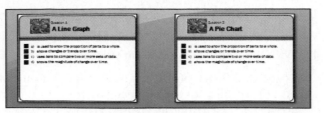

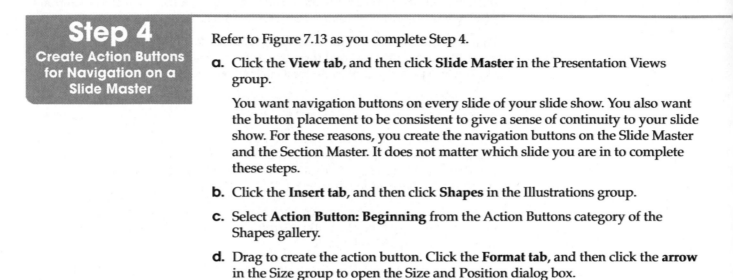

Figure 7.12 Sound Action Buttons Attached to Answers

Refer to Figure 7.13 as you complete Step 4.

Step 4

Create Action Buttons for Navigation on a Slide Master

a. Click the **View tab**, and then click **Slide Master** in the Presentation Views group.

You want navigation buttons on every slide of your slide show. You also want the button placement to be consistent to give a sense of continuity to your slide show. For these reasons, you create the navigation buttons on the Slide Master and the Section Master. It does not matter which slide you are in to complete these steps.

b. Click the **Insert tab**, and then click **Shapes** in the Illustrations group.

c. Select **Action Button: Beginning** from the Action Buttons category of the Shapes gallery.

d. Drag to create the action button. Click the **Format tab**, and then click the **arrow** in the Size group to open the Size and Position dialog box.

e. Set the **Height** to .33″ and the **Width** to .5″.

f. Click the Position tab and set the **Horizontal** position to **3.25″** and the **Vertical** position to **6.25″**. Click **Close**.

g. Click **Shapes** in the Illustrations group on the Insert tab, and then select **Action Button: Back or Previous** from the Action Buttons category of the Shapes gallery. Drag to create the action button. Click the **Format tab**, and then click the **arrow** in the Size group to open the Size and Position dialog box. Set the **Height** to .33″ and the **Width** to .5″. Click the Position tab and set the **Horizontal** position to **4.42″** and the **Vertical** position to **6.25″**. Click **Close**.

h. Click **Shapes** in the Illustrations group on the Insert tab, and then select **Action Button: Forward or Next** from the Action Buttons category of the Shapes gallery. Drag to create the action button. Click the **Format tab**, and then click the **arrow** in the Size group to open the Size and Position dialog box. Set the **Height** to .33″ and the **Width** to .5″. Click the Position tab and set the **Horizontal** position to **5.58″** and the **Vertical** position to **6.25″**. Click **Close**.

i. Click **Shapes** in the Illustrations group on the Insert tab, and then select **Action Button: End** from the Action Buttons category of the Shapes gallery. Drag to create the action button. Click the **Format tab**, and then click the **arrow** in the Size group to open the Size and Position dialog box. Set the **Height** to .33″ and the **Width** to .5″. Click the Position tab and set the **Horizontal** position to **6.75″** and the **Vertical** position to **6.25″**. Click **Close**.

The action buttons for navigation have now been created and positioned on the slide master. Look at the masters on the left pane of the slide master, however, and note that the action buttons do not appear on the Section Header Layout used by Slide (s) 2–3 and 6. Because this layout is not based on the slide master, the buttons have not been applied to it. You want the buttons on all slides.

j. Select the four sound action buttons and press **Ctrl+C** to copy them. Select the Section Header Layout in the left pane, and then press **Ctrl+V** to paste the action buttons into the layout.

k. Click the **Slide Master tab** in the Edit Master group on the Edit Master tab, and then click **Close Master View** in the Close group.

TROUBLESHOOTING: If the action buttons for navigation do not appear on Slides 2, 3, and 6, open the Slide Master View, select the Section Header Layout, and then repeat Steps b through f.

l. Save the *chap7_ho1_review_solution* presentation.

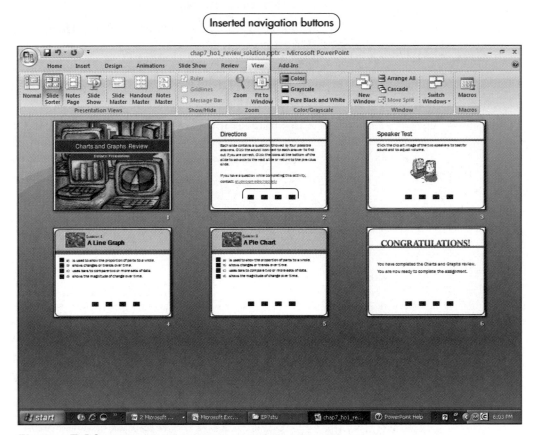

Figure 7.13 Action Buttons for Navigation Inserted in Master

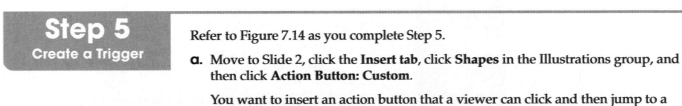

Step 5
Create a Trigger

Refer to Figure 7.14 as you complete Step 5.

a. Move to Slide 2, click the **Insert tab**, click **Shapes** in the Illustrations group, and then click **Action Button: Custom**.

You want to insert an action button that a viewer can click and then jump to a Charts and Graphs Reference Guide that was created in Microsoft Word. Because you want to insert text in the button, you decide to insert an action button you can customize.

b. Drag to create an action button. Click **Hyperlink to**, click the arrow, scroll down, and then click **Other File**.

c. Select the *chap7_ho1_reference.docx* file and click **OK**.

d. Click the **Format tab**, and then click the **arrow** in the Size group to open the Size and Position dialog box. Set the Height to **.75"** and the **Width** to **2.25"**. Click the **Position tab** and set the **Horizontal** position to **6.75"** and the **Vertical** position to .5". Click **Close**.

e. Type **Charts and Graphs Reference Sheet** inside the custom action button.

f. Click the **Animations tab**, and then click **Custom Animation** in the Animations group. Click the **Add Effect** button in the Custom Animation task pane.

g. Click **Entrance**, and then click **More Effects**. Click **Curve Up** in the Exciting category of the Add Entrance Effect list.

h. Click the down arrow next to the selected object in the Custom Animation list, and then click **Timing**.

i. Click **Triggers**, and then click the **Start effect on click of** option. Choose **Directions** and click **OK**.

You added a trigger to launch your action button. To trigger the launch you must click the title **Directions**. You must modify the directions to include information about the trigger.

j. Click in the empty area of the bottom placeholder and type **If you wish to review a Charts and Graphs Reference Guide before beginning this activity, click "Directions."** Delete any extra space if necessary (see Figure 7.14).

k. Save the *chap7_ho1_review_solution* presentation.

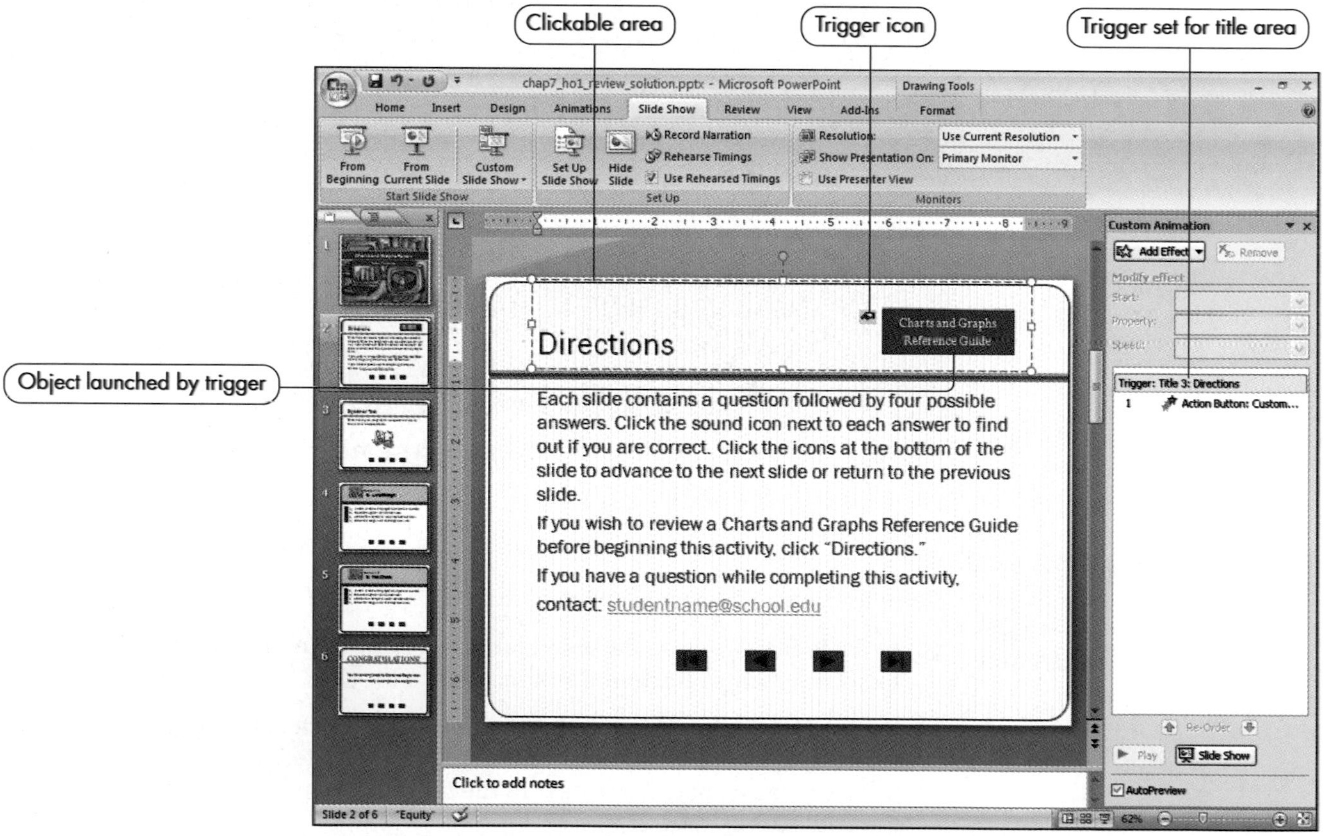

Figure 7.14 Action Button Launched by a Trigger

Step 6
Create a Hyperlink to an Existing File

Refer to Figure 7.15 as you complete Step 6.

a. Move to Slide 6 and select the word *assignment*.

You want the viewer to be able to click on the word *assignment* and have the assignment open. You decide to create a hyperlink to the existing file.

b. Click the **Insert tab**, and then click **Hyperlink** in the Links group.

c. Click **ScreenTip** and type **Click to open assignment**.

d. Click the **Browse for File button**, locate the *chap7_ho1_assignment.docx* file, and then click **OK**.

e. Click **OK** to close the Insert Hyperlink dialog box.

The hyperlinked text changed color and is underlined.

f. Save the *chap7_ho1_review_solution* presentation.

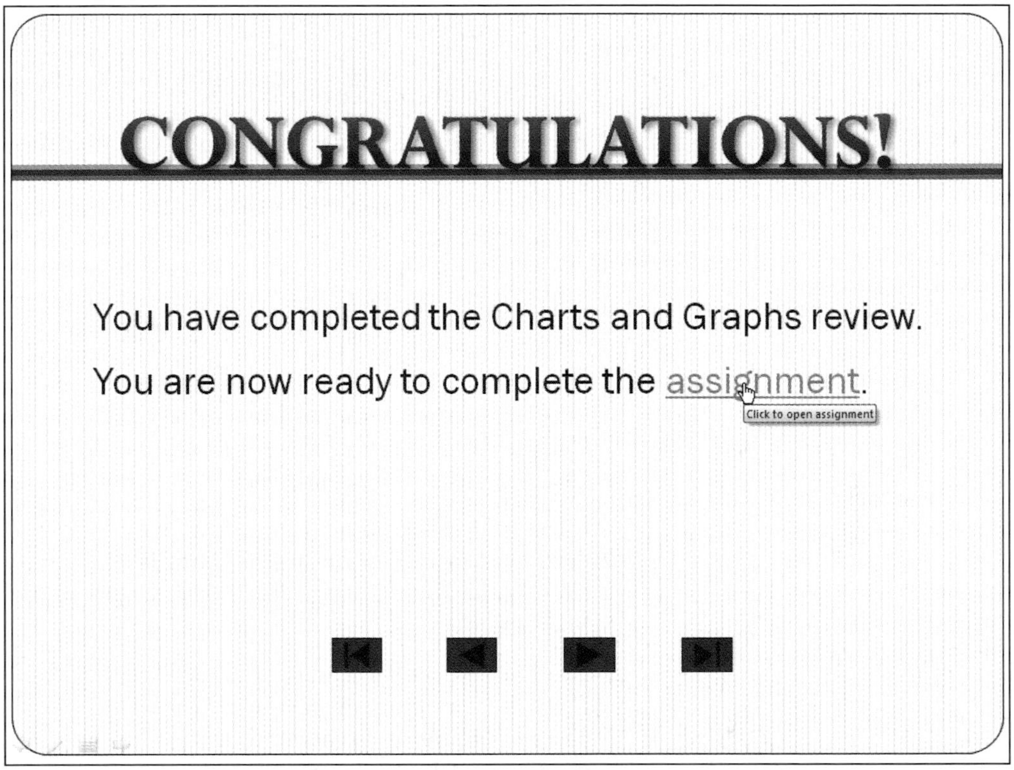

Figure 7.15 Hyperlink and ScreenTip displayed in Slide Show View.

Step 7
Test Hyperlinks and Action Buttons

Refer to Figure 7.16 as you complete Step 7.

a. Click the **Slide Show tab**, and then click **From Beginning** in the Start Slide Show group.

Always test hyperlinks and action buttons in Slide Show view to ensure that they work the way you desire.

b. Advance from the Title Slide to Slide 2, and then click *Directions*. The *Charts and Graphs Reference Guide* action button should curve in. Click the action button to make sure it opens the file.

If the *Charts and Graphs Reference Guide* does not work, delete the action button and repeat Step 5.

c. Click the e-mail hyperlink.

TROUBLESHOOTING: If your hyperlink does not open and your e-mail account is Web-based (Hotmail, Yahoo, AOL, etc.), you may not be connected to the Internet. Exit your slide show, connect to the Internet, and then try the hyperlink again.

d. Advance to Slide 3 and run your mouse pointer over the speakers clip art image.

If the Voltage sound does not play when you mouse over it, try clicking it. If the sound plays with a click, exit the slide show and right-click the clip art image of speakers. Remove the check from Play sound in the Mouse Click tab, move to the Mouse Over tab, and check Play sound. Select Voltage from the list of sounds and click **OK**.

If the sound does not play by either a mouse over or a mouse click, repeat Step 2.

e. While in Slide 3, click the **Action Button: Beginning** and see if it advances you to Slide 1 (Title Slide). Click to advance from the Title Slide to Slide 2. Click the **Action Button: End** while in Slide 2 and see if it advances you to Slide 6 (Congratulations slide). While in Slide 6, click the **Action Button: Back or Previous** to see if it advances you to Slide 5 (Question 2). While in Slide 5, click the **Action Button: Forward or Next** to see if it advances you to Slide 6.

If any of the action buttons do not work, exit the slide show. Click the **View tab**, and then click **Slide Master** in the Presentation Views group. Click the top layout in the list, the Equity Slide Master: used by Slides (s) 1–6, select the button that did not work, and then right-click. Select **Edit Hyperlink**, and then check the slide showing in the Hyperlink to: box. If no slide is showing or if the wrong slide is showing, click the arrow and select the right slide from the list. Click **OK**, and then click **Close Master View** in the Close group on the Edit Master tab.

f. Navigate to Slide 4 (Question 1 slide) and click each of the sound action buttons. Only the sound action button for the b) answer should play the applause sound. The remaining sound action buttons should play a sound that indicates the choice of answer was incorrect.

If any of the sound action buttons plays the wrong sound, exit the slide show. Select the sound action button that plays the wrong sound, right-click, and then click **Hyperlink**. Change the linked sound to the correct choice. Return to Slide Show mode.

g. Navigate to Slide 5 (Question 2 slide) and click each of the sound action buttons. Only the sound action button for the a) answer should play the applause sound. The remaining sound action buttons should play a sound that indicates the choice of answer was incorrect.

If any of the sound action buttons plays the wrong sound, exit the slide show. Select the sound action button that plays the wrong sound, right-click, and then click **Hyperlink**. Change the linked sound to the correct choice. Return to Slide Show mode.

h. Navigate to Slide 6 (Congratulations slide) and click the *assignment* hyperlink.

If Word does not open and display the *chap7_ho1_assignment.docx* file, exit the slide show. Right-click the *assignment* hyperlink and click **Edit Hyperlink**. Click the **Browse for File** button and locate the *chap7_ho1_assignment.docx* file, select the file, and click **OK**. Click **OK** in the Edit Hyperlink dialog box.

i. Save the *chap7_ho1_review_solution* presentation. Close the file and exit PowerPoint if you do not want to continue to the next exercise at this time.

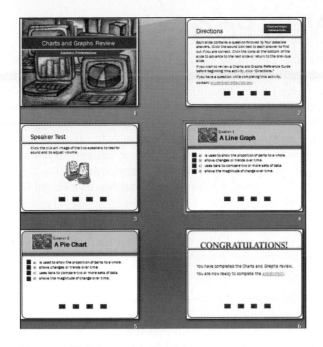

Figure 7.16 Completed Interactive Slide Show

Web Pages

Instead of delivering your presentation to an audience or in a kiosk, you may choose to post it as a Web page on the Internet. Web pages are written in the *HyperText Markup Language (HTML)* authoring language, which defines the structure and layout of the document. Initially, the only way to create a Web page was to learn HTML. Microsoft Office simplifies the process as it lets you create the document in any Office application, then simply save it as a Web page. In other words, you create a PowerPoint slide show in the usual fashion. However, instead of saving the document in the default .pptx format, you use the Save as command to save the presentation as a Web page.

In this section, you save presentations as a single file Web page and as a Web page.

Saving a Presentation as a Single File Web Page

Your presentation can be saved as a single file Web page, which saves all the elements that make up a Web site. This includes the text, slides, sounds, graphics, and other elements in one file. The file format is MHTML, a file format that is supported by Internet Explorer 4.0 and later browsers. The advantage of a single file is that it is easy to manage the Web site. If you have to move the site, you will not forget to move elements of the Web site that may be saved in other locations. You are also able to send a single file as an e-mail attachment if you want to send it to someone else for review.

> The advantage of a single file is that it is easy to manage the Web site.

To save a presentation as a single file Web page, click the Office Button, and then click Save As. Click the Save in list arrow to select the location to store your Web page. Click the Save as type list arrow, and then click Single File Web Page. If you want your Web page title to be different from the title of your presentation, click the Change Title button, type the new title in the Set Page Title box, and then click OK. The Web page title will display in the blue title bar at the top of the browser window. Figure 7.17 displays the Save As dialog box with the Single File Web Page option selected.

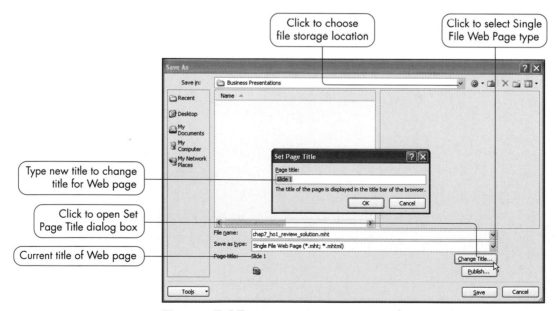

Figure 7.17 Save as Single File Web Page Option

Saving a Presentation as a Web Page

Instead of saving as a single file Web page, you may choose to save as a Web Page.
This option saves the presentation as a Web page that consists of an HTML file and a
folder. Inside the folder are the supporting elements of the presentation such as files
for each slide and each graphic.

To save a presentation as a Web page, click the Office Button, and then click Save
As. Click the Save in list arrow to select the location to store your Web page. Click the
Save as type list arrow, and then click Web Page. Just as in the single file Web page
format, you may change the title by clicking the Change Title button. Figure 7.18 displays the Save As dialog box with Web Page selected.

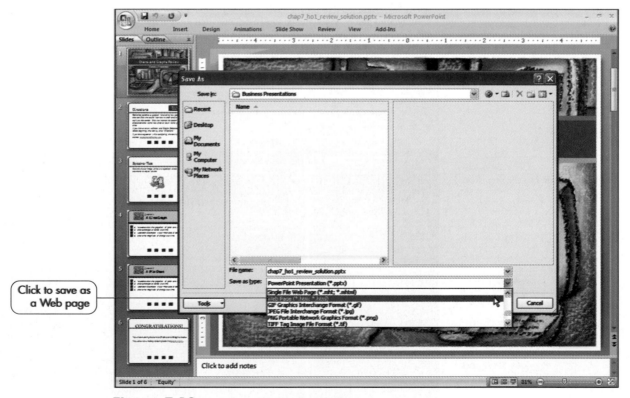

Click to save as
a Web page

Figure 7.18 Save as Web Page Option

Previewing a Web Page

Before you actually publish your Web page to the Web, you should preview it in your browser. That way, you can see how it displays on the Web. To preview the Web page, click the Office Button, and then click Open. Click the Files of type list arrow and click All Web Pages. Click the Open button arrow at the bottom of the dialog box, and then click Open in Browser. The Web page opens in your browser. If you did not change the title of your Web page, Slide 1 will appear on the Title bar.

The left frame displays links to slide titles. Simply click a link to move to that slide. Also, when you display the Web page in a browser, a navigation bar appears at the bottom of the Web page. In the center of the navigation bar are buttons to move you to the Next Slide or Previous Slide. The navigation bar also includes an Expand/Collapse Outline button. You can toggle this button to display the full outline of the presentation or just the titles. To view the Web page in a full-screen mode similar to how you view a standard PowerPoint presentation, click the Full Screen Slide Show button on the far-right side of the navigation bar. Figure 7.19 shows the Charts and Graphs Review Web page in Preview mode.

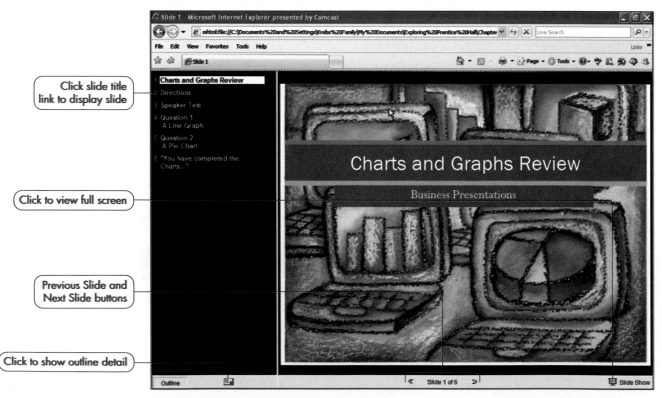

Figure 7.19 Web Page Preview

Hands-On Exercises

2 | Saving Web Pages

Skills covered: 1. Save a Presentation as a Single File Web page **2.** Save a Presentation as a Web Page
3. Preview a Web Page

Refer to Figure 7.20 as you complete Step 1.

a. Open the *chap7_ho1_review_solution* presentation if you closed it after the last exercise.

b. Click the **Office Button**, and then click **Save As**.

c. Click the **Save in** list arrow, and then click the storage location for your file.

d. Click the **Save as type** list arrow, and then click **Single File Web Page**.

e. Change the file name from *chap7_ho1_review_solution* to **chap7_ho2_review_ solution**.

f. Click the **Change Title** button.

g. Type **Charts and Graphs Review** as the new Web page title, and then click **OK**.

h. Click **Save** to save the *chap7_ho2_review_solution* single file Web page, and then close the page.

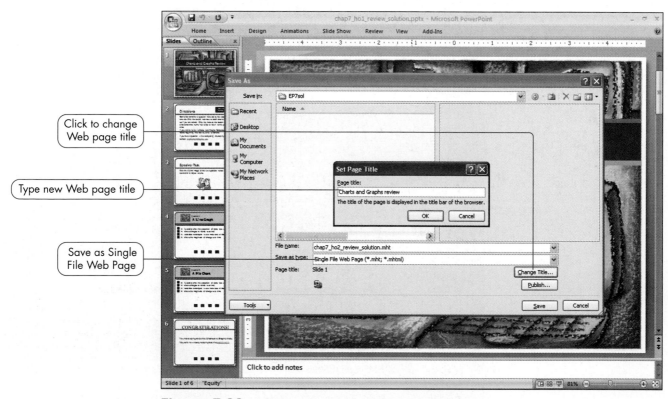

Figure 7.20 Saving as a Single File Web Page

Refer to Figure 7.21 as you complete Step 2.

a. Open the *chap7_ho1_review_solution* presentation.

b. Click the **Office Button**, and then click **Save As**.

c. Click the **Save as type** list arrow and select **Web Page**.

d. Change the file name from *chap7_ho1_review_solution* to **chap7_ho2_review_ solution**.

e. Click **Save**.

f. Click the **Office Button**, and then click **Open**.

g. Click the **Files of type** list arrow, and then click **All Web Pages**.

Note that three items display in the Name list. *Chap7_ho2_review_solution.mht* is the single file Web page that contains the Web page as well as all support elements. *Chap7_ho2_review_solution.htm* is the Web page. The supporting elements have been automatically saved in the folder named *chap7_ho2_review_ solution_files*.

h. Open the *chap7_ho2_review_solution_files* folder, and then change the **Files of type** to **All Files**.

Note that the Name list now displays buttons, masters, images, slides, and sounds along with many other elements. These elements have been saved to the folder to make it easy for you to transfer them to another storage location or Web server if desired.

i. Click **Cancel**.

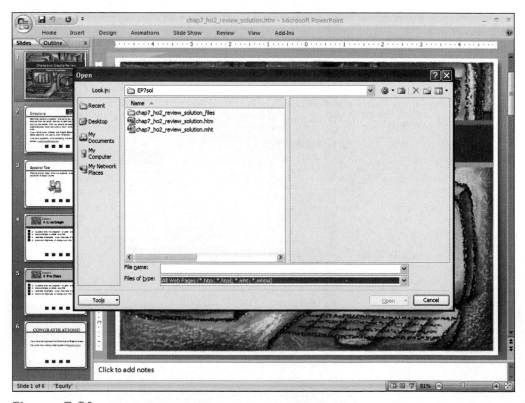

Figure 7.21 Open Dialog Box Displaying All Web Pages

Refer to Figure 7.24, if necessary, as you complete Step 3.

a. Click the **Office Button**, click **Open**, and then change the **Files of type** to **All Web Pages**.

b. Click the *chap7_ho2_review_solution.mht* file, and then click **Open**.

> **TROUBLESHOOTING:** If you have installed Internet Explorer 7, or have changed your security settings, you may have trouble opening the file. Internet Explorer may restrict the Web page from running scripts or ActiveX controls that could access your computer. If this happens, click the yellow bar below the toolbar for options. Click to see the options and click **Allow Blocked Content**. A Security Warning dialog box will appear letting you know that active content may harm your computer. Click **Yes**. The Web page should open at this point. See Figures 7.22 and 7.23.

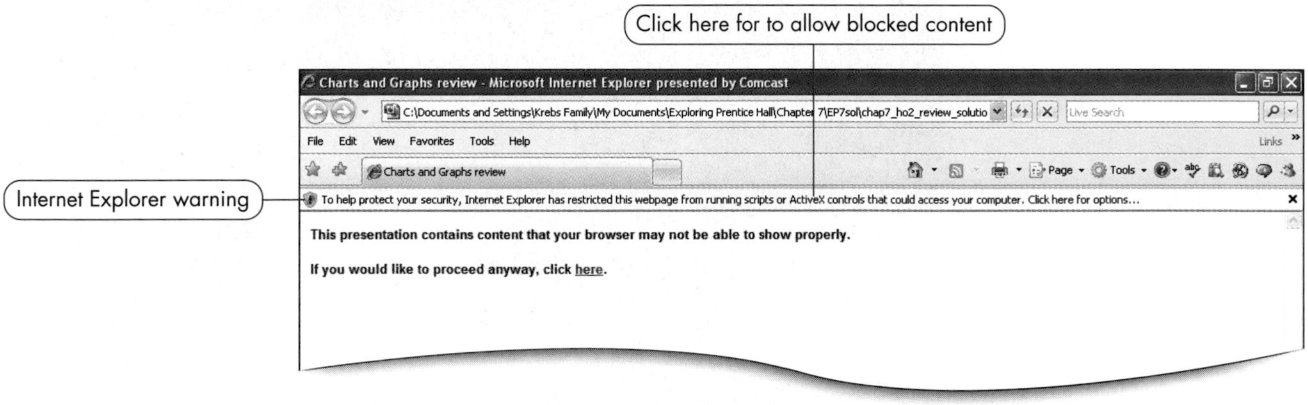

Figure 7.22 Internet Explorer Warning

Figure 7.23 Internet Explorer Security Warning

c. Click the **Expand/Collapse Outline** button on the navigation bar.

The Outline expands to show the detailed text in each slide.

d. Click the **Next Slide** button on the navigation bar to advance to the next slide. Click the **Previous Slide** button to return to the previous slide.

e. Click **Slide Show** on the navigation bar.

The slide show opens in full-screen mode.

f. Click **Esc** to leave slide show mode.

g. Click the **Close** button to close the browser.

h. Close the *chap7_ho2_review_solution.mht* file, and exit PowerPoint if you do not want to continue to the next exercise at this time.

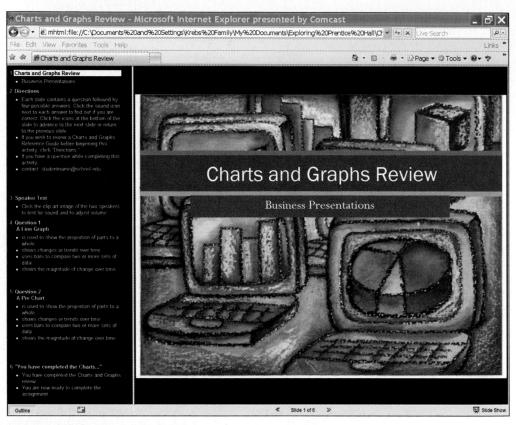

Figure 7.24 Web Page with Outline Displayed

Web Page Publishing

When you publish the Web page, you can customize how it will appear on the Web by using Web options.

To **publish** is to copy a Web page to a Web server so that viewers on the Internet can view the Web page.

Once you save a file in either MHTML format or HTML format, you can *publish* the Web page by copying it to a Web server. This allows it to be viewed on the World Wide Web. When you publish the Web page, you can customize how it will appear on the Web by using Web options.

In this section, you determine what you publish to the Web and how to customize the appearance of the Web page on the Web.

Publishing a Web Page

To publish the Web Page and access the options, open the Save As dialog box and select Single File Web Page or Web Page as the file type. Selecting one of these options changes the dialog box so that the Publish button appears. Click the Publish button and the Publish as a Web Page dialog box opens (refer to Figure 7.25).

The Publish as a Web Page dialog box lets you select what exactly you want to publish. Do you want to publish the complete presentation or just specific slides from the presentation? Did you create a custom slide show based on the presentation and want to publish the custom show? Do you want to publish your speaker notes with the presentation? Do you want a different look to the navigation controls? What language do you want the Web page to display? When you have answered these questions, select the corresponding options in the Publish as a Web Page dialog box.

Another decision you have to make is what type of browser support you want. This can determine your audience in some ways. For example, if you select *Microsoft Internet Explorer 4.0 or Later (high fidelity)*, your viewers can see animations and multimedia features. If your target audience does not have an up-to-date browser, however, you eliminate them as viewers. If you select *Internet Explorer 3.0, Netscape Navigator 3.0, or later*, more people may be able to view your Web page, but some of the features of your presentation will be lost. The *All browsers listed above (creates larger files)* option does just that—it creates larger files which take longer to download. More people can access your page, but you may lose some of them when they have to wait longer for the file to load.

Finally, you can decide where you want a copy of the Web page saved and if you want to open the Web page in your browser when you click the Publish button. You can publish the presentation locally or upload it to a file server. Opening the page in your Web browser lets you see the choices you made in the Web Options dialog box. Because the Web options determine how the Web page is laid out, it is a good idea to immediately open the browser and see how the Web page looks.

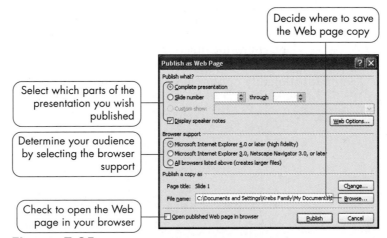

Figure 7.25 Publish as Web Page Dialog Box

Setting Web Page Options

From the Publish as Web Page dialog box, you can click the Web Options button and open the Web Options dialog box. This dialog box includes tabs that give you options to determine the appearance of your Web page, the target browser for your Web page, ways to organize files, your target monitor resolution, the Web page encoding, and the font you want for your Web page. The font options do not refer to a typeface selection, but rather refer to browser support for other languages such as Greek, Hebrew, and Japanese.

Click the General tab of the Web Options dialog box to determine the appearance of your presentation when published to the Web. By default, navigation controls are added to the bottom of the presentation when the presentation is saved as a single file Web page or as a Web page. In the General tab, you can remove the navigation controls or change how the text and frame appear in the browser. You can choose the frame fill color and the color of the text that appears on the frame. You can click each option and view the small sample to determine if that choice gives the effect you want.

You can also determine whether or not a viewer sees slide animations you included in your show by checking or unchecking the Show slide animation while browsing check box. Remember, though—slide animations may be slow on your viewers' browser. You may lose some viewers this way. By default, graphics are resized to fit the browser window. If you deselect this option, you may get unexpected and unattractive pages because shapes may resize or text may resize and no longer fit in a shape.

The Browsers tab expands on the choices you are presented in the Publish as a Web Page dialog box. Click the drop-down arrow to see the list of browsers that are available (see Figure 7.26).

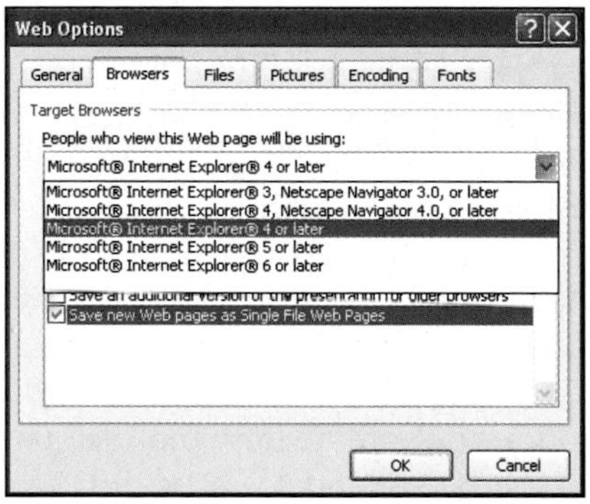

Figure 7.26 Web Options Browser Support Choices

Determine the functionality you need for your Web page, and this will aid you in determining which browser you need to select. The reference table below shows the functionality options available and the browser you will need to select to obtain that functionality.

Browser Options | Reference

Option	Description	Browser Support
Allow PNG as a graphics format	PNG (Portable Network Graphic) is a graphics file format that supports 16 million colors and transparency. It has been approved by the World Wide Web Consortium as a replacement for the GIF graphic file format. Browsers before Internet Explorer 4.0 do not support the PNG format fully.	Microsoft Internet Explorer 4 or later, although default in Web Options is Microsoft Internet Explorer 6 or later
Rely on VML for displaying graphics	VML (Vector Markup Language) is an XML-based high quality vector graphics file format. Because it is XML based, only newer browsers can support it.	Microsoft Internet Explorer 5 or later
Save an additional version of the presentation for older browsers	This option increases the file size and storage space required, but it lets the highest number of viewers view the Web page.	Microsoft Internet Explorer 3, Netscape Navigator 3.0, or later
Save New Web Pages as Single File Web Pages	Uses MHTML file format to save all elements of the Web page in a single file.	Microsoft Internet Explorer 4 or later

When you first create your Web page from your presentation, you save the working file to your hard drive or storage device so that you can work with it and edit it. Once you are satisfied with your presentation and you want to share it on the Internet, you need to locate a Host site for your presentation. You can contact an Internet Service Provider for details about the cost to store the Web page on their Web server, and how to transfer your files from your storage area to the host site. Finally, you must upload your file to the Web server that will host your Web page.

In the next hands-on exercise, you set Web options for the Charts and Graphs Review presentation and publish your Web page.

Hands-On Exercises

3 | Publishing a Web Page

Skills covered: 1. Set Web Options **2.** Publish the Web Page

Refer to Figure 7.27 as you complete Step 1.

a. Open the *chap7_ho1_review_solution* presentation, and then save it as **chap7_ho3_revised_solution**.

b. Change the title on Slide 1 to **Charts and Graphs Web Review**.

c. Click the **Office Button**, and then click **Save As**.

d. Click the **Save as type** list arrow, and then click **Web Page**.

e. Click the **Change Title** button, and then type **Charts and Graphs Web Review** in the Page Title box. Click **OK**.

f. Click the **Publish** button.

The Publish as Web Page dialog box opens.

g. Click the **Web Options** button.

h. Click the list arrow for Colors on the General tab.

i. Select **Presentation colors (accent color)** from the list of available color options.

j. Click the **Browsers** tab, and then select the **Microsoft Internet Explorer 3, Netscape Navigator 3.0, or later** option from the **People who view this Web page will be using** list. Click **OK**.

Choosing this option allows more people to view the Web page, but the file size will be larger and the page will take more time to download. The Web Options dialog box closes and the Publish as Web Page dialog remains open.

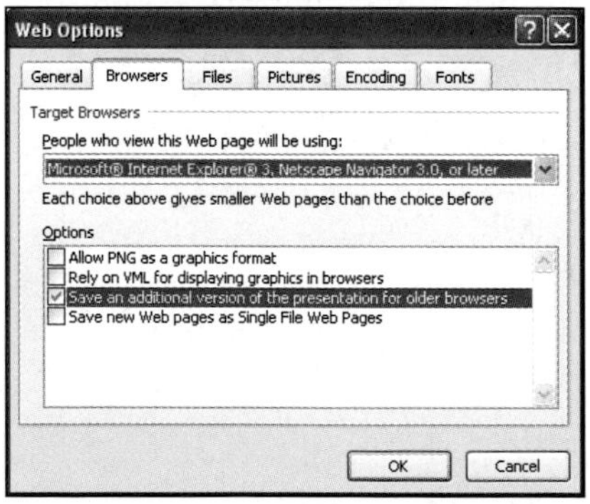

Figure 7.27 Web Options for Browser Selection

Refer to Figure 7.28 as you complete Step 2.

a. In the open **Publish as Web Page**, click the check box for **Display speaker notes**.

The check to display speaker notes is removed. You do not need to display speaker notes because you did not create any speaker notes.

b. Click the check box for **Open published Web page in browser**.

The Web page will now open in the browser as soon as you publish it.

c. Click the **Browse button**, and then locate the place where you will store the copy of the Web page.

d. Click **OK**, and then click **Publish**.

e. Click the **Close** button to close the browser.

f. Save and close the *chap7_ho3_revised_solution.mht* presentation.

TROUBLESHOOTING: If you have installed Internet Explorer 7, or have changed your security settings, you may have trouble opening the file. Internet Explorer may restrict the Web page from running scripts or ActiveX controls that could access your computer. If this happens, click the yellow bar below the toolbar for options. Click to see the options and click **Allow Blocked Content**. A Security Warning dialog box will appear, letting you know that active content may harm your computer. Click **Yes**. The Web page should open at this point.

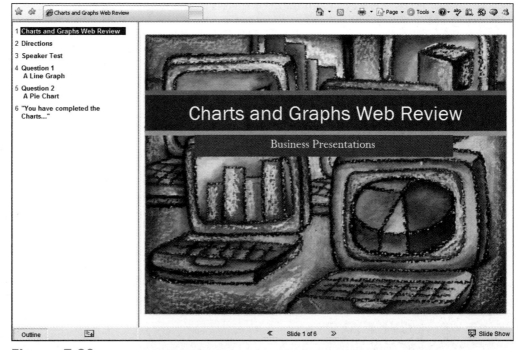

Figure 7.28 Published Web Page

Summary

1. **Insert and use hyperlinks.** Hyperlinks connect two locations and can be used to add interactivity to a slide show. When clicked, hyperlinks can jump to another slide in a slide show, an existing file, a Web page on the Internet, another program, or an e-mail address. ScreenTips can be added to a hyperlink to give the viewer additional information. Hyperlinks can be attached to any selected object. Hyperlinks can be activated by a mouse click or a mouse over.

2. **Add action buttons.** Actions are instructions to PowerPoint to perform a task such as jump to another slide, play a sound, or open another program. Actions can be attached to any object, but PowerPoint includes pre-made icons called action buttons. Action buttons are shapes with actions attached. Action buttons are typically used to navigate in a slide show (Back button, Forward button, Beginning button, End button, Home button, and Return button) or to display some type of information (Information button, Movie button, Document button, Sound button, and Help button). Action buttons can be activated by a mouse click or a mouse over.

3. **Use a trigger.** A trigger is an option that is attached to an animation and controls when an event takes place. In order for the event to take place, a viewer must click an object that has an animation trigger attached.

4. **Save a presentation as a single file Web page.** A presentation can be saved as a single file Web page so that it can be viewed over the World Wide Web. When a presentation is saved as a single file Web page, the file is converted to MHTML format. This saves all elements, such as text, slides, sounds, and graphics, in one file. This makes it easier to maintain a Web site, as all elements are stored in one location. However, only Internet Explorer 4.0 and later browsers can display MHTML formats.

5. **Save a presentation as a Web page.** A presentation also can be saved as a Web page so that it can be viewed over the World Wide Web. When a slide show is saved as a Web page, the file is converted to an HTML format and a folder is created that contains all the elements, such as images and sounds. Thus, saving as a Web page creates a file and a folder, whereas saving as a single file Web page creates only a file. Internet Explorer browsers earlier than Internet Explorer version 4.0 can only display HTML formats.

6. **Preview a Web page.** Web pages can be previewed so that you can see how they will appear when published to the Internet. By default, when the Web page is published, a frame is created on the left side of the page that contains the titles of the slides. The titles are hyperlinked so that when you click a title you jump to the associated slide. A navigation bar appears at the bottom of the slide that enables you to click to view a detailed outline, navigate to the previous or next slide, or view the slide show in a full screen mode.

7. **Publish a Web page.** To be viewed on the World Wide Web, a presentation must be published by copying it to a Web server. The presentation may be copied in either the single file Web page format (MHTML) or in Web page format (HTML).

8. **Set Web page options.** Web page options can be changed before publishing a Web page. These options control the appearance of the slide show on the Web, the browser support, the location files are saved to, picture size, language encoding, and language font.

Key Terms

Multiple Choice

1. The term used for a connection between two locations is:

   (a) Hyperlink
   (b) Trigger
   (c) Browser
   (d) Object

2. Which of the following cannot have an action added to it?

   (a) Clip art image
   (b) Shape
   (c) SmartArt
   (d) WordArt

3. When you attach an object to an animation effect, you create a(n):

   (a) Hyperlink
   (b) Trigger
   (c) Action button
   (d) Mouse over

4. Which of the following refers to an interactive slide show?

   (a) Sequential presentation
   (b) Linear presentation
   (c) Non-linear presentation
   (d) Abstract presentation

5. Which of the following would not be suitable for an interactive slide show?

   (a) A presentation printed on overhead transparencies
   (b) A presentation before an audience
   (c) A World Wide Web presentation
   (d) A kiosk presentation

6. Which of the following cannot have a hyperlink attached?

   (a) An existing file
   (b) A slide in the current presentation
   (c) A new document
   (d) A placeholder

7. To add an action button, which tab do you click to start the process?

   (a) Insert
   (b) Design
   (c) Slide Show
   (d) View

8. When viewing a presentation in Slide Show mode, which of the following does not indicate a shape has an action attached?

   (a) A hand pointer appears when the mouse moves over the object.
   (b) A sound plays when the mouse clicks on the object.
   (c) The object is highlighted on the slide.
   (d) The object spins when the mouse moves over the object.

9. Which is not a good practice when creating buttons for interactivity in a slide show?

   (a) Create buttons that appear on all slides in the slide master.
   (b) Scatter action buttons randomly around the slide to ensure that the viewer concentrates on the slide.
   (c) Create equally sized buttons for navigation.
   (d) Use action button shapes with recognizable icons.

10. Which of the following steps are necessary when publishing a slide show to the Web?

    (a) Saving the slide show as a Web page or as a single file Web page
    (b) Obtaining a host site from an Internet Service Provider
    (c) Uploading the slide show to the Web server
    (d) All of the above

11. A single file Web page is converted to which of the following file formats?

    (a) MHTML
    (b) HTML
    (c) XML
    (d) PNG

12. Which of the following is not a valid consideration when planning a Web presentation?

    (a) The target audience and the browser they will most likely be using
    (b) File size and download time
    (c) Whether the Web page and supporting elements will likely change file servers
    (d) The printed presentation

Multiple Choice

continued

13. By default, the Web page title is:

    (a) Slide 1

    (b) The title displayed in the title placeholder of the presentation

    (c) The file name of the saved .pptx presentation

    (d) Presentation 1

14. An advantage of saving as a single file Web page rather than as a Web page is:

    (a) Internet Explorer browsers can open the Web page.

    (b) The Web page and its associated support elements are saved in one file.

    (c) The file size is larger.

    (d) The Web page support elements are saved in a single folder.

15. To begin the process for changing the appearance of the slide navigation controls and browser support for a Web page, in the Save As dialog box, click:

    (a) Change Options

    (b) General

    (c) Web Options

    (d) Publish

16. Which of the following is not a true statement regarding Web browser support?

    (a) The higher the Web browser version, the greater the functionality of PowerPoint features in the Web page.

    (b) Choosing a lower browser version excludes the portion of your audience that does not have that browser version.

    (c) Selecting All browsers provides for full PowerPoint functionality at a much larger file size.

    (d) The higher the Web browser version, the more you potentially exclude a portion of your audience.

Practice Exercises

1 Adding an E-Mail and a Web Page Hyperlink

As a volunteer in the Campus Health Center, you are often asked to prepare presentations to run at various kiosks located around campus. The presentations are varied, but all have the goal of educating students about health and safety issues. This week, you were asked to prepare a presentation based on information about the Cycle of Abuse provided to the Center from the local City Police Department Crime Victim Advocate Program. In this practice exercise, you include a hyperlink to the Web site of the program on the Resource slide of the presentation. You also create an e-mail hyperlink. Refer to Figure 7.29 to see the completed slide.

a. Open the *chap7_pe1_cycle* presentation, and then save it as **chap7_pe1_cycle_solution**.
b. Move to Slide 9, position your mouse pointer after the colon following *contact:*, and enter your e-mail address.
c. Right-click your e-mail address and click **Edit Hyperlink**. Enter **Cycle of Abuse Question** in the Subject box, and then click **OK**.
d. Select the text *Crime Victim Advocate Program*.
e. Click the **Insert tab**, and then click **Hyperlink** in the Links group.
f. Click **Existing File or Web Page** in the Link to: pane.
g. Click the **ScreenTip** button, and then type **Click to read additional information** in the **ScreenTip text**: box. Click **OK**.
h. Type **http://www.sanjuancounty.org/victim_advocate.htm** in the Address box. Click **OK**.
i. Test the links by clicking the **Slide Show** tab, and then click **From Current Slide** in the Start Slide Show group.
j. Click the *Crime Victim Advocate Program* hyperlink.
k. Click the **Close button** to close the Web page and return to your slide show.
l. If either of the links did not work, right-click the link, click **Edit Hyperlink**, and then compare your setting with the instructions above. Correct any option that is not working.
m. Click the **e-mail** hyperlink, and then close the e-mail dialog box. Press **Esc** to close the Slide Show view.
n. Save the *chap7_pe1_cycle_solution* presentation.

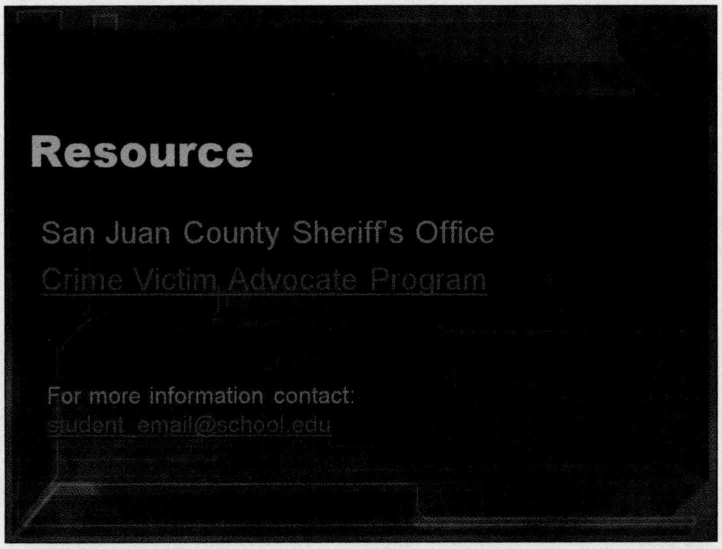

Figure 7.29 Resource Slide with Web Page and E-Mail Hyperlinks

...continued on Next Page

2 Attaching Actions to Shapes

You want to add interactivity to the slide show by allowing the viewer to click a shape in the Cycle illustration and jump to a slide giving detail about the related phase. The illustration was created with shapes because SmartArt cannot have linked actions. You want the detail slides hidden unless the viewer clicks the link. Figure 7.30 shows the presentation after completing this exercise. Note that hidden slides have blocked symbols around the slide number in the slide sorter view.

a. Save the *chap7_pe1_cycle_solution* presentation as **chap7_pe2_cycle_solution**.
b. Click the **View tab**, and then click **Slide Sorter** in the Presentation Views group.
c. Right-click Slide 3 (Phase 1 Tension-Building), and then click **Hide Slide**.
d. Repeat Step C with Slides 4, 5, and 6. Slides 3 through 6 are now hidden.
e. Double-click Slide 2 (The Cycle of Abuse) to open it in Normal view, and then select the shape labeled *Tension*.
f. Click the **Insert tab**, and then click **Action** in the Links group.
g. Click **Hyperlink to**, and then click the list arrow. Scroll down, and then click **Slide**. Click Slide 3 (Phase 1 Tension-Building). Note that the slide number is in parentheses, indicating that this slide is hidden. Click **OK**, and then click **OK**.
h. Select the shape labeled *Violence*. Click **Action** in the Links group on the Insert tab. **Click Hyperlink to**, and then click the list arrow. Scroll down, and then click **Slide**. Click Slide 4 (Phase 2 Violence). Click **OK**, and then click **OK**.
i. Select the shape labeled *Remorse*. Click **Action** in the Links group on the Insert tab. Click **Hyperlink to**, and then click the list arrow. Scroll down, and then click **Slide**. Click Slide 5 (Phase 3 Remorse). Click **OK**, and then click **OK**.
j. Select the shape labeled *Reconciliation*. Click **Action** in the Links group on the Insert tab. Click **Hyperlink to**, and then click the list arrow. Scroll down, and then click **Slide**. Click Slide 6 (Phase 4 Reconciliation). Click **OK**, and then click **OK**.
k. Test the actions assigned to the shapes by clicking the **Slide Show** tab, and then click **From Current Slide** in the Start Slide Show group.
l. Click **Tension**. The attached action is successful if you jump to the Phase 1 Tension-Building slide. Right-click in the slide and click **Last Viewed** to return to the illustration slide.
m. Click **Violence**. The attached action is successful if you jump to the Phase 2 Violence slide. Right-click in the slide and click **Last Viewed**.
n. Click **Remorse**. The attached action is successful if you jump to the Phase 3 Remorse slide. Right-click in the slide and click **Last Viewed**.
o. Click **Reconciliation**. The attached action is successful if you jump to the Phase 4 Reconciliation slide. Press **Esc** to exit the slide show.
p. If the action did not work properly on any of the shapes, right-click the shape and select **Edit Hyperlink**. Compare the setting against the instruction above and make any necessary changes.
q. Save the *chap7_pe2_cycle_solution* presentation.

...continued on Next Page

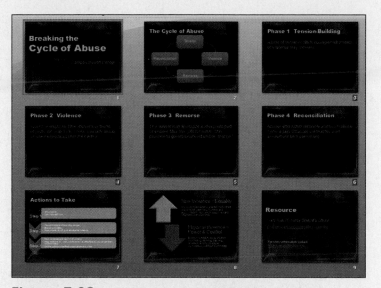

Figure 7.30 Slide Sorter View Showing Slide Number Blocked for Hidden Slides

3 Create a Navigation Bar Using Action Buttons

You are unsure if the viewer will know how to right-click in a slide show to return to the previously viewed slide, so you decide to create a navigation bar for the viewer's use. You want the controls to be easily recognizable, so you decide to use PowerPoint's action buttons that mimic the controls on a VCR or DVD player. Because you want controls on every slide, you create the action buttons on the slide master. Refer to Figure 7.31 when you complete these steps.

a. Save the *chap7_pe2_cycle_solution* presentation as **chap7_pe3_cycle_solution**.

b. Click the **View tab**, and then click **Slide Master** in the Presentation Views group.

c. Click the **Insert tab**, and then click **Shapes** in the Illustrations group.

d. Select **Action Button: Beginning** from the Action Buttons category of the Shapes gallery.

e. Drag to create the action button. Click **OK** to accept the action settings and close the Action Settings dialog box.

f. **Click** the **Format tab**, and then click the **arrow** in the Size group to open the Size and Position dialog box.

g. Set the **Height** to **.33"** and the **Width** to **.5"**.

h. Click the Position tab and set the **Horizontal** position to **2.83"** and the **Vertical** position to **7"**. Click **Close**.

i. Click **Shapes** in the Illustrations group on the Insert tab, and then select **Action Button: Back or Previous** from the Action Buttons category of the Shapes gallery. Drag to create the action button. Click the **Format tab**, and then click the **arrow** in the Size group to open the Size and Position dialog box. Set the **Height** to **.33"** and the **Width** to **.5"**. Click the Position tab and set the **Horizontal** position to **3.81"** and the **Vertical** position to **7"**. Click **Close**.

j. Click **Shapes** in the Illustrations group on the Insert tab, and then select **Action Button: Return** from the Action Buttons category of the Shapes gallery. Drag to create the action button. Click the **Format tab**, and then click the **arrow** in the Size group to open the Size and Position dialog box. Set the **Height** to **.33"** and the **Width** to **.5"**. Click the Position tab and set the **Horizontal** position to **4.79"** and the **Vertical** position **to 7"**. Click **Close**.

k. Click **Shapes** in the Illustrations group on the Insert tab, and then select **Action Button: Forward or Next Slide** from the Action Buttons category of the Shapes gallery. Drag to create the action button. Click the **Format tab**, and then click the **arrow** in the Size group to open the Size and Position dialog box. Set the **Height** to **.33"** and the **Width** to **.5"**. Click the Position tab and set the **Horizontal** position to **5.77"** and the **Vertical** position to **7"**. Click **Close**.

...continued on Next Page

l. Click **Shapes** in the Illustrations group on the Insert tab, and then select **Action Button: End** from the Action Buttons category of the Shapes gallery. Drag to create the action button. Click the **Format tab**, and then click the **arrow** in the Size group to open the Size and Position dialog box. Set the **Height** to **.33"** and the **Width** to **.5"**. Click the Position tab and set the **Horizontal** position to **6.75"** and the **Vertical** position to **7"**. Click **Close**.

m. Click the **Slide Master tab** in the Edit Master group on the Edit Master, and then click **Close Master View**.

n. Test the action buttons by clicking the **Slide Show** tab, and then click **From Current Slide** in the Start Slide Show group.

o. Click each action button as you navigate through the slide show. Press **Esc** to exit the slide show. If any of the action buttons did not work, right-click the button and click **Edit Hyperlink**. Compare the settings to the instructions above and make any necessary changes.

p. Save the *chap7_pe3_cycle_solution* presentation.

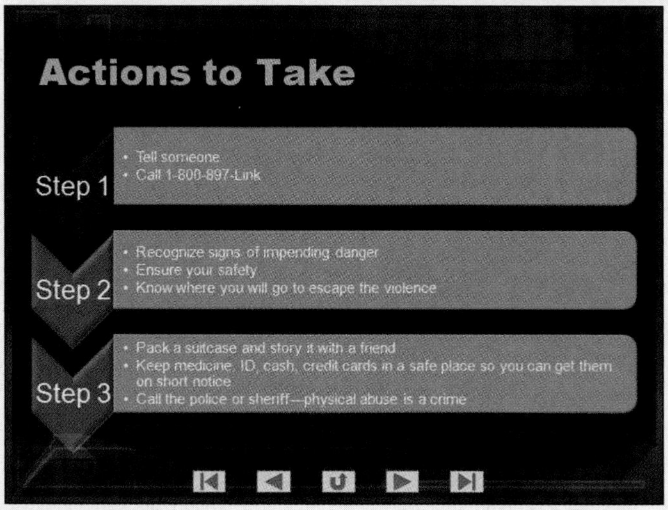

Figure 7.31 Navigation Bar with Action Buttons

4 Create a Custom Action Button

You decide to create a custom action button to cause an explosion sound to emphasize the idea of conflict. You enter text in the custom action button to direct the user to click on the button. Refer to Figure 7.32 when positioning the custom button.

a. Save the *chap7_pe3_cycle_solution* presentation as **chap7_pe4_cycle_solution** and move to Slide 8.

b. Click the **Insert tab**, and then click **Shapes** in the Illustrations group.

c. Click **Action Button: Custom** in the Action Buttons category of the Shapes gallery.

d. Drag to create the action button. In the open Action Settings dialog box, check the **Play Sound** option, and then click **Explosion**. Click **OK**.

e. Click the **Format tab**, and then click the **arrow** in the Size group to open the Size and Position dialog box. Set the **Height** to **.67"** and the **Width** to **.75"**. Click the **Position tab** and set the **Horizontal** position to **.5"** and the Vertical position to **.25"**. Click **Close**.

f. Type **Click Here** in the custom button.

g. Save the *chap7_pe4_cycle_solution* presentation.

...continued on Next Page

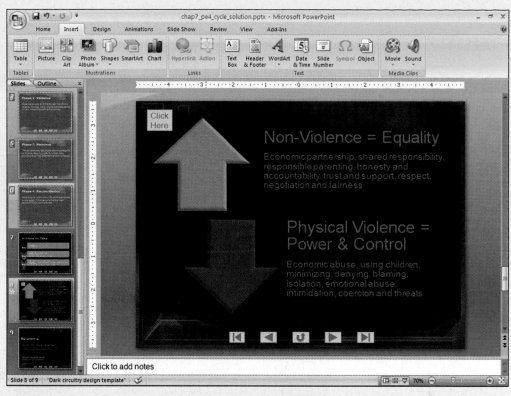

Figure 7.32 Customized Action Button

5 Create a Trigger

You know that you cannot turn the SmartArt shapes on Slide 8 into action buttons, but you can animate the objects. Because the SmartArt displays opposing shapes, you decide to animate them one right after the other and use the *Click Here* button as the trigger to the event. Refer to Figure 7.33 as you complete this exercise.

a. Save the *chap7_pe4_cycle_solution* presentation as **chap7_pe5_cycle_solution.**

b. Click the SmartArt diagram to select it, and then click the **Animations tab**.

c. Click the arrow for **Animate** in the Animations group, and then click **One by One** in the **Wipe** category.

d. Click **Custom Animation** in the Animations group on the Animations tab.

e. Click the arrow for **Direction**, and then click **From Top**.

f. Click the list arrow for the diagram in the Custom Animation list, and then click **Timing**.

g. Click **Triggers**.

h. Click **Start effect on click of**, and then click the list arrow.

i. Click **Action Button: Custom 5: Click**, and then click **OK**.

j. To test the custom action button created in Step 4 and the triggers created in Step 5, click the **Slide Show** tab, and then click **From Current Slide** in the Start Slide Show group.

k. Click the *Click Here* action button. The explosion sound should play and the first shape in the SmartArt diagram should wipe in from the top. Click the *Click Here* action button again to launch the second animation and the explosion sound.

l. If the action button does not trigger the SmartArt shapes, select the Diagram animation in the Custom Animation list, and then click the list arrow. Click **Timing** and then make sure that you have the Triggers Start effect set to **Action Button** and not Diagram 2.

m. Save the *chap7_pe5_cycle_solution* presentation.

...continued on Next Page

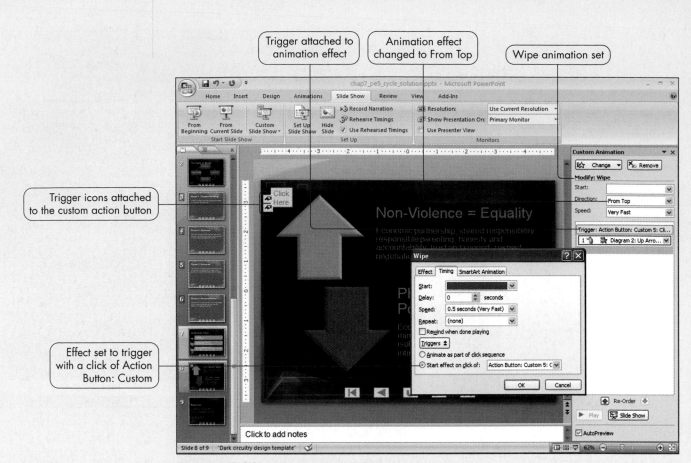

Figure 7.33 Triggers Set for Each SmartArt Shape

6 Create a Hyperlink to an Existing File

You just received an e-mail from a clerk at the San Juan County Sheriff's Office that contains information about obtaining a protective order. You copied the e-mail text into a Word document, and then saved it. You decide to include a hyperlink to this document as an additional resource for viewers. Refer to Figure 7.34 as you complete this exercise.

a. Save the *chap7_pe5_cycle_solution* presentation as **chap7_pe6_cycle_solution**.

b. Move to Slide 9 and change *Resource* to **Resources**.

c. Click after the last word (*Program*) in the body placeholder, and then press **Enter**.

d. Type **Obtaining Protective Orders**, and then select the text.

e. Click the **Insert tab**, and then click **Hyperlink** in the Links group.

f. Navigate to your student files, and then click *chap7_pe6_po.docx*.

g. Click **ScreenTip**, and then type the following text in the ScreenTip text box: **Click to see a list of the requirements for obtaining a protective order**. Click **OK**, and then click **OK**.

h. Click the placeholder border, right-click, and then click **Format Shape**.

i. Click **Text Box** in the Fill pane, and then click the option for **Resize shape to fit text** in the Autofit section. Click **Close**.

j. Drag to select the two hyperlinks, and then drag the **First Line Indent marker** to the 1″ mark on the horizontal ruler.

k. To test the hyperlink to an existing file, click the **Slide Show** tab, and then click **From Current Slide** in the Start Slide Show group.

l. If the hyperlink did not work, right-click the hyperlink and click **Edit Hyperlink**. Check to see if the file location and file name are correct. If not, navigate to locate and select the correct file. Click **OK**, and then click **OK**.

...continued on Next Page

m. Create a Notes and Handouts header and footer with the date and your name in the header and your instructor's name and your class in the footer.

n. Save the *chap7_pe6_cycle_solution* presentation.

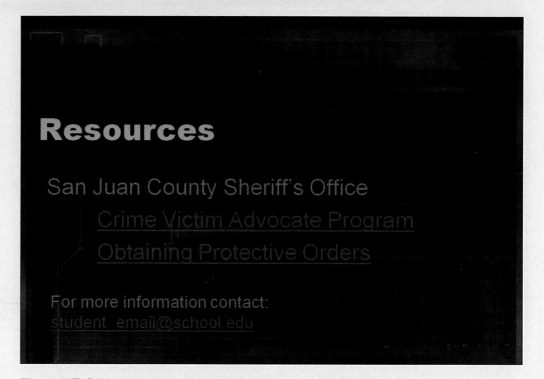

Figure 7.34 Hyperlink to Existing File Added

7 Setting Web Options and Publishing a Web Page

You completed this week's Campus Health Center's safety presentation and need to publish it to the Campus Intranet. After publishing, the presentation will be available for students to view at various kiosks around campus. Before you publish the presentation, you set the Web options. Figure 7.35 displays the Web page.

a. Save the *chap7_pe6_cycle_solution* presentation as **chap7_pe7_cycle_solution**.

b. Click the **Office Button**, and then click **Save As**.

c. Click the **Save as type** list arrow, and then click **Web Page**.

d. Click the **Change Title button**, and then type **Breaking the Cycle of Abuse** in the Page title box. Click **OK**.

e. Click the **Publish button**. Click the option for **Display speaker notes** to remove the check. Click the option for **Open published Web page in browser** to add a check and activate the feature.

f. Click **Web Options**. In the General tab, click **Show slide animation while browsing**. Click **OK**.

g. Click **Publish**. If you get security warnings, click **Allow Blocked Content** to allow ActiveX control.

h. Close the Web browser.

i. Close the presentation and PowerPoint.

...continued on Next Page

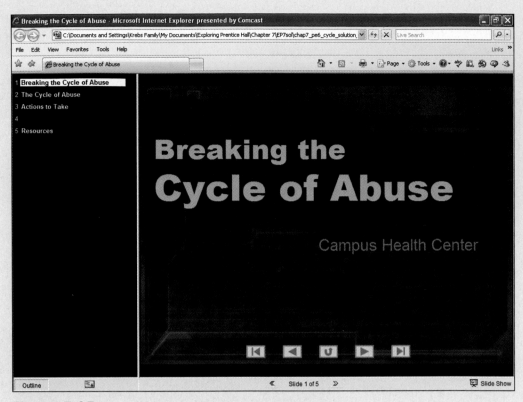

Figure 7.35 Breaking the Cycle of Abuse Web Page

The presentation in Figure 7.36 was created using a Microsoft Office Online template, *Presentation on brainstorming*. Because it is a presentation template, it includes suggested text to "jump start" the creative process. In this exercise, you download the template and modify it. You add a navigation bar using custom action buttons that link to the related slides. Figure 7.36 shows the completed slide show.

a. Click the **Office Button**, and then click **New** to access templates. Open the *Presentations* category in the Microsoft Office Online section, and then open the *Other Presentations* subcategory. You see two presentations with the name *Presentation on brainstorming*. Download the *Presentation on brainstorming* that uses *Creativity Session* as the title and displays a light bulb on the slides. Save the presentation as **chap7_mid1_creativity_solution**.

b. Replace the subtitle *Presenter's Name* with your name.

c. Delete the third slide (Overview) because the information on this slide is redundant with the agenda slide. Delete the overview bullet on the agenda slide as well.

d. Open the Slide Master, and in the Master create a Custom Action Button **.25"** high and **1.2"** wide. Change the **Shape Style to Style 6**. To locate this style, click the Format tab, and click the More button in the Shape Styles group. Shape Style 6 is in the Other Theme Fills category at the bottom of the gallery.

e. Change the Shape Outline color to **Theme Color Gold, Background 2**.

f. Type **Agenda** in the action button, and then change the font size to **12** points.

g. Duplicate the button five times. Change the label of the buttons to: **Objectives**, **Rules**, **Activity**, **Summarize**, **Next Steps**. Position the buttons near the bottom of the slide, align the buttons at their bottoms, and then distribute the buttons horizontally.

h. Add the appropriate hyperlink to each of the action buttons you just created.

i. Hide the Background Graphics on the Title Slide so that the action buttons do not block the light bulb image.

j. Create a Notes and Handouts header and footer with the date and your name in the header, and your instructor's name and your class in the footer.

k. Save the *chap7_mid1_creativity_solution* presentation and close.

...continued on Next Page

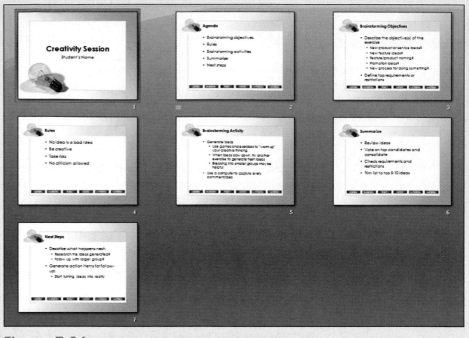

Figure 7.36 Creativity Interactive Slide Show

2 Patient Assessment Flow Chart

In this exercise, you will create hyperlinks for a Patient Assessment Flow Chart for the Fire and Rescue Academy. The flow chart and related slides are already created to save you time. Your instructor may, however, ask you to recreate the flow chart for practice creating and aligning shapes. Your task is to turn each shape in the flow chart into a clickable button with an action assigned. When clicked, the button will link to its associated detail slide. You create a button to return the viewer to the flow chart after viewing a slide. You also add a sound to a slide. Refer to Figures 7.37 and 7.38 as you complete this exercise.

a. Open the *chap7_mid2_assessment* presentation and save it as **chap7_mid2_assessment_ solution**.

b. Move to Slide 2 and select the *Scene Size-Up* shape and open the Action Settings dialog box. Hyperlink the shape to Slide 3 (Scene Size-Up).

c. Continue converting each shape in the Patient Assessment Flow Chart into a button with a hyperlink to the associated slide. Note that the *Focused Assessment* and the *Rapid Trauma Assessment* share a common slide, Slide 5. Each of these buttons, therefore, must link to Slide 5.

d. To enable the viewer to move quickly back to the flow chart slide, create an **Action Button: Return** button on the Slide Master.

e. Create an **Action Button: Sound** button to the left of the Slide Title on Slide 7. Link the sound to the *chap7_mid2_ambulance.wav* file, located in your student files. This is a Microsoft Online sound with the keyword *ambulance*, which has been saved as a file for your convenience in creating the sound button. Size the sound action button so it is the same size as the return button you created to give a sense of balance to your slide.

f. Test each of the buttons you created in Slide Show view.

g. Edit any buttons that do not link correctly.

h. Save the *chap7_mid2_assessment_solution* presentation.

...continued on Next Page

i. Open the Save As dialog box and change the **Save as type** setting to Single File Web Page. Change the title for the Web Page from Slide 1 to Patient Assessment Flow Chart. Change the **Publish** options to include the option to open the published Web page in your browser after publishing.

j. Change your Web options so that the slide navigation controls use the **Presentation Colors (accent color)** color scheme.

k. Publish the *chap7_mid2_assessment_solution* presentation. If you get security warnings, allow blocked content and let the file run active content. Examine the resulting Web Page, and then close your browser and close the file in PowerPoint.

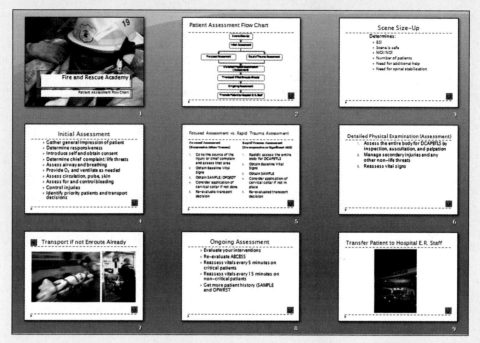

Figure 7.37 Patient Assessment Flow Chart Presentation

Figure 7.38 Patient Assessment Flow Chart Web Page

...continued on Next Page

The presentation in Figure 7.39 was created using a downloaded Microsoft Office Business Presentation template and saved as a Web page. The presentation can be viewed locally as in Figure 7.39 or it can be uploaded to the Web. Either way, it is a sophisticated presentation that can be easily edited to fit your needs. In this exercise, you download the template, save it as a Web page, change the title of the Web page, change the Web options, and then publish the Web page locally. You then view the Web page and use the navigation controls available to move through the slide show.

a. Click the **Office Button**, and then open the **New Presentation** dialog box. Select the **Business Presentations** subcategory of the Presentations category of Microsoft Online Templates. You have multiple Business plan presentations. Select the **Business plan presentation** that looks like Figure 7.39.

b. Save the presentation as **chap7_mid3_sports_solution**. Add your name after *Business Plan* in the subtitle placeholder.

c. Change the title on the Title slide to **Colorado Extreme Sports**.

d. Add a footer to every slide that displays the date, your name, and the slide number. Note: The footer does not apply to the Title Slide and the Section Header Slides (Slides 1 and 2).

e. Save the presentation as a Web page after making the following modifications:

- Web page title as **Colorado Extreme Sports**
- No Speaker Notes
- Open published Web page in browser activated
- Slide navigation controls in Presentation colors (accent color).

f. In the open browser, as shown in Figure 7.39, answer the following questions:

- How do you go to a specific slide?
- The pane on the left side shows only slide titles. How do you see the slide detail in this pane?
- How do you show the slide in full-screen format?
- Where does the Web page title display?

g. Close the Web browser and the *chap7_mid3_sports_solution* presentation.

...continued on Next Page

Figure 7.39 Colorado Extreme Sports Business Plan Web Page

4 Photographs on the Web

Uploading photographs to the Web is very popular. It enables you to share your photographs with family members and friends throughout the world. One method to do so is to place the photographs in a PowerPoint album and publish the album on the Web. You can create a menu with a list of each photograph that the viewer clicks to link to the photo stored alone on a page, or you can create a menu listing categories of photographs with links to the slide on which the photos are stored. In this exercise, you open an album displaying the pictures of activities and trips of two friends through a school year. The album was created using the Classic Photo Album template. You create hyperlinks to slides showing the friends' various activities and trips. You create navigation buttons to aid the viewer to move through the slide show. Finally, you publish the Photo Album as a single file Web page. Refer to Figures 7.40 and 7.41 as you complete this exercise.

a. Open the *chap7_mid4_webalbum* presentation and save it as **chap7_mid4_webalbum _ solution**.

b. Move to Slide 2 (menu slide) and select the text *Fun Times*. Create a hyperlink that links this text to Slide 3 (Fun Times).

c. Continue linking the menu items *Vegas Vacations, Nieces and Nephews*, and *Home in O'ahu* to their respective slides.

d. Create a navigation bar on the slide master that includes buttons to go to the beginning of the slide show, go back one slide, return to the previous slide, go forward one slide, and go to the end of the slide show. Change the fill colors to the colors shown in Figures 7.40 and 7.41.

...continued on Next Page

e. Publish the presentation as a single file Web page after making the following modifications and choosing the following Web options:

- Web Page title as **Lee and Anela's 2008/2009 Photo Album**
- No Speaker Notes
- Open published Web page in browser activated
- Slide navigation controls in Presentation colors (text color).
- Show slide animation while browsing

f. View the slide show in the browser. Depending on your computer system, you may experience considerable lag time when the animations play. Realizing that other viewers may have even slower systems and that the slide show could be frustrating for viewers waiting for animations, you remove the animations. Close the browser and edit the presentation to remove all animations in the Custom Animation task pane. Publish the slide show again.

g. Create a Notes and Handouts header and footer with the date and your name in the header and your instructor's name and your class in the footer.

h. Save the *chap7_mid4_webalbum_solution* presentation.

Figure 7.40 Photograph Album with Hyperlinks and Action Buttons

...continued on Next Page

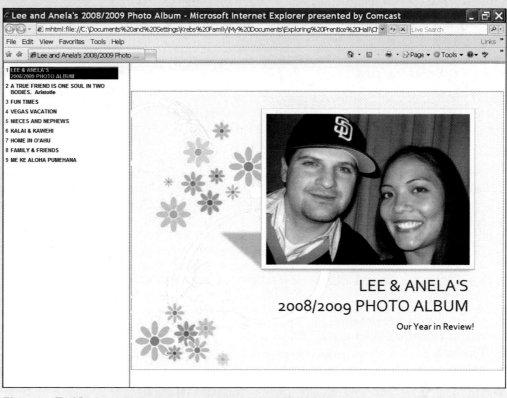

Figure 7.41 Photograph Album Single File Web Page

Capstone Exercise

Copyright and the Law

The IT manager of your company has observed some violations of software copyright in the organization. He immediately removed the offending software and spoke with the employees involved, but feels that perhaps it is a lack of understanding about copyright rather than deliberate theft. He asks you, as a company trainer, to prepare and deliver a presentation about basic copyright principles to company employees. After the presentation, he plans on posting the slide show to the company Intranet so that it can be reviewed as needed in the future.

1. Set Up Slide Show

You locate and download a Microsoft Office Online Template that you feel indicates the importance of this topic. Then, you reuse slides you have created previously to begin the slide show. You make any necessary adjustments to individual slides necessitated by reusing slides, and then save the slide show. Figure 7.42 shows the Title slide of the new slide show.

a. Create a new presentation using one of the Microsoft Office Online templates. Use the *Corinthian columns design template* in the Design category, Business subcategory. Save the slide show as **chap7_cap_copyright_solution**.

b. Create a Notes and Handouts header and footer with the date and your name in the header and your instructor's name and your class in the footer.

c. Use the New Slide feature to reuse all of the slides in the *chap7_cap_copyright* presentation.

d. In the Design tab, change the Fonts theme to the **Equity** theme (Franklin Gothic Bold and Perpetua).

e. Clean up each of the slides in the slide show by adjusting placement of placeholders and objects, and resizing text as necessary to ensure that elements fit on the page. (Example: On Slide 1 move the copyright clip art image above the word *Law*.)

f. Save the *chap7_cap_copyright_solution* presentation.

Figure 7.42 Title Slide Using Corinthian Columns Design Template

2. Create and Format an E-Mail Hyperlink

You create an e-mail hyperlink to yourself so that employees viewing the slide show can contact you for further information. You edit the design theme to change the hyperlink colors. Figure 7.43 shows the e-mail hyperlink in the Title Slide.

a. In the open *chap7_cap_copyright_solution*, move to Slide 1 (if necessary).

b. At the beginning of the Subtitle placeholder, type **For more information contact**, and then press **Enter**.

c. Replace the text *Student Name* with your name, and then type **at**. Press **Enter**.

d. On the new line, type your e-mail address.

e. Because the light blue text color assigned to the hyperlink does not have enough contrast with the background, you decide to change it. Click the **Design tab**, and then click **Colors** in the Themes group.

f. Click **Create New Theme Colors**, and then click the **Color** list arrow next to Hyperlink in the Theme Colors list. Click **Light Blue, Accent 2, Darker 50%** (the color on the sixth row, sixth column), and then exit the dialog box.

g. Save the *chap7_cap_copyright_solution* presentation.

Figure 7.43 Edited E-Mail Hyperlink

3. Assign an Action to a Clip Art Object

To emphasize the message that copying software illegally and installing the software is piracy, you insert a clip art image, modify it, and position it on the slide. Finally, you turn the clip art image into a mouse over button that has a sound action attached to it. Figure 7.43 shows the modified button positioned on the slide.

a. Move to Slide 7 in the open *chap7_cap_copyright_solution* presentation, and then open the Clip Art task pane. Perform a search using **No** as the keyword and locate the pink button labeled with the word *No*. Insert the clip art image in Slide 6.

b. Recolor the clip art using **Accent color 2 Light** in the Light Variations category of the Recolor gallery.

c. Set the button size to **.75"** by **.75"** and set its horizontal position to **4.67"** from the top-left corner and its vertical position to **1.85"** from the top-left corner.

d. From the **Action Settings** dialog box, assign a **Mouse Over** action that inserts the sound file *chap7_cap_no.wav* to the clip art object.

e. Test the mouse over button in Slide Show view and troubleshoot as necessary.

f. Save the *chap7_cap_copyright_solution* presentation.

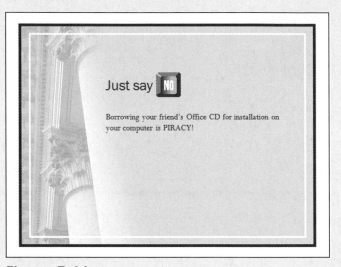

Figure 7.44   Mouse Over Button with a Sound Action Assigned

4. Create Action Buttons for Navigation on the Slide Master

To provide for easy navigation to the viewers of the slide show on the company's Intranet, you create navigation buttons to return to the beginning of the slide show, go back one slide, return to last viewed slide, move forward one slide, and advance to the end of the slide show. You size and position the buttons, and then you test them in the slide show. Figure 7.45 shows the Slide Master with the navigation buttons.

a. In the open *chap7_cap_copyright_solution* presentation, open the slide master.

b. Select the topmost slide master, **Corinthian columns design template Slide Master: used by Slide(s) 1–10**.

c. Move the date placeholder to the top left of the slide, and then move the footer placeholder to the left side of the slide. Position the slide number placeholder next to the footer placeholder. This creates an open area for your navigation bar.

d. Create an **Action Button: Beginning** button and size it so that it is **.25″** by **.25″**. Position it **6.67″** horizontally and **6.5″** vertically from the top left corner.

e. Apply the **Colored Outline – Accent 2** Shape Style to the button. Change the Shape Outline color to **Dark Yellow** to match the color of the slide border.

f. Repeat Steps d and e to create action buttons to return to the previous slide, last slide viewed, next slide, and last slide (four more buttons). Size and format the buttons, but do not worry about the button positions. You position the buttons in the next two steps.

g. Select the **Action Button: Last Slide** button, and then position it at **8.33″** horizontally and **6.5″** vertically from the top left corner.

h. Select all five buttons and align at the bottom. Distribute the buttons horizontally.

i. Close the Master View.

j. Save the *chap7_cap_copyright_solution* presentation.

Capstone

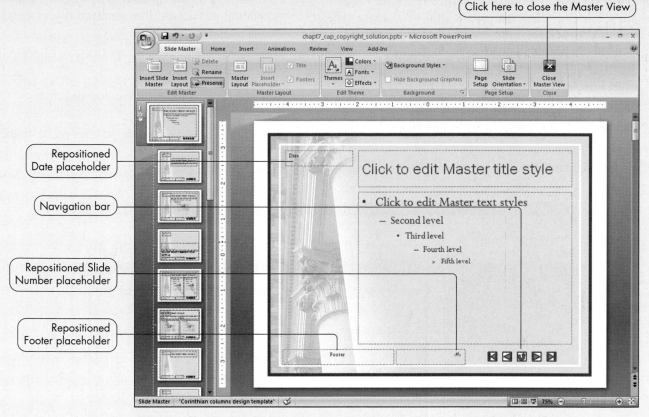

Figure 7.45 Slide Master with Navigation Bar

Labels on figure:
- Click here to close the Master View
- Repositioned Date placeholder
- Navigation bar
- Repositioned Slide Number placeholder
- Repositioned Footer placeholder

5. Hyperlink to an Existing File and Web Pages

You decide that it would help the viewer to see an existing End User License Agreement, so you include a link to an existing Word document with the Microsoft End User License Agreement. So the viewer can read more about site licensing, you include a link to the Microsoft volume licensing site. Finally, you insert hyperlinks that will link the viewer to Web sites with further information about copyright and copyright protection.

a. Move to Slide 4 and select the text *End User License Agreement*. Insert a hyperlink that links to the existing file *chap7_cap_eclu.docx*, which can be located by navigating to your student file location.

b. Select the text *Site License* and then create a hyperlink that links to *www.microsoftvolumelicensing.com*.

c. Move to Slide 10, and then select the text *United States Copyright*. Link the text to *www.loc. gov/copyright*.

d. Select the text *Business Software Alliance* and link the text to *www.bsa.org*.

e. Select the text *Copyright* and link the text to *www.benedict.com*.

f. Save the *chap7_cap_copyright_solution* presentation.

Capstone

6. Saving a Presentation as a Single File Web Page

You are ready to publish the presentation as a single file Web page. Figure 7.46 shows Slide 10 of the Web page which displays the three hyperlinks you created in the above exercise.

a. Select **Single File Web Page** as the file type in the Save As dialog box.

b. Change the Page title to **Copyright and the Law**.

c. Change the Publish options to display the slide navigation controls in **Presentation colors (text color)**.

d. Test each of the links in the slide show, and then close the browser.

e. Edit and repair any broken links, and then publish the slide show again.

f. Save the *chap7_cap_copyright_solution* presentation.

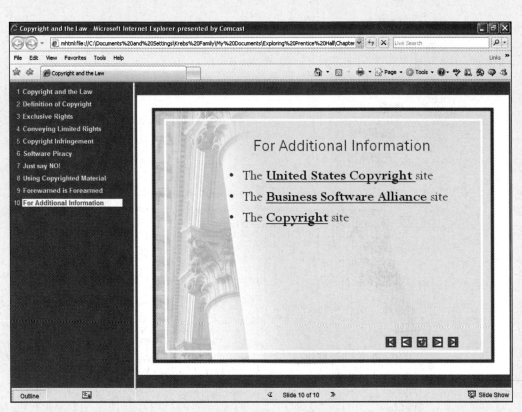

Figure 7.46 Copyright and the Law Web Page, Slide 10

Mini Cases

Use the rubric following the case as a guide to evaluate your work, but keep in mind that your instructor may impose additional grading criteria or use a different standard to judge your work.

Personal Mythology

GENERAL CASE

A myth can be defined as a traditional story accepted as history that serves to explain the world view of a people (WordNet®2.1, Dictionary.com). You can explore your personal myth, or story, to help you creatively examine your feelings and beliefs. Steven Larsen in *The Mythic Imagination* says, "Myths appear interwoven with our feelings and our behavior—and our dreams. We think we know how we feel most of the time, but we may not take the time in daily life to notice all the connections: how our soul life does in fact hang together."

In this case study, you examine your personal myth. You collect sounds, images, and/or hyperlinks to Web sites that appeal to you and represent your feelings and your dreams. Present these items as collages on slides. Create a menu and link the menu items to their associated slides. Add animations if desired. When creating the collages, be sure to go with your instincts—do not think too hard about why the objects you are adding appeal to you. You are not trying to predetermine your myth; you are simply performing a self-exploration. Brainstorm in this activity. If it helps, remember the rules for brainstorming given in the *chap7_mid1_creativity_solution* presentation: no idea is a bad idea, be creative, take risks, and no self-criticism allowed. Do not worry about pleasing anyone else with your selections. "Go with the flow." Remember—**You are the audience!** This does not mean, however, that the slide show should not be done well. You should do your very best work for yourself. In your slide show, answer Carl Jung, the famous Swiss psychologist, when he asks, "What is the myth you are living?" (*Symbols of Transformation*). Save your file as **chap7_mc1_mythology_solution**. Create a single file Web page from your presentation. Figure 7.47 shows one possible solution to this task. The title slide includes words that hyperlink to their associated slides and the Slide Master includes navigation buttons.

Figure 7.47   Sample Solution to Mini Case 1

Performance Elements	Exceeds Expectations	Meets Expectations	Below Expectations
Organization	Menu present with links to associated slides.	Menu available but no links to associated slides are present.	No menu created.
Visual aspects	Multiple objects are added to the slides to demonstrate feelings and dreams.	Some objects added.	Single object on slides to represent feelings and dreams. Little effort demonstrated in creating myth.
Layout	The layout is visually pleasing and contributes to understanding the feelings and dreams.	The layout includes objects representing beliefs or values.	Understanding of the personal mythology is lost in slides showing no discernable layout strategy.
Mechanics	Menu items link to proper slide. Hyperlinks jump to correct location. Presentation text has no errors in spelling, grammar, word usage, or punctuation.	Presentation has no more than two errors in spelling, grammar, word usage, or punctuation. Hyperlinks jump to the correct location.	Hyperlinks do not work. Presentation readability is impaired due to repeated errors in spelling, grammar, word usage, or punctuation. Multiple typographical errors.

Professionalism

RESEARCH CASE

Many professions have support organizations to promote them. These organizations are created to serve the membership and to enhance their professional growth. Belonging to a professional organization can provide members with a sense of unity and a means of networking with others who share the same interests. Laurie Brems, president of the Utah Business and Computer Educators Association and a professional business educator, created a slide to show Utah business educators the two professional routes available for them in their pursuit of professionalism. Following one route, educators join the state and national technical education organizations. Following the other route, educators join the state and national business education organizations. These routes are not mutually exclusive. Joining both sets of organizations ensures a business educator the greatest support and network possible. Figure 7.48 shows the chart President Brems created to illustrate the professional paths. Each path includes hyperlinks to jump to the Web site for each organization. Costs for membership are included.

In this case, you research the professional organizations available to you in your field of interest. Create a slide similar to the one created by President Brems to illustrate the path(s) available to you. Include hyperlinks to the organizations. Include additional information on this slide or on additional slides in the slide show. After creating the slide, publish the slide show as a single file Web page. Save the presentation as **chap7_mc2_professionalism_solution**.

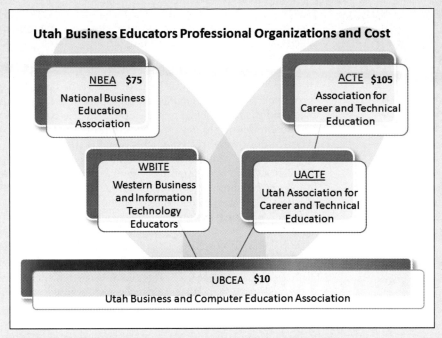

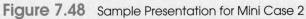

Figure 7.48 Sample Presentation for Mini Case 2

Performance Elements	Exceeds Expectations	Meets Expectations	Below Expectations
Organization	Organization clearly defines the route(s) available for someone entering the profession. Additional information regarding the organizations is presented.	Organization clearly defines the route(s) available for someone entering the profession.	No research into organization structure is indicated. Path to follow is unclear.
Visual aspects	There is a consistent visual theme if multiple slides are created. Shapes and lines used to indicate the paths are easy to read and follow.	The visual theme is inconsistent if multiple slides are created. Shapes are inconsistent. No connecting lines present to indicate the path members would take.	The visual theme is not apparent if multiple slides are created.
Layout	The layout is visually pleasing.	The layout is appropriate for the display of professional choices, but could be improved upon.	The layout is cluttered and confusing.
Mechanics	Hyperlinks added to organizations for field of interest. Hyperlinks link correctly. Any added text has no errors in spelling, grammar, word usage, or punctuation. No typographical errors present.	Web address for organizations added to the page but hyperlinks not created. Any added text has no more than two errors in spelling, grammar, word usage, or punctuation.	No hyperlinks or Web addresses are added. Any added text has impaired readability due to repeated errors in spelling, grammar, word usage, or punctuation. Multiple typographical errors.

Colorful Diet = Healthy Diet Presentation

DISASTER RECOVERY

You are part of a group assigned to create a presentation on healthy eating. Your group was given one hour in a computer lab to prepare, so first you sketched out a storyboard, and then you divided responsibilities. One member of the group researched the benefits of eating fruits and vegetables, and two members created the design of the presentation including locating pictures. As information was located, it was typed into the presentation. Your role in the group is to check the design to make sure all aspects display properly and that the introduction slide, body slides, and conclusion slide appear in the correct order. You must also test hyperlinks and action buttons to ensure they link properly. If they do not, you must edit the links. The action buttons were created quickly, so you must resize them and distribute them horizontally. You make other changes to the slide show as desired. Finally, you carefully proofread the text and check the images carefully, as you know one of the group members has a corny sense of humor. You want to present a professional presentation to the instructor and class and you are not sure of the audience's sense of humor. Save your file as *chap7_mc3_diet_solution*. As the final step, you save the presentation as a Web page.

Performance Elements	Exceeds Expectations	Meets Expectations	Below Expectations
Organization	Slides follow a logical sequence with the multimedia supporting the message.	The message is difficult to understand because sequencing is inconsistent. Multimedia elements do not support the message.	The multimedia elements are not placed in a logical order. The message is lost because the multimedia is distracting.
Visual aspects	The multimedia elements are appealing and enhance the presentation. They are consistent and blend in with the message. Text is easy to read.	The multimedia elements are consistent with the message but they are haphazardly placed on the slide. Text is readable but not consistent throughout the presentation.	The multimedia does not enhance the message. The theme of the multimedia is confusing. Text is difficult to read due to size or color.
Layout	The layout is visually pleasing and contributes to understanding the topic. White space, photographs, and the movie are cohesive.	The layout shows some structure, but placement of some multimedia element is distracting.	The layout is cluttered and confusing. The multimedia elements detract from understanding.
Mechanics	Presentation has no errors in spelling, grammar, word usage, or punctuation. No typographical errors present. Sources of research are shown on an ending slide.	Presentation has no more than two errors in spelling, grammar, word usage, or punctuation. A resource slide is included, but the format of the slide is confusing.	Presentation readability is impaired due to repeated errors in spelling, grammar, word usage, or punctuation. Multiple typographical errors. No resource page is included.

Collaborate and Distribute

Reviewing, Securing, and Publishing a Presentation

Objectives

After you read this chapter, you will be able to:

1. Add and edit comments **(page 558)**.
2. Show and hide markup **(page 560)**.
3. Print comments and ink markup **(page 562)**.
4. View and set document properties **(page 569)**.
5. Inspect the presentation **(page 570)**.
6. Encrypt and set a password **(page 571)**.
7. Restrict permissions **(page 572)**.
8. Add a digital signature **(page 573)**.
9. Check compatibility and mark as final **(page 573)**.
10. Package a presentation **(page 580)**.
11. Create a handout in Microsoft Office Word **(page 582)**.
12. Recognize other publishing options **(page 584)**.

Hands-On Exercises

Exercises	Skills Covered
1. REVIEWING A PRESENTATION (page 563) **Open:** chap8_ho1_protect.pptx **Save as:** chap8_ho1_protect_solution.pptx **Open:** chap8_ho1_safety.pptx **Save as:** chap8_ho1_safety_solution.pptx	• Insert a Comment • Review Comments and Make Changes • Add Ink Annotations • Show and Hide Markup • Print Comments and Ink Markup
2. PREPARING A PRESENTATION FOR DISTRIBUTION (page 575) **Open:** chap8_ho1_safety_solution.pptx (from exercise 1) **Save as:** chap8_ho2_threat_solution.pptx	• Set Document Properties • Inspect the Presentation • Set and Remove a Password • Check for Compatibility • Mark as Final • Add a Personal Digital Signature
3. PACKAGING A PRESENTATION (page 585) **Open:** chap8_ho3_security.pptx **Save as:** chap8_ho3_security_solution.pptx	• Package a Presentation • Use the PowerPoint 2007 Viewer • Create a Microsoft Office Word Handout

CASE STUDY

The Harbor Business Center

ACSL Development is a large, internationally owned commercial real estate development company. It specializes in developing properties to serve as business hubs with access to cutting-edge technology. The centers are designed to meet the demands of leading global companies. You were recently hired by the organization, and the vice president of marketing, Susil Akalushi, has asked you to prepare a presentation under her supervision. The presentation must describe ACSL's latest project.

The Harbor Business Center is a $58.5 million, mixed-use project offering luxurious new office space that includes multiperson office suites and 1-, 2-, or 4-person offices. Office suites are finished to a high standard with imported tile, stylish décor, and a sense of spaciousness and comfort. They include state-of-the-art communication

Case Study

technology. Monthly leases offer fully customizable office space, 24-hour access to the office 365 days a year, high security, access to state-of-the-art meeting facilities, and on-site banking and global messenger services. The project is centrally located two blocks from the city harbor area and one block from the state and federal courthouses.

Vice President Akalushi reviewed your presentation and sent it back to you with comments regarding the changes you need to make. You make the requested changes and hide the markup, but do not delete the markup. Leaving the markup allows the vice president to ensure her instructions were followed. You prepare the presentation for distribution, and then package the presentation as a CD, but rather than burn it to a CD you save it to your student solution folder.

Your Assignment

- Read the chapter, paying special attention to inserting and editing comments, preparing a presentation for distribution, and packaging for CDs.
- Open the *chap8_case_harbor* file and immediately save it as **chap8_case_harbor_solution**.
- Read each comment and follow the instructions. After you have completed the instructions, add a new comment that indicates you have completed the task.
- In Slide 5, move the legend to the bottom and insert a new comment letting Vice President Akalushi know that the grid interfered with the legend when you moved it to the top right. Ask if it is ok at the bottom.
- Make any other formatting or position changes to the presentation you feel are necessary. Add a comment explaining your choice(s). Hide Markup when you have finished.
- Create a Notes and Handouts Header and Footer with your name in the header and your instructor's name and your class in the footer.
- Prepare the presentation by changing Document Properties to include a subject, keywords, status, and comments; by inspecting the document and removing the Presentation Notes; and finally by encrypting the document with the password **cAse8h@b:r**.
- Use Microsoft Office Word to print notes next to slides.
- Package the presentation and media links to a folder. If asked to update file objects, click yes. Name the folder **Harbor Center**. Although your presentation still contains comments, continue the process. The comments are necessary for evaluating the case.

Presentation Review

Collaboration is a process by which a team of people work together to achieve a goal.

(Collaborating with others in a presentation sparks the creativity and problem solving skills of all group members.)

Collaboration is the process by which two or more individuals work together to achieve an outcome, or goal. Many times, a presentation results from the collaborative efforts of a team of people. Collaborating with others in a presentation sparks the creativity and problem solving skills of all group members, which makes the final project a better project than one in which one individual has sole responsibility. Today's technology enables you to collaborate easily with others, and Office 2007 applications include features to facilitate this process. In the next section you examine the reviewing features of PowerPoint 2007.

After you have created your PowerPoint presentation, you may want to route it to others for review. If you and your teammates share a network connection, you can save the presentation to a shared location on that network. Your teammates can then access the network location and download your file for reviewing.

If you do not have a shared location, you can e-mail the presentation to others on your team. You can e-mail the presentation from within PowerPoint if you have an e-mail program such as Microsoft Outlook installed on your computer. This saves you time because you do not have to open your e-mail program separately. PowerPoint allows you to send the presentation as an attachment in the standard PPTX presentation file format or as a PDF or XPS document. Both the *PDF* and *XPS* file formats preserve your presentation format and enable the presentation to be viewed and printed by any platform. This is extremely helpful if you are sending your presentation out to viewers who do not have Microsoft Office 2007. The PDF file format was created by Adobe Systems and the XPS file format was created by Microsoft. If you do not have an e-mail program installed on your computer because you use an Internet e-mail service, simply open your online e-mail client, attach the PowerPoint presentation in whichever document format you choose, and then send it to the individuals you want to view or review it.

In this section, you create a comment, review comments, and modify a presentation based on the comments.

PDF file format (PDF) is a more secure electronic file format created by Adobe Systems that preserves document formatting and is viewable and printable on any platform.

XPS file format (XPS) is an electronic file format created by Microsoft that preserves document formatting and is viewable and printable on any platform.

Downloading and Installing the Publish as PDF or XPS Add-in for Microsoft Office 2007 | Reference

The PDF (created by Adobe Systems) and XPS (created by Microsoft) file formats are excellent file formats to use when distributing files to others. This is because documents saved in either of these formats are fixed file formats—they retain their format regardless of the application used to create them. They look exactly like the original document on any platform. Saving your presentation or document also makes it difficult to modify. When you distribute documents such as instructions, directions, legal forms, or reports, you probably want the document to be easy to read and print, but you do not want the document to be easily modified.

In order to export and save a document in either of these formats, however, you must download a Microsoft Add-in. This is a free download provided by Microsoft if you are running genuine Microsoft Office software.

To download the free Add-in:

Go to **www.microsoft.com**.
Click the hyperlink for **Downloads and Trials**.
Click **Download Center**.
Click **Office** in the **Product Families** category.
Click **2007 Microsoft Office Add-in: Microsoft Save as PDF or XPS**.
Continue following the on-screen instructions on the Microsoft site to validate your software and download the Add-in.

To save a presentation in a PDF or XPS file format:

Click the **Office Button**, point to **Save As**, and then click **PDF** or **XPS**.
Click the **Open file after publishing** check box if you wish to open the presentation in Adobe Reader after saving.
Click **Standard** or **Minimize size** to specify how you want the file optimized.
Click **OK**.
Click **Publish**.

TIP Send a Presentation for Review Using Outlook

To send a presentation for review from within PowerPoint using Microsoft Outlook, click the Office Button, point to Send, click e-mail, and then either e-mail as PDF Attachment or e-mail as XPS Attachment. An Outlook e-mail message opens with your presentation attached. The subject line displays the file name of the presentation. All you need to do is add the recipients and a message for the people you want to view your presentation and add suggestions.

Adding and Editing Comments

A *reviewer* is someone who inserts comments in a slide as part of a collaborative effort.

A *comment* is a text note attached to a slide.

An *ink annotation* is a marking written or drawn on a slide while displaying the slide show.

Markup refers to comments and ink annotations appearing in a presentation.

After receiving your presentation, the *reviewer* can add *comments* (text notes attached to the slide) or *ink annotations* (markings written or drawn on a slide for additional commentary or explanation while displaying a slide show presentation). A presentation or document with comments and ink annotations contains *markup*. When the reviewer returns the presentation to you, you determine the changes you wish to make based on the markup in the presentation.

Think of the comments as onscreen sticky notes that you can insert and remove as needed. Comments can be used in ways other than having another person add them in a review process. You may find comments to be a very useful personal tool: You can insert comments to remind yourself of revisions you want to make or even as reminders of where you are in the project. You insert a comment on the slide by typing it in a comment box. The name of the person inserting the comment is included along with the date. A color is assigned to the box, and each subsequent reviewer is assigned a different color. Comments are positioned at the upper left of the slide, but may be dragged to any location on the slide.

As you review comments, you can edit your presentation to incorporate any suggestions you agree with or to ignore any you do not wish to incorporate. Usually, you would delete a comment after your decision. This helps you determine where you are in the process. If you are part of a work group, you may choose to leave the comments for others to see. If you have reviewed presentations in previous versions of PowerPoint, it is important to know that the Send for Review and the Compare and Merge Presentations features have been removed.

To insert a comment, click the Review tab, and then click New Comment in the Comments group. Type the statement in the comment box, and when you are finished typing your comment, click outside the comment box to close it and display just the comment thumbnail. To view the comment, click the comment thumbnail or roll the mouse over the comment box. If you want to edit an existing comment, click the comment to select it (the comment border changes color to indicate it is the active comment), and then click Edit Comment in the Comments group. Delete a comment by selecting it and clicking Delete in the Comments group. To move between comments, click Previous or Next. Figure 8.1 shows the Comments group and a slide with an open comment box.

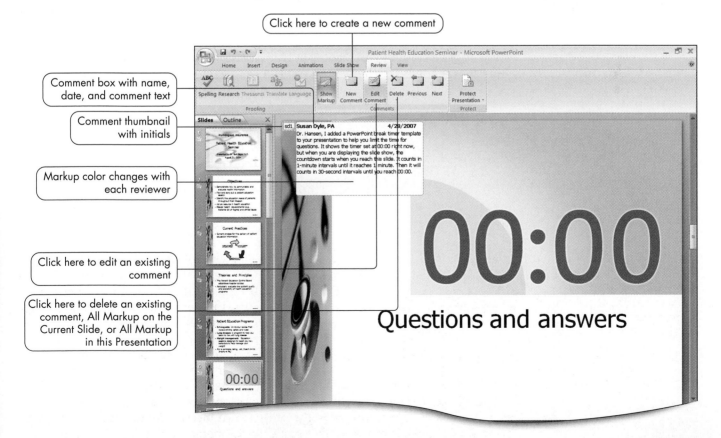

Figure 8.1 The Comments Group

Showing and Hiding Markup

A comment is only visible if you have Show Markup active. Show Markup is in the Comments group of the Review tab. Show Markup is a toggle that displays or hides inserted comments. Figure 8.2 displays the active Show Markup button.

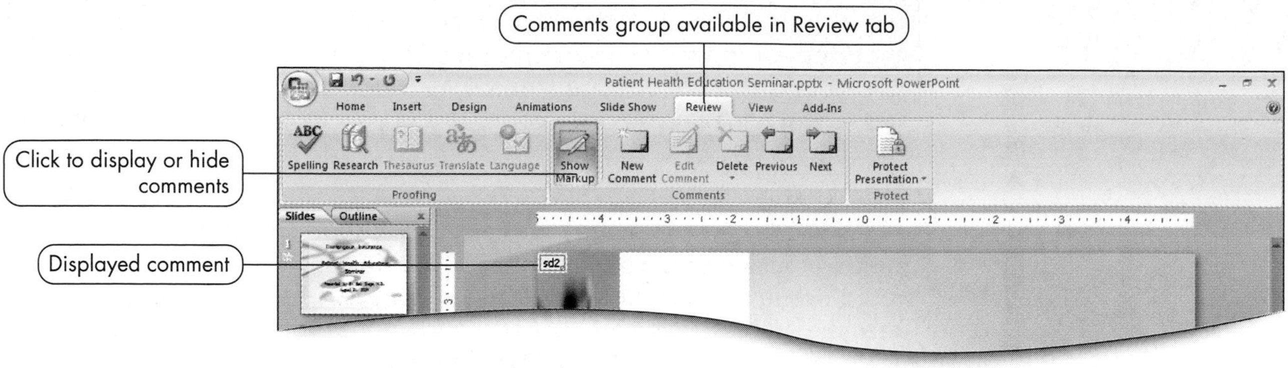

Figure 8.2 The Show Markup Button

The Show Markup feature also displays or hides saved ink annotations. You add an annotation by marking on a slide while playing a presentation. Right-click a slide, select Pointer Options, and choose between Ballpoint Pen, Felt Tip Pen, and Highlighter. Ballpoint Pen creates a thin line, Felt Tip Pen creates a medium width line, and Highlighter creates a thick line behind text or objects. Drag the mouse to draw or write on the slide and continue advancing through the slide show, adding annotations as needed. When you exit the slide show, you will be prompted to keep or discard the ink annotations. Select your preferred option.

Figure 8.3 shows a slide displaying in Slide Show view with the Pointer Options open. The Felt Tip Pen pointer was used to circle the perfect score and add exclamation marks for emphasis. The Highlight pointer was used to emphasize the area needing improvement. Now consider Figure 8.4, which displays the slide in Normal view. The annotations still display in Normal view because they were kept when the slide show ended. The Show Markup feature is active.

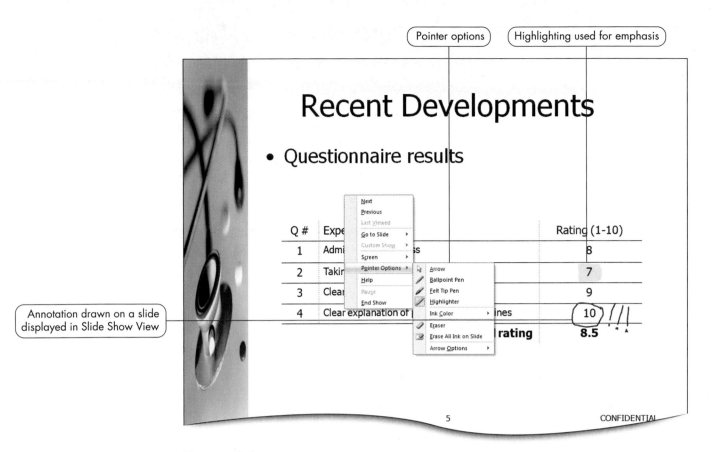

Figure 8.3 Annotations in Slide Show View

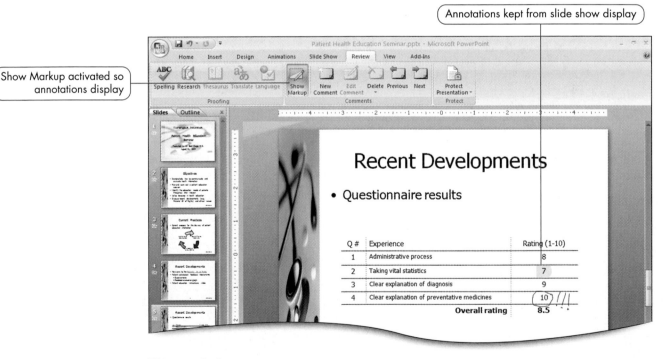

Figure 8.4 Annotations in Normal View

Printing Comments and Ink Markup

Because it is sometimes easier to review comments and ink annotations in print format, you may choose to print the comments and ink annotations that have been stored in your slide. When you choose to print comments and ink annotations (markup), the comments print on a separate page from the slides that display the annotations. To print comments and ink markup, click the Office Button, and then click Print. If your slide show contains comments or ink annotations, the Print comments and ink markup option is active. This option is grayed out if the presentation does not contain comments or ink annotations. Figure 8.5 displays the Print comments and ink markup option.

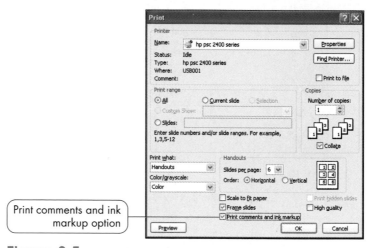

Print comments and ink markup option

Figure 8.5 Print Comments and Ink Markup Option

Hands-On Exercises

1 | Reviewing a Presentation

Skills covered: 1. Insert a Comment **2.** Review Comments and Make Changes **3.** Add Ink Annotations **4.** Show and Hide Markup **5.** Print Comments and Ink Markup

Refer to Figure 8.6 as you complete Step 1.

a. Open the *chap8_ho1_protect* presentation and save it as **chap8_ho1_protect_ solution**.

b. Click the **Office Button**, and then click **PowerPoint Options** at the bottom right of the menu.

The PowerPoint Options dialog box opens and displays the most popular options in PowerPoint.

c. If necessary, change the **User Name** to your name. Change the **Initials** to your initials. Click **OK**.

d. In Slide 1, click the **Review tab**, and then click **New Comment** in the Comments group.

A comment thumbnail with your initials and the number 1 appears on the top left of the slide. An open comment box is attached with your name and the date you are completing the exercise. Figures in this exercise display the initials *stu* for "student," and *Student Name* as the name. Your comment box should display your name, not your school name.

TROUBLESHOOTING: If your school lab has a freeze software program installed to protect software and hardware settings from being changed, you will need to repeat Steps b and c each time you log in to the computer while completing the chapter exercises.

e. Type the following: **JD, Please review this presentation for content and accuracy. When the presentation is complete, the Training Department is going to burn it to CDs and distribute it to employees. Thanks!**

If you were actually creating this on the job, you would now send the presentation file as an attachment in an e-mail to a colleague for review.

f. Create a Notes and Handouts Header and Footer with your name in the header and your instructor's name and your class in the footer.

g. Save and close the *chap8_ho1_protect_solution* presentation.

Figure 8.6 Comment Thumbnail and Box

Step 2
Review Comments and Make Changes

Refer to Figure 8.7 as you complete Step 2.

a. Open the *chap8_ho1_safety* presentation and save it as **chap8_ho1_safety_solution**.

b. Move to Slide 1, click the *jdw1* comment thumbnail to open it, and then read the comment text.

After reading the comment, you decide to try the Module design theme to see if you agree with the suggestion.

c. Click the **Design tab**, and then click the **More** button in the Themes group. Click the **Module** theme.

You decide to keep the Module theme and make note that you need to watch for placeholders that may have shifted and must be moved.

d. Move to Slide 2, click the *jdw2* comment thumbnail to open it, and then read the comment text.

You decide to keep the clip art image. You note that the Title placeholder has shifted and that the hyperlinks are difficult to read. You decide to move the placeholder and change the theme color for the hyperlinks.

e. Drag the Title placeholder (*What Can Harm You*) up approximately ½".

f. Click **Colors** in the Themes group on the Design tab, and then click **Create New Theme Colors**. Click the **Color button** next to *Hyperlink*, and then click **Rose, Accent 3, Lighter 80%**. Click **Save**.

g. Move to Slide 3, click the *jdw3* comment thumbnail to open it, and then read the comment text.

You decide that bullet points would make the slide easier to read.

h. Select the text in the Content Placeholder. Click the **Home tab** and then click **Bullets** in the Paragraph group. Click at the beginning of the sentence reading "A worm spreads without your action and distributes complete copies of itself across networks." Press **Enter**. Click at the beginning of the sentence reading "A trojan horse masks as a useful program but actually does damage." Press **Enter**.

i. Move to Slide 6, click the *jdw4* comment thumbnail to open it, and then read the comment text.

You decide you do not like the added clip art image.

j. Select the clip art image, and then press **Delete** on the keyboard.

k. Move to Slide 7, click the *jdw5* comment thumbnail to open it, and then read the comment text.

You realize that not everyone will know what "spoofed" means, so you decide to add to the bullet point to clarify.

l. Click immediately before the quote mark before *spoofed*, and then type **faked or** and press the **Spacebar**.

The bullet point now reads "links to faked or 'spoofed' Web sites."

m. Move to Slide 10, click the *jdw6* comment thumbnail to open it, and then read the comment text.

You do not like the clip art image so you delete it.

n. Select the clip art image, and then press **Delete** on the keyboard.

o. Move to Slide 11, click the *jdw7* comment thumbnail to open it, and then read the comment text.

The reviewer is right. You should avoid abbreviations and *ID* should be capitalized.

p. Edit the text in the text box to read "Most harmful forms of spyware can record your keystrokes, allowing the capture of passwords, login information, ID numbers, Social Security numbers, and bank information."

q. Create a Notes and Handouts Header and Footer with your name in the header and your instructor's name and your class in the footer.

r. Save the *chap8_ho1_safety_solution* presentation. Close the file if you are not continuing to the next exercise.

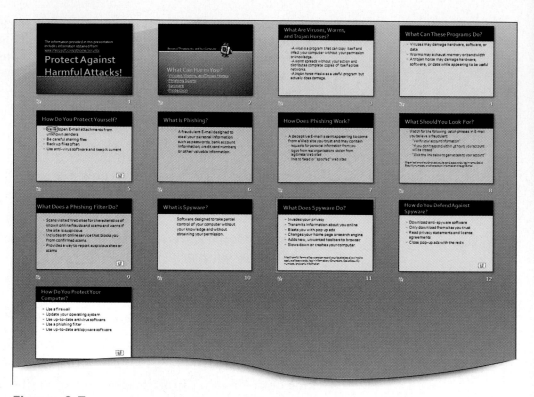

Figure 8.7 Reviewed and Changed Presentation

Refer to Figure 8.8 as you complete Step 3.

a. With the *chap8_ho1_safety_solution* presentation open, click the **Slide Show tab**, and then click **From Beginning** in the Start Slide Show group.

b. Advance to the "What Are Viruses, Worms, and Trojan Horses?" slide, and then right-click anywhere on the slide. Click **Pointer Options**, and then click **Highlighter**.

   You decide to highlight the words *virus, worm,* and *Trojan horse* for additional emphasis.

c. Drag the highlighter over the words *virus, worm,* and *Trojan horse.*

d. Move to the "How Do You Protect Yourself?" slide, and then right-click anywhere on the slide. Click **Pointer Options**, and then click **Felt Tip Pen**.

e. Circle the word *Never* for emphasis.

f. Right-click, and then click **End Show**.

g. When the Microsoft Office PowerPoint box displays, click **Keep** to keep the ink annotations.

h. Save the *chap8_ho1_safety_solution* presentation. Close the file if you are not continuing to the next exercise.

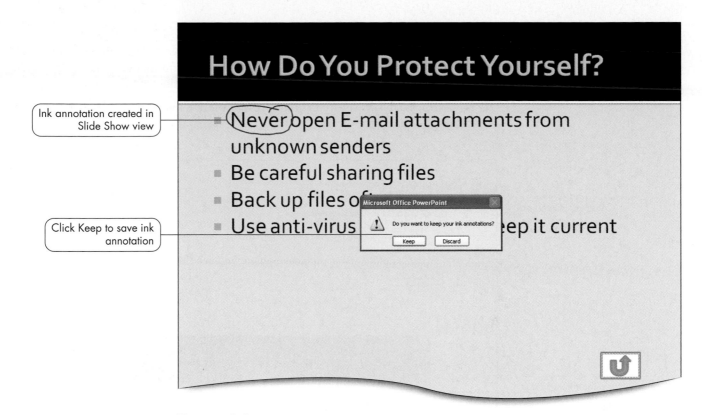

How Do You Protect Yourself?

Ink annotation created in Slide Show view

- Never open E-mail attachments from unknown senders
- Be careful sharing files
- Back up files o
- Use anti-virus ...ep it current

Click Keep to save ink annotation

Microsoft Office PowerPoint

⚠ Do you want to keep your ink annotations?

[Keep]   [Discard]

Figure 8.8 Saving Ink Annotations

Step 4
Show and Hide Markup

a. With the *chap8_ho1_safety_solution* presentation onscreen, move to Slide 3.

Slide 3 shows the *jdw3* comment and the highlighted ink annotations on the words *virus, worm,* and *trojan horse*.

b. Click the **Review tab**, and then click **Show Markup** in the Comments group.

The comment and ink annotations no longer display, but they have not been deleted.

c. Click **Show Markup** in the Comments group once again.

The comment and ink annotations display. The Show Markup button is a toggle button that is used to show and hide markup.

d. Save the *chap8_ho1_safety_solution* presentation. Close the file if you are not continuing to the next exercise.

Step 5
Print Comments and Ink Markup

Refer to Figure 8.9 as you complete Step 5.

a. With the *chap8_ho1_safety_solution* presentation onscreen, move to Slide 3.

b. Click the **Office Button**, and then click **Print**.

c. Select *Current slide* in the *Print range* section.

d. Select *Notes Pages* in the *Print what* category.

e. Check to make sure *Print comments and ink markup* displays a ✓.

TROUBLESHOOTING: If you have comments or ink markup in a presentation, the Print comments and ink markup option should automatically activate. If not, click the check box next to it to activate the feature.

f. Click **OK**.

Two pages will print. One will be the notes page for Slide 3, which includes the annotations you created. The other will show the comment for the slide. Figure 8.9 shows the comment page, overlapped by a portion of the notes page.

g. Save the *chap8_ho1_safety_solution* presentation. Close the file if you are not continuing to the next exercise.

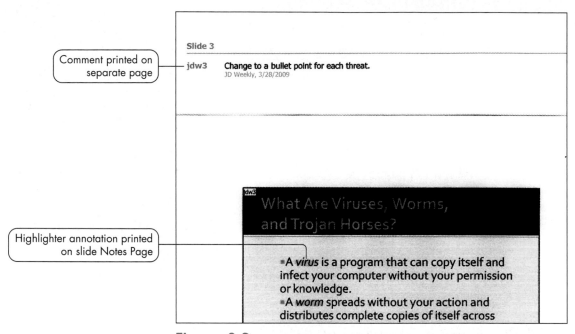

Figure 8.9 Printed Comments and Annotations

Preparations for Presentation Distribution

Once you complete a slide show, you either present it or you distribute it to others to view. If you want to distribute the presentation to others, take advantage of PowerPoint's tools for preparing the presentation for distribution. Using this collection of tools enables you to do the following:

• Add properties to or strip properties from the presentation.

• Add a password.

• Allow people viewing rights but restrict their rights to edit, copy, and print.

• Attach a digital signature.

• Run a compatibility checker to check for features that viewers using previous versions will not be able to see.

• Mark the presentation as read only.

To access the document distribution options, click the Office Button, and then point to Prepare. The options display with descriptions to aid you in selecting which feature(s) you want to use, as shown in Figure 8.10.

In this section, you examine each of these features and how they can help you prepare your presentation for distribution.

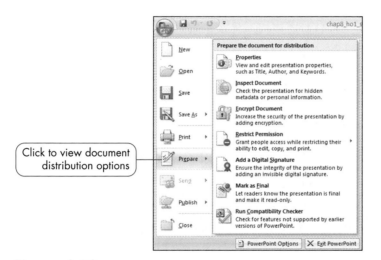

Figure 8.10   Prepare the Document for Distribution Options

Viewing and Setting Document Properties

Metadata are data that describe other data.

The presentation *properties* contain the collection of metadata.

When you create a presentation, *metadata* (data that describe other data) is attached. For example, the text in a presentation is data, whereas the number of words used in the text of the presentation is metadata. The collection of metadata is contained in the presentation *properties*. You can add additional data to the presentation properties to help you identify the presentation, if desired. Adding more data can make it easier to find and organize your presentations.

Whereas your slide show contains presentation properties, PowerPoint refers to the properties as *document properties*. Do not be confused by the terminology, just understand that any file contains properties assigned by the software that creates it. Whether you are creating a worksheet, a database, a report, or a slide show, you have document properties.

> Adding more data can make it easier to find and organize your presentations.

To display the presentation properties in PowerPoint, click the Office Button, point to Prepare, and then click Properties. The Document Properties panel opens and displays the author of the presentation and the presentation storage location. You can add a title for your presentation, a subject, keywords, a category, the status of the presentation, and comments. Figure 8.11 shows the Document Properties dialog box.

Document Properties ▼			Location: C:\Sundance Concrete\Fossil Crete Album.pptx			* Required field ✕
Author:	Title:	Subject:	Keywords:	Category:	Status:	
JDK	Sundance Concrete Design	Design Samples	concrete, custom design, flatw	Marketing	In Progress	
Comments:						
Shows vertical and flatwork designs.						

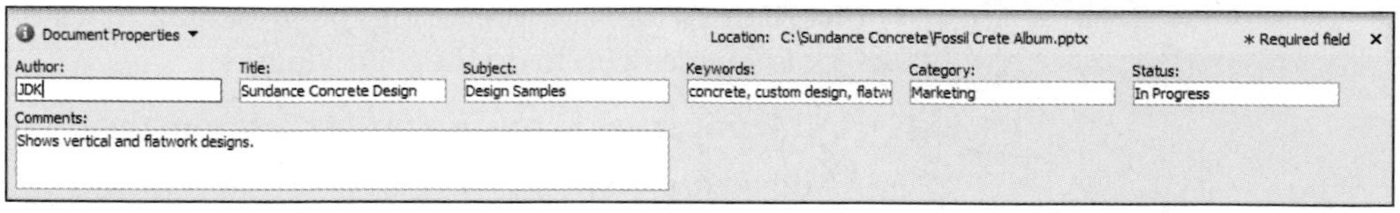

Figure 8.11 The Document Properties Dialog Box

TIP   To Determine Presentation Statistics

To determine the statistics for your presentation, click the arrow to the right of Document Properties in the Document Properties dialog box, and then click the Statistics tab. You can see the number of slides, number of paragraphs, number of words, number of notes, number of hidden slides, number of multimedia clips, and the Presentation format.

Inspecting the Presentation

Adding data to the presentation properties helps you organize and locate your presentations, but you may not wish other people to have access to that data. Other PowerPoint features like comments and annotations may also have information you do not want others to see. PowerPoint lets you inspect your presentation for hidden data and personal information that may be contained in the content of your presentation.

To check your document, click the Office Button, point to Prepare, and then click Inspect Document. When the Document Inspector dialog box appears, click the check box next to the content that you wish to inspect. You can search the following content areas:

- Comments and Annotations
- Document Properties and Personal Information
- Custom XML Data
- Invisible On-Slide Content
- Off-Slide Content
- Presentation Notes

After you check each of the content areas you want inspected, click Inspect. PowerPoint searches your content and then displays the results in the dialog box. Click the Remove All button next to any content you want to remove. Figure 8.12 shows the document inspector after an inspection has been performed.

TIP   Be Cautious Using Document Inspector

If you remove hidden content from your presentation, you may not be able to restore it with the Undo command. To be safe, make a copy of your presentation before using the Document Inspector.

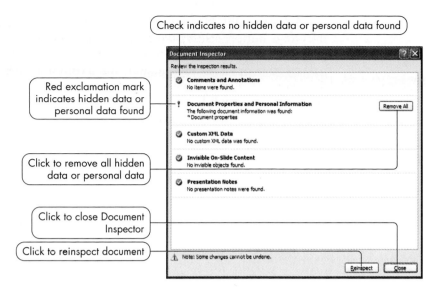

Check indicates no hidden data or personal data found

Red exclamation mark indicates hidden data or personal data found

Click to remove all hidden data or personal data

Click to close Document Inspector

Click to reinspect document

Figure 8.12 Results from Document Inspection

Encrypting and Setting a Password

(Use **encryption** to protect the privacy of your presentation . . .)

Encryption protects the contents of your presentation by converting it into unreadable scrambled text that needs a password to be opened.

Use *encryption* to protect the privacy of your presentation by converting it into unreadable scrambled text that needs a password to be opened. Set a password on your presentation to prevent other people from opening and/or changing your presentation. Once you set a password, you can change it or remove it—if you know the original password! To set a password, click the Office Button, point to Prepare, and then click Encrypt Document. The Encrypt Document dialog box appears. Type your password in the text box, and then click OK. You will then be prompted to reenter the password. This is a security device to ensure you enter the password you desire, with no typographical errors. This is critical because, if you type the password incorrectly or forget the password, you will not be able to open your presentation or change the password. Also be careful about what you type in capital letters and what you type lowercase. Passwords are intentionally case-sensitive. It is a good idea to mix in one or two capital letters in a password for better security. See the reference table for further tips on creating a password.

Password Tips | Reference

Tip	Background	Good Example	Bad Example
Use uppercase and lowercase letters, numbers, and symbols.	A random string of characters is more difficult to steal.	mlp@$&w0r!	mypassword
Use a minimum of 8 characters; 14 characters or longer is best.	Each character you add to your password increases your security.	z2c4=6x8?10k	12345
If your software allows the use of the space bar, use a phrase for your password.	A phrase is easier to remember, and is usually longer.	Alg*bra bEA]s cHemIs]ry	algebra
Use the entire keyboard, not just the common characters and symbols.	Including punctuation marks and any symbols not on the top row of the keyboard makes the password harder to break.	unh>n3	Sunshine3

Source: Microsoft Corporation. Strong passwords: How to create and use them. www.microsoft.com/athome/security/privacy/password.mspx.

Another method you can use to set a password for your presentation is to click the Office Button, select Save As, select Tools, and then select General Options. If you use this method to encrypt your document, you have more options. You can set one password to open the presentation and a different password to modify the presentation. You can also remove automatically generated personal information when you save. This does not, however, remove properties you have added. After setting it, a password takes effect the next time you open the presentation.

Figure 8.13 displays the General Options dialog box.

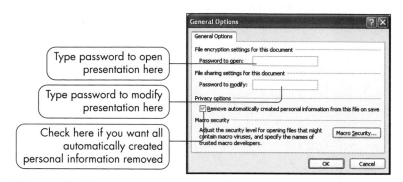

Figure 8.13 General Options for Setting a Password

Restricting Permissions

Office 2007 uses an Information Rights Management feature (IRM) to restrict the access of others. It prevents presentations or other documents from being forwarded, edited, printed, or copied without your authorization. It can also set an expiration date for your presentation so that it can no longer be viewed after a date you select. Using the IRM feature enables you to allow unrestricted access to your presentation or to specify the restrictions you want enabled, such as the permissions an individual user must possess to view the presentation.

IRM uses a server to authenticate the credentials of people who create or receive presentations with restricted permissions. However, to use IRM you have to install the Windows Rights Management Client to access one of the servers. It is unlikely you will have access to IRM in a school lab setting, but you can experiment with this service because Microsoft provides a free trial IRM service if you have a Windows Live ID (.NET Passport).

To access the Restrict Permission feature, click the Office Button, point to Prepare, and then click Restrict Permission. The default allows unrestricted access, but if you select either Restricted Access or Manage Credentials, a Microsoft Information dialog box appears giving you information about IRM with a hyperlink you can click to learn more about Information Rights Management. You can also click a Yes button to download the latest version of the Windows Rights Management client or a No button to close the dialog box.

TIP To Obtain a Windows Live ID (.NET Passport)

Create credentials for Windows Live ID or .Net Passport and you will have access to many more features than just the trial version of IRM. Your Live ID or Passport enables you to log in to such services as Hotmail, Xbox 360's Xbox Live, and MSN Music. If you already have a Hotmail account, you already have a Live ID or Passport! To sign up for a Windows Live ID account, visit **https://accountservices.passport.net**.

Adding a Digital Signature

A **digital signature** is an invisible, electronic signature that authenticates a presentation.

A **digital signature** can be added to authenticate a presentation or other Office document. A digital signature is an invisible, electronic signature stamp that is encrypted and attached to a certificate. The certificate is attached to the presentation. This is similar to signing a paper document. As a student, you probably will not use this feature because it requires you to get a digital ID from a Microsoft partner if you wish others to respect the signature. You can create your own digital ID; however, it will only enable you to verify the authenticity of your signature on the computer you are using, which reassures you that your presentation has not been changed. Other people will not be able to verify your signature.

To create your own digital signature, click the Office Button, point to Prepare, click Add a Digital Signature, and then click OK in the dialog box that appears giving you information about digital signatures. When you click OK, a Sign dialog box appears. Enter the purpose for signing the document, and then click Sign. If the name displayed is not correct, click the Change button and enter the correct name. Adding a digital signature should be the last step you perform when preparing the document because, if you make any changes after the signature is added, your signature is invalidated.

Checking Compatibility and Marking as Final

Whenever you share your presentation with others, you need to consider what software they are using. If they are using an earlier version of PowerPoint, they may not be able to see or use some of the features available in PowerPoint 2007. You can check your presentation for features not supported by PowerPoint 97–2003 by activating the Compatibility Checker. The Microsoft Office PowerPoint Compatibility dialog box appears, showing features not supported by earlier versions of PowerPoint. The dialog box warns you about features you used in your presentation that may be lost or degraded when you save the presentation to an earlier format for distribution. To run the Compatibility Checker, click the Office Button, point to Prepare, and then click Run Compatibility Checker. Figure 8.14 displays the Microsoft Office PowerPoint Compatibility Checker dialog box with two warnings.

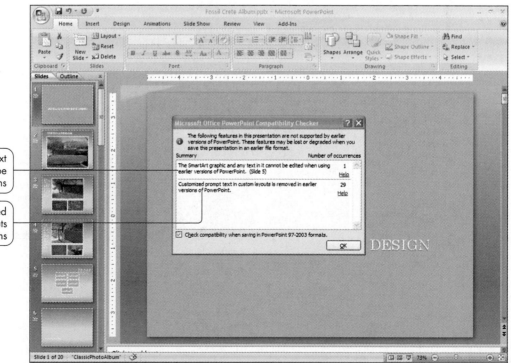

Warning that SmartArt text and graphics cannot be edited in earlier versions

Warning that customized prompt text in custom layouts is removed in earlier versions

Figure 8.14 Microsoft Office PowerPoint Compatibility Checker

After you prepare your presentation for distribution, you can mark it as final. This feature, which is new in PowerPoint 2007, deactivates most PowerPoint tools and converts the presentation to read-only. Doing this allows viewers to watch your presentation but not to edit it unless they turn off the Mark as Final feature. It also lets your viewers know they are viewing a finished presentation. To mark your presentation as final, click the Office Button, point to Prepare, and then click Mark as Final. A Microsoft Office PowerPoint dialog box appears to let you know the presentation will be marked as final and then saved. A Mark as Final icon displays on the status bar, indicating that no changes should be made to the presentation. If you wish to make changes, however, you can do so by turning off the final status. To turn off final status, click the Office Button, point to Prepare, and then click Mark as Final. Figure 8.15 shows a presentation marked as final.

TIP Turn Off Mark as Final

When you mark a presentation as final, it disables typing, editing commands, and proofing features. This prevents accidental changes to the presentation while it is turned on. Mark as Final is **not** a security tool, however. It can be turned off by anyone at any time. The purpose of this tool is to prevent accidental changes, not deliberate changes. To turn off Mark as Final for further editing, a user only has to click the Office Button, point to Prepare, and then click Mark as Final a second time.

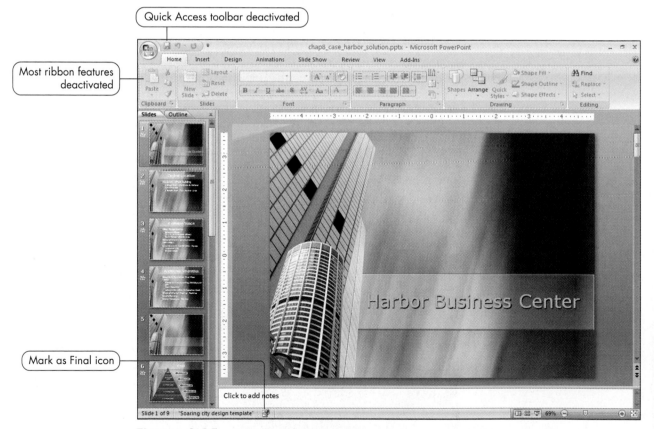

Quick Access toolbar deactivated

Most ribbon features deactivated

Mark as Final icon

Figure 8.15 Presentation Marked as Final

Hands-On Exercises

2 | Preparing a Presentation for Distribution

Skills covered: 1. Set Document Properties **2.** Inspect the Presentation **3.** Set and Remove a Password **4.** Check for Compatibility **5.** Mark as Final **6.** Add a Personal Digital Signature

---

Step 1
Set Document Properties

Refer to Figure 8.16 as you complete Step 1.

a. Open the *chap8_ho1_safety* presentation and save it as **chap8_ho2_threat_solution**.

b. Click the **Office Button**, point to **Prepare**, and then click **Properties**.

> The Document Properties Information Panel opens below the Ribbon and shows the properties currently set for this presentation.

c. Click in the **Author** box and change the author name to your name.

> The Author property is automatically set by PowerPoint, but can be changed if you want.

d. Click in the **Title** box and change the title to **Protect Against Harmful Attacks**.

e. Click in the **Subject** box and type **Threats to Computers and Computer Users**.

f. Click in the **Keywords** box and type **Threat, Virus, Phishing, Spyware**.

g. Click in the **Category** box and type **Education**.

h. Click in the **Status** box and type **Final**.

i. Click in the **Comments** box and type **Presentation for Employee Education Program**.

j. Click **Close** on the top right side of the Document Properties Information Panel.

k. Save the *chap8_ho2_threat_solution* presentation. Close the file if you are not continuing to the next exercise.

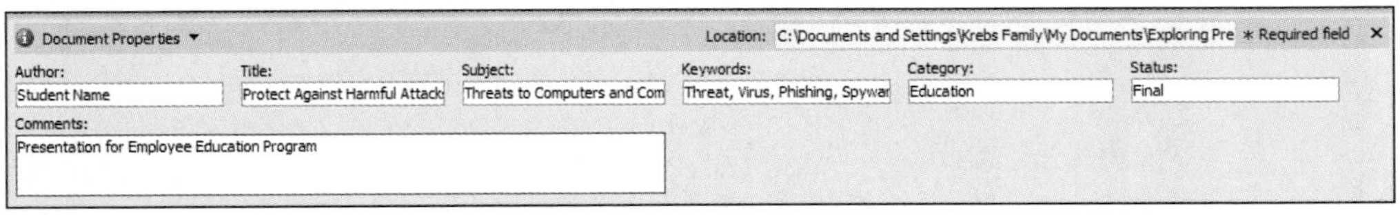

Figure 8.16 Comment Thumbnail and Box

Step 2
Inspect the Presentation

Refer to Figure 8.17 as you complete Step 2.

a. With the *chap8_ho2_threat_solution* presentation onscreen, click the **Office Button**, point to **Prepare**, and then click **Inspect Document**.

b. Clear the **Custom XML Data** check box, and then click **Inspect**.

> The Document Inspector checks for comments and annotations, document properties and personal information, invisible on-slide content, and presentation notes. Then the Document Inspector reports the inspection results.

c. Click **Remove All** for Comments and Annotations, but leave the document properties and personal information.

d. Click **Close**.

e. Save the *chap8_ho2_safety_solution* presentation. Close the file if you are not continuing to the next exercise.

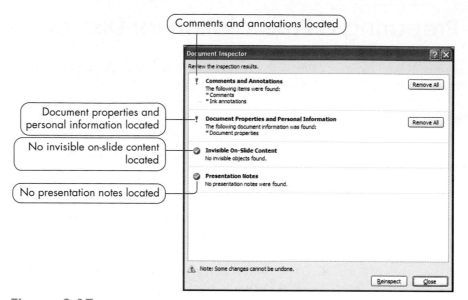

Figure 8.17 Results of Document Inspector

Step 3

Set and Remove a Password

Refer to figure 8.18 as you complete Step 3.

a. With the *chap8_ho2_threat_solution* presentation onscreen, click the **Office Button**, point to **Prepare**, and then click **Encrypt Document**.

b. Type **Th>3@t$**.

This is a moderately secure password because it uses uppercase and lowercase letters and symbols from the upper and lower keyboards. To be more secure, it should be 14 or more characters long.

c. Type **Th>3@t$** when you are prompted to reenter the password.

TROUBLESHOOTING: If you typed the two passwords differently, you will be warned that the passwords did not match and that the password was not created. Repeat the process until the passwords match. **Never** copy a password and paste it into the duplicate password box. If you copy and paste a typographical error, you will not be able to open the document or remove the password.

d. Close the *chap8_ho2_threat_solution* presentation, and then open the presentation.

You open the presentation again so that you can remove the password.

e. When the Password dialog box appears, type **Th>3@t$**.

f. Click the **Office Button**, and then click **Save As**.

g. Click **Tools**, and then click **General Options**.

h. Select the bullets in the **Password to open** box, and then press **Delete**.

The round bullets are masking the password. When you delete the bullets, you delete the password.

i. Click **OK**, and then click **Save** to save the presentation without a password.

j. Save the *chap8_ho2_threat_solution* presentation. Close the file if you are not continuing to the next exercise.

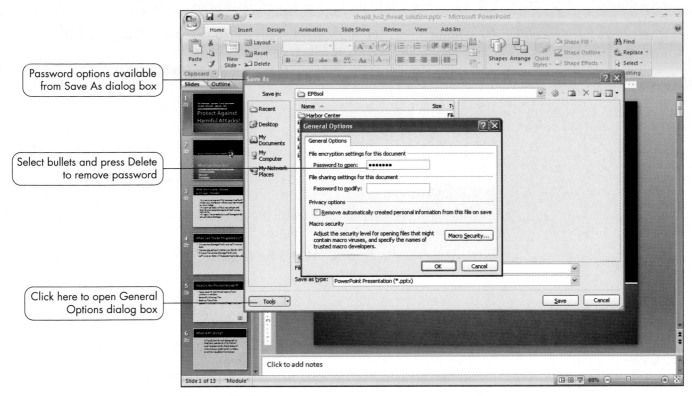

Password options available from Save As dialog box

Select bullets and press Delete to remove password

Click here to open General Options dialog box

Figure 8.18 Add or Delete a Password

Step 4
Check for Compatibility

Refer to Figure 8.19 as you complete Step 4.

a. With the *chap8_ho2_threat_solution* presentation onscreen, click the **Office Button**, point to **Prepare**, and then click **Run Compatibility Checker**.

There will be a slight pause as your presentation is checked for features that are incompatible with earlier versions.

b. When the **Microsoft Office PowerPoint Compatibility Checker** appears, read the summary of the features that cannot be edited in earlier versions. How many slides include text that cannot be edited?

c. Click **OK**.

d. Save the *chap8_ho2_threat_solution* presentation. Close the file if you are not continuing to the next exercise.

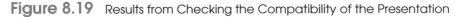

Figure 8.19 Results from Checking the Compatibility of the Presentation

Step 5
Mark as Final

a. With the *chap8_ho2_threat_solution* presentation onscreen, click the **Office Button**, click **Prepare**, and then click **Mark as Final**.

A Microsoft Office PowerPoint dialog box appears to let you know that the presentation will be marked as final.

b. Click **OK**.

A Microsoft Office PowerPoint dialog box appears, letting you know that the presentation has been marked as final to indicate that editing is complete and that this is the final version of the document.

c. Click **OK**.

The Mark as Final icon appears on the status bar, indicating the presentation has been marked as final. Refer to Figure 8.20 to locate this icon.

d. Save the *chap8_ho2_safety_solution* presentation. Close the file if you are not continuing to the next exercise.

Step 6
Add a Personal Digital Signature

Refer to Figure 8.20 as you complete Step 6.

a. With the *chap8_ho2_threat_solution* presentation onscreen, click the **Office Button**, point to **Prepare**, and then click **Add a Digital Signature**.

b. Click **OK** in the Microsoft Office PowerPoint dialog box.

The dialog box cautions users that although a digital signature verifies a document's integrity, it may not be legally enforceable.

c. Type **To verify that I personally completed this exercise** in the *Purpose for signing this document* box.

d. If your name appears next to *Signing as*, move to Step e. If it does not, click **Change**, select your information from the certificates listed, and then click **OK**.

TROUBLESHOOTING: If your name does not appear in the digital certificates available for use, cancel out of the Select Signature and Sign dialog boxes. Then click the Office Button and click PowerPoint Options. Change the User name and Initials to your information and click OK. Repeat Steps a–c to add your personal digital signature.

e. Click **Sign**.

f. Click **OK** in the Signature Confirmation dialog box.

The Signatures task pane opens on the right side of your screen and displays your signature.

g. Save the *chap8_ho2_safety_solution* presentation. Close the file if you are not continuing to the next exercise.

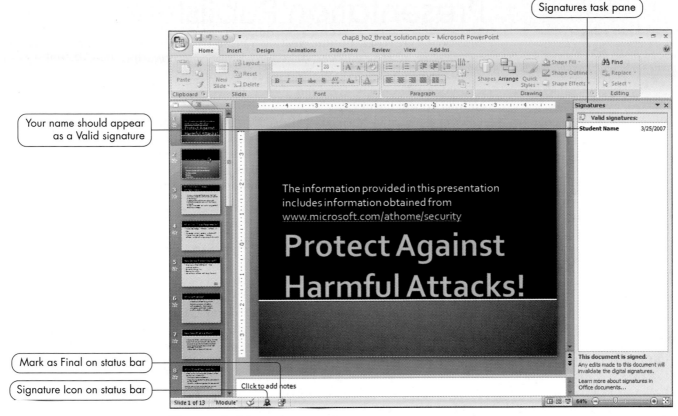

Signatures task pane

Your name should appear as a Valid signature

Mark as Final on status bar

Signature Icon on status bar

Figure 8.20 Signatures Task Pane

Presentation Publishing

You spent a great deal of time creating a professional presentation that delivers your message—now how will you deliver that message to your audience? Will you present it? Will you post it on the Internet for viewing? Will you publish it and distribute it to your audience so they can view it later? If you are going to publish it, what options do you have?

You can turn to Microsoft Office 2007 and PowerPoint 2007 for other distribution options. PowerPoint 2007 provides you with a way to pack your presentation into a compressed file, save slides to a Slide Library, save the presentation to a document management server, or create a document workspace.

In this section, you pack your presentation into a compressed file and send handouts to Microsoft Word for printing.

Packaging a Presentation

After you have packaged your presentation to CD, you can then distribute it to others who will not even need to have PowerPoint installed on their computers to view it.

Package for CD writes a presentation, its fonts and linked files, and a PowerPoint Viewer to a CD or folder for distribution.

Package for CD is a PowerPoint feature that enables you to write your presentation to a CD or a storage location such as a hard drive, network location, or a USB device. You can save the fonts you used, the files you linked to your presentation, and a special PowerPoint Viewer. After you have packaged your presentation to CD, you can then distribute it to others who will not even need to have PowerPoint installed on their computers to view it. You may package your presentation on a CD for your personal use, too. If you are presenting at another location and you are unsure of the system you will be using to present with, you can package your presentation and carry the CD with you. At the new location, you simply play the presentation without worrying about whether the computer you are using to present with has PowerPoint installed.

TIP Saving to a DVD

Although you cannot directly save to a DVD through PowerPoint, you can package your presentation to a folder. Then you can use DVD-burning software to import the presentation files and create a DVD copy.

Set Package for CD Options

To package a presentation on a CD, Click the Office Button, point to Publish, and then click Package for CD. If your presentation uses a template created in an earlier version of PowerPoint, or reuses slides created in an earlier version, you will receive an information prompt telling you that PowerPoint will update the presentation to compatible file formats. This will ensure that your presentation package will run in the PowerPoint Viewer. Click OK to continue. The Package for CD dialog box opens. Click in the Name the CD box and type a name for your CD. If you wish to add other files to the CD, click the Add Files button. Before choosing whether to copy the files to a folder or CD, you can set options. Figure 8.21 displays the Package for CD dialog box.

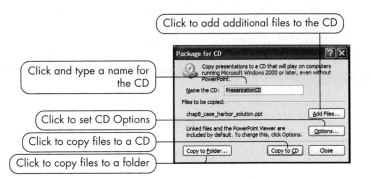

Figure 8.21 The Package for CD Dialog Box

The Package for CD options ensure that your presentation plays properly, includes the features you need for playing, and protects the privacy and security of the presentation. You can choose whether you want the Viewer Package, which updates file formats to run in the PowerPoint Viewer, or whether you want the Archive Package. Choose Viewer Package if you are unsure whether the computer that will play the presentation has PowerPoint. The second option, Archive Package, does not include the PowerPoint Viewer, and thus creates a smaller package, but it should only be used if you are positive the computer that will play back the presentation has PowerPoint.

A **TrueType font** is a digital font that contains alphabetic characters and information about the shape, spacing, and character mapping of the font.

You can choose whether or not you want to include files you have linked to in the presentation and whether you want to embed TrueType fonts. **TrueType fonts** are digital fonts that contain alphabetic characters and information about the characters, such as the shape of the character, how it is horizontally and vertically spaced, and the character mapping that governs the keystrokes you use to access them. This is important if you want the font to display as the font designer created it and as you used it in the presentation. If you have used a nonstandard font in your presentation, you cannot be sure the computer on which you are going to display your presentation has the same font. If it doesn't have the same font, the computer will substitute another font, which can create havoc in your presentation design. If you embed the TrueType fonts you used in your presentation, you will have a larger file, but you can be sure that your presentation displays fonts accurately.

To ensure the security and privacy of your presentation, the Package for CD options also enable you to set a password for opening the presentation, and a second password for modifying the presentation. You can also check the option to inspect the presentation for inappropriate or private information and remove it, a feature you explored earlier in this chapter. Figure 8.22 displays the Options dialog box.

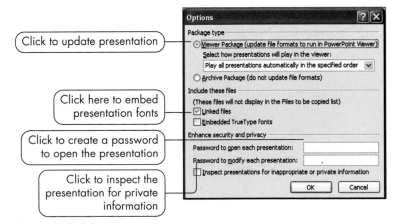

Figure 8.22 Package for CD Options

Copy Presentation to a CD or Folder

Once you have selected the options you want, click either Copy to Folder or Copy to CD. If you click Copy to Folder, you can copy the files to a new folder on your hard drive or a storage location such as a USB drive. You can create a name for the folder, browse to the location you wish to store the folder, and then copy the presentation to that location. If you click Copy to CD, for security purposes you will be asked if you want to include linked files. If you trust the linked files, click Yes. At that point, you see instructions for writing to your CD writer. These instructions will vary depending on the device you use to burn CDs.

Use the PowerPoint Viewer

After you have packaged your presentation for CD and distributed it, the individual receiving the CD simply places the CD in his or her CD drive, and the CD will load and display your presentation. If you included more than one presentation on the CD, the presentations load and display in the order in which you added them to the CD. This is the default setting for Package for CD.

If the presentation was packaged to a folder, locate the folder, and then double-click the pptview.exe file. This starts the Viewer, and a screen will display with a list of the presentations you packaged. Click the presentation you wish to display, and then click Open.

Creating a Handout in Microsoft Office Word

In addition to the excellent handouts you can create in PowerPoint, you can prepare handouts in Microsoft Office Word. When you create your audience handouts through Word, you can take advantage of all of Word's word processing tools. In addition, you are given several helpful layouts not available in PowerPoint. For example, when you create Notes Page handouts in PowerPoint, the handouts consist of a thumbnail of the slide at the top of the page with its related notes beneath it—one slide per sheet of paper. If you have many slides, this can be an inefficient use of paper. By sending your presentation to Word, you can select a layout that puts thumbnails of the slides on the left side of the page and the related notes on the right side. Depending on the length of your notes, you may fit several slides per sheet of paper. This saves paper, but can be time-consuming, as Word has to create the table and insert the slides. Figure 8.23 shows a Notes Page in PowerPoint, and Figure 8.24 shows its counterpart in Word.

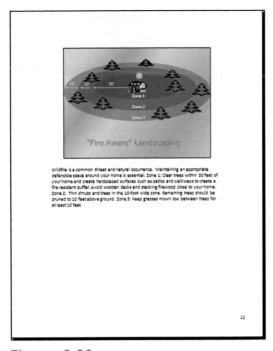

Figure 8.23   PowerPoint Notes Page

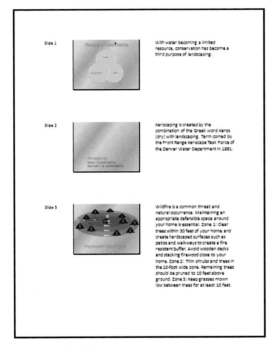

Figure 8.24   Microsoft Office Word Notes Page

To create handouts in Word, click the Office Button, point to Publish, and then click Create Handouts in Microsoft Office Word. The Send to Microsoft Office Word dialog box opens, enabling you to choose the format for the handout you desire. Click the layout you want for your handouts. To create a link between the Word document and the presentation so that changes you make in either one are reflected in the other, click the Paste Link option. Click OK, and then Microsoft Office Word opens, displaying your presentation in the page layout you selected. When you are done making changes in Word and done printing, click Close to quit Word. Figure 8.25 displays the layout options available to you when you send your notes and slides to Microsoft Office Word.

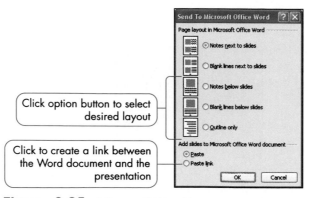

Click option button to select desired layout

Click to create a link between the Word document and the presentation

Figure 8.25 Microsoft Word Layouts for PowerPoint Notes and Slides

Recognizing Other Publishing Options

In an office environment, you may have access to a Microsoft Office SharePoint Server 2007. Access to the SharePoint server allows collaboration between team members on a project and provides additional services unavailable in PowerPoint. All SharePoint team members would be able to save to and obtain files from a centralized browser-based location. Check with your instructor or lab manager to see whether a SharePoint Server is available for your use, but a SharePoint Server is generally found in a corporate environment.

Using SharePoint for collaborating allows you to do the following:

- Store your presentations in a Document Workspace

- Save and reuse presentations in a PowerPoint Slide Library so team members have access to each others' work

- Have online discussions as presentations are being developed

- Track the progress of a presentation using workflow

A Document Workspace enables work teams to work together on a presentation, share files, and discuss presentations in progress. The workspace provides a set of icons to make sharing and updating documents easy. Slides can be saved directly to a Slide Library that has been created on an Office SharePoint 2007 server. Published slides are then available to team members for reuse in other presentations. The slides are available from the Reuse Slides task pane that we explored earlier in this text. Finally, Office SharePoint Servers provide for work flow management by monitoring the start, progress, and completion of a presentation review process.

Hands-On Exercises

3 | Packaging a Presentation

Skills covered: 1. Package a Presentation **2.** Use the PowerPoint 2007 Viewer **3.** Create a Microsoft Office Word Handout

Step 1 **Package a Presentation**	Refer to Figure 8.26 as you complete Step 1.

a. Open the *chap8_ho3_security* presentation and save it as **chap8_ho3_security_solution**.

b. Create a Notes and Handouts Header and Footer with your name in the header and your instructor's name and your class in the footer.

c. Click the **Office Button**, point to **Publish**, and then click **Package for CD**.

A Microsoft Office PowerPoint dialog box appears, telling you that in order for the presentation to show properly in the PowerPoint Viewer, some file formats would have to be converted. These PowerPoint 97–2003 file formats (.ppt, .pot, .pps) have to be converted because the template applied to the presentation is one of Microsoft's earlier templates.

d. Click **OK** in the Microsoft Office PowerPoint dialog box.

e. Type **Security** in the *Name the CD* box.

f. Click **Add Files**, and then navigate to the location of your Chapter 8 solution files.

You have three versions of this slide show, and you wish for the reviewer to see the various backgrounds you have applied. The reviewer can then indicate a preference for the background to be used.

g. Click the *chap8_ho1_safety_solution* file, and then ctrl-click the *chap8_ho2_threat_solution* file. Click **Add**.

The Page for CD dialog box changes and displays a playlist showing the order in which you added the presentations.

h. Click **Options**, and then click **Embedded TrueType fonts.**

Although this creates a larger file size, you ensure your fonts display correctly.

i. Click **OK**.

j. Click **Copy to Folder**.

k. In the *Folder name* box, type **Security**.

l. Click the **Browse** button and navigate to the location where you save your solution files, and then click **Select**.

m. Click **OK**, and then click **Yes** to include linked files.

n. Click **Continue** when PowerPoint prompts you that one or more of your files includes ink annotations and asks if you want to continue.

o. Click **Close** to close the Package for CD dialog box when the packaging process is complete.

p. Save and close the *chap8_ho3_security_solution* presentation. Exit PowerPoint.

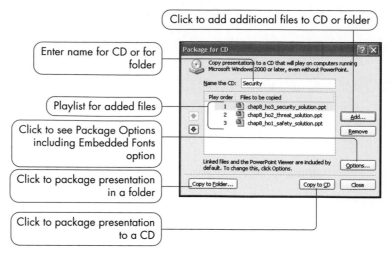

Enter name for CD or for folder

Click to add additional files to CD or folder

Playlist for added files

Click to see Package Options including Embedded Fonts option

Click to package presentation in a folder

Click to package presentation to a CD

Figure 8.26 Package for CD Dialog Box

Step 2
Use the PowerPoint 2007 Viewer

a. With PowerPoint closed, navigate to the location of your solution files, and then open the folder named *Security*.

b. Double-click *PPTVIEW.EXE*.

The playlist appears, showing the three presentations you added to your folder.

c. Select any of the three presentations, and then click **Open**.

PowerPoint 2007 Viewer opens and displays the selected presentation. PowerPoint does not open.

d. Navigate through the presentation and press **Esc** to close.

When the presentation closes, the playlist is visible and you may choose to play a different version of the software if you desire.

e. Close the Microsoft Office PowerPoint Viewer.

Step 3
Create a Microsoft Office Word Handout

Refer to Figure 8.27 as you complete Step 3.

a. Open the *chap8_ho3_safeguard* presentation, and then save it as **chap8_ho3_safeguard_solution**.

b. Create a Notes and Handouts Header and Footer with your name in the header and your instructor's name and your class in the footer.

c. In the *Notes* pane of Slide 1, type **Presentation to Basic Computer Proficiency class**.

d. Click the **Office Button**, point to **Print**, and then click **Print Preview**.

e. Change the *Print what* option to **Notes Pages**.

f. Scroll through the three pages of the presentation to view how they print in PowerPoint, and then click **Close Print Preview**.

Printing your notes in PowerPoint would result in three separate printouts—one for each slide.

g. Click the **Office Button**, point to **Publish**, and then click **Create Handouts in Microsoft Office Word**.

h. Select *Notes next to slide*, and then click **OK**.

Your slides are exported to Microsoft Office Word. Word builds a table with slide numbers, slide thumbnails, and the slide notes.

---

i. In Microsoft Office Word, click the **Insert tab**, and then click **Header**. Select the *Blank* design, and then replace the *Type text* field with your name.

j. Click **Close Header and Footer**.

k. Click the **Page Layout tab**, and then click **Margins** in the Page Setup group.

l. Select *Narrow* from the Margins gallery.

m. Save the Word document as **chap8_ho3_notespage_solution**. Close Microsoft Office Word.

n. Save the *chap8_ho3_safeguard_solution* presentation. Close the file.

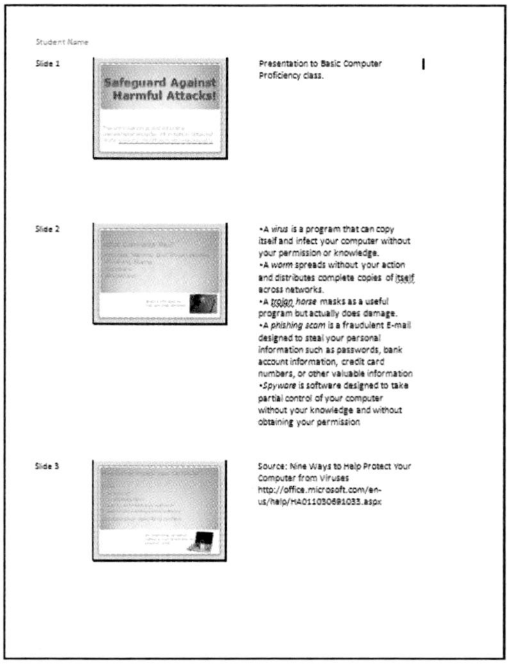

Figure 8.27 Microsoft Office Word Notes Page

Summary

1. **Add and edit comments.** Collaboration is an important part of the workplace. A team may collaborate on the creation of a presentation. To facilitate the collaboration process, PowerPoint provides tools that team members can use to review a presentation. The Review tab contains the Comments group, which has tools for adding a new comment on a slide, for editing or deleting an existing comment, and for moving between comments.

2. **Show and hide markup.** While displaying a slide show, you can add ink annotations, such as high-lighting or drawings made with a pen tool or even with a mouse. These ink annotations can be saved when you exit the Slide Show view. When the ink annotations display on a slide in Normal view, or when comments have been added to a slide, the slide shows the markup. Markup can be hidden or displayed. The tool, Hide markup, toggles between displaying or hiding markup. This tool is contained in the Comments group on the Review tab.

3. **Print comments and ink markup.** You may wish to keep a record of the comments and ink annotations made in a presentation before removing them. You can keep this record by printing the comments and ink annotations. Comments will print on a separate page for each slide, whereas ink annotations print on the slide for which they were created.

4. **View and set document properties.** PowerPoint automatically stores data about your documents as document properties. It automatically stores the name of the author creating the show, as well as data such as the number of slides in the show and the number of words. You can add additional properties such as a subject, keywords, status, and comments.

5. **Inspect the presentation.** Although you may want to create properties for document management purposes, you may not want this information viewed by others. Before distributing the slideshow, you can use the Inspect Document feature to find the document properties and strip out the properties you do not want others to see.

6. **Encrypt and set a password.** For security and privacy reasons, you may want to encrypt a presentation and set a password to open a document. A password can also be set to modify a document so that someone could look at your slide show but not modify it.

7. **Restrict permissions.** Office 2007 uses an Information Rights Management (IRM) feature to restrict the access of others. IRM prevents presentations or other documents from being forwarded, edited, printed, or copied without your authorization. To use IRM, however, you have to install the Windows Rights Management Client to access one of the servers.

8. **Add a digital signature.** Add a digital signature to your presentation if you want to authenticate it. To authenticate your presentation to others, you must sign up with a third-party signature service. To authenticate the presentation to yourself, however, you do not need a third-party signature service. You can create the digital signature for your use to authenticate that the presentation has not been modified since you last worked on it.

9. **Check compatibility and mark as final.** If you plan on distributing your presentation to someone who may be using a different version of PowerPoint, you should check the compatibility of your presentation. By checking the compatibility of your presentation you can tell which PowerPoint 2007 features will not display in previous versions. To indicate that the presentation is completed, use the Mark as Final feature. This is not a security feature, as others can still make changes, but it does prevent accidental changes being made.

10. **Package a presentation.** The Package for CD feature enables you to write your presentation, fonts, linked files, and the PowerPoint 2007 Viewer to a CD. An individual receiving the CD can watch your presentation without needing PowerPoint installed because the packaged presentation includes the viewer. Rather than write to a CD, however, you may choose to package the presentation to a folder, enabling you to burn it to a DVD or place it on a network.

11. **Create a handout in Microsoft Office Word.** Exporting your presentation to Microsoft Office Word to create a handout enables you to use all of the program's word processing features. It also provides you with layouts not available in PowerPoint. After you have selected the layout you want and edited the information as needed, you send the handout to the printer from Word.

12. **Recognize other publishing options.** Microsoft Office SharePoint Server 2007 allows collaboration between team members on a project. It provides a centralized location for file checkout and check-in. It enables slides to be published directly to a Slide Library that has been created on the server and creates a work flow for monitoring the progress of a presentation. Whereas a business may subscribe to a SharePoint Server, your school probably does not.

Key Terms

Multiple Choice

1. The process whereby a team works together to accomplish a goal is referred to as which of the following?

   (a) Unification
   (b) Collusion
   (c) Collaboration
   (d) Deliberation

2. Which of the following is an Adobe electronic file format that preserves document formatting?

   (a) PDF
   (b) XPS
   (c) PDX
   (d) XML

3. Markup may consist of all of the following except:

   (a) Comments inserted by the presentation creator
   (b) Ink annotations
   (c) Comments inserted by a reviewer
   (d) Passwords created for opening and modifying a presentation

4. Which of the following statements regarding comments in a presentation is untrue?

   (a) Comments from the author and each reviewer display in different colors.
   (b) Comments display as a small thumbnail that may be clicked on to open so the comment text can be read.
   (c) Comments display in the lower right side of the presentation by default, but may be dragged to any location.
   (d) Comments include the name of the person creating the presentation and the date the comment was created.

5. The Comments feature is located on which tab?

   (a) Home
   (b) Insert
   (c) References
   (d) Review

6. To access the Prepare options, click the:

   (a) Office Button
   (b) Insert tab
   (c) Review tab
   (d) View tab

7. Before sending a presentation out for a review where comments will be inserted, which of the following tasks should be completed?

   (a) Burn the presentation to a CD.
   (b) Add a digital signature.
   (c) Check the presentation's compatibility.
   (d) Mark the presentation as final.

8. Which of the following document properties is not created automatically by PowerPoint, but can be added?

   (a) Number of slides in the presentation
   (b) Location of the presentation
   (c) Keywords
   (d) Date the presentation was created

9. Which of the following is not a statistic you can check from the Statistics tab under Advanced Properties?

   (a) Number of slides
   (b) Number of notes
   (c) Number of multimedia clips
   (d) Number of ink annotations

10. Which of the following is not checked by the Document Inspector?

    (a) Comments and Annotations
    (b) Version Compatibility
    (c) Document Properties and Personal Information
    (d) Presentation Notes

11. Which of the following is a true statement regarding passwords?

    (a) One password may be set to open a document and a second password may be set to modify a document.
    (b) Mary_Sept18_1990 is a more secure password than M@ryO9LB_L99O.
    (c) A password can only be set through the Encrypt Document feature available from the Prepare gallery.
    (d) If you forget a password you have created, contact www.microsoft.com for a tool that will restore your document without a password.

12. Which of the following is one way to see if a presentation has been marked as final?

(a) The word *Final* will appear on the presentation title.

(b) A *Final* ScreenTip will appear next to the insertion point each time you click in the presentation text.

(c) A Mark As Final icon displays on the Status Bar.

(d) A stamp saying "Final" is inserted in the Title Slide.

13. Which of the following may be packaged with your presentation when you use the Package for CD feature?

(a) All TrueType fonts used in the presentation

(b) Any files linked to the presentation

(c) The PowerPoint Viewer 2007

(d) All of the above

14. All of the following statements about exporting your presentation to Microsoft Office Word are true except:

(a) Create Handouts in Microsoft Word is available from the Insert tab.

(b) Creating handouts in Microsoft Word allows you to use word processing features to format the handouts.

(c) Word provides layouts not available in PowerPoint.

(d) A link can be pasted between PowerPoint and Word so changes can update in either document when made.

15. All of the following statements about Microsoft Office SharePoint Server 2007 are true except:

(a) Microsoft Office SharePoint Server 2007 enables the monitoring of a presentation work flow.

(b) Microsoft Office SharePoint Server 2007 is a free component of PowerPoint 2007.

(c) Microsoft Office SharePoint Server 2007 lets team members reuse slides saved in a Slide Library.

(d) Microsoft Office SharePoint Server 2007 lets team members discuss the progress of a presentation.

1 Insert a Comment

Castle Gardens provides wedding packages that include the use of fabulous gardens or a castle great hall, a wedding planner, pewter tableware, old English décor, photography, and videography. The owners pride themselves on helping brides and grooms create moments and memories to treasure forever. You are a friend of the owner's daughter and offered to create a PowerPoint presentation the owner could burn to a CD to distribute to potential clients. You begin the slide show and realize that you will be collaborating continuously with the owner until the presentation is finalized. In this exercise, you create a comment asking the owner to review the beginnings of the slide show. Refer to Figure 8.28 as a guide.

    a. Open the *chap8_pe1_cg* file and save it as **chap8_pe1_cg_solution**.

    b. Click the **Office Button**, and then click **PowerPoint Options** at the bottom right of the menu.

    c. If necessary, change the **User Name** to your name. Change the **Initials** to your initials. Click **OK**.

    d. In Slide 1, click the **Review tab**, and then click **New Comment** in the Comments group.

    e. Type: **Mrs. Grosscurth, Here is the beginning of the slide show we talked about. Please review it and make suggestions for changes. Thanks!**

    f. Create a Notes and Handouts Header and Footer with your name in the header and your instructor's name and your class in the footer.

    g. Save the *chap8_pe1_cg_solution* file, and then close. Exit PowerPoint if you do not want to continue to the next exercise at this time.

Figure 8.28 Comment Inserted

2 Review Comments and Make Changes

You submitted the beginning of your Castle Gardens slide show to the owner, R. Grosscurth, and she reviewed the slides. She inserted comments detailing changes she would like you to make in some of the slides. Read the comment on each slide and make the requested changes. The changes are displayed in Figures 8.29, 8.30, 8.31, and 8.32.

    a. Open the *chap8_pe2_castle* file and save it as **chap8_pe2_castle_solution**.

    b. In Slide 1, click the comment thumbnail to open it, and then read the comment text.

    c. To respond to the request to change the image to grayscale, click the image of the castle. Click the **Format tab**, and then click **Recolor** in the Adjust group. Because the owner requested that the image look like a cloud, instead of selecting grayscale in the Color Mode category, click **Background color 2 light**, the first option in the Light Variations category. Figure 8.29 shows the open comment and the changed image.

...continued on Next Page

Figure 8.29 Image Changed as Requested by Comment

d. Move to Slide 2, click the comment thumbnail to open it, and then read the comment text. Select and copy the text in the comment box, position the insertion point after the paragraph in the slide text box, and paste. Figure 8.30 displays the open comment and the new text added to the text box.

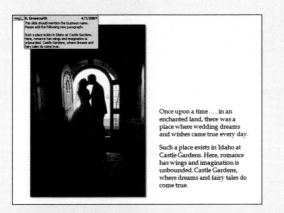

Figure 8.30 Text Added as Requested in Comment

e. Move to Slide 3, click the comment thumbnail to open it, and then read the comment text. Modify the text *The garden* to read **Castle Gardens**. Apply bold and italics to each reference to Castle Gardens in the slide and the notes, except for the title slide and the last slide because they already have special formatting applied. Figure 8.31 displays the open comment and the modified text.

Figure 8.31 Text Modified as Requested in Comment

...continued on Next Page

f. Move to Slide 4, click the comment thumbnail to open it, and then read the comment text. Click the **Design tab**, and then click **Background Styles** in the Background group. Click **Format Background**. Click **File** and locate the *chap8_pe2_carriage.JPG* image. Click **Insert**. Click **Close**. Figure 8.32 displays the open comment and the new background.

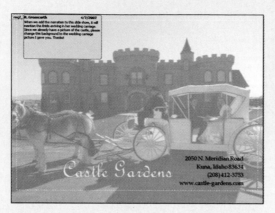

Figure 8.32 Background Changed as Requested in Comment

g. Save the *chap8_pe2_castle_solution* file and keep it onscreen if you plan to continue to the next exercise. Close the file and exit PowerPoint if you do not want to continue to the next exercise at this time.

3 Add Ink Annotations

You watch the slide show, and as you do, you highlight words and phrases that you think create the emotional appeal of Castle Gardens. After watching the show, you keep the ink annotations. Figure 8.33 shows Slide 2 with markup—the ink annotations and the comments previously created.

a. Open the *chap8_pe2_castle_solution* file if you closed it after the last exercise, and then save it as **chap8_pe3_castle_solution**.

b. Click the **Slide Show tab**, and then click **From Beginning** in the Slide Show group.

c. In Slide 1, right-click anywhere on the slide, click **Pointer Options**, and then click **Highlighter**.

d. Right-click anywhere in the slide, click **Pointer Options**, and then click **Ink Color**. Select **Accent 5**, the second color from the end on the top row.

e. Drag across the words *dreams* and *fairy tales*.

f. Advance to the next slide and highlight the following words: *dreams, wishes, romance, imagination, dreams,* and *fairy tales*.

g. Advance to the next slide and highlight the following words: *lavish, intimate,* and *memories*.

h. Press **ESC** to exit the slide show, and then click **Keep** to keep your ink annotations.

i. Save the *chap8_pe3_castle_solution* file and keep it onscreen if you plan to continue to the next exercise. Close the file and exit PowerPoint if you do not want to continue to the next exercise at this time.

...continued on Next Page

Figure 8.33 Slide with Ink Annotations

4 Print Markup and Then Hide Markup

To create a record of the changes you are making, you print a copy of the comments and ink annotations. After printing, you decide to display each slide to several other employees, but you do not want the markup to distract from the display. In this exercise, you print the comments and ink annotations, and then hide the markup. Figure 8.34 shows Slide 2 with the markup hidden.

a. Open the *chap8_pe3_castle_solution* file if you closed it after the last exercise, and then save it as **chap8_pe4_castle_solution**.

b. Click the **Office Button**, and then click **Print**.

c. Select *Handouts* from the *Print what* list. Select *4 Slides per page*.

d. Check to make sure Print comments and ink markup displays a ✓.

e. Click **OK** to print the handout displaying the ink annotations and the sheet displaying all of the comments for each slide.

f. Click the **Review tab**, and then click **Show Markup** in the Comments group.

g. Move through the slides and note that comments and ink annotations do not display.

h. Save the *chap8_pe4_castle_solution* file and keep it onscreen if you plan to continue to the next exercise. Close the file and exit PowerPoint if you do not want to continue to the next exercise at this time.

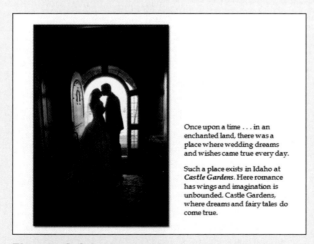

Figure 8.34 Slide with Markup Hidden

...continued on Next Page

In this exercise, you prepare the presentation for distribution by adding presentation properties, inspecting the presentation, checking its compatibility with previous versions of PowerPoint, and marking the presentation as final. Then you remove the Marked as Final designation so you can make further changes. Finally, you add a personal digital signature. Figure 8.36 shows the Signature pane with your valid signature.

a. Open the *chap8_pe4_castle_solution* file if you closed it after the last exercise, and then save it as **chap8_pe5_castle_solution**.

b. Click the **Office Button**, point to **Prepare**, and then click **Properties**. Add the properties listed in the table below to your presentation. Figure 8.35 displays the completed properties.

Author	Your Name
Title	Castle Gardens
Subject	Castle Gardens Overview
Keywords	wedding, gardens, services
Category	Sales Presentation
Status	In progress
Comments	Beginning of slide presentation for Castle Gardens

Figure 8.35 Inserted Document Properties

c. Close the *Document Properties* pane.

d. Click the **Office Button**, point to **Prepare**, click **Inspect Document**, and then click **Yes** if prompted to save changes.

e. Make sure that all content is selected in the Document Inspector dialog box, and then click **Inspect**.

f. Click **Remove All** for Comments and Annotations, and then click **Remove All** for Off-Slide Content. Do **not** remove document properties and personal information or presentation notes. Click **Close**.

g. Click the **Office Button**, point to **Prepare**, and then click **Run Compatibility Checker**. When the Compatibility Checker finds that the earlier versions cannot edit the shape and any text on Slide 4 (the WordArt) and customized prompt text in all slides, click **OK**.

h. Click the **Office Button**, click **Prepare**, and then click **Mark as Final**.

i. Click **OK** when prompted that the presentation will be marked as final and then saved.

j. When prompted that the document has been marked as final, click **OK**.

k. Note the Marked as Final icon on the Status Bar. Move to Slide 2, select the ellipses (. . .) in the text box, and press **Delete** on the keyboard. The ellipses cannot be deleted while the presentation is marked as final.

l. Click the **Office Button**, click **Prepare**, and then click **Mark as Final** to toggle the Mark as Final status off.

m. Press **Delete** to remove the ellipses. Move to Slide 3 and replace the two occurrences of ellipses with commas, making sure there is a blank space after each comma.

n. Click the **Office Button**, point to **Prepare**, and then click **Add a Digital Signature**.

o. Click **OK** in the Microsoft Office PowerPoint dialog box.

...continued on Next Page

p. Type **To verify that I personally completed this exercise** in the **Purpose for signing this document** box, and then click **Sign**. Click **OK**.

q. Save the *chap8_pe5_castle_solution* file and keep it onscreen if you plan to continue to the next exercise. Close the file and exit PowerPoint if you do not want to continue to the next exercise at this time.

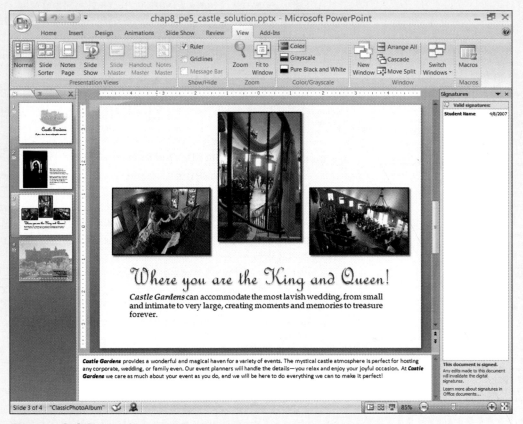

Figure 8.36 Presentation with Valid Document Signature

6 Package a Presentation and Print Handouts in Microsoft Office Word

You decide to use the Package for CD feature to package the presentation to a folder that can be distributed to others. Before you can use the Package for CD feature, however, you must remove the digital signature. You also create a hard copy of the presentation and the presentation notes by exporting the presentation to Microsoft Office Word and printing the handout from Word. Figure 8.37 shows the Word handout.

a. Open the *chap8_pe5_castle_solution* file if you closed it after the last exercise, and then save it as **chap8_pe6_castle_solution**.

b. Changing the name of the presentation and saving a copy will invalidate the signature you created in the previous exercise. Click **OK** to continue.

c. Note the *Signature* pane now indicates that your signature is invalid.

d. Point to your signature in the *Signature* pane, and then click the list arrow that appears. Click **Remove Signature**. Click **Yes** to permanently remove this signature, and then click **OK**.

e. Make sure that all content is selected in the Document Inspector dialog box, and then click **Inspect**.

...continued on Next Page

f. Click **Remove All** for Comments and Annotations, and then click **Remove All** for Off-Slide Content. Do **not** remove document properties and personal information or presentation notes. Click **Close**.

g. Click the **Office Button**, point to **Prepare**, and then click **Run Compatibility Checker**. When the Compatibility Checker finds that the earlier versions cannot edit the shape and any text on Slide 4 (the WordArt) and customized prompt text in all slides, click **OK**. Close the *Signature* pane.

h. Click the **Office Button**, click **Publish**, and then click **Package for CD**.

i. Type **Castle Gardens** in the *Name the CD* box.

j. Click **Options**, and then click **Embedded True Type fonts**. Click **OK**.

k. Click **Copy to Folder**.

l. Click **Browse** and navigate to the location where you save your solution files, and then click **Select**.

m. Click **OK**.

n. Click **Yes** to include lined files in your package.

o. When the Copying Files to Folder dialog box disappears, click **Close**.

p. Click the **Office Button**, point to **Publish**, and then click **Create Handouts in Microsoft Office Word**.

q. Select *Notes next to slide*, and then click **OK**.

r. After Microsoft Office Word completes building the table displaying the thumbnails of your slides and the related notes, click the **Insert tab** in Word, click **Header**, and then select **Blank**.

s. Type your name in the *Type Text* field, and then click **Close** in the Close group on the Design tab.

t. Click the **Office Button**, click **Print**, and then click **OK**.

u. Save the Word document as **chap8_pe6_notespage_solution**. Close Microsoft Office Word.

v. Save the *chap8_pe6_castle_solution* file. Close the file and exit PowerPoint if you do not want to continue to the next exercise at this time.

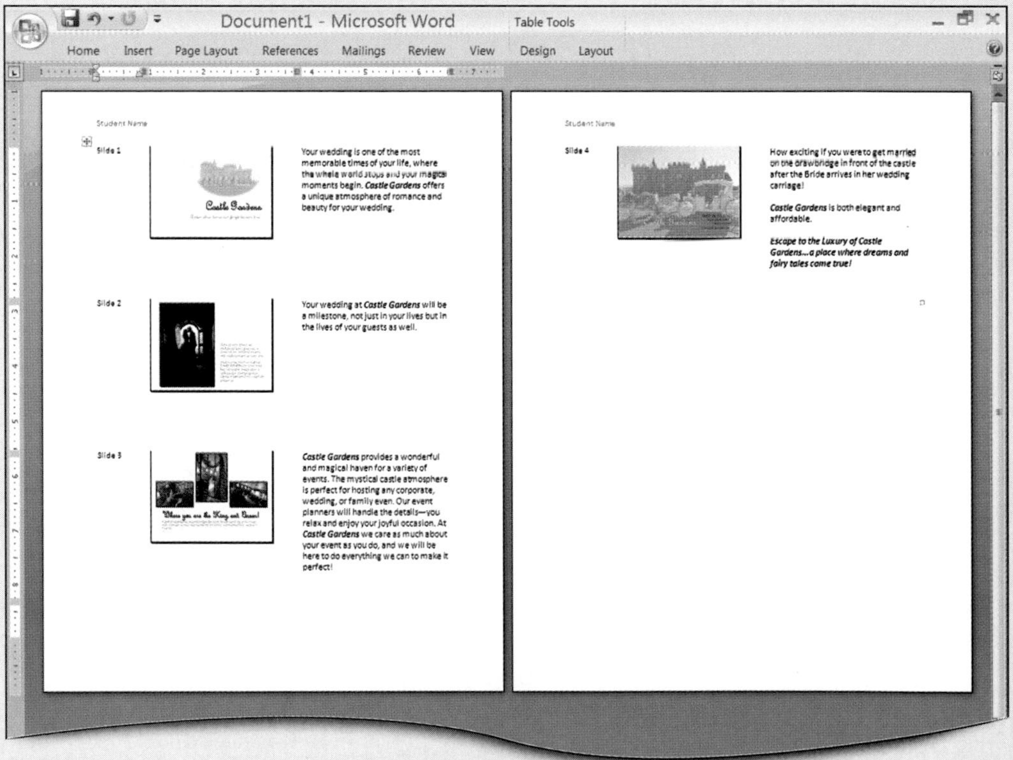

Figure 8.37 Microsoft Office Word Notes Page

Mid-Level Exercises

1 Office 2007 Training

You are a part-time employee of a local regional medical center and work in the Employee Training and Support department. You were asked by the department supervisor to create a presentation that medical office personnel could watch as an introduction to Office 2007. You created the presentation, and then the supervisor reviewed it and added comments. Now you read each of her comments and print a copy of them for tracking purposes. You make her suggested changes, and then delete the comments. You export a copy of the changed presentation to Microsoft Office Word and print the handout. In the last step, you mark the presentation as final. Slides requiring style changes or coloring changes are displayed in Figures 8.38 through 8.40 to help you in your selection. The Microsoft Office Word handout is displayed in Figure 8.41. The final presentation is displayed in Figure 8.42.

a. Open the *chap8_mid1_new* presentation and save it as **chap8_mid1_new_solution**.

b. Create a handout header with your name and a handout footer with your instructor's name and your class.

c. Print a copy of the presentation as handouts, six per page. Make sure that comments and ink markup are also printed.

d. Read the comments on each slide and make the requested changes.

- Slide 2 requires you to hyperlink an external file to each of the compasses on the right side of the slide.
- Slide 3 requires a capitalization change.
- Slide 4 requires a change in the table style.

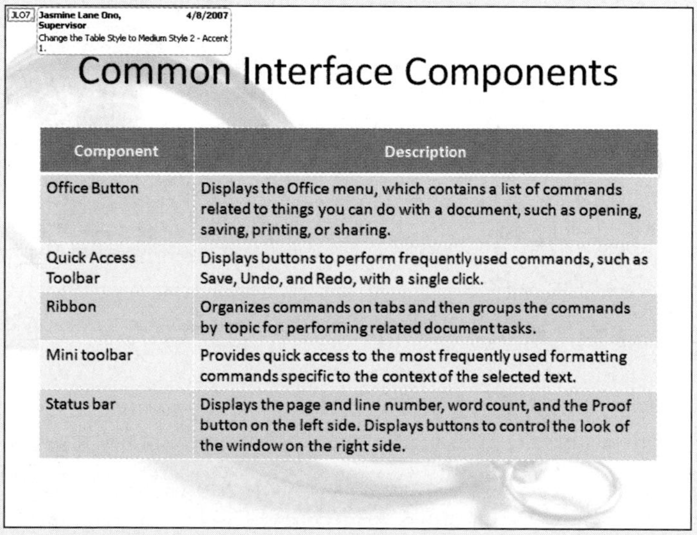

Figure 8.38 Medium Style 2 – Accent 1 Table Style

- Slide 5 requires a capitalization change.
- Slide 6 requires moving a text box.
- Slide 8 requires re-coloring two images.

...continued on Next Page

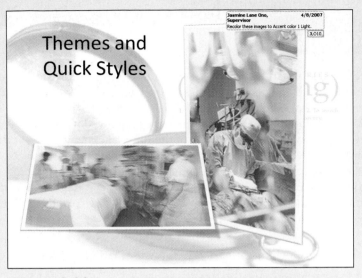

Figure 8.39 Accent Color 1 Light

- Slide 11 requires a change in the table style.

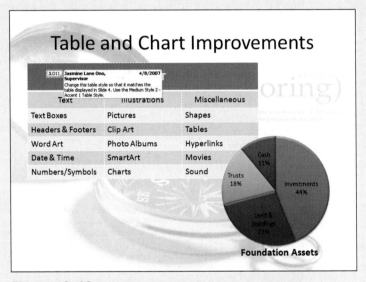

Figure 8.40 Medium Style 2 – Accent 1 Table Style

e. Proofread the presentation carefully to ensure you have made all requested changes, and then delete all markup in the presentation.

f. Export the presentation to Microsoft Office Word to create a handout with the notes next to the slides. Add your name in a header, and then print. Save the Word handout as **chap8_mid1_handout**.

g. Prepare the presentation for distribution by marking it as final.

h. Switch to Slide Sorter view and change the zoom to 100%. Compare your presentation to Figure 8.41. Does your presentation include the Marked as Final icon on the Status bar?

i. Save and close the *chap8_mid1_new_solution* presentation. Exit PowerPoint if you do not want to continue to the next exercise at this time.

...continued on Next Page

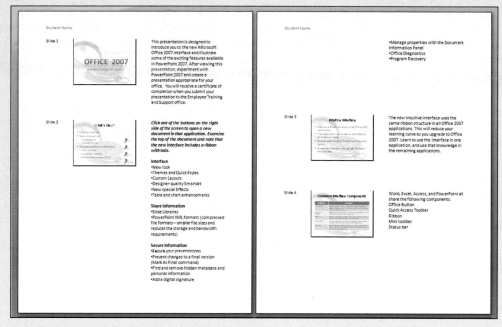

Figure 8.41 Microsoft Office Word Handout with Notes Next to Slides

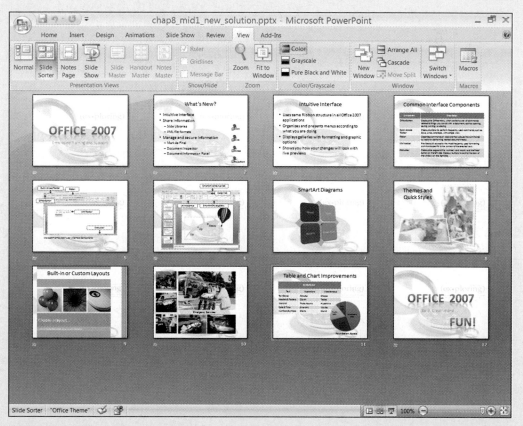

Figure 8.42 Completed Office 2007 Training Presentation with Marked as Final Icon

2 Constitution Quiz

To meet one of your general education requirements for graduation, you register for a U.S. History class. The instructor for this class likes to encourage creativity, and so assigns a creative project to all students. The project requires you to select a topic from the course and to create a personal project to

...continued on Next Page

display to the class related to that topic. Fellow students have done everything from dressing as Abraham Lincoln and delivering the Gettysburg Address to creating a Statue of Liberty out of clay. You decide to create a Constitution Quiz using the Microsoft PowerPoint "QuizShow" template—creating the quiz not only meets the project requirements, but it also helps you review for the final exam! After downloading the QuizShow template and typing your questions, you marked the presentation as final and added a personal digital signature. You realize that you left one question out, so you must remove the digital signature and the Marked as Final designation, add the question, and mark the presentation as final again. You also add a password so that others cannot open the presentation until you are ready to display the quiz to the class. The final presentation is displayed in Figure 8.43.

a. Open the *chap8_mid2_quiz* presentation and save it as **chap8_mid2_quiz_solution**. Continue with the saving process even though it invalidates the digital signature in the copy.

b. Remove the invalid signature, and then close the *Signatures* pane.

c. Remove the Marked as Final designation.

d. Create a handout header with your name and a handout footer with your instructor's name and your class.

e. Display the slide and note how the question and answers animate. This is possible because the QuizShow template includes a layout for multiple-choice questions. The template includes a question placeholder and answer placeholders. The first answer placeholder on the slide is animated to be the last answer left on the page. The template is set up to always show the correct answer last. You type the correct answer in the first answer placeholder, but can then drag the placeholder to another location. Microsoft created the template in this fashion to allow you to change the position of the correct answer.

f. Insert a new slide between Slide 5 and Slide 6 using the Multiple Choice layout.

g. Type **The new Congress met for the first time on April 6, 1789. What else happened on that day?** in the title placeholder.

h. Type **George Washington was elected president** in the first answer placeholder because it is the correct answer.

i. Type the following incorrect answers in the remaining placeholders:

   • **Washington, D.C., was designated the Capitol**

   • **The White House opened**

   • **Thomas Jefferson was elected president**

j. Add **USHistory1110** as a password required for opening the presentation.

k. Mark the presentation as final and save the presentation.

l. Save the *chap8_mid2_quiz_solution* presentation. Close the file and exit PowerPoint if you do not want to continue to the next exercise at this time.

...continued on Next Page

Figure 8.43 Completed Quiz Presentation with Marked as Final Icon

3 Impressionist Artists

You have been refining a presentation on impressionist artists for your Nineteenth Century Art class. You submitted it to your instructor and he returned it to you with comments. You made the changes he requested and are now ready to prepare the presentation for distribution and to copy it to a folder that the instructor will post on the class Web site. The Microsoft Office Word handout is displayed in Figure 8.44. The completed presentation is displayed in Figure 8.45.

a. Open the *chap8_mid3_impressionism* presentation and save it as **chap8_mid3_ impressionism_solution**.

b. Inspect the presentation for hidden metadata or personal information. Check all types of information, including off-slide content.

c. Remove all comments and annotations, document properties and personal information, and off-slide content. Do **not** remove presentation notes.

d. Create a handout header with your name and a handout footer with your instructor's name and your class.

e. Export the presentation to Microsoft Office Word to create a handout with the notes next to the slides. Add your name in a header, and then print. Save the Word handout as **chap8_mid3_notespage**.

f. Run the Compatibility Checker to check for features not supported by earlier versions of PowerPoint.

g. Note that earlier versions cannot change the shape and text in Slide 1, and then click **OK**.

h. Use the Package for CD feature to copy the presentation and media links to the folder where you have saved your solution files. Name the CD **Impressionism**. Change the package options to embed TrueType fonts.

i. Save the *chap8_mid3_impressionism_solution* presentation. Close the file and exit PowerPoint if you do not want to continue to the next exercise at this time.

...continued on Next Page

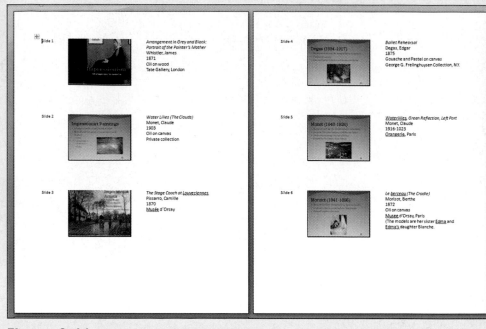

Figure 8.44 Microsoft Office Word Handout

Figure 8.45 Completed Impressionism Presentation

Capstone Exercise

You just returned from your first visit to New York City. Your sister also went on the trip and she combined your digital images and her digital images into a slide show. She wants you to review the presentation and make suggestions. She plans to incorporate your suggestions and then return the presentation to you to burn onto a CD. She will duplicate the CD and send it to your parents, grandparents, and her friends.

Create Ink Annotations and Comments

You open the presentation your sister sent to you and view it in Slide Show mode so you get an overall impression of the presentation. You jot some ink annotations on some slides to remind you about comments you want to make about the presentation, and you keep the annotations when you exit Slide Show mode. Then you move through the presentation slide by slide and make comments.

a. Open the *chap8_cap_ny* presentation and save it as **chap8_cap_ny_solution**.

b. Play the slide show from the beginning. In Slide 2, change your pointer options to *Felt Tip Pen* and circle the existing text by using the mouse. Continue advancing through the slide show, circling any existing text.

c. On Slide 7, circle the text relating to the eternal flame and the actual flame. Connect the two with an arrow.

d. When you reach the end of the presentation, keep the ink annotations as a reminder of changes you want to suggest.

e. Create a comment in Slide 1 that reads **Hey Sis, Why don't you use this spot to identify where we were? That's Battery Park on the southern tip of Manhattan!** Drag the comment thumbnail so it is next to the text placeholder.

f. Refer to Figure 8.46 to create and position a comment in Slide 2.

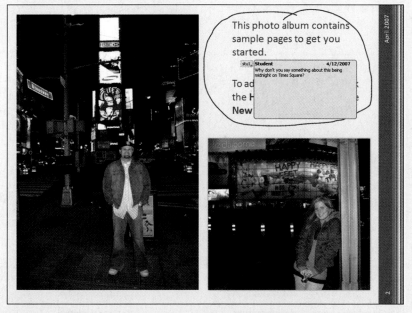

Figure 8.46 Comment Text and Position for Slide 2

g. Refer to Figure 8.47 to create and position a comment in Slide 3.

Figure 8.47 Comment Text and Position for Slide 3

h. Refer to Figure 8.48 to create and position a comment in Slide 5.

Figure 8.48 Comment Text and Position for Slide 5

Capstone

i. Refer to Figure 8.49 to create and position a comment in Slide 7.

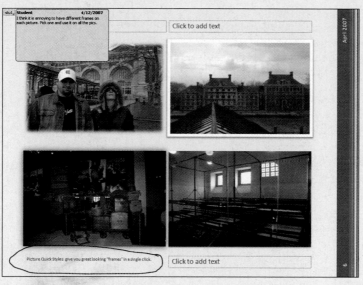

Figure 8.49 Comment Text and Position for Slide 7

j. Print the presentation as handouts, six per page. Also print the comments and ink markup at the same time.

k. Save the *chap8_cap_ny_solution* presentation.

Hide Markup and Print Word Handouts

Your sister added the information you requested, and also added brief notes with Web site addresses. She left your comments in case you want to review them again. You remove the markup and create a handout with notes next to the slide in Microsoft Office Word. Finally, you create presentation properties.

a. Refer to figure 8.50 to create a handout. Open the *chap8_cap_newyork* presentation and save it as **chap8_cap_newyork_solution**.

b. Delete all comments and ink annotations in this presentation.

c. Export the presentation to Microsoft Office Word to create a handout with the notes next to the slides.

d. Add your name in a header, using the Annual format. Insert the current year in the Year field.

e. Print the Microsoft Office Word handout.

f. Save the Word handout as **chap8_cap_notespage**, and then close Word.

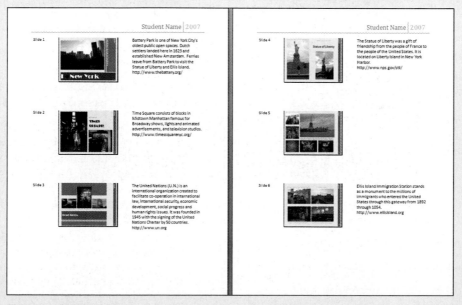

Figure 8.50 First Two Pages of Microsoft Office Word Handout

Capstone

Set Document Properties, Inspect the Presentation, and Check Compatibility

To aid you in organizing your files and make it easy to search for your presentation if necessary, you decide to create additional presentation properties. You also inspect the presentation to ensure that only the metadata you want is retained. You know that your mother or other family members might want to work with the presentation to create printed scrapbook pages, but you also know they have not upgraded to Office 2007 yet. Run the Compatibility Checker to see which features you used that will not be supported by earlier versions of PowerPoint.

a. Create the following presentation properties:

Author	Your name
Title	I Love New York
Subject	New York Trip
Keywords	New York, Times Square, Statue of Liberty, Yankees
Category	Album
Status	Final
Comments	Trip to New York including visits to United Nations, Statue of Liberty, Ellis Island, Ground Zero, Yankee Stadium, Empire State Building

b. Create a handout header with your name and a handout footer with your instructor's name and your class.

c. Inspect the presentation for hidden metadata or personal information. The Document Inspector locates document properties and presentation notes. You decide to retain this information, so you close the Document Inspector.

d. Run the Compatibility Checker to see which features you used that are not supported by earlier versions of PowerPoint. Which slides have shapes with text that cannot be edited if you save the presentation in an earlier file format for your family's use? (Tip: These slides include WordArt that cannot be edited in earlier versions of PowerPoint.)

Set and Remove a Password

In addition to packaging your presentation and burning it to a CD, you plan to copy the presentation to a folder and post it to a family Web site. You do not want anyone other than family members to view the presentation for safety reasons, so you decide to add a password to the presentation. After adding the password, you decide to remove it until you are ready to post the presentation to the Web.

a. Encrypt the document with this password, realizing that it is not a very secure password: **NewYork07.**

b. Close the presentation, saving all changes.

c. Open the *chap8_cap_newyork_solution* presentation.

d. Enter **NewYork07** when prompted for the password.

e. Use the Save As Tools feature available from General Options to remove the password.

f. Save the presentation to ensure that the unencrypted presentation is the version you have available in the future.

Mark as Final and Add a Personal Digital Signature

To indicate that this presentation is complete and make it read only, you mark the presentation as final. To ensure the integrity of the presentation on your computer, you add a personal digital signature.

a. Mark the presentation as Final and save.

b. Verify the presentation has been marked as final by checking the Status bar for the Marked as Final icon.

c. Add a personal Digital Signature, indicating that your purpose for signing the document is to verify that you have personally completed this exercise.

d. Verify that the presentation has been signed by locating the icon that indicates the document contains signatures in the Status bar, and by confirming that your signature appears in the *Signatures* pane.

Package the Presentation and Use the PowerPoint 2007 Viewer

You are ready to package the presentation to a CD. You also want to package to a folder so that it can be uploaded to the family Web site. In order to package the presentation, however, the marked as final designation must be removed. This will invalidate the digital signature.

a. Refer to figure 8.51 as you package your presentation. Toggle the Mark as Final feature so that the marked as final designation is removed and the presentation is no longer read only.

b. Package the presentation for a CD with **New York 2007** as the name.

c. Include the Viewer Package and embed TrueType fonts.

d. Copy the presentation to a CD, following the instructions that are unique to your CD burner. Skip this step if you do not have a CD burner.

e. Repeat the above process to copy the presentation to a folder, saving the folder to the location where you save your solution files.

f. Close the presentation and exit PowerPoint.

g. If you burned the presentation to a CD, insert the CD into your CD player. The presentation uses AutoRun to begin displaying your presentation immediately.

h. Locate the *New York 2007* folder, open *PPTVIEW.EXE*, and then open the *chap8_cap_newyork_solution.ppt* presentation. The presentation plays using the PowerPoint 2007 Viewer.

Figure 8.51 I ♥ New York Presentation

Mini

Use the rubric following the case as a guide to evaluate your work, but keep in mind that your instructor may impose additional grading criteria or use a different standard to judge your work.

Collaborative Pain Presentation

GENERAL CASE

Assume that, in addition to this class where you are learning PowerPoint 2007, you are also registered in a Medical-Surgical I class. Your Medical-Surgical I instructor asks you to prepare a presentation on the Fifth Vital Sign: Pain. You typed your class notes in Microsoft Office Word and saved them as *chap8_mc1_pain.docx*. Create a presentation from your Microsoft Office Word notes, following the guidelines you have learned in this class. Create a hyperlink to the Word notes when you create the presentation. Save the presentation as **chap8_mc1_pain**.

After creating the presentation, e-mail your presentation to another student in this class. Ask your classmate to use the comments feature to make suggestions for improving your presentation. As this student will be completing the same assignment, offer to evaluate his or her presentation in return. When the presentation is returned to you with comments, print the comments so you can retain a record of them. Review the suggestions of your classmate, and then determine which of the suggestions you want to incorporate in your presentation. Modify the presentation as needed. Hide the comments, but do not delete them, as your instructor may wish to review them. Create presentation properties, inspect the document, and remove anything that appears except the properties. Check the compatibility of the presentation with earlier versions of PowerPoint. Export the presentation to Microsoft Office Word using the layout of your choice. Package the presentation to a folder. Figure 8.52 shows one possible solution to this task.

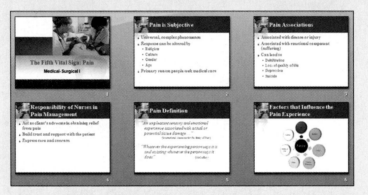

Figure 8.52 Pain Presentation

Performance Elements	Exceeds Expectations	Meets Expectations	Below Expectations
Organization	Concepts can be easily identified. Pain experience factors are easily identified so process is understood.	Concepts are understandable.	Flowchart cannot be understood because there is no sequence of information or because sequencing jumps around.
Visual aspects	SmartArt is appealing and enhances the understanding of factors influencing the pain experience. A consistent visual theme is present.	SmartArt text and shapes are too large/small in size.	The fills, outlines, or shapes are distracting and do not enhance understanding of the factors. Text is too small, making it difficult to read. There is no consistent visual theme.
Layout	The layout is visually pleasing and contributes to the understanding of concepts.	The layout shows some structure, but placement of some shapes, text, and/or white space is distracting.	The layout is cluttered and confusing. Placement of shapes, text, and/or white space detracts from understanding. Understanding of concepts is lost.

Performance Elements	Exceeds Expectations	Meets Expectations	Below Expectations
Mechanics	Presentation has no errors in spelling, grammar, word usage, or punctuation. No typographical errors present.	Presentation has no more than two errors in spelling, grammar, word usage, or punctuation.	Presentation readability is impaired due to repeated errors in spelling, grammar, word usage, or punctuation. Multiple typographical errors.

Get Your Groove On!

RESEARCH CASE

Microsoft Office Groove is a new collaboration software program designed to help teams work together. It promises to help teams work together dynamically and effectively, even if the team members are in different locations or different organizations. Groove doesn't require a centralized server as Office SharePoint Server 2007 does. Instead, it stores all workspaces, tools, and data right on your computer. Research Microsoft Office Groove and create a presentation answering the following questions: How can you use Groove? What is the Document Management task pane? What tools come with Groove? What tools would you find most helpful if you had access to Groove? Save the new presentation as **chap8_mc2_groove_solution**. Figure 8.53 shows one possible solution to this task.

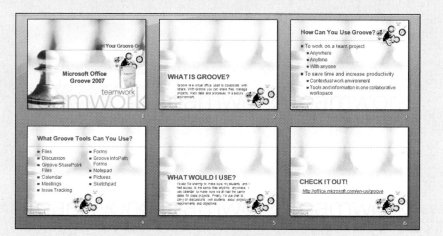

Figure 8.53 Microsoft Office Groove Presentation

Performance Elements	Exceeds Expectations	Meets Expectations	Below Expectations
Organization	Presentation indicates accurate research and significant facts. Evidence exists that information has been evaluated and synthesized, showing an understanding of the topic.	Presentation indicates some research has taken place and that information was included in the content.	Presentation demonstrates a lack of research or understanding of the topic.
Visual aspects	Presentation background, themes, clip art, and animation are appealing and enhance the understanding of presentation purpose and content. There is a consistent visual theme.	Some of the clip art or shapes seem to be unrelated to the presentation purpose and content and do not enhance the overall concepts. Images are too large/small in size. Animation is distracting.	The background or theme is distracting to the topic. Images do not enhance understanding of the content or are unrelated.
Layout	The layout is visually pleasing and contributes to the overall message, with appropriate use of headings, subheadings, bullet points, clip art, and white space.	The layout shows some structure, but placement of some headings, subheadings, bullet points, images, and/or white space is distracting.	The layout is cluttered and confusing. Placement of headings, subheadings, bullet points, images, and/or white space detracts from readability.
Mechanics	Presentation has no errors in spelling, grammar, word usage, or punctuation. Bullet points are parallel.	Presentation has no more than two errors in spelling, grammar, word usage, or punctuation. Bullet points are inconsistent in several slides.	Presentation readability is impaired due to repeated errors in spelling, grammar, word usage, or punctuation. Most bullet points are not parallel.

Sundance Concrete

DISASTER RECOVERY ✚

Sundance Concrete is a concrete design company. It advertises that its designs are only limited by the imagination of the client. It suggests using custom designs to allow you to use your imagination in designing the rooms in your home—for example, using concrete to create a tree with knotholes for stuffed animals in the corner of a child's playroom.

One of the co-owners of the company wanted a presentation on a CD that he could distribute to potential clients. He began the presentation, but was in a hurry and unable to fine-tune it. He needs a copy of the presentation immediately, but he would like to know what changes you suggested and implemented. Review the presentation and insert comments on changes you recommend and changes that are required, such as misspellings and grammatical errors. Save the presentation with comments as **chap8_mc3_concrete_solution**. Print the presentation as handouts, four per page, including comments and ink annotations. After printing the comments and ink annotations, resave the presentation as **chap8_mc3_concrete2_solution**. After resaving the presentation, make the changes you suggested. Make any other changes you feel will help make the presentation become more professional and pleasing. Create relevant presentation properties. Inspect the document and remove comments and ink annotations, but do not remove document properties. Mark the presentation as final. Figure 8.54 shows one possible solution to this task.

Figure 8.54 Sundance Concrete Presentation

Performance Elements	Exceeds Expectations	Meets Expectations	Below Expectations
Organization	Changes and additions enhance the presentation organization.	Changes and additions neither enhance nor detract from the presentation organization.	Changes and additions detract from the overall presentation organization.
Visual aspects	Changes to presentation background or theme are appealing and enhance the understanding of presentation purpose and content. Text can be easily read and understood.	Changes are appealing and enhance the understanding of presentation purpose and content. Text can be easily read.	Changes to the background or theme are distracting and do not enhance understanding of the content. Text is difficult to read.
Layout	Changes to the layout are visually pleasing and contribute to the overall message. If headings, subheadings, bullet points, or clip art are added, they enhance the presentation message.	The changed layout shows some structure, but changes in the placement of some headings, subheadings, bullet points, images, and/or white space are distracting.	The layout is cluttered and confusing. Placement of headings, subheadings, bullet points, images, and/or white space detracts from readability and presentation message.

Performance Elements	Exceeds Expectations	Meets Expectations	Below Expectations
Mechanics	Presentation has no errors in spelling, grammar, word usage, or punctuation.	Presentation has no more than one error in spelling, grammar, word usage, or punctuation.	Presentation readability is impaired due to repeated errors in spelling, grammar, word usage, or punctuation.

Glossary

All key terms appearing in this book (in bold italic) are listed alphabetically in this Glossary for easy reference. If you want to learn more about a feature or concept, use the Index to find the term's other significant occurrences.

Action button a readymade button designed to serve as an icon to which an action can be assigned.

Adjustment handle A control in the shape of a yellow diamond that allows you to modify a shape.

Align To arrange in a line so as to be parallel.

Animation Movement applied to individual elements on a single slide.

Animation scheme A built-in, standard animation effect.

Annotation A note that can be written or drawn on a slide for additional commentary or explanation.

Area chart Emphasizes the magnitude of change over time.

Aspect ratio The ratio of width to height.

Background Styles gallery Provides both solid color and background styles for application to a theme.

Bar chart Shows comparisons between items.

Basic custom show A single presentation file, from which you can create separate presentations.

Bitmap image An image created by bits or pixels placed on a grid that form a picture.

Brightness The ratio between lightness and darkness of an image.

Bubble chart Shows relationships using three values.

Callout A shape that includes a line with a text box that you can use to add notes.

Cell An intersection of a horizontal row and a vertical column in a table.

Chart A visual display of information.

Chart area The entire chart and all its elements.

Clip Any media object that you can insert in a document.

Clipboard A memory location that holds up to 24 items for you to paste into the current document, another file, or another application.

Codec Digital video compression scheme used to compress a video and decompress for playback.

Collaboration A team of people working together to achieve a goal.

Collapsed outline View that displays the title of slides only in the Outline view.

Color schemes The color combinations for the text, lines, background, and graphics in a presentation.

Colors gallery A gallery with a set of colors for every available theme.

Column chart Shows data changes over a period of time or comparisons among items.

Column heading The text in the top row of the table that identifies the contents of a column.

Command An icon on the Quick Access Toolbar or in a group on the Ribbon that you click to perform a task. A command can also appear as text on a menu or within a dialog box.

Comment A text note attached to a slide.

Connector A line that is attached to and moves with shapes.

Contextual tab A specialty tab that appears on the Ribbon only when certain types of objects are being edited.

Contrast The difference between the darkest and lightest areas of a image.

Copy The process of making a duplicate copy of the text or object leaving the original intact.

Copyright The legal protection afforded to a written or artistic work.

Cropping Process of reducing an image size by eliminating unwanted portions of an image.

Custom animation An animation where you determines the animation settings.

Custom dictionary A supplemental dictionary Microsoft Office uses to store items such as proper names, acronyms, or specialized words.

Custom shows Grouped subsets of the slides in a presentation.

Cut Process of removing the original text or an object from its current location.

Data marker A graphical representation of a data point such as a bar, circle, or slice.

Data point A numeric value used in plotting data on a chart.

Data series Contains the data points representing a set of related numbers.

Destination application The application that created the document into which an object is being inserted.

Destination file The file that contains an inserted object.

Dialog box A window that provides an interface for you to select commands.

Dialog Box Launcher A small icon that, when clicked, opens a related dialog box.

Digital signature An invisible, electronic signature that authenticates a presentation.

Distribute To divide or evenly spread over a given area.

Document Properties The collection of metadata about a document, such as author name, keywords, and date.

Doughnut chart Shows proportions to a whole and can contain more than one data series.

Duplex printer A printing device that prints on both sides of the page.

Effects gallery Includes a range of effects for shapes used in a presentation.

Embedded object An object from an external source that is stored within a presentation.

Encryption Protects the contents of your presentation by converting it into unreadable scrambled text that needs a password to be deciphered.

Expanded outline Displays the title and content of slides in the Outline view.

Enhanced ScreenTip Information that displays the name and a brief description of a command when you rest the pointer on a command.

Exploded pie chart A pie chart with one or more slices of the pie separated for emphasis.

Fill The inside of a shape.

Find Locates a word or group of words in a file.

Flowchart An illustration showing the sequence of a project or plan.

Font A complete set of characters—upper- and lowercase letters, numbers, punctuation marks, and special symbols with the same design.

Fonts gallery Contains font sets for title text and body text.

Footer Information printed at the bottom of document pages.

Format Painter Feature that enables you to copy existing text formats to other text to ensure consistency.

Formatting text Changes an individual letter, a word, or a body of selected text.

Freeform shape A shape that combines both curved and straight lines to create a shape.

Gallery Displays a set of predefined options that can be clicked to apply to an object or to text.

Go To Moves the insertion point to a specific location in the file.

Gradient fill A blend of colors and shades.

Graph Displays a relationship between two sets of numbers plotted as a point with coordinates on a grid.

Grid A set of intersecting lines used to align objects.

Gridlines The horizontal and vertical lines that extend from the horizontal and vertical axes of a chart to make the data in the chart easier to read.

Group Categories that organize similar commands together within each tab on the Ribbon.

Grouping Combining two or more objects.

Guide A straight horizontal or vertical line used to align objects.

Handout master Contains the design information for audience handout pages.

Header Information printed at the top of document pages.

Hierarchy Denotes levels of importance in a structure.

HSL A color model in which the numeric system refers to hue, saturation, and luminosity of a color.

Hyperlink A connection between two locations.

Hyperlinked custom shows Slide shows that begin with a main custom show and use hyperlinks to link between other shows.

HyperText Markup Language (HTML) The authoring language used to create pages for the World Wide Web.

Infringement of Copyright Occurs when a right of a copyright owner is violated.

Ink annotation Markup written or drawn on a slide while displaying the slide show.

Insert The process of adding text in a document, spreadsheet cell, database object, or presentation slide.

Insertion point The blinking vertical line in the document, cell, slide show, or database table designating the current location where text you type displays.

Interactivity The ability to branch or interact based upon decisions made by a viewer or audience.

Key Tip The letter or number that displays over each feature on the Ribbon and Quick Access Toolbar and is the keyboard equivalent that you press. Press Alt by itself to display Key Tips.

Kiosk An interactive computer terminal available for public use.

Label Identifies information in a chart.

Landscape orientation Page orientation is wider than it is long, resembling a landscape scene.

Layout Determines the position of objects containing content on a slide, form, report, document, or spreadsheet.

Leader A connecting line between labels and pie slices.

Legend A key in a chart that displays identifying information about a data series connected to the data series name.

Line chart Displays data changes over time.

Line weight The width or thickness of a line.

Linear presentation A presentation that progresses sequentially starting with the first slide and ending with the last slide.

Linked object A representation of data stored in the source file.

Live Preview A feature that provides a preview of how a gallery option will affect the current text or object when the mouse pointer hovers over the gallery option.

Macro Small program that automates tasks in a file.

Manual duplex Operation that enables you to print on both sides of the paper by printing first on one side and then on the other.

Markup Refers to comments and ink annotations appearing in a presentation.

Masters Contain design information that provides for a consistent look to a presentation, handouts, and notes pages.

Metadata Data that describes other data.

Mini toolbar A semitransparent toolbar of often-used font, indent, and bullet commands that displays when you position the mouse over selected text and disappears when you move the mouse away from the selected text.

Movie Video file, or GIF file, containing multiple images that stream to produce an animation.

Multi-series Data for two or more sets of data.

Multimedia Multiple forms of media used to entertain or inform you or an audience.

Narration Spoken commentary that is added to a project.

Non-linear presentation A presentation that progresses sequentially starting with the first slide and ending with the last slide.

Normal view The tri-pane default PowerPoint view.

Notes master Contains design information for speaker's notes.

Notes Page view Used for entering and editing large amounts of text that the speaker can refer to when presenting.

Object Any type of information that can be inserted in slide.

Object linking and embedding (OLE) Inserting an object created in one application into a document created in another application.

Office Button Icon that, when clicked, displays the Office menu.

Office menu List of commands (such as New, Open, Save, Save As, Print, and Options) that work with an entire file or with the specific Microsoft Office program.

Opaque Refers to a solid fill, one without transparency.

Outline A method of organizing text in a hierarchy to depict relationships.

Outline view Displays varying amounts of detail; a structural view of a document that can be collapsed or expanded as necessary.

Overtype mode Replaces the existing text with text you type character by character.

Package for CD A process that writes a presentation, its fonts and linked files, and a PowerPoint Viewer to a CD for distribution.

Paste Places the cut or copied text or object in the new location.

PDF file format An electronic file format created by Adobe Systems that preserves document formatting.

Photo Album A presentation containing multiple pictures organized into album pages.

Picture fill Inserts an image from a file into a shape.

Pie chart Shows proportions to a whole as slices in a circular pie.

Placeholder A container that holds content and is used in the layout to determine the position of objects on the slide.

Plain Text Format (.txt) A file type that retains only text when used to transfer documents between applications or platforms.

Plot area The area representing the data in a chart.

Portrait orientation Page orientation is longer than it is wide—like the portrait of a person.

Presentation graphics software A computer application, such as Microsoft PowerPoint, that is used primarily to create electronic slide shows.

Presenter view Delivers a presentation on two monitors simultaneously.

Properties The collection of metadata in a presentation.

Public domain When the rights to a literary work or property are owned by the public at large.

Publish To copy a Web page to a Web server so that viewers on the World Wide Web can view the Web page.

Quick Access Toolbar A customizable row of buttons for frequently used commands, such as Save and Undo.

Quick Style A combination of formatting options available that can be applied to a shape or graphic.

Radar chart Compares the aggregate values of three or more variables represented on axes starting from the same point.

Redo Command that reinstates or reserves an action performed by the Undo command.

Relational database software A computer application, such as Microsoft Access, that is used to store data and convert it into information.

Repeat A command that duplicates the last action you performed.

Replace The process of finding and replacing a word or group of words with other text.

Reviewer Someone who inserts comments in a slide as part of a collaborative effort.

RGB A numeric system for identifying the color resulting from the combination of red, green, and blue light.

Ribbon The Microsoft Office 2007 GUI command center that organizes commands into related tabs and groups.

Rich Text Format (.rtf) A file type that retains structure and most text formatting when used to transfer documents between applications or platforms.

ScreenTip A small window that describes a command.

Selection net Selects all objects in an area defined by dragging the mouse.

Selection Pane A pane designed to help select objects.

Shape A geometric or nongeometric object such as a rectangle or an arrow.

Shortcut menu A list of commands that appears when you right-click an item or screen element.

Single-series Data representing only one set of data that is plotted in a chart.

Sizing handle The small circles and squares that appear around a selected object and enable you to adjust the height and width of a selected object.

Slide master Contains design information for the slides in a presentation.

Slide Show view Used to deliver the completed presentation full screen to an audience, one slide at a time, as an electronic presentation on the computer.

Slide Sorter view Displays thumbnails of slides.

SmartArt A diagram that presents information visually to effectively communicate a message.

Source application The application used to create the original object.

Source file The file that contains the table or data that is used to create a linked or embedded object.

Spreadsheet software A computer application, such as Microsoft Excel, that is used to build and manipulate electronic spreadsheets.

Stacked The vertical alignment of text.

Stacking order The order of objects placed on top of each other.

Status bar The horizontal bar at the bottom of a Microsoft Office application that displays summary information about the selected window or object and contains View buttons and the Zoom slider. The Word status bar displays the page number and total words, while the Excel status bar displays the average, count, and sum of values in a selected range. The PowerPoint status bar displays the slide number and the Design Theme name.

Stock chart Shows fluctuations or the range of change between the high and low values of a subject over time.

Storyboard A visual plan that displays the content of each slide in the slideshow.

Stub The left column of a table that identifies the data in each row.

Surface chart Plots a surface using two sets of data.

Tab Looks like a folder tab and divides the Ribbon into task-oriented categories.

Table A series of rows and columns that organize data effectively.

Table style A combination of formatting choices available that are based on the theme of the presentation.

Template A file that incorporates a theme, a layout, and content that can be modified.

Text box An object that enables you to place text anywhere on a slide or in a document or within a dialog box.

Text-based chart A chart based on text that is arranged to illustrate a relationship between words, numbers, and/or graphics.

Text pane A special pane that opens up for text entry when a SmartArt diagram is selected.

Texture fill Inserts a texture such as marble into a shape.

Theme A set of design elements that gives the slide show a unified, professional appearance.

Thumbnail A miniature display of an image, page, or slide.

Tick marks Short lines on axes that mark the category and value divisions.

Title bar The shaded bar at the top of every window; often displays the program name and file name.

Transition A movement special effect that takes place as one slide replaces another in Slide Show view.

Transparency Refers to how much you can see through a fill.

Trigger An animation that sets off an action when you click the associated object.

TrueType font A digital font that contains alphabetic characters and information about the shape, spacing, and character mapping of the font.

Undo Command cancels your last one or more operations.

Ungrouping Breaking a combined object into individual objects.

Uniform Resource Locator (URL) The unique address of a resource on the Web.

User interface The meeting point between computer software and the person using it.

Vector graphic An object-oriented graphic based on geometric formulas.

Vertex The point where a curve ends or the point where two line segments me et in a freeform shape.

Virus checker Software that scans files for a hidden program that can damage your computer.

Word processing software A computer application, such as Microsoft Word, that is used primarily with text to create, edit, and format documents.

WordArt Text that has a decorative effect applied.

X-axis The horizontal category axis of a chart.

XPS file format An electronic file format create by Microsoft that preserves document formatting.

XY (scatter) chart Shows distributions, groupings, or patterns.

Y-axis The vertical value axis of a chart.

Z-axis The axis used to plot the depth of a chart.

Zoom slider Enables you to increase or decrease the magnification of the file onscreen.

Multiple Choice Answer Keys

Office Fundamentals, Chapter 1
1. b
2. c
3. d
4. a
5. d
6. c
7. b
8. c
9. d
10. a
11. c
12. d
13. c
14. a
15. d

PowerPoint 2007, Chapter 2
1. d
2. b
3. a
4. d
5. b
6. c
7. c
8. a
9. b
10. a
11. d
12. d
13. a
14. c
15. d

PowerPoint 2007, Chapter 4
1. c
2. a
3. b
4. a
5. b
6. d
7. b
8. d
9. b
10. c
11. a
12. a
13. c
14. d
15. c

PowerPoint 2007, Chapter 1
1. d
2. b
3. d
4. a
5. b
6. d
7. a
8. c
9. d
10. b
11. d
12. d
13. c
14. a
15. c

PowerPoint 2007, Chapter 3
1. b
2. a
3. d
4. b
5. a
6. c
7. b
8. d
9. c
10. d
11. c
12. a
13. a
14. b
15. b

PowerPoint 2007, Chapter 5
1. c
2. b
3. d
4. a
5. d
6. c
7. c
8. b
9. b
10. c
11. d
12. a
13. c
14. c
15. b
16. a
17. b

PowerPoint 2007, Chapter 6

1. b
2. d
3. b
4. a
5. c
6. d
7. b
8. d
9. d
10. a
11. a
12. b
13. c
14. c
15. b

PowerPoint 2007, Chapter 7

1. a
2. c
3. b
4. c
5. a
6. d
7. a
8. a
9. b
10. d
11. a
12. d
13. a
14. a
15. d
16. b

PowerPoint 2007, Chapter 8

1. c
2. a
3. d
4. c
5. d
6. a
7. c
8. c
9. d
10. d
11. a
12. c
13. d
14. a
15. b

Index

U

Underline command, 46
Undo button, 39
Undo command, 39, 53
Ungrouping, 246
  of clip art, 246–248, 258
  of objects, 246–248
Uniform Resource Locator (URL), 497
Universal tasks, in Office 2007, 18
  exercise with, 28–30
  opening files as, 18–21, 28
  printing files as, 18, 24–27
  saving files as, 18, 21–24
University housing exercise, 134–135
UNIX audio, 321
Urban theme, 97, 104
URL. *See* Uniform Resource Locator
User interface, 4

V

Vector clip art, 246, 264
Vector graphics, 246, 289
  Microsoft Windows Metafile
    clip art as, 246
Vector Markup Language (.vml)
    format, 290, 525
Venture capital exercise, 409
Vertexes, 211
  moving of, 211
Vertical alignment, 237
Video file formats, 315
  descriptions of, 315
  extensions for, 315
Video files, 314. *See also* Movies
View(s), 123. *See also specific views*
  default, 76
  individual slide, 82
  Normal, 75, 76, 80–82, 123, 561
  Notes, 80, 82, 83, 123
  Outline, 120, 155–156, 184
  Presenter, 85, 123
  Properties, 87
  Slide Show, 80, 83, 84, 123, 561
  Slide Sorter, 80, 83, 103, 123
View commands, 8
  Word, 9
View tab
  description of, 78
  Word, 9
Viewer, PowerPoint, 582, 586
Vinyl banners, 355
Violet color, associations for, 446
Virus checker, 23

W

Waterwise landscaping
  exercise, 201, 280–281, 347–349
Wave Form, 321
Web address, 497
Web Options Browser
  Support choices, 524
Web pages. *See also* Internet
  Breaking the Cycle of
    Abuse, 537, 538
  Colorado Extreme Sports, 542, 543
  exercise with, 519–522
  file format, 86, 163
  hyperlinks, 497, 531, 549
  opening of, 518
  options, 524, 528, 537
  with outline, 522
  Patient Assessment Flow
    Chart, 540–541
  photographs on, 543–545
  presentation as, 517, 520, 528
  presentation as single file, 516, 517, 519,
    528, 550
  previewing of, 518, 521–522
  publishing, 523–527, 537
Web presentations, 493–554
  multiple choice test for, 529–530
Web sites, PowerPoint
  knowledge and, 284
Weights
  line, 216, 225
  Outline, 217, 225
Wellness Center exercise, 188–193
  content added to presentation
    in, 190–191
  creation of outline in, 188–189
  header/footer creation in, 192–193
  modification of outline in, 189–190
  theme application/modification
    in, 191–192
White color, associations for, 446
Windows Audio files, 321
Windows Bitmap (.bmp, .rle)
    format, 290
Windows Explorer, image
    additions with, 291
Windows Live ID, 572
Windows Media
  audio files, 321
  file format, 315
  video, 315
  video file format, 315
Windows Rights Management
  Client, 572, 588
Windows Video file format, 315

.wmf. *See* Microsoft Windows Metafile format
Word 2007, Microsoft, 3
  file formats for, 23
  handouts in, 582–584, 586–587, 588,
    597–598, 601
  help feature in, 16–17
  Notes Page, 583, 587, 598
  Open dialog box in, 19
  status bar in, 9
  status bar usage in, 15–16
  View commands for, 9
  View tab for, 9
  word processing software and, 3
  Zoom Dialog Box in, 9
Word document format (.docx), 163
Word Options dialog box, 33
Word processing software, 3
  characteristics of, 3
  Word as, 3
WordArt, 105
  alignment options for, 237
  creation of, 237, 242, 264
  definition of, 236
  handout master with, 431, 432
  modification of, 237–238, 243, 264
  Transform options in, 237, 238
WordArt Gallery, ScreenTip and, 79, 107
Worksheets. *See* Excel worksheet

X

X-axis, 387
XML (eXtensible Markup Language) format,
  23, 86, 123
XPS file format, 557, 558
  add-in for, 558
XY (scatter) charts, 383, 385
  creation of, 412, 413
  data for, 413

Y

Y-axis, 387
Yellow color, associations for, 446

Z

Z-axis, 387
Zoo presentation exercise, 341–343
Zoom dialog box
  Excel and, 13
  Word, 9
Zoom slider, 9
  PowerPoint and, 12